Get the eBook FREE!

(PDF, ePub, Kindle, and liveBook all included)

We believe that once you buy a book from us, you should be able to read it in any format we have available. To get electronic versions of this book at no additional cost to you, purchase and then register this book at the Manning website.

Go to https://www.manning.com/freebook and follow the instructions to complete your pBook registration.

That's it!
Thanks from Manning!

Spark in Action

SECOND EDITION

JEAN-GEORGES PERRIN
FOREWORD BY ROB THOMAS

MANNING
SHELTER ISLAND

For online information and ordering of this and other Manning books, please visit
www.manning.com. The publisher offers discounts on this book when ordered in quantity.
For more information, please contact

    Special Sales Department
    Manning Publications Co.
    20 Baldwin Road
    PO Box 761
    Shelter Island, NY 11964
    Email: orders@manning.com

Manning Publications Co.
20 Baldwin Road
PO Box 761
Shelter Island, NY 11964

Development editor:	Marina Michaels
Technical development editor:	Al Scherer
Review editor:	Aleks Dragosavljević
Production editor:	Lori Weidert
Copy editor:	Sharon Wilkey
Proofreader:	Melody Dolab
Technical proofreader:	Rambabu Dosa and Thomas Lockney
Typesetter:	Gordan Salinovic
Cover designer:	Marija Tudor

ISBN 9781617295522
Printed in the United States of America

Liz,
Thank you for your patience, support, and love during this endeavor.

Ruby, Nathaniel, Jack, and Pierre-Nicolas,
Thank you for being so understanding about my lack of availability during this venture.

I love you all.

contents

17 Exporting data and building full data pipelines   373

18 Exploring deployment constraints: Understanding the ecosystem   395

foreword

The analytics operating system

In the twentieth century, scale effects in business were largely driven by breadth and distribution. A company with manufacturing operations around the world had an inherent cost and distribution advantage, leading to more-competitive products. A retailer with a global base of stores had a distribution advantage that could not be matched by a smaller company. These scale effects drove competitive advantage for decades.

The internet changed all of that. Today, three predominant scale effects exist:

- *Network*—Lock-in that is driven by a loyal network (Facebook, Twitter, Etsy, and so forth)
- *Economies of scale*—Lower unit cost, driven by volume (Apple, TSMC, and so forth)
- *Data*—Superior machine learning and insight, driven from a dynamic corpus of data

In *Big Data Revolution* (Wiley, 2015), I profiled a few companies that are capitalizing on data as a scale effect. But, here in 2019, big data is still largely an unexploited asset in institutions around the world. Spark, the analytics operating system, is a catalyst to change that.

Spark has been a catalyst in changing the face of innovation at IBM. Spark is the analytics operating system, unifying data sources and data access. The unified programming model of Spark makes it the best choice for developers building data-rich analytic applications. Spark reduces the time and complexity of building analytic workflows, enabling builders to focus on machine learning and the ecosystem around Spark. As we have seen time and again, an open source project is igniting innovation, with speed and scale.

This book takes you deeper into the world of Spark. It covers the power of the technology and the vibrancy of the ecosystem, and covers practical applications for putting Spark to work in your company today. Whether you are working as a data engineer, data scientist, or application developer, or running IT operations, this book reveals the tools and secrets that you need to know, to drive innovation in your company or community.

Our strategy at IBM is about building on top of and around a successful open platform, and adding something of our own that's substantial and differentiated. Spark is that platform. We have countless examples in IBM, and you will have the same in your company as you embark on this journey.

Spark is about innovation—an analytics operating system on which new solutions will thrive, unlocking the big data scale effect. And Spark is about a community of Spark-savvy data scientists and data analysts who can quickly transform today's problems into tomorrow's solutions. Spark is one of the fastest-growing open source projects in history. Welcome to the movement.

—Rob Thomas

Senior Vice President,
Cloud and Data Platform, IBM

preface

I don't think Apache Spark needs an introduction. If you're reading these lines, you probably have some idea of what this book is about: data engineering and data science at scale, using distributed processing. However, Spark is more than that, which you will soon discover, starting with Rob Thomas's foreword and chapter 1.

Just as Obelix fell into the magic potion,[1] I fell into Spark in 2015. At that time, I was working for a French computer hardware company, where I helped design highly performing systems for data analytics. As one should be, I was skeptical about Spark at first. Then I started working with it, and you now have the result in your hands. From this initial skepticism came a real passion for a wonderful tool that allows us to process data in—this is my sincere belief—a very easy way.

I started a few projects with Spark, which allowed me to give talks at Spark Summit, IBM Think, and closer to home at All Things Open, Open Source 101, and through the local Spark user group I co-animate in the Raleigh-Durham area of North Carolina. This allowed me to meet great people and see plenty of Spark-related projects. As a consequence, my passion continued to grow.

This book is about sharing that passion.

Examples (or labs) in the book are based on Java, but the only repository contains Scala and Python as well. As Spark 3.0 was coming out, the team at Manning and I

---

[1]Obelix is a comics and cartoon character. He is the inseparable companion of Asterix. When Asterix, a Gaul, drinks a magic potion, he gains superpowers that allow him to regularly beat the Romans (and pirates). As a baby, Obelix fell into the cauldron where the potion was made, and the potion has an everlasting effect on him. Asterix is a popular comic in Europe. Find out more at www.asterix.com/en/.

decided to make sure that the book reflects the latest versions, and not as an after-thought.

As you may have guessed, I love comic books. I grew up with them. I love this way of communicating, which you'll see in this book. It's not a comic book, but its nearly 200 images should help you understand this fantastic tool that is Apache Spark.

Just as Asterix has Obelix for a companion, *Spark in Action*, Second Edition has a reference companion supplement that you can download for free from the resource section on the Manning website; a short link is http://jgp.ai/sia. This supplement contains reference information on Spark static functions and will eventually grow to more useful reference resources.

Whether you like this book or not, drop me a tweet at @jgperrin. If you like it, write an Amazon review. If you don't, as they say at weddings, forever hold your peace. Nevertheless, I sincerely hope you'll enjoy it.

Alea iacta est.[2]

---

[2]The die is cast. This sentence was attributed to Julius Caesar (Asterix's arch frenemy) as Caesar led his army over the Rubicon: things have happened and can't be changed back, like this book being printed, for you.

acknowledgments

This is the section where I express my gratitude to the people who helped me in this journey. It's also the section where you have a tendency to forget people, so if you feel left out, I am sorry. Really sorry. This book has been a tremendous effort, and doing it alone probably would have resulted in a two- or three-star book on Amazon, instead of the five-star rating you will give it soon (this is a call to action, thanks!).

I'd like to start by thanking the teams at work who trusted me on this project, starting with Zaloni (Anupam Rakshit and Tufail Khan), Lumeris (Jon Farn, Surya Koduru, Noel Foster, Divya Penmetsa, Srini Gaddam, and Bryce Tutt; all of whom almost blindly followed me on the Spark bandwagon), the people at Veracity Solutions, and my new team at Advance Auto Parts.

Thanks to Mary Parker of the Department of Statistics at the University of Texas at Austin and Cristiana Straccialana Parada. Their contributions helped clarify some sections.

I'd like to thank the community at large, including Jim Hughes, Michael Ben-David, Marcel-Jan Krijgsman, Jean-Francois Morin, and all the anonymous posting pull requests on GitHub. I would like to express my sincere gratitude to the folks at Databricks, IBM, Netflix, Uber, Intel, Apple, Alluxio, Oracle, Microsoft, Cloudera, NVIDIA, Facebook, Google, Alibaba, numerous universities, and many more who contribute to making Spark what it is. More specifically, for their work, inspiration, and support, thanks to Holden Karau, Jacek Laskowski, Sean Owen, Matei Zaharia, and Jules Damji.

During this project, I participated in several podcasts. My thanks to Tobias Macey for Data Engineering Podcast (http://mng.bz/WPjX), IBM's Al Martin for "Making Data Simple" (http://mng.bz/8p7g), and the Roaring Elephant by Jhon Masschelein and Dave Russell (http://mng.bz/EdRr).

As an IBM Champion, it has been a pleasure to work with so many IBMers during this adventure. They either helped directly, indirectly, or were inspirational: Rob Thomas (we need to work together more), Marius Ciortea, Albert Martin (who, among other things, runs the great podcast called Make Data Simple), Steve Moore, Sourav Mazumder, Stacey Ronaghan, Mei-Mei Fu, Vijay Bommireddipalli (keep this thing you have in San Francisco rolling!), Sunitha Kambhampati, Sahdev Zala, and, my brother, Stuart Litel.

I want to thank the people at Manning who adopted this crazy project. As in all good movies, in order of appearance: my acquisition editor, Michael Stephens; our publisher, Marjan Bace; my development editors, Marina Michaels and Toni Arritola; and production staff, Erin Twohey, Rebecca Rinehart, Bert Bates, Candace Gillhoolley, Radmila Ercegovac, Aleks Dragosavljevic, Matko Hrvatin, Christopher Kaufmann, Ana Romac, Cheryl Weisman, Lori Weidert, Sharon Wilkey, and Melody Dolab.

I would also like to acknowledge and thank all of the Manning reviewers: Anupam Sengupta, Arun Lakkakulam, Christian Kreutzer-Beck, Christopher Kardell, Conor Redmond, Ezra Schroeder, Gábor László Hajba, Gary A. Stafford, George Thomas, Giuliano Araujo Bertoti, Igor Franca, Igor Karp, Jeroen Benckhuijsen, Juan Rufes, Kelvin Johnson, Kelvin Rawls, Mario-Leander Reimer, Markus Breuer, Massimo Dalla Rovere, Pavan Madhira, Sambaran Hazra, Shobha Iyer, Ubaldo Pescatore, Victor Durán, and William E. Wheeler. It does take a village to write a (hopefully) good book. I also want to thank Petar Zečević and Marco Banaći, who wrote the first edition of this book. Thanks to Thomas Lockney for his detailed technical review, and also to Rambabu Posa for porting the code in this book. I'd like to thank Jon Rioux (merci, Jonathan!) for starting the PySpark in Action adventure. He coined the idea of "team Spark at Manning."

I'd like to thank again Marina. Marina was my development editor during most of the book. She was here when I had issues, she was here with advice, she was tough on me (yeah, you cannot really slack off), but instrumental in this project. I will remember our long discussions about the book (which may or may not have been a pretext for talking about anything else). I will miss you, big sister (almost to the point of starting another book right away).

Finally, I want to thank my parents, who supported me more than they should have and to whom I dedicate the cover; my wife, Liz, who helped me on so many levels, including understanding editors; and our kids, Pierre-Nicolas, Jack, Nathaniel, and Ruby, from whom I stole too much time writing this book.

about this book

When I started this project, which became the book you are reading, *Spark in Action*, Second Edition, my goals were to

- Help the Java community use Apache Spark, demonstrating that you do not need to learn Scala or Python
- Explain the key concepts behind Apache Spark, (big) data engineering, and data science, without you having to know anything else than a relational database and some SQL
- Evangelize that Spark is an operating system designed for distributed computing and analytics

I believe in teaching anything computer science with a high dose of examples. The examples in this book are an essential part of the learning process. I designed them to be as close as possible to real-life professional situations. My datasets come from real-life situations with their quality flaws; they are not the ideal textbook datasets that "always work." That's why, when combining both those examples and datasets, you will work and learn in a more pragmatic way than a sterilized way. I call those examples *labs*, with the hope that you will find them inspirational and that you will want to experiment with them.

Illustrations are everywhere. Based on the well-known saying, *A picture is worth a thousand words*, I saved you from reading an extra 183,000 words.

Who should read this book

It is a difficult task to associate a job title to a book, so if your title is data engineer, data scientist, software engineer, or data/software architect, you'll certainly be happy. If you are an enterprise architect, meh, you probably know all that, as enterprise architects know everything about everything, no? More seriously, this book will be helpful if you look to gather more knowledge on any of these topics:

- Using Apache Spark to build analytics and data pipelines: ingestion, transformation, and exporting/publishing.
- Using Spark without having to learn Scala or Hadoop: learning Spark with Java.
- Understanding the difference between a relational database and Spark.
- The basic concepts about big data, including the key Hadoop components you may encounter in a Spark environment.
- Positioning Spark in an enterprise architecture.
- Using your existing Java and RDBMS skills in a big data environment.
- Understanding the dataframe API.
- Integrating relational databases by ingesting data in Spark.
- Gathering data via streams.
- Understanding the evolution of the industry and why Spark is a good fit.
- Understanding and using the central role of the dataframe.
- Knowing what resilient distributed datasets (RDDs) are and why they should not be used (anymore).
- Understanding how to interact with Spark.
- Understanding the various components of Spark: driver, executors, master and workers, Catalyst, Tungsten.
- Learning the role of key Hadoop-derived technologies such as YARN or HDFS.
- Understanding the role of a resource manager such as YARN, Mesos, and the built-in manager.
- Ingesting data from various files in batch mode and via streams.
- Using SQL with Spark.
- Manipulating the static functions provided with Spark.
- Understanding what immutability is and why it matters.
- Extending Spark with Java user-defined functions (UDFs).

- Extending Spark with new data sources.
- Linearizing data from JSON so you can use SQL.
- Performing aggregations and unions on dataframes.
- Extending aggregation with user-defined aggregate functions (UDAFs).
- Understanding the difference between caching and checkpointing, and increasing performance of your Spark applications.
- Exporting data to files and databases.
- Understanding deployment on AWS, Azure, IBM Cloud, GCP, and on-premises clusters.
- Ingesting data from files in CSV, XML, JSON, text, Parquet, ORC, and Avro.
- Extending data sources, with an example on how to ingest photo metadata using EXIF, focusing on the Data Source API v1.
- Using Delta Lake with Spark while you build pipelines.

What will you learn in this book?

The goal of this book is to teach you how to use Spark within your applications or build specific applications for Spark.

I designed this book for *data engineers* and *Java software engineers*. When I started learning Spark, everything was in Scala, nearly all documentation was on the official website, and Stack Overflow displayed a Spark question every other blue moon. Sure, the documentation claimed Spark had a Java API, but advanced examples were scarce. At that time, my teammates were confused, between learning Spark and learning Scala, and our management wanted results. My team members were my motivation for writing this book.

I assume that you have basic Java and RDBMS knowledge. I use Java 8 in all examples, even though Java 11 is out there.

You do not need to have Hadoop knowledge to read this book, but because you will need some Hadoop components (very few), I will cover them. If you already know Hadoop, you will certainly find this book refreshing. You do not need any Scala knowledge, as this is a book about Spark and Java.

When I was a kid (and I must admit, still now), I read a lot of *bandes dessinées*, a cross between a comic book and a graphic novel. As a result, I love illustrations, and I have a lot of them in this book. Figure 1 shows a typical diagram with several components, icons, and legends.

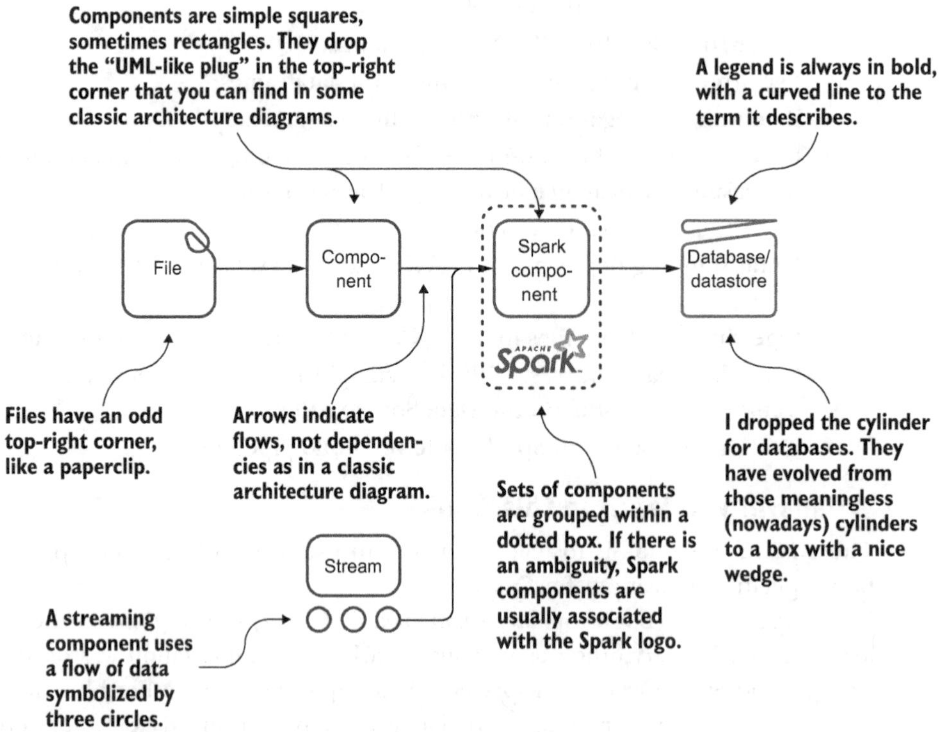

Components are simple squares, sometimes rectangles. They drop the "UML-like plug" in the top-right corner that you can find in some classic architecture diagrams.

A legend is always in bold, with a curved line to the term it describes.

File → Compo-nent → Spark compo-nent → Database/datastore

APACHE Spark

Files have an odd top-right corner, like a paperclip.

Arrows indicate flows, not dependencies as in a classic architecture diagram.

Stream

○ ○ ○

A streaming component uses a flow of data symbolized by three circles.

Sets of components are grouped within a dotted box. If there is an ambiguity, Spark components are usually associated with the Spark logo.

I dropped the cylinder for databases. They have evolved from those meaningless (nowadays) cylinders to a box with a nice wedge.

Figure 1   Iconography used in a typical illustration in this book

How this book is organized

This book is divided into four parts and 18 appendices.

Part 1 gives you the keys to Spark. You will learn the theory and general concepts, but do not despair (yet); I present a lot of examples and diagrams. It almost reads like a comic book.

- Chapter 1 is an overall introduction with a simple example. You will learn why Spark is a distributed analytics operating system.
- Chapter 2 walks you through a simple Spark process.
- Chapter 3 teaches about the magnificence of the dataframe, which combines both the API and storage capabilities of Spark.
- Chapter 4 celebrates laziness, compares Spark and RDBMS, and introduces the directed acyclic graph (DAG).
- Chapters 5 and 6 are linked: you'll build a small application, build a cluster, and deploy your application. Chapter 5 is about building a small application, while chapter 6 is deploying the application.

In part 2, you will start diving into practical and pragmatic examples around ingestion. Ingestion is the process of bringing data into Spark. It is not complex, but there are a lot of possibilities and combinations.

- Chapter 7 describes data ingestion from files: CSV, text, JSON, XML, Avro, ORC, and Parquet. Each file format has its own example.
- Chapter 8 covers ingestion from databases: data will be coming from relational databases and other data stores.
- Chapter 9 is about ingesting anything from custom data sources.
- Chapter 10 focuses on streaming data.

Part 3 is about transforming data: this is what I would call heavy data lifting. You'll learn about data quality, transformation, and publishing of your processed data. This largest part of the book talks about using the dataframe with SQL and with its API, aggregates, caching, and extending Spark with UDF.

- Chapter 11 is about the well-known query language SQL.
- Chapter 12 teaches you how to perform transformation.
- Chapter 13 extends transformation to the level of entire documents. This chapter also explains static functions, which are one of the many great aspects of Spark.
- Chapter 14 is all about extending Spark using user-defined functions.
- Aggregations are also a well-known database concept and may be the key to analytics. Chapter 15 covers aggregations, both those included in Spark and custom aggregations.

Finally, part 4 is about going closer to production and focusing on more advanced topics. You'll learn about partitioning and exporting data, deployment constraints (including to the cloud), and optimization.

- Chapter 16 focuses on optimization techniques: caching and checkpointing.
- Chapter 17 is about exporting data to databases and files. This chapter also explains how to use Delta Lake, a database that sits next to Spark's kernel.
- Chapter 18 details reference architectures and security needed for deployment. It's definitely less hands-on, but so full of critical information.

The appendixes, although not essential, also bring a wealth of information: installing, troubleshooting, and contextualizing. A lot of them are curated references for Apache Spark in a Java context.

About the code

As I've said, each chapter (except 6 and 18) has labs that combine code and data. Source code is in numbered listings and in line with normal text. In both cases, source code is formatted in a `fixed-width font like this` to separate it from ordinary text. Sometimes code is also in **bold** to highlight code that is more important in a block of code.

All the code is freely available on GitHub under an Apache 2.0 license. The data may have a different license. Each chapter has its own repository: chapter 1 will be in https://github.com/jgperrin/net.jgp.books.spark.ch01, while chapter 15 is in https://github.com/jgperrin/net.jgp.books.spark.ch15, and so on. Two exceptions:

- Chapter 6 uses the code of chapter 5.
- Chapter 18, which talks about deployment in detail, does not have code.

As source control tools allow branches, the master branch contains the code against the latest production version, while each repository contains branches dedicated to specific versions, when applicable.

Labs are numbered in three digits, starting at 100. There are two kinds of labs: the labs that are described in the book and the extra labs available online:

- Labs described in the book are numbered per section of the chapter. Therefore, lab #200 of chapter 12 is covered in chapter 12, section 2. Likewise, lab #100 of chapter 17 is detailed in the first section of chapter 17.
- Labs that are not described in the book start with a 9, as in 900, 910, and so on. Labs in the 900 series are growing: I keep adding more. Labs numbers are not contiguous, just like the line numbers in your BASIC code.

In GitHub, you will find the code in Python, Scala, and Java (unless it is not applicable). However, to maintain clarity in the book, only Java is used.

In many cases, the original source code has been reformatted; we've added line breaks and reworked indentation to accommodate the available page space in the book. In rare cases, even this was not enough, and listings include line-continuation markers (➥). Additionally, comments in the source code have often been removed from the listings when the code is described in the text. Code annotations accompany many of the listings, highlighting important concepts.

liveBook discussion forum

Purchase of *Spark in Action* includes free access to a private web forum run by Manning Publications where you can make comments about the book, ask technical questions, and receive help from the author and from other users. To access the forum, go to https://livebook.manning.com/#!/book/spark-in-action-second-edition/discussion. You can also learn more about Manning's forums and the rules of conduct at https://livebook.manning.com/#!/discussion.

Manning's commitment to our readers is to provide a venue where a meaningful dialogue between individual readers and between readers and the author can take place. It is not a commitment to any specific amount of participation on the part of the author, whose contribution to the forum remains voluntary (and unpaid). We suggest you try asking the author some challenging questions lest his interest stray! The forum and the archives of previous discussions will be accessible from the publisher's website as long as the book is in print.

about the author

Jean-Georges Perrin is passionate about software engineering and all things data. His latest projects have driven him toward more distributed data engineering, where he extensively uses Apache Spark, Java, and other tools in hybrid cloud settings. He is proud to have been the first in France to be recognized as an IBM Champion, and to have been awarded the honor for his twelfth consecutive year. As an awarded data and software engineering expert, he now operates worldwide with a focus in the United States, where he resides. Jean-Georges shares his more than 25 years of experience in the IT industry as a presenter and participant at conferences and through publishing articles in print and online media. You can visit his blog at http://jgp.ai.

about the cover illustration

The figure on the cover of *Spark in Action* is captioned "Homme et Femme de Housberg, près Strasbourg" (Man and Woman from Housberg, near Strasbourg). Housberg has become Hausbergen, a natural region and historic territory in Alsace now divided between three villages: Niederhausbergen (lower Hausbergen), Mittelhausbergen (middle Hausbergen), and Oberhausbergen (upper Hausbergen). The illustration is from a collection of dress costumes from various countries by Jacques Grasset de Saint-Sauveur (1757–1810), titled *Costumes de Différents Pays*, published in France in 1797. Each illustration is finely drawn and colored by hand.

This particular illustration has special meaning to me. I am really happy it could be used for this book. I was born in Strasbourg, Alsace, currently in France. I immensely value my Alsatian heritage. When I decided to immigrate to the United States, I knew I was leaving behind a bit of this culture and my family, particularly my parents and sisters. My parents live in a small town called Souffelweyersheim, directly neighboring Niederhausbergen. This illustration reminds me of them every time I see the cover (although my dad has a lot less hair).

The rich variety of Grasset de Saint-Sauveur's collection reminds us vividly of how culturally separate the world's towns and regions were just 200 years ago. Isolated from each other, people spoke different dialects (here, Alsatian) and languages. In the streets or in the countryside, it was easy to identify where someone lived and what their trade or station in life was just by their dress.

The way we dress has changed since then, and the diversity by region, once so rich, has faded away. It's now hard to distinguish the inhabitants of different continents, let alone different towns, regions, or countries. Perhaps we have traded cultural diversity for a more varied personal life—certainly for a more varied and fast-paced technological life.

At a time when it's hard to tell one computer book from another, Manning celebrates the inventiveness and initiative of the computer business with book covers based on the rich diversity of regional life of two centuries ago, brought back to life by Grasset de Saint-Sauveur's pictures.

Part 1

The theory crippled by awesome examples

As with any technology, you need to understand a bit of the "boring" theory before you can deep dive into using it. I have managed to contain this part to six chapters, which will give you a good overview of the concepts, explained through examples.

Chapter 1 is an overall introduction with a simple example. You will learn why Spark is not just a simple set of tools, but a real distributed analytics operating system. After this first chapter, you will be able to run a simple data ingestion in Spark.

Chapter 2 will show you how Spark works, at a high level. You'll build a representation of Spark's components by building a *mental model* (representing your own thought process) step by step. This chapter's lab shows you how to export data in a database. This chapter contains a lot of illustrations, which should make your learning process easer than just from words and code!

Chapter 3 takes you to a whole new dimension: discovering the powerful dataframe, which combines both the API and storage capabilities of Spark. In this chapter's lab, you'll load two datasets and union them together.

Chapter 4 celebrates laziness and explains why Spark uses lazy optimization. You'll learn about the directed acyclic graph (DAG) and compare Spark and an RDBMS. The lab teaches you how to start manipulating data by using the dataframe API.

Chapters 5 and 6 are linked: you'll build a small application, build a cluster, and deploy your application. These two chapters are very hands-on.

So, what is Spark, anyway?

When I was a kid in the 1980s, discovering programming through Basic and my Atari, I could not understand why we could not automate basic law enforcement activities such as speed control, traffic-light violations, and parking meters. Everything seemed pretty easy: the book I had said that to be a good programmer, you should avoid GOTO statements. And that's what I did, trying to structure my code from the age of 12. However, there was no way I could imagine the volume of data (and the booming Internet of Things, or IoT) while I was developing my Monopoly-like game. As my game fit into 64 KB of memory, I definitely had no clue that datasets would become bigger (by a ginormous factor) or that the data would have a speed, or *velocity*, as I was patiently waiting for my game to be saved on my Atari 1010 tape recorder.

A short 35 years later, all those use cases I imagined seem accessible (and my game, futile). Data has been growing at a faster pace than the hardware technology to support it.[1] A cluster of smaller computers can cost less than one big computer. Memory is cheaper by half compared to 2005, and memory in 2005 was five times cheaper than in 2000.[2] Networks are many times faster, and modern datacenters offer speeds of up to 100 gigabits per second (Gbps), nearly 2,000 times faster than your home Wi-Fi from five years ago. These were some of the factors that drove people to ask this question: How can I use distributed memory computing to analyze large quantities of data?

When you read the literature or search the web for information about Apache Spark, you may find that it is a tool for big data, a successor to Hadoop, a platform for doing analytics, a cluster-computer framework, and more. *Que nenni!*[3]

LAB   The lab in this chapter is available in GitHub at https://github.com/ jgperrin/net.jgp.books.spark.ch01. This is lab #400. If you are not familiar with GitHub and Eclipse, appendixes A, B, C, and D provide guidance.

1.1   *The big picture: What Spark is and what it does*

As the Little Prince would say to Antoine de Saint-Exupéry, *Draw me a Spark*. In this section, you will first look at what Spark is, and then at what Spark can do through several use cases. This first section concludes by describing how Spark is integrated as a software stack and used by data scientists.

1.1.1   *What is Spark?*

Spark is more than just a software stack for data scientists. When you build applications, you build them on top of an operating system, as illustrated in figure 1.1. The operating system provides services to make your application development easier; in other words, you are not building a filesystem or network driver for each application you develop.

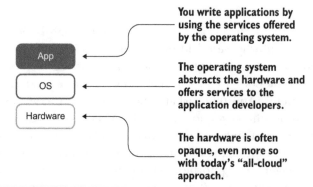

You write applications by using the services offered by the operating system.

The operating system abstracts the hardware and offers services to the application developers.

The hardware is often opaque, even more so with today's "all-cloud" approach.

Figure 1.1   When you write applications, you use services offered by the operating system, which abstracts you from the hardware.

---

[1]See "Intel Puts the Brakes on Moore's Law" by Tom Simonite, MIT Technology Review, March 2016 (http:// mng.bz/gVj8).

[2]See "Memory Prices (1957–2017)" by John C. McCallum (https://jcmit.net/memoryprice.htm).

[3]A medieval French expression meaning *of course not.*

With the need for more computing power came an increased need for distributed computing. With the advent of distributed computing, a distributed application had to incorporate those distribution functions. Figure 1.2 shows the increased complexity of adding more components to your application.

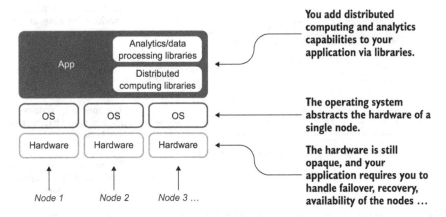

Figure 1.2 One way to write distributed data-oriented applications is to embed all controls at the application level, using libraries or other artifacts. As a result, the applications become fatter and more difficult to maintain.

Having said all that, Apache Spark may appear like a complex system that requires you to have a lot of prior knowledge. I am convinced that you need only Java and relational database management system (RDBMS) skills to understand, use, build applications with, and extend Spark.

Applications have also become smarter, producing reports and performing data analysis (including data aggregation, linear regression, or simply displaying donut charts). Therefore, when you want to add such analytics capabilities to your application, you have to link libraries or build your own. All this makes your application bigger (or *fatter*, as in a fat client), harder to maintain, more complex, and, as a consequence, more expensive for the enterprise.

"So why wouldn't you put those functionalities at the operating system level?" you may ask. The benefits of putting those features at a lower level, like the operating system, are numerous and include the following:

- Provides a standard way to deal with data (a bit like Structured Query Language, or SQL, for relational databases).
- Lowers the cost of development (and maintenance) of applications.
- Enables you to focus on understanding how to use the tool, not on how the tool works. (For example, Spark performs distributed ingestion, and you can learn how to benefit from that without having to fully grasp the way Spark accomplishes the task.)

And this is exactly what Spark has become for me: an *analytics operating system.* Figure 1.3 shows this simplified stack.

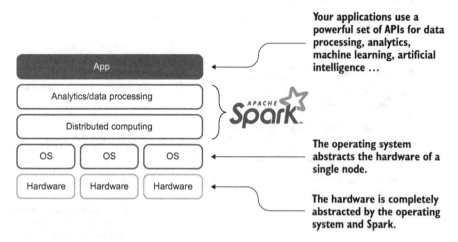

Figure 1.3   Apache Spark simplifies the development of analytics-oriented applications by offering services to applications, just as an operating system does.

In this chapter, you'll discover a few use cases of Apache Spark for different industries and various project sizes. These examples will give you a small overview of what you can achieve.

I am a firm believer that, to get a better understanding of where we are, we should look at history. And this applies to information technology (IT) too: read appendix E if you want my take on it.

Now that the scene is set, you will dig into Spark. We will start from a global overview, have a look at storage and APIs, and, finally, work through your first example.

1.1.2   *The four pillars of mana*

According to Polynesians, *mana* is the power of the elemental forces of nature embodied in an object or person. This definition fits the classic diagram you will find in all Spark documentation, showing four pillars bringing these elemental forces to Spark: Spark SQL, Spark Streaming, Spark MLlib (for machine learning), and GraphX sitting on top of Spark Core. Although this is an exact representation of the Spark stack, I find it limiting. The stack needs to be extended to show the hardware, the operating system, and your application, as in figure 1.4.

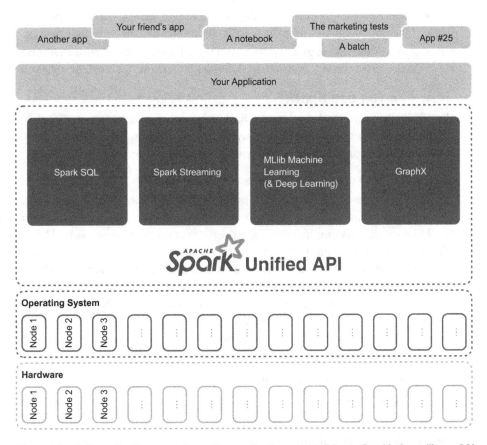

Figure 1.4 Your application, as well as other applications, are talking to Spark's four pillars—SQL, streaming, machine learning, and graphs—via a unified API. Spark shields you from the operating system and the hardware constraints: you will not have to worry about where your application is running or if it has the right data. Spark will take care of that. However, your application can still access the operating system or hardware if it needs to.

Of course, the cluster(s) where Spark is running may not be used exclusively by your application, but your work will use the following:

- *Spark SQL* to run data operations, like traditional SQL jobs in an RDBMS. Spark SQL offers APIs and SQL to manipulate your data. You will discover Spark SQL in chapter 11 and read more about it in most of the chapters after that. Spark SQL is a cornerstone of Spark.
- *Spark Streaming*, and specifically Spark structured streaming, to analyze streaming data. Spark's unified API will help you process your data in a similar way, whether it is streamed data or batch data. You will learn the specifics about streaming in chapter 10.

- *Spark MLlib* for machine learning and recent extensions in deep learning. Machine learning, deep learning, and artificial intelligence deserve their own book.
- *GraphX* to exploit graph data structures. To learn more about GraphX, you can read *Spark GraphX in Action* by Michael Malak and Robin East (Manning, 2016).

1.2 How can you use Spark?

In this section, you'll take a detailed look at how you can use Apache Spark by focusing on typical data processing scenarios as well as a data science scenario. Whether you are a data engineer or a data scientist, you will be able to use Apache Spark in your job.

1.2.1 Spark in a data processing/engineering scenario

Spark can process your data in a number of different ways. But it excels when it plays in a big data scenario, where you ingest data, clean it, transform it, and republish it.

I like to see data engineers as data preparers and data logisticians. They make sure the data is available, that the data quality rules are applied successfully, that the transformations are executed successfully, and that the data is available to other systems or departments, including business analysts and data scientists. Data engineers can also be the ones taking the work of the data scientists and industrializing it.

Spark is a perfect tool for data engineers. The four steps of a typical Spark (big data) scenario performed by data engineering are as follows:

1 Ingestion
2 Improvement of data quality (DQ)
3 Transformation
4 Publication

Figure 1.5 illustrates this process.

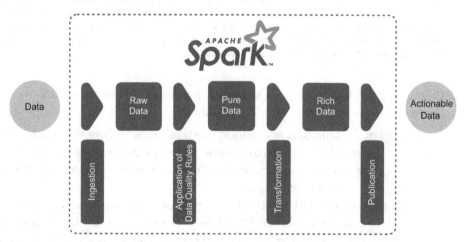

Figure 1.5   Spark in a typical data processing scenario. The first step is ingesting the data. At this stage, the data is raw; you may next want to apply some data quality (DQ). You are now ready to transform your data. Once you have transformed your data, it is richer. It is time to publish or share it so people in your organization can perform actions on it and make decisions based on it.

The process includes four steps, and after each step, the data lands in a *zone*:

1 *Ingesting data*—Spark can ingest data from a variety of sources (see chapters 7, 8, and 9 on ingestion). If you can't find a supported format, you can build your own data sources. I call data at this stage *raw data*. You can also find this zone named the *staging, landing, bronze,* or even *swamp zone.*

2 *Improving data quality (DQ)*—Before processing your data, you may want to check the quality of the data itself. An example of DQ is to ensure that all birth dates are in the past. As part of this process, you can also elect to obfuscate some data: if you are processing Social Security numbers (SSNs) in a health-care environment, you can make sure that the SSNs are not accessible to developers or nonauthorized personnel.[4] After your data is refined, I call this stage the *pure data* zone. You may also find this zone called the *refinery, silver, pond, sandbox,* or *exploration zone.*

3 *Transforming data*—The next step is to process your data. You can join it with other datasets, apply custom functions, perform aggregations, implement machine learning, and more. The goal of this step is to get *rich data*, the fruit of your analytics work. Most of the chapters discuss transformation. This zone may also be called the *production, gold, refined, lagoon,* or *operationalization zone.*

4 *Loading and publishing*—As in an ETL process,[5] you can finish by loading the data into a data warehouse, using a business intelligence (BI) tool, calling APIs, or saving the data in a file. The result is actionable data for your enterprise.

1.2.2 Spark in a data science scenario

Data scientists have a slightly different approach than software engineers or data engineers, as data scientists focus on the transformation part, in an interactive manner. For this purpose, data scientists use different tools, such as notebooks. Names of notebooks include Jupyter, Zeppelin, IBM Watson Studio, and Databricks Runtime.

How data scientists work will definitely matter to you, as data science projects will consume enterprise data, and therefore you may end up delivering data to the data scientists, off-loading their work (such as machine learning models) into enterprise data stores, or industrializing their findings.

Therefore, a UML-like sequence diagram, as in figure 1.6, will explain a little better how data scientists use Spark.

If you want to know more about Spark and data science, you can take a look at these books:

- *PySpark in Action* by Jonathan Rioux (Manning, 2020, www.manning.com/books/pyspark-in-action?a_aid=jgp).
- *Mastering Large Datasets with Python* by John T. Wolohan (Manning, 2020, www.manning.com/books/mastering-large-datasets-with-python?a_aid=jgp).

---

[4]If you are outside the United States, you need to understand how important the SSN is. It governs your entire life. It has almost no connection to its original purpose: once an identifier for social benefits, it has become a tax identifier and financial shadow, following and tracking people. Identity thieves look for SSNs and other personal data so they can open bank accounts or access existing accounts.

[5]Extract, transform, and load is a classic data warehouse process.

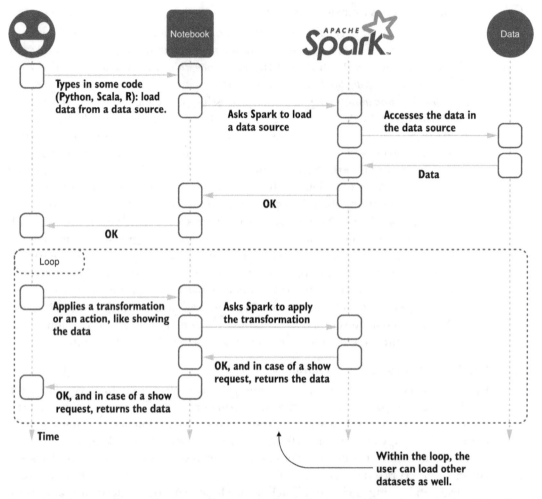

Figure 1.6 Sequence diagram for a data scientist using Spark: the user "talks" to the notebook, which calls Spark when needed. Spark directly handles ingestion. Each square represents a step, and each arrow represents a sequence. The diagram should be read chronologically, starting from the top.

In the use case described in figure 1.6, the data is loaded in Spark, and then the user will play with it, apply transformations, and display part of the data. Displaying the data is not the end of the process. The user will be able to continue in an interactive manner, as in a physical notebook, where you write recipes, take notes, and so on. At the end, the notebook user can save the data to files or databases, or produce (interactive) reports.

1.3   What can you do with Spark?

Spark is used in various kinds of projects, so let's explore a handful of them. All use cases involve data that cannot fit or be processed on a single computer (aka big data) and therefore require a cluster of computers—hence the need for a distributed operating system, specialized in analytics.

The definition of *big data* has evolved over time, from data with characteristics known as the five Vs[6] to "data that cannot fit on a single computer." I dislike this definition; as you probably know, many RDBMSs split data over several servers. As with many concepts, you may have to make your own definition. This book will hopefully help you.

For me, big data is the collection of datasets, available everywhere in the enterprise, aggregated in a single location, on which you can run basic analytics to more advanced analytics, like machine and deep learning. Those bigger datasets can become the basis for artificial intelligence (AI). Technologies, size, or number of computers are irrelevant to this concept.

Spark, through its analytics features and natively distributed architecture, can address big data, whether or not you think it is big, or whether it fits in one or many computers. Simply remember that the traditional report output on a 132-column dot-matrix printer is not a typical use case for Spark. Let's discover a few real-world examples.

1.3.1 Spark predicts restaurant quality at NC eateries

In most of the United States, restaurants require inspections by local health departments in order to operate and are graded based on these inspections. A higher grade does not signify better food, but it might give an indication of whether you are going to die after you have BBQ in a certain shack on your trip to the South. Grades measure the cleanliness of the kitchen, how safely the food is stored, and many more criteria to (hopefully) avoid food-borne illnesses.

In North Carolina, restaurants are graded on a scale of 0 to 100. Each county offers access to the restaurant's grade, but there is no central location for accessing the information statewide.

NCEatery.com is a consumer-oriented website that list restaurants with their inspection grades over time. The ambition of NCEatery.com is to centralize this information and to run predictive analytics on restaurants to see if we can discover patterns in restaurant quality. *Is this place I loved two years ago going downhill?*

In the backend of the website, Apache Spark ingests datasets of restaurants, inspections, and violations data coming from different counties, crunches the data, and publishes a summary on the website. During the crunching phase, several data quality rules are applied, as well as machine learning to try to project inspections and scores. Spark processes 1.6×10^{21} datapoints and publishes about 2,500 pages every 18 hours using a small cluster. This ongoing project is in the process of onboarding more NC counties.

1.3.2 Spark allows fast data transfer for Lumeris

Lumeris is an information-based health-care services company, based in St. Louis, Missouri. It has traditionally helped health-care providers get more insights from their data. The company's state-of-the-art IT system needed a boost to accommodate more customers and drive more powerful insights from the data it had.

---

[6]The five Vs are volume (quantity of generated and stored data), variety (type and nature of the data), velocity (speed at which the data is generated and processed), variability (inconsistency of the dataset), and veracity (data quality can vary greatly)—adapted from Wikipedia and IBM.

At Lumeris, as part of the data engineering processes, Apache Spark ingests thousands of comma-separated values (CSV) files stored on Amazon Simple Storage Service (S3), builds health-care-compliant HL7 FHIR resources,[7] and saves them in a specialized document store where they can be consumed by both the existing applications and a new generation of client applications.

This technology stack allows Lumeris to continue its growth, both in terms of processed data and applications. Down the road, with the help of this technology, Lumeris aims to save lives.

1.3.3   *Spark analyzes equipment logs for CERN*

CERN, or the European Organization for Nuclear Research, was founded in 1954. It is home to the Large Hadron Collider (LHC), a 27-kilometer ring located 100 meters under the border between France and Switzerland, in Geneva.

The giant physics experiments run there generate 1 petabyte (PB) of data per second. After significant filtering, the data is reduced to 900 GB per day.

After experiments with Oracle, Impala, and Spark, the CERN team designed the Next CERN Accelerator Logging Service (NXCALS) around Spark on an on-premises cloud running OpenStack with up to 250,000 cores. The consumers of this impressive architecture are scientists (through custom applications and Jupyter notebooks), developers, and apps. The ambition for CERN is to onboard even more data and increase the overall velocity of data processing.

1.3.4   *Other use cases*

Spark has been involved in many other use cases, including the following:

- Building interactive data-wrangling tools, such as IBM's Watson Studio and Databricks' notebooks
- Monitoring the quality of video feeds for TV channels like MTV or Nickelodeon[8]
- Monitoring online video game players for bad behavior and adjusting the player interaction in quasi real-time to maximize all players' positive experiences, via the company Riot Games

1.4   *Why you will love the dataframe*

In this section, my goal is to make you love the dataframe. You will learn just enough to want to discover more, which you will do as you explore deeper in chapter 3 and throughout the book. A *dataframe* is both a data container and an API.

The concept of a dataframe is essential to Spark. However, the concept is not difficult to understand. You will use dataframes all the time. In this section, you will look at what

---

[7] Health Level Seven International (HL7) is a not-for-profit, ANSI-accredited standards developing organization dedicated to facilitating the exchange, integration, sharing, and retrieval of electronic health information. HL7 is supported by more than 1,600 members from over 50 countries. Fast Healthcare Interoperability Resources (FHIR) is one of the latest specification standards for exchanging health-care information.

[8] See "How MTV and Nickelodeon Use Real-Time Big Data Analytics to Improve Customer Experience" by Bernard Marr, Forbes, January 2017 (http://bit.ly/2ynJvUt).

a dataframe is from a Java (software engineer) and an RDBMS (data engineer) perspective. Once you are familiar with some of the analogy, I will wrap up with a diagram.

> ### A question of spelling
> In most literature, you will find a different spelling for dataframe: DataFrame. I decided to settle for the most English way of writing it, which, I concur, may be odd for a French native. Nevertheless, and despite its majestic grandeur, the dataframe remains a common noun, so no reason to play with uppercase letters here and there. It's not a burger place!

1.4.1 The dataframe from a Java perspective

If your background is in Java and you have some Java Database Connectivity (JDBC) experience, the dataframe will look like a `ResultSet`. It contains data; it has an API . . .

Similarities between a `ResultSet` and a dataframe are as follows:

- Data is accessible through a simple API.
- You can access the schema.

Here are some differences:

- You do not browse through it with a `next()` method.
- Its API is extensible through user-defined functions (UDFs). You can write or wrap existing code and add it to Spark. This code will then be accessible in a distributed mode. You will study UDFs in chapter 16.
- If you want to access the data, you first get the `Row` and then go through the columns of the row with getters (similar to a `ResultSet`).
- Metadata is fairly basic, as there are no primary or foreign keys or indexes in Spark.

In Java, a dataframe is implemented as a `Dataset<Row>` (pronounced "a dataset of rows").

1.4.2 The dataframe from an RDBMS perspective

If you come more from an RDBMS background, you may find that a dataframe is like a table. The following are similarities:

- Data is described in columns and rows.
- Columns are strongly typed.

Here are some differences:

- Data can be nested, as in a JSON or XML document. Chapter 7 describes ingestion of those documents, and you will use those nested constructs in chapter 13.
- You don't update or delete entire rows; you create new dataframes.
- You can easily add or remove columns.
- There are no constraints, indices, primary or foreign keys, or triggers on the dataframe.

1.4.3   *A graphical representation of the dataframe*

The dataframe is a powerful tool you will use throughout the book and your journey with Spark. Its powerful API and storage capabilities make it the key element from which everything radiates. Figure 1.7 shows one way to imagine the API, implementation, and storage.

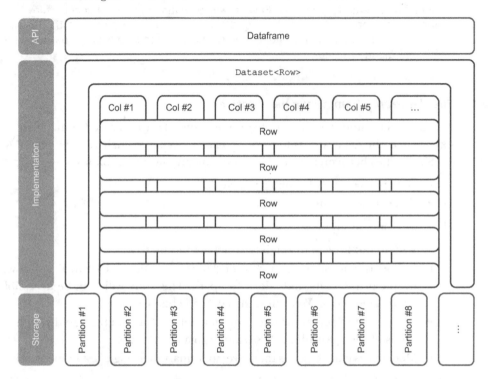

Figure 1.7   **A graphical representation of the dataframe, its implementation in Java (`Dataset<Row>`), the schema, and partitioned storage. As a developer, you will use the dataset API, which will allow you to manipulate columns and rows. The storage in partitions can also be accessed, mainly for optimization; you will learn more about partitions in chapter 2.**

1.5   *Your first example*

It is time for your first example. Your goal is to run Spark with a simple application that will read a file, store its content in a dataframe, and display the result. You will learn how to set up your working environment, which you will be using throughout the book. You will also learn how to interact with Spark and do basic operations.

As you will discover, most chapters contain dedicated labs, which you can hack to experiment with the code. Each lab has a dataset (as often as possible, a real-life one) as well as one or more code listings.

To get started, you will do the following:

- Install basic software, which you may already have: Git, Maven, Eclipse.
- Download the code by cloning it from GitHub.
- Execute the example, which will load a basic CSV file and display some rows.

1.5.1 Recommended software

This section provides the list of software you will be using throughout the book. Detailed installation instructions for the required software are in appendixes A and B.

This book uses the following software:

- Apache Spark 3.0.0.
- Mainly macOS Catalina, but examples also run on Ubuntu 14 to 18 and on Windows 10.
- Java 8 (although you won't use a lot of the constructs introduced in version 8, such as lambda functions). I know that Java 11 is available, but most enterprises are slow at adopting the newer version (and I found Oracle's recent Java strategy a little confusing). As of now, only Spark v3 is certified on Java 11.

The examples will use either the command line or Eclipse. For the command line, you can use the following:

- Maven: the book uses version 3.5.2, but any recent version will work.
- Git version 2.13.6, but any recent version will work as well. On macOS, you can use the version packaged with Xcode. On Windows, you can download from https://git-scm.com/download/win. If you like graphical user interfaces (GUIs), I highly recommend Atlassian Sourcetree, which you can download from www.sourcetreeapp.com.

Projects use Maven's pom.xml structure, which can be imported or directly used in many integrated development environments (IDEs). However, all visual examples will use Eclipse. You could use any earlier version of Eclipse than 4.7.1a (Eclipse Oxygen), but Maven and Git integration have been enhanced in the Oxygen release of Eclipse. I highly recommend that you use at least the Oxygen releases, which are pretty old by now.

1.5.2 Downloading the code

The source code is in a public repository on GitHub. The URL of the repository is https://github.com/jgperrin/net.jgp.books.spark.ch01. Appendix D describes in great detail how to use Git on the command line, and Eclipse to download the code.

1.5.3 Running your first application

You are now ready to run your application! If you have any issues running your first app, appendix R should have you covered.

COMMAND LINE

On the command line, change to the working directory:

```
$ cd net.jgp.books.spark.ch01
```

Then run this:

```
$ mvn clean install exec:exec
```

ECLIPSE

After importing the project (see appendix D), locate CsvToDataframeApp.java in the Project Explorer. Right-click the file and then select Run As > 2 Java Application, as shown in figure 1.8. Look at the result in the console.

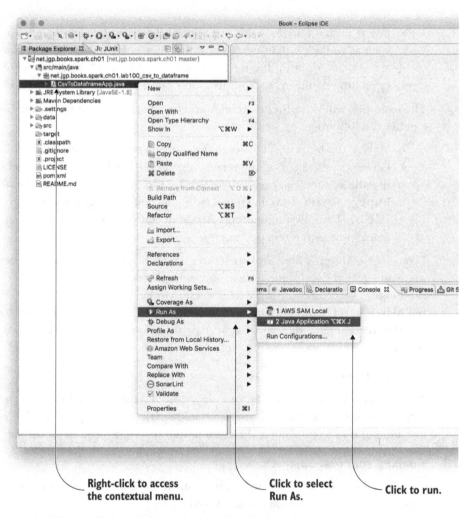

Figure 1.8   Eclipse with the project tree in the Project Explorer

Whether you use the command line or Eclipse, your result should look like this after a few seconds:

```
+---+--------+--------------------+-----------+--------------------+
| id|authorId|               title|releaseDate|                link|
+---+--------+--------------------+-----------+--------------------+
|  1|       1|Fantastic Beasts ...|   11/18/16|http://amzn.to/2k...|
|  2|       1|Harry Potter and ...|    10/6/15|http://amzn.to/2l...|
|  3|       1|The Tales of Beed...|    12/4/08|http://amzn.to/2k...|
|  4|       1|Harry Potter and ...|    10/4/16|http://amzn.to/2k...|
|  5|       2|Informix 12.10 on...|    4/23/17|http://amzn.to/2i...|
+---+--------+--------------------+-----------+--------------------+
only showing top 5 rows
```

Now, let's understand what happened.

1.5.4 Your first code

Finally, you are coding! In the previous section, you saw the output. It's time you run your first application. It will acquire a session, ask Spark to load a CSV file, and then display five rows (at most) of the dataset. Listing 1.1 provides the full program.

When it comes to showing code, two schools of thought exist: one school of thought is to show abstracts, and the other is to present all of the code. I am of the latter school: I like the example to be complete, rather than partial, as I don't want you to have to figure out the missing part or the needed packages, even if they are obvious.

Listing 1.1 Ingesting CSV

```java
package net.jgp.books.spark.ch01.lab100_csv_to_dataframe;

import org.apache.spark.sql.Dataset;
import org.apache.spark.sql.Row;
import org.apache.spark.sql.SparkSession;

public class CsvToDataframeApp {

    public static void main(String[] args) {          // main() is your entry
        CsvToDataframeApp app = new CsvToDataframeApp();  // point to the application.
        app.start();
    }

    private void start() {                             // Creates a session
        SparkSession spark = SparkSession.builder()    // on a local master
                .appName("CSV to Dataset")
                .master("local")
                .getOrCreate();
                                                       // Reads a CSV file with header,
                                                       // called books.csv, and stores
        Dataset<Row> df = spark.read().format("csv")   // it in a dataframe
                .option("header", "true")
                .load("data/books.csv");

        df.show(5);            // Shows at most five rows from the dataframe
    }
}
```

Although the example is simple, you have accomplished the following:

- Installed all the components you need to work with Spark. (Yes, it is that easy!)
- Created a session where code can be executed.
- Loaded a CSV data file.
- Displayed five rows of this dataset.

You are now ready to get deeper into Apache Spark and understand a little more about what is under the hood.

Summary

- Spark is an analytics operating system; you can use it to process workloads and algorithms in a distributed way. And it's not only good for analytics: you can use Spark for data transfer, massive data transformation, log analysis, and more.
- Spark supports SQL, Java, Scala, R, and Python as a programming interface, but in this book, we focus on Java (and sometimes Python).
- Spark's internal main data storage is the dataframe. The dataframe combines storage capacity with an API.
- If you have experience with JDBC development, you will find similarities with a JDBC `ResultSet`.
- If you have experience with relational database development, you can compare a dataframe to a table with less metadata.
- In Java, a dataframe is implemented as a `Dataset<Row>`.
- You can quickly set up Spark with Maven and Eclipse. Spark does not need to be installed.
- Spark is not limited to the MapReduce algorithm: its API allows a lot of algorithms to be applied to data.
- Streaming is used more and more frequently in enterprises, as businesses want access to real-time analytics. Spark supports streaming.
- Analytics have evolved from simple joins and aggregations. Enterprises want computers to think for us; hence Spark supports machine learning and deep learning.
- Graphs are a special use case of analytics, but nevertheless, Spark supports them.

Architecture and flow

This chapter covers

- Building a mental model of Spark for a typical use case
- Understanding the associated Java code
- Exploring the general architecture of a Spark application
- Understanding the flow of data

In this chapter, you will build a mental model of Apache Spark. A *mental model* is an explanation of how something works in the real world, using your thought process and following diagrams. The goal of this chapter is to help you define your own ideas about the thought process I will walk you through. I will use a lot of diagrams and some code. It would be extremely pretentious to build a *unique* Spark mental model; this model will describe a typical scenario involving loading, processing, and saving data. You will also walk through the Java code for these operations.

The scenario you will follow involves distributed loading of a CSV file, performing a small operation, and saving the result in a PostgreSQL database (and Apache Derby). Knowing or installing PostgreSQL is not required to understand the example. If you are familiar with using other RDBMSs and Java, you will easily adapt to this example. Appendix F provides additional help with relational databases (tips, installation, links, and more).

LAB Code and sample data are available on GitHub at https://github
.com/jgperrin/net.jgp.books.spark.ch02.

2.1   *Building your mental model*

In this section, you'll build a mental model of Spark. In terms of software, a mental
model is a conceptual map that you can use to plan, predict, diagnose, and debug your
applications. To start building the mental model, you'll work through a big data scenario. While learning the scenario, you'll explore Spark's overall architecture, flows,
and terminology, and will be well on your way to understanding Spark's big picture.

Imagine the following big data scenario: you are a bookseller who has a list of
authors in a file, and you want to perform a basic operation on the file and then save
it in a database. In technical terms, this process is as follows:

1   *Ingest* a CSV file, as you saw in chapter 1.
2   *Transform* the data by concatenating the last name and first name.
3   *Save* the result in a relational database.

Figure 2.1 illustrates what you and Spark are going to do.

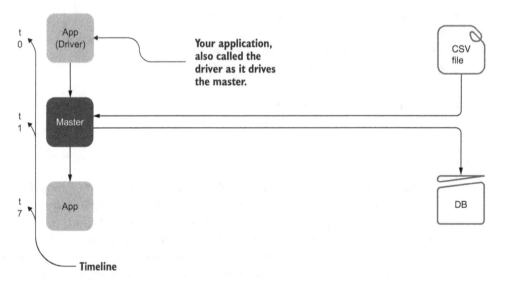

**Figure 2.1   I use specific icons throughout the book; check out "about the book" in the front matter
if they confuse you! Your application (also called the *driver*) connects to Apache Spark (the master),
asks it to load a CSV file, makes a transformation, and saves it to a database. On the left of the
diagram, you can see a timeline (here, t_0, t_1, and t_7); as you probably guessed, these represent steps.
Your application is the first and last element of this flow.**

Your application, or *driver*, connects to a Spark cluster. From there, the application
tells the cluster what to do: the application drives the cluster. In this scenario, the master starts by loading a CSV file and finishes by saving in a database.

EXAMPLE ENVIRONMENT For lab #100, I initially used Spark v2.4.0, PostgreSQL v10.1 with the PostgreSQL JDBC driver v42.1.4, on macOS v10.13.2 with Java 8. Lab #110 uses Apache Derby v10.14.2.0 as a backend. The code is mostly the same, so if you do not want to (or cannot) install PostgreSQL, follow along with lab #110.

2.2   *Using Java code to build your mental model*

Before you delve into each step of building the mental model, let's analyze the application as a whole. In this section, you will set the Java "decorum" before you deconstruct and deep dive into each line of code and its consequence.

Figure 2.2 is a basic representation of the process: Spark reads a CSV file; concatenates the last name, a comma, and the first name; and then saves the entire dataset in the database.

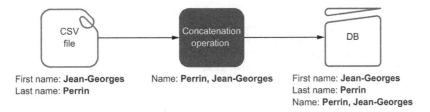

First name: **Jean-Georges**   Name: **Perrin, Jean-Georges**   First name: **Jean-Georges**
Last name: **Perrin**   Last name: **Perrin**
                                                                                                            Name: **Perrin, Jean-Georges**

Figure 2.2   A simple process in three steps: reading the CSV file, performing a simple concatenation operation, and saving the resulting data in the database

When you run this application, you will get a simple *Process complete* message. Figure 2.3 illustrates the result of the process. You have the ch02 table with three columns—fname,

Figure 2.3   The data from your CSV file, along with the additional column, in PostgreSQL. This illustration uses SQLPro, but you could use the standard tools packaged with the database (pgAdmin version 3 or 4).

lname, and the new column you want, name. If you need help with databases, refer to appendix F.

Listing 2.1 is the full application. I try to present the code as completely as possible, including the import statements, to prevent you from using wrong packages or deprecated classes with similar names. This code can be downloaded from GitHub at https://github.com/jgperrin/net.jgp.books.spark.ch02.

Listing 2.1 Ingesting the CSV, transforming, and saving in the database

```
package net.jgp.books.spark.ch02.lab100_csv_to_db;

import static org.apache.spark.sql.functions.concat;
import static org.apache.spark.sql.functions.lit;

import java.util.Properties;

import org.apache.spark.sql.Dataset;
import org.apache.spark.sql.Row;
import org.apache.spark.sql.SaveMode;
import org.apache.spark.sql.SparkSession;

public class CsvToRelationalDatabaseApp {

  public static void main(String[] args) {
    CsvToRelationalDatabaseApp app = new CsvToRelationalDatabaseApp();
    app.start();
  }

  private void start() {
    SparkSession spark = SparkSession.builder()
        .appName("CSV to DB")
        .master("local")
        .getOrCreate();
    Dataset<Row> df = spark.read()
        .format("csv")
        .option("header", "true")
        .load("data/authors.csv");
    df = df.withColumn(
        "name",
        concat(df.col("lname"),
            lit(", "), df.col("fname")));
    String dbConnectionUrl = "jdbc:postgresql://localhost/spark_labs";
    Properties prop = new Properties();
    prop.setProperty("driver", "org.postgresql.Driver");
    prop.setProperty("user", "jgp");
    prop.setProperty("password", "Spark<3Java");
    df.write()
        .mode(SaveMode.Overwrite)
        .jdbc(dbConnectionUrl, "ch02", prop);

    System.out.println("Process complete");
  }
}
```

Creates a session on a local master

Reads a CSV file with header, called authors.csv, and stores it in a dataframe

Creates a new column called "name" as the concatenation of lname, a virtual column containing ", " and the fname column

Both concat() and lit() were statically imported.

The connection URL, assuming your PostgreSQL instance runs locally on the default port, and the database you use is spark_labs.

Properties to connect to the database; the JDBC driver is part of your pom.xml (see listing 2.2).

Overwrites in a table called ch02

If you are curious and already feel comfortable, you can *roast a few steps* (another French colloquialism for getting carried away), and refer to the Spark Javadoc at https://spark.apache.org/docs/latest/api/java/index.html.

You will need the PostgreSQL JDBC driver. Therefore, your pom.xml file should contain the dependencies in the following listing.

Listing 2.2   Properties and dependencies of your pom.xml (abstract)

Spark is built using a specific Scala version. You can use a property in your Maven project file (aka pom.xml or simply pom) to ensure that you have a consistent version across all your Spark libraries. The property scala.version has a value of 2.12 and is reused in both the spark-core and spark-sql artifacts.

```xml
<properties>
    <scala.version>2.12</scala.version>
    <spark.version>2.4.5</spark.version>
    <postgresql.version>42.1.4</postgresql.version>
</properties>

<dependencies>
    <dependency>
        <groupId>org.apache.spark</groupId>
        <artifactId>spark-core_${scala.version}</artifactId>
        <version>${spark.version}</version>
    </dependency>

    <dependency>
        <groupId>org.apache.spark</groupId>
        <artifactId>spark-sql_${scala.version}</artifactId>
        <version>${spark.version}</version>
    </dependency>

    <dependency>
        <groupId>org.postgresql</groupId>
        <artifactId>postgresql</artifactId>
        <version>${postgresql.version}</version>
    </dependency>
</dependencies>
```

The property spark.version, here 2.4.5, is reused in both the spark-core and spark-sql artifacts. With the coming Apache Spark 3.0.0, use 3.0.0.

Reusing the scala.version property as a constant in the artifact's ID

Reusing the spark.version property as a constant in the dependency version

---

Because the pom.xml is shared with all the labs of a chapter, and because lab #110 uses Apache Derby instead of PostgreSQL, the pom.xml in the repository (in GitHub) also includes the dependencies for Derby.

2.3   *Walking through your application*

You have seen a simple use case of Spark ingesting data from a CSV file, performing a simple operation, and then storing the result in the database. In this section, you'll look at what really happens behind the scenes.

To start, you will look a little more closely at the very first operation: the connection to the master. After this nonfunctional step, let's walk through the ingestion, the transformation, and, finally, the publishing of the data in the RDBMS.

2.3.1 *Connecting to a master*

For every Spark application, the first operation is to connect to the Spark master and get a Spark *session*. This is an operation you will do every time. This is illustrated by the code fragment in listing 2.3 and by figure 2.4.

In this context, you are connecting to Spark in local mode. You will discover three ways to connect to and use Spark in chapter 5.

> **Listing 2.3 Getting a Spark session**

```
SparkSession spark = SparkSession.builder()
    .appName("CSV to DB")
    .master("local")
    .getOrCreate();
```

Method chaining makes Java more compact

In recent years, more and more Java APIs have been using *method chaining*, as in `SparkSession.builder().appName(…).master(…).getOrCreate()`. Previously, you may have seen more intermediate objects being created, a bit like this:

```
Object1 o1 = new Object1();
Object2 o2 = o1.getObject2();
o2.set("something");
```

Spark's API uses a lot of method chaining. Method chaining makes your code more compact and more readable. But one major drawback is debugging: imagine a null pointer exception (NPE) in the middle of your chain, and you'll spend more time debugging it.

All the illustrations in this chapter represent a timeline. At t_0, you start your application (your `main()` function), and at t_1, you get your session.

This first step is always to connect to a master. You can now ask Spark to load the CSV file.

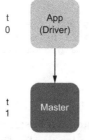

Figure 2.4 The application (or driver) connects to the master and gets a Spark session. The arrow indicates the flow of sequence: at t_0, you start your application, and at t_1, you get your Spark session.

Local mode is not a cluster, but it's much easier

In order for you to be able to run the example in this chapter without setting up a full cluster, I specified `local` as the value for the master because you are running Spark in *local mode*. If you had a cluster, you would give the address of this cluster. You will learn more about clusters in chapters 5 and 6.

For the sake of building your mental model, you will assume you have a cluster instead of the local mode.

2.3.2 Loading, or ingesting, the CSV file

Loading, ingesting, and *reading* are synonyms for what you are going to do now: ask Spark to load the data contained in the CSV file. Spark can use distributed ingestion through the various nodes of the cluster. It's about time to ask Spark to load the file, right? You are several pages into this chapter, learning new concepts, so it's prime time for Spark to do something for you.

But as you can imagine, as with all good masters, Spark does not do much. Spark relies on *slaves*, or *workers*. You will find both terms in the Spark documentation; despite being French and, by nature, indecisive, I will use *worker*.

In our scenario, illustrated in figure 2.5, you have three workers. *Distributed* ingestion means you will ask our three workers to ingest at the same time.

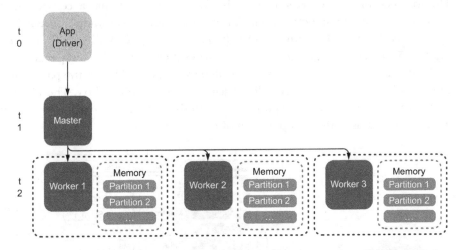

Figure 2.5   The master knows its workers. Here, you have three workers. This is a logical representation: any worker could be on the same physical node as the master. Each worker has memory (of course!), which it will use via partitions.

At t_2, the master tells the workers to load the file, as coded in listing 2.4. You may wonder, "If you have three workers, which one is loading the file?" or "If they load simultaneously, how do they know where to start and finish?" Spark will ingest the CSV file in a distributed way. The file must be on a shared drive, distributed filesystem (like HDFS in chapter 18), or shared via a shared filesystem mechanism such as Dropbox, Box, Nextcloud, or ownCloud. In this context, a *partition* is a dedicated area in the worker's memory.

Listing 2.4   Reading the authors file

```
Dataset<Row> df = spark.read()
    .format("csv")
    .option("header", "true")
    .load("data/authors.csv");
```

Let's take a second to look at our CSV file (see listing 2.5). It is a simple file with two columns: lname for the last name, and fname for the first name. The first line of the file is a header. The file contains six more lines, which will become six rows in our dataframe.

Listing 2.5   A good ol' CSV file

```
lname,fname
Pascal,Blaise
Voltaire,François
Perrin,Jean-Georges
Maréchal,Pierre Sylvain
Karau,Holden
Zaharia,Matei
```

The workers will create tasks to read the file. Each worker has access to the node's memory and will assign a memory partition to the task, as shown in figure 2.6.

At t_4, each task will continue by reading a part of the CSV file, as illustrated in figure 2.7. As the task is ingesting its rows, it stores them in a dedicated partition.

Figure 2.7 shows the record being copied from the CSV file to the partition during the ingestion process, within the R > P (Record to Partition) box. The Memory box shows which records are in which partition. In this example, record 1, which contains Blaise Pascal, is in the first partition of the first worker.

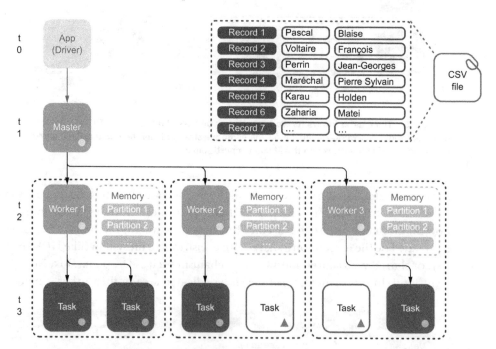

Figure 2.6   The tasks are being created based on available resources. The worker may create several tasks and will assign a memory partition to each task. The solid tasks are running (they also have a dot), to contrast with nonworking tasks (from another application, for example), which are hollow and have a triangle.

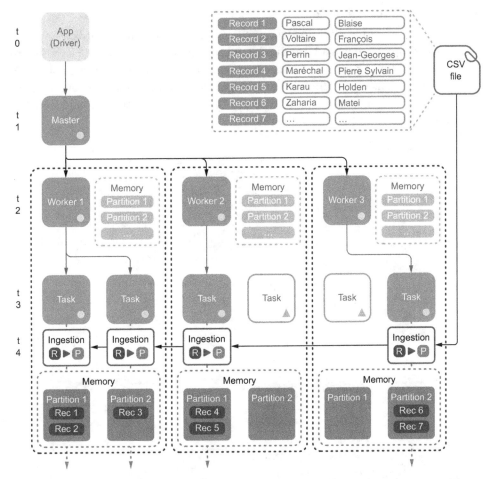

Figure 2.7 As the ingestion is taking place, each task loads records into its own memory partition, as indicated by the R > P (Record to Partition) box. The partition box contains the records after the ingestion has been completed.

Why should you care about partitions and their locations?

Because your operations are pretty simple (for example, concatenating two fields in a third one), Spark will be very fast.

As you will see in chapters 12 and 13, Spark can join data from multiple datasets and can perform data aggregation, exactly as you do those operations with your relational database. Now imagine that you are joining data from the first partition of worker 1 with data in the second partition of worker 2: all that data will have to be transferred, which is a costly operation.

You can repartition the data, which can make your applications more efficient, as you will see in chapter 17.

2.3.3   *Transforming your data*

After the data has been loaded, at t_5, you can process the records. Your operation is fairly simple: you will add to the dataframe a new column, called name. The full name (in the column name) is a concatenation of the last name (from the column lname), a comma, a space, and the first name (from the column fname). So, Jean-Georges (first name) and Perrin (last name) becomes Perrin, Jean-Georges. Listing 2.6 describes the process, and figure 2.8 illustrates it.

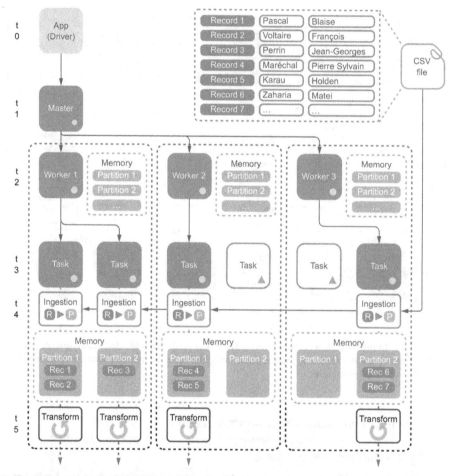

Figure 2.8   At t_5, Spark adds the transformation step to your flow. Each task will continue to perform its work, getting all first and last names from the memory partition to create the new name.

Listing 2.6   Adding a column to your dataframe

```
df = df.withColumn(
    "name",
    concat(df.col("lname"), lit(", "), df.col("fname")));
```

> **Spark is lazy**
>
> As Seth Rogen said, "I am lazy, but for some reason, I am so paranoid that I end up working hard."[1] This is how Spark acts. At this time, you told Spark to concatenate the fields, but it did not do anything.
>
> Spark is lazy: it will work only when asked. Spark will stack up all your requests, and when it needs to, it will optimize the operations and do the hard work. You will look more closely at its laziness in chapter 4. And, like Seth, when you ask nicely, Spark will work very hard.
>
> In this situation, you are using the `withColumn()` method, which is a *transformation*. Spark will start processing only when it sees an *action*, such as the `write()` method in listing 2.7.

You are now ready for the last operation: saving the result in the database.

2.3.4 *Saving the work done in your dataframe to a database*

It's time to save your result to the database, after ingesting the CSV file and transforming the data in the dataframe. The code responsible for this operation is in the following listing and is illustrated in figure 2.9.

Listing 2.7 Saving the data to the database

```
String dbConnectionUrl = "jdbc:postgresql://localhost/spark_labs";

Properties prop = new Properties();
prop.setProperty("driver", "org.postgresql.Driver");
prop.setProperty("user", "jgp");
prop.setProperty("password", "Spark<3Java");

df.write()
    .mode(SaveMode.Overwrite)
    .jdbc(dbConnectionUrl, "ch02", prop);
```

As you are certainly familiar with JDBC, you have probably noticed that Spark expects similar information:

- A JDBC connection URL
- The name of a driver
- A user
- A password

The `write()` method returns a `DataFrameWriter` object on which you can chain a `mode()` method to specify how to write; here, you will overwrite the data in the table.

---

[1]Seth Rogen is a Canadian-American comedian and filmmaker, known for *The Interview* and for being Steve Wozniak in the *Steve Jobs* 2015 documentary; see more at www.imdb.com/name/nm0736622/.

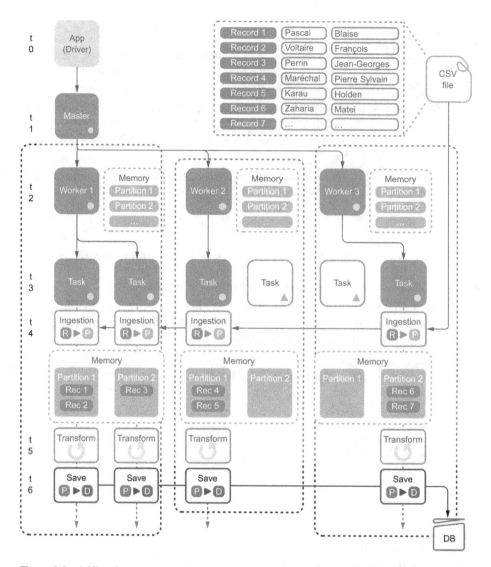

Figure 2.9 Adding the save operation to your workflow, as you copy the data in the partition (P) to the database (D) at t_6, as indicated by the P > D boxes. Each task will open a connection to the database.

Figure 2.10 represents your application's full mental model. It is important to remember the following:

- The whole dataset never hits our application (driver). The dataset is split between the partitions on the workers, not on the driver.
- The entire processing takes place in the workers.
- The workers save the data in their partition to the database. In this scenario, you have four partitions, which means four connections to the database when

you save the data. Imagine a similar scenario with 200,000 tasks trying first to connect to the database and then inserting data. A fine-tuned database server will refuse too many connections, which will require more control in the application. A solution to this load issue is addressed in chapter 17 through repartitioning and the options when exporting to a database.

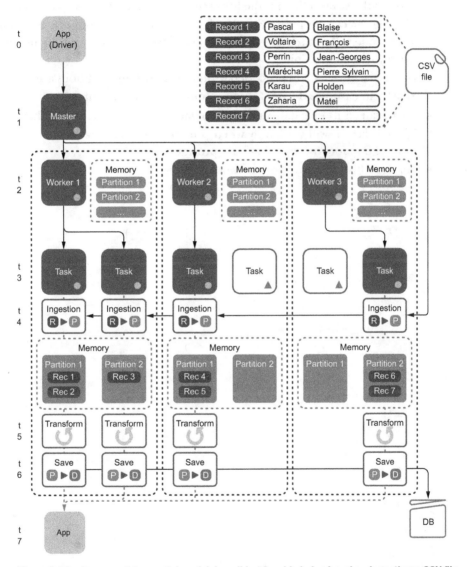

Figure 2.10 Our complete mental model describing Spark's behavior when ingesting a CSV file, transforming its data, and then saving the data to a database. The diagram also illustrates the usage of memory in each worker and the attribution of records in those partitions. The R > P symbol indicates that you are loading records in the partition, and the P > D symbol indicates that you are copying the data in the partition to the database. Finally, the timeline, at *t₇*, returns to the application: no data has ever been transferred from the worker to the application.

Summary

- Your application is the driver. Data may not have to come to the driver; it can be driven remotely. It is important to remember this when you size your deployment (see chapters 5, 6, and 18).
- The driver connects to a master and gets a session. Data will be attached to this session; the session defines the life cycle of the data on the worker's nodes.
- The master can be local (your local machine) or a remote cluster. Using the local mode will not require you to build a cluster, making your life much easier while you are developing.
- Data is partitioned and processed within the partition. Partitions are in memory.
- Spark can easily read from CSV files (more details in chapter 7).
- Spark can easily save data in relational databases (more details in chapter 17).
- Spark is lazy: it will work only when you ask it to do so via an action. This laziness is good for you, and chapter 4 provides more details.
- Spark's APIs rely heavily on method chaining.

The majestic role of the dataframe

This chapter covers

- Using the dataframe
- The essential (majestic) role of the dataframe in Spark
- Understanding data immutability
- Quickly debugging a dataframe's schema
- Understanding the lower-level storage in RDDs

In this chapter, you will learn about using the dataframe. You'll learn that the dataframe is so important in a Spark application because it contains typed data through a schema and offers a powerful API.

As you saw in previous chapters, Spark is a marvelous distributed analytics engine. Wikipedia defines an *operating system* (*OS*) as "system software that manages computer hardware [and] software resources, and provides common services for computer programs." In chapter 1, I even qualify Spark as an operating system, as it offers all the services needed to build applications and manage resources. To use Spark in a programmatic way, you need understand some of its key APIs. To perform analytics and data operations, Spark needs storage, both logical (at the application level) and physical (at the hardware level).

At the logical level, the favorite storage container is the *dataframe*, a data structure similar to a table in the relational database world. In this chapter, you will dig into the structure of the dataframe and learn how to use the dataframe via its API.

Transformations are operations you perform on data, such as extracting a year from a date, combining two fields, normalizing data, and so on. In this chapter, you'll learn how to use dataframe-specific functions to perform transformations, as well as methods directly attached to the dataframe API. You will merge two dataframes into one by using a SQL union-like operation. You'll also see the difference between a dataset and a dataframe, and how to go from one to the other.

Finally, you will look at the resilient distributed dataset (RDD), which was the first generation of storage in Spark. The dataframe is built on top of the RDD concept, and you may encounter RDDs in discussions and projects.

Examples in this chapter are divided into labs. At the end of the chapter, you will ingest two files in two dataframes, modify their schema so they match, and union the result. You will see how Spark handles the storage as you go through those operations. At various steps, you will inspect the dataframes.

LAB   Examples from this chapter are available in GitHub at https://github .com/jgperrin/net.jgp.books.spark.ch03.

3.1   *The essential role of the dataframe in Spark*

In this section, you will learn what a dataframe is and how it is organized. You will also learn about immutability.

A *dataframe* is both a data structure and an API, as illustrated in figure 3.1. Spark's dataframe API is used within Spark SQL, Spark Streaming, MLlib (for machine

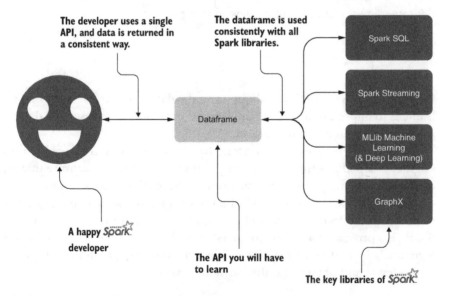

Figure 3.1   By having to learn only one API to do Spark SQL, streaming, machine and deep learning, and graph-based analytics, the developer is happier!

learning), and GraphX to manipulate graph-based data structures within Spark. Using this unified API drastically simplifies access to those technologies. You will not have to learn an API for each sublibrary.

It is probably odd to describe the dataframe as majestic, but this qualifier suits it perfectly. Just as majestic artwork attracts curiosity, a majestic oak dominates the forest, and majestic walls protect a castle, the dataframe is majestic in the world of Spark.

3.1.1 *Organization of a dataframe*

In this section, you will learn how a dataframe organizes data. A *dataframe* is a set of records organized into named columns. It is equivalent to a table in a relational database or a `ResultSet` in Java. Figure 3.2 illustrates a dataframe.

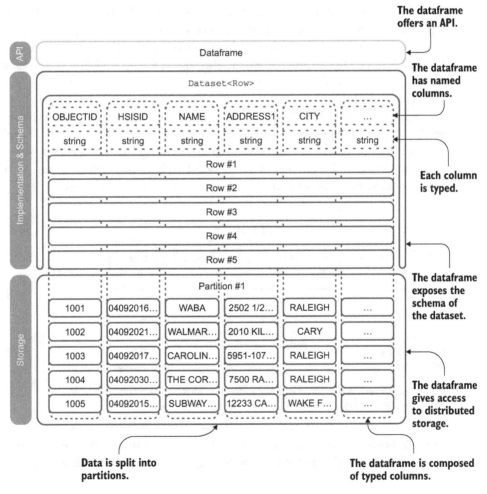

Figure 3.2 A full dataframe with its schema and data: the dataframe is implemented as a dataset of rows (`Dataset<Row>`). Each column is named and typed. The data itself is in partitions. This illustration is based on the ingestion of the Wake County restaurant dataset used in section 3.2.1.

Dataframes can be constructed from a wide array of sources, such as files, databases, or custom data sources. The key concept of the dataframe is its API, which is available in Java, Python, Scala, and R. In Java, a dataframe is represented by a dataset of rows: `Dataset<Row>`.

Storage can be in memory or on disk, based on Spark's strategy at the moment, but it will use memory as much as it can.

Dataframes include the schema in a form of `StructType`, which can be used for introspection. Dataframes also include a `printSchema()` method to more quickly debug your dataframes. Enough theory—let's practice!

3.1.2 *Immutability is not a swear word*

Dataframes, as well as datasets and RDDs (discussed in section 3.4), are considered immutable storage. *Immutability* is defined as *unchangeable*. When applied to an object, it means its state cannot be modified after it is created.

I think this terminology is counterintuitive. When I first started working with Spark, I had a difficult time embracing the concept: *Let's work with this brilliant piece of technology designed for data processing, but the data is immutable. You expect me to process data, but it cannot be changed?*

Figure 3.3 gives an explanation: in its first state, data is immutable; then you start modifying it, but Spark stores only the steps of your transformation, not every step of the transformed data. Let me rephrase that: *Spark stores the initial state of the data*, in an immutable way, and then *keeps the recipe (a list of the transformations)*. The intermediate data is not stored. Chapter 4 digs deeper into transformations.

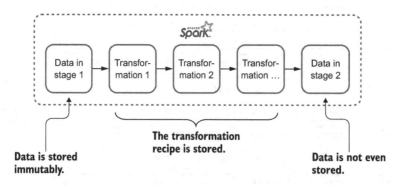

Figure 3.3 A typical flow: data is initially stored in an immutable way. The recipe for transformations is stored, not the various stages of the data.

The *why* becomes easier to understand when you add nodes. Whereas figure 3.3 illustrates a typical Spark flow with one node, figure 3.4 illustrates with more nodes.

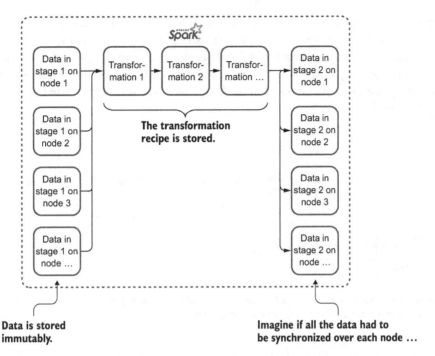

Figure 3.4 As you add nodes, imagine the complexity of data synchronization. By keeping only the recipe (list of transformations), you reduce your dependency on storage and increase your reliability (resilience). No data is stored in stage 2.

Immutability becomes really important when you think in a distributed way. In terms of storage, you have two choices:

- You store data, and each modification is done immediately on every node, as in a relational database.
- You keep the data in sync over the nodes and share only the transformation recipe with the various nodes.

Spark uses the second solution, because it is faster to sync a recipe than all the data over each node. Chapter 4 covers optimization through Catalyst. *Catalyst* is the cool kid in charge of optimization in Spark processing. Immutability and recipes are cornerstones of this optimization engine.

Although immutability is brilliantly used by Spark as the foundation to optimize data processing, you will not have to think too much about it as you develop applications. Spark, like any good operating system, will handle the resources for you.

3.2 Using dataframes through examples

There's nothing like a small example to start with. You ingested files in chapters 1 and 2. But what happens after that?

In this section, you will perform two simple ingestions. Then you will study their schemas and storage in order to understand the behavior of dataframes as they're used in an application. The first ingestion is a list of restaurants in Wake County, North Carolina. The second dataset consists of restaurants in Durham County, North Carolina. You will then transform the datasets so you can combine them via a union.

These are key operations you will be performing as a Spark developer, so understanding the principles behind them will provide the foundation you need. Figure 3.5 illustrates the process.

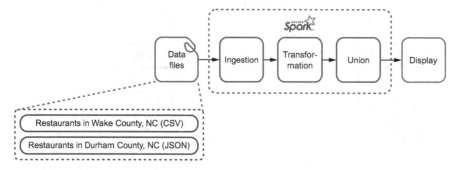

Figure 3.5   This chapter's labs will show ingestion of files, modification of the dataframes through transformation, union of the dataframes, and their display.

The destination (and final) dataframe, after the union operation, needs to have the same schema after both transformations, as illustrated in figure 3.6.

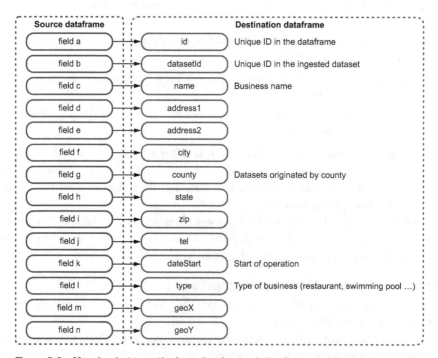

Figure 3.6   Mapping between the incoming (source) dataframe and the destination dataframe

3.2.1 A dataframe after a simple CSV ingestion

In this section, you will first ingest the data, and then you'll look at the data in the dataframe in order to understand the schema. This process is an important step in your understanding of the way Spark works.

The goal of the example is to normalize a dataset so it matches specific criteria, as you just saw in figure 3.6. I bet you like to go to restaurants. Maybe not every day, maybe not every kind, but each of you has preferences: type of food, distance from home, company, noise level, and so forth. Websites such as Yelp or OpenTable have rich datasets, but let's explore some open data. Figure 3.7 illustrates the process in this example.

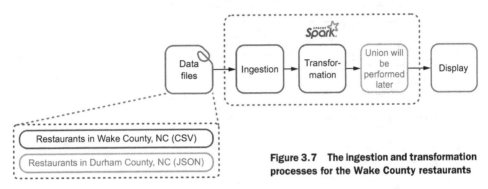

Figure 3.7   The ingestion and transformation processes for the Wake County restaurants

Your first dataset comes from Wake County in North Carolina at http://mng.bz/ 5AM7. It contains a list of restaurants in the county. The data can be downloaded directly from http://mng.bz/Jz2P.

You will now walk through an ingestion and a transformation of the dataframe so it matches the output (by renaming and dropping columns); then you'll scope out data partitions. As you are ingesting and transforming the data, you will also count the number of records. Figure 3.8 illustrates the mapping.

> **LAB** You can download the code from GitHub at https://github.com/jgperrin/ net.jgp.books.spark.ch03. This is lab #200 in package net.jgp.books.spark.ch03 .lab200_ingestion_schema_manipulation.

The visual result you are trying to achieve is a list of restaurants, matching the mapping defined in figure 3.8. Note that the following output has been altered to fit on this page:

```
*** Dataframe transformed
+---------------+-----------+-----+---------------+------+---------------+
|           name|       city|state|           type|county|             id|
+---------------+-----------+-----+---------------+------+---------------+
|           WABA|    RALEIGH|   NC|     Restaurant|  Wake|NC_Wake_0409...|
|WALMART DELI...|       CARY|   NC|     Food Stand|  Wake|NC_Wake_0409...|
|CAROLINA SUS...|    RALEIGH|   NC|     Restaurant|  Wake|NC_Wake_0409...|
|THE CORNER V...|    RALEIGH|   NC|Mobile Food ...|  Wake|NC_Wake_0409...|
|   SUBWAY #3726|WAKE FOREST|   NC|     Restaurant|  Wake|NC_Wake_0409...|
+---------------+-----------+-----+---------------+------+---------------+
only showing top 5 rows
```

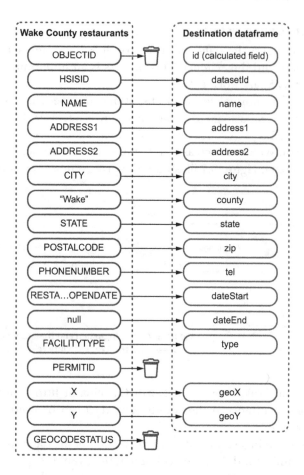

Figure 3.8   Mapping the input dataframe for the Wake County restaurants to the destination dataframe. The little trash cans indicate the fields you are dropping.

Because records spreading over multiple lines are a little difficult to read, I've added the records as a screenshot in figure 3.9.

```
*** Dataframe transformed
+-----------+--------------------+-------------------+--------+------------+---+----------+--------------+---------------------+----------------+------------+-------------+----+---------------------+
| datasetId|                name|  address1|address2|   city|state|       zip|           tel|           dateStart|            type|        geoX|        geoY|county|                   id|
+-----------+--------------------+-------------------+--------+------------+---+----------+--------------+---------------------+----------------+------------+-------------+----+---------------------+
|04092016024|                WABA|2502 1/2 HILLSBOR...|   null|    RALEIGH| NC|    27607|(919) 833-1710|2011-10-18T00:00:...|      Restaurant|-78.66818477|35.78783803| Wake|NC_Wake_04092016024|
|04092021693| WALMART DELI #2247|2010 KILDAIRE FAR...|   null|       CARY| NC|    27518|(919) 852-6651|2011-11-08T00:00:...|      Food Stand|-78.78211173|35.73717591| Wake|NC_Wake_04092021693|
|04092017012|CAROLINA SUSHI &a...|5951-107 POYNER V...|   null|    RALEIGH| NC|    27616|(919) 981-5835|2015-08-28T00:00:...|      Restaurant|-78.57038208|35.86511564| Wake|NC_Wake_04092017012|
|04092030288| THE CORNER VENEZU...|    7500 RAMBLE WAY |   null|    RALEIGH| NC|    27616|          null|2015-09-04T00:00:...|Mobile Food Units|  -78.537511|35.87630712| Wake|NC_Wake_04092030288|
|04092015530|       SUBWAY #3726|1Z233 CAPITAL BLVD |   null|WAKE FOREST| NC|27587-6200|(919) 556-8266|2009-12-11T00:00:...|      Restaurant|-78.54097555|35.98087357| Wake|NC_Wake_04092015530|
+-----------+--------------------+-------------------+--------+------------+---+----------+--------------+---------------------+----------------+------------+-------------+----+---------------------+
only showing top 5 rows
```

Figure 3.9   The first five rows of the Wake County restaurant dataset

To display those datasets (which are also dataframes), your code will look like the following:

> Static functions are a powerful tool in Spark; you will study them more in chapter 13, and appendix G provides a reference.

```
package net.jgp.books.spark.ch03.lab200_ingestion_schema_manipulation;

import static org.apache.spark.sql.functions.concat;
import static org.apache.spark.sql.functions.lit;
```

```
import org.apache.spark.Partition;
import org.apache.spark.sql.Dataset;
import org.apache.spark.sql.Row;
import org.apache.spark.sql.SparkSession;

public class IngestionSchemaManipulationApp {

  public static void main(String[] args) {
    IngestionSchemaManipulationApp app =
        new IngestionSchemaManipulationApp();
    app.start();
  }

  private void start() {
    SparkSession spark = SparkSession.builder()      ◄── Creates a Spark session
        .appName("Restaurants in Wake County, NC")
        .master("local")
        .getOrCreate();                                   Creates a dataframe
                                                          (a Dataset<Row>)
    Dataset<Row> df = spark.read().format("csv")   ◄─┘
        .option("header", "true")                    ◄── The CSV file has a header row.
        .load("data/Restaurants_in_Wake_County_NC.csv");  ◄─
    System.out.println("*** Right after ingestion");      Name of the file in
    df.show(5);                                            the data directory
```

Shows five records/rows (points to `df.show(5);`)

So far, this ingestion is similar to chapter 1's ingestion of a simple list of books, and chapter 2's ingestion of a list of authors. Ingestion is always done the same way, and chapters 7, 8, and 9 provide further details. Let's go a little deeper into the dataframe. You can print the schema to standard output (stdout) by using printSchema(). The result is as follows:

The first column of the schema is always the field name.

The second column (after the colon) is the type.

The third column, in parentheses, indicates nullability. In this example, all fields can be null.

Because schemas can be nested, they are displayed as a tree, with a root.

```
root
 |-- OBJECTID: string (nullable = true)
 |-- HSISID: string (nullable = true)
 |-- NAME: string (nullable = true)
 |-- ADDRESS1: string (nullable = true)
 |-- ADDRESS2: string (nullable = true)
 |-- CITY: string (nullable = true)
 |-- STATE: string (nullable = true)
 |-- POSTALCODE: string (nullable = true)
 |-- PHONENUMBER: string (nullable = true)
 |-- RESTAURANTOPENDATE: string (nullable = true)
 |-- FACILITYTYPE: string (nullable = true)
 |-- PERMITID: string (nullable = true)
 |-- X: string (nullable = true)
 |-- Y: string (nullable = true)
 |-- GEOCODESTATUS: string (nullable = true)
```

Appendix H provides more details on types. Your call is simply as follows:

```
df.printSchema();
```

There is an easy way to count the number of records you have in your dataframe. Say you want to display this:

```
We have 3440 records.
```

You simply use the following:

```
System.out.println("We have " + df.count() + " records.");
```

The goal of this section is for you to merge two dataframes, just as you can perform an SQL union of two tables. To make the union effective, you need similarly named columns in both dataframes. To get there, you can easily imagine that the schema of your first dataset was modified too. This is how it looks:

```
root
 |-- datasetId: string (nullable = true)
 |-- name: string (nullable = true)
 |-- address1: string (nullable = true)
 |-- address2: string (nullable = true)
 |-- city: string (nullable = true)
 |-- state: string (nullable = true)
 |-- zip: string (nullable = true)
 |-- tel: string (nullable = true)
 |-- dateStart: string (nullable = true)
 |-- type: string (nullable = true)
 |-- geoX: string (nullable = true)
 |-- geoY: string (nullable = true)
 |-- county: string (nullable = false)
 |-- id: string (nullable = true)
```

The columns are renamed to match the desired name.

These new columns add the county name and a made-up unique ID, respectively.

Let's walk through the transformation. Note the strong usage of method chaining. As defined in chapter 2, Java APIs can use method chaining, as in `SparkSession .builder().appName(…).master(…).getOrCreate()`, instead of creating an object at each step and passing it to the next operation.

You will use four methods of the dataframe and two static functions. You are likely familiar with static functions: they are those functions that are "grouped" in a class, but do not require the instantiation of the class.

Methods are easy to understand: they are attached to the object itself. Static functions are useful when you work directly with the values in the column. As you read this book, you will see more and more usage of these static functions, and they are described in more detail in chapter 13 and appendix G.

If you do not find a function that does what you want (for example, a specific transformation or a call to an existing library you may have), you can write your own functions. These are called *user-defined functions* (*UDFs*), which you will study in chapter 16.

Let's look at the methods and functions you need now:

- withColumn() method—Creates a new column from an expression or a column.
- withColumnRenamed() method—Renames a column.
- col() method—Gets a column from its name. Some methods will take the column name as an argument, and some require a Column object.
- drop() method—Drops a column from the dataframe. This method accepts an instance of a Column object or a column name.
- lit() functions—Creates a column with a value; literally, a literal value.
- concat() function—Concatenates the values in a set of columns.

You can look at the code now:

```
df = df.withColumn("county", lit("Wake"))
    .withColumnRenamed("HSISID", "datasetId")
    .withColumnRenamed("NAME", "name")
    .withColumnRenamed("ADDRESS1", "address1")
    .withColumnRenamed("ADDRESS2", "address2")
    .withColumnRenamed("CITY", "city")
    .withColumnRenamed("STATE", "state")
    .withColumnRenamed("POSTALCODE", "zip")
    .withColumnRenamed("PHONENUMBER", "tel")
    .withColumnRenamed("RESTAURANTOPENDATE", "dateStart")
    .withColumnRenamed("FACILITYTYPE", "type")
    .withColumnRenamed("X", "geoX")
    .withColumnRenamed("Y", "geoY")
    .drop("OBJECTID")
    .drop("PERMITID")
    .drop("GEOCODESTATUS");
```

Creates a new column called "county" containing the value "Wake" in every record

Simply renames column names to what you need in your new dataset

Columns to be dropped

You may need a unique identifier for each record. You can call this column id and build it by concatenating the following:

1 The state
2 An underscore (_)
3 The county
4 An underscore (_)
5 The identifier within the dataset

The code looks like this:

```
df = df.withColumn("id", concat(
    df.col("state"), lit("_"),
    df.col("county"), lit("_"),
    df.col("datasetId")));
```

Finally, you can display five records and print the schema:

```
System.out.println("*** Dataframe transformed");
df.show(5);
df.printSchema();
```

3.2.2   *Data is stored in partitions*

Now that you have loaded the data, you can see where it is stored. This will show you how Spark stores data internally. Data is not stored physically in the dataframe, but in *partitions,* as shown in figure 3.1 and in a simplified figure 3.10.

Partitions are not directly accessible from the dataframe; you will need to look at partitions through the RDDs. You will learn more about the RDDs a little later in section 3.4.

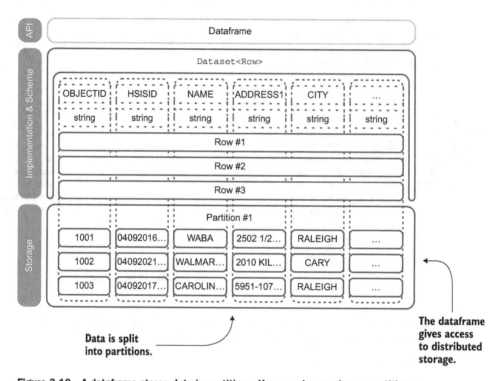

Figure 3.10   A dataframe stores data in partitions. Here, we have only one partition.

Partitions are created, and data is assigned to each partition automatically based on your infrastructure (number of nodes and size of the dataset). Because of the size of the dataset and the laptop I am using, only one partition is used in this scenario. You can find out how many partitions you have with the following code:

```
System.out.println("*** Looking at partitions");
Partition[] partitions = df.rdd().partitions();
int partitionCount = partitions.length;
System.out.println("Partition count before repartition: " +
    partitionCount);
```

**You access the RDD through rdd()
and then get to the partitions.**

You can repartition the dataframe to use four partitions by using the `repartition()` method. Repartitioning can increase performance:

```
df = df.repartition(4);
System.out.println("Partition count after repartition: " +
    df.rdd().partitions().length);
```

3.2.3 Digging in the schema

In the previous section, you learned about accessing the schema by using `printSchema()`. It is important to know the structure of the data, and specifically how Spark sees it. You can learn more details about the schema by calling the `schema()` method.

Look at SchemaIntrospectionApp in the net.jgp.books.spark.ch03.lab210_schema _introspection package for details about `schema()` usage. I limited the next lab's output to the first three fields in each case to simplify reading.

Say you want to output the following:

```
*** Schema as a tree:
root
 |-- OBJECTID: string (nullable = true)
 |-- datasetId: string (nullable = true)
 |-- name: string (nullable = true)
...
```

You can use the dataframe's `printSchema()` method as you did previously, or the `printTreeString()` method of the `StructType`:

```
StructType schema = df.schema();        ◄── Extracts the schema

System.out.println("*** Schema as a tree:");
schema.printTreeString();
```

Displays the schema as a tree

You can also display the schema as a simple string:

```
*** Schema as string:
StructField(OBJECTID,StringType,true)StructField(datasetId,StringType,true)
StructField(name,StringType,true)...
```

To do this, you use the following code:

Extracts the schema as a string

```
String schemaAsString = schema.mkString();      ◄─┘
System.out.println("*** Schema as string: " + schemaAsString);
```

And you can even display the schema as a JSON structure:

```
*** Schema as JSON: {
  "type" : "struct",
  "fields" : [ {
    "name" : "OBJECTID",
    "type" : "string",
```

```
      "nullable" : true,
      "metadata" : { }
    }, {
      "name" : "datasetId",
      "type" : "string",
      "nullable" : true,
      "metadata" : { }
    }, {
      "name" : "name",
      "type" : "string",
      "nullable" : true,
      "metadata" : { }
    }, {
  ...
```

You'd use the following code:

Extracts the schema as a JSON object in a string

```
String schemaAsJson = schema.prettyJson();   ←┘
System.out.println("*** Schema as JSON: " + schemaAsJson);
```

Advanced schema manipulation is possible, as you'll see in chapter 17.

3.2.4   *A dataframe after a JSON ingestion*

JSON documents can be a little more complex than CSVs because of their nested structure. You are going to work on a similar lab as previously, but this time the source of the restaurant data is a JSON file. This section focuses on the differences from the previous lab and assumes you have read it.

Using Spark, you are going to read a JSON file, which contains restaurant data that has a similar structure as the dataset in section 3.2.1. You'll transform the ingested data to match the previous dataset's transformed structure. You are doing that so you can merge them through a union process. Figure 3.11 illustrates this part of the process.

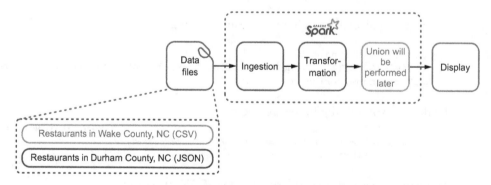

Figure 3.11   The ingestion and transformation processes for the Durham County restaurants

Your second dataset comes from another North Carolina county, Durham. Durham County is a neighbor of Wake, and its dataset can be found at https://live-durhamnc .opendata.arcgis.com/.

LAB   You can download the code from GitHub at https://github.com/jgperrin/
net.jgp.books.spark.ch03. This is lab #220 in package net.jgp.books.spark.ch03
.lab220_json_ingestion_schema_manipulation.

Because JSON can be a little trickier to visualize than CSV, the next listing shows an
excerpt of the dataset with only two restaurants. JSON is definitely more verbose, isn't
it? I removed some of the fields of the second record.

Listing 3.1   Two restaurants in Durham, NC

```
[{
    "datasetid": "restaurants-data",
    "recordid": "1644654b953d1802c3c941211f61be1f727b2951",
    "fields": {
        "status": "ACTIVE",
        "geolocation": [35.9207272, -78.9573299],
        "premise_zip": "27707",
        "rpt_area_desc": "Food Service",
        "risk": 4,
        "est_group_desc": "Full-Service Restaurant",
        "seats": 60,
        "water": "5 - Municipal/Community",
        "premise_phone": "(919) 403-0025",
        "premise_state": "NC",
        "insp_freq": 4,
        "type_description": "1 - Restaurant",
        "premise_city": "DURHAM",
        "premise_address2": "SUITE 6C",
        "opening_date": "1994-09-01",
        "premise_name": "WEST 94TH ST PUB",
        "transitional_type_desc": "FOOD",
        "smoking_allowed": "NO",
        "id": "56060",
        "sewage": "3 - Municipal/Community",
        "premise_address1": "4711 HOPE VALLEY RD"
    },
    "geometry": {
        "type": "Point",
        "coordinates": [-78.9573299, 35.9207272]
    },
    "record_timestamp": "2017-07-13T09:15:31-04:00"
}, {
    "datasetid": "restaurants-data",
    "recordid": "93573dbf8c9e799d82c459e47de0f40a2faa47bb",
    "fields": {
        ...
        "geolocation": [36.0467802, -78.8895483],
        "premise_zip": "27704",
        "rpt_area_desc": "Food Service",
        "est_group_desc": "Nursing Home",
        "premise_phone": "(919) 479-9966",
        "premise_state": "NC",
        "type_description": "16 - Institutional Food Service",
```

**Fields are
nested.**

**The description is in the
form of \<id\> - \<label\>;
you are interested in only
the label, not the ID.**

```
                "premise_city": "DURHAM",
                "opening_date": "2003-10-15",
                "premise_name": "BROOKDALE DURHAM IFS",
                "id": "58123",
                "premise_address1": "4434 BEN FRANKLIN BLVD"
        },
     ...
     }]
```

As with the CSV dataset, let's walk through the JSON transformation. The first part is the JSON ingestion, which will produce the following (as well as figure 3.12):

```
*** Right after ingestion
+---------------+-------------------+-------------------+
➥  -------------------+-------------------+
|      datasetid|             fields|           geometry|
➥         record_timestamp|           recordid|
+---------------+-------------------+-------------------+
➥  -------------------+-------------------+
|restaurants-data|[, Full-Service R...|[[-78.9573299, 35...|
➥ 2017-07-13T09:15:...|1644654b953d1802c...|
     ...
only showing top 5 rows
```

```
*** Right after ingestion
+---------------+-------------------+-------------------+-------------------+-------------------+
|      datasetid|             fields|           geometry|   record_timestamp|           recordid|
+---------------+-------------------+-------------------+-------------------+-------------------+
|restaurants-data|[, Full-Service R...|[[-78.9573299, 35...|2017-07-13T09:15:...|1644654b953d1802c...|
|restaurants-data|[, Nursing Home, ...|[[-78.8895483, 36...|2017-07-13T09:15:...|93573dbf8c9e799d8...|
|restaurants-data|[, Fast Food Rest...|[[-78.9593263, 35...|2017-07-13T09:15:...|0d274200c7cef50d0...|
|restaurants-data|[, Full-Service R...|[[-78.9060312, 36...|2017-07-13T09:15:...|cf3e0b175a6ebad2a...|
|restaurants-data|[,, [36.0556347, ...|[[-78.9135175, 36...|2017-07-13T09:15:...|e796570677f7c39cc...|
+---------------+-------------------+-------------------+-------------------+-------------------+
only showing top 5 rows
```

Figure 3.12   After ingestion, the Durham restaurant data's nested fields and arrays are difficult to read.

The dataframe contains nested fields and arrays. Using the show() method is useful, but the result is not very readable. The schema brings you more information:

```
root
 |-- datasetid: string (nullable = true)                  Nested fields are
 |-- fields: struct (nullable = true)          ◄─────┘    seen as a structure.
 |     |-- closing_date: string (nullable = true)
 |     |-- est_group_desc: string (nullable = true)
 |     |-- geolocation: array (nullable = true)           ◄───── Arrays are seen as such.
 |     |     |-- element: double (containsNull = true)
 |     |-- hours_of_operation: string (nullable = true)
 |     |-- id: string (nullable = true)
 |     |-- insp_freq: long (nullable = true)
 |     |-- opening_date: string (nullable = true)
 |     |-- premise_address1: string (nullable = true)
 |     |-- premise_address2: string (nullable = true)
```

```
|       |-- premise_city: string (nullable = true)
|       |-- premise_name: string (nullable = true)
|       |-- premise_phone: string (nullable = true)
|       |-- premise_state: string (nullable = true)
|       |-- premise_zip: string (nullable = true)
|       |-- risk: long (nullable = true)
|       |-- rpt_area_desc: string (nullable = true)
|       |-- seats: long (nullable = true)
|       |-- sewage: string (nullable = true)
|       |-- smoking_allowed: string (nullable = true)
|       |-- status: string (nullable = true)
|       |-- transitional_type_desc: string (nullable = true)
|       |-- type_description: string (nullable = true)
|       |-- water: string (nullable = true)
|-- geometry: struct (nullable = true) #A
|       |-- coordinates: array (nullable = true)          <---- Arrays are seen as such.
|       |     |-- element: double (containsNull = true)
|       |-- type: string (nullable = true)
|-- record_timestamp: string (nullable = true)
|-- recordid: string (nullable = true)
```

Of course, the structure of this schema tree is similar to that of the JSON document in listing 3.1. And this structure definitely looks more like a tree now than with the CSV file. The code to make this is also similar to the code to ingest and transform your CSV dataset:

```java
SparkSession spark = SparkSession.builder()
    .appName("Restaurants in Durham County, NC")
    .master("local")
    .getOrCreate();

Dataset<Row> df = spark.read().format("json")
    .load("data/Restaurants_in_Durham_County_NC.json");
System.out.println("*** Right after ingestion");
df.show(5);
df.printSchema();
```

Once the data is in the dataframe, APIs to manipulate the data are the same. You can start transforming the dataframe. Your destination structure is flat, so the mapping (as illustrated in figure 3.13) will have to embrace nested fields.

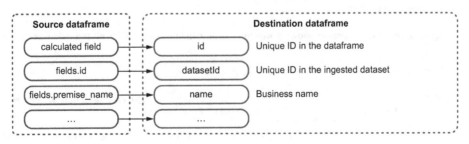

Figure 3.13 Nested fields can be accessed via the dot (.) symbol.

Here is what you will produce (figure 3.14 displays the dataframe's content as a screenshot):

```
*** Dataframe transformed
+---------+--------------------+--------------------+--------------------+...
|datasetId|              fields|            geometry|    record_timestamp|...
+---------+--------------------+--------------------+--------------------+...
|    56060|[, Full-Service R...|[[-78.9573299, 35...|2017-07-13T09:15:...|...
|    58123|[, Nursing Home, ...|[[-78.8895483, 36...|2017-07-13T09:15:...|...
|    70266|[, Fast Food Rest...|[[-78.9593263, 35...|2017-07-13T09:15:...|...
|    97837|[, Full-Service R...|[[-78.9060312, 36...|2017-07-13T09:15:...|...
|    60690|[,, [36.0556347, ...|[[-78.9135175, 36...|2017-07-13T09:15:...|...
+---------+--------------------+--------------------+--------------------+...
only showing top 5 rows
```

Nested fields are difficult to read when using show().

Array fields are equally difficult to read when using show().

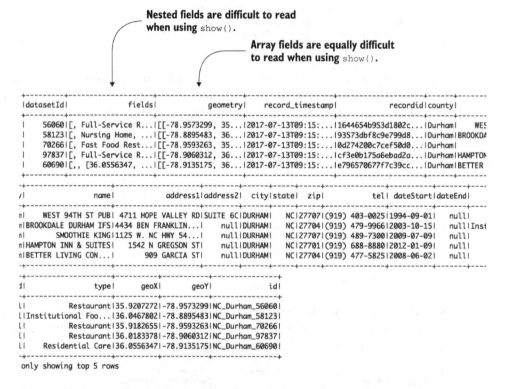

Figure 3.14   The dataframe showing five rows after transformation, with all the columns

The schema with its nested structure is as follows:

```
root
 |-- datasetId: string (nullable = true)              The new fields you will create
 |-- fields: struct (nullable = true)
 |    |-- closing_date: string (nullable = true)      The fields coming from the
 |    |-- est_group_desc: string (nullable = true)    original dataset, before
 |    |-- geolocation: array (nullable = true)        the transformation
```

```
|    |    |-- element: double (containsNull = true)
...
|    |-- premise_name: string (nullable = true)
...
|-- geometry: struct (nullable = true)
...
|-- record_timestamp: string (nullable = true)
|-- recordid: string (nullable = true)
|-- county: string (nullable = false)
|-- name: string (nullable = true)
|-- address1: string (nullable = true)
|-- address2: string (nullable = true)
|-- city: string (nullable = true)
|-- state: string (nullable = true)
|-- zip: string (nullable = true)
|-- tel: string (nullable = true)
|-- dateStart: string (nullable = true)
|-- dateEnd: string (nullable = true)
|-- type: string (nullable = true)
|-- geoX: double (nullable = true)
|-- geoY: double (nullable = true)
|-- id: string (nullable = true)
```

The new fields you will create

To access the fields in a structure, you can use the dot (.) symbol in the path. To access an element in an array, use the getItem() method. Here is the code in action:

Accesses the nested fields with . (dot)

```
df = df.withColumn("county", lit("Durham"))
    .withColumn("datasetId", df.col("fields.id"))
    .withColumn("name", df.col("fields.premise_name"))
    .withColumn("address1", df.col("fields.premise_address1"))
    .withColumn("address2", df.col("fields.premise_address2"))
    .withColumn("city", df.col("fields.premise_city"))
    .withColumn("state", df.col("fields.premise_state"))
    .withColumn("zip", df.col("fields.premise_zip"))
    .withColumn("tel", df.col("fields.premise_phone"))
    .withColumn("dateStart", df.col("fields.opening_date"))
    .withColumn("dateEnd", df.col("fields.closing_date"))
    .withColumn("type",
        split(df.col("fields.type_description"), " - ").getItem(1))
    .withColumn("geoX", df.col("fields.geolocation").getItem(0))
    .withColumn("geoY", df.col("fields.geolocation").getItem(1));
```

As with the CSV, you can add a column with the county name.

The description has the <id> - <label> notation; you can split the field on " - " and get the second element.

Extracts the first element of the array as the latitude (geoX)

Extracts the second element of the array as the longitude (geoY)

Just as you created all the fields and columns, creating the id field is the same operation you did for the CSV file:

```
df = df.withColumn("id",
    concat(df.col("state"), lit("_"),
        df.col("county"), lit("_"),
        df.col("datasetId")));
System.out.println("*** Dataframe transformed");
df.show(5);
df.printSchema();
```

Finally, looking at partitions is also equivalent, as for your CSV file:

```
*** Looking at partitions
Partition count before repartition: 1
Partition count after repartition: 4
```

And here is the code:

```
System.out.println("*** Looking at partitions");
Partition[] partitions = df.rdd().partitions();
int partitionCount = partitions.length;
System.out.println("Partition count before repartition: " +
    partitionCount);

df = df.repartition(4);
System.out.println("Partition count after repartition: " +
    df.rdd().partitions().length);
```

You now have two dataframes, with the same core set of columns. Your next step is to combine them.

3.2.5   Combining two dataframes

In this section, you will learn how to combine two datasets in a SQL-like union in order to build a bigger dataset. This will allow you to perform analytics on more data-points.

In the previous section, you ingested two datasets, transformed them, and analyzed them. As with tables in a relational database, you can do a lot of operations between them: joining them, combining them, and more.

Now, you are going to combine the two datasets so you can later perform analytics on the combined dataset. Figure 3.15 illustrates the details of the process.

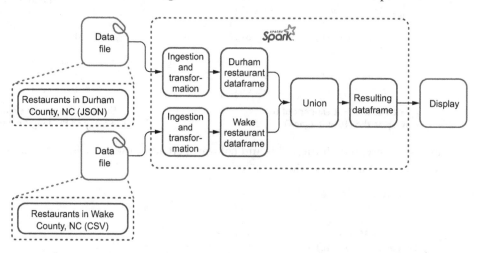

Figure 3.15   The two datasets are being combined in a union operation after their transformation.

LAB You can download the code from GitHub at https://github.com/jgperrin/ net.jgp.books.spark.ch03. This is lab #230 in package net.jgp.books.spark.ch03 .lab230_dataframe_union.

As you can certainly imagine, you can reuse most of the code you wrote for the ingestion and transformation. However, to perform a union, you have to make sure that the schemas are strictly identical. Otherwise, Spark will not be able to perform the union.

Figure 3.16 illustrates the mapping you are going to do.

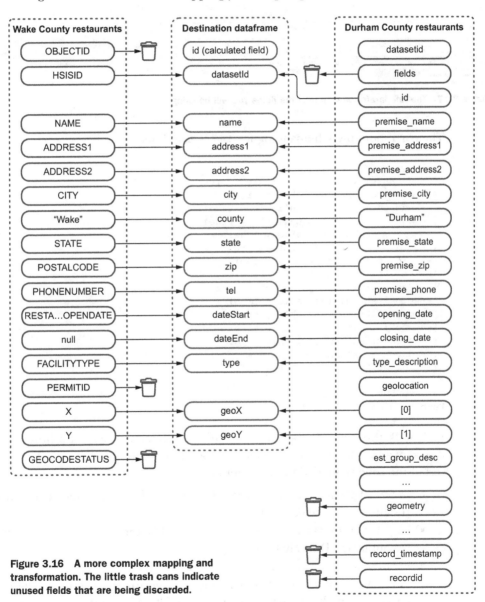

Figure 3.16 A more complex mapping and transformation. The little trash cans indicate unused fields that are being discarded.

The final output of your application is as follows (with figure 3.17 showing a full screenshot):

```
+-----------+--------------------+--------------------+--------+...
|  datasetId|                name|            address1|address2|...
+-----------+--------------------+--------------------+--------+...
|04092016024|                WABA|2502 1/2 HILLSBOR...|    null|...
...
only showing top 5 rows
```

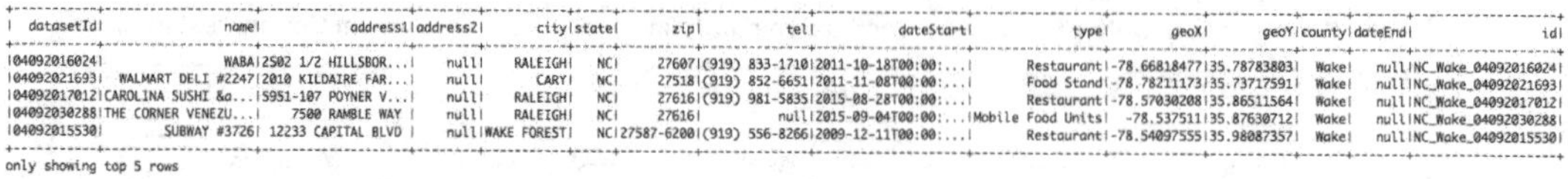

datasetId	name	address1	address2	city	state	zip	tel	dateStart	type	geoX	geoY	county	dateEnd	id
04092016024	WABA	2502 1/2 HILLSBOR...	null	RALEIGH	NC	27607	(919) 833-1710	2011-10-18T00:00:...	Restaurant	-78.66818477	35.78783803	Wake	null	NC_Wake_04092016024
04092021693	WALMART DELI #2247	2010 KILDAIRE FAR...	null	CARY	NC	27518	(919) 852-6651	2011-11-08T00:00:...	Food Stand	-78.78211173	35.73717591	Wake	null	NC_Wake_04092021693
04092017012	CAROLINA SUSHI &a...	5951-107 POYNER V...	null	RALEIGH	NC	27616	(919) 981-5835	2015-08-28T00:00:...	Restaurant	-78.57030208	35.86511564	Wake	null	NC_Wake_04092017012
04092030288	THE CORNER VENEZU...	7500 RAMBLE WAY	null	RALEIGH	NC	27616	null	2015-09-04T00:00:...	Mobile Food Units	-78.537511	35.87630712	Wake	null	NC_Wake_04092030288
04092015530	SUBWAY #3726	12233 CAPITAL BLVD	null	WAKE FOREST	NC	27587-6200	(919) 556-8266	2009-12-11T00:00:...	Restaurant	-78.54097555	35.98087357	Wake	null	NC_Wake_04092015530

only showing top 5 rows

Figure 3.17 The full dataframe with only the fields you will be using

The corresponding schema to figure 3.17 is as follows:

```
root
 |-- datasetId: string (nullable = true)
 |-- name: string (nullable = true)
 |-- address1: string (nullable = true)
 |-- address2: string (nullable = true)
 |-- city: string (nullable = true)
 |-- state: string (nullable = true)
 |-- zip: string (nullable = true)
 |-- tel: string (nullable = true)
 |-- dateStart: string (nullable = true)
 |-- type: string (nullable = true)
 |-- geoX: string (nullable = true)
 |-- geoY: string (nullable = true)
 |-- county: string (nullable = false)
 |-- dateEnd: string (nullable = true)
 |-- id: string (nullable = true)

We have 5903 records.
Partition count: 1
```

Let's walk through the code. Imports are the same. To make it a little easier, the `SparkSession`'s instance is a private member, initialized in the `start()` method. The rest of the code is isolated in three methods:

- `buildWakeRestaurantsDataframe()` builds the dataframe containing the restaurants in Wake County.
- `buildDurhamRestaurantsDataframe()` builds the dataframe containing the restaurants in Durham County.
- `combineDataframes()` combines the two dataframes by using a SQL-like union. For now, do not worry about memory usage for the resulting dataframe. In chapter 4, you'll see that the dataframe is self-optimizing.

Let's analyze the code:

```
package net.jgp.books.spark.ch03.lab400_dataframe_union;
...
  private void start() {
    this.spark = SparkSession.builder()
        .appName("Union of two dataframes")
        .master("local")
        .getOrCreate();

    Dataset<Row> wakeRestaurantsDf = buildWakeRestaurantsDataframe();
    Dataset<Row> durhamRestaurantsDf = buildDurhamRestaurantsDataframe();
    combineDataframes(wakeRestaurantsDf, durhamRestaurantsDf);
  }
```

Builds the dataframe containing the restaurants in Wake County

Builds the dataframe containing the restaurants in Durham County

Combines the two dataframes by using a SQL-like union

That was the easy part, right? Let's analyze the methods, starting with `buildWake-RestaurantsDataframe()`, which reads the dataset from a CSV file. This should be familiar to you, as you saw this previously in section 3.2.1:

```
  private Dataset<Row> buildWakeRestaurantsDataframe() {
    Dataset<Row> df = this.spark.read().format("csv")
        .option("header", "true")
        .load("data/Restaurants_in_Wake_County_NC.csv");
    df = df.withColumn("county", lit("Wake"))
        .withColumnRenamed("HSISID", "datasetId")
        .withColumnRenamed("NAME", "name")
        .withColumnRenamed("ADDRESS1", "address1")
        .withColumnRenamed("ADDRESS2", "address2")
        .withColumnRenamed("CITY", "city")
        .withColumnRenamed("STATE", "state")
        .withColumnRenamed("POSTALCODE", "zip")
        .withColumnRenamed("PHONENUMBER", "tel")
        .withColumnRenamed("RESTAURANTOPENDATE", "dateStart")
        .withColumn("dateEnd", lit(null))
        .withColumnRenamed("FACILITYTYPE", "type")
        .withColumnRenamed("X", "geoX")
        .withColumnRenamed("Y", "geoY")
        .drop(df.col("OBJECTID"))
        .drop(df.col("GEOCODESTATUS"))
        .drop(df.col("PERMITID"));
    df = df.withColumn("id", concat(
        df.col("state"),
        lit("_"),
        df.col("county"), lit("_"),
        df.col("datasetId")));
    return df;
  }
```

Your target schema includes a dateEnd column; this is a way to add the column.

These columns are no longer needed.

You are now ready to work on your second dataset:

```
private Dataset<Row> buildDurhamRestaurantsDataframe() {
  Dataset<Row> df = this.spark.read().format("json")
      .load("data/Restaurants_in_Durham_County_NC.json");
  df = df.withColumn("county", lit("Durham"))
      .withColumn("datasetId", df.col("fields.id"))
      .withColumn("name", df.col("fields.premise_name"))
      .withColumn("address1", df.col("fields.premise_address1"))
      .withColumn("address2", df.col("fields.premise_address2"))
      .withColumn("city", df.col("fields.premise_city"))
      .withColumn("state", df.col("fields.premise_state"))
      .withColumn("zip", df.col("fields.premise_zip"))
      .withColumn("tel", df.col("fields.premise_phone"))
      .withColumn("dateStart", df.col("fields.opening_date"))
      .withColumn("dateEnd", df.col("fields.closing_date"))
      .withColumn("type",
          split(df.col("fields.type_description"), " - ").getItem(1))
      .withColumn("geoX", df.col("fields.geolocation").getItem(0))
      .withColumn("geoY", df.col("fields.geolocation").getItem(1))
      .drop(df.col("fields"))                    These columns are
      .drop(df.col("geometry"))                  no longer needed.
      .drop(df.col("record_timestamp"))
      .drop(df.col("recordid")));
  df = df.withColumn("id",
      concat(df.col("state"), lit("_"),
          df.col("county"), lit("_"),
          df.col("datasetId")));
  return df;
}
```

Note that when you drop a parent column, all the nested columns are dropped as well. The nested columns under the `fields` and `geometry` fields are dropped because you dropped the parent. So, when you drop the `fields` column, all subfields such as risk, seats, sewage, and so on are being dropped at the same time.

You now have two dataframes with the same number of columns. Therefore, you can union them in the `combineDataframes()` method. There are two ways of combining two dataframes in a SQL-like union: you can use the `union()` or `unionByName()` method.

The `union()` method does not care about the names of the columns, just their order. This method will always union column 1 from the first dataframe with column 1 from the second dataframe, and then move to column 2, and then 3—regardless of the names. After a few transformative operations (in which you create new columns, rename them, dump them, or combine them), it can be difficult to remember whether the columns are in the right order. If fields don't match, you could have inconsistent data in the worst case, or a program stop at best. On the other hand, `unionByName()` matches columns by names, which is safer.

Both methods require you to have the same number of columns on both sides of the dataset. The following code shows the union operation and looks at the resulting partitions:

This is all it takes to make a union.

```
private void combineDataframes(Dataset<Row> df1, Dataset<Row> df2) {
    Dataset<Row> df = df1.unionByName(df2);
    df.show(5);
    df.printSchema();
    System.out.println("We have " + df.count() + " records.");

    Partition[] partitions = df.rdd().partitions();
    int partitionCount = partitions.length;
    System.out.println("Partition count: " + partitionCount);
}
```

The record count of the two combined datasets: 5,903 records

Can you explain why you have two partitions? You had two datasets in two partitions, so Spark keeps this structure.

You can union more datasets, but not at the same time.

When you load a small (typically, under 128 MB) dataset in a dataframe, Spark will create only one partition.[1] However, in this scenario, Spark creates a partition for the CSV-based dataset and one for the JSON-based dataset. Two datasets in two distinct dataframes result in at least two partitions (at least one for each dataset). Joining them will create a unique dataframe, but it will rely on the two original partitions (or more). You can try to modify the example by playing with repartition() to see how Spark will create the datasets and the partitions. Playing with partitions will not provide great benefits. In chapter 17, you'll see that partitions can improve performance on larger datasets that are split over several nodes, specifically (but not only) in join operations.

3.3   The dataframe is a Dataset<Row>

In this section, you will learn more about the implementation of the dataframe. You can have datasets of almost any Plain Old Java Object (POJO), but only the dataset of rows (Dataset<Row>) is called a *dataframe*. Let's explore the benefits of the dataframes and have a closer look at how to manipulate those specific datasets.

It is important to understand that you can have datasets with other POJOs, as you can reuse the POJOs that you might already have in your libraries or that are more specific to your applications. Chapter 9 even illustrates how to ingest data based on existing POJOs.

However, the dataframe, implemented as a dataset of rows (Dataset<Row>), has a richer API. You will see how to convert back and forth, from dataframe to dataset, when needed.

---

[1]Source: Spark RDD Programming Guide, http://mng.bz/6waR.

LAB You can download the code from GitHub at https://github.com/jgperrin/ net.jgp.books.spark.ch03. You will start with lab #300 in the package net.jgp .books.spark.ch03.lab300_dataset.

3.3.1 *Reusing your POJOs*

Let's explore the benefits of reusing POJOs directly in your dataset API and learn a bit more about Spark storage. The main benefit of using a dataset instead of a dataframe is that you can reuse your POJOs directly in Spark. Using a dataset with your POJOs allows you to use your familiar objects without any limitations that Row may bring, such as extracting the data from it.

When you look at the dataset API (http://mng.bz/qXYE), you will see a lot of references to Dataset<T>, where T stands for a generic type, not specifically a Row. However, beware that some operations will lose the strong typing of your POJO and will return a Row: an example of that is joining two datasets or performing aggregation on a dataset.

This is not a problem at all, but should be an expected feature. Consider a dataset based on books, for instance. If you group by to count the number of books published by year, you will not have a count field in your book POJO, so Spark will automatically create a dataframe to store the result.

Finally, a Row uses efficient storage called *Tungsten*. This is not the case with your POJOs.

Tungsten: Crazy fast storage for Java

Performance optimization is a never-ending story. *Project Tungsten* is an integrated part of Apache Spark that focuses on enhancing three key areas: memory management and binary processing, cache-aware computation, and code generation. Let's have a quick look at the first area and the way Java stores objects.

One of the first things I loved in Java (coming from C++) is that you do not have to track memory usage and object life cycles: all of that is done by the garbage collector (GC). Although the GC is performing pretty well in most cases, it may be quickly overwhelmed by the creation of millions of objects as you play with your datasets.

Storing a four-character string, such as Java in Java (8 and below) will take 28 bytes;[2] storing this string should take only 4 bytes when using UTF-8/ASCII encoding. The Java Virtual Machine (JVM) native String implementation stores this differently by encoding each character using 2 bytes with UTF-16 encoding, and each String object also contains a 12-byte header and 8-byte hash code. When you call a Java (or any other JVM-based language) .length() operation, the JVM will still return 4 because that is the length of the string in characters, not its physical representation in memory. Check out the Java Object Layout (JOL) tool at http://openjdk.java .net/projects/code-tools/jol/ to understand more about physical storage.

---

[2]The design has slightly changed in Java 9 with compactStrings: https://openjdk.java .net/jeps/254.

> Both the GC and the object storage are not bad per se. However, in high-performance and predictable workloads, progress could have been made. Therefore, a more efficient storage system was born. Tungsten directly manages blocks of memory, compresses data, and has new data containers that use low-level interaction with the operating system and offer performance enhancements from 16 times to 100 times.[3]
>
> You can read more about Project Tungsten at http://mng.bz/7zyg.

3.3.2 Creating a dataset of strings

To understand how to use datasets and not dataframes, let's look at creating a simple dataset of String. This will illustrate the usage of datasets by using a simple object we are all familiar with, the string. You will then be able to create datasets of more-complex objects.

Your application is going to create a dataset of String from a simple Java array containing strings, and then display the result—nothing fancy. Here is the expected output:

```
+------+
| value|
+------+
|  Jean|
|   Liz|
|Pierre|
|Lauric|
+------+

root
 |-- value: string (nullable = true)
```

And you can reproduce this output by using the following application:

```
package net.jgp.books.spark.ch03_lab300_dataset;

import java.util.Arrays;          What could you do in Java without these? Let's
import java.util.List;            use a simple List and a method of Arrays.

import org.apache.spark.sql.Dataset;
import org.apache.spark.sql.Encoders;        Encoders help build the
import org.apache.spark.sql.SparkSession;    dataset for conversion.

public class ArrayToDatasetApp {
...
  private void start() {
    SparkSession spark = SparkSession.builder()
      .appName("Array to Dataset<String>")
```

---

[3]Source: Apache Spark project and Databricks, one of the companies behind Apache Spark.

Creates a static array with four values

```
                .master("local")
                .getOrCreate();

        String[] stringList =
            new String[] { "Jean", "Liz", "Pierre", "Lauric" };
        List<String> data = Arrays.asList(stringList);
        Dataset<String> ds = spark.createDataset(data, Encoders.STRING());
        ds.show();
        ds.printSchema();
    }
}
```

Converts the array to a list

Creates the dataset of strings from the list and specifies the encoder

To use the extended methods of the dataframe instead of the dataset, you can easily convert a dataset into a dataframe by calling the toDF() method. Look at lab #310 (net.jgp .books.spark.ch03.lab310_dataset_to_dataframe.ArrayToDatasetToDataframeApp). It adds the following snippet at the end of the start() method:

```
        Dataset<Row> df = ds.toDF();
        df.show();
        df.printSchema();
```

The output is identical to the previous lab in this section (lab #300), but now you have a dataframe!

3.3.3   *Converting back and forth*

In this section, you will learn how to convert a dataframe to a dataset and back. This conversion is useful if you want to manipulate your existing POJOs and the extended API that apply to only the dataframe.

You will read a CSV file containing books in a dataframe. You will convert the dataframe to a dataset of books and then back to a dataframe. Although it sounds like an obnoxious flow, as a Spark engineer, you could be involved in part or all of those operations.

Imagine the following use case. You have an existing bookProcessor() method in your arsenal of libraries. This method takes a Book POJO and publishes it, via APIs, on a merchant website such as Amazon, Fnac, or Flipkart. You definitely do not want to rewrite this method to work only with Spark. You want to continue sending a Book POJO. You can load thousands of books, store them in a dataset of books, and when you are going to iterate over them, you can use distributed processing to call your existing bookProcessor() method without modification.

CREATE THE DATASET

Let's focus on the first part: ingesting the file and turning the dataframe into a dataset of books. The output will be as follows:

```
*** Books ingested in a dataframe
+---+--------+--------------------+-----------+--------------------+
| id|authorId|               title|releaseDate|                link|
+---+--------+--------------------+-----------+--------------------+
|  1|       1|Fantastic Beasts ...|   11/18/16|http://amzn.to/2k...|
|  2|       1|Harry Potter and ...|    10/6/15|http://amzn.to/2l...|
...
only showing top 5 rows
```

root   ⟵ **The order of fields is the order in the file.**

```
 |-- id: integer (nullable = true)
 |-- authorId: integer (nullable = true)
 |-- title: string (nullable = true)
 |-- releaseDate: string (nullable = true)    ⟵  Seen as a string
 |-- link: string (nullable = true)               when parsed
```

```
*** Books are now in a dataset of books
+--------+---+------------------+-----------------+-----------------+
|authorId| id|              link|      releaseDate|            title|
+--------+---+------------------+-----------------+-----------------+
|       1|  1|http://amzn.to...|[18, 0, 0, 10,...|Fantastic Beas...|
|       1|  2|http://amzn.to...|[6, 0, 0, 9, 0...|Harry Potter a...|
...
only showing top 5 rows
```

root   ⟵ **The fields are now alphabetically sorted (same for nested fields); this is Spark behavior.**

```
 |-- authorId: integer (nullable = true)
 |-- id: integer (nullable = true)
 |-- link: string (nullable = true)
 |-- releaseDate: struct (nullable = true)
 |    |-- date: integer (nullable = true)
 |    |-- hours: integer (nullable = true)
 |    |-- minutes: integer (nullable = true)
 |    |-- month: integer (nullable = true)
 |    |-- seconds: integer (nullable = true)
 |    |-- time: long (nullable = true)
 |    |-- year: integer (nullable = true)
 |-- title: string (nullable = true)
```

Day of the date ⟶ (points to `date:`)

"Exploded" as the components of a date when converted to a Dataset<Books>

The fields are sorted after you convert your dataframe to a dataset. This is not something you asked the application to do; it is a bonus (or "malus," depending on the day). However, remember to use unionByName() (instead of union()) if you plan on combining datasets after that, because fields *may have shifted during take-off* (an analogy to things being moved around in the overhead compartment when you're flying, meaning you don't know what you're going to get when you open the cover).

Your application is in the following listing.

Listing 3.2   CsvToDatasetBookToDataframeApp

```
package net.jgp.books.spark.ch03.lab320_dataset_books_to_dataframe;

import static org.apache.spark.sql.functions.concat;
import static org.apache.spark.sql.functions.expr;
import static org.apache.spark.sql.functions.lit;
import static org.apache.spark.sql.functions.to_date;
```

> As you are progressing, you will use more of those static functions and will get familiar with them; they are used later in the application.

```
import java.io.Serializable;
import java.text.SimpleDateFormat;

import org.apache.spark.api.java.function.MapFunction;
import org.apache.spark.sql.Dataset;
import org.apache.spark.sql.Encoders;
import org.apache.spark.sql.Row;
import org.apache.spark.sql.SparkSession;

import net.jgp.books.spark.ch03.x.model.Book;
```

> The subpackage named x contains extra packages, shared among the different applications.

```
public class CsvToDatasetBookToDataframeApp implements Serializable {
...
  private void start() {
    SparkSession spark = SparkSession.builder()
      .appName("CSV to dataframe to Dataset<Book> and back")
      .master("local")
      .getOrCreate();

    String filename = "data/books.csv";
    Dataset<Row> df = spark.read().format("csv")
      .option("inferSchema", "true")
      .option("header", "true")
      .load(filename);

    System.out.println("*** Books ingested in a dataframe");
    df.show(5);
    df.printSchema();

    Dataset<Book> bookDs = df.map(
        new BookMapper(),
        Encoders.bean(Book.class));

    System.out.println("*** Books are now in a dataset of books");
    bookDs.show(5, 17);
    bookDs.printSchema();
```

Creates a session (annotation for SparkSession block)

Ingests the data in a dataframe (annotation for read block)

> When dealing with maps, a lot of objects may need to become Serializable. Spark will tell you, at runtime, when this is required.

> Converts the dataframe into a dataset by using a map() function

The map() method is an interesting animal that seems a little intimidating at first but is as sweet as a puppy. The map() method can be intimidating because it requires a little more coding and it is not always an easy concept to understand. This method will

- Go through every record of the dataset
- Do something in the call() method of the MapFunction class
- Return a dataset

Let's have a deeper look at the map() method signature. Generics are not always straightforward in Java:

```
Dataset<U> map(MapFunction<T, U>, Encoder<U>)
```

In your scenario, U is Book, and T is Row. So the map() method signature looks like this:

```
Dataset<Book> map(MapFunction<Row, Book>, Encoder<Book>)
```

When called, the map() method will

- Go through every record of the dataframe.
- Call an instance of a class implementing MapFunction<Row, Book>; in your case, BookMapper. Note that it is instantiated only once, whatever the number of records you have to process.
- Return a Dataset<Book> (your goal).

When you implement your method, make sure you have the right signature and implementation, as this could be tricky. The skeleton, including the signature and required method, is as follows:

```
class AnyMapper implements MapFunction<T, U> {
  @Override
  public U call(T value) throws Exception {
...
  }
}
```

The following listing applies this skeleton to the BookMapper mapper class you are building. Appendix I lists the references for these types of transformations, including class signature.

Listing 3.3 BookMapper

Make sure your method signature is right.

```
class BookMapper implements MapFunction<Row, Book> {
  private static final long serialVersionUID = -2L;

  @Override
  public Book call(Row value) throws Exception {
    Book b = new Book();
    b.setId(value.getAs("id"));
    b.setAuthorId(value.getAs("authorId"));
    b.setLink(value.getAs("link"));
    b.setTitle(value.getAs("title"));

    String dateAsString = value.getAs("releaseDate");
    if (dateAsString != null) {
```

As previously stated, you are building a new book instance for every record; these objects will not benefit from Tungsten's optimization.

Simple extraction from the row object to the POJO, similar to manipulating a JDBC ResultSet

As always, dates are a little trickier; you will have to convert the string to a date.

```
      SimpleDateFormat parser = new SimpleDateFormat("M/d/yy");    ◄─────┐
      b.setReleaseDate(parser.parse(dateAsString));                     │
    }                                                                    │
    return b;                                                           
  }                                          You can also turn this into a static
}                                            field to increase performance.
```

You will also need a simple POJO representing a book (the Book POJO), which is the next listing. I removed most getters and setters to simplify readability; I am pretty sure you can mentally add the missing methods. I store all common artifacts in an x subpackage to increase project readability; in Eclipse, *x* stands for *extra*.

Listing 3.4   Book POJO

```
package net.jgp.books.spark.ch03.x.model;

import java.util.Date;

public class Book {
  int id;
  int authorId;
  String title;
  Date releaseDate;
  String link;
...
  public String getTitle() {
    return title;
  }

  public void setTitle(String title) {
    this.title = title;
  }
...
}
```

CREATE THE DATAFRAME

Now that you have the dataset, you can convert it back to a dataframe, so you could, for example, perform join or aggregation operations.

So, let's convert the dataset back to a dataframe to study this part of the mechanism. You will study an interesting case with the date, as the date is split in a nested structure. The following listing shows the output.

Listing 3.5   Output and schema

```
*** Books are back in a dataframe
+--------+---+------------+-------------+-------------+-----------------+
|authorId| id|        link|  releaseDate|        title|releaseDateAsDate|
+--------+---+------------+-------------+-------------+-----------------+
|       1|  1|http://amz...|[18, 0, 0,...|Fantastic ...|       2016-11-18|
|       1|  2|http://amz...|[6, 0, 0, ...|Harry Pott...|       2015-10-06|
...
only showing top 5 rows
```

```
root
 |-- authorId: integer (nullable = true)
 |-- id: integer (nullable = true)
 |-- link: string (nullable = true)
 |-- releaseDate: struct (nullable = true)
 |    |-- date: integer (nullable = true)
 |    |-- hours: integer (nullable = true)
 |    |-- minutes: integer (nullable = true)
 |    |-- month: integer (nullable = true)
 |    |-- seconds: integer (nullable = true)
 |    |-- time: long (nullable = true)
 |    |-- year: integer (nullable = true)
 |-- title: string (nullable = true)
 |-- releaseDateAsDate: date (nullable = true)  ◁———
```

In the process of converting the dataset to a dataframe, you are building the date, which has become a set of nested fields, to a real date.

You are now ready to convert the dataset to a dataframe, and then perform a few transformations, such as changing the date from this abominable structure to a date column in your dataframe:

```
Dataset<Row> df2 = bookDs.toDF();
```

Okay, that wasn't hard, right? To convert a dataset to a dataframe, you simply use the toDF() method. However, you still have this strange date format, so let's correct that. The first step is to transform the date to a string with a representation of the date. In this situation, you will use the ANSI/ISO format: *YYYY-MM-DD*, as in 1971-10-05.

Remember that years in Java start in 1900, so 1971 is 71, while 2004 is 104. Similarly, months start at 0, making October, the tenth month of the year, month 9. Using the Java methods to build the date would require using a mapping function as you did in listing 3.3. This is the way to build a dataset or a dataframe through iteration over the data. You could also use UDFs, defined in chapter 16:

Creates a column . . .

called releaseDateAsString . . .

```
  └─▷ df2 = df2.withColumn(
          "releaseDateAsString",   ◁———
          concat(                            ◁———
            expr("releaseDate.year + 1900"), lit("-"),
            expr("releaseDate.month + 1"), lit("-"),   ◁———
            df2.col("releaseDate.date")));   ◁———
```

the expression that is the sum of the release year and 1900 . . .

whose value is the concatenation of . . .

the expression that is the month plus one . . .

and the day of the month

The expr() static function will compute an SQL-like expression and return a column. It can use field names. The expression releaseDate.year + 1900 will be evaluated by Spark during this transformation and turned into a column containing the value. The dot notation in releaseDate.year indicates the path to the data, as you can see in the schema of listing 3.5. You will see more static functions through the examples and will study transformations in chapter 13, as well as in appendix G.

Once you have a date as a string, you can convert it to a date as a date, using the `to_date()` static function:

```
df2 = df2
    .withColumn(
        "releaseDateAsDate",
        to_date(df2.col("releaseDateAsString"), "yyyy-MM-dd"))
    .drop("releaseDateAsString");
System.out.println("*** Books are back in a dataframe");
df2.show(5);
df2.printSchema();
    }
}
```

to_date() transforms a text representation of a date to a real date.

Drops the column you do not need anymore

You could also `drop()` the `releaseDate` column with its weird structure; it is not very useful. Now you should be able to build a dataset containing any POJO and transform it into a dataframe.

3.4   *Dataframe's ancestor: the RDD*

In the previous sections, you studied the dataset and dataframe extensively. However, Spark was not born with those components. Let's understand why it is important to remember the role of the resilient distributed dataset.

Prior to dataframes, Spark exclusively used RDDs. Unfortunately, you will still find some old guards that swear *only* by the RDD and disregard or ignore dataframes. To avoid insane discussions, you should know what the RDD is and why dataframes are most certainly easier to use in most applications, but that they would not work without the RDD.

One of Spark's most famous founders, Matei Zaharia, defines the RDD as *a distributed memory abstraction that lets programmers perform in-memory computations on large clusters in a fault-tolerant manner.*[4]

The first implementation of RDDs was in Spark. The idea was to enable in-memory computation through a reliable (resilient) set of nodes: if one fails, no biggie; another takes the relay, like a RAID 5 disk architecture. The RDD was born with the immutability concept in mind (defined in section 3.1.2).

Despite major efforts around the dataframe, RDDs are not disappearing. And nobody wants them to disappear; they remain the low-level storage tier used by Spark. Check out my friend Jules Damji's article on comparing Spark's various storage structures at http://mng.bz/omdD—but be careful, he is biased toward Scala.

One way you can see dataframes and RDDs is that dataframes are an extension of RDDs.

If dataframes are majestic, RDDs are definitely not ugly and wimpy. RDDs bring all their presence to the storage layer. You should consider RDDs when

---

[4] Source: "Resilient Distributed Datasets: A Fault-Tolerant Abstraction for In-Memory Cluster Computing" by Matei Zaharia et al, http://mng.bz/4e9v.

- You do not need a schema.
- You are developing lower-level transformation and actions.
- You have legacy code.

RDDs are the foundation blocks for dataframes. As you saw, dataframes are easier to use and perform more optimally than RDDs in many use cases, but don't tease fans of RDD over the majestic quality of dataframes, okay?

Summary

- A dataframe is an immutable distributed collection of data, organized into named columns. Basically, a dataframe is an RDD with a schema.
- A dataframe is implemented as a dataset of rows—or in code: `Dataset<Row>`.
- A dataset is implemented as a dataset of anything except rows—or in code: `Dataset<String>`, `Dataset<Book>`, or `Dataset<SomePojo>`.
- Dataframes can store columnar information, like a CSV file, and nested fields and arrays, like a JSON file. Whether you are working with CSV files, JSON files, or other formats, the dataframe API remains the same.
- In a JSON document, you can access nested fields by using a dot (`.`).
- The API for the dataframe can be found at http://mng.bz/qXYE; see the reference section for details on how to use dataframes.
- The API for the static methods can be found at http://mng.bz/5AQD (and in appendix G); see the reference section for details on how to use static methods.
- If you do not care about column names when you union two dataframes, use `union()`.
- If you care about column names when you union two dataframes, use `unionBy-Name()`.
- You can reuse your POJOs directly in a dataset in Spark.
- An object must be serializable if you want to have it as part of a dataset.
- The dataset's `drop()` method removes a column in the dataframe.
- The dataset's `col()` method returns a dataset's column based on its name.
- The `to_date()` static function transforms a date as a string to a date.
- The `expr()` static function will compute the result of expressions by using field names.
- The `lit()` static function returns a column with a literal value.
- A resilient distributed dataset (RDD) is an immutable distributed collection of elements of your data.
- You should use a dataframe over an RDD when performance is critical.
- Tungsten storage relies on dataframes.
- Catalyst is the transformation optimizer (see chapter 4). It relies on dataframes to optimize actions and transformations.
- APIs across Spark libraries (graph, SQL, machine learning, or streaming) are becoming unified under the dataframe API.

Fundamentally lazy

This chapter is not only about celebrating laziness. It also teaches, through examples and experiments, the fundamental differences between building a data application the traditional way and building one with Spark.

There are at least two kinds of laziness: sleeping under the trees when you've committed to doing something else, and thinking ahead in order to do your job in the smartest possible way. Although, at this precise moment, my mind is thinking of lying in the shade of a tree, largely inspired by *Asterix in Corsica*, in this chapter I will show how Spark makes your life easier by optimizing its workload. You will learn about the essential roles of transformations (each step of the data process) and actions (the trigger to get the work done).

You will work on a real dataset from the US National Center for Health Statistics. The application is designed to illustrate the reasoning that Spark goes through when it processes data. The chapter focuses on only one application, but it contains three execution modes, which correspond to three experiments that you will run to get a better sense of Spark's "way of thinking."

I cover transformations and actions from a Java perspective. A lot of the online documentation is about Scala; here, I think I improved the information to better cover Java.

Finally, you will have a deeper look at Catalyst, Spark's built-in optimizer. Like an RDBMS query optimizer, it can dump the query plan, which is useful for debugging. You will learn how to analyze its output.

Appendix I is the reference companion to this chapter; it contains the list of transformations and the list of actions.

LAB Examples from this chapter are available in GitHub at https://github .com/jgperrin/net.jgp.books.spark.ch04.

4.1 A real-life example of efficient laziness

Most of the time, laziness is associated with a negative behavior. When I mention laziness, you might instantly think sloth, siesta under a tree, goofing around instead of working. But is there more to it? In this section, let's see whether there is a link between being lazy and being smart.

I've always wondered whether smart people are lazier than others. This theory is based on the idea that smart people think more before doing something.

Let's think of this in the following way. Your boss (or product manager) asks you to build version 1.1 of your great feature, and then he modifies his request to something slightly different. Now you are going to build version 1.2. Finally, he asks you to remember the first version, and do a slight modification of the original version feature. This is version 1.3. Of course, this is a work of fiction. Names, businesses, events, excuses for being agile, and features are the products of my imagination. Any resemblance to actual persons, living or dead, or actual events is purely coincidental. It never happened to you either, right? Nevertheless, figure 4.1 illustrates the thought process.

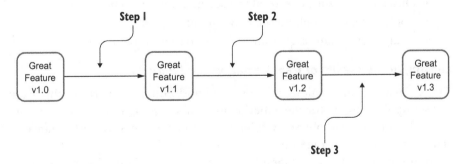

Figure 4.1   While building the next evolution of the great feature, you follow the requests your boss or product manager asks you to perform.

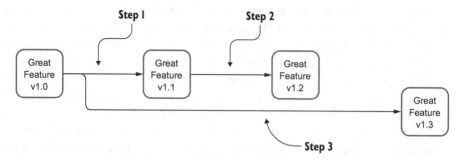

Figure 4.2   Sometimes, depending on the requests from your product manager, it is easier to rewind to the first version and start over, even if step 1 and step 2 are done.

Another way to do it is to get back to version 1.0 and modify from there, as illustrated in figure 4.2.

This is probably why source control tools like Git (or even cvs or sccs) were invented.

If you knew about your boss's changing requests beforehand, you would agree that the second way to work, as illustrated in figure 4.2, would be preferred, right? It is a lazier, yet smarter, way to proceed. In the next section, you will see how to apply that to Spark. Actually, even if you did not know the features in v1.3 before starting, you would probably still be safer starting with v1.0 just to make sure you wouldn't deal with induced bugs.

4.2   A Spark example of efficient laziness

In the previous section, you learned what smart laziness could look like in your day-to-day life. This section transposes that to Apache Spark through a specific example.

Most importantly, you will understand why Spark is lazy and why that's good for you. You will also do the following:

- Understand the experiments you will run to understand Spark's transformations and actions
- Observe the results of several transformations and actions
- Look at the code behind the experiments
- Analyze the results closely and see where time is spent

4.2.1   Looking at the results of transformations and actions

Transformations and actions are the bread and butter of Spark. In this section, you will set up the context for the experiments you are going to perform (or at least walk through). In this example, you will load a dataset and measure performance to understand where work is being done.

In this book, I end most examples with a show() method. This is an efficient way to quickly see the result, but it is not really the typical end goal. A collection action (collect() in your code) allows you to retrieve, as a Java list, the entire dataframe, allowing further processing such as creating a report, sending an email, and so on. This is often one of the final operations as you finalize your application. In Spark's vocabulary, this is called an *action.*

To understand the concepts of transformations and actions, and through that the concept of lazy operations, you will perform three experiments in lab #200:

- *Experiment 1*—Load a dataset and perform a collection action.
- *Experiment 2*—Load a dataset, perform a transformation (creating three columns through duplication and mathematical operations), and perform a collection action.
- *Experiment 3*—Load a dataset, perform a transformation (creating three columns through duplication and mathematical operations), drop the newly created columns, and perform a collection action. This experiment will illustrate Spark's laziness.

Your dataset contains about 2.5 million records. The detailed results are in table 4.1.

Table 4.1 Analyzing the results of your three experiments with transformations and actions

	Experiment 1: Load and collect	Experiment 2: Load, create columns, and collect	Experiment 3: Load, create columns, delete the columns, and collect
Load (get a Spark session, load the dataset, build the dataset, clean up)	5,193 ms		
Transformation	0 ms	182 ms	185 ms
Notes on transformations	None done	Creation of three columns: duplication and mathematical expression	Creation of the same three columns as in experiment 2, then deletion of those columns
Action	20,770 ms	34,061 ms	24,909 ms
Notes on action	Performed a `collect()`		

I hope that some of the results in table 4.1 seem odd to you. If not, here are a few hints:

- Through transformations, you just created three columns of 2.5 million records, so about 7.5 million datasets, in 182 milliseconds. That's fast, no?
- While performing the action, if you do not do any transformation, the action takes about 21 seconds. If you create three columns, the action takes 34 seconds. But if you create and then delete the columns, the action takes about 25 seconds. Isn't that odd? As you already guessed, this is due to laziness.

Let's look at the process in more detail as well as the code you can build to fill table 4.1. Then you will have the clues to resolve these two mysteries.

4.2.2   *The transformation process, step by step*

In the previous section, you saw the results of the transformation process and the anomalies in the results. In this section, you will explore the process in more detail, before looking at the code and then delving deeper into the mysteries.

The process itself is pretty basic. You do the following:

1 Get a new Spark session.
2 Load a dataset. In this example, you will work with data from the US National Center for Health Statistics (NCHS), a division of the Centers for Disease Control and Prevention (CDC), accessible at www.cdc.gov/nchs/index.htm. The dataset contains mean teen birth rates by year for each county and state in the United States. You can find more information at http://mng.bz/yz6e, and the dataset is included in the lab's data directory.
3 Duplicate the dataset several times to make it a little bigger. The file included in the example contains 40,781 records. That number is a little low: when you study a particular mechanism or processing, you may see side-effect conditions. Spark is designed to be distributed and to process a huge number of records, not a mere 40,000. Therefore, you will increase the dataset by performing a union of the dataset with itself. I know that does not have a lot of business value, but I did not find a dataset that was bigger but not huge (thereby breaking the 100 MB limit of GitHub).
4 Clean up. There is always a little cleanup to do on an external dataset. In this case, you will rename some columns.
5 Perform transformations. These are divided into three types: no transformation, creation of the additional columns, and, finally, creation of the columns and deletion.
6 Finally, take the action.

Figure 4.3 illustrates the process. Note that the transformations will be run in step 5, which will vary according to our three experiments.

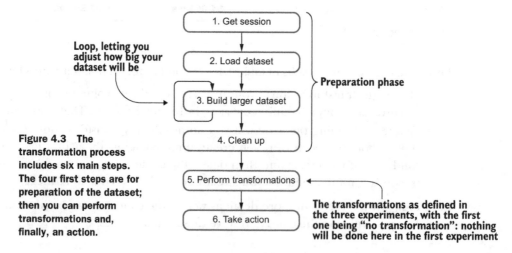

Figure 4.3   The transformation process includes six main steps. The four first steps are for preparation of the dataset; then you can perform transformations and, finally, an action.

Table 4.2 details the dataset structure. The NCHS dataset you are using contains birth rates for teens of ages 15 to 19 in the United States, divided by county, from 2003 to 2015. The tone of this dataset is a bit serious, but during the course of the book, I want to use meaningful and real-life datasets. Each dataset serves as a base, and you can also work with it beyond this chapter.

Table 4.2 Structure of the NHCS birth rate dataset used throughout the chapter

Column name in the dataset	Type	Comment
Year	Numeric	
State	String	
County	String	
State FIPS Code	Integer	State code in the US Federal Information Processing Standards
County FIPS Code	Integer	County code in the US FIPS
Combined FIPS Code	Integer	Combination of the state and county FIPS code in one
Birth Rate	Decimal	Teen birth rate: births per 1,000 females ages 15–19 in a given year
Lower Confidence Limit	Decimal	Column renamed `lcl` later
Upper Confidence Limit	Decimal	Column renamed `ucl` later

Standardizing government data with FIPS

Federal Information Processing Standards (FIPS) are publicly announced standards developed by the US federal government for use in computer systems by nonmilitary government agencies and government contractors.

You can read more about FIPS at the National Institute of Standards and Technology (NIST) website (www.nist.gov/itl/fips-general-information) and on Wikipedia (https://en.wikipedia.org/wiki/Federal_Information_Processing_Standards).

In this dataset, the two last columns are the lower and upper confidence limits, respectively. These indicate the confidence level in the birth rate.

Confidence limits are part of statistics

As you probably figured out, all the larger datasets used in this book are from the real world and are not made up just for the sake of learning. Therefore, sometimes you will find odd (or unusual) terms.

(continued)

This dataset contains lower and upper confidence limits. *Confidence limits* are the numbers at the upper and lower end of a confidence interval. The interval is computed from the statistics of the observed data and should contain the true value of an unknown population parameter, based on the observed data. You are not going to calculate it; it is part of the dataset you are using.

For more explanation of the confidence limit and confidence interval, see the *Handbook of Biological Statistics* by John H. McDonald (Sparky House Publishing, 2014, www.biostathandbook.com/confidence.html) and Wikipedia (https://en.wikipedia .org/wiki/Confidence_interval).

4.2.3   *The code behind the transformation/action process*

In previous sections, you saw the results of the process (table 4.1), went through the details of the process used in the experiments, and looked at the structure of the dataset. Now, it is time to look at the code and how to run it.

You will execute the code three times, with three different arguments on the command line. The code will automatically adapt, based on the arguments. Using the command line will allow you to more easily chain the commands, run the tests several times to compare the results, average the results, and more easily try other platforms. You will use Maven. Check appendix B for installation if needed.

By no means is this section a scientific description of how to perform a benchmark; however, it illustrates where time is spent.

You can run the three experiments in one command by using command-line arguments. You are going to run `clean` and compile/install, and then run each experiment. The first experiment is the default, so it does not require an argument. The command line looks like this:

```
mvn clean install &&
mvn exec:exec && \
mvn exec:exec -DexecMode=COL && \
mvn exec:exec -DexecMode=FULL
```

The result of the execution is as follows:

First experiment: execution without transformation

```
...
[INFO] --- exec-maven-plugin:1.6.0:exec (default-cli) @ spark-chapter04 ---
1. Creating a session ............. 1791
2. Loading initial dataset ........ 3287
3. Building full dataset .......... 242
4. Clean-up ...................... 8
5. Transformations .............. 0
6. Final action .................. 20770

# of records .................... 2487641
...
```

Preparation time (items 1–3)

Transformation (item 5)

Action (item 6)

```
[INFO] --- exec-maven-plugin:1.6.0:exec (default-cli) @ spark-chapter04 ---
1. Creating a session ............. 1553
2. Loading initial dataset ......... 3197          Second experiment:
3. Building full dataset ........... 208    Preparation time    creation of the
4. Clean-up ........................ 8                                  columns
5. Transformations ................ 182    ◄──── Transformation
6. Final action ................... 34061  ◄───
                                                  │ Action
# of records ...................... 2487641              Third experiment: full
...                                                      process—creation and
[INFO] --- exec-maven-plugin:1.6.0:exec (default-cli) @ spark-chapter04 ---  deletion of the columns
1. Creating a session ............. 1903
2. Loading initial dataset ......... 3184
3. Building full dataset ........... 213    Preparation time
4. Clean-up ........................ 8
5. Transformations ................ 205    ◄──── Transformation
6. Final action ................... 24909  ◄───
                                                  │ Action
# of records ...................... 2487641
...
[INFO] Total time: 37.659 s        ◄───  Total execution time for the whole
                                          Maven process, safe to ignore
```

If you want to build the same table as table 4.1, you can copy the values in Microsoft Excel. The Excel sheet is attached to the project. It is called Analysis results.xlsx and is in the data folder of the chapter's repository.

Listing 4.1 is a little long but should not be difficult to understand.

Your main() method will ensure that you pass an argument to the start() method, where all the work is. Expected arguments are as follows (the arguments are not case-sensitive):

- noop for no operation/transformation, used in experiment 1
- col for column creation, used in experiment 2
- full for the full process, used in experiment 3

The start() method will create a session, read the file, increase the dataset, and perform a little cleanup as part of the preparation phase. You will then perform the transformations and action.

LAB Lab #200 is available in the net.jgp.books.spark.ch04.lab200_transformation_and_action package. The application is TransformationAndAction-App.java.

Listing 4.1 TransformationAndActionApp.java

```java
package net.jgp.books.spark.ch04.lab200_transformation_and_action;

import static org.apache.spark.sql.functions.expr;   ◄───  You will use this function
import org.apache.spark.sql.Dataset;                         to calculate an expression
import org.apache.spark.sql.Row;                             on a column.
```

```
import org.apache.spark.sql.SparkSession;

public class TransformationAndActionApp {

  public static void main(String[] args) {
    TransformationAndActionApp app = new TransformationAndActionApp();
    String mode = "noop";
    if (args.length != 0) {
      mode = args[0];
    }
    app.start(mode);
  }
```

← Make sure that you have an argument to pass to start().

The first step is to get a session, as usual:

```
  private void start(String mode) {
    long t0 = System.currentTimeMillis();        ← Sets the timer

    SparkSession spark = SparkSession.builder()  ← Creates the sessions
        .appName("Analysing Catalyst's behavior")
        .master("local")
        .getOrCreate();                              Measures the time spent
    long t1 = System.currentTimeMillis();        ← creating the session
    System.out.println("1. Creating a session .......... " + (t1 - t0));
```

The second step is to ingest the data from a CSV file:

```
    Dataset<Row> df = spark.read().format("csv")  ← Reads the file
        .option("header", "true")
        .load(
            "data/NCHS_-_Teen_Birth_Rates_for_Age_Group_15-19_in_the_United
    _States_by_County.csv");
    Dataset<Row> initalDf = df;                   ← Creates a reference dataframe
    long t2 = System.currentTimeMillis();            to use in the copy
    System.out.println("2. Loading initial dataset ...... " + (t2 - t1));
```

Measures the time spent reading the file and creating the dataframe

In step 3, you union the dataframe onto itself to create a bigger dataset (otherwise, Spark would be too fast, and you could not measure the benefits):

Measures the time needed to build a bigger dataset

```
    for (int i = 0; i < 60; i++) {               ←
      df = df.union(initalDf);                       Loops to make the
    }                                                dataset bigger
    long t3 = System.currentTimeMillis();
    System.out.println("3. Building full dataset ........ " + (t3 - t2));
```

Step 4 renames the columns:

Basic cleanup: makes the column names shorter for easier manipulation

Measures the time for cleanup

```
    df = df.withColumnRenamed("Lower Confidence Limit", "lcl");
    df = df.withColumnRenamed("Upper Confidence Limit", "ucl");
    long t4 = System.currentTimeMillis();
    System.out.println("4. Clean-up .................... " + (t4 - t3));
```

Step 5 is the actual data transformation, with the different modes:

**If mode is "noop," skips all transformations;
otherwise, creates new columns**

**Creates a new column
containing the average
between the upper and
lower confidence limit**

**Creates a
duplicate
column of lcl
called lcl2**

**Creates a duplicate
column of ucl called ucl2**

**If mode is "full," deletes
the newly created columns**

**Measures the
time used for
transformation**

```
if (mode.compareToIgnoreCase("noop") != 0) {
    df = df
        .withColumn("avg", expr("(lcl+ucl)/2"))
        .withColumn("lcl2", df.col("lcl"))
        .withColumn("ucl2", df.col("ucl"));
    if (mode.compareToIgnoreCase("full") == 0) {
        df = df
            .drop(df.col("avg"))
            .drop(df.col("lcl2"))
            .drop(df.col("ucl2"));
    }
}
long t5 = System.currentTimeMillis();
System.out.println("5. Transformations ........... " + (t5 - t4));
```

Step 6 is the last step of the application, which calls the action:

**Measures
the time
needed for
the action**

```
df.collect();                                    ← Performs the collection action
long t6 = System.currentTimeMillis();
System.out.println("6. Final action ............... " + (t6 - t5));

System.out.println("");
System.out.println("# of records ................. " + df.count());
    }
}
```

The `collect()` action returns an object. The method's full signature is shown here:

```
Object collect()
```

You can ignore the return, as you are not interested in further processing. However, in cases outside benchmarks, you will most likely use the returned value. In the next sections, you will take a closer look at what happened.

4.2.4 *The mystery behind the creation of 7 million datapoints in 182 ms*

In the previous sections, you saw that the transformation process created over 7 million datapoints in about 182 milliseconds. Let's look at what you did and what Spark did.

Your original dataset contains 40,781 records. You copy the dataset itself 60 times, which creates a new dataset of 2,487,641 records (about 2.5 million records). In listing 4.1, this was done via the following code:

```
for (int i = 0; i < 60; i++) {
  df = df.union(df0);
}
```

After building this dataset, you create three columns: one containing the average of the lower and upper confidence limits, and two duplicate columns. This results in creating 3 × 2,487,641 = 7,462,923 datapoints. You started the timer just before creating the columns and stopped it right after: did you really create about 7.5 million datapoints in 182 milliseconds?

Spark is only *creating the recipe* and will execute the recipe when you call an action. This is why Spark is lazy, a little bit like when you ask your kids to do something, as illustrated in figure 4.4.

What do I mean by *recipe*? Is it a job?

Spark defines a *job* as a parallel computation consisting of multiple tasks that gets spawned in response to a Spark action (such as `save()`, `collect()`, and more).

Spark does not have a term describing a list of transformations, which is an essential part of a job. You will see more about jobs in chapter 5.

Being French, I have this strong relationship with food, and, of course, analogies with food related-terms are numerous. It makes sense to me to call this list of transformations a *recipe*. A term used in cooking is *mise en place*: having all your ingredients measured, cut, peeled, sliced, grated, and more, before you start cooking. If you want to push the analogy a little bit, you could say that all the data ingestion is the *mise en place*, but this is not a cookbook, is it?

To summarize: Spark handles jobs, and a job consists of a certain number of transformations assembled in a recipe.

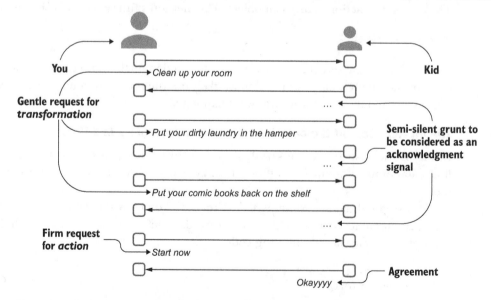

Figure 4.4 Explaining *transformations* and *action* in real life: you create a recipe, or work order, and then call for action.

Spark implements this recipe as a directed acyclic graph (DAG).

> **What is a directed acyclic graph?**
>
> One of my promises in this book was to skip the complex mathematical concepts, so if you are allergic to math, feel free to skip to the next section.
>
> In mathematics and computer science, a *directed acyclic graph* (DAG) is a finite directed graph with no directed cycles. The graph consists of finitely many vertices and edges, with each edge directed from one vertex to another, such that there is no way to start at any vertex *v* and follow a consistently directed sequence of edges that eventually loops back to *v* again.
>
> Equivalently, a DAG is a directed graph that has a topological ordering, a sequence of the vertices such that every edge is directed from earlier to later in the sequence. Basically, a DAG is a graph that never goes back.
>
> This information is adapted from Wikipedia at https://en.wikipedia.org/wiki/Directed _acyclic_graph.

In the next section, you will analyze how Spark is cleaning (or optimizing) the recipe.

4.2.5 *The mystery behind the timing of actions*

In the previous sections, you learned about Spark's laziness and how, like a kid, it waits for you to tell it to do all the transformations when you call for action. All moms and dads reading this book should be able to relate. You also learned that Spark stores the recipe of transformations in a DAG, which, basically, is a graph that never rewinds.

So, as you remember, you worked on three experiments. Table 4.3 summarizes the recipe and timing.

Table 4.3 Detailing the recipe of your three experiments with transformations and actions

	Experiment 1: Load and collect	**Experiment 2:** Load, create columns, and collect	**Experiment 3:** Load, create columns, delete the columns, and collect
Recipe	Load an initial dataset and copy it 60 times.	Load an initial dataset, copy it 60 times, create one column based on an expression (computation of an average), and duplicate two columns.	Load an initial dataset, copy it 60 times, create one column based on an expression (computation of an average), duplicate two columns, and delete the three columns.
See figure	4.5	4.6	4.7
Action	**20,770 ms**	**34,061 ms**	**24,909 ms**

Figure 4.5 describes the recipe of transformations for the first experiment. You load the dataset, copy it 60 times onto itself, and clean up. This process took about 21 seconds on my laptop.

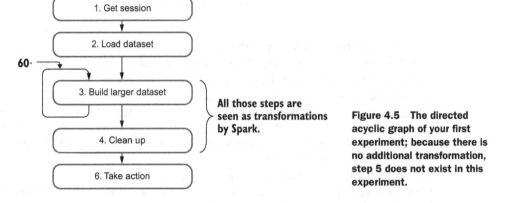

Figure 4.5   The directed acyclic graph of your first experiment; because there is no additional transformation, step 5 does not exist in this experiment.

Figure 4.6 describes the recipe used in the second experiment: the fifth step appears with transformations. It makes sense that the action takes more time, as it will perform all the transformations at this point:

1. Build the larger dataset.
2. Clean up.
3. Compute the average.
4. Duplicate the lcl column.
5. Duplicate the ucl column.

This process took about 34 seconds on my laptop.

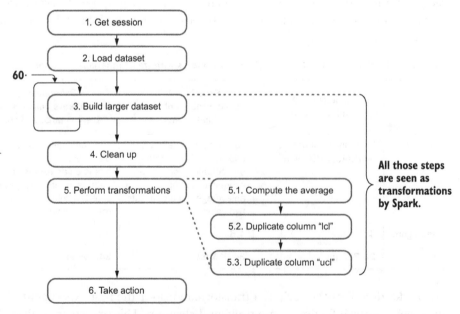

Figure 4.6   The second experiment's DAG extends the first experiment, by adding the average computation and the creation of the two duplicate columns.

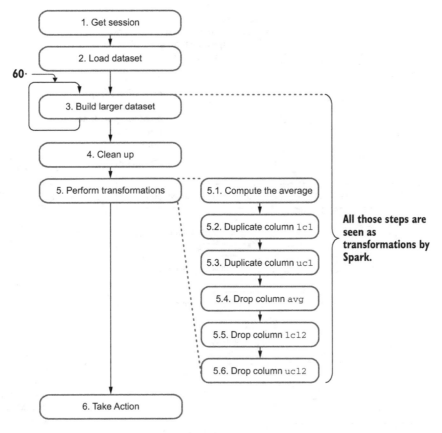

Figure 4.7 The third experiment's DAG before any optimization, with the following transformations: build a larger dataset, clean up, create the columns, and then delete them.

Figure 4.7 illustrates the third experiment with the additional transformations, before any optimization.

When you look at figure 4.7, it makes sense that the third experiment should take more than 34 seconds to complete. That number of seconds is the duration of the second experiment, where fewer transformations were done. So why does it take only 25 seconds to perform? Spark embeds an optimizer, called *Catalyst*. Before performing the action, Catalyst looks at the DAG and makes a better one. Figure 4.8 shows the Catalyst process.

Catalyst will still build the larger dataset (through union()) and perform the cleanup, but it will optimize the other transformations:

- Computing the average is canceled by dropping the column.
- Duplicating the lc1 and uc1 columns and then dropping the duplicated columns cancels the operation.

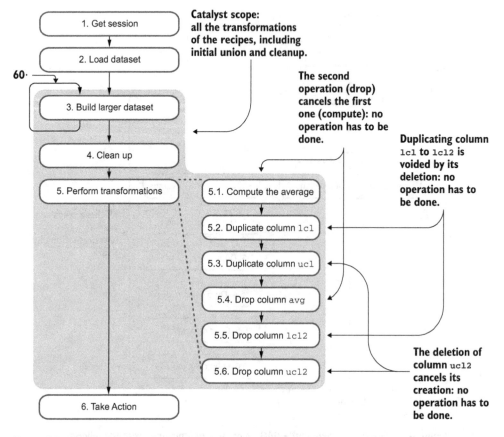

Figure 4.8   Catalyst, the Spark optimizer, is having a serious look at what you ask it to do. And then it optimizes.

After the optimization process, the DAG is simplified, as illustrated in figure 4.9.

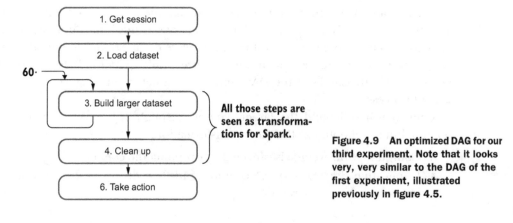

Figure 4.9   An optimized DAG for our third experiment. Note that it looks very, very similar to the DAG of the first experiment, illustrated previously in figure 4.5.

Hopefully, you get a sense of what Catalyst can do in terms of optimization. Let's just, for the fun of it, compare this to a standard application using JDBC that would do the same operations using a database.

4.3 Comparing to RDBMS and traditional applications

In the previous sections, you read about the differences between a transformation (a step of the recipe) and an action (the trigger that starts the job). You also read about how Spark builds and optimizes the DAG, which represents the recipe, or process of manipulating your data.

In this section, you will compare Spark's process to that of a traditional application. You will briefly review the context of the application, detailed in the previous section. Then you'll compare a traditional application to a Spark application and draw a few conclusions.

4.3.1 Working with the teen birth rates dataset

Setting the context of your application is important: you are working with a dataset containing mean teen birth rates by year for each county and state in the United States. It comes from the NCHS. Table 4.4 describes the structure of the dataset (identical to table 4.2).

Table 4.4   Structure of the NCHS birth rate dataset used throughout the chapter

Column name in the dataset	Type	Comment
Year	Numeric	
State	String	
County	String	
State FIPS Code	Integer	State code in the US Federal Information Processing Standards
County FIPS Code	Integer	County code in the US FIPS
Combined FIPS Code	Integer	Combination of the state and county FIPS code in one
Birth Rate	Decimal	Teen birth rate: births per 1,000 females ages 15–19 in a given year
Lower Confidence Limit	Decimal	Column renamed `lcl` later
Upper Confidence Limit	Decimal	Column renamed `ucl` later

In the previous section, you ran three incremental experiments. However, in this section, you will limit your approach to the third experiment, which consists of the following steps:

1   Get a Spark session.
2   Load an initial dataset.

  3 Build a larger dataset.
  4 Clean up: rename the Lower Confidence Limit column to `lcl`, and the Upper
     Confidence Limit column to `ucl`.
  5 Compute the average in a new column.
  6 Duplicate the `lcl` column.
  7 Duplicate the `ucl` column.
  8 Drop the three columns.

4.3.2 Analyzing differences between a traditional app and a Spark app

Now that you have the context in mind, you can analyze the paths taken for a traditional application and a Spark application. For a traditional application, you can assume that the original data is already in a database table, and there is no need to create a bigger dataset.

Figure 4.10 compares the two processes, and table 4.5 details each step.

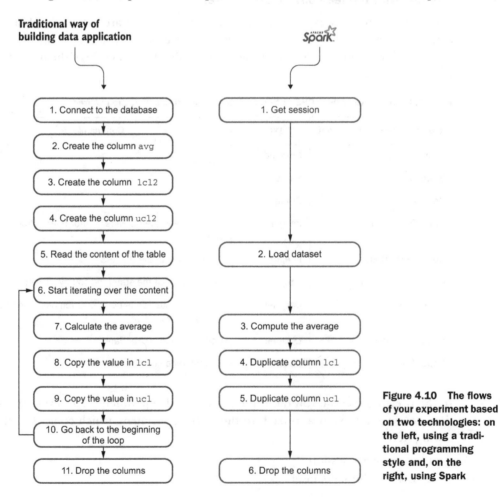

Figure 4.10 The flows of your experiment based on two technologies: on the left, using a traditional programming style and, on the right, using Spark

Table 4.5 reuses figure 4.10's flow, but describes each step and explains the difference between a traditional application and a Spark application.

Table 4.5   Comparing the steps in a traditional Java/RDBMS application and a Spark application

\multicolumn{3}{|c|}{Traditional app}			\multicolumn{3}{c|}{Spark app}		
Step	**Description**	**Notes**	**Step**	**Description**	**Notes**
1	Connect to the database.		1	Get a session from the Spark server/cluster.	
2	Create the column `avg`, which will contain the average.	Modification of table's structure is not trivial in an RDBMS world.		Not needed	This is not needed by Spark, as the schema of the dataframe is less constrained.
3	Create the column `lc12`, which will contain the values of column `lc1`.			Not needed	
4	Create the column `uc12`, which will contain the values of column `uc1`.			Not needed	
5	Read the content of the table in a `ResultSet`.		2	Load the data in the dataframe from the CSV file.	
6	Iterate over the content of the `ResultSet`.			Not needed	There is no need to iterate over the data within Spark.
7	Calculate the average of two cells.		3	Calculate the average for the column.	
8	Copy the value in column `lc1` to column `lc12`.		4	Duplicate the entire column `lc1` to `lc12`.	
9	Copy the value in column `uc1` to column `uc12`.		5	Duplicate the entire column `uc1` to `uc12`.	
10	Go back to step 6 until iteration is over.			Not needed	No need for iteration
11	Drop columns `avg`, `lc12`, and `uc12`.	Modification of the table structure	6	Drop columns `avg`, `lc12`, and `uc12`.	

Based on this comparison, you can see that the lazy approach of Spark saves processing time.

4.4   *Spark is amazing for data-focused applications*

In the previous sections, you looked at a real-life example of transformations and actions, and then you drilled into Spark's vision of this mechanism and its implementation as a DAG. Finally, you compared the traditional way of building data-centric applications to the way Spark allows you to implement those applications. This section summarizes the Spark way of building data-centric applications.

I must concede that the application you built during your experiments in this chapter does not make much sense: you do something and then you delete what you just did. However, in big data and analytics, those operations happen a lot. If you are not a big data guru yet (agreed, this is only chapter 4), you can think of building formulas with Excel or any other spreadsheet: sometimes (often!) you need to use a cell as a pivot. Big data transformations are similar. You can compare this mechanism to a variable or a list (column) of variables.

You can transform your data by using the following:

- The built-in methods on the dataframe, such as `withColumn()`
- The built-in column-level methods, such as `expr()` (refer to the list in appendix G)
- The lower-level methods, such as `map()`, `union()`, and more (see appendix I)
- Your own transformations using UDFs, detailed in chapter 16

Appendix I presents two tables containing the list of transformations and the list of actions, respectively. Although these lists are available online, the ones in the appendix add the important class signature that makes it possible for you to write easy and maintainable Java code for your project.

Your transformations will be applied only when you call an action.

4.5   *Catalyst is your app catalyzer*

In the previous sections, you learned that Spark turns your process of manipulating data into a DAG. Catalyst is in charge of optimizing this graph. In this section, you will learn more about Catalyst.

In one of my projects, the team needed and developed a join between two dataframes that resulted in the second dataframe being a nested document, as a column of the first dataframe. When we needed to add a third dataframe, the team considered developing a method that would take three dataframes, a master and two subdocuments, and so on. Because the operation was fairly heavy, the team wanted to optimize the number of steps. Rather than developing a method to take three dataframes as parameters, the team used the first method several times: each step was simply added to the DAG. At the end, Catalyst took the liberty of optimizing, making the code "lighter" and more readable (and cheaper to maintain).

What Catalyst does is similar to what a query optimizer does with a query plan in the relational database world. Let's have a closer look at a Catalyst plan.

To access the plan, you can use the `explain()` method of the dataframe to display it, as in the following listing. I added line breaks to make the output more readable.

Listing 4.2   Execution plan for ingestion, transformation, and action

The union operation

```
   == Physical Plan ==
-> Union
    :- *(1) Project  <
      [
        Year#10,
        State#11,
        County#12,
        State FIPS Code#13,
        County FIPS Code#14,
        Combined FIPS Code#15,
        Birth Rate#16,
        Lower Confidence Limit#17 AS lcl#37,
        Upper Confidence Limit#18 AS ucl#47,
        ((cast(Lower Confidence Limit#17 as double) + cast(Upper Confidence
        Limit#18 as double)) / 2.0) AS avg#57,  <
        Lower Confidence Limit#17 AS lcl2#68,
        Upper Confidence Limit#18 AS ucl2#80
      ]
```

The second set of operations: manipulating the columns through renaming, operations, and duplication

Original fields from the CSV file

Renamed fields

Duplicated columns

Average column

The operations are in reverse order. The first part of this execution plan is the union. The initial operations, such as ingestion, occur after the union operation:

```
    :  +- *(1) FileScan csv   <---- Reads the CSV file
      [
        Year#10,
        State#11,
        County#12,
        State FIPS Code#13,
        County FIPS Code#14,
        Combined FIPS Code#15,
        Birth Rate#16,
        Lower Confidence Limit#17,
        Upper Confidence Limit#18
      ]
      Batched: false,
      Format: CSV,
      Location: InMemoryFileIndex[file:/Users/jgp/Workspaces/Book/net.jgp.
      books.spark.ch04/data/NCHS_-_Te...,
      PartitionFilters: [],
      PushedFilters: [],
      ReadSchema: struct<Year:string,State:string,County:string,
      State FIPS Code:string,County FIPS Code:string,Comb...  <
    +- *(2) Project [Year#10, State#11, County#12, State FIPS Code#13,
      County FIPS Code#14, Combined FIPS Code#15, Birth Rate#16,
      Lower Confidence Limit#17 AS lcl#37,
      Upper Confidence Limit#18 AS ucl#47,
      ((cast(Lower Confidence Limit#17 as double) +
      cast(Upper Confidence Limit#18 as double)) / 2.0) AS avg#57,
      Lower Confidence Limit#17 AS lcl2#68,
      Upper Confidence Limit#18 AS ucl2#80]
        +- *(2) FileScan csv [Year#10,State#11,County#12,State FIPS Code#13,
```

Fields from the CSV file

Format of the file

Note that the file is in memory.

The schema inferred by Spark

➥ County FIPS Code#14,Combined FIPS Code#15,Birth Rate#16,
➥ Lower Confidence Limit#17,Upper Confidence Limit#18]
➥ Batched: false, Format: CSV, Location: InMemoryFileIndex[file:/Users/
➥ jgp/Workspaces/Book/net.jgp.books.spark.ch04/data/NCHS_-_Te...,
➥ PartitionFilters: [], PushedFilters: [],
➥ ReadSchema: struct<Year:string,State:string,County:string,
➥ State FIPS Code:string,County FIPS Code:string,Comb...

Listing 4.3 shows the code that produces this output. This code is similar to the second experiment:

- Load the dataset.
- Union it (only once here).
- Rename the columns.
- Add the three columns: the average and the two duplicate columns.

Listing 4.3 Basic transformation application

```
package net.jgp.books.spark.ch04.lab500_transformation_explain;

import static org.apache.spark.sql.functions.expr;

import org.apache.spark.sql.Dataset;
import org.apache.spark.sql.Row;
import org.apache.spark.sql.SparkSession;

public class TransformationExplainApp {
...
  private void start() {
    SparkSession spark = SparkSession.builder()
        .appName("Showing execution plan")
        .master("local")
        .getOrCreate();

    Dataset<Row> df = spark.read().format("csv")
        .option("header", "true")
        .load(
            "data/NCHS_-_Teen_Birth_Rates_for_Age_Group_15-19_
➥ in_the_United_States_by_County.csv");
    Dataset<Row> df0 = df;

    df = df.union(df0);

    df = df.withColumnRenamed("Lower Confidence Limit", "lcl");
    df = df.withColumnRenamed("Upper Confidence Limit", "ucl");

    df = df
        .withColumn("avg", expr("(lcl+ucl)/2"))
        .withColumn("lcl2", df.col("lcl"))
        .withColumn("ucl2", df.col("ucl"));

    df.explain();
  }
}
```

The result can be useful for debugging your applications.

If you are interested in the details of how Catalyst works, Matei Zaharia and other Spark engineers published "Spark SQL: Relational Data Processing in Spark," a paper available at http://mng.bz/MOA8. Another interesting paper on DAG and its representation, "Understanding your Apache Spark Application Through Visualization" comes from Andrew Or, and you can read it at http://mng.bz/adYX. Although the original design comes from Databricks, for Spark v2.2, IBM contributed query optimization techniques from its database engines to the Spark code base. If you are interested in adding your own rules to Catalyst, check out "Learn the Extension Points in Apache Spark and Extend the Spark Catalyst Optimizer" by Sunitha Kambhampati at http://mng.bz/gVjG, with examples in Scala.

Summary

- Spark is efficiently lazy: it will build the list of transformations as a directed acyclic graph (DAG), which it will optimize using Catalyst, Spark's built-in optimizer.
- When you apply a transformation on a dataframe, the data is not modified.
- When you apply an action on a dataframe, all the transformations are executed, and, if it needs to be, the data will be modified.
- Modification of the schema is a natural operation within Spark. You can create columns as placeholders and perform operations on them.
- Spark works at the column level; there is no need to iterate over the data.
- Transformations can be done using the built-in functions (see appendix G), lower-level functions (appendix I), dataframe methods, and UDFs (see chapter 16).
- You can print the query plan by using the dataframe's explain() method, which is useful for debugging—and very verbose!

5
Building a simple app for deployment

This chapter covers

- Building a simple application that will not require data ingestion
- Using Java lambdas with Spark
- Building an application with or without lambdas
- Interacting with Spark in local mode, cluster mode, and interactively
- Calculating an approximation of π by using Spark

In the previous chapters, you discovered what Apache Spark is and how to build simple applications, and, hopefully, understood key concepts including the dataframe and laziness. Chapters 5 and 6 are linked: you will build an application in this chapter and deploy it in chapter 6.

In this chapter, you will start from scratch by building an application. You built applications previously in this book, but they always needed to ingest data at the very beginning of the process. Your lab will generate data within and by Spark, avoiding the need to ingest data. Ingesting data in a cluster is a bit more complex than creating a self-generated dataset. The goal of this application is to approximate a value of π (pi).

You will then learn about the three ways to interact with Spark:

- Local mode, which you are already familiar with through the examples in the previous chapters
- Cluster mode
- Interactive mode

LAB　Examples from this chapter are available in GitHub at https://github .com/jgperrin/net.jgp.books.spark.ch05.

5.1　*An ingestionless example*

In this section, you will work on an example that does not need to ingest data. Ingestion is a key part of an overall big data process, as you've seen in this book's many examples. However, this chapter will bring you to deployment, including deployment on a cluster, so I do not want you to be distracted by ingestion.

Working on a cluster implies that the data is available to all nodes. To understand deployment on a cluster, you need to spend a lot of time focusing on data distribution. You will learn more about data distribution in chapter 6.

Therefore, to simplify the understanding of deployment, I skip the ingestion and focus on understanding all the components, the flow of data, and the hands-on deployment. Spark will generate a large dataset (self-generation) of random data that can be used to calculate π.

5.1.1　*Calculating π*

In this small theoretical section, I explain how to compute π by using darts and how to implement the process within Spark. If you hate math, you will see that this section is not that terrible (and you can skip it if you are allergic). Nevertheless, I'd like to dedicate this section to my older son, Pierre-Nicolas, who is certainly more appreciative than me of the beauty of this algorithm.

You're still reading? Fine! In this short section, you will learn how to get an approximation of π by throwing darts and then implement the code in Spark. The result and actual code are in the next section.

There are many ways of calculating π (see more on Wikipedia at https://en.wikipedia.org/wiki/Approximations_of_%CF%80). The one most adapted to our scenario is called *summing a circle's area*, illustrated in figure 5.1.

This code estimates π by "throwing darts" at a circle: as points (the darts' impact) are randomly scattered inside the unit square, some fall within the unit circle. The fraction of points inside the circle approaches π/4 as points are added.

You will simulate throwing millions of darts. You will randomly generate the abscissa (x) and the ordinate (y) of each throw. From these coordinates, using the Pythagorean theorem, you can calculate whether the dart is *in* or *out*. Figure 5.2 illustrates this measure.

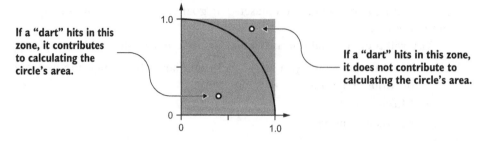

If a "dart" hits in this zone, it contributes to calculating the circle's area.
If a "dart" hits in this zone, it does not contribute to calculating the circle's area.
1.0
0
0
1.0

Figure 5.1 A graphical representation of throwing darts to approximate π by using a circle's area

Based on figure 5.2, you can look at two throws, *t1* and *t2*, and see that the first throw, *t1*, is out of the circle. Its coordinates are $x1 = 0.75$ and $y1 = 0.9$. The distance *d1* is the distance between *t1* and the origin, whose coordinates are (0, 0). This is represented by the following equation:

y1 = 0.9
t1
d1
t2
y2 = 0.2
d2
0
0
x2 = 0.4
x1= 0.75

Figure 5.2 With the use of the Pythagorean theorem, you can easily determine whether the throw is in the circle.

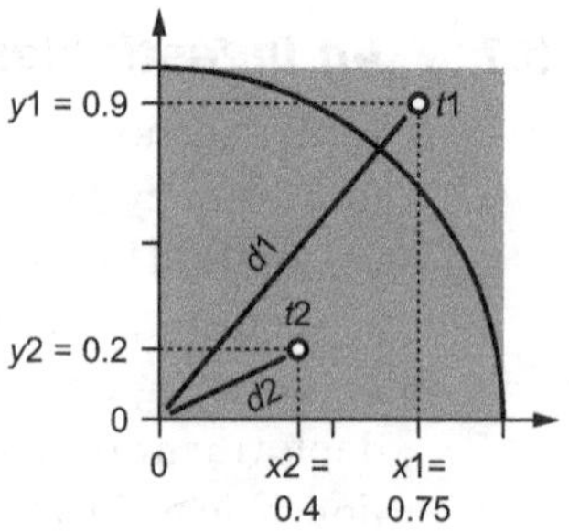

$$d1 = \sqrt{x1^2 + y1^2}$$

$$d1 = \sqrt{0.75^2 + 0.9^2}$$

$$d1 \cong 1.17$$

$$d1 > 1$$

You can do the same exercise for the second throw, where *d2* represents the distance between the origin and *t2*:

$$d2 = \sqrt{x2^2 + y2^2}$$

$$d2 = \sqrt{0.4^2 + 0.2^2}$$

$$d2 \cong 0.44$$

$$d2 \leq 1$$

This means that the second throw is in the circle.

Spark will create the data, apply transformations, and then apply an action—a classic modus operandi for Spark. The process (shown in figure 5.3) is as follows:

1. Open a Spark session.
2. Spark creates a dataset containing one row per dart throw. The bigger the number of throws, the more precise your approximation of π will be.

3   Create a dataset containing the result of each throw.

4   Sum the count of throws contributing to the circle's area.

5   Compute the ratio of throws in both zones and multiply it by 4, which approximates π.

While summarizing the process, figure 5.3 introduces the *methods* being used as well as which *components* are involved. You learned about some of those components in chapter 2. Chapter 6 will also detail each component further.

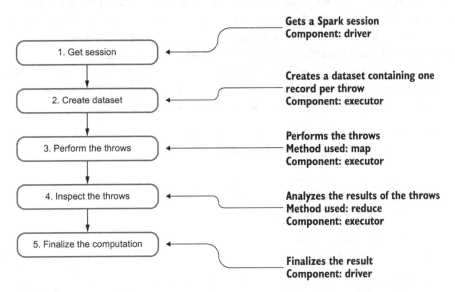

Figure 5.3   The process of approximating π, illustrating the Spark components (driver and executor) as well as the methods. The executor is controlled by the worker.

Enough math—let's look at Java code, okay?

5.1.2   *The code to approximate* π

In this section, you'll walk through the code, which you will use throughout this chapter in various examples. You will first run the code in local mode. You will then modify this version of the code to use Java lambda functions.

Java 8 introduced lambda functions, which can exist without belonging to a class and can be passed around as parameters, and are executed on demand. You will discover how lambda functions can help you (or not) to write transformation code.

Let's first look at the output of your application in the following listing.

Listing 5.1   Result of throwing darts to approximate π

```
About to throw 1000000 darts, ready? Stay away from the target!
Session initialized in 1685 ms
Initial dataframe built in 5083 ms
```

```
Throwing darts done in 21 ms
100000 darts thrown so far
200000 darts thrown so far
...
900000 darts thrown so far
1000000 darts thrown so far
Analyzing result in 6337 ms
Pi is roughly 3.143304
```

◄——— **You just threw I million darts in 2I ms.**

**The throws start only
when you call the action.**

The application tells you that 1 million darts were thrown in 21 milliseconds. However, Spark will *throw* the darts only when you ask it to, as you call an action to analyze the results. This is coming from Spark's lazy attitude you learned about in chapter 4; remember those darn kids who need to be reminded by an action!

In this lab, you will slice the processing into separate batches. I call those *slices* and, after you run the labs, you can play with the values of slices at different locations to better understand how Spark can deal with this kind of processing.

LAB   The code of lab #100 is in net.jgp.books.spark.ch05.lab100_pi_compute
.PiComputeApp and in the following listing.

Listing 5.2   Code to compute π

```
package net.jgp.books.spark.ch05.lab100_pi_compute;

import java.io.Serializable;
import java.util.ArrayList;
import java.util.List;
import org.apache.spark.api.java.function.MapFunction;     ◄——┐  Used for the mapper
import org.apache.spark.api.java.function.ReduceFunction;   ◄——— Used for the reducer
import org.apache.spark.sql.Dataset;
import org.apache.spark.sql.Encoders;
import org.apache.spark.sql.Row;
import org.apache.spark.sql.SparkSession;
...
  private void start(int slices) {
    int numberOfThrows = 100000 * slices;
    System.out.println("About to throw " + numberOfThrows
        + " darts, ready? Stay away from the target!");

    long t0 = System.currentTimeMillis();
    SparkSession spark = SparkSession
        .builder()
        .appName("Spark Pi")
        .master("local[*]")
        .getOrCreate();
    long t1 = System.currentTimeMillis();
    System.out.println("Session initialized in " + (t1 - t0) + " ms");
```

**You can use the number of slices
as a multiplier; it will be useful
later when you run it on a cluster.**

**Uses all the possible
threads on this system**

Up to this point, the code is pretty standard: it uses the usual imported Spark classes and is getting a session. You will notice the calls to currentTimeMillis() to measure where time is spent:

```
List<Integer> listOfThrows = new ArrayList<>(numberOfThrows);
for (int i = 0; i < numberOfThrows; i++) {
  listOfThrows.add(i);
}
Dataset<Row> incrementalDf = spark
    .createDataset(l, Encoders.INT())
    .toDF();
long t2 = System.currentTimeMillis();
System.out.println("Initial dataframe built in " + (t2 - t1) + " ms");
```

In this snippet, you create a dataset from a list of integers, which you convert to a dataframe. When you create a dataset from a list, you need to provide Spark a hint about the type of data—hence the `Encoders.INT()` parameter.

The purpose of this dataframe is solely to dispatch the processing over as many nodes as possible in an operation called a *map*. In traditional programming, if you want to throw 1 million darts, you use a loop in a single thread, on a single node. This cannot scale. In a highly distributed environment, you map the process of throwing darts over your nodes. Figure 5.4 compares the processes.

In other words, every row of `incrementalDf` is passed to an instance of a `DartMapper`, which is on all physical nodes of the cluster:

```
Dataset<Integer> dartsDs = incrementalDf
    .map(new DartMapper(), Encoders.INT());      <── Call to the mapper
long t3 = System.currentTimeMillis();
System.out.println("Throwing darts done in " + (t3 - t2) + " ms");
```

You will see `DartMapper()` in listing 5.3.

The reduce operation brings back the result: the number of darts in the circle. In a similar way, the reduce operation is transparent in your application and consists of only one line of code:

```
int dartsInCircle = dartsDs.reduce(new DartReducer());  <── Call to the reducer
long t4 = System.currentTimeMillis();
System.out.println("Analyzing result in " + (t4 - t3) + " ms");
```

Shows the estimation of π ⎰ `System.out.println("Pi is roughly " + 4.0 * dartsInCircle / numberOfThrows);`

You will see `DartReducer()` in listing 5.3.

I can summarize the application's process as follows:

1 Create a list, which will be used for mapping the data.
2 Map the data (throw the darts).
3 Reduce the result.

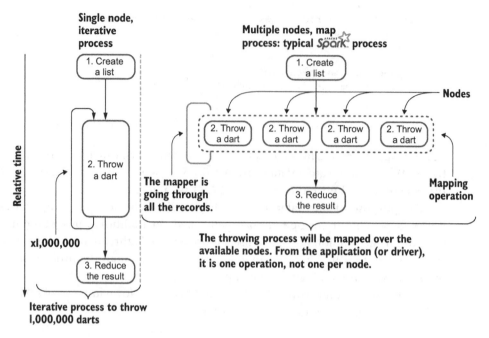

Figure 5.4   Comparing a process of throwing 1 million darts in an iterative process versus mapping them over four nodes (but it could be more)

Let's have a look at the code for the mapping and reducing operations in listing 5.3.

GOING FURTHER   You can practice this lab by changing `numberOfThrows` type from `int` to `long`. If you use an IDE such as Eclipse, you will see directly where it impacts the rest of your code. Another twist to this example: try to incorporate the `slices` variable (or a fraction of it) when you call your master, as in `.master("local[*]")` to see how it impacts performance (this will be more obvious as you use more cores).

Listing 5.3   Code to compute π: map and reduce classes

```
private final class DartMapper              ⟵── The mapper
    implements MapFunction<Row, Integer> {
  private static final long serialVersionUID = 38446L;

  @Override
  public Integer call(Row r) throws Exception {
    double x = Math.random() * 2 - 1;
    double y = Math.random() * 2 - 1;
    counter++; #C
    if (counter % 100000 == 0) {
      System.out.println("" + counter + " darts thrown so far");
    } #C
    return (x * x + y * y <= 1) ? 1 : 0;
  }
}
```

Returns 1 if it's in the circle and 0 if not (see note on square root that follows)

You're randomly throwing darts; x and y are coordinates.

Simple counter to see what's going on; you never reset it.

```
    }

    private final class DartReducer implements ReduceFunction<Integer> {
        private static final long serialVersionUID = 12859L;

        @Override
        public Integer call(Integer x, Integer y) throws Exception {
            return x + y;
        }
    }
```

Returns the sum of every throw's result

The reducer sums the results; note that the types are matching. The generic exception comes from the method's signature.

WHY DIDN'T I RETURN A SQUARE ROOT? Take a look at the return value of the `call()` method in the mapper. If you follow the Pythagorean theorem, you would need to return the square root of the sum of the squares of x and y. However, as those values are under 1, it does not matter: the dart is in the circle (or not), and we do not care about the exact distance from the origin to the throw, just that it's the square. Therefore, we can spare the expensive square root operation.

Let's analyze the plumbing (or supporting code) needed to make this class work. I will remove all the business logic from listing 5.3 and walk you through the plumbing code.

To be used, the mapper needs to implement a `MapFunction<Row, Integer>`, which means that the mapping function, `call()`, will get a `Row` and return an `Integer`. In listing 5.2, you saw that the return of the call to the `map()` function was a `Dataset<Integer>`:

```
Dataset<Integer> dartsDs = incrementalDf
        .map(new DartMapper(), Encoders.INT());
```

Your class looks like this:

```
private final class DartMapper
        implements MapFunction<Row, Integer> {
    ...
    public Integer call(Row r) throws Exception {...}
    ...
}
```

Types (in bold) must match: you are using integers, and integers are used in the dataset, in the implemented type, and the method.

When you call the reducer, in listing 5.2, you use the following:

```
int dartsInCircle = dartsDs.reduce(new DartReducer());
```

The class looks like this:

```
private final class DartReducer implements ReduceFunction<Integer> {
    ...
    public Integer call(Integer x, Integer y) throws Exception {...}
    ...
}
```

Types must match.

Did I just use MapReduce?

Yes, you just did! But what exactly is MapReduce? *MapReduce* is a way to spread workloads over a cluster of servers in a distributed environment.

A MapReduce application is composed of a mapping operation, which performs filtering and sorting (such as sorting students by first name into queues, one queue for each name), and a reduce method, which performs a summary operation (such as counting the number of students in each queue, yielding name frequencies). The MapReduce framework orchestrates the processing by marshalling the distributed servers, running the various tasks in parallel, managing all communications and data transfers between the various parts of the system, and providing for redundancy and fault tolerance. It works the same way if you have only one server, as you still have numerous tasks.

The following diagram illustrates the principle of MapReduce:

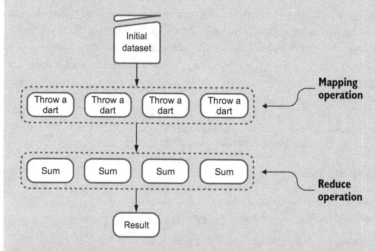

Summary of a MapReduce process: mapping distributes the data and reduces it. MapReduce is not only about throwing darts and summing up the result.

The original MapReduce idea was published in a Google paper in 2004. It has since been implemented in various products. The most popular implementation remains Apache Hadoop.

In this chapter's example, the use of MapReduce is easy, as we perform simple and atomic operations. In a more complex scenario, the complexity can become exponential. This is one of the reasons Hadoop is complex: everything is a MapReduce job (some tools can mask the complexity). With Apache Spark, the complexity is hidden from the beginning, but Spark lets you go low-level if you want, as you did in this chapter.

In summary, Spark simplifies the MapReduce processing and, often, you do not even realize you're doing MapReduce operations.

The internet has more resources on MapReduce. YouTube has a fun explanation of MapReduce that uses playing cards: www.youtube.com/watch?v=bcjSeOxCHbE. (Hint: Double the playback speed if you don't want to fall asleep.)

Of course, you can also check out the Wikipedia page, slightly too scientific for an introduction (but you just got one, right?) at https://en.wikipedia.org/wiki/MapReduce.

So, as surprising or shocking at it may seem, Spark does MapReduce, but does not require you to do MapReduce.

Information in this sidebar was loosely adapted from Wikipedia.

In the next sections, you will see how to write this application's code (listings 5.2 and 5.3) differently with Java lambda functions and reduce a bit of the plumbing code. There is no preference in how you write the code in the end; the ultimate implementation may be driven by habit, guidelines, perceived difficulties, and more.

5.1.3 What are lambda functions in Java?

In the previous section, you ran an approximation of π by using classes for the mapping and reducing steps. In this section, you will (re)discover a bit about lambda functions in Java. In the next section (5.1.4), you will run the same application to approximate π with lambda functions instead of classes. If you are familiar with lambda functions in Java, jump directly to section 5.1.4.

Writing a class or a lambda function is often a question of taste or comfort for the software engineer. It is important that you recognize one when you see it.

Despite Java's current version of 11, I keep seeing younger developers coming into the workforce with Java 7 knowledge, and more-recent features, including lambda functions, are still not popular. The goal of this book is not to teach you Java 8, but I provide some Java reminders for some of the less visible (but nevertheless great) features.

WHAT ARE JAVA LAMBDA FUNCTIONS? You may be familiar with lambda functions in Java. If you are not, Java 8 introduced a new type of function, which can be created without belonging to a class. *Lambda functions* can be passed around as a parameter and are executed on demand. It's Java's first step toward functional programming. The notation for a lambda function is `<variable> -> <function>`.

In the source code repository, net.jgp.books.spark.ch05.lab900_simple_lambda.SimpleLambdaApp contains an example of lambda functions using a list. It will iterate twice over a list of French first names and build their composed form, such as the following:

```
Georges and Jean-Georges are different French first names!
Claude and Jean-Claude are different French first names!
...
Louis and Jean-Louis are different French first names!
-----
Georges and Jean-Georges are different French first names!
...
Luc and Jean-Luc are different French first names!
Louis and Jean-Louis are different French first names!
```

The first iteration is done in one line, and the second iteration is done in several lines of code, showing the block syntax in lambda functions. The following listing illustrates the process.

Listing 5.4   A basic lambda function

```
package net.jgp.books.spark.ch05.lab900_simple_lambda;

import java.util.ArrayList;
import java.util.List;

public class SimpleLambdaApp {

  public static void main(String[] args) {
    List<String> frenchFirstNameList = new ArrayList<>();
    frenchFirstNameList.add("Georges");
    frenchFirstNameList.add("Claude");
...
    frenchFirstNameList.add("Luc");
    frenchFirstNameList.add("Louis");

    frenchFirstNameList.forEach(
        name -> System.out.println(name + " and Jean-" + name
          + " are different French first names!"));

    System.out.println("-----");

    frenchFirstNameList.forEach(
        name -> {
          String message = name + " and Jean-";
          message += name;
          message += " are different French first names!";
          System.out.println(message);
        });
  }
}
```

Builds a list of first names

A simple instruction accesses the content of the list through the variable at the left of -> (name).

The list's forEach() method iterates over the list.

When a simple instruction is not enough, you can have a block; each instruction must end with a semicolon (;).

Lambda functions allow you to write more-compact code and avoid repeating some of the boring statements; you did not need a loop in listing 5.4. However, readability might suffer. Nevertheless, whether you like or hate lambda functions, you will see more and more of them in the code you will deal with, both in this book and in your professional life. In the next section, you will rewrite the code to approximate π by using a couple of lambda functions.

5.1.4 Approximating π by using lambda functions

In the previous sections, you saw how to compute an approximation of π by using classes, and then you read about lambda functions. In this section, you will combine both: approximating π with Spark through Java lambdas and implementing a basic MapReduce application.

You will discover an alternate way to write the code in listings 5.2 and 5.3: by replacing the mapper and reducer classes with Java lambda functions. Figure 5.5, which is similar to figure 5.3, describes the process. Listing 5.5 drills into the code.

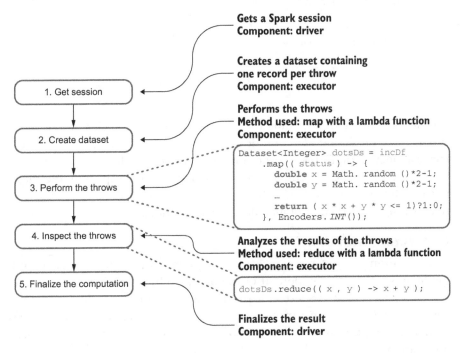

Figure 5.5 Computing π by using lambda functions in Java: the code is more compact, but the process is the same as the class-based process in figure 5.3.

Listing 5.5 Computing π by using lambda functions

```
package net.jgp.books.spark.ch05.lab101_pi_compute_lambda;

...
public class PiComputeLambdaApp implements Serializable {

...
  private void start(int slices) {

...
    long t2 = System.currentTimeMillis();
```

```
System.out.println("Initial dataframe built in " + (t2 - t1) + " ms");

Dataset<Integer> dotsDs = incrementalDf
    .map((MapFunction<Row, Integer>) status -> {         Beginning of the lambda
        double x = Math.random() * 2 - 1;                 function in a block
        double y = Math.random() * 2 - 1;
        counter++;
        if (counter % 100000 == 0) {
            System.out.println("" + counter + " darts thrown so far");
        }
        return (x * x + y * y <= 1) ? 1 : 0;
    }, Encoders.INT());

    long t3 = System.currentTimeMillis();
    System.out.println("Throwing darts done in " + (t3 - t2) + " ms");

    int dartsInCircle =
        dotsDs.reduce((ReduceFunction<Integer>) (x, y) -> x + y);

    long t4 = System.currentTimeMillis();
    System.out.println("Analyzing result in " + (t4 - t3) + " ms");
...
```

Reduce as a lambda function (annotation pointing to `int dartsInCircle`)

The lambda functions are doing the same operations as the classes in listing 5.3. The first lambda throws the darts randomly, doing the mapping operation. The second lambda function performs a reduce operation by adding the results together.

The source code is definitely more compact (I also kept only the major differences). However, the code may be a little more difficult to read for a software engineer whose Java skills do not include lambda functions.

5.2   *Interacting with Spark*

In all the examples so far, you have used only one way to connect to Spark: using local mode, in which each component of the Spark architecture is running seamlessly on the same machine. There are at least three ways to connect to Spark. In this section, you will read about the various interactions, their strengths, and their use cases. Understanding this information is important, as you are on your way to deploy your application.

You will study three ways of interacting with Spark:

- *Local mode,* which is certainly the developers' preferred way, as everything runs on the same computer and does not need any configuration
- *Cluster mode,* through a resource manager, which deploys your applications in a cluster
- *Interactive mode,* either directly or via a computer-based notebook, which is probably the preferred way for data scientists and data experimenters

Are we going back to school with notebooks?

When I was a kid, I loved the end of summer because I would go with my mom to get new notebooks. Being raised in France and Morocco, my sisters and I had access to such a variety of notebooks: text, drawing, science, music, math with graphing paper, and all of that in various paper weights. The science notebooks were probably my favorite, with alternating pages, a squared page (like graph paper) with a blank page. You could take notes on the squared page and draw schemas, flowers, parts of the body, and more on the blank page. (I could also tell you how disappointed I am at the lack of offerings in the United States, but that's not really the point.)

Computer notebooks are exactly like the science notebooks of my youth: you can take notes, execute code, display graphs, and much more on a single "page." Of course, because they are digital, you can easily share these notebooks. Some tools offer collaborative capabilities. Notebooks are extensively used by data scientists to experiment with data, while taking notes and, in some cases, displaying graphs.

Notebooks are available as software products. Two open source products are Jupyter (http://jupyter.org/) and Apache Zeppelin (https://zeppelin.apache.org/). A few hosted commercial products are available too: IBM has Watson Studio (www.ibm .com/cloud/watson-studio) and Databricks offers Unified Data Analytics Platform (https://databricks.com/product/unified-analytics-platform).

5.2.1 Local mode

Spark's *local mode* is one of the things I like the most about Spark. Local mode enables all Spark components on the same machine, whether a laptop or a server.

You do not have any software to install. Local mode allows onboarding of engineers on a development team in a matter of minutes: download Eclipse, clone a project, and your new software engineer is ready to work with Spark and big data. Local mode allows your developer to develop and debug on a single machine.

Figure 5.6 summarizes the stack.

Behind the scenes, Spark starts the required machinery to stand up a master and worker. In local mode, you will not have to submit a JAR file; Spark will set the right class path, so you do not even have to deal with *JAR hell.*

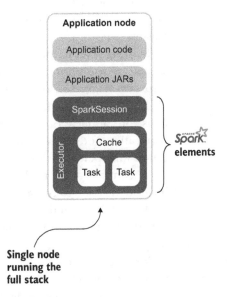

Figure 5.6 In local mode, all the components are running on a single node.

To start Spark in local mode, as you have done in previous examples, you simply start a session by specifying the master node to be local:

```
.master("local")
```

Here is the full code to get or create a session in local mode:

```
SparkSession spark = SparkSession.builder()
    .appName("My application")
    .master("local")
    .getOrCreate();
```

You can request the number of threads by specifying them between brackets ([..]):

```
SparkSession spark = SparkSession.builder()
    .appName("My application")
    .master("local[2]")
    .getOrCreate();
```

By default, the local mode will run with one thread.

5.2.2   *Cluster mode*

In *cluster mode*, Spark behaves in a multinode system with a master and workers, as you saw in chapter 2. As you may remember, the master dispatches the workload to the worker, which then processes it. The goal of the cluster is to offer more processing power, as each node brings its CPU, memory, and storage (when needed) to the cluster.

Starting several workers on the same worker node is possible too, but I did not find a good use case nor see the benefits; the worker will use the configured or available resources. Figure 5.7 describes the cluster stack.

Let's walk through this cluster stack. On the left is your application node. It contains your application code, which is called the *driver program*, as it drives Spark. The application node also contains the additional JARs your application needs. The application will open a session on Spark by using the Spark libraries.

The master node, in the center of the diagram, contains the Spark libraries, which include the code to run as a master.

The workers, on the right, have the application JARs and the Spark libraries to execute the code. The workers also have the binaries to connect to the master: the worker scripts.

You are learning all those concepts because you are on your way to deploying your work, and deployment has consequences on your build strategy.

In some cases, to ease deployment, you will want to create an uber JAR containing your application and its dependencies. In this scenario, your uber JAR should never include Hadoop or Spark libraries; those are already deployed because they are contained in the Spark distribution. Building an uber JAR can be automated via Maven.

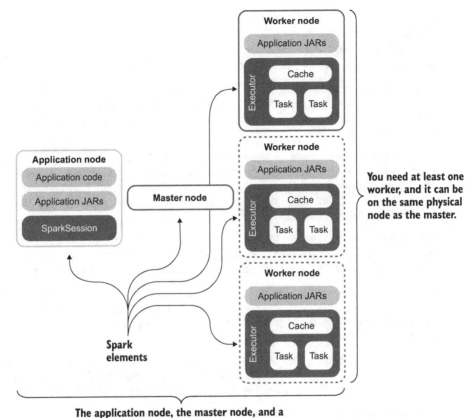

You need at least one worker, and it can be on the same physical node as the master.

The application node, the master node, and a worker node could be the same physical node.

Figure 5.7 Spark in a cluster configuration, in which each component can be on a separate node

What's Hadoop?

Hadoop is an elephant. *Hadoop* is also a popular implementation of MapReduce. Like Spark, it is open source, governed by the Apache Foundation. Unlike Spark, it is a complex ecosystem to get into and has constraints on the types of algorithms (mainly MapReduce) and storage (mainly disk). Everything is slowly changing in the Hadoop world to make it easier, but Spark is already here.

Spark uses some Hadoop libraries, which are contained in the Spark runtime you are deploying on each node.

And yes, Hadoop is the name of an elephant. The son of Hadoop cocreator Doug Cutting named a yellow elephant plush Hadoop—hence the Hadoop logo being a yellow pachyderm.

What's an uber JAR?

A *JAR* is a Java archive file. When you compile all your .java files into .class, you combine them all in a JAR file. You probably know that already.

An *uber JAR* (also known as *super JAR* or *fat JAR*) is a JAR above (literally the German translation of *über*) the other JARs. The uber JAR contains most, if not all, the dependencies of your application. Logistics are then *uber* simplified because you will handle only one JAR.

The JAR system is sometimes nicknamed *JAR hell* among Java developers because it can become very confusing with multiple versions of JARs as you combine more and more libraries with different dependencies. For example, Elasticsearch client library v6.2.4 uses Jackson core v2.8.6 (a common parser). Spark v2.3.1 uses the same library, but in v2.9.6.

Package managers, such as Maven, try to manage those dependencies, but sometimes later versions of a library are incompatible with an older one. Those version discrepancies can bring you to JAR hell. And sometimes getting out is difficult.

As you know, a JAR is a Java archive. Java comes with a tool called `jar`, which works like the UNIX `tar` command. You can *jar*, or archive, your classes into a JAR. You can extract, or *unJAR*, the files, and, of course, you can rebuild your archive, or *reJAR*. I hope I am not being too jarring here . . . .

Let's get back to building the uber JAR. The uber JAR is rebuilt every time you deploy. The process of building an uber JAR involves unJARring all the JARs of your project in the same directory. Then Maven will reJAR all the classes in one bigger, uber JAR.

This creates many problems. Here are the two most common problems:

- Some JARs can be signed, and unJARring them and reJARring them as part of a different archive will break the signature. A similar issue will happen with the manifest files, which will be overwritten.
- Case sensitivity can be a problem. As you know, `MyClass` and `Myclass` are different. But when you unJAR on a filesystem that is not case-sensitive (for example, Windows), one will overwrite the other one, and one will not be available afterward, producing random `ClassNotFoundException` exceptions in your code. This can happen when developers use Windows for building and then deploying from their workstation—crazy, but true. That's another reason for continuous integration and continuous delivery (CICD) processes using (Linux) build servers.

Uber JARs are a powerful tool for deploying your work, but make sure you have the build operation on a case-sensitive filesystem, do not package the Spark libraries, and be extremely careful about the problems I just described.

Chapter 6 will walk you through the various steps of deploying your application; at this stage, you are still discovering the key concepts to deploy an app. The details will come.

There are two ways to run an application on a cluster:

- You submit a job by using the `spark-submit` shell and a JAR of your application.
- You specify the master in your application and then run your code.

SUBMITTING A JOB TO SPARK

One way to execute an application on a cluster is to submit a job, as a packaged JAR, to Spark. This is similar to submitting jobs on a mainframe. To do so, make sure of the following:

- You build a JAR with your application.
- All the JARs that your application depends on are on each node or in the uber JAR.

SETTING THE CLUSTER'S MASTER IN YOUR APPLICATION

The other way to run an application on a cluster is simply to specify the master's Spark URL in your application. You have the same requirements as when you submit a job:

- You build a JAR with your application.
- All the JARs that your application depends on are on each node or in the uber JAR (assuming you submit the uber JAR).

5.2.3   *Interactive mode in Scala and Python*

In the previous subsections, you saw how to interact with Spark programmatically or via submitting a job. There is a third way to interact with Spark. You can also run Spark in full interactive mode, which allows you to manipulate big data in a shell.

In addition to the shell, you can use notebooks such as Jupyter and Zeppelin. However, those tools are targeted more toward data scientists.

Spark offers two shells, which accept Scala, Python, and R. In this section, you will see how to run the Scala and Python shells. (Teaching those languages is beyond the scope of this book.)

Figure 5.8 illustrates the architecture when using Spark in interactive mode. It is similar to cluster mode and figure 5.7. The only difference is in the way you start your work session.

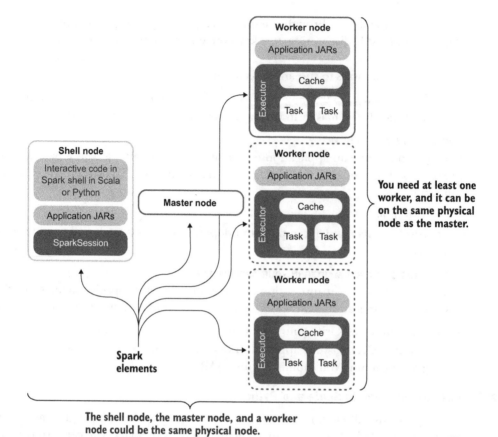

Figure 5.8   The Spark stack when running in interactive mode is similar to cluster mode; the only difference is in the way you start working.

SCALA SHELL

Spark offers an interactive Scala shell. As with any shell, you can type in commands. Let's see how to run it, check Spark's version, and run the approximation of the π application in Scala.

To run interactive mode in local mode, go to your Spark's bin directory and run this:

```
$ ./spark-shell
```

If you have a cluster, you can specify your cluster's master URL on the command line by using --master <Master's URL>. You can see the help by using the --help parameter on the command line.

And you should get the following:

**The shell is initialized with an
instance of SparkContext called sc.**

```
To adjust logging level use sc.setLogLevel(newLevel). For SparkR, use
    setLogLevel(newLevel).
Spark context Web UI available at http://un.oplo.io:4040
Spark context available as 'sc'
    (master = local[*],
    app id = local-1534641339137).
Spark session available as 'spark'.
Welcome to
      ____              __
     / __/__  ___ _____/ /__
    _\ \/ _ \/ _ `/ __/  '_/
   /___/ .__/\_,_/_/ /_/\_\   version 2.3.1
      /_/

Using Scala version 2.11.8 (Java HotSpot(TM) 64-Bit Server VM, Java
     1.8.0_181)
Type in expressions to have them evaluated.
Type :help for more information.

scala>
```

**Runs in local mode on all
your local machine's cores**

**An instance of SparkSession
is available as spark.**

Of course, to go further with the shell, you need to know Scala, which is not at all required in the context of this book (refer to appendix J to learn a little more). The rest of this subsection will show you basic operations in Scala, and you will see the similarities with Java. If you want to leave now (I would understand), you can exit the shell by pressing Ctrl-C.

You can try a few things, such as displaying the version of Spark

```
scala> sc.version
res0: String = 2.3.1
```

or

```
scala> spark.sparkContext.version
res1: String = 2.3.1
```

Because calculating an approximation of π is the theme of this chapter, here is how you can do it in the interactive shell. This is the Scala snippet you can type in the interpreter:

```
import scala.math.random
val slices = 100
val n = (100000L * slices).toInt
val count = spark.sparkContext.parallelize(1 until n, slices).map { i =>
     val x = random * 2 - 1
     val y = random * 2 - 1
```

**Map operation: throwing the darts randomly
and checking whether they're in the circle**

```
        if (x*x + y*y <= 1) 1 else 0
}.reduce(_ + _)
println(s"Pi is roughly ${4.0 * count / (n - 1)}")
```

Reduce operation: summing the results

When you run the snippet in the shell, this is the output you get:

```
Welcome to
      ____              __
     / __/__  ___ _____/ /__
    _\ \/ _ \/ _ `/ __/  '_/
   /___/ .__/\_,_/_/ /_/\_\   version 2.3.1
      /_/

Using Scala version 2.11.8 (Java HotSpot(TM) 64-Bit Server VM, Java 1.8.0_181)
Type in expressions to have them evaluated.
Type :help for more information.

scala> import scala.math.random
import scala.math.random

scala> val slices = 100
slices: Int = 100

scala> val n = (100000L * slices).toInt
n: Int = 10000000

scala> val count = spark.sparkContext.parallelize(1 until n, slices).map { i =>
     |          val x = random * 2 - 1
     |          val y = random * 2 - 1
     |          if (x*x + y*y <= 1) 1 else 0
     |        }.reduce(_ + _)
count: Int = 7854580

scala> println(s"Pi is roughly ${4.0 * count / (n - 1)}")
Pi is roughly 3.1418323141832314
```

As you can see, you run similar code in Scala as you did in Java. And without digging into the syntax, you must definitely recognize some elements of your Java application in the previous section. You can also see the MapReduce operation.

If you want to know more about Scala, have a look at *Get Programming with Scala* by Daniela Sfregola (Manning, 2017, www.manning.com/books/get-programming-with-scala).

Let's have a look at the Python shell.

PYTHON SHELL

Spark also offers an interactive Python shell. As with any shell, you can type in commands. Let's see how to run it, check Spark's version, and run the Python application for approximating π.

To run interactive mode in local mode, go to your Spark's bin directory and run this:

```
$ ./pyspark
```

If you have a cluster, you can specify your cluster's master URL on the command line by using --master <Master's URL>. You can see the help by using the --help parameter on the command line. And you should get the following:

```
Python 2.7.15rc1 (default, Apr 15 2018, 21:51:34)
[GCC 7.3.0] on linux2
Type "help", "copyright", "credits" or "license" for more information.
2018-10-01 06:35:23 WARN  NativeCodeLoader:62 - Unable to load
▬▶ native-hadoop library for your platform... using builtin-java classes
▬▶ where applicable
Setting default log level to "WARN".
To adjust logging level use sc.setLogLevel(newLevel). For SparkR, use
▬▶ setLogLevel(newLevel).
Welcome to
      ____              __
     / __/__  ___ _____/ /__
    _\ \/ _ \/ _ `/ __/  '_/
   /__ / .__/\_,_/_/ /_/\_\   version 2.3.1
      /_/

Using Python version 2.7.15rc1 (default, Apr 15 2018 21:51:34)
SparkSession available as 'spark'.
>>>
```

The shell uses the Python 2 version on your system; here, it is v2.7.l5rcl.

An instance of SparkSession is available as spark.

To exit the shell, you can use Ctrl-D or call quit(). If you prefer Python v3, before starting the PySpark shell, set the PYSPARK_PYTHON environment variable to python3:

```
$ export PYSPARK_PYTHON=python3
$ ./pyspark
```

And you should get this:

Now shell uses the Python version on your system; here, it is v3.6.5.

```
Python 3.6.5 (default, Apr  1 2018, 05:46:30)
[GCC 7.3.0] on linux
Type "help", "copyright", "credits" or "license" for more information.
2018-10-01 06:40:22 WARN  NativeCodeLoader:62 - Unable to load
▬▶ native-hadoop library for your platform... using builtin-java classes
▬▶ where applicable
Setting default log level to "WARN".
To adjust logging level use sc.setLogLevel(newLevel). For SparkR, use
▬▶ setLogLevel(newLevel).
Welcome to
      ____              __
     / __/__  ___ _____/ /__
    _\ \/ _ \/ _ `/ __/  '_/
   /__ / .__/\_,_/_/ /_/\_\   version 2.3.1
      /_/

Using Python version 3.6.5 (default, Apr  1 2018 05:46:30)
SparkSession available as 'spark'.
>>>
```

The rest of the chapter assumes you're running Python v3. From this point, you need to know a little bit of Python. You can display the version of Spark:

```
>>> spark.version
'2.3.1'
```

The approximation of π in Python can be done this way:

```
import sys
from random import random
from operator import add
from pyspark.sql import SparkSession

spark = SparkSession\
  .builder\
  .appName("PythonPi")\
  .getOrCreate()
n = 100000

def throwDarts(_):
  x = random() * 2 - 1
  y = random() * 2 - 1
    return 1 if x ** 2 + y ** 2 <= 1 else 0

count = spark.sparkContext.parallelize(range(1, n + 1),
  1).map(throwDarts).reduce(add)
print("Pi is roughly %f" % (4.0 * count / n))
spark.stop()
```

The throwDarts function will be used in the mapping process.

Python enforces indentation to delimit blocks; this is the operation done in the throwDarts method.

The small application will first throw all the darts. When you type your code in the shell, this is how the shell behaves:

```
>>> import sys
>>> from random import random
>>> from operator import add
>>> from pyspark.sql import SparkSession
>>>
>>> spark = SparkSession\
...     .builder\
...     .appName("PythonPi")\
...     .getOrCreate()
>>> n = 100000
>>> def throwDarts(_):
...     x = random() * 2 - 1
...     y = random() * 2 - 1
...     return 1 if x ** 2 + y ** 2 <= 1 else 0
...
>>> count = spark.sparkContext.parallelize(range(1, n + 1),
    1).map(throwDarts).reduce(add)
>>> print("Pi is roughly %f" % (4.0 * count / n))
Pi is roughly 3.138000
>>> spark.stop()
>>>
```

If you want to know more about Python, have a look at *The Quick Python Book* by Naomi Ceder (Manning, 2018), now in its third edition (www.manning.com/books/the-quick-python-book-third-edition).

Summary

- Spark can work without ingesting data; it can generate its own data.
- Spark supports three execution modes: local mode, cluster mode, and interactive mode.
- Local mode allows developers to get started on Spark development in minutes.
- Cluster mode is used for production.
- You can submit a job to Spark or connect to the master.
- The driver application is where your `main()` method is.
- The master node knows about all the workers.
- The execution takes place on the workers.
- Sparks handles the distribution of your application JAR in cluster mode, to each worker node.
- MapReduce is a common method to work on big data in distributed systems. Hadoop is its most popular implementation. Spark masks its complexity.
- Continuous integration and continuous delivery (CICD) is an agile methodology that encourages frequent integration and delivery.
- Lambda functions, introduced in Java 8, allow you to have functions outside the scope of a class.
- An uber JAR contains all the classes (including the dependencies) of an application in a single file.
- Maven can build an uber JAR automatically.
- Maven can deploy your source code at the same time it deploys your JAR file.
- Spark's map and reduce operations can use classes or lambda functions.
- Spark provides a web interface to analyze the execution of jobs and applications.
- Interactive mode allows you to type Scala, Python, or R commands directly in a shell. Interaction can also be achieved with the help of notebooks such as Jupyter or Zeppelin.
- π (pi) can be estimated by throwing darts at a board and measuring the ratio of the darts within the circle and outside the circle.

Deploying
your simple app

6

This chapter covers

- Deploying a Spark application
- Defining the roles of the critical components in a Spark cluster environment
- Running an application on a cluster
- Calculating an approximation of π (pi) using Spark
- Analyzing the execution logs

In the previous chapters, you discovered what Apache Spark is and how to build simple applications, and, hopefully, understood key concepts like the dataframe and laziness. This chapter is linked with the preceding one: you built an application in chapter 5 and will deploy it in this chapter. Reading chapter 5 before this one is not required but is highly recommended.

In this chapter, you will leave code production aside to discover how to interact with Spark as you move toward deployment and production. You could ask, "Why are we talking deployment so early in the book? Deployment is at the end, no?"

A little over 20 years ago, when I was building applications using Visual Basic 3 (VB3), toward the end of the project, I would run the Visual Basic Setup wizard that would help build 3.5-inch floppy disks. In those days, my bible was the 25-chapter *Microsoft Visual Basic 3.0 Programmer's Guide*, and deployment was covered in chapter 25.

Fast-forward to today. Your shop is running DevOps or is about to, you (may) have heard of terms like *continuous integration and continuous delivery* (*CICD*), and deployment happens now much earlier in the process than it used to. On one of my last projects, the team implemented a prototype of a data pipeline using Spark; CICD was a full part of the realization of the prototype. Deployment is important. Understanding the deployment's constraints is key, and I encourage you to do so as early as possible in the project.

Continuous integration and continuous deployment

CICD, or *CI/CD*, refers to the combined practices of continuous integration and continuous delivery.

Continuous integration (CI) is the practice of merging all developers' working copies to a shared mainline at frequent intervals. It could be several times a day. Grady Booch (cofounder of UML, IBMer, Turing lecturer, and more) coined *CI* in his 1991 software engineering method. Extreme programming (XP) adopted the concept of CI and advocated integrating more than once per day.

CI's main goal is to prevent integration problems. CI is intended to be used in combination with automated unit tests written thanks to test-driven development (TDD). Initially, this was conceived of as running and passing all unit tests in the developer's local environment before committing to the mainline. This helps prevent one developer's work in progress from breaking another developer's copy. More recent elaborations of the concept introduced build servers, which automatically ran the unit tests periodically or even after every commit and reported the results to the developers.

Continuous delivery (CD) allows teams to produce software in short cycles, ensuring that the software can be reliably released at any time. It aims at building, testing, and releasing software with greater speed and frequency. The approach helps reduce the cost, time, and risk of delivering changes by allowing for more incremental updates to applications in production. A straightforward and repeatable deployment process is important for continuous delivery.

Continuous delivery is sometimes confused with continuous deployment. In *continuous deployment*, any change to production that passes a series of tests is deployed to production, automatically. In contrast, under continuous delivery, the software needs to be reliably released at any time, but it is up to a human to decide when to release, usually based on business reasons.

Both definitions were adapted from Wikipedia.

Therefore, unlike me in 1994 working with VB3, you started exploring deployment in chapter 5. However, don't worry: the tradition is respected, as advanced deployment (including managing clusters, resources, sharing files, and more) is still in chapter 18.

You will first look at an example in which data is generated within and by Spark, avoiding the need to ingest data. Ingesting data in a cluster is a bit more complex than creating a self-generated dataset.

You will then learn about the three ways to interact with Spark:

- Local mode, which you are already familiar with through the examples in previous chapters
- Cluster mode (more than one computer or node)
- Interactive mode (through a shell)

You will set the environment for your lab. You will understand what constraints are coming in the game as you split the computing resources on several nodes. It is important to gather this experience now so you have a better awareness when you plan to deploy your apps. Finally, you will run your application on a cluster.

> **LAB** Examples from this chapter are linked with chapter 5, so they share the same repository. They are available in GitHub at https://github.com/jgperrin/ net.jgp.books.spark.ch05.

6.1   *Beyond the example: The role of the components*

In the previous chapter, you read about how to calculate an approximation of π by using Spark with classes and lambda functions. You ran the application, but you did not really look at what was going on in your infrastructure, nor did you consider the role of each element of the architecture.

A *component* is a logical representation that encapsulates a set of related functions. The component can be physically a package, a web service, or more. A great benefit of identifying a component is that you can more easily identify its interface, which is the way to communicate with it.

In the chapter's introduction, you read about the three ways to interact with Spark. However, whether you run Spark in local, cluster, or interactive mode, Spark uses a set of components.

Each component has a unique role. It is important to understand what is going on with each component so you can more easily debug or optimize your processes. You will first have a quick overview of the components and their interactions and will then dive into more details.

6.1.1   *Quick overview of the components and their interactions*

This subsection gives you a high-level overview of each component in a Spark architecture, including the links between them. You will follow the flows based on the chapter 5 example application that approximates π. Figure 6.1 places the components in an architectural diagram.

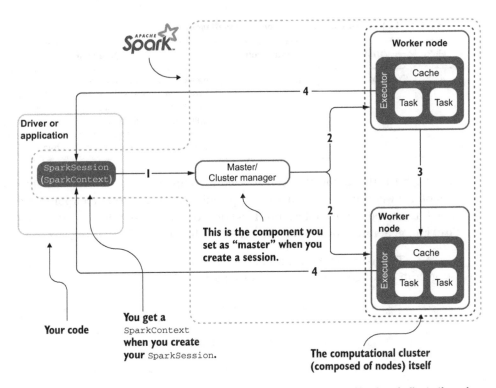

Figure 6.1 Spark components and interactions among the components. Numbers indicate the order in which the network calls are most likely to be initiated.

From an application standpoint, the only connection you will establish is by creating the session in the master/cluster manager, link 1 in figure 6.1. Table 6.1 describes the links. The "Care level" column explains why you should care about this specific item in Spark architecture: this will be useful when it comes to securing, debugging, or deploying Spark.

Table 6.1   Links between Spark components

Link	Origin	Destination	Care level
1	Driver	Cluster manager/master	You do care about this link; your application connects to the master or cluster manager this way.
2	Cluster manager/master	Executor	This link establishes a connection between the workers and the master. The workers initiate the connection, but data is passed from the master to the workers. If this link is broken, your cluster manager will not be able to communicate with the executors.
3	Executor	Executor	Internal link between the executors; as developers, we do not care that much about it.

Table 6.1 Links between Spark components *(continued)*

Link	Origin	Destination	Care level
4	Executor	Driver	The executor needs to be able to get back to the driver, which means the driver cannot be behind a firewall (which is a rookie mistake when your first application tries to connect to a cluster in the cloud). If the executors cannot communicate with the driver, they will not be able to send data back.

Listing 6.1 is the application you studied in chapter 5, where you calculate π. In this chapter, I will not explain what the application does, but what components are being used/triggered by the application. This code will run on your driver node, but it will control and generate activities on other nodes. The numbers link listing 6.1 to figure 6.1.

LAB   This is lab #200, from chapter 5. It is available in GitHub at https://github.com/jgperrin/net.jgp.books.spark.ch05.

Listing 6.1 Calculating an approximation of π

```
package net.jgp.books.spark.ch05.lab200_pi_compute_cluster;
...
public class PiComputeClusterApp implements Serializable {
...
  private final class DartMapper
      implements MapFunction<Row, Integer> {
...
  }

  private final class DartReducer implements ReduceFunction<Integer> {
...
  }

  public static void main(String[] args) {
    PiComputeClusterApp app = new PiComputeClusterApp();
    app.start(10);
  }

  private void start(int slices) {
    int numberOfThrows = 100000 * slices;
...
    SparkSession spark = SparkSession
        .builder()
        .appName("JavaSparkPi on a cluster")          Link I: The session resides
        .master("spark://un:7077")                    on the cluster manager.
        .config("spark.executor.memory", "4g")
        .getOrCreate();
...
    List<Integer> l = new ArrayList<>(numberOfThrows);
    for (int i = 0; i < numberOfThrows; i++) {
      l.add(i);
```

```
    }
    Dataset<Row> incrementalDf = spark
        .createDataset(1, Encoders.INT())
        .toDF();
```
| Link 2: The first dataframe is created in the executor.

...

```
    Dataset<Integer> dartsDs = incrementalDf
        .map(new DartMapper(), Encoders.INT());
```
| This step is added to the DAG, which sits in the cluster manager.

...

```
    int dartsInCircle = dartsDs.reduce(new DartReducer()); ◄─┐
```
...
```
    System.out.println("Pi is roughly " +
➡ 4.0 * dartsInCircle / numberOfThrows);
```
Link 4: The result of the reduce operation is brought back to the application.

```
    spark.stop();
  }
}
```

Spark applications run as independent processes on a cluster. The SparkSession object in your application (also called the *driver*) coordinates the processes. There is a unique SparkSession for your application, whether you are in local mode or have 10,000 nodes. The SparkSession is created when you build your session, as in the following:

```
SparkSession spark = SparkSession.builder()
    .appName("An app")
    .master("local[*]")
    .getOrCreate();
```

As part of your session, you will also get a context: SparkContext. The context was your only way to deal with Spark prior to v2. You mostly do not need to interact with the SparkContext, but when you do (accessing infrastructure information, creating accumulators, and more, described in chapter 17), this is how you access it:

```
SparkContext sc = spark.sparkContext();
System.out.println("Running Spark v" + sc.version());
```

Basically, the cluster manager allocates resources across applications. However, to run on a cluster, the SparkSession can connect to several types of cluster managers. This might be dictated from your infrastructure, enterprise architects, or know-it-all guru. You may not have a choice here. Chapter 18 discusses more cluster manager options, including YARN, Mesos, and Kubernetes.

Once connected, Spark acquires executors on nodes in the cluster, which are JVM processes that run computations and store data for your application. Figure 6.2 illustrates the acquisition of resources by the cluster manager.

Next, the cluster manager sends your application code to the executors. There is no need for you to deploy your application on each node. Finally, SparkSession sends tasks to the executors to run.

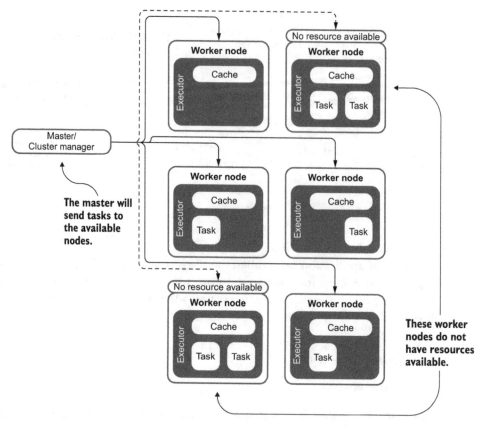

Figure 6.2   One of the roles of the cluster manager is to find resources in the worker nodes.

6.1.2   *Troubleshooting tips for the Spark architecture*

Spark's architecture, as described in section 6.1.1, may seem unusual but hopefully remains easy to understand, at least at the level that data and software engineers need to understand it (performance tuning will certainly require a deeper knowledge). In this section, you will look at the details and constraints of the architecture.

Among the typical things that can go wrong are that Spark takes too much time or you never get your results back. If something goes wrong after deployment, consider these points:

- Even if your action does not bring back results to your application, which is the case when you export data, you must always ensure that the executor can talk to the driver. Talking to the driver means that the executor and the driver should not be isolated by a firewall, on another network, exposing multiple IP addresses, and so on. Those issues in communications can happen when your application runs locally (in development, for example) and tries to connect to a remote cluster. The driver program must listen for and accept incoming connections from its executors throughout its lifetime (see `spark.driver.port` in the "Application configuration" section of appendix K).

- Each application gets its own executor processes, which stay up for the duration of the entire application and run tasks in multiple threads. This has the benefit of isolating applications from each other, on both the scheduling side (each driver schedules its own tasks) and executor side (tasks from different applications run in different JVMs). However, it also means that data cannot be shared across different Spark applications (instances of `SparkSession` or `Spark-Context`) without writing it to an external storage system.

- Spark is agnostic to the underlying cluster manager, as long as it can acquire executor processes, and these communicate with each other. It is possible to run on a cluster manager that supports other applications, like Mesos or YARN (see chapter 18).

- As the driver schedules tasks on the cluster, it should run physically close to the worker nodes, preferably on the same local area network. Processes are network intensive, and you reduce latency when the boxes are closer together. Maintaining the physical nodes together is not easy to know how to do or demand when you use cloud services. If you plan on running Spark in the cloud, check with your cloud operator about having the machines physically located close to one another.

Appendix R lists common issues and solutions, as well as where to find help.

6.1.3 Going further

In section 6.1, I introduced you to Spark architecture, which is the essential minimum for deployment. As you can imagine, there is more to it.

The book's inside cover lists the terms in your driver logs when you are executing your applications. To go further, you can read the Spark documentation, available at https://spark.apache.org/docs/latest/cluster-overview.html.

6.2 Building a cluster

In section 6.1, you went through building an ingestionless application, read about the three ways to interact with Spark, and explored the various components and links between them.

This should have provided enough appetite for your next task: deploying your application on a real cluster. In this section, you will see how to do the following:

- Build a cluster
- Set its environment
- Deploy your application (either by building an uber JAR or using Git and Maven)
- Run your application
- Analyze the execution logs

6.2.1   *Building a cluster that works for you*

I realize that it is not easy to set up a distributed environment at home or at the office, but as you know, Spark is designed to work in a distributed environment. In this section, I will describe your options; some are more realistic than others, depending on your time and budget. I will describe the deployment using four nodes, but you can work on a single node if you wish. I highly recommend that you have at least two; this will allow you to understand the network issues and how to share data, configuration, and binaries (application, JARs).

So, what are your options for working on a cluster? You have several options for building a distributed environment at home:

- The easiest one is probably to use the cloud: get two or three virtual machines in a cloud provider such as Amazon EC2, IBM Cloud, OVH, or Azure. Note that this option has a cost that can be difficult to estimate. I do not recommend Amazon EMR at this point, as it has some constraints (you will discover more about that in chapter 18). You will not need huge servers; target a bit more than 8 GB of memory and 32 GB of disk. CPU does not matter that much for this lab.

- A second option is to have a *slightly bigger* server-like machine at home, on which you will install the virtual machines or containers. This option carries the same requirements for each machine as the first option; this means at least 32 GB of RAM in the physical machine if you plan on having four nodes. This option can be done for free with Docker or VirtualBox. *Hint: your teenager's gaming machine used for Fortnite is probably a good candidate for Spark, and you could use the GPU for something useful like TensorFlow on Spark.*

- Your third alternative is to use all your *old stuff* you may have around your house and build a cluster with it, with the exception of computers with less than 8 GB of RAM. This excludes your Atari 800XL, your Commodore 64, your ZX81, and a few others.

- Lastly, you can do it *my way* and buy and build four nodes from scratch. My cluster is called CLEGO, and you can find a how-to (and why I named it this way) on my blog at http://jgp.ai/clego.

In this chapter, I will use CLEGOS's four nodes, as the hardware was designed for distributed processing. Figure 6.3 shows the architecture used for this lab.

If you do not have more than one node, you can still follow along and perform the operations for only node *un*.

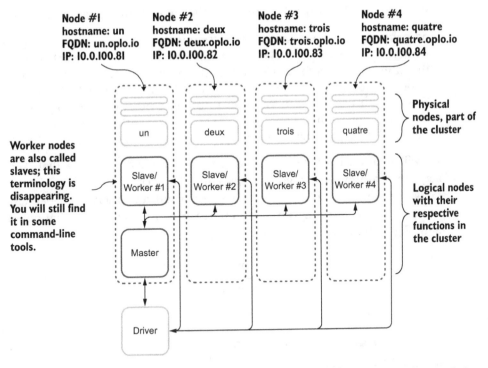

Figure 6.3 Architecture used for deployment in this lab: you will use four nodes. Hosts are called un, deux, trois, and quatre (one, two, three, and four in French). *FQDN* **stands for** *fully qualified domain name.*

6.2.2 Setting up the environment

Now that you have defined your environment, you will need to do the following:

- Install Spark.
- Configure and run Spark.
- Download/upload your application.
- Run it.

You need to install Spark on each node (refer to appendix K for details). Installation is pretty straightforward. You do not have to install your application on every node. In the rest of this chapter, I will assume you installed Spark in /opt/apache-spark.

On the master node (in this case, un) go to /opt/apache-spark/sbin.

Run the master:

```
$ ./start-master.sh
```

Remember that the master does not do much, but it will always require workers. To run your first worker, type this:

```
$ ./start-slave.sh spark://un:7077
```

In this scenario, the worker is running on the same physical node as the master.

BE CAREFUL WITH YOUR NETWORK CONFIGURATION   As you are building your cluster, the network plays a key role here. Each node should be able to talk to the other, back and forth. Check that the ports you need are accessible and hopefully not used by something else; typically, they are 7077, 8080, and 4040. You will not have those ports open to the internet, just internally. You can check with ping, telnet (using the `telnet <host> <port>` command). Do not use *localhost* as a hostname in any of the commands.

You will always start your master first, then your workers. To check that everything is okay, open a browser and go to http://un:8080/. This web interface is provided by Spark; you do not need to start a web server or link a web server to Spark. Make sure you do not have anything running on port 8080, or modify the configuration accordingly. Figure 6.4 shows the result.

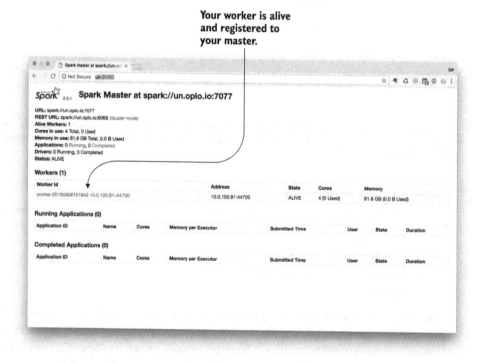

Figure 6.4   The master node has a single worker. As you can also see, there are no running or completed applications.

As you run more applications, this interface will populate itself, and you will be able to discover more information about the applications, their execution, and so on. In section 6.4.1, you will see how to access your application's logs.

You can now go to the next node (in this example, deux). Go to /opt/apache-spark/sbin. Do not run another master, but start your second worker:

```
$ ./start-slave.sh spark://un:7077
```

You can refresh your browser. Figure 6.5 illustrates the result.

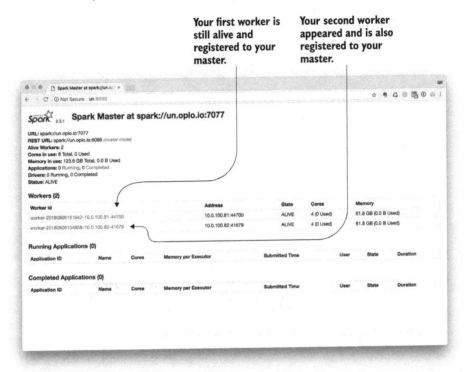

Figure 6.5 Your Spark dashboard now displays your two first workers.

Because I have four nodes, I will repeat this operation for the third and fourth nodes. My master is running on the same node as my first node. At the end, the browser should display figure 6.6.

You now have a working cluster, composed of one master and four workers, ready to execute your work. The physical cluster is using four nodes.

Your first worker is registered to your master.

Your second worker is registered to your master.

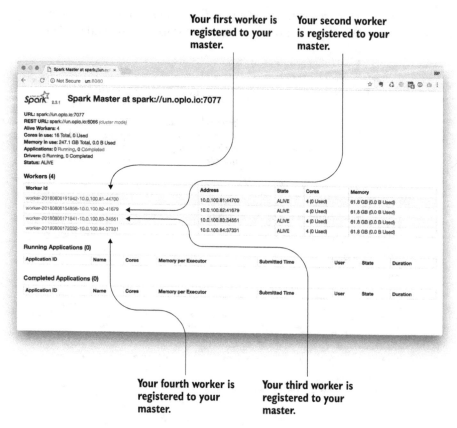

Your fourth worker is registered to your master.

Your third worker is registered to your master.

Figure 6.6   Your Spark dashboard now displays the four workers.

6.3   *Building your application to run on the cluster*

We've almost reached the grand finale. You have deployed Spark and built your cluster. I am pretty sure you can't wait to deploy your π approximation code on the cluster to see how it performs.

But hold your horses—you first need to deploy your code to the cluster. To deploy your application, you have several options:

- Build an uber JAR with your code and all your dependencies.
- Build a JAR with your app and make sure all the dependencies are on every worker node (not recommended).
- Clone/pull from your source control repository.

SPARK DEPLOYS YOUR CODE TO THE WORKERS   This is a pretty cool feature. You will have to deploy it only once; the copy to each worker node is taken care of by Spark itself.

The deployment choice between the uber JAR and the download from Git and local rebuild will probably be made by the department in charge of deployment/infrastructure in your organization. It can be driven by a security policy such as "no compilation on production servers."

What about the data?

When it comes to deploying the application to each node, Spark will do it for you from the master node. However, Spark will not make sure all your executors have access to the data. Remember that in the process described in this chapter, you are not deploying any data, as Spark self-generates the dataframes containing the data needed to compute π. When you work with external data, all workers will need to access the data as well. The Hadoop Distributed File System (HDFS) is a distributed filesystem and is a popular choice for sharing data in a replicated way. To deploy the data, you can use the following:

- A shared drive accessible from all the workers, such as Server Message Block/Common Internet File System (SMB/CIFS), Network File System (NFS), and many more. I highly recommend that the mount point is the same on every worker.
- A file-sharing service like Nextcloud/ownCloud, Box, Dropbox, or any other. Data will be automatically replicated on each worker. This solution limits data transfer: data is copied only once. As with the shared drive, I highly recommend that the mount point is the same on every worker.
- A distributed filesystem such as HDFS.

Those techniques and technologies are covered in more detail in chapter 18.

6.3.1 Building your application's uber JAR

On your journey to deployment, one of your options is to package your application in an uber JAR. As you may recall from chapter 5, an uber JAR is an archive containing all the classes needed by your application, regardless of the number of JARs you had on your class path. The uber JAR contains most, if not all, the dependencies of your application. Logistics are then uber simplified, as you will handle only one JAR. Let's build an uber JAR with Maven.

To build the uber JAR, you will use the Maven Shade build plugin. You can read its full documentation at http://maven.apache.org/plugins/maven-shade-plugin/index.html.

Open your project's pom.xml file. Locate the build/plugins section and add the contents of the following listing.

Listing 6.2 Using the Shade build plugin to build an uber JAR with Maven

```
<build>
  <plugins>
    ...
```

```
<plugin>
  <groupId>org.apache.maven.plugins</groupId>      Definition of
  <artifactId>maven-shade-plugin</artifactId>       the plugin
  <version>3.1.1</version>
  <executions>
    <execution>
      <phase>package</phase>        Shade will be executed during
      <goals>                       packaging (when you call mvn package).
        <goal>shade</goal>
      </goals>
      <configuration>
        <minimizeJAR>true</minimizeJAR>       Removes all classes that
        <artifactSet>                         are not used by the project,
Exclusions ──>  <excludes>                    reducing the size of the JAR
            <exclude>org.apache.spark</exclude>
            <exclude>org.apache.hadoop</exclude>
...
            <exclude>junit:junit</exclude>
            <exclude>jmock:*</exclude>
            <exclude>*:xml-apis</exclude>
            <exclude>log4j:log4j:jar:</exclude>
Allows a suffix   </excludes>
for name of     </artifactSet>
the uber JAR └─> <shadedArtifactAttached>true</shadedArtifactAttached>
        <shadedClassifierName>uber</shadedClassifierName>     Suffix
      </configuration>                                        added to the
    </execution>                                              generated
  </executions>                                               uber JAR
</plugin>
</plugins>
</build>
```

Exclusions are key; you do not want to carry all your dependencies. If you do not have exclusions, all your dependent classes will be transferred in your uber JAR. This includes all the Spark classes and artifacts. They are indeed needed, but because they are included with Spark, they will be available in your target system. If you bundle them in your uber JAR, that uber JAR will become really big, and you may encounter conflicts between libraries.

Because Spark comes with more than 220 libraries, you don't need to bring, in your uber JAR, the dependencies that are already available on the target system. You can specify them by package name, as in this Hadoop exclusion:

```
<exclude>org.apache.hadoop</exclude>
```

Or by artifact, with wildcards, as in this mocking library for tests:

```
<exclude>jmock:*</exclude>
```

Tests, even if they are crucial, and their libraries are not needed in deployment.

Listing 6.2 has an excerpt of the exclusions. The pom.xml available in the GitHub repository for chapter 5 has an almost exhaustive exclusion list that you can use as a base in your projects.

In your project directory (where your pom.xml is located), you can build the uber JAR by calling the following:

```
$ mvn package
```

The result is in the target directory:

```
$ ls -l target
...
-rw-r--r--   ...   748218 ... spark-chapter05-1.0.0-SNAPSHOT-uber.JAR
-rw-r--r--   ...    25308 ... spark-chapter05-1.0.0-SNAPSHOT.JAR
```

Although the size of the uber JAR is much larger (about 750 KB instead of about 25 KB), try to temporarily remove the exclusions and the `minimizeJAR` parameter to see the effect of those parameters on the size of the uber JAR.

6.3.2 Building your application by using Git and Maven

When it comes to deploying your application, another option is to transfer the source code and recompile locally. I must admit this is my favorite way, because you can adjust parameters on the server and push back your code to your source control.

Security experts will probably not let you do this on a production system (those days are probably gone for good). However, I strongly support it in a development environment.

You can make the call on a testing environment, depending on your company's maturity in DevOps. If you completely master your CICD processes, there is almost no need for a local recompilation on the development server. If your deployment still involves a lot of manual processes or if your CICD pipeline is cumbersome, local compilation can help.

Appendix H offers a few critical tips to simplify your life with Maven.

ACCESS TO THE SOURCE CONTROL SERVER Deploying the code to your target system requires that your target system has access to your source code repository, which can be tricky in some cases. I worked on a project in which users were identified via Active Directory/LDAP to the source control system, so you could not leave your login and password exposed on a development server. Thankfully, products like Bitbucket support public and private keys.

In this scenario, the code is freely available on GitHub, so you can pull it pretty easily. On the node, you want to run your driver application. In this scenario, this node is *un*. You will not have to run the application on each node. Type the following:

```
$ git clone https://github.com/jgperrin/
➥ net.jgp.books.spark.ch05.git
remote: Counting objects: 296, done.
remote: Compressing objects: 100% (125/125), done.
remote: Total 296 (delta 72), reused 261 (delta 37), pack-reused 0
Receiving objects: 100% (296/296), 38.04 KiB | 998.00 KiB/s, done.
Resolving deltas: 100% (72/72), done.
$ cd net.jgp.books.spark.ch05
```

You can now compile and install your artifacts by simply calling `mvn install`. Note that this process may take a little while on your first call, as Maven will download all the dependencies:

```
$ mvn install
[INFO] Scanning for projects...
[INFO]
[INFO] -----------------------------------------------------------------
[INFO] Building spark-chapter05 1.0.0-SNAPSHOT
[INFO] -----------------------------------------------------------------
Downloading from central:
     https://repo.maven.apache.org/maven2/org/apache/maven/plugins/
➥ maven-resources-plugin/2.6/maven-resources-plugin-2.6.pom
...
Downloaded from central:
     https://repo.maven.apache.org/maven2/org/codehaus/plexus/
➥ plexus-utils/3.0.5/plexus-utils-3.0.5.JAR (230 kB at 2.9 MB/s)
[INFO] Installing /home/jgp/net.jgp.books.spark.ch05/target/                  Builds and
➥ spark-chapter05-1.0.0-SNAPSHOT.JAR to                                       installs the
➥ /home/jgp/.m2/repository/net/jgp/books/spark-chapter05/                     application
➥ 1.0.0-SNAPSHOT/spark-chapter05-1.0.0-SNAPSHOT.JAR         ◁————            JAR
[INFO] Installing /home/jgp/net.jgp.books.spark.ch05/pom.xml to
➥ /home/jgp/.m2/repository/net/jgp/books/spark-chapter05/
➥ 1.0.0-SNAPSHOT/spark-chapter05-1.0.0-SNAPSHOT.pom
[INFO] Installing /home/jgp/net.jgp.books.spark.ch05/target/                  Builds and
➥ spark-chapter05-1.0.0-SNAPSHOT-sources.JAR to                              installs the
➥ /home/jgp/.m2/repository/net/jgp/books/spark-chapter05/                     application's
➥ 1.0.0-SNAPSHOT/spark-chapter05-1.0.0-SNAPSHOT-sources.JAR ◁————            source code
[INFO] -----------------------------------------------------------------
[INFO] BUILD SUCCESS
[INFO] -----------------------------------------------------------------
[INFO] Total time: 52.643 s
[INFO] Finished at: 2018-08-19T14:39:29-04:00
[INFO] Final Memory: 50M/1234M
[INFO] -----------------------------------------------------------------
```

Note that a package containing the source code has been built and installed. In this scenario, I used my personal account on *un*, but you could use a common account or share your Maven repository with all the users. You can check it in your local Maven repository:

```
$ ls -1 ~/.m2/repository/net/jgp/books/spark-chapter05/1.0.0-SNAPSHOT/
...
spark-chapter05-1.0.0-SNAPSHOT-sources.JAR
spark-chapter05-1.0.0-SNAPSHOT-uber.JAR
spark-chapter05-1.0.0-SNAPSHOT.JAR
spark-chapter05-1.0.0-SNAPSHOT.pom
```

Are you really deploying the source code?

I can hear some people: "Are you nuts? Why are you deploying the source code, our most precious asset?" I would argue that your most precious asset is probably not your source code, but your data. However, that's beyond the point.

For most of my professional life, I have been using source control software: Concurrent Versions System (CVS), Apache Subversion (SVN), Git, even Microsoft Visual SourceSafe. However, as the saying goes about a chain and its links, a process is only as strong as the weakest of the elements. The weak element is usually the part between the keyboard and the chair: the human. Numerous times, despite processes, rules, and automation, the team and I could not recover the source code that matched the deployed version: the tag was not set, the branch was not created, the archive was not built . . .

And as Murphy's law says, you always have production problems with the application that you lost the source code for. Well, that's not exactly Murphy's law, but you get the gist.

So, my answer to those people's questions is, "Who cares?" Because in the emergency of a down production system, the priority is to make sure that *the team has access to the right assets,* and deploying the matching source code ensures part of this. Maven can ensure that the deployed application has the corresponding source code, as illustrated in listing 6.3.

You can easily instruct Maven to automatically package the source code.

Listing 6.3   Ensuring that Maven deploys the source code with the application

```
<build>
  <plugins>
  ...
    <plugin>
      <groupId>org.apache.maven.plugins</groupId>      Definition of
      <artifactId>maven-source-plugin</artifactId>     the plugin
      <version>3.0.1</version>
      <executions>
        <execution>
          <id>attach-sources</id>
          <phase>verify</phase>
          <goals>
            <goal>jar-no-fork</goal>      ◁──┐ No forking during
          </goals>                            the packaging
        </execution>
      </executions>
    </plugin>
  </plugins>
</build>
```

You have the JAR file and can now run it on the cluster.

6.4   Running your application on the cluster

So here we are. After going through all the key concepts of how Spark works, learning how to interact with it, building all those JARs, and digging deep into Maven, you can finally run your application on the cluster. No jokes!

In section 6.3, you built two artifacts that you can execute:

- The uber JAR that you will submit to Spark
- The JAR from the compiled source

Let's deploy and execute them. Your choice of execution depends on how you built your application.

6.4.1   Submitting the uber JAR

Your first option is to run the uber JAR you built via `spark-submit`. This is the uber JAR you prepared in section 6.3.1. You do not need anything other than your JAR.

To upload your uber JAR to the server:

```
$ cd /opt/apache-spark/bin
```

Then submit your application to the master:

```
$ ./spark-submit \
  --class net.jgp.books. spark.ch05.lab210.
  piComputeClusterSubmitJob.PiComputeClusterSubmitJobApp \
  --master "spark://un:7077" \
  <path to>/spark-chapter05-1.0.0-SNAPSHOT.JAR
```

Spark will be verbose, but through the log, you will see your messages:

```
...
About to throw 100000 darts, ready? Stay away from the target!
...
2018-08-20 11:52:14 INFO  SparkContext:54 - Added JAR
      file:/home/jgp/.m2/repository/net/jgp/books/spark-chapter05/
  1.0.0-SNAPSHOT/spark-chapter05-1.0.0-SNAPSHOT.JAR at
      spark://un.oplo.io:42805/JARs/spark-chapter05-1.0.0-SNAPSHOT.JAR
  with timestamp 1534780334746
...
2018-08-20 11:52:14 INFO  StandaloneAppClient$ClientEndpoint:54 - Executor
  added: app-20180820115214-0006/2 on
  worker-20180819144804-10.0.100.83-44763 (10.0.100.83:44763)
  with 4 core(s)
...
Initial dataframe built in 3005 ms
Throwing darts done in 49 ms
...
Analyzing result in 2248 ms
Pi is roughly 3.14448
...
```

Spark makes your JAR available for download by the workers.

The executor has been successfully created.

6.4.2 Running the application

Your second option for running the application is to run it directly via Maven. This is the continuation of your local compilation in section 6.3.2.

Go to the directory where you have your source code:

```
$ cd ~/net.jgp.books.spark.ch05
```

Then run the following:

```
$ mvn clean install exec:exec
[INFO] Scanning for projects...
...
[INFO] --- exec-maven-plugin:1.6.0:exec (default-cli) @ spark-chapter05 ---
About to throw 100000 darts, ready? Stay away from the target!
Session initialized in 1744 ms
Initial dataframe built in 3078 ms
Throwing darts done in 23 ms
Analyzing result in 2438 ms
Pi is roughly 3.14124
...
[INFO] BUILD SUCCESS
...
```

Maven will clean, recompile, and then execute the code.

You have successfully executed an application in two ways. Let's look at what happened behind the scenes.

6.4.3 Analyzing the Spark user interface

In section 6.2, as you were building your cluster, you saw that Spark has a user interface, which you can access on port 8080 (by default) of your master node. Now that you have run your first applications, you can go back to these views, which show the status of your cluster and the applications, both running and completed.

Go to your master's web interface (in this example, it is http://un:8080). Figure 6.7 shows the interface after running a few tests.

When you refresh your screen, the application will be moved to the Completed Applications section. If you click the link, you will access the details of the execution, including the standard out and standard error output. If you look in the log file, as illustrated in figure 6.8, you will find more information about the execution of the application.

Here, you can see that the connection to the master was successful and the executor is starting to work.

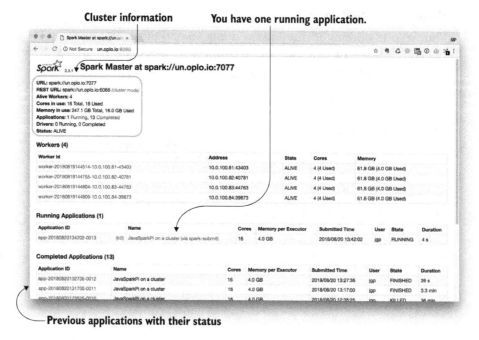

Figure 6.7   Spark's user interface showing your application running as well as the cluster's status

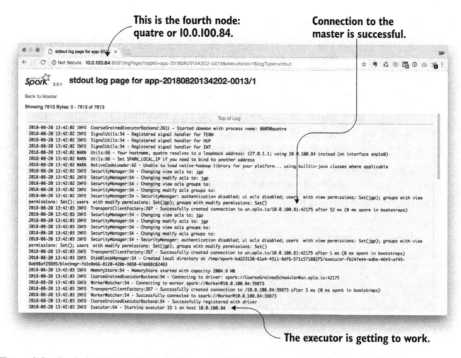

Figure 6.8   Analyzing the worker's node log can bring precious debugging information.

Summary

- Spark supports three execution modes: local mode, cluster mode, and interactive mode.
- Local mode allows developers to get started on Spark development in minutes.
- Cluster mode is used for production.
- You can submit a job to Spark or connect to the master.
- The driver application is where your `main()` method is.
- The master node knows about all the workers.
- The execution takes place on the workers.
- Spark handles the distribution of your application JAR in cluster mode to each worker node.
- CICD (continuous integration and continuous delivery) is an agile methodology that encourages frequent integration and delivery.
- Spark provides a web interface to analyze the execution of jobs and applications.
- I started my career as a VB3 developer.

Part 2

Ingestion

I*ngestion* is a fancy name for *putting the data into the system.* I agree with you: it sounds a little too much like *digestion* and may, at first, scare you.

Nevertheless, don't be fooled by the apparent small size of this part—four chapters. These chapters are crucial to starting your big data journey, as they really explain how Spark will digest your data, from files to streams. Figure 1 shows the topics that these chapters focus on.

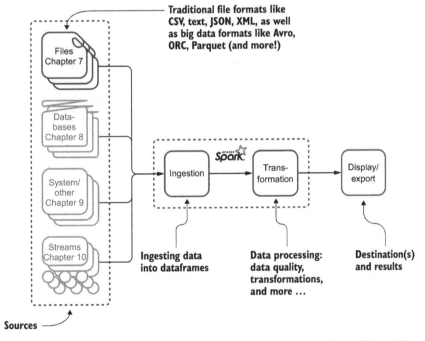

Overall process for ingestion explained over the next four chapters, starting with ingestion from files, then databases, systems, and streams

Chapter 7 focuses on ingestion of files. These files can be not only the well-known types such as CSV, text, JSON, and XML, but also the new generation of file formats that have appeared for big data. You will learn why, as well as more about Avro, ORC, and Parquet. Each file format has its own example.

Chapter 8 covers ingestion from databases, whether from one of the databases supported by Spark or not. This chapter also shows how to ingest data from Elasticsearch. I provide plenty of examples to illustrate those processes.

Chapter 9 is about ingesting anything else. Data is not always in files and databases, right? Chapter 9 talks about convenient places to look for data sources and how to build your own data source. The example in this chapter shows you how to ingest all the data contained in your photos.

Chapter 10 focuses on streaming data. After a quick explanation of what streaming data is, you will ingest data coming from one stream—no, let's be ambitious—two streams! The example uses a streaming data generator available exclusively to you!

Ingestion from files

7

This chapter covers

- Common behaviors of parsers
- Ingesting from CSV, JSON, XML, and text files
- Understanding the difference between one-line and multiline JSON records
- Understanding the need for big data-specific file formats

Ingestion is the first step of your big data pipeline. You will have to onboard the data in your instance of Spark, whether it is in local mode or cluster mode. As you know by now, data in Spark is transient, meaning that when you shut down Spark, it's all gone. You will learn how to import data from standard files including CSV, JSON, XML, and text.

In this chapter, after learning about common behaviors among various parsers, you'll use made-up datasets to illustrate specific cases, as well as datasets coming from open data platforms. It will be tempting to start performing analytics with those datasets. As you see the data displayed onscreen, you will start thinking, "What happens if I join this dataset with this other one? What if I start aggregating this field . . . ?" You will learn how to do those actions in chapters 11 through 15 and chapter 17, but first you need to get all that data into Spark!

The examples in this chapter are based on Spark v3.0. Behaviors have evolved over time, especially when dealing with CSV files.

Appendix L accompanies this chapter as a reference for data ingestion options. After you learn how to ingest files in this chapter, you can use that appendix as a reference for options so you can develop more quickly by finding all the formats and options in one convenient location.

For each format studied in this chapter, you will find, in this order

- A description of the file you want to ingest
- The desired output that illustrates the result of our application
- A detailed walk-through of the application so you understand precisely how to use and fine-tune the parser

New file formats are used in the world of bigger data, as CSV or JSON could not make the cut anymore. Later in this chapter, you'll learn about these new, popular file formats (such as Avro, ORC, Parquet, and Copybook).

Figure 7.1 illustrates where you are on your journey to data ingestion.

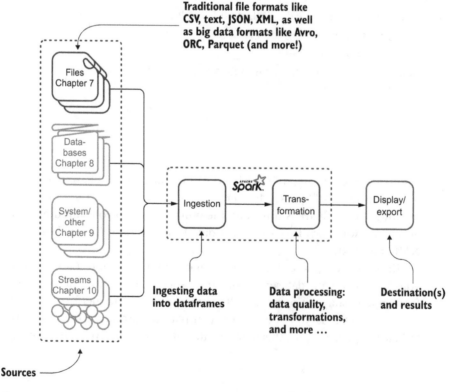

Figure 7.1   On your journey to file ingestion, this chapter focuses on files.

LAB All the examples of this chapter are available on GitHub at https://github.com/jgperrin/net.jgp.books.spark.ch07. Appendix L is a reference for ingestion.

7.1 Common behaviors of parsers

Parsers are the tools that transfer data from an unstructured element, such as a file, to an internal structure; in Spark's case, the dataframe. All the parsers you are going to use have similar behaviors:

- The input of the parser is a file, which you can locate through its path. You can use regex (regular expressions) in the path when reading a file, so when you specify, for example, a*, you will ingest all the files starting with an a.
- Options are not case-sensitive, so `multiline` and `multiLine` are the same.

These behaviors are implementation-dependent, so when you use third-party ingestion libraries (see chapter 9), you may not have the same behaviors. If you have a specific file format to ingest, you can build custom data sources (also explained in chapter 9); however, keep these generic behaviors in mind as you build the component.

7.2 Complex ingestion from CSV

Comma-separated values (*CSV*) is probably the most popular data-exchange format around.[1] Because of its age and wide use, this format has many variations in its core structure: separators are not always commas, some records may span over multiple lines, there are various ways of escaping the separator, and many more creative considerations. So when your customer tells you, "I'll just send you a CSV file," you can certainly nod and slowly start to freak out.

Fortunately for you, Spark offers a variety of options for ingesting CSV files. Ingesting CSV is easy, and the schema inference is a powerful feature.

You already ingested CSV files in chapters 1 and 2, so here you'll look at more-advanced examples with more options that illustrate the complexity of CSV files in the outside world. You will first look at the file you will ingest and understand its specifications. You will then look at the result and, finally, build a mini application to achieve the result. This pattern will repeat for each format.

LAB This is lab #200. The example you are going to study is net.jgp.books .spark.ch07.lab200_csv_ingestion.ComplexCsvToDataframeApp.

Figure 7.2 illustrates the process you are going to implement.

In listing 7.1, you will find an excerpt of a CSV file with two records and a header row. Note that *CSV* has become a generic term: nowadays, the *C* means *character* more than *comma*. You will find files in which values are separated by semicolons, tabs, pipes

---

[1] For more information, see Wikipedia's page on CSV at https://en.wikipedia.org/wiki/Comma-separated _values. In the History section, you'll learn that CSV has been around for quite some time.

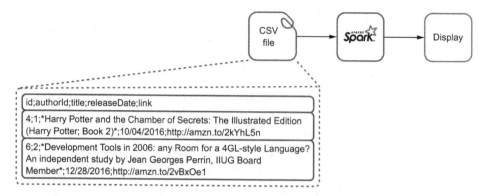

Figure 7.2   Spark ingests a complex CSV-like file with nondefault options. After ingesting the file, the data will be in a dataframe, from which you can display records and the schema—in this case, the schema is inferred by Spark.

(|), and more. For the purist, the acronym may matter, but for Spark, all these separators fall into the same category.

A few observations:

- Your file is not comma-separated but semicolon-separated.
- I manually added the end-of-paragraph symbol (¶) to show the end of each line. It is not in the file.
- If you look at the record with ID 4, you will see that there is a semicolon in the title. This would break the parsing, so this field is surrounded by stars. Keep in mind that this example is a stretch to illustrate some of Spark's features.
- If you look at the record with ID 6, you will see that the title is split over two lines: there is a carriage return after Language? and before An.

Listing 7.1   Complex CSV file (abstract of books.csv)

```
id;authorId;title;releaseDate;link ¶
4;1;*Harry Potter and the Chamber of Secrets: The Illustrated Edition (Harr
➥ y Potter; Book 2)*;10/04/2016;http://amzn.to/2kYhL5n ¶
6;2;*Development Tools in 2006: any Room for a 4GL-style Language? ¶
An independent study by Jean Georges Perrin, IIUG Board Member*;12/28/2016;
➥ http://amzn.to/2vBxOe1 ¶
```

7.2.1   Desired output

The following listing shows the possible output. I added the paragraph marks to illustrate the new lines, as long records are really not easy to read.

Listing 7.2   Desired output after ingestion of the complex CSV file

```
Excerpt of the dataframe content:
+---+---------+------------------------------------------------------------
➥ ------------------------------------+----------+------------------------+¶
```

```
| id|authorId|
                                title|releaseDate|                              link|¶
+---+--------+-----------------------------------------------------------------------
 ------------------------------------+----------+---------------------+¶
    ...
|  4|       1|   Harry Potter and the Chamber of Secrets: The Illustrated E
 dition (Harry Potter; Book 2)|   10/14/16|http://amzn.to/2kYhL5n|¶
...
|  6|       2|Development Tools in 2006: any Room for a 4GL-style Language? ¶
 An independent study by...|   12/28/16|http://amzn.to/2vBxOe1|¶                    <──
...
+---+--------+-----------------------------------------------------------------------
 ------------------------------------+----------+---------------------+¶
only showing top 7 rows
```

The line break that was in your CSV file is still here.

```
Dataframe's schema:
root
 |-- id: integer (nullable = true)
 |-- authorId: integer (nullable = true)
 |-- title: string (nullable = true)
 |-- releaseDate: string (nullable = true)     <──
 |-- link: string (nullable = true)
```

The datatype is an integer. In CSV files, everything is a string, but you will ask Spark to make an educated guess!

Note that the release date is seen as a string, not a date!

7.2.2   Code

To achieve the result in listing 7.2, you will have to code something similar to listing 7.3. You will first get a session, and then configure and run the parsing operation in one call using method chaining. Finally, you will show some records and display the schema of the dataframe. If you are not familiar with schemas, you can read more about them in appendix E.

Listing 7.3   ComplexCsvToDataframeApp.java: Ingesting and displaying a complex CSV

```java
package net.jgp.books.spark.ch07.lab200_csv_ingestion;

import org.apache.spark.sql.Dataset;
import org.apache.spark.sql.Row;
import org.apache.spark.sql.SparkSession;

public class ComplexCsvToDataframeApp {

  public static void main(String[] args) {
    ComplexCsvToDataframeApp app = new ComplexCsvToDataframeApp();
    app.start();
  }

  private void start() {
    SparkSession spark = SparkSession.builder()
        .appName("Complex CSV to Dataframe")
        .master("local")
        .getOrCreate();

    Dataset<Row> df = spark.read().format("csv")
        .option("header", "true")
        .option("multiline", true)
```

Format to ingest is CSV

First line of your CSV file is a header line

Some of our records split over multiple lines; you can use either a string or a Boolean, making it easier to load values from a configuration file.

Quote character is a star (*)

Spark will infer (guess) the schema.

```
       .option("sep", ";")                    ←——— Separator between values is a semicolon (;)
   ├─▷ .option("quote", "*")
       .option("dateFormat", "M/d/y") ◁
   ┌─▷ .option("inferSchema", true)            Date format matches the month/day/year
       .load("data/books.csv");                format, as commonly used in the US

   System.out.println("Excerpt of the dataframe content:");
   df.show(7, 90);
   System.out.println("Dataframe's schema:");
   df.printSchema();
 }
}
```

As you probably guessed, you will need to know what your file looks like (separator character, escape character, and so on) before you can configure the parser. Spark will not infer those. This format is part of the contract that comes with your CSV files (though most of the time you never get a clear description of the format, so you have to guess).

The *schema inference* feature is a pretty neat one. However, as you can see here, it did not infer that the releaseDate column was a date. One way to tell Spark that it is a date is to specify a schema.

7.3 Ingesting a CSV with a known schema

As you just read, ingesting CSV is easy, and the schema inference is a powerful feature. However, when you know the structure (or schema) of the CSV file, it can be useful to specify the datatypes by telling Spark what schema to use. Inferring the schema is a costly operation, and specifying enables you to have better control of the datatypes (see appendix L for a list of datatypes and more hints on ingestion).

> **LAB** This is lab #300. The example you are going to study is net.jgp.books .spark.ch07.lab300_csv_ingestion_with_schema.ComplexCsvToDataframeWith SchemaApp.

In this example, similar to the previous one, you will start a session, define a schema, and parse the file with the help of the schema. Figure 7.3 illustrates this process.

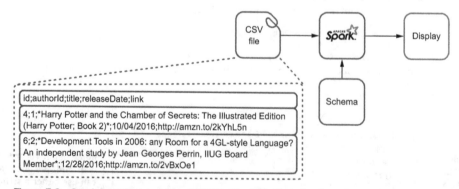

Figure 7.3 Spark ingests a complex CSV-like file, with the help of a schema. Spark does not have to infer the schema. After the ingestion, Spark will display some records and the schema.

Unfortunately, you cannot specify whether the columns can be `null` (nullability). The option exists, but it is ignored by the parser (listing 7.5 shows this option). You are going to ingest the same file as in listing 7.1.

7.3.1 Desired output

The desired output is similar to listing 7.2. However, the schema will look like the following listing, as you are using your schema instead of the one that Spark could infer.

Listing 7.4 Specified schema

```
+---+---------+---------------+-----------+---------------+
| id|authordId|      bookTitle|releaseDate|            url|
+---+---------+---------------+-----------+---------------+
|  1|        1|Fantastic Be...| 2016-11-18|http://amzn....|
|  2|        1|Harry Potter...| 2015-10-06|http://amzn....|
|  3|        1|The Tales of...| 2008-12-04|http://amzn....|
|  4|        1|Harry Potter...| 2016-10-04|http://amzn....|
|  5|        2|Informix 12....| 2017-04-23|http://amzn....|
+---+---------+---------------+-----------+---------------+
only showing top 5 rows

root
 |-- id: integer (nullable = true)
 |-- authordId: integer (nullable = true)
 |-- bookTitle: string (nullable = true)
 |-- releaseDate: date (nullable = true)
 |-- url: string (nullable = true)
```

The column headers are different from the ones in the original CSV files.

◁—— **You have a date!**

7.3.2 Code

Listing 7.5 shows you how to build a schema, ingest a CSV file with a specified schema, and display the dataframe.

To keep the example small, I removed some imports (they are similar to the ones in listing 7.3), and the `main()` method, whose only purpose is to create an instance and call the `start()` method (as in listing 7.3 and many other examples in this book). Blocks of code have been replaced by an ellipsis (...).

Listing 7.5 ComplexCsvToDataframeWithSchemaApp.java (abstract)

```java
package net.jgp.books.spark.ch07.lab300_csv_ingestion_with_schema;
...
import org.apache.spark.sql.types.DataTypes;
import org.apache.spark.sql.types.StructField;
import org.apache.spark.sql.types.StructType;

public class ComplexCsvToDataframeWithSchemaApp {
...

  private void start() {
    SparkSession spark = SparkSession.builder()
```

Name of the field; it will overwrite the column's name in the file.

The datatype; see listing 7.3 for a list of values with explanations

```
    .appName("Complex CSV with a schema to Dataframe")
    .master("local")
    .getOrCreate();

StructType schema = DataTypes.createStructType(new StructField[] {
    DataTypes.createStructField(
        "id",
        DataTypes.IntegerType,
        false),
    DataTypes.createStructField(
        "authordId",
        DataTypes.IntegerType,
        true),
    DataTypes.createStructField(
        "bookTitle",
        DataTypes.StringType,
        false),
    DataTypes.createStructField(
        "releaseDate",
        DataTypes.DateType,
        true),
    DataTypes.createStructField(
        "url",
        DataTypes.StringType,
        false) });

Dataset<Row> df = spark.read().format("csv")
    .option("header", "true")
    .option("multiline", true)
    .option("sep", ";")
    .option("dateFormat", "MM/dd/yyyy")
    .option("quote", "*")
    .schema(schema)
    .load("data/books.csv");

df.show(5, 15);
df.printSchema();
    }
}
```

This is one way to create a schema; in this example, our schema is an array of StructField.

Is this field nullable? Equivalent to: can this field accept a null value?

This value is ignored by the parser.

Tells the reader to use your schema

If you unchain the method chain, you can see that the read() method returns an instance of DataFrameReader. This is the object you configure using the option() methods, the schema() method, and finally the load() method.

As I previously said, CSV has an impressive number of variants, so Spark has an equally impressive number of options—and they keep growing. Appendix L lists those options.

7.4   Ingesting a JSON file

Over the last few years, *JavaScript Object Notation* (*JSON*) has become the new cool kid in town in terms of data exchange, mainly after representational state transfer (REST) supplanted Simple Object Access Protocol (SOAP) and Web Services Description Language (WSDL, written in XML) in web services-oriented architecture.

JSON is easier to read, less verbose, and brings fewer constraints than XML. It supports nested constructs such as arrays and objects. You can find out more about JSON at https://www.json.org. Nevertheless, JSON is still very verbose!

A subformat of JSON is called *JSON Lines*. JSON Lines (http://jsonlines.org) stores a record on one line, easing parsing and readability. Here is a small example copied from the JSON Lines website; as you can see, it supports Unicode:

```
{"name": "Gilbert", "wins": [["straight", "7♣"], ["one pair", "10♥"]]}
{"name": "Alexa", "wins": [["two pair", "4♠"], ["two pair", "9♠"]]}
{"name": "May", "wins": []}
{"name": "Deloise", "wins": [["three of a kind", "5♣"]]}
```

Before Spark v2.2.0, JSON Lines was the only JSON format that Spark could read. Figure 7.4 illustrates JSON ingestion.

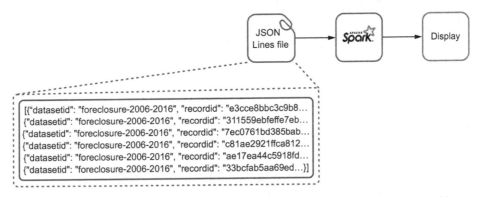

Figure 7.4 Spark ingests a JSON Lines file. The records are in JSON but on one line each. After the ingestion, Spark will display some records and the schema.

For your first JSON ingestion, you are going to use the foreclosure dataset from the city of Durham, NC, for 2006 to 2016. You can download this dataset for free from the city's recently changed portal at https://live-durhamnc.opendata.arcgis.com/.

> **LAB** This is lab #400. The example you are going to study is net.jgp.books.spark .ch07.lab400_json_ingestion.JsonLinesToDataframeApp. The data comes from Open Durham, the open data portal of the city and county of Durham, NC. The data being used comes from the former open data portal using Opendatasoft's solution, which provides data as JSON Lines.

As shown in figure 7.4, each record appears on one line. The following listing shows three records (the first two and the last).

Listing 7.6 Foreclosure data: two first records and the last record

```
[{"datasetid": "foreclosure-2006-2016", "recordid": "629979c85b1cc68c1d4ee8
➥  cc351050bfe3592c62", "fields": {"parcel_number": "110138", "geocode": [
➥  36.0013755, -78.8922549], "address": "217 E CORPORATION ST", "year": "2
```

➥ 006"}, "geometry": {"type": "Point", "coordinates": [-78.8922549, 36.00
➥ 13755]}, "record_timestamp": "2017-03-06T12:41:48-05:00"},
{"datasetid": "foreclosure-2006-2016", "recordid": "e3cce8bbc3c9b804cbd87e2
➥ 67a6ff121285274e0", "fields": {"parcel_number": "110535", "geocode": [3
➥ 5.995797, -78.895396], "address": "401 N QUEEN ST", "year": "2006"}, "g
➥ eometry": {"type": "Point", "coordinates": [-78.895396, 35.995797]},
...
{"datasetid": "foreclosure-2006-2016", "recordid": "1d57ed470d533985d5a3c3d
➥ fb37c294eaa775ccf", "fields": {"parcel_number": "194912", "geocode": [3
➥ 5.955832, -78.742107], "address": "2516 COLEY RD", "year": "2016"}, "ge
➥ ometry": {"type": "Point", "coordinates": [-78.742107, 35.955832]}, "re
➥ cord_timestamp": "2017-03-06T12:41:48-05:00"}]

The following listing shows an indented version of the first record (pretty printed via JSONLint [https://jsonlint.com/] and Eclipse), so you can see the structure: field names, arrays, and nested structure.

Listing 7.7   Foreclosure data: pretty print of the first record

```
[
  {
    "datasetid": "foreclosure-2006-2016",
    "recordid": "629979c85b1cc68c1d4ee8cc351050bfe3592c62",
    "fields": {
      "parcel_number": "110138",
      "geocode": [
        36.0013755,
        -78.8922549
      ],
      "address": "217 E CORPORATION ST",
      "year": "2006"
    },
    "geometry": {
      "type": "Point",
      "coordinates": [
        -78.8922549,
        36.0013755
      ]
    },
    "record_timestamp": "2017-03-06T12:41:48-05:00"
  }
  ...
]
```

7.4.1   Desired output

The following listing shows the output of a dataframe's data and schema after ingesting a JSON Lines document.

```
+-------------+-------------+-------------+-----------------+-------------+
|    datasetid|       fields|     geometry|record_timestamp|     recordid|
+-------------+-------------+-------------+-----------------+-------------+
|foreclosur...|[217 E COR...|[WrappedAr...|    2017-03-06...|629979c85b...|
|foreclosur...|[401 N QUE...|[WrappedAr...|    2017-03-06...|e3cce8bbc3...|
|foreclosur...|[403 N QUE...|[WrappedAr...|    2017-03-06...|311559ebfe...|
|foreclosur...|[918 GILBE...|[WrappedAr...|    2017-03-06...|7ec0761bd3...|
|foreclosur...|[721 LIBER...|[WrappedAr...|    2017-03-06...|c81ae2921f...|
+-------------+-------------+-------------+-----------------+-------------+
only showing top 5 rows
```

Listing 7.8 Displaying foreclosure records and schema

The "fields" field is a structure with nested fields.

```
root
 |-- datasetid: string (nullable = true)
 |-- fields: struct (nullable = true)
 |    |-- address: string (nullable = true)
 |    |-- geocode: array (nullable = true)
 |    |    |-- element: double (containsNull = true)
 |    |-- parcel_number: string (nullable = true)
 |    |-- year: string (nullable = true)
 |-- geometry: struct (nullable = true)
 |    |-- coordinates: array (nullable = true)
 |    |    |-- element: double (containsNull = true)
 |    |-- type: string (nullable = true)
 |-- record_timestamp: string (nullable = true)
 |-- recordid: string (nullable = true)
 |-- year: string (nullable = true)
```

The dataframe can contain arrays.

For every field that Spark cannot precisely identify the datatype, it will use a string.

When you see a piece of data like that, aren't you tempted to group by the year to see the evolution of foreclosures or display each event on a map to see if there are areas more subject to foreclosures, and compare with average incomes in this area? This is good—let your inner data-scientist spirit come out! Data transformations are covered in part 2 of this book.

7.4.2 Code

Reading JSON is not much more complex that ingesting a CSV file, as you can see in the following listing.

Listing 7.9 JsonLinesToDataframeApp.java

```java
package net.jgp.books.spark.ch07.lab400_json_ingestion;

import org.apache.spark.sql.Dataset;
import org.apache.spark.sql.Row;
import org.apache.spark.sql.SparkSession;

public class JsonLinesToDataframeApp {

  public static void main(String[] args) {
    JsonLinesToDataframeApp app =
        new JsonLinesToDataframeApp();
    app.start();
  }
```

```
private void start() {
  SparkSession spark = SparkSession.builder()
      .appName("JSON Lines to Dataframe")
      .master("local")
      .getOrCreate();

  Dataset<Row> df = spark.read().format("json")
      .load("data/durham-nc-foreclosure-2006-2016.json");

  df.show(5, 13);
  df.printSchema();
  }
}
```

That's it! This is the only change you have to do to ingest JSON.

7.5   *Ingesting a multiline JSON file*

Starting with v2.2, Spark can ingest more-complex JSON files and is not constrained to the JSON Lines format. This section will show you how to process these files.

For this JSON ingestion, you'll use travel advisory data from the Bureau of Consular Affairs at the US Department of State.

> **LAB**   This is lab #500. The example you are going to study is net.jgp.books .spark.ch07.lab500_json_multiline_ingestion.MultilineJsonToDataframeApp. The Bureau of Consular Affairs runs an open data portal based on CKAN. CKAN is an open source open data portal; you can learn more about CKAN at https://ckan.org/. You can access the bureau's portal at https://cadatacatalog .state.gov/. Click the Travel link and then the countrytravelinfo link; then click the Go to Resource button to download the file.

Figure 7.5 illustrates the process.

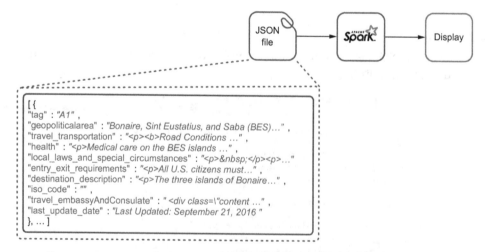

Figure 7.5 Spark ingests a JSON file, in which records are spread over multiple lines. After the ingestion, Spark will display some records and the schema.

The following listing shows an excerpt of the file. For readability purposes, I have shortened the long descriptions.

Listing 7.10   Abstract of the travel advisory from the Department of State

```
[ {
  "tag" : "A1",
  "geopoliticalarea" : "Bonaire, Sint Eustatius, and Saba (BES) (Dutch Cari
⇒ bbean)",
  "travel_transportation" : "<p><b>Road Conditions …",
  "health" : "<p>Medical care on the BES islands …",
  "local_laws_and_special_circumstances" : "<p> </p><p><b>…",
  "entry_exit_requirements" : "<p>All U.S. citizens must…",
  "destination_description" : "<p>The three islands of Bonaire…",
  "iso_code" : "",
  "travel_embassyAndConsulate" : "    <div class=\"content …",
  "last_update_date" : "Last Updated: September 21, 2016          "
}, {
  "tag" : "A2",
  "geopoliticalarea" : "French Guiana",
  "travel_transportation" : "<p><b>Road Conditions and …",
  "local_laws_and_special_circumstances" : "<p><b>Criminal Penalties…",
  "safety_and_security" : "<p>French Guiana is an overseas department…",
  "entry_exit_requirements" : "<p>Visit the…",
  "destination_description" : "<p>French Guiana is an overseas…",
  "iso_code" : "GF",
  "travel_embassyAndConsulate" : "    <div class=\"content…",
  "last_update_date" : "Last Updated: October 12, 2017          "
}, … ]
```

As you can see, this is a rather basic JSON file with an array of objects. Each object has simple key/value pairs. The content of some fields contains rich text in HTML or dates in a nonstandard format (JSON dates should match RFC 3339), which makes extracting information a little more complex. But I am pretty sure you have seen similar examples in your day-to-day projects.

7.5.1   *Desired output*

The following listing shows the output of the travel advisory as it is digested. I removed some columns to fit the code on this page.

Listing 7.11   Abstract of the travel advisory from the Department of State

```
+---------------------+----------------------+---------------------+---…
|destination_description|entry_exit_requirements|   geopoliticalarea|   …
+---------------------+----------------------+---------------------+---…
|   <p>The three isla...|   <p>All U.S. citiz...|Bonaire, Sint Eus...|<p>…
|   <p>French Guiana ...|   <p>Visit the ...|     French Guiana|<p>…
|   <p>See the Depart...|   <p><b>Passports a...|     St Barthelemy|<p>…
|   <p>Read the Depar...|   <p>Upon arrival i...|             Aruba|<p>…
|   <p>See the Depart...|   <p><b>Passports a...| Antigua and Barbuda|<p>…
+---------------------+----------------------+---------------------+---…
```

```
only showing top 5 rows

root
 |-- destination_description: string (nullable = true)
 |-- entry_exit_requirements: string (nullable = true)
 |-- geopoliticalarea: string (nullable = true)
 |-- health: string (nullable = true)
 |-- iso_code: string (nullable = true)
 |-- last_update_date: string (nullable = true)      ◄──
 |-- local_laws_and_special_circumstances: string (nullable = true)
 |-- safety_and_security: string (nullable = true)
 |-- tag: string (nullable = true)
 |-- travel_embassyAndConsulate: string (nullable = true)
 |-- travel_transportation: string (nullable = true)
```

> **Your date is not really a date! You will learn how to turn this nonstandard field into a date as you work on data quality in chapters 12 and 14.**

7.5.2   Code

The following listing shows the Java code needed to process the Department of State's travel advisory.

Listing 7.12   MultilineJsonToDataframeApp.java

```java
package net.jgp.books.spark.ch07.lab500_json_multiline_ingestion;

import org.apache.spark.sql.Dataset;
import org.apache.spark.sql.Row;
import org.apache.spark.sql.SparkSession;

public class MultilineJsonToDataframeApp {

  public static void main(String[] args) {
    MultilineJsonToDataframeApp app =
        new MultilineJsonToDataframeApp();
    app.start();
  }

  private void start() {
    SparkSession spark = SparkSession.builder()
        .appName("Multiline JSON to Dataframe")
        .master("local")
        .getOrCreate();

    Dataset<Row> df = spark.read()
        .format("json")
        .option("multiline", true)              ◄──┐  The key to processing
        .load("data/countrytravelinfo.json");         multiline JSON!

    df.show(3);
    df.printSchema();
  }
}
```

If you forget the `multiline` option, your dataframe will be composed of a single column called _corrupt_record:

```
+--------------------+
|     _corrupt_record|
+--------------------+
|                [ {|
|       "tag" : "A1",|
|   "geopoliticalar...|
+--------------------+
only showing top 3 rows
```

7.6 *Ingesting an XML file*

In this section, you will ingest an *Extensible Markup Language* (*XML*) document containing National Aeronautics and Space Administration (NASA) patents and then display some patents and the dataframe's schema. Note that, in this context, the schema is not an XML Schema (or XSD), but the dataframe schema. Quite a few years ago, when I discovered XML, I really thought it could become a unified lingua franca of data exchange. XML can be described as follows:

- Structured
- Extensible
- Self-describing
- Embeds validation rules through document type definition (DTD) and XML Schema Definition (XSD)
- A W3 standard

You can read more about XML at https://www.w3.org/XML/. XML looks like HTML and any other markup language since SGML:

```
<rootElement>
  <element attribute="attribute's value">
    Some payload in a text element
  </element>
  <element type="without sub nodes"/>
</rootElement>
```

Unfortunately, XML is verbose and harder to read than JSON. Nevertheless, XML is still widely used, and Apache Spark ingests it nicely.

LAB This is lab #600. The example you are going to study is net.jgp.books .spark.ch07.lab600_xml_ingestion.XmlToDataframeApp.

Figure 7.6 shows a fragment of the XML file and illustrates the process.

For this XML example, you are going to ingest the NASA patents. NASA offers various open datasets at https://data.nasa.gov. Listing 7.13 shows a record of this file.

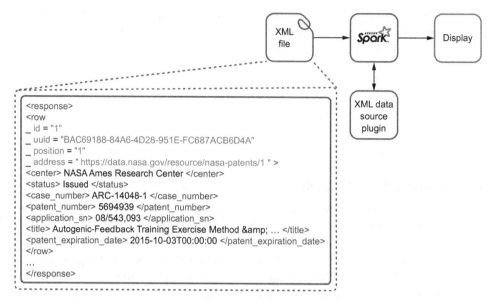

Figure 7.6   Spark ingests an XML file containing NASA patents. Spark uses an external plugin, provided by Databricks, to perform the ingestion. Spark will then display records and the dataframe schema (not to be confused with an XML Schema).

LAB   You can download the NASA patents dataset from https://data.nasa .gov/Raw-Data/NASA-Patents/gquh-watm. For this example, I used Spark v2.2.0 on Mac OS X v10.12.6 with Java 8 as well as the Databricks XML parser v0.4.1. The dataset was downloaded in January 2018.

Listing 7.13   NASA patents (excerpt)

**Root element of
your list of patents**

```
⤷ <response>              ┌ Element (or tag)
     <row         ⤺       └ designing our record
         _id="1"
         _uuid="BAC69188-84A6-4D28-951E-FC687ACB6D4A"              Attributes are
         _position="1"                                             prefixed by one
         _address="https://data.nasa.gov/resource/nasa-patents/1"> underscore (_).
     <center>NASA Ames Research Center</center>
     <status>Issued</status>
     <case_number>ARC-14048-1</case_number>
     <patent_number>5694939</patent_number>
     <application_sn>08/543,093</application_sn>
     <title>Autogenic-Feedback Training Exercise Method &amp; System</title>
     <patent_expiration_date>2015-10-03T00:00:00</patent_expiration_date>
     </row>
   ...
</response>
```

7.6.1 *Desired output*

Listing 7.14 shows the output of a dataframe's data and schema after ingesting the NASA patents as an XML document. You can see that the attributes are prefixed by an underscore (attributes already had an underscore as a prefix in the original document, so now they have two), and the element's name is used as a column name.

Listing 7.14 NASA patents in a dataframe

```
+-------------------+----+----------+--------------------+-------------+...
|          __address|__id|__position|              __uuid|application_sn|...
+-------------------+----+----------+--------------------+-------------+...
|https://data.nasa...| 407|       407|2311F785-C00F-422...|   13/033,085|...
|https://data.nasa...|   1|         1|BAC69188-84A6-4D2...|   08/543,093|...
|https://data.nasa...|   2|         2|23D6A5BD-26E2-42D...|   09/017,519|...
|https://data.nasa...|   3|         3|F8052701-E520-43A...|   10/874,003|...
|https://data.nasa...|   4|         4|20A4C4A9-EEB6-45D...|   09/652,299|...
+-------------------+----+----------+--------------------+-------------+...
only showing top 5 rows

root
 |-- __address: string (nullable = true)
 |-- __id: long (nullable = true)
 |-- __position: long (nullable = true)
 |-- __uuid: string (nullable = true)
 |-- application_sn: string (nullable = true)
 |-- case_number: string (nullable = true)
 |-- center: string (nullable = true)
 |-- patent_expiration_date: string (nullable = true)
 |-- patent_number: string (nullable = true)
 |-- status: string (nullable = true)
 |-- title: string (nullable = true)
```

7.6.2 *Code*

As usual, our code will start with a main() method, which calls a start() method to create a Spark session. The following listing is the Java code needed to ingest the NASA XML file and then display five records and its schema.

Listing 7.15 XmlToDataframeApp.java

```java
package net.jgp.books.spark.ch07.lab600_xml_ingestion;

import org.apache.spark.sql.Dataset;
import org.apache.spark.sql.Row;
import org.apache.spark.sql.SparkSession;

public class XmlToDataframeApp {

  public static void main(String[] args) {
    XmlToDataframeApp app = new XmlToDataframeApp();
    app.start();
```

```
    }

    private void start() {
        SparkSession spark = SparkSession.builder()
            .appName("XML to Dataframe")
            .master("local")
            .getOrCreate();

        Dataset<Row> df = spark.read().format("xml")
            .option("rowTag", "row")
            .load("data/nasa-patents.xml");

        df.show(5);
        df.printSchema();
    }
}
```

Element or tag that indicates a record in the XML file → (points to `.option("rowTag", "row")`)

Specifies XML as the format. Case does not matter. → (points to `.format("xml")`)

I had to modify the original NASA document because it contained an element with the same name as the record, wrapping the records. Unfortunately, as of now, Spark cannot change this element's name for us. The original structure was as follows:

```
<response>
  <row>
    <row _id="1" …>
      …
    </row>
    …
  </row>
</response>
```

If the first child of `response` had been `rows`, or anything else other than `row`, I wouldn't have had to remove it (another option is to rename it).

Because the parser is not part of the standard Spark distribution, you will have to add it to the pom.xml file, as described in the following listing. To ingest XML, you will use spark-xml_2.12 (the artifact) from Databricks, in version 0.7.0.

Listing 7.16   pom.xml to ingest XML (excerpt)

```
…
<properties>
    …
    <scala.version>2.12</scala.version>
    <spark-xml.version>0.7.0</spark-xml.version>
</properties>

<dependencies>
    …
    <dependency>
        <groupId>com.databricks</groupId>
        <artifactId>spark-xml_${scala.version}</artifactId>
        <version>${spark-xml.version}</version>
        <exclusions>
```

Scala version on which the XML is built → (points to `<scala.version>2.12</scala.version>`)

Version of the XML parser → (points to `<spark-xml.version>0.7.0</spark-xml.version>`)

Equivalent to spark-xml_2.12 (points to `<artifactId>spark-xml_${scala.version}</artifactId>`)

Equivalent to 0.7.0 → (points to `<version>${spark-xml.version}</version>`)

Optional: I excluded the logger from other packages to have better control over the one I use. → (points to `<exclusions>`)

```
    <exclusion>
      <groupId>org.slf4j</groupId>
      <artifactId>slf4j-simple</artifactId>
    </exclusion>
  </exclusions>
</dependency>
...
  </dependencies>
...
```

More details on Spark XML can be found at https://github.com/databricks/spark-xml.

7.7 Ingesting a text file

Although text files are less popular in enterprise applications, they are still used, so you'll see them from time to time. The growing popularity of deep learning and artificial intelligence also drives more natural language processing (NLP) activities. In this section, you will not do any NLP, but simply ingest text files. To learn more about NLP, see *Natural Language Processing in Action* by Hobson Lane, Cole Howard, and Hannes Max Hapke (Manning, 2019).

In lab #700, you are going to ingest Shakespeare's *Romeo and Juliet*. Project Gutenberg (http://www.gutenberg.org) hosts numerous books and resources in digital format.

Each line of the book will become a record of our dataframe. There is no feature to cut by sentence or word. Listing 7.17 shows an excerpt of the file you'll work on.

> **LAB** This is lab #700. The example you are going to study is net.jgp.books .spark.ch07.lab700_text_ingestion.TextToDataframeApp. You can download *Romeo and Juliet* from www.gutenberg.org/cache/epub/1777/pg1777.txt.

Listing 7.17 Abstract of Project Gutenberg's version of *Romeo and Juliet*

```
This Etext file is presented by Project Gutenberg, in
cooperation with World Library, Inc., from their Library of the
Future and Shakespeare CDROMS.  Project Gutenberg often releases
Etexts that are NOT placed in the Public Domain!!
...
ACT I. Scene I.
Verona. A public place.

Enter Sampson and Gregory (with swords and bucklers) of the house
of Capulet.

  Samp. Gregory, on my word, we'll not carry coals.
  Greg. No, for then we should be colliers.
  Samp. I mean, an we be in choler, we'll draw.
  Greg. Ay, while you live, draw your neck out of collar.
  Samp. I strike quickly, being moved.
  Greg. But thou art not quickly moved to strike.
  Samp. A dog of the house of Montague moves me.
...
```

7.7.1 *Desired output*

The following listing shows the first five rows of *Romeo and Juliet* after it has been ingested by Spark and transformed into a dataframe.

Listing 7.18 *Romeo and Juliet* in a dataframe

```
+--------------------+
|               value|
+--------------------+
|                    |
|This Etext file i...|
|cooperation with ...|
|Future and Shakes...|
|Etexts that are N...|
...
root
 |-- value: string (nullable = true)
```

7.7.2 *Code*

The following listing is the Java code needed to turn *Romeo and Juliet* into a dataframe.

Listing 7.19 TextToDataframeApp.java

```java
package net.jgp.books.spark.ch07.lab700_text_ingestion;

import org.apache.spark.sql.Dataset;
import org.apache.spark.sql.Row;
import org.apache.spark.sql.SparkSession;

public class TextToDataframeApp {

  public static void main(String[] args) {
    TextToDataframeApp app = new TextToDataframeApp();
    app.start();
  }

  private void start() {
    SparkSession spark = SparkSession.builder()
        .appName("Text to Dataframe")
        .master("local")
        .getOrCreate();

    Dataset<Row> df = spark.read().format("text")        Specify "text" when you
        .load("data/romeo-juliet-pg1777.txt");           want to ingest a text file.

    df.show(10);
    df.printSchema();
  }
}
```

Unlike with other formats, there are no options to set with text.

7.8 File formats for big data

Big data brings its own set of file formats. If you haven't seen an Avro, ORC, or Parquet file yet, you will definitely see one (if not all of them) on your journey with Spark. It is important to understand what those files are before you ingest them.

I hear you: "Why do I need more file formats?" In this section, I answer this question. Then I discuss these three newer formats. In section 7.9, I'll show you how to ingest data in these newer formats.

7.8.1 The problem with traditional file formats

In the context of big data, traditional files formats such as text, CSV, JSON, and XML have limitations you should be aware of.

In most big data projects, you will have to pull the data from *somewhere* (the sources) and you may have to put it back *somewhere else* (the destinations). Figure 7.7 describes this process.

The sources can be files (studied in this chapter), databases (chapter 8), complex systems or APIs (chapter 9), or even streams (chapter 10). Even if you can access all

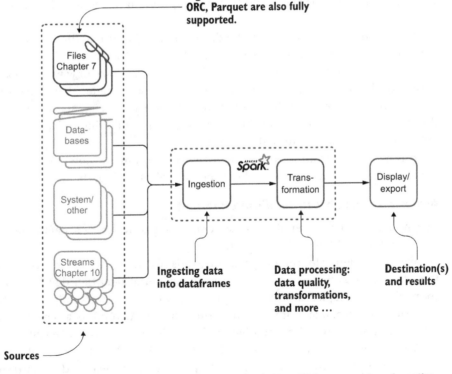

Figure 7.7 A classic big data scenario with ingestion from multiple sources, transformation, and export. This section is about understanding the limit of traditional file formats as well as the benefits of Avro, ORC, and Parquet in the context of big data.

those resources in a more efficient way than files, for some odd reason you still have to deal with files and their annoying life cycles.

"So why can't I just use JSON, XML, or CSV?" Here are some reasons:

- JSON and XML (and in some measure CSV) are not easy to split. When you want your nodes to read a part of the file, it's easier if you can split it. Node 1 will read the first 5,000 records, node 2 the second 5,000, and so on. Because of its root element, XML will need rework, which may break the document. Big data files need to be splittable.
- CSV cannot store hierarchical information as JSON or XML can.
- None are designed to incorporate metadata.
- None of these formats support easy column addition, deletion, or insertion (although you will probably not need those operations, as Spark will do them).
- These formats are all quite verbose (especially JSON and XML), which inflates the file size drastically.

"Okay, so why not use a binary format like the ones used by RDBMSs?" Because every vendor has its own format, you would end up with a myriad of formats. Other formats, such as COBOL Copybook or its Programming Language One (PL/I), or IBM's High Level Assembler (HLASM), would be too complex and linked to IBM's mainframe to be used generically.

Therefore, new formats had to be developed, and as usual, the industry created a plethora. The most popular ones are Avro, ORC, and Parquet.

In most organizations, you probably will not have a choice of which format you will have to deal with. That choice has probably already been made. Some file formats may have been inherited from the Hadoop distribution your team started working with. But if your organization has not made a choice, the following quick definitions can help you make a more educated decision.

You may also encounter other file formats from time to time, but the ones I just mentioned are the most popular. Let's have a look at each of them.

7.8.2 *Avro is a schema-based serialization format*

Apache Avro is a data serialization system, which provides rich data structures in a compact, fast, and binary data format.

Avro was designed for remote procedure calls (RPCs) in a similar way as Protocol Buffers (Protobuf), a popular method for transferring serializable data developed and open sourced by Google; learn more at https://developers.google.com/protocol-buffers/. Avro supports dynamic modification of the schema. Avro offers a schema, written in JSON. Because an Avro file is row-based, the file is easier to split, like CSV.

Avro is available in Java, C, C++, C#, Go, Haskell, Perl, PHP, Python, Ruby, and Scala. The reference for Avro can be found at https://avro.apache.org/docs/current/.

7.8.3 *ORC is a columnar storage format*

Apache Optimized Row Columnar (ORC), along with its predecessor RCFile, is a columnar storage format. ORC is ACID-compliant (atomicity, consistency, isolation, durability).

Beyond the standard datatypes, ORC supports compound types including structs, lists, maps, and unions. ORC supports compression, which reduces file size and network transfer time (always a bonus for big data).

Apache ORC is backed by Hortonworks, which means that all Cloudera-based tools, such as Impala (a SQL query engine for data stored in a Hadoop cluster), may not fully support ORC. With the merger of Hortonworks and Cloudera, it is not yet known what to expect for the support of those file formats.

ORC is available in Java and C++. The reference for ORC can be found at https://orc.apache.org/.

7.8.4 *Parquet is also a columnar storage format*

Like ORC, Apache Parquet is a columnar file format. Parquet supports compression, and you can add columns at the end of the schema. Parquet also supports compound types such as lists and maps.

Parquet seems to be the most popular format among big data practitioners. Apache Parquet is backed by Cloudera, in collaboration with Twitter. Once more, with the merger of Hortonworks and Cloudera, it is not yet known what to expect for the support of those file formats. Parquet seems more popular nevertheless.

Parquet is available in Java. The reference for Parquet can be found at https://parquet.apache.org/.

7.8.5 *Comparing Avro, ORC, and Parquet*

Big data file formats add a layer of complexity. Nevertheless, I hope you understand their necessity and the differences between them. The following are qualities that ORC, Parquet, and Avro share:

- They are binary formats.
- They embed their schema. Avro's use of JSON for its schema gives the most flexibility.
- They compress their data. Parquet and ORC are better at compression than Avro.

Based on popularity, if you have a choice to make, Parquet is probably the way to go. Remember that your organization may already have a standard for big data file formats, and even if it is not Parquet, it is probably a good idea to stick with that choice.

If you are interested in more technical details, you can read "Big Data File Formats Demystified" by Alex Woodie (http://mng.bz/2JBa) and "Hadoop File Formats: It's Not Just CSV Anymore" by Kevin Hass (http://mng.bz/7zAQ). Both articles were written prior to the Hortonworks and Cloudera merger.

7.9   Ingesting Avro, ORC, and Parquet files

In this last section, I'll show you how to ingest Avro, ORC, and Parquet files. Earlier in this chapter, you learned about traditional formats including CSV, JSON, XML, and text files. As you may recall, the constructs of those file formats are similar. As expected, the ingestion process will be similar for the big data file format.

In all the examples, I used sample datafiles from the Apache projects themselves. They are, unfortunately, not as inspiring for creative analytics as you might have expected, considering all the other datasets I used in this book.

7.9.1   Ingesting Avro

To ingest an Avro file, you need to add a library to your project, as Avro is not natively supported by Spark. After that, the ingestion is straightforward, like any file ingestion.

> **LAB** The example you are going to study is net.jgp.books.spark.ch07 .lab910_avro_ingestion.AvroToDataframeApp. The sample file comes from the Apache Avro project itself.

The following listing shows the expected output of this example.

Listing 7.20   Output of AvroToDataframeApp.java

```
+------------+--------------+----+
|     station|          time|temp|
+------------+--------------+----+
|011990-99999|-619524000000|   0|
|011990-99999|-619506000000|  22|
|011990-99999|-619484400000| -11|
|012650-99999|-655531200000| 111|
|012650-99999|-655509600000|  78|
+------------+--------------+----+

root
 |-- station: string (nullable = true)
 |-- time: long (nullable = true)
 |-- temp: integer (nullable = true)

The dataframe has 5 rows.
```

Since Spark v2.4, Avro is part of the Apache community. Prior to this version, it was maintained by Databricks (as the XML data source). You will still need to manually add the dependency to your pom.xml file. The additional library is available through Maven Central, and you can add the library definition in your pom.xml:

```
...
  <properties>
    <scala.version>2.12</scala.version>
    <spark.version>3.0.0</spark.version>
...
  </properties>
```

```
<dependencies>
  <dependency>
    <groupId>org.apache.spark</groupId>
    <artifactId>spark-avro_${scala.version}</artifactId>
    <version>${spark.version}</version>
  </dependency>
...
</dependencies>
```

This resolves as follows:

```
<dependency>
  <groupId>org.apache.spark</groupId>
  <artifactId>spark-avro_2.12</artifactId>
  <version>3.0.0</version>
</dependency>
```

After you have added the library, you can write your code, as in the following listing.

Listing 7.21 AvroToDataframeApp.java

```
package net.jgp.books.spark.ch07.lab900_avro_ingestion;

import org.apache.spark.sql.Dataset;          You do not need any special
import org.apache.spark.sql.Row;              imports; the library will be
import org.apache.spark.sql.SparkSession;     dynamically loaded.

public class AvroToDataframeApp {
  public static void main(String[] args) {
    AvroToDataframeApp app = new AvroToDataframeApp();
    app.start();
  }

  private void start() {
    SparkSession spark = SparkSession.builder()
        .appName("Avro to Dataframe")
        .master("local")
        .getOrCreate();

    Dataset<Row> df = spark.read()            Specifies the format; no
        .format("avro")                       short code is available.
        .load("data/weather.avro");

    df.show(10);
    df.printSchema();
    System.out.println("The dataframe has " + df.count()
        + " rows.");
  }
}
```

To learn more about Avro's support in Spark prior to v2.4, you can refer to the Databricks GitHub repository at https://github.com/databricks/spark-avro.

7.9.2   *Ingesting ORC*

Ingesting ORC is a straightforward process. The format code needed by Spark is orc.
In Spark versions prior to Spark v2.4, you also need to configure your session by specifying the implementation if you do not already use Apache Hive.

> **LAB** The example you are going to study is net.jgp.books.spark.ch07
> .lab920_orc_ingestion.OrcToDataframeApp. The sample file comes from the
> Apache ORC project itself.

The following listing shows the expected output of this example.

Listing 7.22   Output of OrcToDataframeApp.java

```
+-----+-----+-----+-------+-----+-----+-----+-----+-----+
|_col0|_col1|_col2|  _col3|_col4|_col5|_col6|_col7|_col8|
+-----+-----+-----+-------+-----+-----+-----+-----+-----+
|    1|    M|    M|Primary|  500| Good|    0|    0|    0|
|    2|    F|    M|Primary|  500| Good|    0|    0|    0|
...
|   10|    F|    U|Primary|  500| Good|    0|    0|    0|
+-----+-----+-----+-------+-----+-----+-----+-----+-----+
only showing top 10 rows

root
 |-- _col0: integer (nullable = true)
 |-- _col1: string (nullable = true)
 |-- _col2: string (nullable = true)
 |-- _col3: string (nullable = true)
 |-- _col4: integer (nullable = true)
 |-- _col5: string (nullable = true)
 |-- _col6: integer (nullable = true)
 |-- _col7: integer (nullable = true)
 |-- _col8: integer (nullable = true)

The dataframe has 1920800 rows.
```

The following listing provides the sample code to read an ORC file.

Listing 7.23   OrcToDataframeApp.java

```java
package net.jgp.books.spark.ch07.lab910_orc_ingestion;

import org.apache.spark.sql.Dataset;
import org.apache.spark.sql.Row;
import org.apache.spark.sql.SparkSession;

public class OrcToDataframeApp {

  public static void main(String[] args) {
    OrcToDataframeApp app = new OrcToDataframeApp();
    app.start();
```

```
    }

    private void start() {
        SparkSession spark = SparkSession.builder()
            .appName("ORC to Dataframe")
            .config("spark.sql.orc.impl", "native")    ◁
            .master("local")
            .getOrCreate();

        Dataset<Row> df = spark.read()
            .format("orc")
            .load("data/demo-11-zlib.orc");    ◁

        df.show(10);
        df.printSchema();
        System.out.println("The dataframe has " + df.count() + " rows.");
    }
}
```

Use the native implementation to access the ORC file, not the Hive implementation.

The format to use for ORC

A standard file that comes from the Apache ORC project

The implementation parameter can have either the `native` value or the `hive` value. The native implementation means that it uses the implementation that comes with Spark. It is the default value starting with Spark v2.4.

7.9.3　Ingesting Parquet

In this section, you'll look at how Spark ingests Parquet. Spark will easily ingest Parquet files natively: there is no need for an additional library or configuration. It is important to remember that Parquet is also the default format used by Spark and Delta Lake (in chapter 17).

LAB　The example you are going to study is net.jgp.books.spark.ch07 .lab930_parquet_ingestion.ParquetToDataframeApp. The sample file comes from the Apache Parquet Testing project itself, available at https://github .com/apache/parquet-testing.

The following listing shows the expected output of this example.

Listing 7.24　Output of ParquetToDataframeApp.java

```
+---+--------+-----------+------------+-------+----------+---------+...
| id|bool_col|tinyint_col|smallint_col|int_col|bigint_col|float_col|...
+---+--------+-----------+------------+-------+----------+---------+...
|  4|    true|          0|           0|      0|         0|      0.0|...
|  5|   false|          1|           1|      1|        10|      1.1|...
|  6|    true|          0|           0|      0|         0|      0.0|...
|  7|   false|          1|           1|      1|        10|      1.1|...
|  2|    true|          0|           0|      0|         0|      0.0|...
|  3|   false|          1|           1|      1|        10|      1.1|...
|  0|    true|          0|           0|      0|         0|      0.0|...
|  1|   false|          1|           1|      1|        10|      1.1|...
+---+--------+-----------+------------+-------+----------+---------+...
```

```
root
 |-- id: integer (nullable = true)
 |-- bool_col: boolean (nullable = true)
 |-- tinyint_col: integer (nullable = true)
 |-- smallint_col: integer (nullable = true)
 |-- int_col: integer (nullable = true)
 |-- bigint_col: long (nullable = true)
 |-- float_col: float (nullable = true)
 |-- double_col: double (nullable = true)
 |-- date_string_col: binary (nullable = true)
 |-- string_col: binary (nullable = true)
 |-- timestamp_col: timestamp (nullable = true)

The dataframe has 8 rows.
```

The following listing provides the sample code to read a Parquet file.

Listing 7.25   ParquetToDataframeApp.java

```java
package net.jgp.books.spark.ch07.lab930_parquet_ingestion;

import org.apache.spark.sql.Dataset;
import org.apache.spark.sql.Row;
import org.apache.spark.sql.SparkSession;

public class ParquetToDataframeApp {
  public static void main(String[] args) {
    ParquetToDataframeApp app = new ParquetToDataframeApp();
    app.start();
  }

  private void start() {
    SparkSession spark = SparkSession.builder()
        .appName("Parquet to Dataframe")
        .master("local")
        .getOrCreate();

    Dataset<Row> df = spark.read()            // Spark code for
        .format("parquet")                    // reading Parquet
        .load("data/alltypes_plain.parquet");

    df.show(10);
    df.printSchema();
    System.out.println("The dataframe has " + df.count() + " rows.");
  }
}
```

7.9.4 Reference table for ingesting Avro, ORC, or Parquet

Table 7.1 summarizes the Spark format code for each file type you want to ingest.

Table 7.1 Spark format code for each file format

File format	Code	Things to remember
Avro (before Spark v2.4)	`com.databricks.spark.avro`	You will need to add the Spark-Avro library to your project.
Avro (after Spark v2.4)	`avro`	
ORC	`orc`	Make sure you specify the implementation. The recommended option is the native implementation, which you set with `.config("spark.sql.orc.impl", "native")` when you get your Spark session, if you use Spark prior to v2.4.
Parquet	`parquet`	Nothing extra (makes my day for once)!

Summary

- Ingestion is a key part of your big data pipeline.
- When ingesting files, you can use a regular expression (regex) to specify the path.
- CSV is more complex than it looks, but a rich set of options allows you to tune the parser.
- JSON exists in two forms: the one-line form called JSON Lines, and multiline JSON. Spark ingests both forms of JSON (since v2.2.0).
- All options for file ingestion that are described in this chapter are not case-sensitive.
- Spark can ingest CSV, JSON, and text out of the box.
- To ingest XML, Spark needs a plugin provided by Databricks.
- The pattern for ingesting any document is fairly similar: you specify the format and simply read.
- Traditional file formats, including CSV, JSON, and XML, are not well suited for big data.
- JSON and XML are not considered splittable file formats.
- Avro, ORC, and Parquet are popular big data file formats. They embed the data and the schema in a file and compress the data. They are easier and more efficient to manipulate than CSV, JSON, and XML when it comes to big data.
- ORC and Parquet files are in a columnar format.
- Avro is row-based, which is more suitable for streaming.
- ORC and Parquet's compression is better than Avro's.

Ingestion from databases

In the big data and enterprise context, relational databases are often the source of the data on which you will perform analytics. It makes sense to understand how to extract data from those databases, both through the whole table or through SQL SELECT statements.

In this chapter, you'll learn several ways to ingest data from those relational databases, ingesting either the full table at once or asking the database to perform some operations before the ingestion. Those operations could be filtering, joining, or aggregating data at the database level to minimize data transfer.

You will see in this chapter which databases are supported by Spark. When you work with a database not supported by Spark, a custom *dialect* is required. The dialect is a way to inform Spark of how to communicate with the database. Spark comes with a few dialects and, in most cases, you won't need to even think about them. However, for those special situations, you'll learn how to build one.

Finally, many enterprises use document stores and NoSQL databases. In this chapter, you'll also learn how to connect to Elasticsearch and go through a complete ingestion scenario. Elasticsearch is the only NoSQL database that you will study.

In this chapter, you will work with MySQL, IBM Informix, and Elasticsearch.

Figure 8.1 illustrates where you stand on your road to ingestion.

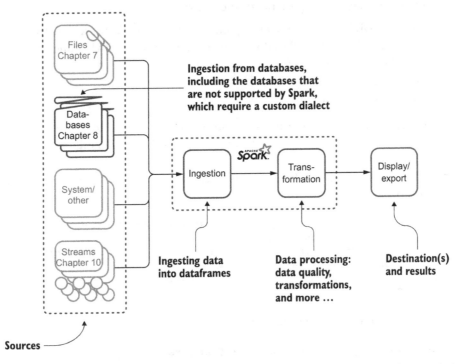

Figure 8.1   This chapter focuses on ingestion from databases, whether the database is supported by Spark, or is not supported and requires a custom dialect to be used.

> **LAB** Examples from this chapter are available in GitHub at https://github
> .com/jgperrin/net.jgp.books.spark.ch08. Appendix F provides links, tips, and
> help with installing relational databases. Appendix L is a reference for ingestion.

8.1   Ingestion from relational databases

As you probably know, relational databases are a cornerstone of the transactional data stores you'll find in any enterprise. In most cases, as soon as a transaction happens, it involves an existing relational database somewhere.

Let's imagine you have a relational database containing film actors and want to display them alphabetically. To accomplish that, you'll learn about the elements Spark needs to establish a database connection (and, spoiler alert, if you are familiar with JDBC, it's the same). You'll then learn a bit about the sample database, its data, and its schema; play with the sample database; look at the output; and, finally, dig into the code.

8.1.1   Database connection checklist

Spark needs a small list of information to connect to a database. Spark connects directly to relational databases by using Java Database Connectivity (JDBC) drivers. To connect to a database, Spark needs the following:

- The JDBC driver in the class path of the workers (You learned about workers in chapter 2: basically, they do all the work and will deal with loading the JDBC driver.)
- The connection URL
- The username
- The user password

The driver may need other information that is driver-specific. For example, Informix needs DELIMIDENT=Y, and MySQL server expects SSL by default, so you may want to specify useSSL=false.

Naturally, the JDBC driver needs to be provided to the application. It can be in your pom.xml file:

```
<dependency>                              Driver definition for MySQL
  <groupId>mysql</groupId>            ◁──┘
  <artifactId>mysql-connector-java</artifactId>   ◁──── Artifact ID
  <version>8.0.8-dmr</version>        ◁──┐
  ...                                      │  Version
</dependency>
```

Listing 8.3 describes the pom.xml file in more detail.

8.1.2   Understanding the data used in the examples

For your first ingestion from a database, you are going to use the Sakila database in MySQL. *Sakila* is a standard sample database that comes with MySQL; a lot of tutorials are available, and you may even have learned MySQL with it. This section describes what the database is about—its purpose, structure, and data. Figure 8.2 will summarize our operation.

The Sakila sample database is designed to represent a DVD rental store. Okay, I get it—some of you are probably wondering what a DVD is and why you would even rent such a thing. *DVD* stands for *digital video* (or *versatile*) *disc.* A DVD is a shiny disk, 12 cm (about 5 inches) in diameter, which is used to store digital information. In the early days (1995), it was used to store movies in digital format. People could buy or rent those objects and watch the movie on their TV by using a device called a DVD player.

If you did not want to buy the DVD, you could rent it from small shops or larger chains like Blockbuster in the United States. Those stores needed people to check in and out the disks and other artifacts like VHS tapes (as much as I recognize that this is even more obscure than a DVD, it is really beyond the scope of this book). In 1997, an innovative firm, Netflix, started to rent DVDs via mail.

You will use the demo database, which includes about 15 tables and a few views (figure 8.2) for this scenario.

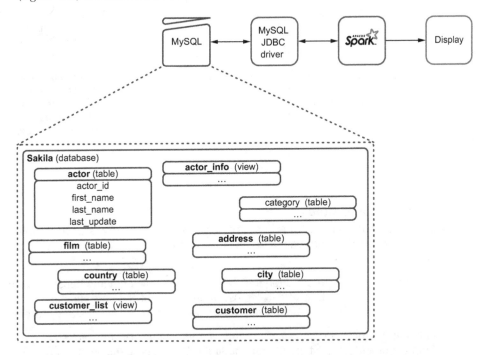

Figure 8.2   Spark ingests the database, stored in a MySQL instance. Spark needs a JDBC driver, like any Java application. MySQL stores the sample database, called Sakila, which contains 23 tables and views. Some are represented here, such as `actor`, `actor_info`, `category`, and so on. You'll focus on `actor`.

As you can see in figure 8.2, you're going to use the `actor` table for this project, which is described in more detail in table 8.1. You'll notice that `last_update` implements change data capture (CDC).

Table 8.1   The `actor` table as it is defined in the Sakila database in MySQL

Column	Type	Attributes	Comment
actor_id	SMALLINT	Primary key, not null, unique, auto-increment. In MySQL, an integer with autoincrement will automatically get a new value when you insert a new row. Informix and PostgreSQL use a SERIAL and SERIAL8 datatype; other databases use stored procedures or sequences.	The actor's unique identifier.

Table 8.1   The `actor` table as it is defined in the Sakila database in MySQL *(continued)*

Column	Type	Attributes	Comment
first_name	VARCHAR(45)	Not null.	The actor's first name.
last_name	VARCHAR(45)	Not null.	The actor's last name. As you can see, the database modeler did not think of movies starring Cher or Madonna.
last_update	TIMESTAMP	Not null, CURRENT_TIMESTAMP ON UPDATE CURRENT_TIMESTAMP.	A timestamp that is automatically updated each time you do an update. This is a good practice: if you are using and designing RDBMSs, it is a good thing to integrate. It will allow you to implement CDC.

Change data capture

Change data capture (*CDC*) is a set of software design patterns used to determine (and track) the data that has changed so that action can be taken using the changed data.

CDC solutions occur most often in data-warehouse environments because capturing and preserving the state of data across time is one of the core functions of a data warehouse, but CDC can be utilized in any database or data repository system.

Although Spark is not designed for data warehousing, CDC techniques can be used from incremental analytics. Overall, adding a `last_update` column as a timestamp (or similar) is a good practice.

Information in this sidebar was adapted from Wikipedia.

8.1.3   Desired output

Let's look at the output you'll render. The following listing shows the result you will achieve programmatically: five actors from the `actor` table, as well as the metadata.

Listing 8.1   List of actors and metadata

```
+--------+----------+---------+-------------------+          ⟵─── A sample of the data
|actor_id|first_name|last_name|        last_update|
+--------+----------+---------+-------------------+
|      92|   KIRSTEN|   AKROYD|2006-02-14 22:34:33|
|      58| CHRISTIAN|   AKROYD|2006-02-14 22:34:33|
|     182|    DEBBIE|   AKROYD|2006-02-14 22:34:33|
|     118|      CUBA|    ALLEN|2006-02-14 22:34:33|
|     145|       KIM|    ALLEN|2006-02-14 22:34:33|
+--------+----------+---------+-------------------+
```

```
only showing top 5 rows
```

```
root                                    ⟵—— Schema
 |-- actor_id: integer (nullable = false)
 |-- first_name: string (nullable = false)
 |-- last_name: string (nullable = false)
 |-- last_update: timestamp (nullable = false)
```

Datatypes are directly converted from the table's type to Spark's datatype.

```
The dataframe contains 200 record(s).  ⟵——
```

Counting the number of records in the dataframe

Watch out for errors

You may see an error similar to the following:

```
Exception in thread "main" java.sql.SQLException: No suitable driver
    at java.sql.DriverManager.getDriver(DriverManager.java:315)
    at org.apache.spark.sql.execution.datasources.jdbc.JDBCOptio
    ns$$anonfun$7.apply(JDBCOptions.scala:84)
```

If so, you are missing the JDBC driver on your class path, so check your pom.xml. See listing 8.2.

8.1.4 Code

Let's look at the code to produce the output you want. You'll see three options for doing that, and you'll get to choose your favorite. You'll also learn how to modify your pom.xml file to load the JDBC driver, by simply adding it in the dependencies section.

The first thing to do is to identify the column by using the dataframe's col() method, and then you can use its orderBy() method. An introduction to the dataframe is in chapter 3. (You'll study more transformation and manipulation in chapters 11 to 13.)

Finally, you can sort the output by using a single line:

```
df = df.orderBy(df.col("last_name"));
```

LAB This is lab #100. It is available on GitHub at https://github.com/jgperrin/net.jgp.books.spark.ch08. It requires a MySQL or MariaDB connection.

The following listing shows you the first option.

Listing 8.2 MySQLToDatasetApp.java

```java
package net.jgp.books.spark.ch08.lab100_mysql_ingestion;

import java.util.Properties;

import org.apache.spark.sql.Dataset;
```

```
import org.apache.spark.sql.Row;
import org.apache.spark.sql.SparkSession;

public class MySQLToDatasetApp {

  public static void main(String[] args) {
    MySQLToDatasetApp app = new MySQLToDatasetApp();
    app.start();
  }

  private void start() {
    SparkSession spark = SparkSession.builder()         ←──── Gets a session
        .appName(
            "MySQL to Dataframe using a JDBC Connection")
        .master("local")
        .getOrCreate();

    Properties props = new Properties();
    props.put("user", "root");
    props.put("password", "Spark<3Java");
    props.put("useSSL", "false");          ←──

    Dataset<Row> df = spark.read().jdbc(
        "jdbc:mysql://localhost:3306/sakila?serverTimezone=EST",
        "actor",
        props);                            ←──
    df = df.orderBy(df.col("last_name"));

    df.show(5);
    df.printSchema();
    System.out.println("The dataframe contains " +
        df.count() + " record(s).");
  }
}
```

Creates a Properties object, which is going to be used to collect the properties needed

Password property

JDBC URL ──▷

Sorts by last name

Username property—you may not want to use root on a production system

Custom property—here, MySQL needs to be told that it won't use SSL in its communication

Table you are interested in

Properties you just defined

NOTE   If you read chapter 7, you'll notice that the ingestion mechanism is similar, whether you ingest files or databases.

PASSWORDS   I know you know, and you know I know you know, right? A small reminder is always useful: do not hardcode a password in your code; anyone can extract it from the JAR file in a matter of seconds (especially if your variable is called password!). In the repository, lab #101 uses the same code as listing 8.2 (lab #100) but gets the password from an environment variable.

You'll also need to ensure that Spark has access to your JDBC driver, as shown in listing 8.3. One of the easiest ways to do that is to list the database drivers you need in your project's pom.xml file.

NOTE   We'll use MySQL, Informix, and Elasticsearch in this chapter: MySQL because it is a fully supported database, Informix because it will require a dialect, and Elasticsearch because it is a NoSQL database.

Listing 8.3 Your modified pom.xml for database access

You are using MySQL JDBC
driver v8.0.8-dmr.

You are going to use
Informix JDBC driver
v4.I0.8.I.

You are using
Elasticsearch
v6.2.I.

```
...
    <properties>
...
        <mysql.version>8.0.8-dmr</mysql.version>
        <informix-jdbc.version>4.10.8.1</informix-jdbc.version>
        <elasticsearch-hadoop.version>6.2.1</elasticsearch-hadoop.version>
    </properties>

    <dependencies>
...
        <dependency>
            <groupId>mysql</groupId>
            <artifactId>mysql-connector-java</artifactId>
            <version>${mysql.version}</version>
        </dependency>

        <dependency>
            <groupId>com.ibm.informix</groupId>
            <artifactId>jdbc</artifactId>
            <version>${informix-jdbc.version}</version>
        </dependency>

        <dependency>
            <groupId>org.elasticsearch</groupId>
            <artifactId>elasticsearch-hadoop</artifactId>
            <version>${elasticsearch-hadoop.version}</version>
        </dependency>
...
```

In this example, you
are using MySQL.

You are using MySQL
JDBC driver v8.0.8-dmr.

You are
going to
use Informix
JDBC driver
v4.I0.8.I.

Later in this chapter, you'll use
Informix to build a custom dialect.

You are using
Elasticsearch
v6.2.I.

Toward the end of this chapter,
you'll connect to Elasticsearch.

Note that the version numbers are different in the repository, as I keep up with, as much as possible, the latest versions.

8.1.5 Alternative code

As is often the case, there are various ways to write the same operations. Let's look at how you can tweak the parameters and URL to connect to the database. In listing 8.2, you used the following:

```
Properties props = new Properties();
props.put("user", "root");
props.put("password", "Spark<3Java");
props.put("useSSL", "false");

Dataset<Row> df = spark.read().jdbc(
    "jdbc:mysql://localhost:3306/sakila?serverTimezone=EST",
    "actor",
    props);
```

You can replace this code with one of two options (you can find the full code in MySQLToDatasetWithLongUrlApp.java in this chapter's repository). The first option is to build a longer URL. You may already have a library in your application or platform with a JDBC URL generator, so you can reuse it easily. Note that you need to give the Spark reader object an empty list of properties, materialized by new Properties():

```
String jdbcUrl = "jdbc:mysql://localhost:3306/sakila"   ◄─── Longer URL
    + "?user=root"
    + "&password=Spark<3Java"
    + "&useSSL=false"
    + "&serverTimezone=EST";
Dataset<Row> df = spark.read()                           │ Empty properties
    .jdbc(jdbcUrl, "actor", new Properties());  ◄─┘        are still required.
```

The second option is to use only the options; this may be useful if you read the properties from a configuration file. The following code snippet shows you how to do that:

```
Dataset<Row> df = spark.read()
    .option("url", "jdbc:mysql://localhost:3306/sakila")
    .option("dbtable", "actor")
    .option("user", "root")
    .option("password", "Spark<3Java")
    .option("useSSL", "false")
    .option("serverTimezone", "EST")
    .format("jdbc")
    .load();
```

You can find the full code in MySQLToDatasetWithOptionsApp.java in this chapter's repository.

Note that in this version, you are not using the jdbc() method of the object returned by read()—an instance of DataFrameReader. You are using the format() and load() methods. As you can see, the table is only a property called dbtable. There is no preference in the syntax to use; however, you may encounter them all, and it could appear confusing. If you are working on a project with a team, I advise you to set a standard for the team, knowing that, most likely, those parameters will be read from a configuration file.

As a reminder, properties are case-insensitive. Note that the values are interpreted by the driver, and they might be case-sensitive.

Let's have a look at how Spark can handle nonsupported databases with custom dialects.

8.2   *The role of the dialect*

The dialect is the translation block between Spark and the database. In this section, you'll examine the role of a dialect, the dialects that are provided with Spark, and in which situation you'll have to write your own dialect.

8.2.1 What is a dialect, anyway?

The *dialect* is a small software component, often implemented in a single class, that bridges Apache Spark and the database; see figure 8.3.

When Spark imports the data and stores it, Spark needs to know what database types map to a Spark type. For example, Informix and PostgreSQL have a `SERIAL` type, which is an integer type that automatically increments when you insert new values in the database. It is convenient for defining unique identifiers. However, Spark needs to be told that this datatype is an integer when it hits the Tungsten storage. Tungsten is the storage manager that optimizes memory usage for objects, bypassing the JVM's storage mechanism for more efficiency.

The dialect defines Spark's behavior when communicating with the database.

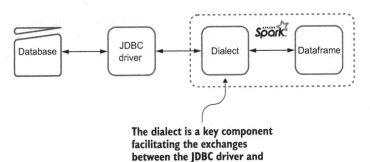

The dialect is a key component facilitating the exchanges between the JDBC driver and the dataframe.

Figure 8.3 Within Spark, the dataframe communicates with the database via a dialect acting as a complementary driver.

8.2.2 JDBC dialects provided with Spark

Spark comes with a few database dialects as part of the standard distribution. This means you can connect to those databases directly out of the box. As of Spark v3.0.0, those dialects are the following:

- IBM Db2
- Apache Derby
- MySQL
- Microsoft SQL Server
- Oracle
- PostgreSQL
- Teradata Database

If your database is not in this list, you can have a look at the Spark Packages website at https://spark-packages.org/?q=tags%3A%22Data%20Sources%22 or write/build your own.

8.2.3 Building your own dialect

If you are using a relational database that is not in the list, you may want to contact your database vendor before implementing your own dialect. If the vendor does not offer a dialect, don't panic. Implementing your own is relatively easy; you'll learn how to do it here. The example you are going to see is based on IBM Informix, but you can easily adapt the code to your own database. No knowledge of Informix is required here, although it is a wonderful RDBMS.

The reason I picked IBM Informix is that it does not have a dialect of its own, compared to all the other ones. Nevertheless, it remains a vibrant database, especially in the IoT sphere.

LAB   This is lab #200. It is available on GitHub at https://github.com/jgperrin/ net.jgp.books.spark.ch08. It requires an Informix database; you can download and use the Developer Edition for free from https://www.ibm.com/products/ informix.

The dialect is one class, extending `JdbcDialect`, as shown in listing 8.4. The `can-Handle()` method is the entry point to the dialect; this method acts as a filter to know whether Spark should use this dialect. It receives the JDBC URL as input, and you can filter based on the URL. In this situation, you'll filter on the beginning of the URL, looking for the distinctive pattern of the Informix JDBC driver: `informix-sqli`. Each JDBC driver has a unique signature through its URL.

The `getCatalystType()` method will convert a JDBC type to a Catalyst type.

Listing 8.4   A minimalist dialect allowing Spark to communicate with your database

JdbcDialect is serializable, hence a unique ID for this class.

```
package net.jgp.books.spark.ch08.lab_200_informix_dialect;

import org.apache.spark.sql.jdbc.JdbcDialect;
import org.apache.spark.sql.types.DataType;
import org.apache.spark.sql.types.DataTypes;
import org.apache.spark.sql.types.MetadataBuilder;

import scala.Option;

public class InformixJdbcDialect extends JdbcDialect {
  private static final long serialVersionUID = -672901;

  @Override
  public boolean canHandle(String url) {
    return url.startsWith("jdbc:informix-sqli");
  }

  @Override
  public Option<DataType> getCatalystType(int sqlType,
      String typeName, int size, MetadataBuilder md) {
    if (typeName.toLowerCase().compareTo("serial") == 0) {
      return Option.apply(DataTypes.IntegerType);
    }
    if (typeName.toLowerCase().compareTo("calendar") == 0) {
```

Converts a SQL type to a Spark type

Returning the value, Scala-style

The filter method that will allow Spark to know which driver to use in which context

The signature of the Informix JDBC driver is Informix-sqli.

In this case, Spark does not know what a SERIAL datatype is, but, for Spark, it is simply an integer. Do not worry about testing typeName for null.

```
    return Option.apply(DataTypes.BinaryType);
  }
...
  return Option.empty();
  }
}
```

Returning the value, Scala-style

I could have used `equalsIgnoreCase()` or many other ways to compare strings, but over my many years of dealing with Java developers, I've seen that there is never a consensus. Defining the proper methods to use (or settling the eternal debate on naming conventions) is not my mission here.

Make sure your driver's signature is sufficient. If I had used something like `return url.contains("informix");`, it could have been too broad. You could add the colon after `sqli` too. I could have written this example using a switch/case statement, but I wanted to leave a little room for improvement, right?

The return type is what is expected by Spark. As you may know, Spark is written in Scala, so, at some touchpoints, you will need to return Scala types. In this situation, the return type corresponds to an empty option.

As a reminder, Catalyst is the optimization engine built in Spark (see chapter 4). The `getCatalystType()` method receives four arguments:

- The SQL type as an integer, as defined in `java.sql.Types` (see http://mng.bz/6wxR). However, note that complex datatypes, for which you may be writing this conversion, will probably not be in the list; you will have to see how they are seen in this method.
- The type name as a string. This is the "real name" you would have used to create the table in SQL. In this example, I used the `SERIAL` datatype, an integer with automatic incrementing you'll find in Informix and PostgreSQL.
- The size for numeric, string, and binary types. This argument is useful for avoiding side effects in conversions.
- The last argument is a metadata builder, which you can use to augment the information about the conversion (more on that in chapter 17).

The `getCatalystType()` method return type is one of the following:

- A datatype, as listed at http://mng.bz/omgD: `BinaryType`, `BooleanType`, `ByteType`, `CalendarIntervalType`, `DateType`, `DoubleType`, `FloatType`, `IntegerType`, `LongType`, `NullType`, `ShortType`, `StringType`, or `TimestampType`
- A subtype of `org.apache.spark.sql.types.DataType` and can be `ArrayType`, `HiveStringType`, `MapType`, `NullType`, `NumericType`, `ObjectType`, or `StructType`

Appendix L covers the datatypes in more detail. It also describes additional methods you may need in order to implement a full dialect (such as a reverse conversion, from a Spark type to a SQL type), how to truncate a table, and so on.

8.3   *Advanced queries and ingestion*

Sometimes you don't want to copy all the data from a table to a dataframe. You know that you won't use some data, and you don't want to copy the rows you won't use, because transfer is an expensive operation. A typical use case would be to run analytics on yesterday's sales, compare month-to-month sales, and so on.

In this section, you'll learn about ingesting data from relational databases by using SQL queries, avoiding superfluous data transfer. This operation is called *filtering the data*. You'll also learn about partitioning while ingesting.

8.3.1   *Filtering by using a WHERE clause*

In SQL, one way to filter data is to use a WHERE clause as part of your SELECT statement. Let's see how to integrate such a clause in your ingestion mechanism. As with full table ingestion, Spark still uses JDBC underneath.

> **LAB**   This is lab #300. It is available on GitHub at https://github.com/jgperrin/ net.jgp.books.spark.ch08. It requires a MySQL or MariaDB database.

The syntax is similar to what we have been using for ingesting a full table. However, the dbtable option (if you use the load() method) or table parameter (if you use the jdbc() method) must use the following syntax:

```
(<SQL select statement>) <table alias>
```

Let's look at a few examples:

1 Cheap movies:

```
(SELECT * FROM film WHERE rental_rate = 0.99) film_alias
```

This returns all films with a rental rate of 99 cents.

2 Specific movies:

```
(SELECT * FROM film WHERE (title LIKE "%ALIEN%"
➥ OR title LIKE "%victory%" OR title LIKE "%agent%"
➥ OR description LIKE "%action%") AND rental_rate>1
➥ AND (rating="G" OR rating="PG")) film_alias
```

In this query, you're looking for movies with a title containing *alien, victory*, or *agent*, or with a description containing *action*; with a rental rate of more than $1; and with a rating of either G (General audience) or PG (Parental Guidance suggested). Note that, because we use LIKE, the case does not matter: you will get all movies with alien, Alien, and ALIEN. The last keyword (film_alias) is simply an alias. Figure 8.4 illustrates the process.

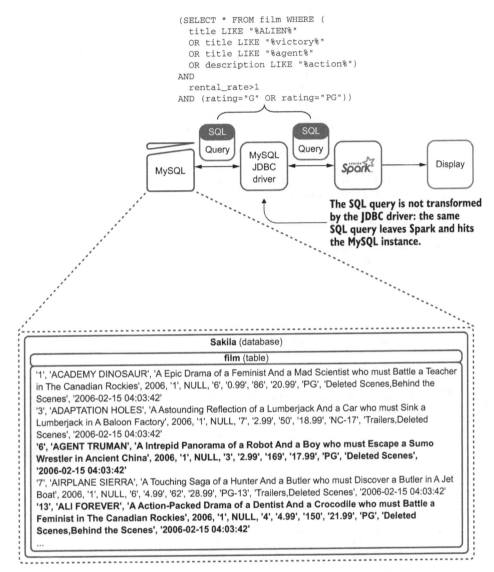

```
(SELECT * FROM film WHERE (
  title LIKE "%ALIEN%"
  OR title LIKE "%victory%"
  OR title LIKE "%agent%"
  OR description LIKE "%action%")
AND
  rental_rate>1
AND (rating="G" OR rating="PG"))
```

The SQL query is not transformed by the JDBC driver: the same SQL query leaves Spark and hits the MySQL instance.

Sakila (database)

film (table)

'1', 'ACADEMY DINOSAUR', 'A Epic Drama of a Feminist And a Mad Scientist who must Battle a Teacher in The Canadian Rockies', 2006, '1', NULL, '6', '0.99', '86', '20.99', 'PG', 'Deleted Scenes,Behind the Scenes', '2006-02-15 04:03:42'

'3', 'ADAPTATION HOLES', 'A Astounding Reflection of a Lumberjack And a Car who must Sink a Lumberjack in A Baloon Factory', 2006, '1', NULL, '7', '2.99', '50', '18.99', 'NC-17', 'Trailers,Deleted Scenes', '2006-02-15 04:03:42'

'6', 'AGENT TRUMAN', 'A Intrepid Panorama of a Robot And a Boy who must Escape a Sumo Wrestler in Ancient China', 2006, '1', NULL, '3', '2.99', '169', '17.99', 'PG', 'Deleted Scenes', '2006-02-15 04:03:42'

'7', 'AIRPLANE SIERRA', 'A Touching Saga of a Hunter And a Butler who must Discover a Butler in A Jet Boat', 2006, '1', NULL, '6', '4.99', '62', '28.99', 'PG-13', 'Trailers,Deleted Scenes', '2006-02-15 04:03:42'

'13', 'ALI FOREVER', 'A Action-Packed Drama of a Dentist And a Crocodile who must Battle a Feminist in The Canadian Rockies', 2006, '1', NULL, '4', '4.99', '150', '21.99', 'PG', 'Deleted Scenes,Behind the Scenes', '2006-02-15 04:03:42'

...

Figure 8.4 **The ingestion process from MySQL, using the MySQL JDBC driver. In this scenario, you are interested in only some films matching the SQL query—the ones highlighted in bold.**

The following listing shows the desired output, which is the records that are highlighted in figure 8.4.

Listing 8.5   Desired output of the query with a WHERE clause

```
+-------+--------------+--------------------+------------+-----------+...
|film_id|         title|         description|release_year|language_id|...
+-------+--------------+--------------------+------------+-----------+...
|      6|  AGENT TRUMAN|A Intrepid Panora...|  2005-12-31|          1|...
|     13|   ALI FOREVER|A Action-Packed D...|  2005-12-31|          1|...
...

+-------+--------------+--------------------+------------+-----------+...
only showing top 5 rows

root
 |-- film_id: integer (nullable = true)
 |-- title: string (nullable = true)
 |-- description: string (nullable = true)
 |-- release_year: date (nullable = true)
 |-- language_id: integer (nullable = true)
 |-- original_language_id: integer (nullable = true)
 |-- rental_duration: integer (nullable = true)
 |-- rental_rate: decimal(4,2) (nullable = true)
 |-- length: integer (nullable = true)
 |-- replacement_cost: decimal(5,2) (nullable = true)
 |-- rating: string (nullable = true)
 |-- special_features: string (nullable = true)
 |-- last_update: timestamp (nullable = true)

The dataframe contains 16 record(s).
```

The following listing shows the code that enables the ingestion through an SQL query.

Listing 8.6   MySQLWithWhereClauseToDatasetApp.java

```java
package net.jgp.books.spark.ch08.lab300_advanced_queries;

import java.util.Properties;

import org.apache.spark.sql.Dataset;
import org.apache.spark.sql.Row;
import org.apache.spark.sql.SparkSession;

public class MySQLWithWhereClauseToDatasetApp {

  public static void main(String[] args) {
    MySQLWithWhereClauseToDatasetApp app =
        new MySQLWithWhereClauseToDatasetApp();
    app.start();
  }

  private void start() {
    SparkSession spark = SparkSession.builder()
        .appName(
            "MySQL with where clause to Dataframe using a JDBC Connection")
        .master("local")
```

```
            .getOrCreate();

    Properties props = new Properties();
    props.put("user", "root");
    props.put("password", "Spark<3Java");
    props.put("useSSL", "false");
    props.put("serverTimezone", "EST");

    String sqlQuery = "select * from film where "
        + "(title like \"%ALIEN%\" or title like \"%victory%\" "
        + "or title like \"%agent%\" or description like \"%action%\") "
        + "and rental_rate>1 "
        + "and (rating=\"G\" or rating=\"PG\")";

    Dataset<Row> df = spark.read().jdbc(
        "jdbc:mysql://localhost:3306/sakila",
        "(" + sqlQuery + ") film_alias",
        props);

    df.show(5);
    df.printSchema();
    System.out.println("The dataframe contains " + df
        .count() + " record(s).");
    }
}
```

> Your SQL query can be built like any other string or can come from a configuration file, a generator, and so on.

The SQL query

> The syntax is respected; the SQL query is between parentheses, and the table alias is at the end.

The following are important things to remember:

- You can nest parentheses in the `select` statement.
- The table alias must not be an existing table in your database.

8.3.2 Joining data in the database

Using a similar technique, you can join data in the database prior to ingesting it in Spark. Spark can join data between dataframes (for more information, see chapter 12 and appendix M), but for performance and optimization reasons, you may want to ask your database to perform the operation. In this section, you'll learn how to perform a join at the database level and ingest the data from the join.

LAB This is lab #310. It is available on GitHub at https://github.com/jgperrin/net.jgp.books.spark.ch08. It requires a MySQL or MariaDB database.

The SQL statement you will run is as follows:

```
SELECT actor.first_name, actor.last_name, film.title, film.description
FROM actor, film_actor, film
WHERE actor.actor_id = film_actor.actor_id
  AND film_actor.film_id = film.film_id
```

Figure 8.5 illustrates the operation.

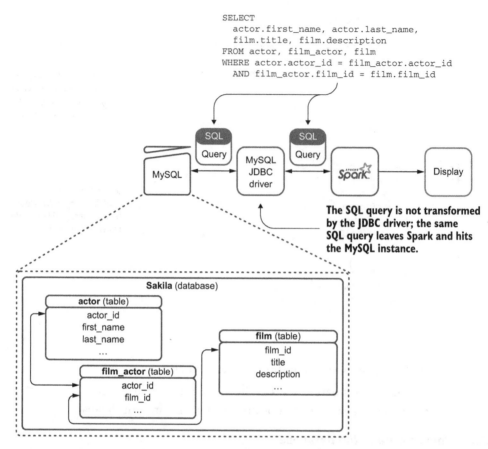

Figure 8.5   Spark ingests the data stored in the MySQL database after the database server performs the joins between the three tables.

The following listing illustrates the result. Note that the dataframe contains more records as you join tables.

Listing 8.7   Output of join performed at database level, ingested by Spark

```
+----------+---------+--------------------+--------------------+
|first_name|last_name|               title|         description|
+----------+---------+--------------------+--------------------+
|  PENELOPE|  GUINESS|     ACADEMY DINOSAUR|A Epic Drama of a...|
|  PENELOPE|  GUINESS|ANACONDA CONFESSIONS|A Lacklusture Dis...|
|  PENELOPE|  GUINESS|          ANGELS LIFE|A Thoughtful Disp...|
|  PENELOPE|  GUINESS|BULWORTH COMMANDM...|A Amazing Display...|
|  PENELOPE|  GUINESS|        CHEAPER CLYDE|A Emotional Chara...|
+----------+---------+--------------------+--------------------+
only showing top 5 rows
```

```
root
 |-- first_name: string (nullable = true)
 |-- last_name: string (nullable = true)
 |-- title: string (nullable = true)
 |-- description: string (nullable = true)

The dataframe contains 5462 record(s).
```

The next listing shows the code. As you would expect, it is similar to the simple filtering in listing 8.6. I have removed the superfluous lines of code.

> **Listing 8.8 MySQLWithJoinToDatasetApp.java (excerpt)**

```
package net.jgp.books.spark.ch08_lab310_sql_joins;
...
public class MySQLWithJoinToDatasetApp {
...
  private void start() {
...
    String sqlQuery =
        "select actor.first_name, actor.last_name, film.title, "
          + "film.description "
          + "from actor, film_actor, film "
          + "where actor.actor_id = film_actor.actor_id "
          + "and film_actor.film_id = film.film_id";

    Dataset<Row> df = spark.read().jdbc(
        "jdbc:mysql://localhost:3306/sakila",
        "(" + sqlQuery + ") actor_film_alias",
        props);
...
  }
}
```

A basic SQL query joining three tables ⟶ (the SQL query lines)

Except for the alias name, this is the same call as in listing 8.6. ⟵

If we had used SELECT * FROM actor, film_actor... in the query in listing 8.7, Spark would have been confused by columns having the same name and would have returned the following error: Duplicate column name 'actor_id'. Spark will not build a fully qualified name (<table>.<column>) for you; you will have to explicitly name the columns and alias them. The code producing this exception is available in GitHub at http://mng.bz/KEOO.

> **NOTE** The SQL you are writing here is directly sent to MySQL. It will not be interpreted by Spark, and, as a consequence, if you write specific Oracle SQL, it will not work with PostgreSQL (although it should work with IBM Db2, as it understands Oracle syntax).

8.3.3 *Performing Ingestion and partitioning*

In this section, you'll have a quick look at an advanced feature of Spark: ingesting from a database and automatically assigning to the partitions. Figure 8.6 shows the dataframe after you ingest the film table, as in listing 8.9.

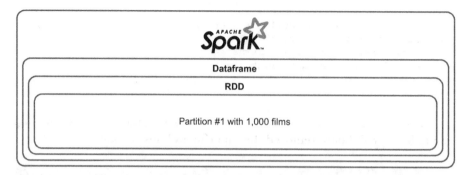

Figure 8.6   Looking at the dataframe, after ingesting 1,000 films from the film table. They are all in one partition.

Figure 8.7 illustrates the partitions in the resilient distributed dataset (RDD) in the dataframe after using partitions. You may recall that the RDD is the data storage part of the dataframe (see chapter 3). The process of ingesting by partition is detailed in listing 8.11.

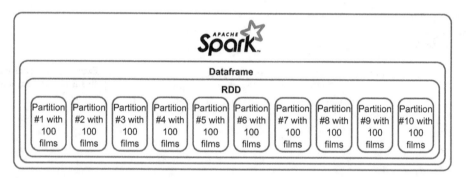

Figure 8.7   In this scenario, you asked Spark to split the data into 10 partitions. You still have one dataframe and one RDD. Physical nodes are not represented, but this diagram could split over several nodes.

LAB   This is lab #320. It is available on GitHub at https://github.com/jgperrin/net.jgp.books.spark.ch08. It requires a MySQL or MariaDB database.

The following listing is similar to listing 8.2, but you are going to ingest movies from the `film` table.

Listing 8.9   MySQLToDatasetWithoutPartitionApp.java

```
package net.jgp.books.spark.ch08.lab320_ingestion_partinioning;
...
public class MySQLToDatasetWithoutPartitionApp {
...
  private void start() {
```

```
...
    Properties props = new Properties();
    props.put("user", "root");
    props.put("password", "Spark<3Java");
    props.put("useSSL", "false");
    props.put("serverTimezone", "EST");

    Dataset<Row> df = spark.read().jdbc(          <──── Ingesting the film table
        "jdbc:mysql://localhost:3306/sakila",
        "film",
        props);

    df.show(5);
    df.printSchema();
    System.out.println("The dataframe contains " + df
        .count() + " record(s).");
    System.out.println("The dataframe is split over " + df.rdd()
        .getPartitions().length + " partition(s).");
  }
}
```

The output is shown in the following listing.

Listing 8.10   Output of MySQLToDatasetWithoutPartitionApp.java

```
+-------+----------------+--------------------+------------+-----------+--...
|film_id|           title|         description|release_year|language_id|or...
+-------+----------------+--------------------+------------+-----------+--...
|      1|ACADEMY DINOSAUR|A Epic Drama of a...|  2005-12-31|          1| ...
|      2|   ACE GOLDFINGER|A Astounding Epis...|  2005-12-31|          1| ...
|      3|ADAPTATION HOLES|A Astounding Refl...|  2005-12-31|          1| ...
|      4|AFFAIR PREJUDICE|A Fanciful Docume...|  2005-12-31|          1| ...
|      5|     AFRICAN EGG|A Fast-Paced Docu...|  2005-12-31|          1| ...
+-------+----------------+--------------------+------------+-----------+--...
only showing top 5 rows

root
 |-- film_id: integer (nullable = true)
 |-- title: string (nullable = true)
 |-- description: string (nullable = true)
 |-- release_year: date (nullable = true)
 |-- language_id: integer (nullable = true)
 |-- original_language_id: integer (nullable = true)
 |-- rental_duration: integer (nullable = true)
 |-- rental_rate: decimal(4,2) (nullable = true)
 |-- length: integer (nullable = true)
 |-- replacement_cost: decimal(5,2) (nullable = true)
 |-- rating: string (nullable = true)
 |-- special_features: string (nullable = true)
 |-- last_update: timestamp (nullable = true)

The dataframe contains 1000 record(s).
The dataframe is split over 1 partition(s).
```

You can focus on the last line of the output of listing 8.10. Data is in one partition. The following listing adds the partitioning code. Chapter 17 talks more about partitioning.

Listing 8.11   MySQLToDatasetWithPartitionApp.java

```
package net.jgp.books.spark.ch08.lab320_ingestion_partinioning;
...
public class MySQLToDatasetWithPartitionApp {
...
    Properties props = new Properties();        ←⎤ Properties to set up the
    props.put("user", "root");                   ⎦ database connection
    props.put("password", "Spark<3Java");
    props.put("useSSL", "false");
    props.put("serverTimezone", "EST");

    props.put("partitionColumn", "film_id");    ←⎤ Column to partition on
    props.put("lowerBound", "1");               ←── Lower bound of the stride
    props.put("upperBound", "1000");
    props.put("numPartitions", "10");           ←── Number of partitions

    Dataset<Row> df = spark.read().jdbc(        ←── Ingesting the film table
        "jdbc:mysql://localhost:3306/sakila",
        "film",
        props);
...
```

Upper bound of the stride → (annotation to `props.put("upperBound", "1000");`)

In this scenario, the data is split into 10 partitions, and the following is the last line of the output:

```
...
The dataframe is split over 10 partition(s).
```

8.3.4   *Summary of advanced features*

In these sections, you have learned how to better ingest data from your RDBMS. Because you probably won't perform those operations all the time, appendix L provides reference tables to help your ingestion operations.

8.4   *Ingestion from Elasticsearch*

In this section, you'll learn how to ingest data directly from Elasticsearch. Elasticsearch has been growing in popularity since 2010 (the year I started using it) as a scalable document store and search engine. A bidirectional communication with Elasticsearch helps Spark store and retrieve complex documents.

I know that some purists will argue that Elasticsearch is not a database, but it is an incredible data store, which makes it a prime candidate for this chapter on ingestion from data stores.

NOTE   See appendix N for help installing Elasticsearch and adding a sample dataset for the examples we are using. If you want to know more about this search engine, you can read *Elasticsearch in Action* by Radu Gheorghe et al. (Manning, 2015), available at https://www.manning.com/books/elasticsearch-in-action.

You'll first have a look at the architecture and then run your first Elasticsearch ingestion.

8.4.1   Data flow

Figure 8.8 illustrates the flows between Spark and Elasticsearch. For Spark, Elasticsearch is like a database, and it needs a driver, like a JDBC driver.

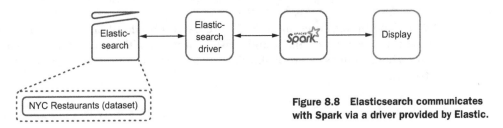

Figure 8.8   Elasticsearch communicates with Spark via a driver provided by Elastic.

As you may remember from listing 8.3, we modified the pom.xml file. This is the abstract required by Elasticsearch:

```
<dependency>
  <groupId>org.elasticsearch</groupId>
  <artifactId>elasticsearch-hadoop</artifactId>
  <version>6.2.1</version>
</dependency>
```

This entry defines the driver needed by Elasticsearch and provided by Elastic (the company behind Elasticsearch), allowing a bidirectional communication between Elasticsearch and Spark, as well as Hadoop.

8.4.2   The New York restaurants dataset digested by Spark

Let's look at the result of the code you're going to create. Elasticsearch stores documents in JSON format; therefore, it should not a be a surprise to see nested constructs such as those in listing 8.12. In this output, I added timings, so you can visualize where time is spent. Time is summarized in table 8.2.

LAB   This is lab #400. It is available on GitHub at https://github.com/jgperrin/ net.jgp.books.spark.ch08. It requires Elasticsearch.

Table 8.2   Timings in ingesting Elasticsearch data

Step	Time (ms)	Sum (ms)	Description
1	1524	1524	Getting a session
2	1694	3218	Connecting to Elasticsearch

Table 8.2   Timings in ingesting Elasticsearch data *(continued)*

Step	Time (ms)	Sum (ms)	Description
3	10450	13668	Getting some records, enough to display 10 and infer the schema
4	1	13669	Displaying the schema
5	33710	47379	Getting the rest of the records
6	118	47497	Counting the number of partitions where the records are stored

NOTE The timings used in table 8.2 are based on a local laptop (this is also one of the beauties of Spark and Elasticsearch: everything can run on a laptop). Those timings will probably differ markedly on your system, but not the proportion.

Listing 8.12   Result of ingesting New York restaurants in Spark from Elasticsearch

```
Getting a session took: 1524 ms
Init communication and starting to get some results took: 1694 ms
+-------------------+-------------------+--------+--------+--------+---...
|             Action|            Address|    Boro|Building|  Camis |...
+-------------------+-------------------+--------+--------+--------+...
|Violations were c...|10405 METROPOLITA...|  QUEENS|   10405|40704305| [-7...
|Violations were c...|10405 METROPOLITA...|  QUEENS|   10405|40704305| [-7...
|Violations were c...|10405 METROPOLITA...|  QUEENS|   10405|40704305| [-7...
|Violations were c...|10405 METROPOLITA...|  QUEENS|   10405|40704305| [-7...
|Violations were c...|181 WEST 4 STREET...|MANHATTAN|    181|40704315| [-7...
|Violations were c...|181 WEST 4 STREET...|MANHATTAN|    181|40704315| [-7...
|Violations were c...|181 WEST 4 STREET...|MANHATTAN|    181|40704315| [-7...
|Violations were c...|181 WEST 4 STREET...|MANHATTAN|    181|40704315| [-7...
|Violations were c...|1007 LEXINGTON AV...|MANHATTAN|   1007|40704453| [-7...
+-------------------+-------------------+--------+--------+--------+---...
only showing top 10 rows

Showing a few records took: 10450 ms
root
 |-- Action: string (nullable = true)
 |-- Address: string (nullable = true)
 |-- Boro: string (nullable = true)
 |-- Building: string (nullable = true)
 |-- Camis: long (nullable = true)
 |-- Coord: array (nullable = true)
 |    |-- element: double (containsNull = true)
 |-- Critical_Flag: string (nullable = true)
 |-- Cuisine_Description: string (nullable = true)
 |-- Dba: string (nullable = true)
 |-- Grade: string (nullable = true)
 |-- Grade_Date: timestamp (nullable = true)
 |-- Inspection_Date: array (nullable = true)
 |    |-- element: timestamp (containsNull = true)
```

```
|-- Inspection_Type: string (nullable = true)
|-- Phone: string (nullable = true)
|-- Record_Date: timestamp (nullable = true)
|-- Score: double (nullable = true)
|-- Street: string (nullable = true)
|-- Violation_Code: string (nullable = true)
|-- Violation_Description: string (nullable = true)
|-- Zipcode: long (nullable = true)
```

```
Displaying the schema took: 1 ms
The dataframe contains 473039 record(s).
Counting the number of records took: 33710 ms
The dataframe is split over 5 partition(s).
Counting the # of partitions took: 118 ms
```

As you can conclude from the timings, Spark does not require the whole dataset to be in memory before it can infer the schema and display a few rows. However, when you ask Spark to count the number of records, it needs to have everything in memory, hence the 33 seconds to download the rest of the data.

8.4.3 *Code to ingest the restaurant dataset from Elasticsearch*

Let's walk through the following code to ingest the New York City restaurants dataset from Elasticsearch into Spark.

Listing 8.13 ElasticsearchToDatasetApp.java

```java
package net.jgp.books.spark.ch08.lab400_es_ingestion;

import org.apache.spark.sql.Dataset;
import org.apache.spark.sql.Row;
import org.apache.spark.sql.SparkSession;

public class ElasticsearchToDatasetApp {

  public static void main(String[] args) {
    ElasticsearchToDatasetApp app =
        new ElasticsearchToDatasetApp();
    app.start();
  }

  private void start() {
    long t0 = System.currentTimeMillis();

    SparkSession spark = SparkSession.builder()
        .appName("Elasticsearch to Dataframe")
        .master("local")
        .getOrCreate();
    long t1 = System.currentTimeMillis();
    System.out.println("Getting a session took: " + (t1 - t0) + " ms");

    Dataset<Row> df = spark
        .read()
        .format("org.elasticsearch.spark.sql")
```

Introducing timing after major step to understand where time is spent

Name of the format, which can be a short name like csv, jdbc, or a full class name (more in chapter 9)

As with any ingestion, we start with read().

Introducing timing after major step to understand where time is spent

Elasticsearch port (optional, as you use 9200)

Query (here, you want all; can be omitted)

Name of the dataset

You need to convert the Inspection_Date field.

```
    .option("es.nodes", "localhost")
    .option("es.port", "9200")
    .option("es.query", "?q=*")
    .option("es.read.field.as.array.include", "Inspection_Date")
    .load("nyc_restaurants");

long t2 = System.currentTimeMillis();
System.out.println(
    "Init communication and starting to get some results took: "
        + (t2 - t1) + " ms");

df.show(10);
long t3 = System.currentTimeMillis();
System.out.println("Showing a few records took: " + (t3 - t2) + " ms");
 #A

df.printSchema();
long t4 = System.currentTimeMillis();
System.out.println("Displaying the schema took: " + (t4 - t3) + " ms");
 #A

System.out.println("The dataframe contains " +
    df.count() + " record(s).");
long t5 = System.currentTimeMillis();
System.out.println("Counting the number of records took: " + (t5 - t4)
    + " ms"); #A

System.out.println("The dataframe is split over " + df.rdd()
    .getPartitions().length + " partition(s).");
long t6 = System.currentTimeMillis();
System.out.println("Counting the # of partitions took: " + (t6 - t5)
    + " ms"); #A
  }
}
```

As you can see, data ingestion from Elasticsearch follows the same principles as files (chapter 7) and databases. You can find the list of options for importing data in appendix L.

Summary

- To connect to a database from Spark, you'll need its JDBC drivers.
- You can use properties or long URLs to connect to the database, as with JDBC.
- You can build a dedicated dialect to connect to data sources that are not available, and it's not very difficult.
- Spark comes with out-of-the-box support for IBM Db2, Apache Derby, MySQL, Microsoft SQL Server, Oracle, PostgreSQL, and Teradata Database.

- You can filter the data you are ingesting by using the (`<select statement>`) `<table alias>` syntax instead of the table name.
- You can perform joins at the database level, prior to ingesting in Spark, but you can also do joins in Spark!
- You can automatically assign data from the database in multiple partitions.
- Connecting to Elasticsearch is as easy as connecting to a database.
- Ingesting data from Elasticsearch follows the same principle as any other ingestion.
- Elasticsearch contains JSON documents, which are ingested as is in Spark.

Advanced ingestion: finding data sources and building your own

In a lot of use cases, I had to get data from nontraditional data sources to use in Apache Spark. Imagine that your data is in an enterprise resource planning (ERP) package, and you want to ingest it via the ERP's REST API. Of course, you could create a standalone application, dumping all the data in a CSV or JSON file and ingesting the file or files, but you don't want to deal with the life cycle of each file. When will you be able to delete it? Who has access to it? Can the disk be full at some time? Do I need all the data at once?

Another use case you could be facing is ingesting a specific format.

Imagine this simple scenario . . . You saw a computer numerical control (CNC) router in the Hillsborough workshop. It really outputs status reports in weird formats. And more recently, you saw those digital imaging and communications in medicine (DICOM) files from the X-ray machine you just installed at Duke. Once more, you may be able to extract the data you need from those files and have them ready in CSV or JSON.

But you would still have to handle those files and their life cycles. And, sometimes, the data cannot be easily converted to CSV or JSON because you would lose a lot of the metadata.

What if I could tell you (or more like write you, to be fair) that Spark can be extended to natively support any data source? You can now build an analytics pipeline that natively talks to your ERP, gathers the job status from the CNC router, and analyzes the metadata of the medical images. As a result, although it may not make sense to us humble data engineers, our friends, the data scientists, could find some correlation on quality of parts produced for those MedTech devices between the ERP, the CNC, and the X-ray machine that controls welding.

Data is available in many forms, and sometimes the ingestion is more complex when the data comes from a complex format. This is the kind of problem you will solve in this chapter.

First, you will have a look at Spark Packages, which is a site where you can find additional packages to extend Spark. In the second part of this chapter, you will build your own interface to a data source. The supporting example is about ingesting photo metadata. As you may know, all digital photos contain a block of metadata describing the photo in a format called EXIF. You will read EXIF data from all your photos and be ready to perform some analytics!

Understanding EXIF

As you know, cameras take pictures and store them in flash memory. Now imagine that every camera manufacturer has its own format. That would become a nightmare. Thankfully, except for what manufacturers call *raw format* on higher-end cameras, they all store photos in Joint Photographic Experts Group (JPEG) format.

JPEG (or JPG, but definitely not my initials, JGP) can embed metadata in the file itself: the date and time the picture was taken (according to the camera, so don't forget to change the camera's time when you travel), the size, text (for example, copyright information), or even GPS coordinates. This additional block of information is in *Exchangeable Image File Format* (*EXIF*).

To read EXIF in a JPEG file, you'll use an open source library called Metadata Extractor from Drew Noakes (https://github.com/drewnoakes/metadata-extractor). It is a fairly easy-to-use library. The library is inserted in the lab's pom.xml, so you do not have anything to download. The library's URL is provided if you want to learn more about EXIF and metadata extraction.

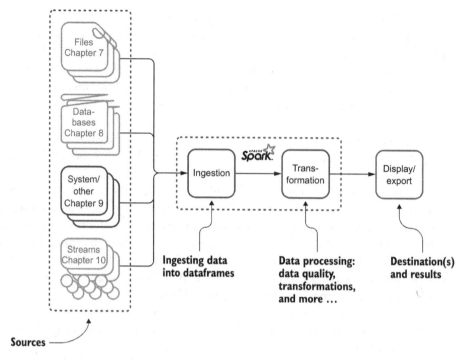

Figure 9.1   This chapter is about other data sources, including building your own.

Figure 9.1 illustrates where you are on your journey to ingestion.

> **LAB**   Examples from this chapter are available in GitHub at https://github.com/
> jgperrin/net.jgp.books.spark.ch09. Appendix L is a reference for ingestion.

9.1   What is a data source?

A *data source* provides data to Spark. Once data is ingested in Spark from this data source, all the traditional data processing (transformations, machine learning, and more) can start. A data source could be any of the following:

- A file (CSV, JSON, XML, and more, as you saw in chapter 7)
- Other file formats including Avro, Parquet, and ORC (defined in chapter 7)
- A relational database (as you saw in chapter 8)
- A nonrelational database such as Elasticsearch (also covered in chapter 8)
- Any other data provider: a representational state transfer (REST) service, unsupported file formats, and so on

As you know, Spark will store the data and schema in the dataframe. The "guy" in charge of reading and creating the dataframe is the dataframe reader. However, the reader needs to have a way to communicate with the data source itself. Figure 9.2 illustrates the data sources and the components involved.

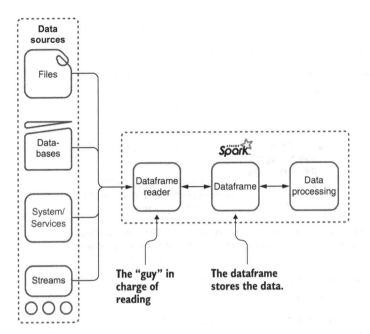

Figure 9.2   Data sources can be files, databases, services, and so on. The dataframe reader needs to understand how to communicate with the source.

9.2   *Benefits of a direct connection to a data source*

Before implementing a solution, you usually study several options. In this section, you will compare a direct connection to a data source to a process whereby you dump the data in a file and then ingest this file. As you learned in previous chapters, Spark can ingest data from many file formats.

But here's an obvious question: *Why bother? I can export my ERP data in a CSV file and then ingest it in Spark this way. In the worst-case scenario, I can run a Perl or Python script to tune the data.*

That is indeed a valid option, as illustrated by figure 9.3. On the other hand, figure 9.4 illustrates a direct connection.

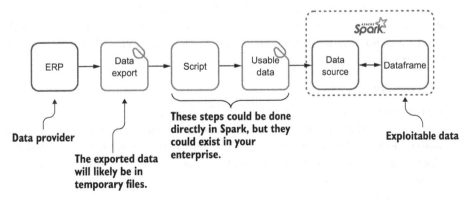

Figure 9.3   An example of getting data from an ERP through a file: export the data, clean it via a script, and obtain usable data you can ingest via a standard data source such as Spark's built-in CSV parser.

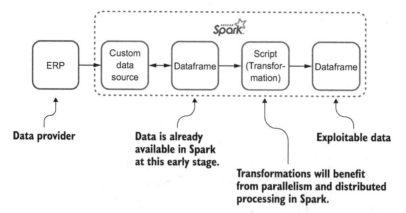

Figure 9.4   **A custom data source can connect directly to the ERP. The cleaning process can be done within Spark too and benefits from the scalable architecture.**

A direct connection to a data source has benefits, so let's go over them. First, let's look at the components of this architecture:

- Temporary files are generated as the export of your data provider.
- Data quality scripts are there to ensure that your data is valid and usable.
- On-demand data is available to optimize massive data transfer.

9.2.1   Temporary files

You will not have to deal with exported files from your data provider. Files can be large and fill up your storage volumes. If your permissions are inadequate, people could eavesdrop on the content of your files as they are copied locally; in some cases, such as with protected health information (PHI), you could be legally responsible. Using a custom data source will pull all the data in Spark, avoiding extra storage or eavesdropping.

Imagine you have 20 million records with about 3,000 bytes per record; this will result in a 55 GB file, which you will extract and transform via scripts. You may need two or three times the space on disk. In Spark, a 55 GB file usually takes about 44 GB of space, thanks to compression. A rule of thumb is that data takes 80% of the space when ingested. Spark will pull data in memory, and, when it does not have room anymore, it will use the disk.

9.2.2   Data quality scripts

Scripts can be used for cleaning the data, validation, and so on: the idea is to perform some level of data quality before the data hits Spark. The scripts have to be maintained and have their own life cycles. Often those scripts are written in Perl or Python, which will have to be maintained, deployed, and so on. Cleaning scripts in Spark will enable them to do the following:

- Perform faster, benefitting from the cluster architecture
- Use the same dataframe API as your application, making maintenance easier

9.2.3 *Data on demand*

A custom data source can also offer filtering options, allowing you to get only the data you want. This process can optimize data transfer and performance. You will see that in this chapter's lab.

9.3 *Finding data sources at Spark Packages*

When you're looking for something, it is always useful to have an entry point for your search. Sometimes, that is not Google. In 2014, Databricks opened Spark Packages, an index of third-party packages for Apache Spark. All packages are not data sources; you will find tutorials including work from your *humble serviteur* (*humble servant*, or *yours truly*, in French). The website is available at https://spark-packages.org/, and packages are organized around the following:

- Core
- Data sources
- Machine learning
- Streaming
- Graph

- PySpark (interfacing Spark with Python)
- Applications
- Deployment
- Examples
- Tools

As you've read in chapter 7, some of those packages are written by third-party vendors and may not respect the common behaviors of parsers, such as regex in paths or no case sensitivity in option names. Therefore, be careful as you use them.

> **COMMUNITY SITE** Spark Packages is a community site. If you have developed something of interest for the community, you can also share your own examples, tutorials, packages, and more there.

9.4 *Building your own data source*

You've looked desperately around the internet for a way to ingest this particular format in a dataframe. Google and Spark Packages could not help you. You realize you need to build your own data source.

Well, you're in luck. This section will walk you through all the steps of building your own data source. You will first learn what you're going to build, why you're building it (the benefits), and, finally, study the code. The code is about creating all the classes and resources in Java to connect to and read your data source.

> **FOCUS ON DATA SOURCE API V1** Although this book covers Apache Spark v3.*x*, this and the following sections cover the Data Source API v1. Spark 2.3 and later started to include an evolution of this API, called Data Source API v2 (also known as DSv2), but I did not feel it was mature enough to document in this book, and v1 of the API is supported and not marked at deprecated. Nevertheless, being a good plumber will also guarantee that switching to a new API will not impact your code too much.

Having read chapter 7 and 8 on ingestion may be helpful but is not required.

9.4.1   Scope of the example project

Let's understand the lab that is the focus of this section. You will extract metadata from photos, store the data in beans, and then turn the beans into a dataframe. Figure 9.5 illustrates the process: the data source will use Java introspection to discover the properties of the bean to build the dataframe.

You will build a data source that will extract the metadata of photos stored on a local disk. *Metadata* is data about the data: for data in a table of a relational database,

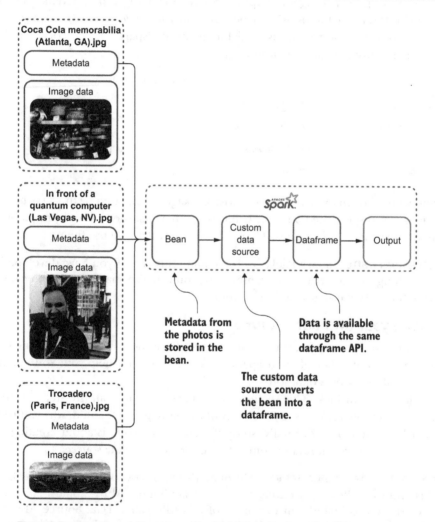

Figure 9.5   From your pictures, you will extract the metadata. You will store the metadata in a JavaBean. Then you'll use Java introspection (aka reflection) to extract the data from the bean by using a bean data source provider, put it in the dataframe, and display the result.

the metadata could include the table name, the name of an index, the type of a column, and so on. In the good ol' days of paper photography, you had a photo, printed on a piece of photo paper, and sometimes, on the back, you were lucky to have a date or a sequence number of the photo in the roll. However, the printed date would be the date the photo was printed on paper, not the date you shot the photo.

With the popularization of digital photography, it has become easier to find, sort, and remember where pictures were taken—even if my mom misses the days of photos printed on paper (and I too, in some ways).

You're going to store the result of the EXIF data you've extracted in a JavaBean (or Plain Old Java Object, POJO). The JavaBean is a perfect container for receiving a list of key/value pairs in which the keys are predefined.

What's a JavaBean?

I know you know what a bean is, and you know I know you know, right? But in this crazy-paced world, I sometimes forget my basics.

A *JavaBean* is a class encapsulating objects and primitive types into a single object (the bean). It is serializable, has a zero-argument constructor, and allows access to properties by using getter and setter methods. The name *bean* was given to encompass this standard, which aims to create reusable software components for Java (and because it sounded coffee-like).

Information in this sidebar was adapted from Wikipedia.

But the challenge does not stop here: your data source will use *reflection* to automatically build the columns in your dataframe from the getters in your class.

What's reflection?

Reflection is one of my favorite Java features: it allows a running Java application to examine, or "introspect," itself. For example, a Java app can obtain the names of all its members through reflection, store them in a list, and display them.

One benefit is being able to see all the getters of a class to build a generic prettyprinter. Imagine a utility class to which you give a POJO or a JavaBean, and it looks at the properties and prints them all, whatever the object is.

You can find an example of this code in this chapter's lab; check out net.jgp .books.spark.ch09.lab900_generic_pretty_printer.GenericPrettyPrinterApp. As this is not the topic of this book, I will not detail the example here, but it is documented and self-sustained.

To learn more, visit Glen McCluskey's introduction to "Using Java Reflection" at http://mng.bz/nvad.

In previous chapters, you used small examples. This project is a little more complete and complex; you will be able to reuse a lot of this code directly in your future project, but you will also have to deal with more classes of various importance. The JavaBean reader is designed in a pretty generic way.

9.4.2   Your data source API and options

Now that you have set the scene, let's see how you can use the new data source. Using the data source is as easy as using the CSV or JSON from chapter 7. There are 14 photos in the project. You will first look at the output result and then dig into the usage code. You're now ready to use the API.

The final result will be as follows:

```
I have imported 14 photos.
root
 |-- Name: string (nullable = true)
 |-- Size: long (nullable = true)
 |-- Extension: string (nullable = true)
 |-- MimeType: string (nullable = true)
 |-- GeoY: float (nullable = true)
 |-- GeoZ: float (nullable = true)
 |-- Width: integer (nullable = true)
 |-- GeoX: float (nullable = true)
 |-- Date: timestamp (nullable = true)
 |-- Directory: string (nullable = true)
 |-- FileCreationDate: timestamp (nullable = true)
 |-- FileLastAccessDate: timestamp (nullable = true)
 |-- FileLastModifiedDate: timestamp (nullable = true)
 |-- Filename: string (nullable = false)
 |-- Height: integer (nullable = true)
```

> **The metadata contains the properties from the photos you decided to expose via your JavaBean.**

	Name	Size	Extension	MimeType	GeoY	GeoZ	Wi...
A pal of mine (Mi...	1851384		jpg	image/jpeg	-93.24203	254.95032	3...
Coca Cola memorab...	589607		jpg	image/jpeg	null	null	1...
Ducks (Chapel Hil...	4218303		jpg	image/jpeg	null	null	5...
Ginni Rometty at ...	469460		jpg	image/jpeg	null	null	1...
Godfrey House (Mi...	511871		jpg	image/jpeg	-93.239494	233.0	1...

only showing top 5 rows

> **The dataframe contains the EXIF information from the pictures in the lab's data directory.**

To produce this output, the code is similar to your previous ingestion examples. From the session, you call a reader and then specify the format and the options, as shown in the following listing.

Listing 9.1   The application code calling the new data source

```
package net.jgp.books.spark.ch09.lab400_photo_datasource;

import org.apache.spark.sql.Dataset;
import org.apache.spark.sql.Row;
import org.apache.spark.sql.SparkSession;
```
> The packages are the same ones that you've been using for any ingestion.

```
public class PhotoMetadataIngestionApp {
  public static void main(String[] args) {
    PhotoMetadataIngestionApp app = new PhotoMetadataIngestionApp();
    app.start();
  }

  private boolean start() {
    SparkSession spark = SparkSession.builder()
```
⟵ Creates a Spark session
```
      .appName("EXIF to Dataset")
      .master("local").getOrCreate();
```
> Option specific to the EXIF data source: you want it to be able to read recursively through the directories.

```
    String importDirectory = "data";

    Dataset<Row> df = spark.read()
```
This is new: you can specify the EXIF format to the reader. ⟶
```
      .format("exif")
      .option("recursive", "true")    ⟵
```
> Option specific to the EXIF data source: the data source reads only files with the JPG or JPEG extensions.

Option specific to the EXIF data source: you want to limit to 100,000 files. ⟶
```
      .option("limit", "100000")
      .option("extensions", "jpg,jpeg")   ⟵
      .load(importDirectory);    ⟵
```
> The data source needs to know from which directory to start importing the data.

```
    System.out.println("I have imported " + df.count() + " photos.");
    df.printSchema();    ⟵
    df.show(5);   ⟵ Shows five rows
```
> As with any dataframe, you can print the schema.

```
    return true;
  }
}
```

The custom data source is used exactly like any other data sources: you specify the format by using the format() method and all the options as key/value pairs using the option() method. Finally, you call the load() method with a path or a filename to start the process. The usage code is compact, easy to read, and easy to maintain.

The questions you should ask yourself now are as follows: How does Spark know what to do with an EXIF data source? And where is this code? The next sections answer these questions, provide the code, and describe in detail the implementation.

9.5   Behind the scenes: Building the data source itself

Now that you've used your data source API and its associated options, let's look at what happens behind the scenes and build the data source. In the following sections, you will write the following:

- The registration file and the short name advertiser file, allowing the data source to be called by a short name: exif in listing 9.1.

- The data source code is a relation between the data and its associated schema.
- The relation between the buildScan() and schema() methods.

Figure 9.6 describes the process graphically. Each step of the process will be detailed using a similar illustration, making the process easier to follow.

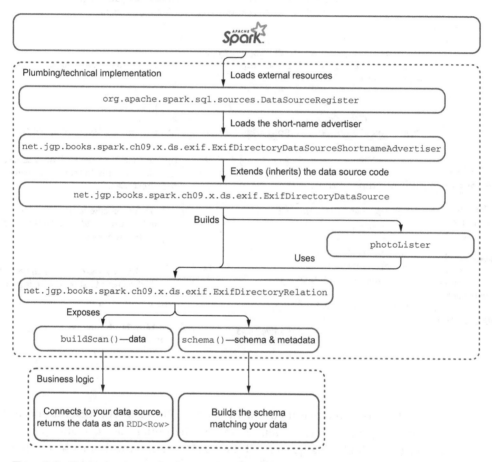

Figure 9.6 The journey to your business logic follows a bit of plumbing code, which involves writing a simple class to advertise your data source short name, the data source, and the relation.

9.6 *Using the register file and the advertiser class*

In the previous section, you read and loaded data in your dataframe, and you specified a format:

```
Dataset<Row> df = spark.read()
    .format("exif")
    .load(importDirectory);
```

You will need to tell Spark what to do with this format. This is the role of the register and the advertiser class you are going to write.

Spark requires a resource file to tell it what to do with a short name (as opposed to a full class name). This is the *advertiser* (in this example, exif). This file contains the list of external data sources that need to be registered. Those classes advertise a short name; in this case, exif. The file contains the class name where the loading process happens: net.jgp.books.spark.ch09.x.ds.exif.ExifDirectoryDataSourceShort-nameAdvertiser. This is done in a resource file called org.apache.spark.sql.sources .DataSourceRegister, as illustrated in figure 9.7. The register file must be in the resources/META-INF/services directory of your project.

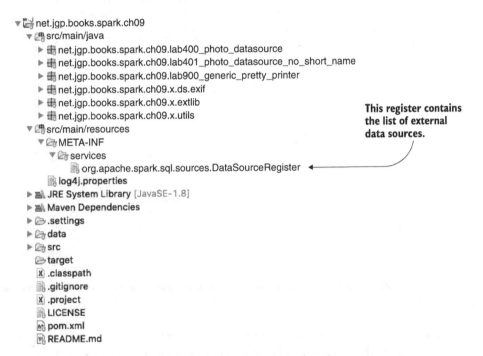

Figure 9.7 Location of the register file, which tells Spark where the data sources' advertisers are. The advertiser will tell Spark the short name of the data source (in this lab, exif).

The advertiser class uses a standard Java mechanism called *Service Loader,* making services available to your application. You can read more about this Java 8 feature at http://mng.bz/vl0a.

Figure 9.8 illustrates where you are in the full process.

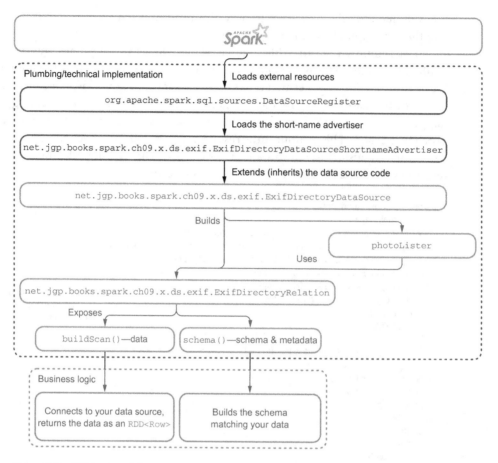

Figure 9.8   At this step of the process, you're defining the short name in the data source register and the advertiser.

As I said before, the advertiser is in charge of exposing (advertising) the short name by which the data source can be called. Let's have a look at the advertiser:

You need to import the DataSourceRegister interface as you're implementing it.

```
package net.jgp.books.spark.ch09.x.ds.exif;

import org.apache.spark.sql.sources.DataSourceRegister;

public class ExifDirectoryDataSourceShortnameAdvertiser
    extends ExifDirectoryDataSource
    implements DataSourceRegister {

  @Override
  public String shortName() {
    return "exif";
  }
}
```

Your data source code is in this class; the advertiser extends it.

Implements the shortName() method to return the short name you wish to use for your data source

Note that the short name is optional: you do not need to advertise a short name. In the call to read() in your application, you used this:

```
Dataset<Row> df = spark.read()
    .format("exif")
    .option("recursive", "true")
    .option("limit", "100000")
    .option("extensions", "jpg,jpeg")
    .load(importDirectory);
```

That is equivalent to the following:

```
Dataset<Row> df = spark.read()
    .format("net.jgp.books.spark.ch09.x.ds.exif.
    ExifDirectoryDataSourceShortnameAdvertiser")
    .option("recursive", "true")
    .option("limit", "100000")
    .option("extensions", "jpg,jpeg")
    .load(importDirectory);
```

You will have to admit that the first form is a little easier to read, right? The second example is also available in the repository as net.jgp.books.spark.ch09.lab101_photo _datasource_no_short_name.PhotoMetadataIngestionNoShortNameApp. This may be useful for debugging.

9.7 *Understanding the relationship between the data and schema*

In the previous section, you saw how to use the API and how to advertise the data source's short name. Now, you will look at the relation between the data and schema, which is what the data source is building. You will first look at how the data source is building this relation object and then at what composes the relation.

9.7.1 *The data source builds the relation*

You can now analyze ExifDirectoryDataSource. The data source has one goal: create the relation. The relation will give you the data and the schema, but to do so, it needs to process the options defined in the application.

Figure 9.9 illustrates where you are in the process. As you would expect, the code is available in the GitHub repository. The code in the repository has additional logging features, which I removed here to condense the example to its core (and enhance readability).

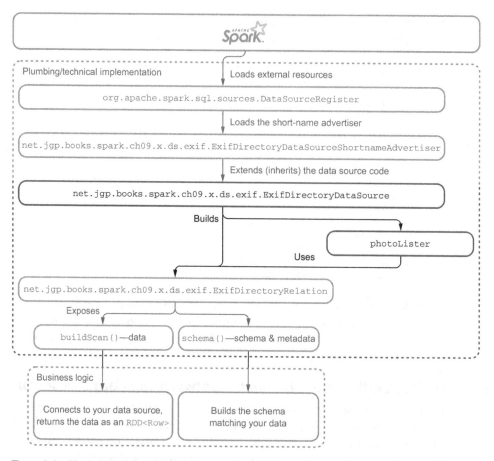

Figure 9.9 The `ExifDirectoryDataSource` builds the relation and the photo lister based on the options you gave in the application code.

Let's analyze the code in the following listing block by block, starting with the import.

Listing 9.2 The data source code with detailed explanation

```
package net.jgp.books.spark.ch09.x.ds.exif;

import static scala.collection.JavaConverters.mapAsJavaMapConverter;

import org.apache.spark.sql.SQLContext;
import org.apache.spark.sql.sources.BaseRelation;
import org.apache.spark.sql.sources.RelationProvider;

import net.jgp.books.spark.ch09.x.extlib.
    RecursiveExtensionFilteredLister;
import net.jgp.books.spark.ch09.x.utils.K;
import scala.collection.immutable.Map;
```

Static method to convert Scala map to a Java map

The Spark packages you will need

This class is actually going to list the files for us.

A map container/collection, but the Scala implementation

I love constants: constants bring rigor, rigor is German, K stands for Konstant in German—elementary, my dear Watson!

More details on Scala can be found in appendix J; you do not need to learn Scala. However, because Spark is built with it, you may have to interact with some Scala objects. Scala offers converters between the data structures in both languages to make our life easier.

As you're getting to the lower level in Spark, you will not see methods offering this dual implementation using both the Java and the Scala types. This is why you see this Scala map collection; however, you're going to convert it to a Java map and use the Java map you are familiar with:

```java
public class ExifDirectoryDataSource implements RelationProvider {
  @Override
  public BaseRelation createRelation(
      SQLContext sqlContext,
      Map<String, String> params) {          Note the Scala map
                                             containing the parameters.
    java.util.Map<String, String> optionsAsJavaMap =    And now you
        mapAsJavaMapConverter(params).asJava();         have a Java map.
```

Because you're programming in Java and using Java collections, you just converted the Scala map to a Java map. Appendix J gives more information about Scala and about Scala-to-Java conversion.

A relation is a resilient distributed dataset, or RDD (for more information, see chapter 3), a known schema, and a few other methods:

```java
                                                            The relation
Your implementation of the relation,                        needs to access
which you will do in the next section                        the SQL Context.
    ExifDirectoryRelation br = new ExifDirectoryRelation();
    br.setSqlContext(sqlContext);
    RecursiveExtensionFilteredLister photoLister =   Analyzes all options passed from the
        new RecursiveExtensionFilteredLister();      application and calls the right setter
    for (java.util.Map.Entry<String, String> entry : optionsAsJavaMap
        .entrySet()) {
      String key = entry.getKey().toLowerCase();
      String value = entry.getValue();              Don't forget that keys
      switch (key) {                                defining options should
        case K.PATH:                                be case insensitive; the
          photoLister.setPath(value);               best way is to compare
          break;                 Note the use       the lowercase version
                                 of constants.      of them.
        case K.RECURSIVE:
          if (value.toLowerCase().charAt(0) == 't') {
            photoLister.setRecursive(true);
          } else {
            photoLister.setRecursive(false);
          }                                          Constants are great: they
          break;                                     bring rigor, rigor is German,
      ...                                            and naturally the class name
        }                                            K stands for Konstant in
      }                                              German.
    br.setPhotoLister(photoLister);
    return br;
  }
}
```

The utility class doing all the metadata extraction work

The path, although set by the load() method, is just another option.

The next class you will study is the implementation of the relation; the class is `Exif-DirectoryRelation`.

The `photoLister` is an instance of `RecursiveExtensionFilteredLister`, which is a generic file lister with a few options including filtering by extensions, support for recursivity, and maximum number of files. The goal of this class is to give you a list of files based on the parameters; reading files is beyond the scope of this book, but you can read the commented file in GitHub at http://mng.bz/4erQ.

Here you assign only the values you got from the application regarding whether the list should support recursivity, file extensions, maximum number of files, and the initial path.

9.7.2   *Inside the relation*

As you saw in the previous section, the relation links the schema and the data. The main goal of the relation is to give you two critical pieces of information:

- The data schema via the `schema()` method, returning a `StructType`
- The data via the `buildScan()` method, returning an `RDD<Row>`

This code will be called by Spark when you trigger the data source. My experience shows that the `schema()` method is called first, but that order is not guaranteed, so I would not assume that one is called before the other in your logic. To prevent this potential issue, you can cache the schema. Figure 9.10 illustrates this part of the process.

The following listing, in net.jgp.books.spark.ch09.x.ds.exif.ExifDirectoryRelation, uses logging, which I did not keep here for readability. This class uses a lot of Spark dependencies. I removed the non-Spark dependencies from this listing.

Listing 9.3   `ExifDirectoryRelation`: your relation with the schema and data

```
package net.jgp.books.spark.ch09.x.ds.exif;
...
import org.apache.spark.api.java.JavaRDD;
import org.apache.spark.api.java.JavaSparkContext;
import org.apache.spark.rdd.RDD;
import org.apache.spark.sql.Row;
import org.apache.spark.sql.SQLContext;
import org.apache.spark.sql.sources.BaseRelation;
import org.apache.spark.sql.sources.TableScan;
import org.apache.spark.sql.types.StructType;
...
```

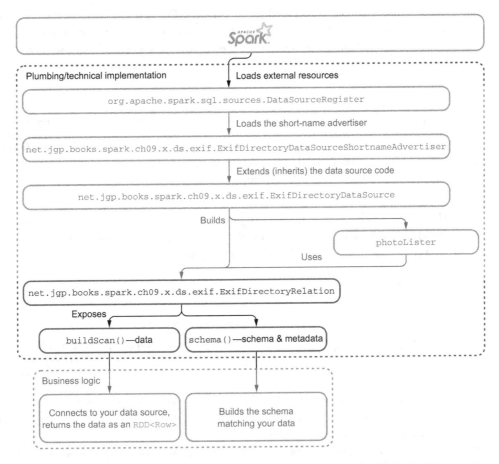

Figure 9.10 Focus on the `ExifDirectoryRelation` with the two key methods: `buildScan()` and `schema()`.

As previously stated, the relation is a (base) relation: it inherits a `BaseRelation`, is serializable (it needs to be eventually passed to the workers), and is a `TableScan`. There is another "Scan," but because your data is represented as a table, this is the one to pick:

Your relation is a BaseRelation and needs to implement sqlContext() and schema().

TableScan brings the buildScan() method, needed to return the data.

Consequence of Serializable, unique identifier (here autogenerated by Eclipse)

```
public class ExifDirectoryRelation
    extends BaseRelation
    implements Serializable, TableScan {
  private static final long serialVersionUID = 4598175080399877334L;
  private SQLContext sqlContext;
  private Schema schema = null;
  private RecursiveExtensionFilteredLister photoLister;
```

Serializable, as the class can be shared

Caches the schema to avoid recalculation

The photo lister you built previously

You will need the application SQL context and must implement the getter.

You can use a simple getter and setter for the SQL context. The SQL context will be needed to create an RDD in the `buildScan()` method, and the getter is a constraint of `BaseRelation`. Even if this is a getter, it does not start with `get` (imposed by the superclass):

```
@Override
public SQLContext sqlContext() {
  return this.sqlContext;
}

public void setSqlContext(SQLContext sqlContext) {
  this.sqlContext = sqlContext;
}
```

The way you obtain a SQL context is not constrained by the superclass.

The `schema()` method returns the schema as a `StructType`. A `StructType` was used in the same way when you ingested a CSV file with a predetermined schema (see chapter 7). Types supported by Spark are listed in appendix L.

```
@Override
public StructType schema() {
  if (schema == null) {
    schema = SparkBeanUtils.getSchemaFromBean(PhotoMetadata.class);
  }
  return schema.getSparkSchema();
}
```

The Schema object used here is a superset of a Spark schema; hence you're asking for the specific information required by Spark.

To simplify the comprehension of those methods, I isolated the functional part in a different class called `SparkBeanUtils`. You will discover `getSparkSchema()` and `getRowFromBean()` in the next section.

You can finally start working on the `buildScan()` method, whose goal is to return the data as an RDD. Remember, a dataframe is basically an RDD with a schema; you have the schema, and you simply need the data now. You'll notice the use of a lambda expression in the code. A lambda expression is easily recognizable by its arrow token, `->`, as in the following:

```
.map(photo -> SparkBeanUtils.getRowFromBean(schema, photo));
```

```
@Override
public RDD<Row> buildScan() {
  schema();

  List<PhotoMetadata> table = collectData();

  JavaSparkContext sparkContext =
    new JavaSparkContext(sqlContext.sparkContext());
  JavaRDD<Row> rowRDD = sparkContext.parallelize(table)
    .map(photo -> SparkBeanUtils.getRowFromBean(schema, photo));

  return rowRDD.rdd();
}
```

Extracts the Spark context from the SQL context

You want to be sure you have the latest schema.

The role of collectData() is to build a list with all your photos' metadata.

Builds the RDD in a parallel way

Creates a JavaRDD<Row> from the table by using a lambda function

I admit it: I am not the greatest fan of lambda expressions. I find them hard to read and understand, so I seldom use them. Here, their use makes sense because you're calling the map() method on each element of the table (each photo).

The collectData() method gets all the files from the lister and goes through them to extract the metadata:

Builds a list of all the files by using
the options defined previously

```
    private List<PhotoMetadata> collectData() {
        List<File> photosToProcess = this.photoLister.getFiles();
        List<PhotoMetadata> list = new ArrayList<>();
        PhotoMetadata photo;
        for (File photoToProcess : photosToProcess) {
            photo = ExifUtils.processFromFilename(
                photoToProcess.getAbsolutePath());
            list.add(photo);
        }
        return list;
    }
    ...
```

Extracts the metadata from the file

Loops through all the photos

Adds the metadata to the list, which you will return when the loop is completed

As you can see in this method, you used simple Java code; you did not have to use a Spark-specific API.

9.8 *Building the schema from a JavaBean*

You went through all the plumbing required to build a data source. You will now learn how to build a schema from a JavaBean through introspection.

The data source requires both the data and the schema. In Spark, the schema is an instance of StructType. If you build it from scratch, it would look like the following (adapted from chapter 7, when you ingested a CSV file with a schema):

```
StructType schema = DataTypes.createStructType(new StructField[] {
    DataTypes.createStructField(
        "id",
        DataTypes.IntegerType,
        false),
    DataTypes.createStructField(
        "bookTitle",
        DataTypes.StringType,
        false),
    DataTypes.createStructField(
        "releaseDate",
        DataTypes.DateType,
        true) });
```

Your goal is to build the schema directly from a JavaBean by using Java introspection, as in figure 9.11.

Using this process means you can turn any JavaBean into a dataframe. Your goal for any future data sources is to get the data in a JavaBean; the utility class (Spark-BeanUtils) will then take care of building the right schema. This also means that if

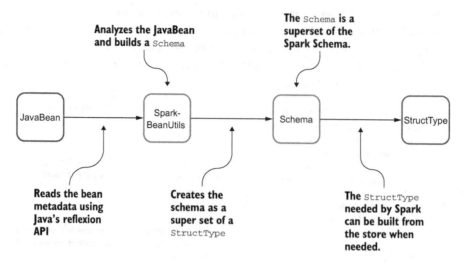

Figure 9.11   SparkBeanUtils **introspects the JavaBean and builds an instance of** Schema, **a superset of what is needed for Spark, which can be used to build the required** StructType.

you want to add or remove columns from your bean, the utility class will do so automatically. *Et voila.*

ANNOTATIONS   In Java, annotations provide additional metadata on an object. This project creates an @SparkColumn annotation to provide a hint about the conversion from a JavaBean to a dataframe.

You can have a look at the JavaBean used for the EXIF ingestion. This class is PhotoMetadata from the net.jgp.books.spark.ch09.x.extlib package. For your sanity, I limited the class to a few properties and removed the logging, setters, and extra imports. The following listing details this POJO.

Listing 9.4   PhotoMetadata: storing your photo's properties

```
package net.jgp.books.spark.ch09.x.extlib;
...
import net.jgp.books.spark.ch09.x.utils.SparkColumn;

public class PhotoMetadata implements Serializable {
...
  private Timestamp dateTaken;
  private String directory;
  private String filename;
  private Float geoX;
  private int width;

  @SparkColumn(name = "Date")
  public Timestamp getDateTaken() {
    return dateTaken;
  }
}
```

The SparkColumn annotation, hinting at the JavaBean-to-dataframe conversion

Some of the properties you will map to Spark columns

Using the annotation, you can specify the name of the column; otherwise, it would use the property name in upper camel case (here, DateTaken).

```
public String getDirectory() {      ◄——— Annotation is not required.
  return directory;
}
                                      |  Forces the nullable property to false; the
@SparkColumn(nullable = false)       |  filename is required at the data source API level.
public String getFilename() {      ◄——
  return filename;                     The annotation can force a type, but be careful about
}                                      the conversion, as Spark will not know how to
                                       convert types from one to another. Here, forcing the
@SparkColumn(type = "float")  ◄—————— type is not useful; this is to illustrate how to do it.
public Float getGeoX() {      ◄—
  return geoX;
}                              Types can be objects or primitives, as long
                               as Spark knows how to deal with them.

public int getWidth() {       ◄—
  return width;
}
...
```

The code that builds and manages the annotation (@SparkColumn) is fairly easy and defines the default values:

```
package net.jgp.books.spark.ch09.x.utils;

import java.lang.annotation.Retention;
import java.lang.annotation.RetentionPolicy;

@Retention(RetentionPolicy.RUNTIME)
public @interface SparkColumn {            Overrides the column name
  String name() default "";      ◄—
  String type() default "";      ◄—
  boolean nullable() default true; ◄—  Overrides the column type—remember that
}                                        Spark will not do the data conversion for you.
        Sets the nullable property, as there is
        no way to infer that from a JavaBean
```

BUILDING YOUR OWN ANNOTATIONS Building you own annotation is not complicated. It involves writing an @interface, similar to an interface.

In the next section, you will transform your JavaBean in a Spark schema and start building rows for your dataframe.

9.9 *Building the dataframe is magic with the utilities*

You went through building your application, calling the new data source. You built all the plumbing, as well as a Spark schema from a JavaBean. You now need to get the data and put it in your dataframe.

The utility class is responsible for building the schema and rows. It is doing a little magic for you:

- It converts the JavaBean to a Spark schema.
- It builds a data row from values.

In general, I recommend that you keep the technical implementation (the plumbing code you just went through) to a minimum. This code uses a lot of low-level interfaces to Spark, so if the interfaces change, you will have to heavily change your code; by limiting the interface code to the simplest possible, changes will affect you, but in a lesser way. For the real business logic (the heavy lifting), you can call services or utility classes to perform the work.

> **BE A GOOD PLUMBER**   We can define *plumbing* as the connection between two or more components in a software diagram, in a similar way as you would connect your faucet to your water line. As a rule of thumb, for any product that you want to interface with, limiting the technical interface (which you do not control) helps minimize the impact of the changes as you shield your business logic in those services. You may find some similarities with the separation of concerns (SoC) design principle.

Figure 9.12 shows this final step of the process.

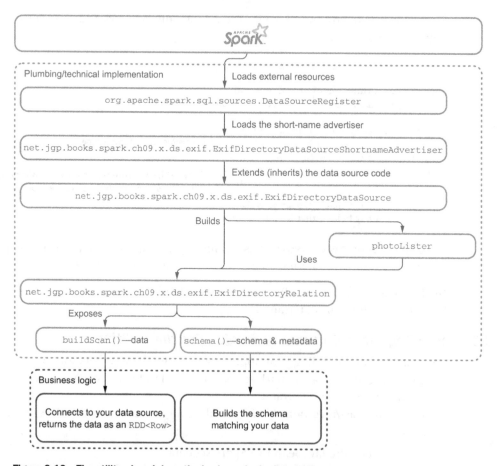

Figure 9.12   The utility class brings the business logic data to the process.

As I did with previous listings in this chapter, I removed some import statements, logging, extra case statements, exception handling, and so on to increase readability. But don't worry; the full listing (with comments!) is available in GitHub at http://mng.bz/Q094.

Listing 9.5 `SparkBeanUtils`: bringing the business logic

```
package net.jgp.books.spark.ch09.x.utils;

import java.lang.reflect.InvocationTargetException;      Packages used
import java.lang.reflect.Method;                         for reflection

import org.apache.spark.sql.Row;
import org.apache.spark.sql.RowFactory;
import org.apache.spark.sql.types.DataType;              Spark package to build
import org.apache.spark.sql.types.DataTypes;             the rows and schema
import org.apache.spark.sql.types.StructField;
import org.apache.spark.sql.types.StructType;
```

The `buildColumnName()` method builds the column name used in the schema and row. It does so by picking the column name in the annotation, or, if there is no annotation, extracts the name from the method name, by removing the `get`. If the process of building the column name fails, the column will be named _c999, where 999 is an incremented integer, starting at _c0. Here is an example based on your bean:

```
@SparkColumn(name = "Date")      ◄───── The resulting column name is Date.
public Timestamp getDateTaken() {

...
public Float getGeoX() {      ◄───── The resulting column name is GeoX.
...
```

And here is the method:

```
public class SparkBeanUtils {
  private static int columnIndex = -1;      ◄─┐ Initialization at –I, as you're going
                                               │ to increment it before using it
  private static String buildColumnName(
      String columnName,
      String methodName) {
    if (columnName.length() > 0) {
      return columnName;                        If the method has fewer than four characters (has
    }                                           three or fewer characters), you could not extract
    if (methodName.length() < 4) {     ◄─────   a name from it even if it starts with "get."
      columnIndex++;
      return "_c" + columnIndex;
    }
    columnName = methodName.substring(3);   ◄─┐ Removes the "get" part
    if (columnName.length() == 0) {            │ from the method name
      columnIndex++;
      return "_c" + columnIndex;
    }
    return columnName;
  }
```

The getSchemaFromBean() method takes an object (it really expects a JavaBean or a POJO) and uses Java reflection to extract the metadata from the class. It also reads the annotation you may have added to the bean:

```
public static Schema getSchemaFromBean(Class<?> c) {          Expects a class,
  Schema schema = new Schema();                                not an object
  List<StructField> sfl = new ArrayList<>();          StructField is needed for Spark.

  Method[] methods = c.getDeclaredMethods();          Extracts the list of methods
                                                      from the class as a static array
```

The code will now loop over each method of the class. If the method is a getter, it will extract the information to build the schema:

```
for (int i = 0; i < methods.length; i++) {
  Method method = methods[i];
  if (!isGetter(method)) {          Simple method to check whether a method
    continue;                       is a getter; if not, skips to the next column
  }

  String methodName = method.getName();          The SchemaColumn is a simple container
  SchemaColumn col = new SchemaColumn();         used to store extra information—the
  col.setMethodName(methodName);                 name of the getter method—that cannot
                                                 be added to the Spark schema (and that
                                                 is not required by Spark).
  String columnName;
  DataType dataType;       The properties for each
  boolean nullable;        column of the dataframe
```

You can first check if the method has a SparkColumn annotation. You built this annotation in the previous section, and it helps determine the properties. It is not compulsory:

```
SparkColumn sparkColumn = method.getAnnotation(SparkColumn.class);
if (sparkColumn == null) {
  log.debug("No annotation for method {}", methodName);
  columnName = "";
  dataType = getDataTypeFromReturnType(method);          The column's type is
  nullable = true;                                       extracted from the
} else {                                                 return type.
```

When a SparkColumn annotation is available, it takes precedence:

```
  columnName = sparkColumn.name();          Gets the name from the annotation

  switch (sparkColumn.type().toLowerCase()) {     ← Gets
    case "stringtype":                              the type
    case "string":                                  from the      Example of case
      dataType = DataTypes.StringType;              annotation     statement for two
      break;                                                       types, but there
    case "integertype":                                            are a lot more
    case "integer":
    case "int":
```

```
            dataType = DataTypes.IntegerType;
            break;

...

        default:
            dataType = getDataTypeFromReturnType(method);    ◁─┐

        }

    nullable = sparkColumn.nullable();    ◁─┐

    }
```

> The column's type is not explicit, so it'll be extracted from the return type.

> Checks if the column is required from the annotation

You now have all the elements to build the final column metadata and add it to the schema object:

```
    String finalColumnName = buildColumnName(columnName, methodName);
    sfl.add(DataTypes.createStructField(    ◁─┐
        finalColumnName, dataType, nullable));
    col.setColumnName(finalColumnName);

    schema.add(col);

    }
```

> Spark method to create a StructField, which is the definition of a field/column

You finally create the StructType schema from all the StructField instances and store it in the schema, just before returning it. You're done!

```
    StructType sparkSchema = DataTypes.createStructType(sfl);
    schema.setSparkSchema(sparkSchema);
    return schema;
}
```

getDataTypeFromReturnType() is a simple method that returns the Spark datatype from a Java type:

```
private static DataType getDataTypeFromReturnType(Method method) {
  String typeName = method.getReturnType().getSimpleName().toLowerCase();
  switch (typeName) {
    case "int":
    case "integer":
      return DataTypes.IntegerType;
    case "string":
      return DataTypes.StringType;
...
    default:
      return DataTypes.BinaryType;
  }
}
```

The isGetter() method checks whether a method is a getter. The definition and constraints of a getter are as follows:

- The method name should start with the word get.
- The method should not have any parameters/arguments.
- The method return type cannot be void.

Checking that a method is indeed a getter:

```
private static boolean isGetter(Method method) {
  if (!method.getName().startsWith("get")) {
    return false;
  }
  if (method.getParameterTypes().length != 0) {
    return false;
  }
  if (void.class.equals(method.getReturnType())) {
    return false;
  }
  return true;
}
```

I realize it was a long class (pun intended), but you just reached your last method! In this method, you're building a Spark Row (the same Row you're using in your Dataset to build the dataframe, or in your RDD). It is definitely good to see a more familiar type, no?

You need a basic container to store all the values that will be composing your Row.

Gets the method name from the schema: this is why you needed the Schema object.

Gets the list of fields in your Spark schema

```
public static Row getRowFromBean(Schema schema, Object bean) {
  List<Object> cells = new ArrayList<>();

  String[] fieldName = schema.getSparkSchema().fieldNames();
  for (int i = 0; i < fieldName.length; i++) {
    String methodName = schema.getMethodName(fieldName[i]);
    Method method;
    method = bean.getClass().getMethod(methodName);
    cells.add(method.invoke(bean));
  }

  Row row = RowFactory.create(cells.toArray());
  return row;
  }
}
```

Adds each value to the cells by dynamically invoking the method

The RowFactory helps you transform a static array into a Row! RowFactory is a Spark class.

9.10 *The other classes*

In this project, you built a complete new data source, and each class was described extensively. However, a few additional classes are used that do not need a detailed walk-through. Those classes are described in table 9.1, along with their package names, which are subpackages of net.jgp.books.spark.ch09.

Table 9.1   Additional ancillary classes used by the data source project

Class	Package	Description
Schema	.x.utils	A simple container to store the Spark schema and additional information.

Table 9.1 Additional ancillary classes used by the data source project *(continued)*

Class	Package	Description
SchemaColumn	.x.utils	The object you use to store additional metadata about a column.
ExifUtils	.x.extlib	The utility functions that extract the EXIF data from each photo and store the extracted data in the PhotoMetadata JavaBean.
RecursiveExtensionFilteredLister	.x.extlib	A generic and reusable file lister supporting extension filtering, threshold (maximum number of files to gather), and optional recursivity. Not limited to photos.

Summary

This chapter is definitely one of the hardest of the book. Nevertheless, in this chapter, you learned the following:

- The Spark Packages website provides a list of extensions to Spark. It is accessible at https://spark-packages.org/.
- Direct connection to a data source from Spark offers these benefits: temporary files are not needed, data quality/cleansing scripts can be written directly in Spark, you get only the data you need, and there's no need for JSON/CSV conversion.
- EXIF is an extension to JPEG (and other graphic formats) to store metadata about the image.
- A JavaBean is a small class that contains properties and accessor methods.
- Reflection allows a running Java application to examine, or "introspect," itself, so the developer can find out the details about a class, including the names of methods, fields, and so on.
- When you develop a new data source, the ingestion code remains similar to generic data sources you've used with files or databases.
- A data source needs to deliver a schema of the data that's as long as the data.
- A data source can be identified by a short name (defined in a resource file and an advertiser class) or by a full class name.
- A schema in Spark is implemented using the StructType object. It contains one or more StructField instances.
- Data structures and collections may be different between Java and Scala, but conversion methods exist.
- The RowFactory class offers a method to convert a static array to a Spark Row.

Ingestion through structured streaming

10

This chapter covers

- Understanding streaming
- Building your first streaming ingestions
- Capturing the various sources of data in streaming
- Building an application that takes two streams
- Differentiating discretized streaming and structured streaming

Look at your data from a few thousand meters (or feet, if you are stuck with the imperial system) and focus on the data-generation part. Do you see systems that generate batches of data, or do you see systems that generate data continuously? Systems delivering a flow of data, also known as *streams*, were less popular a few years ago. Streams are definitely getting more traction, and understanding streams is the focus of this chapter.

Your mobile phone regularly pings cell towers, for example. If it's a smartphone (highly probable, based on the audience of this book), it will also check email and more.

The bus travelling through (smart) cities sends its GPS coordinates.

The cash register at your supermarket's checkout counter generates data as the cashier (or you) pass the items in front of the scanner. A transaction is processed as you pay.

As you bring your car to the garage, a flow of information is collected, stored, and sent to various other recipients such as the manufacturers, insurance companies, or reporting companies.

In the United States, when patients enter a medical facility, messages, called *admissions, discharges, and transfers (ADTs)*, are generated containing atomic pieces of information.

Businesses like streaming data; it gives them better acuity about what's going on than after overnight processing. In North Carolina, where I live, and probably in the rest of the United States, as soon as a catastrophe is announced, people rush to their stores to get milk, water, and spongy bread (don't ask me what they do with it). In terms of business, getting a live feed of what is being sold can actually trigger a faster response from the distribution center to supply more of those items to the grocery stores that sell the most. In this context, I am not talking about while disasters are happening or even disaster recovery, but enabling a faster reaction to market demands. In 2019, data should be seen more as a flow than as silos being filled.

In this chapter, you will discover what streaming is and how it differs (so little) from batch mode. You will then build your first streaming application.

To make streaming a little easier to simulate, I built and added to the chapter's source code repository a streaming data generator, which is useful for simulating a stream. You can tailor this generator to your needs. Appendix O covers the details of the data generator, which is not a prerequisite to this chapter. Nevertheless, we are going to use the generator with the labs in the chapter.

Starting with this chapter, the examples and labs will use more logging instead of a simple print to the screen. Logging simplifies reading and is an industry standard, which is more along the lines of what is expected from you in your day-to-day job (and `println` is a bad development practice). The logging settings will still dump information on the console; no need to look for log files in an obscure place!

You will also experiment with a more complex example, where you will work with two streams. Finally, to wrap up this chapter, you will learn the differences between structured streams (from Apache Spark v2 on) and discretized streams (started in Apache Spark v1). Appendix P provides additional resources on streaming.

Figure 10.1 shows where you are on your journey to ingestion in Apache Spark. Good news! It's the final chapter on data ingestion.

LAB Examples from this chapter are available in GitHub at https://github .com/jgperrin/net.jgp.books.spark.ch10. Appendix L is a reference for ingestion. Appendix P also provides additional resources on streaming.

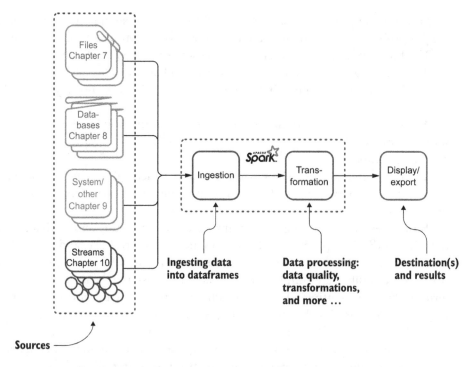

Figure 10.1   Your journey to data ingestion is nearing an end; this chapter covers structured streaming and ends the series on ingestion.

10.1   *What's streaming?*

In this section, let's look at streaming computing in the context of Apache Spark. This will give you the required fundamentals to understand the examples and integrate streaming into your projects.

Processing data through streams is not a novel idea. However, it has increased in popularity in recent years. Nobody wants to wait for anything anymore. As a society, we have grown to expect immediate results all the time. You go see your doctor, and you expect to see your claim in your health-care provider's portal as you go home. You return the TV you bought by accident to Costco, and you expect to see the credit on your credit card statement right away. You finish your Lyft ride, and you expect to see your SkyMiles bonus online right away. In a world where data is accelerating, streaming definitely has its place: nobody wants to wait for overnight batch processing.

Another reason to use streaming is that as the volume of data increases, it's also a pretty good idea to cut it into small chunks to reduce the load at peak time.

Overall, streaming computing is more natural than traditional batch computing, as it happens in a flow. However, because it is a different paradigm than you may be accustomed to, you may have to shift the way you're thinking. Figure 10.2 illustrates the system.

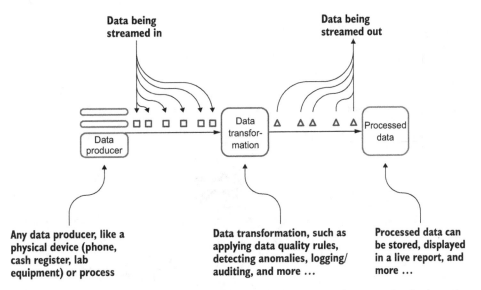

Figure 10.2   In this typical streaming scenario, data is being produced, sent as atomic elements, transformed on the fly, and finally is available in processed form for live reporting, storage, and more.

Streams are usually available in two forms: files and network streams. In a file streaming scenario, files are dropped in a directory (sometimes called a *landing zone* or *staging area*; see chapter 1) and Spark takes the files from this directory as they come in. In the second scenario, data is sent over the network.

The way Apache Spark handles streaming is by regrouping operations over a small window of time. This is called *microbatching*.

10.2   Creating your first stream

For your first stream ingestion, you will use files. Files are generated in a folder. Spark takes them as they are generated. This simpler scenario avoids dealing with potential network issues and will illustrate the core principle of streaming, which is to consume data as soon as it is available.

File streaming is a common use case in the health-care industry. A hospital (a provider) can dump files on an FTP server that are then picked up by an insurance company (a payer).

In this scenario, you are going to run two applications. The order in which you start the application does not matter for file streams. One application will produce the stream, which contains records describing people. The other application will use Spark to consume the generated stream. You will start with the data generator and then build the consumer. Figure 10.3 illustrates the process.

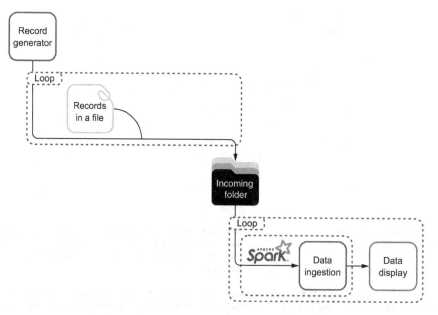

Figure 10.3 In this streaming scenario, one application (the generator) generates records in a file and places those files in a folder. A Spark application (the consumer) reads the files in that folder and displays the data.

10.2.1   *Generating a file stream*

To simulate a steady stream of data, you will first start the record generator. In this section, you will look at the output of the generator, learn how to compile and run it, and then briefly look at its code.

To make things a little easier, I have added a record generator in the chapter's repository. The record generator is designed to create files with random records that describe people: they have a first name, a middle name, a last name, an age, and a US Social Security number. Hey, it's fake data, so don't think you can use it to impersonate anyone!

In this section, you are going to run the generator, but you won't modify it too much. Appendix O describes how to modify the generator or build your own based on the easy API that the generator has been built on.

When run, the output of RecordsInFilesGeneratorApp looks like the following listing.

Listing 10.1   Output of the stream generator

```
[INFO] Scanning for projects...
...
[INFO] --- exec-maven-plugin:1.6.0:java (write-file-in-stream) @
 sparkInAction-chapter10 ---
2020-11-13 12:14:12.496 -DEBUG --- [treamApp.main()]
 ure.getRecords(RecordStructure.java:131): Generated data:
```

```
Aubriella,Silas,Gillet,62,373-69-4505
Reese,Clayton,Kochan,2,130-00-2393
Trinity,Sloan,Vieth,107,202-34-4161
Daphne,Forrest,Huffman,77,250-50-6797
Emmett,Heath,Golston,41,133-17-2450
Alex,Orlando,Courtier,32,290-51-1937
Titan,Deborah,Mckissack,89,073-83-0162
```

Generated records

```
2020-11-13 12:14:12.498 - INFO --- [treamApp.main()]
erUtils.write(RecordWriterUtils.java:21): Writing in: /var/folders/v7/
3jv0[…]/T/streaming/in/contact_1542129252485.txt
…
```

Temporary path and file where the records are saved

Running two applications at the same time is not easy in an IDE such as Eclipse. Therefore, I made sure you could run all the labs from the command line, using Maven. If you are not familiar with Maven, appendix B covers its installation, and appendix H provides some tips for using it.

Once you have cloned the repository locally, go to the folder where you have the project's pom.xml file. In this example, it is as follows:

```
$ cd /Users/jgp/Workspaces/Books/net.jgp.books.spark.ch10
```

Then clean and compile your data generation application. At first, you will not modify it, but simply compile and run it. Cleaning will make sure that no compiled artifacts are left. It is definitely not needed the first time, as there is nothing to clean. Compiling will simply build the application:

```
$ mvn clean install
```

If Maven starts downloading a lot of packages (or if it does not), don't freak out, unless you are paying for your internet service based on the amount of data you are consuming. Then run this:

```
$ mvn exec:java@generate-records-in-files
```

This command will execute the application in the pom.xml file defined by the generate -records-in-files ID, as excerpted in listing 10.2. Examples in this chapter rely on IDs in your pom.xml to distinguish between the different applications. Of course, you can run all the applications in your IDE as well.

Listing 10.2 Excerpt of pom.xml

```
…
<build>
  <plugins>
   <plugin>
    <groupId>org.codehaus.mojo</groupId>
    <artifactId>exec-maven-plugin</artifactId>
    <version>1.6.0</version>
```

```
<executions>
 <execution>
  <id>generate-records-in-files</id>          ◁─┐ Unique identifier defining
  <goals>                                         the "block" being called
   <goal>java</goal>
  </goals>
  <configuration>
   <mainClass>net.jgp.books.spark.ch10.x.utils.streaming.
➥ app.RecordsInFilesGeneratorApp</mainClass>   ◁─┐
  </configuration>                                 Application to execute
 </execution>
...
```

The following listing shows the generator code. Appendix O covers the generator, the
generator's API, and its extensibility in greater detail.

Listing 10.3   RecordsInFilesGeneratorApp.java

```
package net.jgp.books.spark.ch10.x.utils.streaming.app;

import net.jgp.books.spark.ch10.x.utils.streaming.lib.*;

public class RecordsInFilesGeneratorApp {   ┐ Streaming duration
  public int streamDuration = 60;         ◁─┘ in seconds
  public int batchSize = 10;
  public int waitTime = 5;                ◁─┐ Wait time between two batches of records,
                                              in seconds, with an element of variability
  public static void main(String[] args) {
    RecordStructure rs = new RecordStructure("contact")
        .add("fname", FieldType.FIRST_NAME)
        .add("mname", FieldType.FIRST_NAME)
        .add("lname", FieldType.LAST_NAME)       Structure of the record:
        .add("age", FieldType.AGE)               first, middle, and last name,
        .add("ssn", FieldType.SSN);              as well as age and SSN

    RecordsInFilesGeneratorApp app = new RecordsInFilesGeneratorApp();
    app.start(rs);
  }
                                                        Generates records for
  private void start(RecordStructure rs) {              streamDuration seconds
    long start = System.currentTimeMillis();
    while (start + streamDuration * 1000 > System.currentTimeMillis()) {  ◁─┘
      int maxRecord = RecordGeneratorUtils.getRandomInt(batchSize) + 1;
      RecordWriterUtils.write(
          rs.getRecordName() + "_" + System.currentTimeMillis() + ".txt",
          rs.getRecords(maxRecord, false));   ◁─┐ Writes the record in a file
      try {
        Thread.sleep(RecordGeneratorUtils.getRandomInt(waitTime * 1000)
            + waitTime * 1000 / 2);   ◁─┐ Waits a random time
      } catch (InterruptedException e) {
      }
    }
  }
}
```

Annotations:
- *Maximum number of records sent at the same time* → `.add("fname", FieldType.FIRST_NAME)` section
- *Will generate up to batchSize records in the file* → `int maxRecord = RecordGeneratorUtils.getRandomInt(batchSize) + 1;`

You can modify the parameters (streamDuration, batchSize, and waitTime) and the record's structure to study various behaviors:

- streamDuration defines the duration of the stream in seconds. The default value is 60 seconds (1 minute).
- batchSize defines the maximum number of records in a single event. The default of 10 means that you will get at most 10 records dropped by the generator.
- waitTime is the duration the generator waits between two events. There is a bit of randomness associated to this value: the default value of 5 ms means that the application will wait between 2.5 ms (= 5 / 2) and 7.5 ms (= 5 × 1.5).

10.2.2 Consuming the records

Now that the folder is getting filled by records in files, you can ingest them with Spark. You will first have a look at the way records are displayed and then dig into the code.

LAB This is lab #200. It is available on GitHub at https://github.com/jgperrin/ net.jgp.books.spark.ch10. The application is ReadLinesFromFileStreamApp .java in the net.jgp.books.spark.ch10.lab200_read_stream package.

The lab will simply ingest the records, store them in a dataframe (yes, the same dataframe you previously used), and show the result on the console. Figure 10.4 illustrates this process.

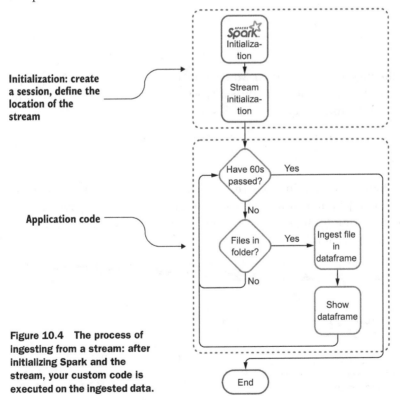

Figure 10.4 The process of ingesting from a stream: after initializing Spark and the stream, your custom code is executed on the ingested data.

The following listing shows the output of the application.

Listing 10.4   Output from ReadLinesFromFileStreamApp

```
2020-11-16 14:13:54.924 -DEBUG --- [            main]
   tart(ReadLinesFromFileStreamApp.java:29): -> start()
-----------------------------------------
Batch: 0                                        <--- Batch #0
-----------------------------------------
+-----------------------------------+
|value                              |           <--| Only one column in our
+-----------------------------------+              | dataframe called "value"
|Mara,Jamison,Acy,52,492-23-4955    |
|Ariel,Raegan,Abend,104,007-31-2841|            Three rows of your dataframe
|Kynlee,Ari,Bevier,106,439-70-9576 |
+-----------------------------------+
only showing top 3 rows


-----------------------------------------
Batch: 1                                        <--- Batch #1 (and so on)
-----------------------------------------
+-----------------------------------+
|value                              |
+-----------------------------------+
|Conrad,Alex,Gutwein,34,998-04-4584|
|Aldo,Adam,Ballard,6,996-95-8983    |
+-----------------------------------+
...
2020-11-16 14:14:59.648 -DEBUG --- [            main]
   tart(ReadLinesFromFileStreamApp.java:58): <- start()
```

To start the ingestion application, you can run it directly in the IDE (Eclipse, in this case) or via Maven. In the same directory where you cloned the project, in another terminal, run the following:

```
$ cd /Users/jgp/Workspaces/Book/net.jgp.books.spark.ch10
$ mvn clean install
$ mvn exec:exec@lab200
```

Note that here, you are using exec:exec, not exec:java. By using exec:exec, Maven is starting a new JVM to run your application. This way, you can pass arguments to the JVM. The following listing shows the section of the pom.xml responsible for the execution of the application.

Listing 10.5   Section of pom.xml to execute lab #200, ReadLinesFromFileStreamApp

```
...
    <execution>
     <id>lab200</id>
     <configuration>
      <executable>java</executable>
      <arguments>
       <argument>-classpath</argument>
       <classpath />
```

```
        <argument>net.jgp.books.spark.ch10.lab200_read_stream.
ReadLinesFromFileStreamApp</argument>
        </arguments>
      </configuration>
    </execution>
```
...

Let's analyze the code in the ReadLinesFromFileStreamApp application, in the net.jgp.books.spark.ch10.lab200_read_stream package in listing 10.6. I know that having this big block of imports at the beginning of the source code is not always appealing, but with the various evolutions of the underlying framework (here, Apache Spark), I like to make sure that you will be using the right packages.

From this point in the book, I will use logging (the SLF4J package) rather than println. Logging is an industry standard, while println may scare some of us (as in dumping information onto the console that you would not like the user to see). I will not describe the initialization of logging in each lab, to keep code clarity a priority, while describing it in the book. However, in the repository, you will find the initialization for each example (otherwise, it would not work, right?).

There is no difference in creating a Spark session, whether you plan on using streaming or batch data processing.

Once you have your session, you can ask the session to read from a stream by using the readStream() method. Based on the type of stream, it will require additional parameters. Here you are reading a text file (as specified with the format() method) from a directory (as defined by the load() method). Note that the format()'s parameter is a String value, not an Enum, but nothing forbids you from having a little utility class somewhere (with, for example, constants).

So far, it is fairly easy, no? You start a session and, in order to build a dataframe, you read it from a stream. However, in a stream, data may or may not be there and may or may not come. Therefore, the application needs to wait for data to come, a bit like a server waiting for requests. Writing your data is done through the dataframe's writeStream() method and the StreamingQuery object.

You first define your streaming query object from the dataframe you use as your stream. The query will start to fill a *result table*, as illustrated in figure 10.5. The result table grows with the data coming in.

To build your query, you will need to specify the following:

- The output mode (see appendix P for a list of output modes). In this lab, you are displaying only the updates between two receptions.
- The format, which basically says what you are going to do with the data you receive. In this lab, you are displaying it on the console (and not through logging). In the literature, you will often read about *sink* when referring to the output format. You can also refer to appendix P for the different sinks and their descriptions.
- Options. In the case of displaying to the console, truncate set to false means that the records will not be truncated to a certain length, and numRows specifies that you will display at most three records. It is the equivalent of calling show(3, false) on a dataframe in nonstreaming (batch) mode.

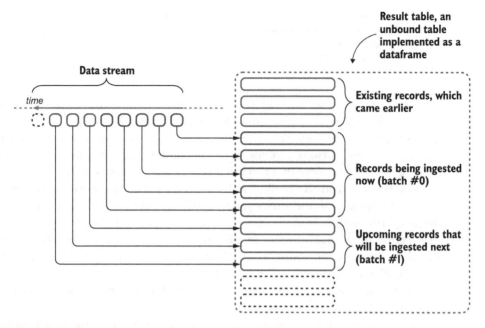

Figure 10.5   As the data stream receives data, the data is added to the result table. The result table is an unbound table, which can grow as much as a dataframe can grow (based on your cluster's physical capacity, of course).

After specifying the output mode, format, and options, you can start the query.

Of course, now, your application needs to wait for data to come in. It does so through the awaitTermination() method on the query. awaitTermination() is a blocking method. It is available with and without parameters. Without a parameter, the method will wait forever. With a parameter, you can specify the duration the method will wait for. In those labs, I used one minute consistently.

You've achieved your first ingestion from a stream. In the next section, you will extract a full record from the stream, not just a raw line of data.

Listing 10.6   ReadLinesFromFileStreamApp.java

```
package net.jgp.books.spark.ch10.lab200_read_stream;

import java.util.concurrent.TimeoutException;

import org.apache.spark.sql.Dataset;
import org.apache.spark.sql.Row;
import org.apache.spark.sql.SparkSession;
import org.apache.spark.sql.streaming.OutputMode;
import org.apache.spark.sql.streaming.StreamingQuery;
import org.apache.spark.sql.streaming.StreamingQueryException;
import org.slf4j.Logger;                                        Log imports
import org.slf4j.LoggerFactory;                                 for SLF4J
```

```
import net.jgp.books.spark.ch10.x.utils.streaming.lib.StreamingUtils;

public class ReadLinesFromFileStreamApp {
  private static transient Logger log = LoggerFactory.getLogger(
      ReadLinesFromFileStreamApp.class);
```
◄── Initialization of the logger

```
  public static void main(String[] args) {
    ReadRecordFromFileStreamApp app = new ReadRecordFromFileStreamApp();
    try {
      app.start();
    } catch (TimeoutException e) {
      log.error("A timeout exception has occured: {}", e.getMessage());
    }
  }
```

```
  private void start() {
    log.debug("-> start()");
```
◄── **Log, at a debug level, that you are getting in the start() method**

```
    SparkSession spark = SparkSession.builder()
        .appName("Read lines over a file stream")
        .master("local")
        .getOrCreate();
```
Creates a Spark session, as you did previously

The file's format is text. →
```
    Dataset<Row> df = spark
        .readStream()
        .format("text")
        .load(StreamingUtils.getInputDirectory());
```
◄── **Specifies that you are going to read from a stream**

◄── **And this is the directory to read from.**

As an append to the output →
```
    StreamingQuery query = df
        .writeStream()
        .outputMode(OutputMode.Append())
        .format("console")
        .option("truncate", false)
        .option("numRows", 3)
        .start();
```
◄── **You are now ready to write in a stream.**

◄── **The output is the console.**

With options, records are not truncated, and at most three will be displayed.

◄── **And you start.**

```
    try {
      query.awaitTermination(60000);
    } catch (StreamingQueryException e) {
      log.error(
          "Exception while waiting for query to end {}.",
          e.getMessage(),
          e);
    }
```
◄── **Waits for data to come, here, for one minute**

```
    log.debug("<- start()");
  }
}
```
◄── **Logs message for leaving the start() method**

Note that with Spark v3.0 preview 2, the `start()` from `StreamingQuery` now throws a time-out exception, which needs to be managed. The code in the repository behaves accordingly in the appropriate branches.

10.2.3 Getting records, not lines

In the previous example, you ingested lines, such as Conrad,Alex,Gutwein,34,998-04-4584. Although the data is in Spark, it is not convenient to use. It's raw, you would have to reparse it, there are no datatypes. . . . Let's turn the raw line into a record by using a schema.

> **LAB**   This is lab #210 in the net.jgp.books.spark.ch10.lab210_read_record _from_stream package. The app is ReadRecordFromFileStreamApp.

The following listing shows output from ReadRecordFromFileStreamApp. The output has clearly separated records. Getting output like this is fairly easy.

Listing 10.7   Output showing structured records

```
...
-----------------------------------------
Batch: 0
-----------------------------------------
+---------+--------+------------+---+-----------+
|   fname |  mname |      lname |age|        ssn|
+---------+--------+------------+---+-----------+
|  Daniela|    Lara|     Clayton| 65|853-73-5075|
|     Niko|   Romeo|     Dunmore| 37|400-54-1312|
|   Austin|   Aliya|     Thierry| 44|988-42-0723|
|  Taliyah|  Caiden|       Hyson| 47|781-05-7373|
|  Roselyn|   Juelz|     Whidbee|102|463-55-3667|
|    Amani| Brendan|      Massey|110|576-90-3460|
...
```

You can execute this lab directly in Eclipse (or your favorite IDE) or on the command line via the following:

```
$ mvn clean compile install
$ mvn exec:exec@lab210
```

The record ingestion application, shown in listing 10.8, is a bit different from the raw line ingestion application from listing 10.5. You will have to tell Spark that you want records and specify the schema.

Listing 10.8   ReadRecordFromFileStreamApp.java

```
...
    SparkSession spark = SparkSession.builder()
        .appName("Read records from a file stream")
        .master("local")
        .getOrCreate();

    StructType recordSchema = new StructType()    ⟵——— Schema definition
        .add("fname", "string")
        .add("mname", "string")
```

```
                      .add("lname", "string")
                      .add("age", "integer")
                      .add("ssn", "string");

             Dataset<Row> df = spark
                      .readStream()
Specifies            .format("csv")          <──── The record is a CSV file.
the schema       └─▷ .schema(recordSchema)
                      .load(StreamingUtils.getInputDirectory());

             StreamingQuery query = df
                      .writeStream()
                      .outputMode(OutputMode.Append())
                      .format("console")
                      .start();
```

The schema must match the one you are using for the generator, or, of course, your real schema on your system.

10.3 *Ingesting data from network streams*

Data may also come in a network stream. Spark's structured streaming can handle a network stream as easily as handling file streaming, as you read in the previous section. In this section, you will set up the network system, start the application, and discover the code.

> **LAB** This is lab #300. It is available on GitHub at https://github.com/jgperrin/ net.jgp.books.spark.ch10. The application is ReadLinesFromNetworkStreamApp in the net.jgp.books.spark.ch10.lab300_read_network_stream package.

The lab application will display results as it receives them on the stream, as illustrated in the following listing. At the end of the processing, you can see a small status of the query.

Listing 10.9 Output of ReadLinesFromNetworkStreamApp

```
…main] t(ReadLinesFromNetworkStreamApp.java:23): -> start()
…
Batch: 1
-------------------------------------------                      │
+-------------------+                                            │
|              value|                                    Batch I │
+-------------------+                                            │
|Jean-Georges Perrin|                                            │
…
Batch: 2
-------------------------------------------                      │
+------------+                                                   │
|       value|                                           Batch 2 │
+------------+                                                   │
|Holden Karau|                                                   │
…
```

```
Batch: 3
-------------------------------------------
+-------------+
|        value|                                           Batch 3
+-------------+
|Matei Zaharia|
...
```

```
...main] t(ReadLinesFromNetworkStreamApp.java:53): Query status: {   <--- Status
  "message" : "Waiting for data to arrive",
  "isDataAvailable" : false,
  "isTriggerActive" : false
}
...main] t(ReadLinesFromNetworkStreamApp.java:54): <- start()
```

To build network streaming, you will require a little tool called NetCat (or nc), which comes with any UNIX (including macOS) distribution. If you are running Windows and if nc.exe is not part of the system, consider looking at https://nmap.org/ncat/.

nc is a versatile tool for manipulating TCP and UDP. It is often described as the Swiss Army knife of network utilities. For your mental sanity, I will not cover all the options for the tool. You will start nc on port 9999 as a server.

You need to start nc before you start anything else! To do so, simply type this:

```
$ nc -lk 9999
```

The -l option specifies that nc should listen, and -k indicates that you can have more connections.

Once nc runs, you can start your Spark application. A common mistake is to start Spark before you start nc. You can run it using mvn exec:exec@lab300.

After you have started the Spark application, you can return to the terminal running nc and start typing in the terminal window. If you want the same display as listing 10.9, you will have to type *Jean-Georges Perrin*, *Holden Karau*, and *Matei Zaharia* (but I am sure you got that). The following listing shows the code.

Listing 10.10   ReadLinesFromNetworkStreamApp.java

```java
package net.jgp.books.spark.ch10.lab300_read_network_stream;
...
public class ReadLinesFromNetworkStreamApp {
...
  public static void main(String[] args) {
    ReadLinesFromNetworkStreamApp app = new ReadLinesFromNetworkStreamApp();
    try {
      app.start();
    } catch (TimeoutException e) {
      log.error("A timeout exception has occured: {}", e.getMessage());
    }
  }
```

```
private void start() throws TimeoutException {
...
    Dataset<Row> df = spark                    The format is socket,
        .readStream()                          telling Spark to read
        .format("socket")              ◄──┘    on a socket.
        .option("host", "localhost")
        .option("port", 9999)          ◄────── Port, your local port
        .load();

    StreamingQuery query = df
        .writeStream()
        .outputMode(OutputMode.Append())
        .format("console")
        .start();

    try {
      query.awaitTermination(60000);
    } catch (StreamingQueryException e) {
      log.error(
          "Exception while waiting for query to end {}.",
          e.getMessage(),
          e);
    }
                                                    Code executed
    log.debug("Query status: {}", query.status()); ◄┘ after a nice kill
    log.debug("<- start()");
  }
}
...
```

Host—here, your local machine → (points to `.option("host", "localhost")`)

As you can see, you do not need to modify too much from the first example of this chapter (listing 10.5); you need to specify only the format, host, and port.

10.4 Dealing with multiple streams

Of course, in real life, you never have only one stream of data coming in, as in the previous sections, right? This section shows you how to use two streams of data coming at the same time.

> **LAB** This lab uses ReadRecordFromMultipleFileStreamApp in the net.jgp
> .books.spark.ch10.lab400_read_records_from_multiple_streams package. This
> is lab #400.

In this example, data will come in two streams from two directories. For simplification, the two streams contain the same record. The same processor ingests each stream and processes each record. The operation is a simple segmentation of the population between kids, teens, and seniors. Figure 10.6 illustrates the process.

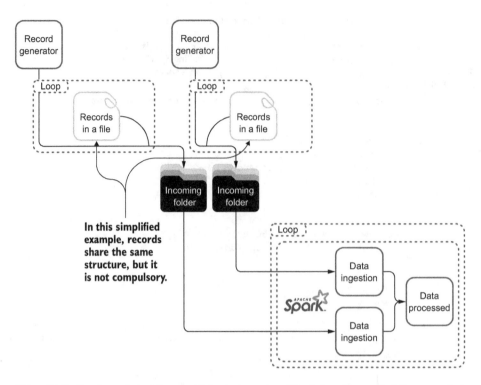

In this simplified
example, records
share the same
structure, but it
is not compulsory.

Figure 10.6   Spark can ingest from multiple streams at once and share the same data processing.

The output looks like the following listing.

Listing 10.11   Output of ReadRecordFromMultipleFileStreamApp

```
...     main] RecordFromMultipleFileStreamApp.java:25): -> start()
...     main] RecordFromMultipleFileStreamApp.java:70): Pass #1
...     main] RecordFromMultipleFileStreamApp.java:70): Pass #2
...task 158] s.AgeChecker.process(AgeChecker.java:43): On stream #2: Aminah
→ is a senior, they are 92 yrs old.
...task 158] s.AgeChecker.process(AgeChecker.java:43): On stream #2: Brinley
→ is a senior, they are 72 yrs old.
...task 158] s.AgeChecker.process(AgeChecker.java:43): On stream #2: Camila
→ is a senior, they are 68 yrs old.
...task 159] s.AgeChecker.process(AgeChecker.java:43): On stream #2: Toby is
→ a senior, they are 67 yrs old.
...task 161] s.AgeChecker.process(AgeChecker.java:38): On stream #1: Jaziel
→ is a teen, they are 17 yrs old.
...task 161] s.AgeChecker.process(AgeChecker.java:43): On stream #1: Tatum is
→ a senior, they are 73 yrs old.
...task 161] s.AgeChecker.process(AgeChecker.java:43): On stream #1: Hallie
→ is a senior, they are 91 yrs old.
...task 161] s.AgeChecker.process(AgeChecker.java:43): On stream #1: Ellie is
→ a senior, they are 74 yrs old.
...     main] RecordFromMultipleFileStreamApp.java:70): Pass #3
```

```
...
...     main] RecordFromMultipleFileStreamApp.java:70): Pass #7
...task 163] s.AgeChecker.process(AgeChecker.java:43): On stream #1: Alisa is
⇒ a senior, they are 76 yrs old.
...task 163] s.AgeChecker.process(AgeChecker.java:43): On stream #1: Khaleesi
⇒ is a senior, they are 93 yrs old.
...task 163] s.AgeChecker.process(AgeChecker.java:43): On stream #1: Grey is
⇒ a senior, they are 65 yrs old.
...     main] RecordFromMultipleFileStreamApp.java:70): Pass #8
...
...     main] RecordFromMultipleFileStreamApp.java:82): <- start()
```

Let's focus on one log line to fully understand what's going on. You may be aware of how Log4j works, but as everybody customizes it a little bit, I wanted to make sure you would be comfortable with the format I used. I split a log entry on several lines:

```
                  2020-11-30 15:30:19.034   <── Timestamp
Thread's          -DEBUG ---                    <─┐
name              [er for task 158]              │  Log level—here, debug
                  s.AgeChecker.process(AgeChecker.java:33):
                  On stream #2: Dimitri is a kid, they are 7 yrs old.   <── Message
```

Class, method, file,
and line number

As you can see from the output in listing 10.11, several threads are active at the same time, processing the data in parallel: the thread called main is the driver, and tasks 158, 159, 161, and 163 are responsible for processing. Results will differ on your system, but you can analyze those to see how many tasks Spark has started. You do not control the number of threads.

Let's go through the code in the following listing.

Listing 10.12   ReadRecordFromMultipleFileStreamApp.java

```java
package net.jgp.books.spark.ch10.lab400_read_records_from_multiple_streams;

import org.apache.spark.sql.Dataset;
import org.apache.spark.sql.Row;
import org.apache.spark.sql.SparkSession;
import org.apache.spark.sql.streaming.OutputMode;
import org.apache.spark.sql.streaming.StreamingQuery;
import org.apache.spark.sql.types.StructType;
import org.slf4j.Logger;
import org.slf4j.LoggerFactory;

import net.jgp.books.spark.ch10.x.utils.streaming.lib.StreamingUtils;

public class ReadRecordFromMultipleFileStreamApp {
  private static transient Logger log = LoggerFactory.getLogger(
      ReadRecordFromMultipleFileStreamApp.class);

  public static void main(String[] args) {
    ReadRecordFromMultipleFileStreamApp app =
        new ReadRecordFromMultipleFileStreamApp();
```

```
        app.start();
    }

    private void start() {
        log.debug("-> start()");

        SparkSession spark = SparkSession.builder()          ⟵ Creates the
            .appName("Read lines over a file stream")            Spark session
            .master("local")
            .getOrCreate();                                   Defines the schema,
                                                              which will be shared
        StructType recordSchema = new StructType()   ⟵      for the two streams
            .add("fname", "string")
            .add("mname", "string")
            .add("lname", "string")
            .add("age", "integer")
            .add("ssn", "string");
```

The first
directory ⟶
```
        String landingDirectoryStream1 = StreamingUtils.getInputDirectory();
        String landingDirectoryStream2 = "/tmp/dir2";   ⟵
```
The second directory—
make sure it exists and
matches the generator

Defines
the first
stream
```
        Dataset<Row> dfStream1 = spark
            .readStream()
            .format("csv")
            .schema(recordSchema)
            .load(landingDirectoryStream1);
```
Defines the
second stream
```
        Dataset<Row> dfStream2 = spark          ⟵
            .readStream()
            .format("csv")
            .schema(recordSchema)
            .load(landingDirectoryStream2);

        StreamingQuery queryStream1 = dfStream1          ⟵
            .writeStream()
            .outputMode(OutputMode.Append())
            .foreach(new AgeChecker(1))
            .start();
```
The records will be processed
by the same writer, a class
called AgeChecker.
```
        StreamingQuery queryStream2 = dfStream2          ⟵
            .writeStream()
            .outputMode(OutputMode.Append())
            .foreach(new AgeChecker(2))
            .start();

        long startProcessing = System.currentTimeMillis();       Loops while
        int iterationCount = 0;                                  the queries
        while (queryStream1.isActive() && queryStream2.isActive()) {  ⟵ are live
            iterationCount++;
            log.debug("Pass #{}", iterationCount);
            if (startProcessing + 60000 < System.currentTimeMillis()) {  ⟵
                queryStream1.stop();
                queryStream2.stop();   │ Stops the queries      Makes sure the process
            }                                                   is running for a minute
            try {
```

```
        Thread.sleep(2000);
      } catch (InterruptedException e) {
        // Simply ignored
      }
    }
    log.debug("<- start()");
  }
}
```

Spark will load the data as it appears in the two directories, and will ask the Age-Checker class to process each row.

The next listing shows the AgeChecker class. It is a fairly simple class that inherits ForeachWriter<Row>. In this lab, the key method to understand is process(), which receives a single row, or record, of the dataframe to be processed.

Listing 10.13   Checking the age with AgeChecker.java

```
package net.jgp.books.spark.ch10.lab300_read_records_from_multiple_streams;

import org.apache.spark.sql.ForeachWriter;
import org.apache.spark.sql.Row;
import org.slf4j.Logger;
import org.slf4j.LoggerFactory;

public class AgeChecker extends ForeachWriter<Row> {
  private static final long serialVersionUID = 8383715100587612498L;
  private static Logger log = LoggerFactory.getLogger(AgeChecker.class);
  private int streamId = 0;
```
In this scenario, you can keep a simple identifier of which stream your data is coming from.
```
  public AgeChecker(int streamId) {   ◁───
    this.streamId = streamId;
  }

  @Override
```
Implement this method when you close your writer; not applicable here.
```
  public void close(Throwable arg0) {   ◁──┘
  }

  @Override
```
Implement this method when you open your writer; not applicable here.
```
  public boolean open(long arg0, long arg1) {   ◁──┘
    return true;
  }

  @Override
```
Method to process a row
```
  public void process(Row arg0) {   ◁───
    if (arg0.length() != 5) {   ◁───
      return;
    }
```
Simple (too simple) quality check to ensure that the record has five columns
```
    int age = arg0.getInt(3);
    if (age < 13) {
      log.debug("On stream #{}: {} is a kid, they are {} yrs old.",
```
Segmentation on the age, then logs the segmentation
```
        streamId,
        arg0.getString(0),
        age);
```

```
    } else if (age > 12 && age < 20) {
      log.debug("On stream #{}: {} is a teen, they are {} yrs old.",
        streamId,
        arg0.getString(0),
        age);
    } else if (age > 64) {
      log.debug("On stream #{}: {} is a senior, they are {} yrs old.",
        streamId,
        arg0.getString(0),
        age);
    }
  }
}
```

To run this application, you need to run two generators at the same time. In two separate terminals, run each generator. You could also run it in your IDE by running each application, but I really recommend having it in a terminal because your output can be messy and hard to read in your IDE.

In the first terminal, run this:

```
$ mvn install exec:java@generate-records-in-files-alt-dir
```

And in the second terminal window, run the exact same generator you used in the first example of this chapter, in subsection 10.2.1:

```
$ mvn install exec:java@generate-records-in-files
```

You can now start your Spark application. The order in which you start the applications does not matter. However, each will run for only one minute. You can also run the lab through mvn clean exec:exec@lab400.

Compared to the previous examples in this chapter, note that you are not using awaitTermination() anymore; it is a blocking operation. You will use a loop to check whether the stream is active, using the isActive() method.

10.5 *Differentiating discretized and structured streaming*

Spark offers two ways of streaming. In this chapter, you have discovered structured streaming. However, Spark started with another type of streaming called *discretized streaming* (or DStream).

In short, Spark v1.*x* used discretized streaming, which relied on RDDs. However, Spark v2.*x* is now focusing on the dataframe (see chapter 3). It made sense to have an evolution of the streaming API to follow the dataframe as well. This switch drastically enhanced performance.

Structured streaming is definitely the way to go, as this API will be enhanced over time. It is expected that the DStream API will be stagnant or made obsolete at some point.

Structured streaming was introduced in alpha status in Spark v2.1.0. Structured streaming has been considered production-ready since Spark v2.2.0.

For more information on *discretized* streaming, check out http://mng.bz/XplE. For more information on *structured* streaming, check out http://mng.bz/yzje.

Summary

- Starting a Spark session is the same whether you are in batch or streaming mode.
- Streaming is a different paradigm from batch processing. One way to see streaming, especially in Spark, is as microbatching.
- You define a stream on a dataframe by using the readStream() method followed by the start() method.
- You can specify ingestion format by using format(), and options by using option().
- The streaming query object, StreamingQuery, will help you query the stream.
- The destination of the data in the query is called a sink. It can be specified by using the format() method or the forEach() method.
- The streamed data is stored in a result table.
- To wait for the data to come, you can use awaitTermination(), which is a blocking method, or check whether the query is active by using the isActive() method.
- You can read from multiple streams at the same time.
- The forEach() method will require a custom writer that lets you process records in a distributed way.
- Streaming as it was done in Spark v1.*x* is called discretized streaming.

Part 3

Transforming
your data

Spark is clearly about transforming data, and I barely touched the surface in the first two parts. It's about time to do some heavy data lifting.

You'll start working with SQL in chapter 11. SQL is not only the de facto standard for manipulating data, but also the lingua franca of all data engineers and data scientists. It seems that SQL has always been around and will clearly be around for a long time. Adding SQL support was a smart move by the creators of Spark. Let's dive into it and understand how it works.

Chapter 12 will teach you how to perform transformations. After an explanation of what transformations are, you'll start by performing record transformations and understanding the classic process of data discovery, data mapping, application engineering, execution, and review. I believe that innovation comes from the intersection of culture, science, and art. This applies to data: it is by joining datasets that you will discover more insightful data. This will be an important part of this chapter.

Just as chapter 12 covers individual records, chapter 13 explores transformation at the document level. You will also build nested documents. Static functions are very helpful in all transformations, and you will learn more about them.

Chapter 14 is all about extending Spark by using user-defined functions. Spark is not a finite system; it can be extended, and you can leverage your existing work.

Aggregations allow us to have this macro vision of data, resulting in more global insights. Getting to use existing and custom aggregation functions is the goal of chapter 15.

Working with SQL

This chapter covers

- Using SQL within Spark
- Determining the local or global scope of your views
- Mixing both the dataframe API and SQL
- Deleting records in a dataframe

Structured Query Language (*SQL*) is the golden standard for manipulating data. Introduced in 1974, it has since evolved to become an ISO standard (ISO/IEC 9075). The latest revision is SQL:2016.

It seems that SQL has been around forever as a way to extract and manipulate data in relational databases. And SQL will be around forever. When I was in college, I clearly remember asking my database professor, "Who do you expect will use SQL? A secretary making a report?" His answer was simply, "Yes." (Based on that answer, I might just figure that you are a secretary who wants to use Spark.)

I realized that SQL was becoming a powerful tool when, a few months later, I used it with Oracle Pro*C. Pro*C is an embedded SQL programming language allowing you to embed SQL in your C applications. Fast-forward to more recent

247

technologies such as Java and JDBC, and you can still contemplate the massive presence SQL has. SQL is still filling your JDBC `RecordSet`.

Based on SQL's popularity and widespread usage, embedding SQL in Spark makes complete sense, especially because you are manipulating structured and semistructured data. In this chapter, you will use SQL with Spark and Java. I will not teach SQL; if your SQL is a little rusty, you will still be able to follow the examples.

You will first manipulate a `SELECT` statement in Spark. You will decide on the scope of a global or local view. You will mix both SQL and the dataframe API. After this, you will see how you can `DROP`/`DELETE` data in an immutable context. Finally, I will share a few external resources to help you go further.

LAB   Examples from this chapter are available in GitHub at https://github .com/jgperrin/net.jgp.books.spark.ch11.

11.1 Working with Spark SQL

In this section, you will discover how to use SQL directly in your application. Spark's SQL is based on standard SQL. You will execute a simple `SELECT` statement, with basic `WHERE`, `ORDER BY`, and `LIMIT` clauses.

In relational databases, the view resides in the database, and your application code invokes the view. In this case, the view is a logical construct that represents the dataframe. The trick to remember when you want to use SQL with Spark is that you need to *define a view*, and the view is the element you are going to query. Let's jump into an example.

In this example, you are going to perform several analytic operations on countries of the world. To help you in this journey, you'll use a dataset containing the world population by territories (countries, continents, and some country subdivisions) from 1980 to 2010. The dataset comes from the US Department of Energy and can be downloaded from https://openei.org/doe-opendata/dataset/population-by-country-1980-2010 or https://catalog.data.gov/dataset/population-by-country-1980-2010.

The file containing the data is populationbycountry19802010millions.csv and is available in the data directory of this chapter's project. It is composed of a first unnamed column and 31 columns for each year from 1980 to 2010. Values for population are in millions. The following listing shows an abstract of the first 15 lines of the file.

Listing 11.1   Abstract of the CSV dataset containing the world's population

```
,1980,1981,1982,1983,1984,1985,1986,1987,1988,1989,1990,1991,1992,…
North America,320.27638,324.44694,328.62014,332.72487,336.72143,34…
Bermuda,0.05473,0.05491,0.05517,0.05551,0.05585,0.05618,0.05651,0.…
Canada,24.5933,24.9,25.2019,25.4563,25.7018,25.9416,26.2038,26.549…
Greenland,0.05021,0.05103,0.05166,0.05211,0.05263,0.05315,0.05364,…
Mexico,68.34748,69.96926,71.6409,73.36288,75.08014,76.76723,78.442…
Saint Pierre and Miquelon,0.00599,0.00601,0.00605,0.00607,0.00611,…
United States,227.22468,229.46571,231.66446,233.79199,235.8249,237…
```

```
Central & South America,293.05856,299.43033,305.95253,312.51136,31…
Antarctica,NA,NA,NA,NA,NA,NA,NA,NA,NA,NA,NA,NA,NA,NA,NA,NA,NA,N…
Antigua and Barbuda,0.06855,0.06826,0.06801,0.06562,0.06447,0.0644…
Argentina,28.3698,28.84806,29.32988,29.79355,30.23064,30.67176,31.…
Aruba,--,--,--,--,--,--,0.0598,0.05918,0.0595,0.06069,0.06303,0.06…
"Bahamas, The",0.20976,0.21345,0.21713,0.22086,0.22462,0.2282,0.23…
Barbados,0.25197,0.25236,0.25348,0.25485,0.25611,0.25725,0.25827,0…
     …
```

I look at an abstract of the data as much as possible, even (or especially) before the ingestion. When you look at listing 11.1, you can see the following:

- Even if the dataset is called *countries*, it mixes continents (for example, North America), territories (for example, Saint Pierre and Miquelon, a French territory strategically placed in front of Canada), and countries (for example, Mexico, Canada, and the United States).
- Data is not always consistent. You'll see NA when data is not available for Antarctica, and -- for Aruba.
- The Bahamas is in quotation marks because of the use of the comma.

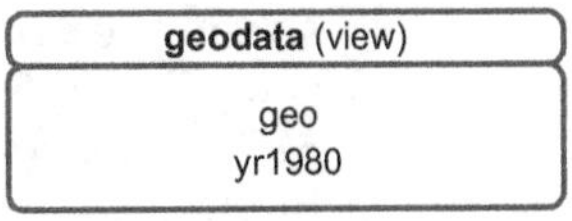

Figure 11.1 illustrates the view as you are going to use it.

Let's display the five smallest territories in ascending order, as of 1980, with population under 1 million, in the following listing.

Figure 11.1 The view used in this lab, with its two columns: geo and yr1980

Listing 11.2 The five smallest territories in 1980

```
Root
 |-- geo: string (nullable = true)        ◄─┐  I also added the schema to get a
 |-- yr1980: double (nullable = true)       │  sense of the structure of the data.


     +---------------------------------+-------+
  ┌─► |geo                              |yr1980 |    ◄─┐  The second (and last)
  │   +---------------------------------+-------+      │  column is yrl980.
  │   |Falkland Islands (Islas Malvinas)|0.002  |
  │   |Niue                             |0.002  |
  │   |Saint Pierre and Miquelon        |0.00599|
  │   |Saint Helena                     |0.00647|
  │   |Turks and Caicos Islands         |0.00747|
  │   +---------------------------------+-------+
  │
The first column is geo.
```

Before you dig into the code, think for a second about the SQL you would generate to get such a result. You have a table or view (let's call it geodata) and two columns (geo and yr1980). To get the first five smallest territories, with a population under 1 million, would you agree with me on the following SQL statement?

```
SELECT * FROM geodata WHERE yr1980 < 1 ORDER BY 2 LIMIT 5
```

Note that this SQL example may not work on all databases. Recent Oracle databases will use FIRST_ROWS, and Informix (prior to v12.1) will use FIRST. If your SQL skills are a little rusty, the following listing splits the action for you.

Listing 11.3   SQL statement to get the smallest five countries under 1 million

The view containing the table

```
SELECT * FROM geodata
    WHERE yr1980 < 1
    ORDER BY 2
    LIMIT 5
```

The column containing the population of 1980, in millions

Ordering by the second column, yr1980

Getting at most five records

> ### Which flavor of SQL?
>
> As you know, despite normalization efforts, every database vendor has subtle differences in the SQL norm. Apache Spark is no different. It is based on Apache Hive's SQL syntax (http://mng.bz/ad2X), but with limitations. Apache Hive's SQL, or HiveQL, is based on SQL-92.
>
> As of now, there is no official Apache Spark SQL reference manual.

Let's see what happens to this query when we have to use it in Spark, as illustrated in listing 11.4. What's noticeable in this example? You're ingesting a file, as in chapter 7, using a schema. Despite the number of columns in the file, the schema defines only the first two; this will give Spark a hint to drop the other columns.

To enable a table-like SQL usage in Spark, you have to create a view. The scope can be local (to the session) as you just did, or global (to the application). You can find more details on local versus global scopes in the next section.

Note that in this lab, the data will be loaded in Spark, and then you will limit the data displayed by the query.

Listing 11.4   SimpleSelectApp.java: executing a SELECT statement

```java
package net.jgp.books.spark.ch11_lab100_simple_select;

import org.apache.spark.sql.Dataset;
import org.apache.spark.sql.Row;
import org.apache.spark.sql.SparkSession;
import org.apache.spark.sql.types.DataTypes;
import org.apache.spark.sql.types.StructField;
import org.apache.spark.sql.types.StructType;

public class SimpleSelectApp {

  public static void main(String[] args) {
    SimpleSelectApp app = new SimpleSelectApp();
```

```
        app.start();
    }

    private void start() {
        SparkSession spark = SparkSession.builder()      <─── Gets a session
            .appName("Simple SELECT using SQL")
            .master("local")
            .getOrCreate();                                           Creates a schema

        StructType schema = DataTypes.createStructType(new StructField[] {  <──┘
            DataTypes.createStructField(
                "geo",
                DataTypes.StringType,
                true),
            DataTypes.createStructField(
                "yr1980",
                DataTypes.DoubleType,
                false) });
                                                          Ingests from the CSV
                                                          file to a dataframe
        Dataset<Row> df = spark.read().format("csv")   <──┘
            .option("header", true)
            .schema(schema)
            .load("data/populationbycountry19802010millions.csv");
        df.createOrReplaceTempView("geodata");
        df.printSchema();                              <─
                                                          Prints the schema,
                                                          showing two columns
        Dataset<Row> smallCountries =
            spark.sql(
                "SELECT * FROM geodata WHERE yr1980 < 1 ORDER BY 2 LIMIT 5");

        smallCountries.show(10, false);          <─── Displays the new dataframe
    }
}
```

Creates a session-scoped temporary view points to `df.createOrReplaceTempView("geodata");`

Executes the query points to `spark.sql(`

Creating a local temporary view is fairly simple: use the `createOrReplaceTempView()` dataframe's method. The argument will be your table/view name. As I said earlier, you can use `geodata` (or anything you like).

Your next operation is to use the `sql()` method of the Spark session. There you can use the very same SQL statement you designed in listing 11.3. No modification is needed. The result is available as a dataframe, so you can use the `show()` method for debugging, as well as other APIs.

In the next section, you will learn a bit about the difference between local and global views.

11.2 The difference between local and global views

In the previous section, you ran your first Spark statement against a local view. Spark also offers global views. Let's see what the differences are.

LAB The lab (lab #200) reflecting this section is called SimpleSelect-GlobalViewApp and is in the net.jgp.books.spark.ch11.lab200_simple_select _global_view package.

The next listing illustrates the result you want: display the five smallest territories with fewer than 1 million inhabitants (as in the previous section). You will also display the five smallest territories with more than 1 million inhabitants.

```
Listing 11.5   Small countries
```
```
root
 |-- geo: string (nullable = true)
 |-- yr1980: double (nullable = true)

+-------------------------------+-------+
|geo                            |yr1980 |
+-------------------------------+-------+
|Falkland Islands (Islas Malvinas)|0.002  |
|Niue                           |0.002  |
|Saint Pierre and Miquelon      |0.00599|
|Saint Helena                   |0.00647|
|Turks and Caicos Islands       |0.00747|
+-------------------------------+-------+


+--------------------+-------+
|geo                 |yr1980 |
+--------------------+-------+
|United Arab Emirates|1.00029|
|Trinidad and Tobago |1.09051|
|Oman                |1.18548|
|Lesotho             |1.35857|
|Kuwait              |1.36977|
+--------------------+-------+
```

Whether you are using a local or global view, views are only temp (for temporary). When the session ends, the local views are removed; when all sessions end, the global views are removed.

The first part of the code in listing 11.6 is similar to listing 11.4. You open a session and ingest the file, but when it comes to creating the view, you will use the create-OrReplaceGlobalTempView() dataframe method (instead of createOrReplace-TempView()). When you use the view in your SQL statement, you will have to prefix the table name with the global_temp table space because you are in the global space. In this scenario, it means that you will use global_temp.geodata.

Figure 11.2 shows the view as a global view.

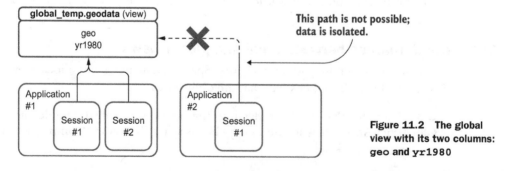

Figure 11.2   The global view with its two columns: geo and yr1980

Listing 11.6　Abstract of SimpleSelectGlobalViewApp.java

Creates the global view

```
df.createOrReplaceGlobalTempView("geodata");
Dataset<Row> smallCountriesDf =
    spark.sql(
        "SELECT * FROM global_temp.geodata "
        + "WHERE yr1980 < 1 ORDER BY 2 LIMIT 5");
smallCountriesDf.show(10, false);

SparkSession spark2 = spark.newSession();
Dataset<Row> slightlyBiggerCountriesDf =
    spark2.sql(
        "SELECT * FROM global_temp.geodata "
        + "WHERE yr1980 > 1 ORDER BY 2 LIMIT 5");
slightlyBiggerCountriesDf.show(10, false);
```

SQL query using the global_temp tablespace

Creates a new session

As you create a new session, your data is still available in both sessions, and this is where you can use global views.

> **Why would you need multiple Spark sessions?**
>
> When you start a new session with `newSession()`, you will get isolated SQL configurations, temporary tables, and registered functions. You will still share the underlying `SparkContext` and cached data.
>
> Use cases could be increased isolation of your data, isolation of a process, having a server in front of Spark handling different requests for different users, specific session tuning, and more. Needless to say, running multiple sessions is not a common case.

11.3　*Mixing the dataframe API and Spark SQL*

In the previous sections, you saw how to use SQL with a dataframe. Now, you will see that you do not have to compromise; you can easily combine SQL and the dataframe API, in order to build more powerful applications.

LAB　The lab (lab #300) reflecting this section is called SqlAndApiApp and is in the net.jgp.books.spark.ch11.lab300SqlAndApi package.

In this lab, you will prepare the data by using the dataframe API, which you saw in previous examples and will see more of in chapter 12. Then, you will apply SQL queries to do some basic analytics:

- You will find out which countries lost the most population between 1980 and 2010.
- You will find out the top growth in territories during the same period.

The output is similar to the following listing.

Listing 11.7   Output of combining API and SQL to deliver analytics

```
+----------------------------+---------+---------+-----------+
|geo                         |yr1980   |yr2010   |evolution  |
+----------------------------+---------+---------+-----------+
|Bulgaria                    |8.84353  |7.14879  |-1694740.0|
|Hungary                     |10.71112 |9.99234  |-718780.0 |
|Romania                     |22.13004 |21.95928 |-170760.0 |
|Guyana                      |0.75935  |0.74849  |-10860.0  |
|Montserrat                  |0.01177  |0.00512  |-6650.0   |
|Cook Islands                |0.01801  |0.01149  |-6520.0   |
|Netherlands Antilles        |0.23244  |0.22869  |-3750.0   |
|Dominica                    |0.07389  |0.07281  |-1080.0   |
|Saint Pierre and Miquelon|0.00599  |0.00594  |-50.0     |
+----------------------------+---------+---------+-----------+

+----------------------------+----------+----------+------------+
|geo                         |yr1980    |yr2010    |evolution   |
+----------------------------+----------+----------+------------+
|World                       |4451.32679|6853.01941|2.40169262E9|
|Asia & Oceania              |2469.81743|3799.67028|1.32985285E9|
|Africa                      |478.96479 |1015.47842|5.3651363E8 |
|India                       |684.8877  |1173.10802|4.8822032E8 |
|China                       |984.73646 |1330.14129|3.4540483E8 |
|Central & South America|293.05856 |480.01228 |1.8695372E8 |
|North America               |320.27638 |456.59331 |1.3631693E8 |
|Middle East                 |93.78699  |212.33692 |1.1854993E8 |
|Pakistan                    |85.21912  |184.40479 |9.918567E7  |
|Indonesia                   |151.0244  |242.96834 |9.194394E7  |
|United States               |227.22468 |310.23286 |8.300818E7  |
|Brazil                      |123.01963 |201.10333 |7.80837E7   |
|Nigeria                     |74.82127  |152.21734 |7.739607E7  |
|Europe                      |529.50082 |606.00344 |7.650262E7  |
|Bangladesh                  |87.93733  |156.11846 |6.818113E7  |
+----------------------------+----------+----------+------------+
only showing top 15 rows
```

Let's see how you, as a data engineer, can extract those results and give them to an analyst (even a political analyst) using Spark. The process of combining API and SQL is illustrated in the following listing.

Listing 11.8   SqlAndApiApp.java

```java
package net.jgp.books.spark.ch11_lab300_sql_and_api;

import org.apache.spark.sql.Dataset;
import org.apache.spark.sql.Row;
import org.apache.spark.sql.SparkSession;
import org.apache.spark.sql.functions;
import org.apache.spark.sql.types.DataTypes;
import org.apache.spark.sql.types.StructField;
```

```java
import org.apache.spark.sql.types.StructType;

public class SqlAndApiApp {

  public static void main(String[] args) {
    SqlAndApiApp app = new SqlAndApiApp();
    app.start();
  }

  private void start() {
    SparkSession spark = SparkSession.builder()
        .appName("Simple SQL")
        .master("local")
        .getOrCreate();

    StructType schema = DataTypes.createStructType(new StructField[] {
        DataTypes.createStructField(
            "geo",
            DataTypes.StringType,
            true),
        DataTypes.createStructField(
            "yr1980",
            DataTypes.DoubleType,
            false),
        DataTypes.createStructField(
            "yr1981",
            DataTypes.DoubleType,
            false),

...

        DataTypes.createStructField(
            "yr2010",
            DataTypes.DoubleType,
            false) });
```

Creates the schema for the whole dataset

```java
    Dataset<Row> df = spark.read().format("csv")
        .option("header", true)
        .schema(schema)
        .load("data/populationbycountry19802010millions.csv");

    for (int i = 1981; i < 2010; i++) {
      df = df.drop(df.col("yr" + i));
    }
```

Removes the extra columns by using the dataframe API

```java
    df = df.withColumn(
        "evolution",
        functions.expr("round((yr2010 - yr1980) * 1000000)"));
    df.createOrReplaceTempView("geodata");

    Dataset<Row> negativeEvolutionDf =
        spark.sql(
            "SELECT * FROM geodata "
            + "WHERE geo IS NOT NULL AND evolution<=0 "
            + "ORDER BY evolution "
            + "LIMIT 25");
```

Creates a new column called evolution

```
    negativeEvolutionDf.show(15, false);

    Dataset<Row> moreThanAMillionDf =
        spark.sql(
            "SELECT * FROM geodata "
            + "WHERE geo IS NOT NULL AND evolution>999999 "
            + "ORDER BY evolution DESC "
            + "LIMIT 25");
    moreThanAMillionDf.show(15, false);
  }
}
```

The application drops a few columns we do not want (basically, all the columns from 1981 to 2009, as we focus on 1980 and 2010), using the dataframe API. It then creates a new column with the evolution of the population between 1980 and 2010, once more, using the dataframe API.

At this stage, you have a cleaned and formatted dataset. You can query it by using SQL and display the result.

11.4 *Don't DELETE it!*

When you deal with data and SQL, it's not only about SELECTing them, it's also about DELETing them. Basically, you can refer to the CRUD (create, read, update, and delete) acronym for all data operations. This section covers deleting the data in a dataframe.

In the previous sections, you used geographical data from the US Department of Energy. The dataset mixes countries, local territories, continents, and the world, so it's not perfect for analytics. The previous lab's output (listing 11.7, partially copied here as listing 11.9) illustrates this situation.

Listing 11.9 Consistency issues in the dataset

```
+----------------------+----------+----------+------------+
|geo                   |yr1980    |yr2010    |evolution   |
+----------------------+----------+----------+------------+
|World                 |4451.32679|6853.01941|2.40169262E9|     ⟵── The world!
|Asia & Oceania        |2469.81743|3799.67028|1.32985285E9|
|Africa                |478.96479 |1015.47842|5.3651363E8 |     │  Continents
|India                 |684.8877  |1173.10802|4.8822032E8 |
|China                 |984.73646 |1330.14129|3.4540483E8 |     │  Countries
...

+----------------------+----------+----------+------------+
only showing top 15 rows
```

As you read in chapter 3, a dataframe in Spark is immutable; the data doesn't change. If you do not remember all the subtleties precisely, that's okay; data does not change; Spark keeps track of the changes in the data, like a cooking recipe, and stores it in a directed acyclic graph (DAG), as you read about in chapter 4.

So, if the data is immutable, how can you alter a dataframe? You certainly cannot use a DELETE SQL statement; you cannot modify the data (it's immutable!). The following listing illustrates what you want: a cleaned dataset, which includes only countries and territories and no continents.

Listing 11.10   Desired dataset without continents

Number of entries in original dataset

Number of entries in cleaned dataset

```
...op.DropApp.start(DropApp.java:36): -> start()
...op.DropApp.start(DropApp.java:193): Territories in orginal dataset: 232
...op.DropApp.start(DropApp.java:206): Territories in cleaned dataset: 215
+----------------+--------+---------+----------+
|geo             |yr1980  |yr2010   |evolution |
+----------------+--------+---------+----------+
|China           |984.73646|1330.14129|3.4540483E8|
|India           |684.8877 |1173.10802|4.8822032E8|
|United States   |227.22468|310.23286|8.300818E7 |
|Indonesia       |151.0244 |242.96834|9.194394E7 |
|Brazil          |123.01963|201.10333|7.80837E7  |
|Pakistan        |85.21912 |184.40479|9.918567E7 |
|Bangladesh      |87.93733 |156.11846|6.818113E7 |
|Nigeria         |74.82127 |152.21734|7.739607E7 |
|Japan           |116.80731|126.80443|9997120.0  |
|Mexico          |68.34748 |112.46886|4.412138E7 |
|Philippines     |50.94018 |99.90018 |4.896E7    |
|Vietnam         |53.7152  |89.57113 |3.585593E7 |
|Ethiopia        |38.6052  |88.01349 |4.940829E7 |
|Egypt           |42.63422 |80.47187 |3.783765E7 |
|Turkey          |45.04797 |77.80412 |3.275615E7 |
|Iran            |39.70873 |76.9233  |3.721457E7 |
|Congo (Kinshasa)|29.01255 |70.91644 |4.190389E7 |
|Thailand        |47.02576 |67.0895  |2.006374E7 |
|France          |53.98766 |63.33964 |9351980.0  |
|United Kingdom  |56.51888 |62.61254 |6093660.0  |
+----------------+--------+---------+----------+
only showing top 20 rows
```

Only countries (and territories)

The way to go is pretty simple: you are going to create a new dataframe that does not include the data you do not want.

LAB   Based on the lab of section 11.3, you can look at lab #400, DeleteApp, in the net.jgp.books.spark.ch11_lab400_delete package.

Listing 11.11 focuses on the changes from the previous lab (#300). When you want to delete the rows, here is what is happening:

- As you did in the previous examples, you load/ingest the data in a first dataframe (not shown in listing 11.10). This dataframe is called df.
- You create a view, called geodata.

- You run your SQL statement on geodata, which acts as a filter. Here, it will exclude the world and all the continents, creating a new dataset with countries and territories.
- The result is stored in a new dataframe called cleanedDf.

Listing 11.11 Deleting data from a dataframe

```
package net.jgp.books.spark.ch11_lab400_drop;
...
public class DeleteApp {
...
    df.createOrReplaceTempView("geodata");

    log.debug("Territories in orginal dataset: {}", df.count());
Dataset<Row> cleanedDf =
        spark.sql(
            "select * from geodata where geo is not null "
            + "and geo != 'Africa' "
            + "and geo != 'North America' "
            + "and geo != 'World' "
            + "and geo != 'Asia & Oceania' "
            + "and geo != 'Central & South America' "
            + "and geo != 'Europe' "
            + "and geo != 'Eurasia' "
            + "and geo != 'Middle East' "
            + "order by yr2010 desc");
    log.debug("Territories in cleaned dataset: {}",
        cleanedDf.count());
    cleanedDf.show(20, false);
    }
}
```

Counts the number of entries in the ingested (and transformed) dataframe

Creates a new dataframe

SQL query to "clean" the initial dataframe

Counts the number of entries in the cleaned dataframe

11.5 *Going further with SQL*

In the previous sections, you saw how to use basic SQL statements and the general mechanics for dropping rows from one dataset to another. This section provides information about resources to help you learn more about using SQL with Spark.

The SparkSession.table() method is worth mentioning. The method returns the specified view as a dataframe, directly from the session, enabling you to avoid passing references to the dataframe itself.

You can find a Spark SQL guide at http://mng.bz/gVnG. Databricks also provides a guide on SQL at http://mng.bz/eD6q. However, it mixes SQL for Apache Spark and Delta Lake, the Databricks database (used in chapter 17).

Spark's SQL is based on Apache Hive's syntax. Apache Hive's syntax can be found at http://mng.bz/ad2X. Limits to the compatibility are described at http://mng.bz/O90a.

Summary

- Spark supports Structured Query Language (SQL) as a query language to inter-rogate data.
- Spark's SQL is based on Apache Hive's SQL (HiveQL), which is based on SQL-92.
- You can mix API and SQL in your application.
- Data is manipulated through views on top of a dataframe.
- Views can be local to the session, or global/shared among sessions in the same application. Views are never shared between applications.
- Because data is immutable, you cannot drop or modify records; you will have to re-create a new dataset.
- To drop records from the dataframe, however, you can build a new dataframe based on a filtered dataframe.

Transforming your data

This chapter is probably the cornerstone of the book. All the knowledge you gathered through the first 11 chapters has brought you to these key questions: "Once I have all this data, how can I transform it, and what can I do with it?"

Apache Spark is all about data transformation, but what precisely is data transformation? How can you perform such transformations in a repeatable and procedural way? Think of it as an industrial process that will ensure that your data is adequately and reliably transformed.

In this chapter, you will perform record-level transformation: manipulating the data at an atomic level, cell by cell, column by column. To perform your labs, you will use the US Census Bureau's report of population in all the counties of all the states and territories of the United States. You will extract information so you can build a different dataset.

Once you know how to transform data within a single dataset, you will join the datasets by using joins, just as you do with an SQL database. You will briefly see the various types of joins. Appendix M details all the kinds of joins for your reference. You will work with two additional datasets: a list of higher education institutions coming from the US Department of Education and a convenient mapping file maintained by the US Department of Housing and Urban Development.

Finally, I will point you to more transformations present in the repository but not described in the book.

I believe that using real-life datasets from official sources can help you understand the concepts more thoroughly. This process definitely simulates issues like the ones you are or will be facing in your day-to-day job. However, as with real data, you will have to go through the hurdle of formatting and understanding the data. Teaching you this process adds to the length of this chapter.

LAB Examples from this chapter are available in GitHub at https://github .com/jgperrin/net.jgp.books.spark.ch12.

12.1 *What is data transformation?*

Data transformation is the process of converting data from one format or structure into another. In this short section, you will read more about the types of data that can be transformed as well as the types of transformations you will be able to perform. Data can be of several types:

- Data can be structured and well organized, like tables and columns in relational databases.
- Data can be in the form of documents, in a semistructured way. Those documents are often seen in NoSQL databases.
- Data can be raw, completely unstructured, like a *binary large object* (*blob*) or document.

Data transformations change the data either from one type to another or within the same type. Transformations can apply to several aspects of the data:

- At the record level: you can modify the values directly in the record (or row).
- At the column level: you can create and drop columns in the dataframe.
- In the metadata/structure of the dataframe.

Figure 12.1 summarizes where transformations can take place.

Apache Spark is a good candidate for any data transformations; the size of the data does not really matter. Spark shines when data is structured and organized, but can be easily extended for more blobby (from *blob*) and obscure data. Chapter 9 gave you an idea of this when you ingested metadata from photos.

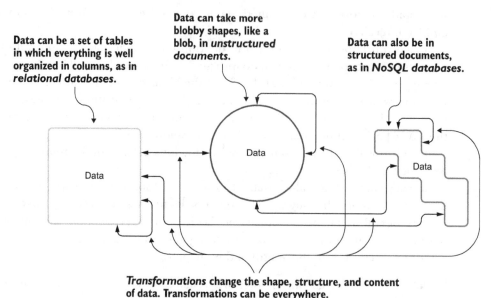

Data can be a set of tables in which everything is well organized in columns, as in *relational databases.*

Data can take more blobby shapes, like a blob, in *unstructured documents.*

Data can also be in structured documents, as in *NoSQL databases.*

Transformations change the shape, structure, and content of data. Transformations can be everywhere.

Figure 12.1   Data can take many shapes, whether structured or unstructured. Transformations can happen between the shapes or within the same shape.

In the next section, you will transform data at a record level and then at a larger document level.

12.2   *Process and example of record-level transformation*

In this section, you will transform data at a record level. This means you'll be extracting raw data from a dataframe and generating new data from calculations. To do so, you will follow a proper methodology: data discovery, data mapping, the data transformation itself (design of the transformation and execution), and finally data validation.

To fully grasp this process of transformation, you will perform some analytics on the population data coming from the US Census Bureau (https://factfinder.census .gov).

> **LAB**   The data is available in the repository in the data/census directory. The lab is #200 and can be found in the net.jgp.books.sparkInAction.ch12.lab200 _record_transformation package.

You are going to transform the Census Bureau's dataset from the raw data to a new dataset, which does the following:

- Makes the counties and states more apparent
- Measures the difference between the population counted in 2010 and the population estimated for the same year
- Estimates the population growth between 2010 and 2017

Table 12.1 illustrates the expected result. I turned the ugly ASCII-art-like output into a nicer, more readable table! In this output table, you can see the following:

- States and counties very clearly
- The difference between the counted population in 2010 and its estimation in the diff column
- The estimated growth between 2010 and 2017

Table 12.1 End result showing renamed columns, difference between counted and estimated data, and growth between 2010 and 2017

stateId	countyId	state	county	diff
growth	13	11	Georgia	Banks County
26	213	13	195	Georgia
Madison County	43	1139	13	213
Georgia	Murray County	–85	239	17
17	Illinois	Cass County	–7	–1130
18	63	Indiana	Hendricks County	436
17801				

Let's run this lab using Apache Spark. However, before we jump into the code, we need to follow a simple five-step process. Data transformation can be divided into these steps:

1. Data discovery
2. Data mapping
3. Application engineering/writing
4. Application execution
5. Data review

Figure 12.2 illustrates the process in a graphical way and gives a few hints about each step.

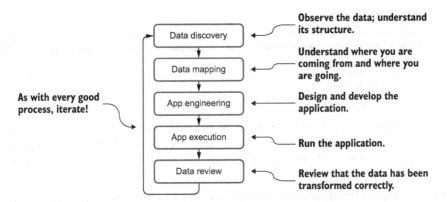

Figure 12.2 Full data transformation process in five steps, with a highlight of each major step. Do not forget to iterate to enhance the quality of your transformation.

Let's detail all these steps by following an example.

12.2.1 Data discovery to understand the complexity

In this subsection, you will perform a typical data discovery: you'll look at the data and understand its structure. This is an essential operation before data mapping. By looking at the data (for example, opening a CSV or JSON file), you'll get the gist of what its complexity could be. Ideally, the data will come with an explanation about the structure, saying what field represents what. If there is no explanation, ask for it; but, unfortunately, based on my experience, be ready to reverse engineer.

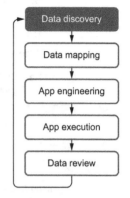

Figure 12.3 Data discovery is the first step of the data transformation process.

Figure 12.3 shows where we are in the process of data transformation.

As with every data transformation project, you start by looking at the data and its structure (also called *data discovery*). After that, you will build the mapping, write the transformation code, run the code, and finally analyze the result.

The following listing shows a small abstract of the data in its raw form, CSV. The file is in /data/census/PEP_2017_PEPANNRES.csv.

Listing 12.1 Abstract of the census data

```
GEO.id,GEO.id2,GEO.display-label,rescen42010,resbase42010,respop72010,
respop72011,respop72012,respop72013,respop72014,respop72015,
➥ respop72016, respop72017
...
0500000US37135,37135,"Orange County, North Carolina",133801,133688,133950,
➥ 134962,137946,139430,140399,141563,142723,144946
```

Table 12.2 shows the data as a table. It definitely helps, but to go to the next step, we need the schema.

Table 12.2 Table representation

GEO.id	GEO.id2	GEO.display-label	rescen42010	resbase42010	respop72010	...	respop72017
0500000U S37135	37135	Orange County, North Carolina	133801	133688	133950	...	144946

Table 12.3 provides the schema (or metadata). This table was built by looking at the metadata description file provided by the Census Bureau. This file is in the repository: /data/census/PEP_2017_PEPANNRES_metadata.csv. The first column (field name) and second column (definition) come with the dataset from the Census Bureau. The third column contains comments that will help you build the mapping.

Table 12.3 Structure of the raw data coming from the US Census Bureau

Field name	Definition	Comment
GEO.id	ID	Will not be used
GEO.id2	ID 2	Five-digit code, see figure 12.1
GEO.display-label	Geography	Label using the "county, state" format
rescen42010	April 1, 2010 - Census	
resbase42010	April 1, 2010 - Estimates Base	Will not be used
respop72010	Population Estimate (as of July 1) - 2010	
respop72011	Population Estimate (as of July 1) - 2011	
respop72012	Population Estimate (as of July 1) - 2012	
respop72013	Population Estimate (as of July 1) - 2013	
respop72014	Population Estimate (as of July 1) - 2014	
respop72015	Population Estimate (as of July 1) - 2015	
respop72016	Population Estimate (as of July 1) - 2016	
respop72017	Population Estimate (as of July 1) - 2017	

Figure 12.4 explains the structure of the id2 field used by the Census Bureau.

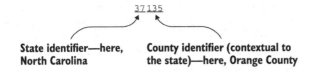

State identifier—here, North Carolina

County identifier (contextual to the state)—here, Orange County

Figure 12.4 Understanding the US Census Bureau's id2 field: the two first digits indicate the state, and the last three indicate the county.

12.2.2 Data mapping to draw the process

Now that you have analyzed the data and its structure, it is time to map the data between the origin and the destination. This operation, called *data mapping*, is essential before you can develop the application: it maps the origin to the destination data and structure. You are literally drawing the transformation process. Figure 12.5 shows where you are in the process.

Before starting the mapping process, let's look at the expected result in table 12.4 (similar to table 12.1). In this table, you see states and counties, the difference between the measured (by the agents of the Census Bureau) data and their initial estimation in the diff column, and the growth between 2010 and 2017.

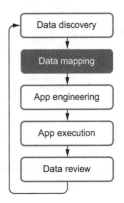

Figure 12.5 Data mapping explains where the data is coming from and where it is going, like a map.

Table 12.4   End result showing new column names, states and counties, difference between counted and estimated data, and growth between 2010 and 2017

stateId	countyId	state	county	diff	growth
13	11	Georgia	Banks County	26	213
18	63	Indiana	Hendricks County	436	17801

The mapping process helps you figure out what you are going to do with the data. The process is illustrated in figure 12.6.

In this scenario, I am using an intermediate dataframe. The intermediate dataframe is like any other dataframe but does not provide direct business value. Using an intermediate dataframe is a good idea, as it can provide the following:

- A cleaner version of the data, formatted as you like
- A dataframe where you can have all your data quality rules applied (more on data quality in chapter 14)
- A cacheable or checkpointed dataframe, which you will be able to reuse faster (more on caches and checkpoints in chapter 16)

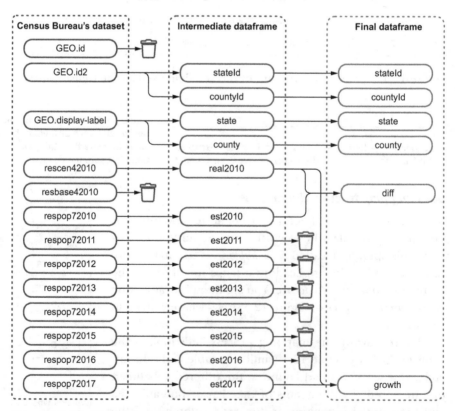

Figure 12.6   Mapping of the Census Bureau's data to an intermediate dataframe and then to the final dataframe with our analytics. From there, you will be able to build your application.

Performance is not affected negatively by using an intermediate dataframe. Performance can be boosted if you cache or checkpoint the data. Chapter 16 provides more details on performance tuning.

What's the point of caching when everything is in memory?

If you have enough memory, everything is stored in memory, right? So why would you cache data? This seems a legitimate question you could ask.

Remember: Spark is lazy and does not perform all the operations (the transformations), unless you ask it explicitly (through an action).

If you plan on reusing a dataframe for different analyses, it is a good idea to cache your data by using the cache() method. It will increase performance. Chapter 16 details those operations.

The following image illustrates what happens when you do not cache your data: operations 1, 2, 3, and 4 are done again each time.

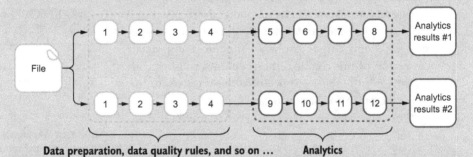

The data preparation steps are executed each time you run an analytics pipeline; this can be optimized by using the cache() method.

The following image illustrates the effect of caching your dataframe: operations 1, 2, 3, and 4 are done only once.

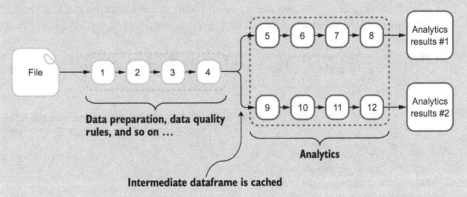

The data preparation steps are done only once. Both analytics pipelines will use the cached dataframe, resulting in better performance.

Table 12.5 shows the content of the intermediate dataframe, with quality data.

Table 12.5   Intermediate dataframe representation

stateId	countyId	state	county	real2010	est2010	est2011	...	est2017
37	135	North Carolina	Orange County	133801	133950	134962	...	144946

Now that the mapping is done, you are ready to write your application.

12.2.3 *Writing the transformation code*

I know—this is the subsection you have been waiting for. Let's write code, manipulate more APIs, and stop the analysis, as illustrated in figure 12.7. I could have jumped directly to producing code, but I feel strongly that good professionals do not take shortcuts, especially when it comes to developing good habits. Therefore, although this is probably the most important subsection of this chapter when it comes to pure coding, it is not the most important when it comes to the entire data transformation process.

The first step is to build this intermediate dataframe:

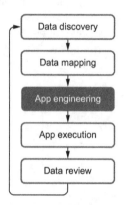

1 Remove the columns you do not want: GEO.id and resbase42010.

2 Split the ID (GEO.id2) and GEO.display-label columns.

3 Rename the columns.

Figure 12.7   Application engineering is the third step of five in data transformation. Nevertheless, developers tend to jump to the phase of application engineering, although the previous two phases are critical to the success of your transformation.

The following listing shows the code to build the intermediate dataframe. As usual, I left out the import statements, so you are not confused by which library you are using.

Listing 12.2   RecordTransformationApp.java: Creating the intermediate dataframe

```
package net.jgp.books.spark.ch12.lab200_record_transformation;

import static org.apache.spark.sql.functions.expr;        Static methods for
import static org.apache.spark.sql.functions.split;       data transformation

import org.apache.spark.sql.Dataset;
import org.apache.spark.sql.Row;
import org.apache.spark.sql.SparkSession;

public class RecordTransformationApp {
  ...
  private void start() {
```

```
SparkSession spark = SparkSession.builder()    ⟵ Creates the session
    .appName("Record transformations")
    .master("local")
    .getOrCreate();

Dataset<Row> intermediateDf = spark       ⟵ Ingests the census data
    .read()
    .format("csv")
    .option("header", "true")
    .option("inferSchema", "true")
    .load("data/census/PEP_2017_PEPANNRES.csv");

intermediateDf = intermediateDf            ⟵ Renames and drops columns
    .drop("GEO.id")
    .withColumnRenamed("GEO.id2", "id")
    .withColumnRenamed("GEO.display-label", "label")
    .withColumnRenamed("rescen42010", "real2010")
    .drop("resbase42010")
    .withColumnRenamed("respop72010", "est2010")
    .withColumnRenamed("respop72011", "est2011")
    .withColumnRenamed("respop72012", "est2012")
    .withColumnRenamed("respop72013", "est2013")
    .withColumnRenamed("respop72014", "est2014")
    .withColumnRenamed("respop72015", "est2015")
    .withColumnRenamed("respop72016", "est2016")
    .withColumnRenamed("respop72017", "est2017");
```

Creates the additional columns ⟶

```
intermediateDf = intermediateDf
    .withColumn(
        "countyState",
        split(intermediateDf.col("label"), ", "))    ⟵
    .withColumn("stateId", expr("int(id/1000)"))
    .withColumn("countyId", expr("id%1000"));    ⟵
intermediateDf.printSchema();
```

Extracts the state's ID from the ID ⟶

Splits the column label using the ", " regular expression, allowing you to split county and state from the "county, state"

Extracts the county's ID from the ID

Let's stop here for a moment and analyze the data and structure you have built. At this stage, the schema looks like this:

```
root
 |-- id: integer (nullable = true)
 |-- label: string (nullable = true)
 |-- real2010: integer (nullable = true)
 |-- est2010: integer (nullable = true)
...
 |-- est2017: integer (nullable = true)
 |-- countyState: array (nullable = true)
 |    |-- element: string (containsNull = true)
 |-- stateId: integer (nullable = true)
 |-- countyId: integer (nullable = true)
```

Representation of the structure of an array

Representation of the array's elements

The label column has been split using the split() static method. split() will apply a regular expression on a column's value and create an array of values. Figure 12.8 illustrates the use of split().

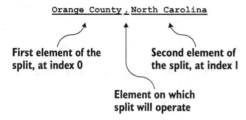

Figure 12.8   You can use the `split()` function to extract the county and the state, and the result is stored in an array.

When you ingest the initial file, the data looks like this:

```
|1007|Bibb County, Alabama|   22915|  22872|  22745|  22658|…
```

Look at how the county and state name is represented: `Bibb County, Alabama`. After you use the `split()` function, the string is transformed to an array, as indicated by the square brackets (`[]`) around the value: `[Bibb County, Alabama]`. Therefore, the ASCII table representation resembles this:

```
+-----+…+-------+----------------------------+-------+--------+
|id   |…|est2017|countyState                 |stateId|countyId|
+-----+…+-------+----------------------------+-------+--------+
|4021 |…|430237 |[Pinal County, Arizona]     |4      |21      |    | Representation
|12019|…|212230 |[Clay County, Florida]      |12     |19      |    | of an array
|12029|…|16673  |[Dixie County, Florida]     |12     |29      |    | using [ ]
…
```

Figure 12.9 reminds you of how the `id` is composed. To extract the `stateId` from the `id` column, you can simply divide by 1,000 and cast to an int. To ask Spark to do it, you will call the `expr()` method, which computes an SQL-like expression in this case:

```
.withColumn("stateId", expr("int(id/1000)"))
```

Similarly, to extract the county's `id`, you can retrieve the modulo (rest of the division) by 1,000:

```
.withColumn("countyId", expr("id%1000"))
```

Listing 12.3 continues building the intermediate dataframe, by extracting the countyState array's elements. Therefore, your dataset will not have nested elements but only linearized data to build, like a basic table. You see that the county (or parish in Louisiana) is the first (index 0) element of the countyState array, and the state is the second (index of 1) element in the same array.

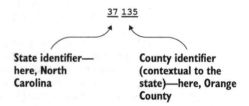

Figure 12.9   Decomposition of the county's ID: the two first digits represent the state, while the last three represent the county.

Listing 12.3   Next steps in creating the intermediate dataframe

```
intermediateDf = intermediateDf
    .withColumn(                              Extracts the second element
        "state",                              of the array at index I
        intermediateDf.col("countyState").getItem(1))  ⟵
    .withColumn(                                                        Extracts the
        "county",                                                      second element
        intermediateDf.col("countyState").getItem(0))  ⟵              of the array at
    .drop("countyState");                                              index 0
intermediateDf.printSchema();
intermediateDf.sample(.01).show(5, false);        ⟵  Shows a sample of the data
...
```

Drops unneeded column

As you see, the getItem() method returns an element of an array in a column. If you ask for an item that does not exist in an array (for example, the fourth one), getItem() will return null—which, I hope you will agree, is nicer than having to handle an ArrayIndexOutOfBoundsException.

You may have noticed the use of the sample() method before show(): this allows you to extract a random sample (without statistical replacement; see the following sidebar) of your dataset. The parameter is a double between 0 and 1, indicating the percentage of rows you want to shuffle. The sample() method has other forms, where you can specify whether you want replacement (see sidebar) or specify a random seed. For more information, jump to http://mng.bz/dxQX.

The following listing illustrates the result of the sampling on two executions.

Listing 12.4   Sampling results

First execution:
```
+-----+...+-------+-------+--------+--------+----------------------------+
|id   |...|est2017|stateId|countyId|state   |county                      |
+-----+...+-------+-------+--------+--------+----------------------------+
|2090 |...|99703  |2      |90      |Alaska  |Fairbanks North Star Borough|
|8113 |...|7967   |8      |113     |Colorado|San Miguel County           |
|13237|...|21730  |13     |237     |Georgia |Putnam County               |
|16059|...|7875   |16     |59      |Idaho   |Lemhi County                |
|17011|...|33243  |17     |11      |Illinois|Bureau County               |
+-----+...+-------+-------+--------+--------+----------------------------+
only showing top 5 rows
```
Second execution:
```
+-----+...+-------+-------+--------+----------+-----------------+
|id   |...|est2017|stateId|countyId|state     |county           |
+-----+...+-------+-------+--------+----------+-----------------+
|5033 |...|62996  |5      |33      |Arkansas  |Crawford County  |
|5145 |...|79016  |5      |145     |Arkansas  |White County     |
|6069 |...|60310  |6      |69      |California|San Benito County|
|13063|...|285153 |13     |63      |Georgia   |Clayton County   |
|13191|...|14106  |13     |191     |Georgia   |McIntosh County  |
+-----+...+-------+-------+--------+----------+-----------------+
only showing top 5 rows
```

To replace or not to replace? This is a statistical question!

Mary Parker, an associate professor in the Department of Statistics and Data Science at the University of Texas at Austin, offers the following human-intelligible explanation of replacement in statistics.

Sampling with replacement: Consider a population of potato sacks, each of which has 12, 13, 14, 15, 16, 17, or 18 potatoes, and all the values are equally likely. Suppose that, in this population, there is exactly one sack with each number: the whole population has seven sacks. If I sample two *with replacement*, then I first pick one (say, 14). I had a 1/7 probability of choosing that one. Then I replace it. Then I pick another. Every one of them still has a 1/7 probability of being chosen. And there are exactly 49 possibilities here (assuming we distinguish between the first and second). They are (12,12), (12,13), (12,14), (12,15), (12,16), (12,17), (12,18), (13,12), (13,13), (13,14), and so on.

Sampling without replacement: Consider the same population of potato sacks, each of which has 12, 13, 14, 15, 16, 17, or 18 potatoes, and all the values are equally likely. Suppose that, in this population, there is exactly one sack with each number: the whole population has seven sacks. If I sample two *without replacement*, then I first pick one (say, 14). I had a 1/7 probability of choosing that one. Then I pick another. At this point, there are only six possibilities left: 12, 13, 15, 16, 17, and 18. So there are only 42 possibilities here (again, assuming that you distinguish between the first and the second). They are (12,13), (12,14), (12,15), (12,16), (12,17), (12,18), (13,12), (13,14), (13,15), and so on.

What's the difference?

When you sample with replacement, the two sample values are independent. Practically, this means that what *you get on the first one doesn't affect what you get on the second*. This also means that, with replacement, you could get the same row of data twice when you sample a dataframe. Spark's `sample()` method is without replacement by default.

To learn more, jump to https://web.ma.utexas.edu/users/parker/sampling/repl.htm.

You now have your intermediate dataframe, with cleaned and formatted values. At this stage, your data is consistent. You can start running analytics applications, algorithms, or pipelines (all more or less synonyms). So, let's finalize this lab to extract growth and the difference between the estimated population and the counted population in 2010.

The last part of our lab is indeed to create a new dataframe, which will contain the columns and the requested data.

Listing 12.5   RecordTransformationApp.java: Performing the analytics

Creates the diff column as the result of est2010-real2010

```
Dataset<Row> statDf = intermediateDf
    .withColumn("diff", expr("est2010-real2010"))
    .withColumn("growth", expr("est2017-est2010"))
```

Creates the growth column as the result of est2017-est2010

```
        .drop("id")
        .drop("label")
        .drop("real2010")
        .drop("est2010")
        .drop("est2011")
        .drop("est2012")      Drops unused
        .drop("est2013")      columns
        .drop("est2014")
        .drop("est2015")
        .drop("est2016")
        .drop("est2017");
    statDf.printSchema();
    statDf.sample(.01).show(5, false);
```

As you can see, once more, you used the expr() method to compute the values we needed in an SQL-like syntax.

The fourth step of a data transformation is to run your application (as illustrated in figure 12.10), which is fairly easy through your IDE. There is no need to describe it here.

After execution, you should get something similar to the following listing.

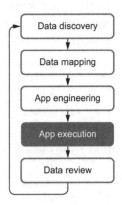

Figure 12.10   At the end of engineering, you will run your application. As you definitely know, be ready to go back a few steps if the execution is not producing the expected results.

Listing 12.6   Tail of the transformation's output

```
...
root
 |-- stateId: integer (nullable = true)
 |-- countyId: integer (nullable = true)
 |-- state: string (nullable = true)
 |-- county: string (nullable = true)
 |-- diff: integer (nullable = true)
 |-- growth: integer (nullable = true)


+-------+--------+----------+-------------------------+----+------+
|stateId|countyId|state     |county                   |diff|growth|
+-------+--------+----------+-------------------------+----+------+
|2      |275     |Alaska    |Wrangell City and Borough|2   |150   |
|5      |19      |Arkansas  |Clark County             |-68 |-634  |
|6      |7       |California|Butte County             |-43 |9337  |
|10     |3       |Delaware  |New Castle County        |352 |20962 |
|13     |195     |Georgia   |Madison County           |43  |1139  |
+-------+--------+----------+-------------------------+----+------+
only showing top 5 rows
```

Let's go to the final step of the process and validate the data after the transformation.

12.2.4 *Reviewing your data transformation to ensure a quality process*

In this short subsection, let's see how Spark can help you in reviewing your data, as illustrated in figure 12.11. Quality is such an important component in a process that it should not be undermined.

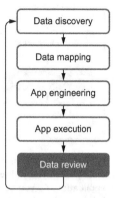

Figure 12.11   **The last step of the data transformation includes the review of the transformed data to ensure it is matching your goal. You may have to go back to the drawing board if the transformation does not produce the expected results. Any good process is iterative by nature, so you will certainly have to go back to data discovery.**

Spark does not come with tools dedicated to reviewing your data. I encourage you to build data unit tests to ensure that the transformation is behaving the way you want. Nevertheless, as printed in the following listing, running the application several times will produce different output, thanks to the `sample()` method.

Listing 12.7   Output of RecordTransformationApp.java

```
Output of first execution:
+-------+--------+----------+-----------------+----+------+
|stateId|countyId|state     |county           |diff|growth|
+-------+--------+----------+-----------------+----+------+
|6      |29      |California|Kern County      |1485|52003 |
|8      |87      |Colorado  |Morgan County    |75  |-42   |
|13     |13      |Georgia   |Barrow County    |329 |9365  |
|17     |177     |Illinois  |Stephenson County|-105|-2552 |
|18     |75      |Indiana   |Jay County       |-74 |-234  |
+-------+--------+----------+-----------------+----+------+
only showing top 5 rows
Output of second execution:
+-------+--------+--------+-----------------+----+------+
|stateId|countyId|state   |county           |diff|growth|
+-------+--------+--------+-----------------+----+------+
|1      |75      |Alabama |Lamar County     |-70 |-548  |
|1      |89      |Alabama |Madison County   |1291|24944 |
|4      |17      |Arizona |Navajo County    |246 |1261  |
|5      |11      |Arkansas|Bradley County   |-36 |-608  |
|12     |109     |Florida |St. Johns County |1197|52576 |
+-------+--------+--------+-----------------+----+------+
only showing top 5 rows
```

Output of third execution:

```
+-------+--------+--------+--------------+----+------+
|       |stateId|countyId|state   |county       |diff|growth|
+-------+--------+--------+--------------+----+------+
|1      |119    |Alabama |Sumter County |-33 |-1043 |
|8      |117    |Colorado|Summit County |74  |2517  |
|12     |131    |Florida |Walton County |170 |13163 |
|13     |117    |Georgia |Forsyth County|1256|51200 |
|13     |187    |Georgia |Lumpkin County|353 |2554  |
+-------+--------+--------+--------------+----+------+
only showing top 5 rows
```

In those examples, I only show() the data. If you want to have a finer look at the data, you will need to export it. Chapter 17 explains how to export data to files and databases.

12.2.5 *What about sorting?*

Before we wrap up this formal transformation, let's look at another way to review your data and prepare a report: sorting.

Of course, Apache Spark supports sorting on any number of columns, whether ascending (default) or descending. Listing 12.8 illustrates how you can sort data. The sort() method is applied on the dataframe. sort() can take multiple columns, and each column can be sorted in the following ways:

- Ascending order, using asc()
- Ascending with null values first, using asc_nulls_first()
- Ascending with null values last, using asc_nulls_last()
- Descending order, using desc()
- Descending with null values first, using desc_nulls_first()
- Descending with null values last, using desc_nulls_last()

Listing 12.8 Sorting your dataframe

```
statDf = statDf.sort(statDf.col("growth").desc());
System.out.println("Top 5 counties with the most growth:");
statDf.show(5, false);

statDf = statDf.sort(statDf.col("growth"));
System.out.println("Top 5 counties with the most loss:");
statDf.show(5, false);
```

The source code in the example is commented. To limit interference with the application, feel free to uncomment and see the data more clearly.

12.2.6 *Wrapping up your first Spark transformation*

If you've been following through the book in order, this is not your first data transformation. However, it is your first formal, process-oriented, step-by-step data transformation. This is the perfect moment to remind you of those five steps:

1 Data discovery
2 Data mapping
3 Application engineering/writing
4 Application execution
5 Data review

In the next chapter, you will learn how to transform entire documents as easily as you transformed records.

12.3 Joining datasets

One of the best ideas of relational databases is joins. *Joins* are the exploitation of the relations between the tables. This idea of building relations and joining the data is not really new (it was introduced in the great year of 1971) but has evolved. Joins are an integral part of the Spark API, as you would expect from any relational database. The support of joins enables relations between dataframes.

In this section, you will build a list of higher education institutions (colleges, universities) in the United States with their ZIP code, county name, and the county's population. One usage of this resulting dataset could be to list the counties with the most colleges and calculate a ratio of colleges per inhabitant. Then, if you like this university atmosphere and culture, you can more easily pick the place you'd like to live.

The lab associated with this section is #300 and can be found in the net.jgp.books .sparkInAction.ch12.lab300_join package.

12.3.1 A closer look at the datasets to join

This subsection describes the datasets you will use in this lab. As in our previous section, let's start with data discovery. You have three datasets at your disposal:

- The list of higher education institutions in the United States, provided by the Office of Postsecondary Education (OPE) of the US Department of Education. This list is called the Database of Accredited Postsecondary Institutions and Programs (DAPIP).
- A list of all the US counties and states, with their population estimates, managed by the US Census Bureau. This list contains a unique identifier for each county, based on the Federal Information Processing Standards (FIPS, https://en.wikipedia.org/wiki/FIPS_county_code). Each county has a FIPS ID.
- A mapping list assigning each ZIP code to a county ID. This list comes from the US Department of Housing and Urban Development (HUD).

Figure 12.12 gives you a relational representation of the three datasets and the links between them.

During the data discovery phase, you can look at the shape of the data. This is where you notice that you do not have a ZIP code in the higher education institutions dataset: you have to extract it from the address. Figure 12.13 illustrates how to extract the ZIP code from the address.

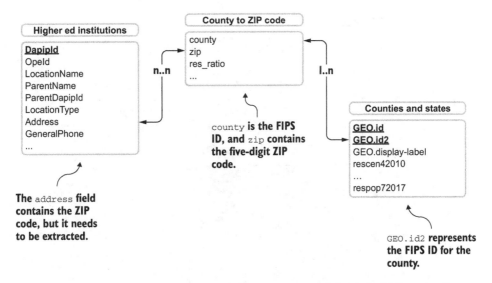

Figure 12.12 Relational representation of the three datasets with their links: higher education institutions (DAPIP), counties and states (Census Bureau), and mapping (HUD). As a reminder, $1..n$ and $n..n$ indicate the cardinality of the relation between the tables (or datasets).

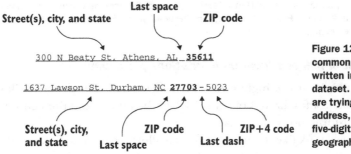

Figure 12.13 The two most common ways addresses are written in the higher education dataset. The ZIP code is what you are trying to extract from the address, and it has two forms: the five-digit code and the more geographically precise ZIP+4 code.

Another discovery makes things a little bit more complicated: a ZIP code is established by the US Postal Service (USPS) and is not a subdivision of a county. Therefore, sometimes a ZIP code covers several counties. Figure 12.14 shows a map of three counties sharing a ZIP code.

The HUD datasets give you a mapping between a county and several ZIP codes. The only way you could distinguish more precisely is to check against the USPS geographic information system (GIS), but this is not available publicly. Therefore, I will assume that an institution in one ZIP code area will benefit all the counties linked to this ZIP code; as an example, the English Learning Institute located in ZIP code 27517 will be listed in all three counties of Orange, Durham, and Chatham. It is not totally accurate, but one could argue that the influence of the institute is in the three counties.

Now that you have analyzed the data and completed data discovery, you can start transforming the data.

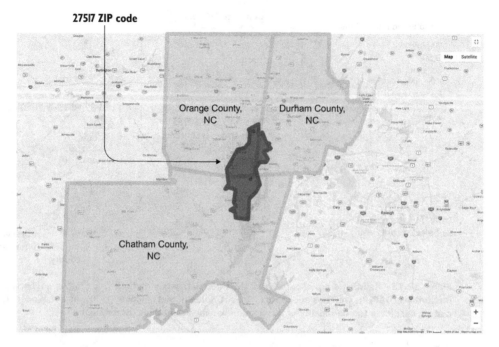

Figure 12.14   Map of three counties in North Carolina (Orange, Durham, and Chatham). Each county shares a piece of the 27517 ZIP code. Knowing the ZIP code alone does not guarantee the exact determination of the county.

12.3.2 *Building the list of higher education institutions per county*

You will now build the list of higher education institutions per county, following the data discovery you just finalized. Let's first look at the output and then go step by step through the transformations of the data.

The final list will look like the next listing. To allow the table to fit and still be readable, I used an ellipsis at the end of the columns.

Listing 12.9   Final list of higher education with name, ZIP code, county, and population

```
+------------------------------+-----+--------------------------...+--------+
|location                   ...|zip  |county                   ...|pop2017 |
+------------------------------+-----+--------------------------...+--------+
|California State University - S...|95819|Sacramento County, Calif...|1530615 |
|Clearwater Christian College   ...|33759|Pinellas County, Florida |970637  |
|Florida Southern College       ...|33801|Polk County, Florida     |686483  |
|Darton State College           ...|31707|Lee County, Georgia      |29470   |
|Southern Polytechnic State Univ...|30060|Cobb County, Georgia     |755754  |
...
```

I will decompose the application into small fragments, so you can focus on each fragment. You will do the following:

1   Load and clean each dataset.

2 Perform the first join between the institution dataset and the mapping file.

3 Perform the second join between the resulting dataset and the census data to get the name of the counties.

INITIALIZATION OF SPARK

The first step of building our list is to import the needed libraries and initialize Spark. You will also import several static functions to help you in your transformations. This is done in the next listing.

If you have read the book in sequence, this is probably the millionth time you have done this operation. Nevertheless, look at the static functions you are going to use.

Listing 12.10 HigherEdInstitutionPerCountyApp, part 1: Initialization

```
package net.jgp.books.sparkInAction.ch12.lab300_join;

import static org.apache.spark.sql.functions.element_at;    Static functions
import static org.apache.spark.sql.functions.size;          you will use to
import static org.apache.spark.sql.functions.split;         transform the data

import org.apache.spark.sql.Dataset;
import org.apache.spark.sql.Row;
import org.apache.spark.sql.SparkSession;

public class HigherEdInstitutionPerCountyApp {

  public static void main(String[] args) {
    HigherEdInstitutionPerCountyApp app =
        new HigherEdInstitutionPerCountyApp();
    app.start();
  }

  private void start() {
    SparkSession spark = SparkSession.builder()
        .appName("Join")
        .master("local")
        .getOrCreate();
```

LOADING AND PREPARING THE DATA

The second step of building our higher education list is to load and prepare all the datasets. This operation is really about ingesting all the data in Spark. You will load and clean the following:

- The census data (listing 12.11)
- The higher education institutions (listing 12.12)
- The mapping between the county code and the ZIP code (listing 12.13)

The census data should look like this:

```
+--------+-------------------------+-------+
|countyId|county                   |pop2017|
+--------+-------------------------+-------+
|1057    |Fayette County, Alabama  |16468  |
|1077    |Lauderdale County, Alabama|92538 |
...
```

Listing 12.11 loads the census CSV file, drops the column you do not need, and renames the columns to friendlier names.

Note that the file encoding is Windows/CP-1252, as some counties have accentuated characters (for example, Cataño Municipio in Puerto Rico). You are also inferring the schema, which becomes important when you join the columns (joins are more efficient with similar datatypes).

Listing 12.11 Loading and cleaning the census data

```
Dataset<Row> censusDf = spark
    .read()
    .format("csv")
    .option("header", "true")
    .option("inferSchema", "true")
    .option("encoding", "cp1252")
    .load("data/census/PEP_2017_PEPANNRES.csv");
censusDf = censusDf
    .drop("GEO.id")
    .drop("rescen42010")
    .drop("resbase42010")
    .drop("respop72010")
...
    .drop("respop72016")
    .withColumnRenamed("respop72017", "pop2017")
    .withColumnRenamed("GEO.id2", "countyId")
    .withColumnRenamed("GEO.display-label", "county");
System.out.println("Census data");
censusDf.sample(0.1).show(3, false);
```

Infers the schema → `.option("inferSchema", "true")`

Specifies the file encoding; cp1252 means Microsoft Windows. → `.option("encoding", "cp1252")`

Table 12.6 shows the schema.

Table 12.6 Schema of the census data after ingestion and preparation

Column	Type	Note
countyId	Integer	You will use this column for joining with the county/zip dataset.
county	String	
pop2017	Integer	

Let's load the second dataset, the higher education institutions. After ingestion and preparation, your dataset should look like this:

```
+----------------------------------+-----+
|location                          |zip  |
+----------------------------------+-----+
|Central Alabama Community College |35010|
|Concordia College Alabama         |36701|
...
```

In this dataset, you will have to extract the ZIP code from the address. Figure 12.15 illustrates the process of extracting the correct information by using the dataframe API and functions. To extract the ZIP code from the address, you will do the following:

1. Isolate the `Address` field.
2. Split (separate) each element of the field at each space. This will create an array that will be stored in the `addressElements` column.
3. Count the number of elements in the array and store the result in the `addressElementCount` column.
4. The last element of a well-formed address (in this dataset) is the ZIP code. You will store it in the `zip9` column. At this step, you can have a ZIP code using five digits or a ZIP code using nine digits (also called ZIP+4).
5. Split the `zip9` column based on the dash character and store the result in the `zips` column.
6. Finally, take the first element of the `zips` column.

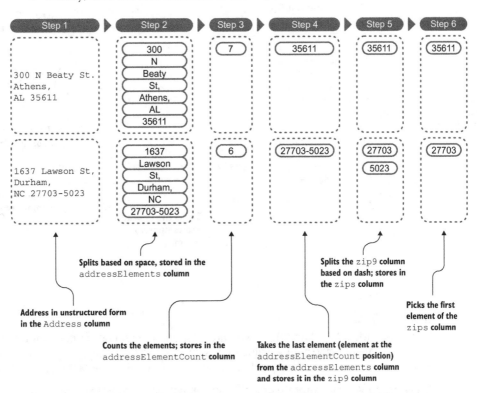

Figure 12.15 **Step-by-step approach to extracting both types of ZIP code from a raw address by using Spark's static functions**

The following listing shows the process of loading and preparing the data.

Listing 12.12   HigherEdInstitutionPerCountyApp, part 2: Cleaning data

```
Dataset<Row> higherEdDf = spark
    .read()
    .format("csv")
    .option("header", "true")
    .option("inferSchema", "true")
    .load("data/dapip/InstitutionCampus.csv");
higherEdDf = higherEdDf
    .filter("LocationType = 'Institution'")          Filters on the
    .withColumn(                                      institution
        "addressElements",
        split(higherEdDf.col("Address"), " "));       Step 1 and 2: Splits the
higherEdDf = higherEdDf                               address on spaces
    .withColumn(
        "addressElementCount",
        size(higherEdDf.col("addressElements")));     Step 3: Counts the
higherEdDf = higherEdDf                               number of elements
    .withColumn(
        "zip9",
        element_at(
            higherEdDf.col("addressElements"),        Step 4: Takes the last
            higherEdDf.col("addressElementCount"))); element in the array
higherEdDf = higherEdDf
    .withColumn(
        "splitZipCode",                               Step 6: Extracts the first
        split(higherEdDf.col("zip9"), "-"));          part of the ZIP code
higherEdDf = higherEdDf
    .withColumn("zip", higherEdDf.col("splitZipCode").getItem(0))
    .withColumnRenamed("LocationName", "location")
    .drop("DapipId")
                                                      Renames a column for
...                                                   naming consistency

    .drop("zip9")                        Drops the unused
    .drop("addressElements")            and temporary
    .drop("addressElementCount")        columns
    .drop("splitZipCode");
```

Step 5: Splits the nine-digit ZIP code

It's an SQL array

Yes, it is a trick! In listing 12.11, you are counting the number of elements and you use this value directly, not the value minus one. This is because element_at() uses an *SQL array*, whose first element is at index 1, not 0 (like a Java array).

If you try to get the zeroth element, you will get an exception: java.lang.Array-IndexOutOfBoundsException: SQL array indices start at 1. However, this is obvious in the case of the zeroth element; be extremely careful for other elements!

Table 12.7 give the schema of the resulting dataframe.

Table 12.7 Schema of the higher education institution dataset after ingestion and preparation

Column	Type	Note
location	Integer	
zip	String	The ZIP code is a string, which makes sense after all the transformations on the address, which was originally a string.

Finally, you can load the last dataset: the mapping of the ZIP code to the county, provided by HUD. The output of the dataframe will look like this:

```
+------+-----+
|county|zip  |
+------+-----+
|1001  |36701|
|1001  |36703|
...
```

This dataset is fairly easy to ingest, as you can see in the following listing.

Listing 12.13 HigherEdInstitutionPerCountyApp, part 3: Loading the mapping file

```
Dataset<Row> countyZipDf = spark
    .read()
    .format("csv")
    .option("header", "true")
    .option("inferSchema", "true")
    .load("data/hud/COUNTY_ZIP_092018.csv");
countyZipDf = countyZipDf
    .drop("res_ratio")
    .drop("bus_ratio")
    .drop("oth_ratio")
    .drop("tot_ratio");
```

The schema associated with this dataframe is in table 12.8.

Table 12.8 Schema of the mapping data after ingestion

Column	Type	Note
county	Integer	County identifier matching FIPS
zip	Integer	

12.3.3 Performing the joins

In the previous subsections, you loaded the data and prepared it so it can be used. In this subsection, you will perform the joins and analyze how they work. You are in the final step of building a list of US higher education institutions associated with a county.

You will first perform a join between the higher education dataset and the mapping of the ZIP code to the county, to add the FIPS county ID to the list. Your second join will be between the newly created dataframe and the census database to add the county name. You will finally perform cleaning operations to match the expected result.

JOINING THE FIPS COUNTY IDENTIFIER WITH THE HIGHER ED DATASET USING A JOIN

You will first perform a join between the higher education dataset, on the left, and the county/ZIP code mapping file on the right. This join will use the ZIP code, and the result will associate the institution with the FIPS county identifier.

The resulting dataframe should look like this:

```
+--------------------------+-----+------+
|location                  |zip  |county|
+--------------------------+-----+------+
|English Learning Institute|27517|37135 |
|English Learning Institute|27517|37063 |
|English Learning Institute|27517|37037 |
...
```

During the data discovery phase, you may have noticed that some addresses do not have a ZIP code. You may not want to carry over those institutions; you also do not want areas without institutions. Therefore, you can do an inner join, as illustrated in figure 12.16.

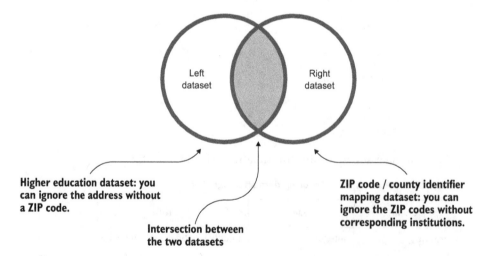

Figure 12.16   Graphical representation of the inner join between the higher education dataset and the ZIP code/county mapping dataset.

The following listing shows the code to perform the join.

```
     Dataset<Row> institPerCountyDf = higherEdDf.join(        Right part of the join
         countyZipDf,
Left part    higherEdDf.col("zip").equalTo(countyZipDf.col("zip")),   ←— Condition
of the join  "inner");            ←
                         Type of join
```

That's it! I admit there was a lot of preparation to come to this point, but the join remains pretty simple. The `join()` method has several forms (see appendix M and http://mng.bz/rP9Z). There are also quite a few join types. Join types are summarized in table 12.9. Lab #940 in this chapter's repository executes all possible joins on a couple of dataframes. A full reference on the join operation is available in appendix M.

Table 12.9   Join types in Spark

Join type	Aliases	Description	
Inner		Default type of join. Selects all rows from the left dataset and the right dataset, where the join condition is met.	
Outer	`full, fullouter, full_outer`	Selects data from both datasets based on the join condition and adds `null` when data is missing from the left or right.	
Left	`leftouter, left_outer`	Selects all rows from the left dataset, as well as all rows from the right dataset for which the join condition is met.	
Right	`rightouter, right_outer`	Selects all rows from the right dataset, as well as all rows from the left dataset for which the join condition is met.	
Left-semi	`left_semi`	Selects rows from only the left dataset for which the join condition is met.	

Table 12.9   Join types in Spark *(continued)*

Join type	Aliases	Description	
Left-anti	`left_anti`	Selects rows from only the left data-set for which the join condition is *not* met.	
Cross		Performs a Cartesian join of both datasets. As a reminder, a *Cartesian join* (also sometimes called a *Cartesian product*) is a join of every row of one table to every row of another table. As an example, if table `institution` with 100 rows is joined with table `subject` with 1,000 rows, the cross-join will return 100,000 rows.	

At this stage, your `institPerCountyDf` dataframe looks like this:

```
+--------------------------+-----+------+-----+
|location                  |zip  |county|zip  |
+--------------------------+-----+------+-----+
|English Learning Institute|27517|37135 |27517|
|English Learning Institute|27517|37063 |27517|
|English Learning Institute|27517|37037 |27517|
...
```

> There are two
> columns called zip.

If you look at the schema, as in table 12.10, you will see that you still have two columns named zip. This oddity continues, as you can see that they have different datatypes: one is of type string and the other is of type integer.

Table 12.10   Schema of the mapping data after ingestion

Column	Type	Note
location	String	
zip	String	First ZIP code column as a string
county	Integer	
zip	Integer	Second ZIP code column as an integer

As you can see, it is perfectly okay for Spark to do the following:

- Have two (or more) columns with the same name when they are the result of a join, as much as it seems counterintuitive
- Join on columns with different datatypes

Now, if you want to delete one of the `zip` columns, you will have to specify the origin of the column to delete it. If you perform

```
institPerCountyDf.drop("zip");
```

you will lose all the columns called `zip` and get this:

```
+------------------------------------+------+
|location                            |county|
+------------------------------------+------+
|Alabama State University            |1101  |
|Chattahoochee Valley Community College|1113  |
|Enterprise State Community College  |1035  |
...
```

If you want to delete only one of the `zip` columns, you can specify the origin dataframe and use the `col()` method:

```
institPerCountyDf.drop(higherEdDf.col("zip"));
```

Figure 12.17 illustrates the origin of the columns.

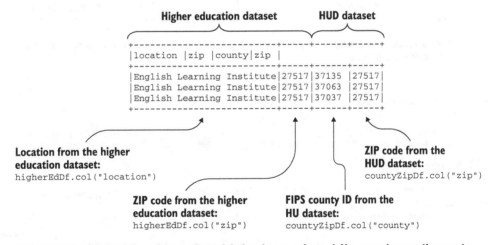

Figure 12.17   Origin of the columns after a join has been performed. You can also see the way to access them using the `col()` method of the original dataframe.

JOINING THE CENSUS DATA TO GET THE COUNTY NAME

Your dataframe now contains the location, the ZIP code, and the FIPS county ID. To add the name, you will have to join the census data to the existing dataset. After this join operation, you will have to drop the extra columns and, as you just saw, pick the right column.

Our final result will look like this:

```
+-------------------------------...+-----+--------------------...+--------+
|location                         |zip  |county                 |pop2017 |
+-------------------------------...+-----+--------------------...+--------+
|California State University - Sacr...|95819|Sacramento County, Ca...|1530615 |
|Clearwater Christian College     |33759|Pinellas County, Flor...|970637  |
|Florida Southern College         |33801|Polk County, Florida   |686483  |
|Mercy School of Nursing          |28273|Mecklenburg County, No |1076837 |
...
```

To perform this, you will perform a left join, as illustrated in figure 12.18.

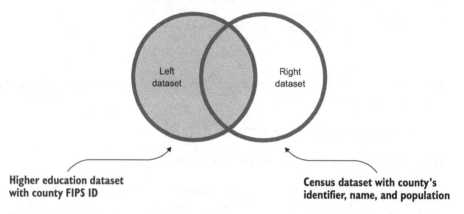

Higher education dataset with county FIPS ID

Census dataset with county's identifier, name, and population

Figure 12.18   Performing a left join to add the county's name and population to the list of higher education institutions

The following listing shows the code to perform the join.

Listing 12.15   Joining the higher education dataset with the Census Bureau dataset

Left part of the join

```
instatPerCountyDf = institPerCountyDf.join(
    censusDf,
    institPerCountyDf.col("county").equalTo(censusDf.col("countyId")),
    "left");
```

Right part of the join

Condition

Type of join

Once more, you can see that a join is not more complicated in Spark than it is with a relational database. Finally, you can clean up the extra columns, which are not required in this lab. You can remove these columns:

- The zip column from the higher education dataset.
- The county column from the mapping/HUD dataset.
- The countyId column; there is no confusion about which dataset it originates from.

The following listing shows you how to do that as well as how to remove duplicate rows by using `distinct()`.

Listing 12.16   **HigherEdInstitutionPerCountyApp: Cleaning the list**

```
institPerCountyDf = institPerCountyDf
    .drop(higherEdDf.col("zip"))
    .drop(countyZipDf.col("county"))
    .drop("countyId")
    .distinct();
```

You're done! You can now use this new dataset to perform analytics and other data discovery. The lab contains commented code on how to group data (aggregation is in chapter 13) or filter on specific geographies, and more.

12.4   *Performing more transformations*

This chapter is long, but it is a real cornerstone of this book. It was really hard to choose the right examples and not turn this chapter into a full book! There are many more labs in this chapter's repository, and this section describes those applications.

Table 12.11 summarizes additional labs that you will find in the GitHub repository.

Table 12.11   Additional examples to perform more transformations

Lab #	Application	Description
900	LowLevelTransformationAndActionApp	Performs lower-level (less abstract) transformations and actions on the data. Very useful to see the class and method signatures you will need. Appendix I is a reference for those.
920	QueryOnJsonApp	Performs a SQL query directly on a JSON document.
930	JsonInvoiceDisplayApp	Processing of invoices formatted using the schema.org format.
940	AllJoinsApp	All types of joins in one single application! Run it when in doubt.
941	AllJoinsDifferentDataTypesApp	Similar to lab #940 but uses different datatypes for joins.

Summary

- A data transformation can be divided into five steps:
  1 Data discovery
  2 Data mapping
  3 Application engineering/writing
  4 Application execution
  5 Data review
- Data discovery looks at both the data and its structure.

- Data mapping builds a map of the data between the origin and the destination of the transformation.
- To help with data discovery and mapping, a definition of the origin data and structure should be available.
- Static functions are key to data transformation. They are described in appendix G.
- The dataframe's `cache()` method allows caching and can help improve performance.
- `expr()` is a convenient function that allows you to compute an SQL-like statement when you are transforming the data.
- A dataframe can contain arrays of values.
- Dataframes can be joined together, like tables in a relational database.
- Spark supports the following kinds of joins: inner, outer, left, right, left-semi, left-anti, and cross (Cartesian).
- When manipulated in dataframes, arrays follow the SQL standard and start their indexing at 1.
- You can extract a sample of the data from a dataframe by using `sample()`.
- The `sample()` method supports the replacement concept from statistics.
- Data can be sorted in a dataframe by using `asc()`, `asc_nulls_first()`, `asc_nulls_last()`, `desc()`, `desc_nulls_first()`, and `desc_nulls_last()`.
- Spark can join dataframes, two at a time, and supports inner, outer, left, right, left-semi, left-anti, and cross joins.
- More examples of transformation are available in the GitHub repository at https://github.com/jgperrin/net.jgp.books.spark.ch12.

13

Transforming
entire documents

This chapter covers

- Transforming entire documents for better analytics or condensing
- Navigating the catalog of static functions
- Using static functions for data transformation

This chapter focuses on the transformation of entire documents: Spark will ingest a complete document, transform it, and make it available in another format.

In the previous chapter, you read about data transformations. The next logical step is to transform entire documents and their structure. As an example, JSON is great for transporting data, but a real pain when you have to traverse it to do analytics. In a similar way, joined datasets have so much data redundancy that it is painful to have a synthetic view. Apache Spark can help with those cases.

Before I wrap up the chapter, I'll teach you a bit more about all those static functions Spark offers for data transformation. There are so many of them that giving you an example for each would require another book! Therefore, I want you to have the tools to navigate them. Appendix G will be your companion.

Finally, I will point you to more transformations that are present in the repository but not described in the book.

As in previous chapters, I believe that using real-life datasets from official sources will help you understand the concepts more thoroughly. In this chapter, I also used simplified datasets where it made sense.

LAB   Examples from this chapter are available in GitHub at https://github .com/jgperrin/net.jgp.books.spark.ch13.

13.1   *Transforming entire documents and their structure*

In this section, you will start transforming entire documents. First, you will flatten a JSON document, which is a useful operation when you want to perform analytics. The nested composition of a JSON document will make analytics more difficult. Flattening will break this structure. Later in this section, you'll work through the reverse operation: building a nested document based on two CSV files. This use case is pretty common when building data pipelines—for example, fetching data from one system/database, building a JSON document from it, and storing the document in a NoSQL database.

Figure 13.1 illustrates a typical scenario: you can extract order data from a transaction-oriented database such as IBM Db2 and store a document representing the order in a document/search-oriented database such as Elasticsearch. Such a system could be used to ease order retrieval by end users, without increasing the load on the transaction database server.

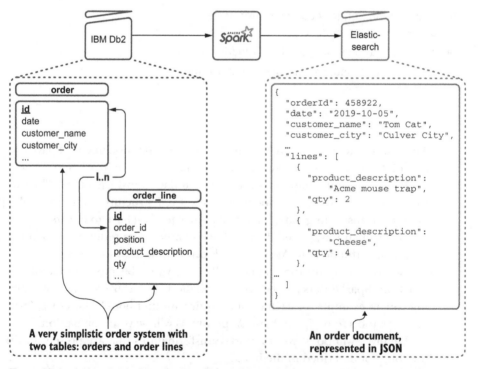

Figure 13.1   A very simple data pipeline, whereby Spark fetches the order data in an IBM Db2 database server, transforms the data into a JSON document, and saves the result into Elasticsearch for easy retrieval, while lowering the overall load on Db2

13.1.1 *Flattening your JSON document*

As you know, JSON is a hierarchical format; in short, the data is organized into a tree-like structure. In this subsection, you will practice *flattening* a JSON document: transforming JSON and its hierarchical data elements into tabular formats.

JSON documents can contain arrays, structures, and, of course, fields. This makes JSON pretty powerful, but when you want to perform an analytical operation, the process can become complex. Therefore, flattening turns the nested structure into a flat, table-like structure.

Why would you want to flatten a JSON document? JSON is not ideal if you want to perform aggregates (group by) or joins; it is not easy to access the nested data.

Let's look at this (fake) shipment receipt. As you can see, the document starts with two fields, followed by two structures (or objects), and an array of three books:

```
{
  "shipmentId": 458922,        | Field
  "date": "2019-10-05",        |
  "supplier": {                           <─┐
    "name": "Manning Publications",         │
    "city": "Shelter Island",               │   Structure
    "state": "New York",                    │   (or object)
    "country": "USA"                        │
  },                                        │
  "customer": {                           <─┘
    "name": "Jean-Georges Perrin",
    "city": "Chapel Hill",
    "state": "North Carolina",
    "country": "USA"
  },
  "books": [        <──── Array
    {
      "title": "Spark with Java",
      "qty": 2
    },
    {
      "title": "Spark in Action, 2nd Edition",
      "qty": 25
    },
    {
      "title": "Spark in Action, 1st Edition",
      "qty": 1
    }
  ]
}
```

If you ingest this document in Spark, and then show the dataframe and display its schema, you will get only one record, as illustrated in the following listing.

Listing 13.1   Ingestion of document returns only one record

```
+----------------+----------------+----------+----------+----------------+
|          books|        customer|      date|shipmentId|        supplier|
+----------------+----------------+----------+----------+----------------+
|[[2, Spark wi...|[Chapel Hill,...|2019-10-05|    458922|[Shelter Isla...|
+----------------+----------------+----------+----------+----------------+

root
 |-- books: array (nullable = true)
 |    |-- element: struct (containsNull = true)
 |    |    |-- qty: long (nullable = true)
 |    |    |-- title: string (nullable = true)
 |-- customer: struct (nullable = true)
 |    |-- city: string (nullable = true)
 |    |-- country: string (nullable = true)
 |    |-- name: string (nullable = true)
 |    |-- state: string (nullable = true)
 |-- date: string (nullable = true)
 |-- shipmentId: long (nullable = true)
 |-- supplier: struct (nullable = true)
 |    |-- city: string (nullable = true)
 |    |-- country: string (nullable = true)
 |    |-- name: string (nullable = true)
 |    |-- state: string (nullable = true)
```

LAB   You can reproduce this output by using lab #100, in the net.jgp.books .sparkInAction.ch13.lab100_json_shipment package. Check JsonShipment-DisplayApp.java.

Flattening this document consists of converting the structures into fields and exploding the arrays into distinct rows.

Denormalizing the document

In its JSON form, the document is normalized, just as a relational database can be normalized. For example, you can use the third normal form (3NF) to reduce the duplication of data. This mainly works by using more tables, identifiers, and relations between the tables. These concepts were introduced in 1971 by E.F. Codd; for more information, jump to https://en.wikipedia.org/wiki/Third_normal_form.

Denormalizing consists of the opposite operation to ease analytics. Flattening JSON is a denormalizing operation.

Figure 13.2 illustrates the parallel between JSON and relational tables.

Based on figure 13.2, if you wanted to count the number of titles sent in this shipment by using SQL, you would perform something like this:

```
SELECT COUNT(*) AS titleCount FROM shipment_detail
```

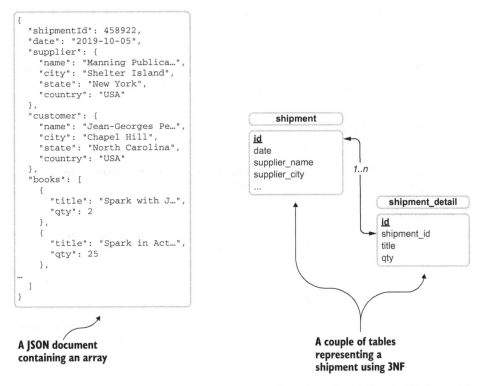

```
{
  "shipmentId": 458922,
  "date": "2019-10-05",
  "supplier": {
    "name": "Manning Publica…",
    "city": "Shelter Island",
    "state": "New York",
    "country": "USA"
  },
  "customer": {
    "name": "Jean-Georges Pe…",
    "city": "Chapel Hill",
    "state": "North Carolina",
    "country": "USA"
  },
  "books": [
    {
      "title": "Spark with J…",
      "qty": 2
    },
    {
      "title": "Spark in Act…",
      "qty": 25
    },
    …
  ]
}
```

A JSON document containing an array

shipment

id
date
supplier_name
supplier_city
…

1..n

shipment_detail

id
shipment_id
title
qty

A couple of tables representing a shipment using 3NF

Figure 13.2   Comparing a JSON document to a relational database: both follow the third normal form.

Using Spark, one way of doing it is to flatten the document first, to obtain something like the following listing.

Listing 13.2   Flattened shipment document

```
+----------+----------+…+----------------+---+---------------------------+
|      date|shipmentId|…|customer_country|qty|                      title|
+----------+----------+…+----------------+---+---------------------------+
|2019-10-05|    458922|…|             USA|  2|            Spark with Java|
|2019-10-05|    458922|…|             USA| 25|Spark in Action, 2nd Edition|
|2019-10-05|    458922|…|             USA|  1|Spark in Action, 1st Edition|
+----------+----------+…+----------------+---+---------------------------+

root
 |-- date: string (nullable = true)
 |-- shipmentId: long (nullable = true)
 |-- supplier_name: string (nullable = true)
 |-- supplier_city: string (nullable = true)
 |-- supplier_state: string (nullable = true)
 |-- supplier_country: string (nullable = true)
 |-- customer_name: string (nullable = true)
 |-- customer_city: string (nullable = true)
 |-- customer_state: string (nullable = true)
```

```
|-- customer_country: string (nullable = true)
|-- qty: long (nullable = true)
|-- title: string (nullable = true)
```

Now that you have seen the goal, let's look at how to perform this operation. Figure 13.3 describes how you will transform this document with Spark.

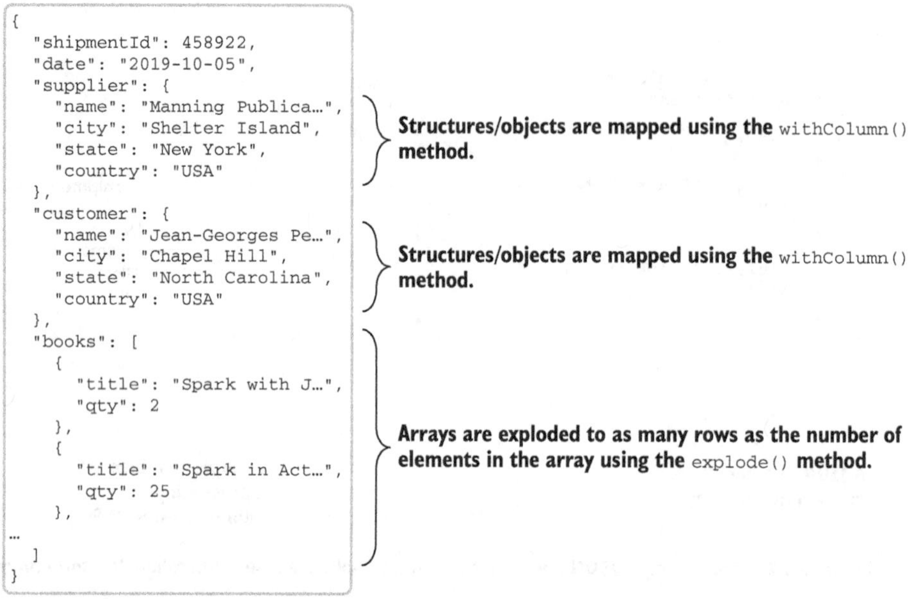

```
{
  "shipmentId": 458922,
  "date": "2019-10-05",
  "supplier": {
    "name": "Manning Publica…",        Structures/objects are mapped using the withColumn()
    "city": "Shelter Island",           method.
    "state": "New York",
    "country": "USA"
  },
  "customer": {
    "name": "Jean-Georges Pe…",        Structures/objects are mapped using the withColumn()
    "city": "Chapel Hill",              method.
    "state": "North Carolina",
    "country": "USA"
  },
  "books": [
    {
      "title": "Spark with J…",
      "qty": 2
    },
                                        Arrays are exploded to as many rows as the number of
    {                                   elements in the array using the explode() method.
      "title": "Spark in Act…",
      "qty": 25
    },
    …
  ]
}
```

Figure 13.3   To flatten a JSON document containing structures and arrays, you will use `withColumn()` and `explode()`.

Listing 13.3 shows the code to perform this transformation. After you created a session and ingested the file, you would do the following to prepare the data:

1 Map the columns in the structure to the top level of your document. This will break the nesting.
2 Drop the columns you do not need.
3 Explode the books column so that each book becomes a single record.

Now that your dataset is ready, you can apply the SQL query to count the number of titles, as you learned in chapter 11.

Listing 13.3   FlattenShipmentDisplayApp flattens a shipment

```
package net.jgp.books.sparkInAction.ch13.lab110_flatten_shipment;

import static org.apache.spark.sql.functions.explode;
```

```
import org.apache.spark.sql.Dataset;
import org.apache.spark.sql.Row;
import org.apache.spark.sql.SparkSession;

public class FlattenShipmentDisplayApp {
...
  private void start() {
    SparkSession spark = SparkSession.builder()
        .appName("Flatenning JSON doc describing shipments")
        .master("local")
        .getOrCreate();

    Dataset<Row> df = spark.read()
        .format("json")
        .option("multiline", true)
        .load("data/json/shipment.json");

    df = df
        .withColumn("supplier_name", df.col("supplier.name"))
        .withColumn("supplier_city", df.col("supplier.city"))
        .withColumn("supplier_state", df.col("supplier.state"))
        .withColumn("supplier_country", df.col("supplier.country"))
        .drop("supplier")
        .withColumn("customer_name", df.col("customer.name"))
        .withColumn("customer_city", df.col("customer.city"))
        .withColumn("customer_state", df.col("customer.state"))
        .withColumn("customer_country", df.col("customer.country"))
        .drop("customer")
        .withColumn("items", explode(df.col("books")));
```

Maps the structure's elements to a field

Drops the unused fields

Explodes the array

In this context, you will need to split your transformation in two. Spark will not be aware of the items column that you just created and that is needed to continue:

```
    df = df
        .withColumn("qty", df.col("items.qty"))
        .withColumn("title", df.col("items.title"))
        .drop("items")
        .drop("books");

    df.show(5, false);
    df.printSchema();

    df.createOrReplaceTempView("shipment_detail");
    Dataset<Row> bookCountDf =
        spark.sql("SELECT COUNT(*) AS titleCount FROM shipment_detail");
    bookCountDf.show(false);
  }
}
```

Note that explode() is a useful method: it creates a new row for each element in the given array or map column, which is really the easiest way to manipulate nested fields in a dataframe. Now that you have successfully flattened a JSON document, let's look at how to create a nested document.

13.1.2 *Building nested documents for transfer and storage*

In the previous subsection, you flattened a JSON document to ease analytics. In this section, you are going to do the opposite: build a nested document out of two linked datasets. This is useful when you have to send structured documents—for example, a claim matching the Fast Healthcare Interoperability Resources (FHIR) standard.

You are going to build a method that you will be able to reuse to easily combine datasets in a nested way. The method is called `nestedJoin()`. Nested documents can be used for transfer and storage, but there are many other use cases.

In lab #120, you are not going to work with health care, but restaurant data. You are going to build a master document defining a restaurant and detailing all the inspections in a nested way. The data comes from North Carolina's Orange County. It adheres to the Local Inspector Value-Entry Specification (LIVES) format defined by Yelp. Figure 13.4 illustrates the document you are going to build.

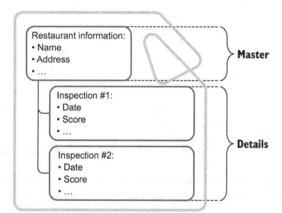

Figure 13.4 **The nested document with the restaurant information (as the master) and the inspection information (as the details)**

The schema of the dataset and the dataset to build will look like the following listing.

Listing 13.4 Schema and examples of nested document

```
root
 |-- business_id: string (nullable = true)
 |-- name: string (nullable = true)
 |-- address: string (nullable = true)          Master document:
 |-- city: string (nullable = true)             info about the
 |-- state: string (nullable = true)            restaurant
 ...
 |-- phone_number: string (nullable = true)
 |-- inspections: array (nullable = true)
 |    |-- element: struct (containsNull = true)
 |    |    |-- business_id: string (nullable = true)   Details of the
 |    |    |-- score: string (nullable = true)         inspections
 |    |    |-- date: string (nullable = true)
 |    |    |-- type: string (nullable = true)
```

```
+-----------+---------------------+...+-------------+...+-------------------+
|business_id|                 name|...|         city|...|         inspections|
+-----------+---------------------+...+-------------+...+-------------------+
| 4068011069|       FIREHOUSE SUBS|...| CHAPEL HILL |...|[[4068011069, 99,...|
| 4068010196|AMANTE GOURMET PIZZA |...|     CARRBORO|...|[[4068010196, 94,...|
| 4068010460|       COSMIC CANTINA |...| CHAPEL HILL |...|[[4068010460, 97,...|
...
```

The inspections appear as a nested document in the cell. Figure 13.5 describes the process.

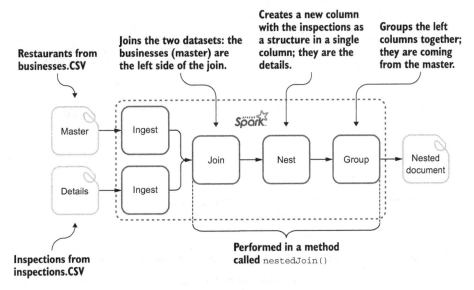

Figure 13.5   Creating a nested document from two datasets

The first part of the code is easy. As you can see in the following listing, you load both datasets in a dataframe and then call the nestedJoin() method.

> **Listing 13.5   RestaurantDocumentApp: Java imports and loads the data**

```java
package net.jgp.books.sparkInAction.ch13.lab120_restaurant_document;

import static org.apache.spark.sql.functions.col;
import static org.apache.spark.sql.functions.collect_list;
import static org.apache.spark.sql.functions.struct;

import java.util.Arrays;

import org.apache.spark.sql.Column;
import org.apache.spark.sql.Dataset;
import org.apache.spark.sql.Row;
import org.apache.spark.sql.SparkSession;
```

```
public class RestaurantDocumentApp {
  public static final String TEMP_COL = "temp_column";
  ...
  private void start() {
    SparkSession spark = SparkSession.builder()          ◁──── Creates a session
        .appName("Building a restaurant fact sheet")
        .master("local")
        .getOrCreate();
                                                         ┌── Ingests the
    Dataset<Row> businessDf = spark.read()           ◁──┘   restaurant dataset
        .format("csv")
        .option("header", true)
        .load("data/orangecounty_restaurants/businesses.CSV");

    Dataset<Row> inspectionDf = spark.read()         ◁──┐
        .format("csv")                                  │  Ingests the
        .option("header", true)                         │  inspection dataset
        .load("data/orangecounty_restaurants/inspections.CSV");

    Dataset<Row> factSheetDf = nestedJoin(           ◁──┐
        businessDf,                                     │  Performs the
        inspectionDf,                                   │  nested join
        "business_id",
        "business_id",
        "inner",
        "inspections");
    factSheetDf.show(3);                 │  Displays the result
    factSheetDf.printSchema();           │  and the schema
  }
```

Let's study the nestedJoin() method. Spark will do the following:

- Perform a join between the two dataframes
- Create a nested structure for each inspection
- Group the rows from the restaurant together

Before going into detail on those operations, let's look at a helper function that you can use in your lab. This function, getColumns(), builds an array of Column instances from a dataframe:

**The columns() method returns
the fieldnames in an array.**

```
    private static Column[] getColumns(Dataset<Row> df) {    │  Creates an array
┌─▷  String[] fieldnames = df.columns();                     │  big enough for
    Column[] columns = new Column[fieldnames.length];   ◁──┘  all the columns
    int i = 0;
    for (String fieldname : fieldnames) {          ◁──┐
      columns[i++] = df.col(fieldname);               │  Copies the columns
    }                                                 │  in the array
    return columns;
  }
```

Listing 13.6 will use this function and build the nested document. You will use a few static functions:

- `struct(Column... cols)` creates a `Column` whose datatype is a structure built from the columns passed as parameters.
- `collect_list(Column col)`, as an aggregate function, returns a list of objects. It will contain duplicates.
- `col(String name)` returns columns based on the name, equivalent to the dataframe's `col()` method.

Listing 13.6 RestaurantDocumentApp: Building the nested dataset

```
public static Dataset<Row> nestedJoin(
    Dataset<Row> leftDf,
    Dataset<Row> rightDf,
    String leftJoinCol,
    String rightJoinCol,
    String joinType,
    String nestedCol) {

    Dataset<Row> resDf = leftDf.join(          ◄── Performs the join
        rightDf,
        rightDf.col(rightJoinCol).equalTo(leftDf.col(leftJoinCol)),
        joinType);
                                                          Makes a list of
                                                          the left columns
    Column[] leftColumns = getColumns(leftDf);  ◄──┘
    Column[] allColumns =
        Arrays.copyOf(leftColumns, leftColumns.length + 1);
    allColumns[leftColumns.length] =
        struct(getColumns(rightDf)).alias(TEMP_COL);   ◄──

    resDf = resDf.select(allColumns);
    resDf = resDf
        .groupBy(leftColumns)
        .agg(
            collect_list(col(TEMP_COL)).as(nestedCol));  ◄──

    return resDf;
}
```

Copies all the columns from the left/master — `Column[] allColumns = Arrays.copyOf(leftColumns, leftColumns.length + 1);`

Adds a column, which is a structure containing all the columns from the details — `struct(getColumns(rightDf)).alias(TEMP_COL);`

Performs a select on all columns — `resDf = resDf.select(allColumns);`

Performs a group by on the columns from the left — `.groupBy(leftColumns)`

Performs the aggregation by using the aggregate function

The aggregate function — `collect_list(col(TEMP_COL)).as(nestedCol));`

Chapter 15 covers aggregations in more detail.

13.2 The magic behind static functions

This section describes, at a high level, the static functions that helped you in this chapter and the previous ones. Function such as `expr()`, `split()`, `element_at()`, and so many more are helping Spark developers daily.

This section emphasizes the importance of static functions. But it isn't a reference to those functions; for reference material, see appendix G and the online supplements.

FAVORITE BOOKMARK   You can find static functions described at https://spark .apache.org/docs/latest/api/java/org/apache/spark/sql/functions.html. This is one of the five pages on Spark I have bookmarked.

The general syntax for functions, since Spark v2.x, uses snake case (keywords are separated by underscores); for example, `format_string()`, which formats a column. This is in opposition to Java and Scala functions, which use camel case, as in `toString()`.

Functions work on a *column* as a whole, not only a cell. Functions are *polymorphic*, which means they can have several signatures.

Table 13.1 illustrates categories in which the functions can be grouped.

Table 13.1   Additional examples of function categories

Group	Description	Example of functions
Array	Manipulates arrays stored in columns	`element_at()`, `greatest()`
Conversion	Converts data from one format to another	`from_json()`
Date	Performs date manipulation such as adding days or months, or calculating differences between dates	`add_months()`, `hour()`, `next_day()`
Mathematics	Performs mathematical operations, including trigonometry and statistics	`acos()`, `exp()`, `hypot()`, `rand()`
Security	Performs security-related computations such as MD5 and hash	`md5()`, `hash()`, `sha2()`
Streaming	Streams specific functions to manipulate, such as windows in time	`lag()`, `row_number()`
String	Performs string manipulation, padding, trimming, concatenation, and more	`lpad()`, `ltrim()`, `regexp_extract()`, `upper()`
Technical	Provides technical information on the data itself	`spark_partition_id()`

13.3   *Performing more transformations*

As you can imagine, transformations are endless. There are probably even more transformations than there are use cases. The examples listed in table 13.2 come from my teams, various customer questions and problems, and questions on Stack Overflow. The GitHub repository contains more labs, illustrating some common operations you may need.

Table 13.2 summarizes the additional examples linked to this chapter and available in the GitHub repository at https://github.com/jgperrin/net.jgp.books.spark.ch13.

Table 13.2 Additional examples to perform more transformations

Lab #	Application	Description
900	FlattenJsonApp	Based on the use case you studied in section 13.1.1, this application automatically flattens any kind of JSON without having to specify any argument; it introspects the schema.
950	CsvWithEmbdeddedJsonApp	Ingestion of a CSV file, which embeds a JSON fragment. This version is based on a static JSON schema.
951	CsvWithEmbdeddedJsonAutomaticJsonifierApp	Ingestion of a CSV file, which embeds a JSON fragment. This version dynamically extracts the JSON schema.
999	Several	Growing list of small applications illustrating the use of the static functions.

13.4 Summary

- Apache Spark is a great tool for building data pipelines using transformations.
- Spark can be used to flatten JSON documents.
- You can build nested documents between two (or more) dataframes.
- Static functions are key to data transformation. They are described in appendix G and in the downloadable supplement available on this book's online catalog page at http://jgp.ai/sia.
- The GitHub repository includes more examples of document transformations to help you with some common cases.

Extending transformations with user-defined functions

Whether you have patiently read the first 13 chapters of this book, or hopped from chapter to chapter using a helicopter reading approach, you are definitely convinced that Spark is great, but . . . is Spark extensible? You may be asking, "How can I bring my existing libraries into the mix? Do I have to use solely the dataframe API and Spark SQL to implement all the transformations I want?"

From the title of this chapter, you can imagine that the answer to the first question is yes: Spark is extensible. The rest of the chapter answers the other questions by teaching you how to use *user-defined functions* (*UDFs*) to accomplish those tasks. Let's look at what this chapter articulates.

You'll first see how Spark is extensible by looking at the architecture involving UDFs and at the impact UDFs have on your deployment.

Then, in section 14.2, you'll dive into using a UDF to solve a problem: finding when the libraries in South Dublin (Ireland) are open. You will register, call, and implement the UDF. One way to extend Spark is to use your existing libraries, using UDFs as the means, just as a plumber connects your water heater to your shower. This section also contains a reminder about being a good plumber, as, I am sure, you are (of course, as a software plumber, we will skip the part where you may need plumber's tape).

UDFs are an excellent choice for performing data quality rules, whether you build the rules yourself or use external resources such as libraries. In section 14.3, I'll teach you how to use UDFs for better data quality.

Finally, in section 14.4, you'll learn the constraints associated with UDFs, though there aren't many and the constraints aren't drastic. However, it's always good to keep those constraints in mind before you design and implement these new user-defined functions.

LAB Examples from this chapter are available in GitHub at https://github .com/jgperrin/net.jgp.books.spark.ch14.

14.1 Extending Apache Spark

In this section, let's review the need for extending Spark and how those extensions materialize. Of course, as with all things, you'll look at the few drawbacks that come with the extensions. This section provides a little theory before diving into the code.

Apache Spark offers a fairly rich set of functions, of which we barely scratched the surface in the previous chapters. However, as you can imagine, those functions don't cover every possible use case. Therefore, Spark has a provision for adding your own functions: user-defined functions.

UDFs work on columns in your dataframe. A custom function remains a function: it has arguments and a return type. They can take from 0 to 22 arguments and always return one. The returned value will be the value stored in the column.

Figure 14.1 illustrates the basic mechanism of calling a UDF from Spark.

As you may remember from chapter 6 and deployment, code is executed on the worker nodes. This means that your UDF code must be serializable (to be transported to the node). Spark takes care of the transport part for you. If you have

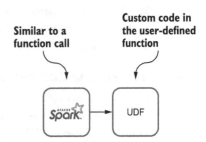

Figure 14.1 A UDF is a simple extension to Spark. Spark calls a UDF in almost the same way it calls a static function.

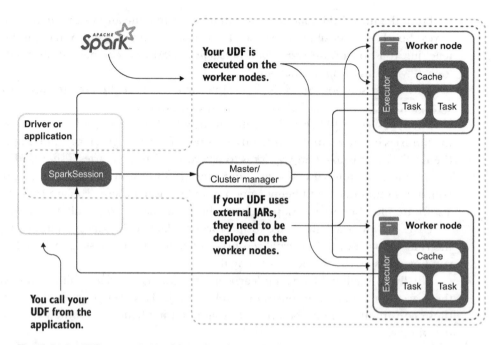

Figure 14.2 UDFs are called in your application (or driver), but the execution is done on the worker nodes. As a consequence, if your UDF requires external JARs, those JARs will need to be deployed on those worker nodes.

a UDF requiring external libraries, you must make sure that they are deployed on the worker nodes, as illustrated in figure 14.2.

As you learned in chapter 4, Spark stacks all your transformations in a directed acyclic graph (DAG) before you call an action. At the time you call the action, Spark asks Catalyst (a Spark internal component) to optimize the DAG before executing the tasks.

As the UDF's internals are not visible to Catalyst, the UDF is treated as a black box for the optimizer. Spark won't be able to optimize the UDF. Equally, Spark won't be able to analyze the context where the UDF is called; if you make dataframe API calls before or after, Catalyst can't optimize the full transformation.

Be cautious of that when you think about performance: I recommend, when possible, having your UDFs at the beginning or the end of your transformations.

14.2 Registering and calling a UDF

In the previous section, you learned what a UDF is. Now, let's go through a typical use case involving code. In this section, I describe the problem to solve and show the data. Then you'll use a UDF to implement the solution. To do that, you register the UDF, use it via the dataframe API, use it via Spark SQL, implement the UDF, and write the service code.

Here is our use case: you have a list of timestamps and would like to know which libraries in the city of South Dublin, Ireland, were open at a given date and time (or timestamp). To do that, you have several possible solutions to choose from:

- You could go to the Apache Spark project management committee (PMC) and ask them to add the `is_south_dublin_library_open()` static function.[1]
- You could implement the function yourself (in Scala) and have a customized version of Spark.
- You could use or create a UDF.

Of course, the only credible option is to implement it as a user-defined function (you probably knew that, as this is the topic of the chapter).

LAB This is lab #200, OpenedLibrariesApp, from the net.jgp.books.spark .ch14.lab200_library_open package.

The library dataset comes from the Smart Dublin open data portal; more specifically, the South Dublin County Council. You can download the dataset from https://data .smartdublin.ie/dataset/libraries.

The following listing shows the desired output: a list of libraries with a date and whether the library was or will be open on that date.

Listing 14.1 South Dublin libraries with opening hours

```
+---------+--------------------+-------------------+-----+
|Council_ID|                Name|               date| open|
+---------+--------------------+-------------------+-----+
|      SD1|      County Library|2019-03-11 14:30:00| true|
|      SD1|      County Library|2019-04-27 16:00:00| true|
...
|      SD2|    Ballyroan Library|2020-01-26 05:00:00|false|
|      SD3| Castletymon Library|2019-03-11 14:30:00| true|
|      SD3| Castletymon Library|2019-04-27 16:00:00| true|
...
|      SD6| Whitechurch Library|2020-01-26 05:00:00|false|
|      SD7|The John Jennings...|2019-03-11 14:30:00| true|
|      SD7|The John Jennings...|2019-04-27 16:00:00|false|
+---------+--------------------+-------------------+-----+
```

Listings 14.2 and 14.3 show excerpts of the two datasets you are going to use in this scenario. Listing 14.2 shows the opening hours of the South Dublin libraries. Every day has its column, from `Opening_Hours_Monday` to `Opening_Hours_Saturday` (South Dubliners don't have access to culture on Sundays). Values for this column can be like `09:45-20:00`, `14:00-17:00` and `18:00-20:00`, or `10:00-17:00 (16:00 July and August) - closed for lunch 12:30-13:00`. As you can see, determining whether a library is open is not a super-obvious operation.

---

[1] Each Apache project is managed by a project management committee called the PMC.

Listing 14.2   South Dublin libraries with opening hours

```
Council_ID,Administrative_Authority,Name,Address1,Address2,Town,Postcode,
    County,Phone,Email,Website,Image,Opening_Hours_Monday,
    Opening_Hours_Tuesday,Opening_Hours_Wednesday,Opening_Hours_Thursday,
    Opening_Hours_Friday,Opening_Hours_Saturday,WGS84_Latitude,
    WGS84_Longitude
SD1,South Dublin County Council,County Library,Library Square,
    Belgard Square North,Tallaght,24,Dublin,+353 1 462 0073,
    talib@sdublincoco.ie,
    http://www.southdublinlibraries.ie/.../county-library-tallaght,
    http://www.southdublinlibraries.ie/.../Images/Tallaght_Library-51.jpg,
    09:45-20:00,09:45-20:00,09:45-20:00,09:45-20:00,09:45-16:30,
    09:45-16:30,53.28846552,-6.373348296
SD2,South Dublin County Council,Ballyroan Library,Orchardstown Avenue,,
    Rathfarnham,14,Dublin,+353 1 494 1900,ballyroan@sdublincoco.ie,
    http://www.southdublinlibraries.ie/find-library/ballyroan,
    http://www.southdublinlibraries.ie/.../interior_retouched.jpg,
    09:45-20:00,09:45-20:00,09:45-20:00,09:45-20:00,09:45-16:30,
    09:45-16:30,53.29067806,-6.299321629
...
```

The timestamp dataset does not come from a file but is built programmatically, as illustrated in the following listing. The `createDataframe()` method directly returns a dataframe of the timestamp to analyze.

Listing 14.3   Building the timestamp dataset

Creates a schema for the initial data   Creates a field in the schema

```
    private static Dataset<Row> createDataframe(SparkSession spark) {
 └─▷ StructType schema = DataTypes.createStructType(new StructField[] {
            DataTypes.createStructField(                                  ◁─────────
The field name  ─▷  "date_str",
                    DataTypes.StringType,           Indicates whether the
The field type      false) });                      field is required (does
                                                    not matter here)
        List<Row>rows = new ArrayList<>();
        rows.add(RowFactory.create("2019-03-11 14:30:00"));   Adds dates to check to
        rows.add(RowFactory.create("2019-04-27 16:00:00"));   the list, as strings; those
        rows.add(RowFactory.create("2020-01-26 05:00:00"));   dates are random
Creates the
dataframe   return spark
by using the   ─▷  .createDataFrame(rows, schema)
list of rows       .withColumn("date", to_timestamp(col("date_str")))  ◁──┐
and the            .drop("date_str");                                      Turns the date
schema  }                                                                  as strings into
    }                                                                      timestamps
                                                                           (no time zone)
```

Now that you have the timestamp dataset, you're ready to dig into the application. Figure 14.3 shows the process of this lab.

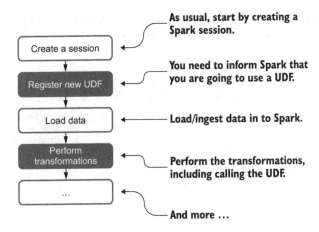

Figure 14.3   Adding a UDF to your application is as easy as registering it and then calling it as part of your transformations. The serialization and transport of the UDF is done behind the scenes.

14.2.1   Registering the UDF with Spark

When you want to use a UDF, the first operation is to register it. This is what this subsection is all about: informing Spark that you are going to use a UDF. So, let's get started.

Figure 14.4 illustrates the registration process, which is as follows:

1 You first need to access the UDF registration functions by calling the `udf()` method from the Spark session.

2 Then you `register()` by using the name of the function, an instance of the class implementing the UDF, and the return type. Upon calling the UDF, any new column that needs to be created will have this datatype. The name should be a valid Java method name.

You can find a list of valid datatypes in appendix L. Note that you don't need to specify the function's parameters at this point.

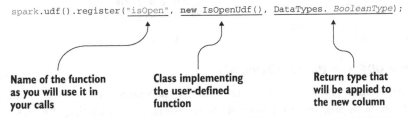

Figure 14.4   Registering a user-defined function in the Spark session that it will be used in requires the UDF's name, an instance of the class implementing the UDF, and the return type that will be used to create the new column.

UDFs have no formal reference documentation. Nevertheless, these Javadoc links offer more details on UDFs:

- The `UDFRegistration` class at http://mng.bz/ANe7; the page lists the methods to register the UDF.
- The static functions at http://mng.bz/Ze1a, with a focus on `callUDF()` and `udf()`.

In the next listing, you will see the creation of the session (somewhat of a known thing at this stage) and the registration of the UDF. As usual, I left all the imports in the code to avoid any confusion.

Listing 14.4   OpenedLibrariesApp: Registration of the UDF

```
package net.jgp.books.spark.ch14.lab200_library_open;        Imports the callUDF
                                                             function, which is
import static org.apache.spark.sql.functions.callUDF;   ◁─── required to call a UDF
import static org.apache.spark.sql.functions.col;
import static org.apache.spark.sql.functions.lit;
import static org.apache.spark.sql.functions.to_timestamp;

import java.util.ArrayList;
import java.util.List;

import org.apache.spark.sql.Dataset;
import org.apache.spark.sql.Row;
import org.apache.spark.sql.RowFactory;
import org.apache.spark.sql.SparkSession;
import org.apache.spark.sql.types.DataTypes;
import org.apache.spark.sql.types.StructField;
import org.apache.spark.sql.types.StructType;

publicclass OpenedLibrariesApp {
...
  privatevoid start() {                                    Creates a session
    SparkSession spark = SparkSession.builder()      ◁──┘  on a local master
        .appName("Custom UDF to check if in range")
        .master("local[*]")
        .getOrCreate();
    spark
         .udf()          ◁──── Accesses the UDFs
         .register(                         Instance of the class
           "isOpen",                        implementing the UDF
           new IsOpenUdf(),          ◁─────┘
           DataTypes.BooleanType);  ◁──── UDF's return type
```

Registers the UDF

UDF's name as you are going to use it

14.2.2   *Using the UDF with the dataframe API*

In this subsection, you will use the UDF with the dataframe API. You will first load and clean the data to use, and then start some transformations. Calling the UDF on your data is part of those transformations.

Now that Spark is aware of your new UDF, let's ingest the data and perform the transformation, as illustrated in listing 14.5. The part about calling the UDF is in bold.

The next step is to ingest the library dataset. As you ingest the dataset, in the same operation, you can drop a lot of the columns you are not going to use, including Town, Phone, or Postcode (that's the ZIP code outside the United States). You will create the second dataset thanks to the createDataframe() method, as shown in listing 14.3.

Once you have the two datasets, you can cross-join (also called a Cartesian join) them. You studied joins in chapter 12, and they are detailed in appendix M. The resulting dataset will contain all the libraries associated to all the timestamps. There are seven libraries and three timestamps; this means that the new dataframe, resulting from the join, contains 21 records (as in 21 = 7 × 3). Yes, Cartesian joins can become pretty big.

Finally you can create a column called open, using the withColumn() method and the callUDF() static function.

The UDF function takes eight parameters: the seven first columns are the opening hours from Monday to Sunday, and the last one is the timestamp.

Listing 14.5 OpenedLibrariesApp: Using the UDF

```
Dataset<Row> librariesDf = spark.read().format("csv")          ◁─┐ Reads the
    .option("header", true)                                        │ first dataset
    .option("inferSchema", true)                                   │ and performs
    .option("encoding", "cp1252")                                  │ cleanup
    .load("data/south_dublin_libraries/sdlibraries.csv")           │ operations
    .drop("Administrative_Authority")                            ◁─┘
    .drop("Address1")
    .drop("Address2")
    .drop("Town")
    .drop("Postcode")
    .drop("County")
    .drop("Phone")
    .drop("Email")
    .drop("Website")
    .drop("Image")
    .drop("WGS84_Latitude")
    .drop("WGS84_Longitude");
librariesDf.show(false);
librariesDf.printSchema();
                                                     Creates the dataframe
Dataset<Row> dateTimeDf = createDataframe(spark);  ◁─ with timestamps
dateTimeDf.show(false);
dateTimeDf.printSchema();                             Performs a cross-
                                                     join between the
Dataset<Row> df = librariesDf.crossJoin(dateTimeDf);  ◁─ two datasets
df.show(false);
                                               Call to the UDF;
Dataset<Row> finalDf = df.withColumn(          the result will be
    "open",                                    in column "open."
    callUDF(                         ◁─────────
        "isOpen",
                col("Opening_Hours_Monday"),
                col("Opening_Hours_Tuesday"),
                col("Opening_Hours_Wednesday"),
                col("Opening_Hours_Thursday"),       Parameters
                col("Opening_Hours_Friday"),         to the UDF
                col("Opening_Hours_Saturday"),
                lit("Closed"),
                col("date")));
```

Creates a column → Dataset<Row> finalDf = df.withColumn(

The new column is called "open." → "open",

Name of the function to call, as registered → "isOpen",

Hours for Sunday as a literal value → lit("Closed"),

```
      .drop("Opening_Hours_Monday")
      .drop("Opening_Hours_Tuesday")
      .drop("Opening_Hours_Wednesday")
      .drop("Opening_Hours_Thursday")
      .drop("Opening_Hours_Friday")
      .drop("Opening_Hours_Saturday");
finalDf.show();
```

Note that the library dataset does not have hours for Sunday, but the UDF processes any day of the week. Therefore, you can use lit() with a specific (or literal) value to pass the value to the function. This is important to keep your function as generic as possible.

14.2.3 *Manipulating UDFs with SQL*

In the previous section, you used a UDF with the dataframe API. Now, in this section, you will use SQL to manipulate a UDF. The lab is #210, almost a fork of lab #200, which uses a lot of the same resources.

Here is the SQL statement itself, without any double quotes or formatting, so you can better understand what you will have to do:

```
SELECT
  Council_ID, Name, date,
  isOpen(
    Opening_Hours_Monday, Opening_Hours_Tuesday, Opening_Hours_Wednesday,
    Opening_Hours_Thursday, Opening_Hours_Friday, Opening_Hours_Saturday,
'closed', date) AS open
FROM libraries
```

Note that you will not have to use lit() for the Sunday hours, as you had to in lab #200 using the dataframe API. In SQL, you simply pass the value (as a literal). The following listing shows how to use your function in a SQL statement within the code to leverage the UDF function.

Listing 14.6 Using a UDF in SQL

```
...
    spark
      .udf()
      .register(              You still need the
        "isOpen",             registration, just as you
        new IsOpenUdf(),      did for the dataframe API.
        DataTypes.BooleanType);
...
        Dataset<Row>df = librariesDf.crossJoin(dateTimeDf);
        df.createOrReplaceTempView("libraries");      Creates the view to
SQL                                                    manipulate via SQL
statement   Dataset<Row>finalDf = spark.sql(
          "SELECT Council_ID, Name, date, "
        + "isOpen("
        + "Opening_Hours_Monday, Opening_Hours_Tuesday, "
```

```
        + "Opening_Hours_Wednesday, Opening_Hours_Thursday, "
        + "Opening_Hours_Friday, Opening_Hours_Saturday, "
        + "'closed', date) AS open FROM libraries ");
    ...
```

14.2.4 Implementing the UDF

You just registered and started using the UDF; you even started using the UDF with both the dataframe API and SQL. However, you have not implemented it. In this subsection, you'll build the class that implements the UDF.

As you saw when you registered the function in Spark's session, a UDF is implemented as a class. The class implements a UDF base class, as illustrated in listing 14.7.

When you are building a UDF, you write a class that implements `org.apache` `.spark.sql.api.java.UDF0` to `org.apache.spark.sql.api.java.UDF22`, depending on the number of parameters you need. In this lab, you will need eight parameters: the hours of the seven days of the week and the timestamp. Remember, the opening hours are just a string containing the opening and closing time.

As Java is strongly typed, you need to specify the types of each argument and the return type, as illustrated in figure 14.5.

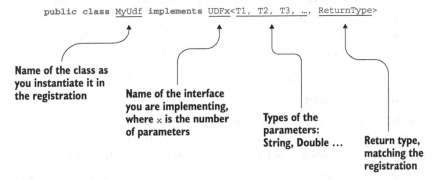

Figure 14.5 Anatomy of a UDF class with the interface it implements, the different types for the parameters, and the return type

The key method you need to implement is `call()`, which takes the parameters and returns the declared type. In this lab, this means seven parameters of type `String`, one parameter of type `Timestamp`, and the return type is `Boolean`.

> **Listing 14.7 `IsOpenUdf` UDF code**

```
package net.jgp.books.spark.ch14.lab200_library_open;

import java.sql.Timestamp;

import org.apache.spark.sql.api.java.UDF8;     Imports for a UDF
                                                with 8 parameters

public class IsOpenUdf implements
```

```
                  UDF8<String, String, String, String, String, String, String, Timestamp,
   The                 Boolean> {
interface             private static final long serialVersionUID = -216751L;
is typed.
                      @Override
                      public Boolean call(
Required                  String hoursMon, String hoursTue,
implementation            String hoursWed, String hoursThu,
of call() with            String hoursFri, String hoursSat,
matching                  String hoursSun,
return type               Timestamp dateTime) throws Exception {

                      return IsOpenService.isOpen(hoursMon, hoursTue, hoursWed, hoursThu,
                          hoursFri, hoursSat, hoursSun, dateTime);
                  }
              }
```

Class must be serializable

Parameters, matching the type interface

Call to the service doing the processing

As you may remember, in chapter 9 I talked about being a good plumber. A good plumber makes sure the processing code is distinct from the "glue" (or plumbing code). Therefore, the actual code, which checks whether the library (or any business) is open, is isolated in its own service class. As a direct consequence of this design, if any changes occur in the UDF API itself, your business logic code is shielded from them. Additionally, you can reuse this service elsewhere and be able to more easily use unit tests. This is why the business logic of this UDF isn't in the UDF but is in the IsOpen-Service class (and in listing 14.8). This plumbing paradigm is part of the broader *separation of concerns* (*SoC*) design principle

14.2.5 *Writing the service itself*

Now, with all the plumbing done, you still need to write the service code itself. Hopefully, you can reuse service code from an existing library in your current organization (and if not, it's a good time to start doing so). This subsection is more in the category of the "nice to read" rather than the "must read" (although that categorization is subjective).

The IsOpenService service is a basic parser that supports the following syntaxes:

- `09:45-20:00`
- `14:00-17:00 and 18:00-20:00`
- `closed`

Remember that hours are based on 24 hours in Ireland, what is called *military time* in the United States. The IsOpenService service doesn't support the more complex syntax like `10:00-17:00 (16:00 July and August) - closed for lunch 12:30-13:0`. The IsOpenService service is described in listing 14.8.

The isOpen() method takes all the opening hours and timestamp as parameters. Then the method does the following:

1 Finds the day of the week from the timestamp
2 Focuses only on the opening hours of that day
3 Checks whether the specific day is not a closed day
4 Attempts to parse the string to check whether the time is within the range

For those time and date manipulations, I relied on Java's `Calendar` object. You can also use `LocalDate` if you wish.

Listing 14.8 IsOpenService code

```
package net.jgp.books.spark.ch14.lab200_library_open;

import java.sql.Timestamp;          ◁─────┐  Spark uses the SQL data types
import java.util.Calendar;                 │  for dates, as in java.sql.* not the
...                                        │  java.util.*

public abstract class IsOpenService {
...
public static boolean isOpen(String hoursMon, String hoursTue,
        String hoursWed, String hoursThu, String hoursFri, String hoursSat,
        String hoursSun, Timestamp dateTime) {

    Calendar cal = Calendar.getInstance();              Instantiates and sets a
    cal.setTimeInMillis(dateTime.getTime());            value to the calendar
    int day = cal.get(Calendar.DAY_OF_WEEK);
    String hours;
    switch (day) {
      case Calendar.MONDAY:
        hours = hoursMon;
        break;                                    Assigns the day of
      case Calendar.TUESDAY:                      the week's hours to
        hours = hoursTue;                         the opening hours
        break;
    ...
    }

                                                       If it's closed on that
                                                       day, exits quickly
    if (hours.compareToIgnoreCase("closed") == 0) {  ◁──┘
      return false;
    }

    int event = cal.get(Calendar.HOUR_OF_DAY) * 3600
        + cal.get(Calendar.MINUTE) * 60             Calculates an
        + cal.get(Calendar.SECOND);                 event in seconds

    String[] ranges = hours.split(" and ");
    for (inti = 0; i<ranges.length; i++) {
      String[] operningHours = ranges[i].split("-");  ◁─── Splits the range on
      int start = #I                                       "-", giving two strings
      Integer.valueOf(operningHours[0].substring(0, 2)) * 3600 +    containing "HH:mm"
      Integer.valueOf(operningHours[0].substring(3, 5)) * 60;
```

Gets the day of the week from the calendar

Splits the opening hours on " and " to iterate on each range

Extracts the opening time in seconds

```
                    int end = #J
Extracts the closing │   Integer.valueOf(operningHours[1].substring(0, 2)) * 3600 +
   time in seconds  │   Integer.valueOf(operningHours[1].substring(3, 5)) * 60;
             if (event>= start && event<= end) {  ◄
               return true;
             }
           }
         }

     return false;
       }
     }
```

Checks if the event is within the opening hours, all in seconds

You have now built your service, connected it to Apache Spark, and called it via the dataframe API. You can also call your UDF via SQL.

14.3   *Using UDFs to ensure a high level of data quality*

One of my favorite use cases for user-defined functions is achieving better data quality. In this section, you will learn about this important step of your analytics journey with Apache Spark.

From chapter 1, you may remember figure 14.6. Before you can start transformation, or any form of analytics, including machine learning (ML) and artificial intelligence (AI), you need to ensure that your raw data is purified through a data quality process.

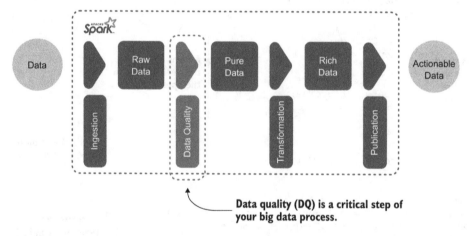

Data quality (DQ) is a critical step of your big data process.

Figure 14.6   Spark in a typical data processing scenario, with an emphasis on achieving better data quality

Achieving data quality can be done in many ways, including scripts and external applications. Figure 14.7 illustrates an aggregation process whereby data quality rules are performed outside Spark, and figure 14.8 shows the flow within Apache Spark.

When the data quality process is external to Spark, you need to manage files and their potential issues with eavesdropping as you interact with them. In the example in figure 14.7, you will need 45 GB of storage (20 + 3 + 19 + 3) just to get the data ready before the ingestion. Do you know when you can delete those files? For security purposes, do you know who can access those files?

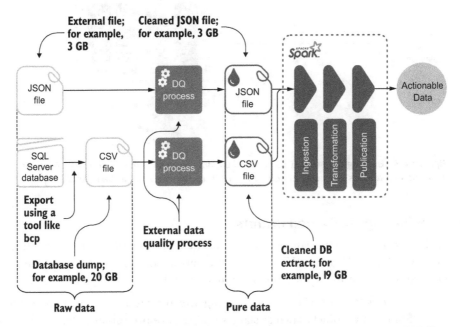

Figure 14.7 A big data process, ingesting data from a SQL Server instance and a JSON file, with an external data quality process, performed before the ingestion: you'll need more storage, more time, and more processes to handle this data.

When you ingest the data first, as in figure 14.8, you can still use external data quality processes. You can also have your data quality (DQ) processes through UDF, and there are great benefits to that:

- Avoiding a potentially complex and onerous file life cycle (copy, delete, backup, and extra security)
- Using parallelized/distributed computing, as the data quality process will be run on each node
- Reusing existing Java (or Scala) scripts and libraries you may already have in your organization

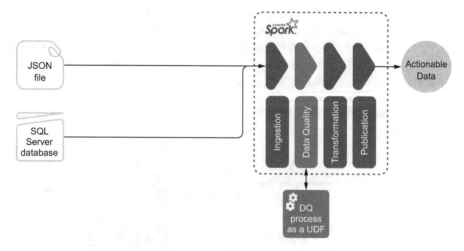

Figure 14.8   Building data quality as part of a big data process within Spark: simplifying the life cycle of data files and using distributed computing are your two key benefits.

14.4   *Considering UDFs' constraints*

In the previous sections, you learned about the benefits and uses of user-defined functions with Spark. However, UDFs aren't the perfect solution for every problem, so let's go through the most important constraints with UDFs:

- *Serializable*—The class implementing the function itself must be serializable. Some Java artifacts, such as static variables, are not serializable.
- *Executed on the worker nodes*—The function itself is executed on the worker nodes, which means that the resources, environment, and dependencies needed by the function to operate must be located on the worker node. As an example, if your function checks values against a database, the worker nodes must have access to this database. If they preload a table of values to compare to, each node will do that; meaning that if you have 10,000 workers, 10,000 connections to the database will happen.
- *Black box for the optimizer*—Catalyst is the key component, which optimizes the DAG. Catalyst does not know anything about what your function is doing.
- *No polymorphism* (specifically, method/function overloading)—You cannot have two functions with the same name and different signatures, even if the return type is the same. In the source code repository, you can study labs #910, #911, and #912, where I wanted to add either two strings or two integers, but they fail with exceptions as the method signature will not match.

A UDF cannot have more than 22 parameters. However, it is possible to pass a column to a UDF. This is illustrated by lab #920 in the repository.

Summary

- You can extend the Spark function set by using UDFs.
- Spark executes UDFs on the worker node.
- To use a UDF is to register your UDF with a unique name, an instance of the class implementing the UDF, and a return type.
- A UDF can have from 0 to 22 parameters.
- You can call a UDF via the `callUDF()` method of the dataframe API or directly in Spark SQL.
- You can implement a UDF via a Java class that implements an interface, based on the number of parameters, from `UDF0` to `UDF22`, from the org.apache.spark.sql.api.java package.
- A good practice is to avoid any business logic code in the UDF itself, leaving the implementation in a service: be a good plumber by shielding the service code and leaving the interface between the service and Spark code in the UDF.
- UDFs are a good way to implement data quality in Spark, because by using a UDF, you avoid manipulating files, use distributed computing, and potentially reuse existing libraries and tools.
- A UDF implementation must be serializable.
- A UDF is a black box for Catalyst, Spark's optimizer.
- You can't apply polymorphism to UDFs.

Aggregating your data

Aggregating is a way to group data so you can view it at a macro level rather than an atomic, or micro, level. Aggregations are an essential step to better analytics, and down the road from machine learning and artificial intelligence.

In this chapter, you will start slow, with a small reminder of what aggregations are. Then you'll perform basic aggregations with Spark. You will be using both Spark SQL and the dataframe API.

Once you go through the basics, you will analyze open data from New York City public schools. You will study attendance, absenteeism, and more through aggregations. Of course, prior to this real-life scenario, you will have to *onboard* (a synonym of *ingest*) the data, clean it, and prepare it for the aggregations.

Finally, when the standard aggregations do not suffice, you will need to write your own. This is what you will be doing in section 15.3. You will build a user-defined aggregation function (UDAF), a custom function to perform your unique aggregation.

LAB Examples from this chapter are available in GitHub at https://github .com/jgperrin/net.jgp.books.spark.ch15.

15.1 Aggregating data with Spark

This section teaches you how to perform an aggregation by using Apache Spark. You'll first look at what an aggregation is. You may already know and use aggregations in your job, so this might be just a reminder for you. If this is the case, you can safely skim through this section; Apache Spark's aggregations are standard. The second part of this section shows you how to transform a SQL aggregation statement to Spark.

15.1.1 A quick reminder on aggregations

In this section, you will go through a quick lesson on what aggregations are as well as the types of aggregations. If you feel comfortable with aggregations, skim through this section and go to section 15.1.2; aggregations in Spark are similar to those in any relational database.

As I stated previously, aggregations are a way to group data so you can look at it from a higher level, as illustrated in figure 15.1. Aggregations can be performed on tables, joined tables, views, and more.

Imagine an order system. You have thousands of orders from a few hundred customers and want to identify your best customer.

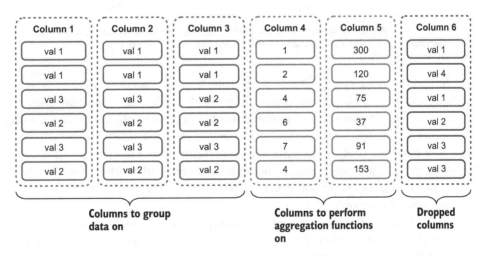

Figure 15.1 A look at the data before you perform an aggregation. An aggregation is all about performing one or more functions on grouped columns. Columns can also be dropped in the process.

Without using aggregations, you could go through each customer, query all the orders for this customer, sum the amount, store this sum somewhere, and go on. This would mean a lot of I/O and interaction with the database. Let's see how an aggregation can help us perform this task faster.

Figure 15.2 puts "real data" in the table: the table now contains first name, last name, and state of the customer; the ordered quantity; the generated revenue; and a timestamp of when the ordered was placed. A customer is defined by their first and last name, as well as their state, so in this example, you have four customers. Therefore, you can see six orders from four customers.

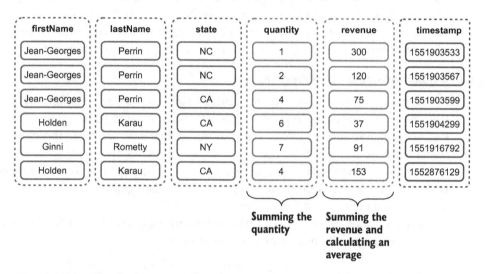

firstName	lastName	state	quantity	revenue	timestamp
Jean-Georges	Perrin	NC	1	300	1551903533
Jean-Georges	Perrin	NC	2	120	1551903567
Jean-Georges	Perrin	CA	4	75	1551903599
Holden	Karau	CA	6	37	1551904299
Ginni	Rometty	NY	7	91	1551916792
Holden	Karau	CA	4	153	1552876129

Summing the quantity   Summing the revenue and calculating an average

Figure 15.2 A table containing order data before aggregation. You can see four distinct customers, as a customer is defined by their name and state, and six orders.

In this scenario, your goal is to study your best customers. Therefore, you are going to focus on the customer rather than on the individual elements composing the order. You'll focus on the aggregation of data around the customer. A unique customer is defined by their first name, last name, and state from which they placed their order and will receive it from shipping. You are going to group on these three criteria. You will aggregate on both the quantity and the revenue. On the revenue data, you will calculate both the total revenue and the average to determine the average revenue per order.

You can also safely drop the timestamp column, which is not needed in this use case. You do not explicitly drop it; you simply do not integrate it in your query. Figure 15.3 shows this process.

The final result shows only the aggregate results, as in figure 15.4.

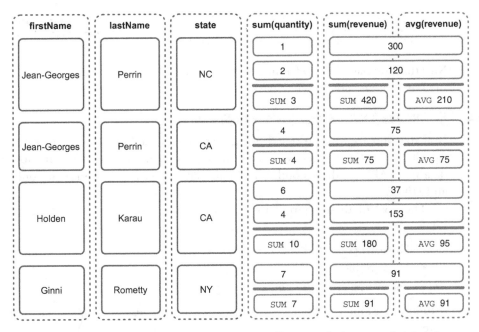

Figure 15.3 Details of the grouping operations done on first name, last name, and state columns. The quantity and revenue columns have morphed into three new columns. The timestamp column is not needed anymore.

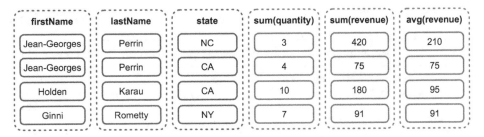

Figure 15.4 Final result of the aggregation, with only one row per unique customer and their related statistical data.

If you turn that into SQL, the following listing shows a PostgreSQL-based SELECT statement.

Listing 15.1 An aggregation using a SQL statement

```
SELECT
    "firstName",
    "lastName",
    "state",                              Sums the quantities
    SUM(quantity) AS sum_qty,      ◁──┘
    SUM(revenue) AS sum_rev,       ◁──── Sums the revenue
```

```
    AVG(revenue::numeric::float8) AS avg_rev       ◄────┐  Converts to a float before
FROM public.ch13                                        │  computing the average
GROUP BY ("firstName", "lastName", "state");
```

Now that you have been refreshed on the aggregation mechanisms, let's see how to do the same things with Apache Spark.

15.1.2 Performing basic aggregations with Spark

Now that you are fully groomed on aggregations, let's do the same aggregations with Apache Spark. You will see two ways of doing aggregations: one using the now-familiar dataframe API and the second using Spark SQL, in a similar way as you would do with an RDBMS.

The goal of these aggregations is to compute, for an individual customer, the following:

- The total count of items the customer bought
- The revenue
- The average revenue per order

A unique customer is defined, in this scenario, by their first name, last name, and state.

Let's start by looking at the desired output. The following listing shows the expected dataframe. No surprise, it is similar to figure 15.4.

Listing 15.2   Result of an aggregation with Spark

```
+------------+--------+-----+-------------+------------+------------+
| firstName|lastName|state|sum(quantity)|sum(revenue)|avg(revenue)|
+------------+--------+-----+-------------+------------+------------+
|       Ginni| Rometty|   NY|            7|          91|        91.0|
|Jean Georges|  Perrin|   NC|            3|         420|       210.0|
|      Holden|   Karau|   CA|           10|         190|        95.0|
|Jean Georges|  Perrin|   CA|            4|          75|        75.0|
+------------+--------+-----+-------------+------------+------------+
```

> **LAB**   This lab, called OrderStatisticsApp, is available in the net.jgp.books .spark.ch13.lab100_orders package.

The raw data is a simple CSV file, as shown in the following listing.

Listing 15.3   Raw order data to perform the aggregation

```
firstName,lastName,state,quantity,revenue,timestamp
Jean Georges,Perrin,NC,1,300,1551903533
Jean Georges,Perrin,NC,2,120,1551903567
Jean Georges,Perrin,CA,4,75,1551903599
Holden,Karau,CA,6,37,1551904299
Ginni,Rometty,NY,7,91,1551916792
Holden,Karau,CA,4,153,1552876129
```

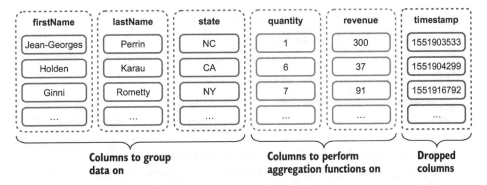

firstName	lastName	state	quantity	revenue	timestamp
Jean-Georges	Perrin	NC	1	300	1551903533
Holden	Karau	CA	6	37	1551904299
Ginni	Rometty	NY	7	91	1551916792
...	...	...	...	...	...

Columns to group data on — Columns to perform aggregation functions on — Dropped columns

Figure 15.5 Structure, sample data, and grouping of the dataset user in this Spark-based aggregation

Figure 15.5 shows the data and metadata you are working on. It is the same dataset as you used in the previous subsection.

As is usual with Spark, you will initialize the session and load the data, as illustrated in the next listing. As is done throughout the book, this code includes all the `import` statements so you will know precisely which packages, classes, and functions you will use.

Listing 15.4 Initializing Spark and loading the dataset

```java
package net.jgp.books.spark.ch13.lab100_orders;

import static org.apache.spark.sql.functions.avg;
import static org.apache.spark.sql.functions.col;
import static org.apache.spark.sql.functions.sum;

import org.apache.spark.sql.Dataset;
import org.apache.spark.sql.Row;
import org.apache.spark.sql.SparkSession;

public class OrderStatisticsApp {

  public static void main(String[] args) {
    OrderStatisticsApp app = new OrderStatisticsApp();
    app.start();
  }

  private void start() {
    SparkSession spark = SparkSession.builder()          // ◁—— Starts a session
        .appName("Orders analytics")
        .master("local[*]")
        .getOrCreate();

    Dataset<Row> df = spark.read().format("csv")         // ◁—— Ingests a CSV file with header and automatic inference of the schema
        .option("header", true)
        .option("inferSchema", true)
        .load("data/orders/orders.csv");
```

There are two ways to perform this aggregation:

- You can use the dataframe API, as in listing 15.5.
- You can use Spark SQL, as in listing 15.6.

Both solutions provide the same results.

PERFORMING AN AGGREGATION USING THE DATAFRAME API

Let's have a look at the dataframe API to perform an aggregation in listing 15.5. You will use the dataframe as your source and use the `groupBy()` method. Using method chaining, you can directly apply an aggregate method such as `agg()`, `avg()`, `count()`, and so on.

The `agg()` method does not perform aggregations but uses functions to do the aggregations at the column level. Appendix G lists the aggregation methods.

Listing 15.5   Aggregation using the dataframe API

```
Dataset<Row> apiDf = df
    .groupBy(col("firstName"), col("lastName"), col("state"))
    .agg(
        sum("quantity"),
        sum("revenue"),
        avg("revenue"));
apiDf.show(20);
```

- **Sums the quantity column**
- **Columns to group by** (`.groupBy(...)`)
- **Starts the aggregation process** (`.agg(`)
- **Sums the revenue column**
- **Calculates the average of the revenue column** (`avg("revenue")`)

Note that the `groupBy()` method has several signatures; the columns can be specified by name, sequence, or using the column objects. You will see the various usages in the code snippets. I find this one rather elegant in this context.

PERFORMING AN AGGREGATION USING SPARK SQL

The alternate way to perform a GROUP BY operation is to directly use Spark SQL, just as you would do with your RDBMS. Listing 15.6 uses the Spark SQL version of the SQL statement I wrote for PostgreSQL in listing 15.1.

Because you will manipulate data through SQL, you will need a view. You can then build your SQL statement and execute it from the Spark session.

Listing 15.6   Aggregation using Spark SQL

```
df.createOrReplaceTempView("orders");
String sqlStatement = "SELECT " +
    "    firstName, " +
    "    lastName, " +
    "    state, " +
    "    SUM(quantity), " +
    "    SUM(revenue), " +
    "    AVG(revenue) " +
    "  FROM orders " +
    "  GROUP BY firstName, lastName, state";
Dataset<Row> sqlDf = spark.sql(sqlStatement);
sqlDf.show(20);
    }
}
```

- **Creates the view to allow the execution SQL statements** (`df.createOrReplaceTempView("orders");`)
- **Creates the SQL statements**
- **Spark does not allow parentheses around the GROUP BY part.**
- **Executes the SQL statement** (`Dataset<Row> sqlDf = spark.sql(sqlStatement);`)

Note that, contrary to PostgreSQL and other RDBMSs, Spark does not want the GROUP BY columns to be within parentheses.

15.2 *Performing aggregations with live data*

In this section, you will perform various kinds of aggregations using Spark, to practice and learn the tools available to you, directly out of the box.

You will explore real-life datasets and perform meaningful statistical operations. You will use a few datasets coming from the school district of New York City (NYC). NYC's school district is the largest in the United States. You will work on the historical daily attendance by school from 2006 to now. The data comes from the open data platform from the city of New York at https://data.cityofnewyork.us. The entire dataset is divided into six files (roughly three years of school data per set).

> **LAB**   This lab uses an app called NewYorkSchoolStatisticsApp, which is available in the net.jgp.books.spark.ch13.lab300_nyc_school_stats package.

15.2.1 *Preparing your dataset*

Before you can perform any kind of aggregation on your data, the first step is ingesting and cleaning your data. This is covered in this subsection. You will perform ingestion of multiple CSV files at once, union the dataframes, and then apply data quality rules using Spark's static functions. This is the required preamble, so you can use the datasets efficiently for analytical operations.

The following listing shows an excerpt of the dataset with the right structure and formatting that will ease your work.

Listing 15.7   Desired dataframe and schema

```
+--------+----------+--------+-------+------+--------+----+
|schoolId|      date|enrolled|present|absent|released|year|
+--------+----------+--------+-------+------+--------+----+
|  01M015|2012-09-07|     168|    144|    24|       0|2012|
|  01M015|2012-09-10|     167|    154|    13|       0|2012|
|  01M015|2012-09-12|     170|    159|    11|       0|2012|
|  01M015|2012-09-13|     172|    157|    15|       0|2012|
|  01M015|2012-09-14|     172|    158|    14|       0|2012|
...
root
 |-- schoolId: string (nullable = true)
 |-- date: date (nullable = true)
 |-- enrolled: integer (nullable = true)
 |-- present: integer (nullable = true)
 |-- absent: integer (nullable = true)
 |-- released: integer (nullable = true)
 |-- year: integer (nullable = true)
```

Before ingesting the data, let's have a look at it. You have five CSV files:

- 2006-2009_Historical_Daily_Attendance_By_School.csv
- 2009-2012_Historical_Daily_Attendance_By_School.csv
- 2012_-_2015_Historical_Daily_Attendance_By_School.csv
- 2015-2018_Historical_Daily_Attendance_By_School.csv
- 2018-2019_Daily_Attendance.csv

The common pattern between these filenames is *20*.csv*. You could use this pattern for Spark to load all the files in one dataframe. However, because the data structure is not the same, you may end up having a serious data quality issue. Remember to look inside the files to see what the data looks like as well.

The 2018–2019 dataset looks like listing 15.8. The school identifier is called School DBN, the date uses the yyyyMMdd format, and the dataset does not include the school year.

Listing 15.8   The 2018–2019 dataset

```
School DBN,Date,Enrolled,Absent,Present,Released
01M015,20180905,172,19,153,0
01M015,20180906,171,17,154,0
01M015,20180907,172,14,158,0
...
```

Listing 15.9 shows how the 20012–2015, 2009–2012, and 2006–2009 datasets are designed. The school identifier is called School; the date uses the yyyyMMdd format; and the dataset includes a SchoolYear field, which is a string containing the starting year, concatenated to the ending year, using the yyyy format.

Listing 15.9   The 20012–2015, 2009–2012, and 2006–2009 datasets

```
School,Date,SchoolYear,Enrolled,Present,Absent,Released
01M015,20120906,20122013,165,140,25,0
01M015,20120907,20122013,168,144,24,0
01M015,20120910,20122013,167,154,13,0
01M015,20120911,20122013,169,154,15,0
...
```

In 2015, the structure changed for the date; it uses the traditional US MM/dd/yyyy format, as illustrated in the following listing.

Listing 15.10   The 2015–2018 dataset

```
School,Date,SchoolYear,Enrolled,Present,Absent,Released
01M015,01/04/2016,20152016,168,157,11,0
01M015,01/05/2016,20152016,168,153,15,0
01M015,01/06/2016,20152016,168,163,5,0
01M015,01/07/2016,20152016,168,154,14,0
...
```

In order to ingest this data, I decided to use methods. Listing 15.11 shows the beginning of the app, where you create the session and load the files. Listing 15.12 shows only one function to load the 2006 dataset.

Listing 15.11 NewYorkSchoolStatisticsApp: Starting the app

```
package net.jgp.books.spark.ch13.lab300_nyc_school_stats;

import static org.apache.spark.sql.functions.avg;
import static org.apache.spark.sql.functions.col;
import static org.apache.spark.sql.functions.expr;           Functions to be used
import static org.apache.spark.sql.functions.floor;          to perform the data
import static org.apache.spark.sql.functions.lit;            preparation and
import static org.apache.spark.sql.functions.max;            aggregations
import static org.apache.spark.sql.functions.substring;
import static org.apache.spark.sql.functions.sum;

import org.apache.spark.sql.Dataset;
import org.apache.spark.sql.Row;
import org.apache.spark.sql.SparkSession;
import org.apache.spark.sql.types.DataTypes;
import org.apache.spark.sql.types.StructField;
import org.apache.spark.sql.types.StructType;
import org.slf4j.Logger;
import org.slf4j.LoggerFactory;

public class NewYorkSchoolStatisticsApp {
  private static Logger log = LoggerFactory
      .getLogger(NewYorkSchoolStatisticsApp.class);

  private SparkSession spark = null;

  public static void main(String[] args) {
    NewYorkSchoolStatisticsApp app =
        new NewYorkSchoolStatisticsApp();
    app.start();
  }

  private void start() {
    spark = SparkSession.builder()
        .appName("NYC schools analytics")
        .master("local[*]")
        .getOrCreate();

    Dataset<Row> masterDf =
        loadDataUsing2018Format("data/nyc_school_attendance/2018*.csv");

    masterDf = masterDf.unionByName(
        loadDataUsing2015Format("data/nyc_school_attendance/2015*.csv"));

    masterDf = masterDf.unionByName(
        loadDataUsing2006Format(
            "data/nyc_school_attendance/200*.csv",        Loading multiple
            "data/nyc_school_attendance/2012*.csv"));      files at once

    log.debug("Datasets contains {} rows", masterDf.count());
```

At this stage, your application should tell you that the dataset is a little less than 4 million records.

The next listing illustrates how to load the 2006 to 2012 datasets. The process is similar for the 2015 and 2018 formats. You can check out the full class directly on GitHub at http://mng.bz/yy1G.

Listing 15.12   NewYorkSchoolStatisticsApp: Starting the app

```
private Dataset<Row> loadDataUsing2006Format(String... fileNames) {
    return loadData(fileNames, "yyyyMMdd");
}

private Dataset<Row> loadData(String[] fileNames, String dateFormat) {
    StructType schema = DataTypes.createStructType(new StructField[] {
        DataTypes.createStructField(
            "schoolId",
            DataTypes.StringType,
            false),
        DataTypes.createStructField(
            "date",
            DataTypes.DateType,
            false),
        DataTypes.createStructField(
            "schoolYear",
            DataTypes.StringType,
            false),
        DataTypes.createStructField(
            "enrolled",
            DataTypes.IntegerType,
            false),
        DataTypes.createStructField(
            "present",
            DataTypes.IntegerType,
            false),
        DataTypes.createStructField(
            "absent",
            DataTypes.IntegerType,
            false),
        DataTypes.createStructField(
            "released",
            DataTypes.IntegerType,
            false) });

    Dataset<Row> df = spark.read().format("csv")
        .option("header", true)
        .option("dateFormat", dateFormat)
        .schema(schema)
        .load(fileNames);

    return df.withColumn("schoolYear", substring(col("schoolYear"), 1, 4));
}
}
```

The difference between the 2006 and 2015 structure is the date format; it makes sense to use a common method.

Definition of the schema

Setting the reader to CSV

Specifies the date format

Specifies the schema

Loads a list of files

Table 15.1 shows the structure of the resulting dataset.

Table 15.1   Result of the data exploration for the attendance datasets

Column name	Description	Type	Notes
schoolId	School identification number.	Plain text	Called `School DNB` in the 2018–2019 datasets.
date	Date using the `YYYYMMDD` format; for example: `20090921`.	Date	
schoolYear	Fiscal school year. Starting year concatenated to ending year; for school year 2009–10, the value is `20092010`.	Plain text	In the lab's dataset, you kept only the four first digits. For school year 2009–10, it is 2009.
enrolled	Number of students enrolled in school on the date that the data is being reported.	Integer	
present	Count of students present in school on the day and date that data is being reported.	Integer	
absent	Count of students absent in school on the day and date that data is being reported.	Integer	
released	Count of students absent in school on the day and date that data is being released.	Integer	

Now is a good time for a quick sanity check on your ingestion. How many schools are in New York City? The fast way to answer the question using Spark is as follows:

```
Dataset<Row> uniqueSchoolsDf = masterDf.select("schoolId").distinct();
```

You should find 1,865 rows. Let's compare that to information on the web. Wikipedia says NYC has "more than 1,700 public schools."[1] The NYC department of education found 1,840 schools.[2] I would say it's probably okay to lose 25 schools. With an average of 608 students per school, it's probably okay to lose 15,218 kids (it's New York after all, no?). But seriously, the data covers over 18 years, so closing schools, changing identifiers, splitting schools, or other justifications are plausible. Let's continue with our 1,865 rows.

Now that you have a clean dataset, let's do some aggregations!

---

[1]For more details, see "Education in New York City" at https://en.wikipedia.org/wiki/Education_in_New_York_City.

[2]See "DOE Data at a Glance" at the NYC Department of Education website, www.schools.nyc.gov/about-us/reports/doe-data-at-a-glance.

15.2.2 Aggregating data to better understand the schools

In this subsection, you will use aggregations to answer questions about the NYC school system. Imagine you are moving to New York and want to understand a little bit more about how the local public schools perform. In the previous subsection, you formatted and cleaned all the data.

At your disposal, you have about 4 million rows, with the following fields:

- schoolId (string)—The school identifier
- date (date)
- schoolYear (string)—The school year matching the YYYY format
- enrolled (integer)—The number of students enrolled
- present (integer)—The count of students who are present
- absent (integer)—The count of students who are absent
- released (integer): The count of students who are released

You are now ready to answer the questions!

WHAT IS THE AVERAGE ENROLLMENT FOR EACH SCHOOL?

To compute the average enrollment for each school, per year, you will have to group the dataset by school and year. In the same operation, you can also add the average presence and absence for the school.

Your output could look like the following listing.

Listing 15.13 Average enrollment for each NYC school

```
…YorkSchoolStatisticsApp.java:80): Average enrollment for each school
+--------+----------+-----------------+-----------------+----------------+
|schoolId|schoolYear|   avg(enrolled) |   avg(present)  |   avg(absent)  |
+--------+----------+-----------------+-----------------+----------------+
|  01M015|      2006|248.68279569892|223.90860215053|24.774193548387|
|  01M015|      2007| 251.5837837837|225.72972972972|24.843243243243|
|  01M015|      2008|243.82967032967|215.57692307692|28.071428571428|
  …
```

The following listing explains the process of calculating those averages.

Listing 15.14 Code to compute the average enrollment for each NYC school

```
                Dataset<Row> averageEnrollmentDf = masterDf                Columns part
Columns  ┌──         .groupBy(col("schoolId"), col("schoolYear")) ◄──┘   of the group
   part  └──►        .avg("enrolled", "present", "absent")
                     .orderBy("schoolId", "schoolYear");          ◄──┐
                                                                     │ Sorting columns; sorting will be
                                                                     │ first on the school, then the year
```

Note that you can calculate an average by using avg() on multiple columns.

WHAT IS THE EVOLUTION OF THE NUMBER OF STUDENTS?

Let's look at the evolution of students enrolled in the NYC school district over the years 2006 to 2018. In the process, let's also find which year was the busiest and how many students attended this year.

Your output could look like the following listing.

Listing 15.15   Evolution of enrollment in NYC schools

```
...YorkSchoolStatisticsApp.java:93): Evolution of # of students per year
+----------+--------+
|schoolYear|enrolled|
+----------+--------+
|      2006|  994597|
|      2007|  978064|
|      2008|  976091|
|      2009|  987968|
|      2010|  990097|
|      2011|  990235|
|      2012|  986900|
|      2013|  985040|
|      2014|  983189|
...
...YorkSchoolStatisticsApp.java:100): 2006 was the year with most students,
   the district served 994597 students.
```

To build this aggregated dataset, you can start from the previous question, which contains the school ID, the school year, and the average enrollment per year.

Spark automatically renames the columns to include the aggregation function in the column name after the aggregation. This can be annoying at times, so let's first rename the column, and then perform an aggregation on the school year, where you will sum all the enrollments per school.

Because the result is a decimal number, you can `floor()` the sum to keep the integer part and cast it to a long. Finally, you can sort the result by school year.

To find out the maximum value, simply set the `enrolled` column in descending order, take the first row, and get the values. Remember that, in this lab, the year is a string. Columns start at 0.

The following listing shows the code of the process I just described.

Listing 15.16   Code to compute the evolution of enrollment in NYC schools

```
Dataset<Row> studentCountPerYearDf = averageEnrollmentDf
    .withColumnRenamed("avg(enrolled)", "enrolled")
    .groupBy(col("schoolYear"))
    .agg(sum("enrolled").as("enrolled"))
    .withColumn(
        "enrolled",
        floor("enrolled").cast(DataTypes.LongType))
    .orderBy("schoolYear");
log.info("Evolution of # of students per year");
```

Annotations:
- **Performs the sum and renames the column** → `.agg(sum("enrolled").as("enrolled"))`
- **Renames the column** → `.withColumnRenamed("avg(enrolled)", "enrolled")`
- **Groups on the school year column** → `.groupBy(col("schoolYear"))`
- **Takes the integer part and casts to long** → `floor("enrolled").cast(DataTypes.LongType))`
- **Orders by the school year** → `.orderBy("schoolYear");`

```
studentCountPerYearDf.show(20);
Row maxStudentRow = studentCountPerYearDf
    .orderBy(col("enrolled").desc())
    .first();
String year = maxStudentRow.getString(0);
long max = maxStudentRow.getLong(1);
log.debug(
    "{} was the year with most students, "
    + "the district served {} students.",
    year, max);
```

Takes the first row

Sorts the dataframe on the enrolled column

Gets the year in the first column

Gets the max value in the second column

With some versions of Spark, the aggregated column would be renamed; for example, the sum of the enrolled column could be named sum(enrolled). Forcing the name of the aggregated column ensures that you have no surprises when you manipulate the column after the aggregation takes place.

As you can see, using

```
.agg(sum("enrolled").as("enrolled"))
```

directly renames the column to enrolled, without the use of another renaming operation, where you would have to know the name of the column (using withColumn-Renamed(), for example).

As a bonus, imagine you want to compare the variation from the maximum every year, to display something like the following. The variation is in the delta column:

```
+----------+--------+-----+
|schoolYear|enrolled|delta|
+----------+--------+-----+
|      2006|  994597|    0|
|      2007|  978064|16533|
|      2008|  976091|18506|
|      2009|  987968| 6629|
|      2010|  990097| 4500|
|      2011|  990235| 4362|
|      2012|  986900| 7697|
|      2013|  985040| 9557|
|      2014|  983189|11408|
|      2015|  977576|17021|
|      2016|  971130|23467|
|      2017|  963861|30736|
|      2018|  954701|39896|
+----------+--------+-----+
```

You could do this by adding a max column and calculate the difference between this max and the enrolled population, as follows:

```
Dataset<Row> relativeStudentCountPerYearDf = studentCountPerYearDf
    .withColumn("max", lit(max))
    .withColumn("delta", expr("max - enrolled"))
```

```
        .drop("max")
        .orderBy("schoolYear");
    relativeStudentCountPerYearDf.show(20);
```

The lit() method will create a literal value, here based on max. The delta column is the result of the expression, expr(), of max-enrolled.

WHAT IS THE HIGHER ENROLLMENT PER SCHOOL AND YEAR?

This question will allow you to figure out, for each school, the maximum enrollment, per year. The output will look like the following listing.

Listing 15.17   Maximum enrollment for each NYC school, per year

```
...YorkSchoolStatisticsApp.java:120): Maximum enrollement per school and year
+--------+----------+-------------+
|schoolId|schoolYear|max(enrolled)|
+--------+----------+-------------+
|  01M015|      2006|          256|
|  01M015|      2007|          263|
|  01M015|      2008|          256|
|  01M015|      2009|          222|
|  01M015|      2010|          210|
|  01M015|      2011|          197|
|  01M015|      2012|          191|
|  01M015|      2013|          202|
...
|  01M019|      2007|          338|
|  01M019|      2008|          335|
|  01M019|      2009|          326|
|  01M019|      2010|          329|
|  01M019|      2011|          331|
...
```

The max() aggregation method will take the maximum value in the set, as illustrated in the following listing.

Listing 15.18   Code to compute the maximum enrollment for each NYC school, per year

```
Dataset<Row> maxEnrolledPerSchooldf = masterDf
    .groupBy(col("schoolId"), col("schoolYear"))        Extracts the maximum
    .max("enrolled")                                     value in the set
    .orderBy("schoolId", "schoolYear");
log.info("Maximum enrollement per school and year");
maxEnrolledPerSchooldf.show(20);
```

WHAT IS THE MINIMAL ABSENTEEISM PER SCHOOL?

Extracting the minimal absenteeism from our dataset is similar to finding the maximum enrollment. Let's calculate the minimal absenteeism for each school of the NYC public schools, per year. The output will look like the following listing.

Listing 15.19   Minimum absenteeism for each NYC school, per year

```
...YorkSchoolStatisticsApp.java:128): Minimum absenteeism per school and year
+--------+----------+----------+
|schoolId|schoolYear|min(absent)|
+--------+----------+----------+
|  01M015|      2006|         9|
|  01M015|      2007|        10|
|  01M015|      2008|         7|
|  01M015|      2009|         8|
...
|  01M015|      2017|         1|
|  01M015|      2018|       150|
|  01M019|      2006|         9|
|  01M019|      2007|         9|
|  01M019|      2008|        11|
...
```

The following listing shows you the code for computing this absenteeism.

Listing 15.20   Code to compute the min. absenteeism for each NYC school, per year

```
Dataset<Row> minAbsenteeDf = masterDf
    .groupBy(col("schoolId"), col("schoolYear"))
    .min("absent")
    .orderBy("schoolId", "schoolYear");
log.info("Minimum absenteeism per school and year");
minAbsenteeDf.show(20);
```

WHICH ARE THE FIVE SCHOOLS WITH THE LEAST AND MOST ABSENTEEISM?

This final question is about finding the five schools with the least absenteeism and the five schools with the most absenteeism. However, absenteeism should not be a straight value, right? An absenteeism of five absentees in a fifty-student school is more than ten absentees in an eighty-student school. So, let's look at the percentage.

When you run the app to answer this question, you should get something similar to the following listing.

Listing 15.21   Five schools with the least and most absenteeism

```
...YorkSchoolStatisticsApp.java:148): Schools with the least absenteeism
+--------+-----------------+--------------------+-------------------+
|schoolId|     avg_enrolled|         avg_absent|                  %|
+--------+-----------------+--------------------+-------------------+
|  11X113|             16.0|                 0.0|                0.0|
|  29Q420|             20.0|                 0.0|                0.0|
|  11X416|21.333333333333332|                 0.0|                0.0|
|  19K435|33.333333333333336|                 0.0|                0.0|
|  27Q481|26.333333333333332|0.010810810810810811|0.04105371193978789|
...
```

```
…YorkSchoolStatisticsApp.java:151): Schools with the most absenteeism
+--------+-----------+-------------------+----------------+
|schoolId|avg_enrolled|        avg_absent|               %|
+--------+-----------+-------------------+----------------+
|  25Q379|      154.0| 148.0810810810811|96.15654615654617|
|  75X596|      407.0|371.27027027027026|91.22119662660204|
|  16K898|       46.0| 41.4054054054054| 90.0117508813161|
|  19K907|       41.0| 36.4054054054054|88.79367172050098|
|  09X594|      198.0|174.54054054054055|88.15178815178815|
…
```

I definitely do not want my kids to be in a school where there is over 96% absenteeism. Nevertheless, let's see how you can build the app.

The first step is to create a dataset for which you collect the average absenteeism by school for each year. You can then work from this dataset to calculate averages over the years. The process is detailed in listing 15.22.

You can combine several columns in the agg() method, and the aggregation does not have to be of the same type. Here, you will be doing a max() aggregation as well as an avg() aggregation at the same time.

A column name can include any character. Here, I used the percent (%) symbol to name the absenteeism percentage column.

The method to filter over a greater value does start with a $. The following listing shows the use of $greater(). This syntax may seem confusing at first.

Listing 15.22 Code to compute the five schools with the least and most absenteeism

```
Dataset<Row> absenteeRatioDf = masterDf
    .groupBy(col("schoolId"), col("schoolYear"))
    .agg(
        max("enrolled").alias("enrolled"),        ← alias() is a
        avg("absent").as("absent"));                 synonym of as().
absenteeRatioDf = absenteeRatioDf
    .groupBy(col("schoolId"))
    .agg(                                          Calculates the absenteeism
        avg("enrolled").as("avg_enrolled"),        percent and stores it in a
        avg("absent").as("avg_absent"))            column called %
    .withColumn("%", expr("avg_absent / avg_enrolled * 100"))  ←
    .filter(col("avg_enrolled").$greater(10))   ←
    .orderBy("%");                                Filters to make sure that
log.info("Schools with the least absenteeism");  the enrollment is over 10
absenteeRatioDf.show(5);                          students

log.info("Schools with the most absenteeism");
absenteeRatioDf
    .orderBy(col("%").desc())    ←          Changes the order to display the
    .show(5);                               schools with the most absenteeism
```

Changing the order is simple, using orderBy() and optionally desc() for descending.

Appendix G lists the available aggregation functions, as you did not use all of them in these labs. Available functions are approx_count_distinct(), collect_list(),

```
collect_set(), corr(), count(), countDistinct(), covar_pop(), covar_samp(),
first(), grouping(), grouping_id(), kurtosis(), last(), max(), mean(), min(),
skewness(), stddev(), stddev_pop(), stddev_samp(), sum(), sumDistinct(),
var_pop(), var_samp(), and variance().
```

As you've seen in these examples, aggregations can be performed by methods chained after the `groupBy()` method, or by static functions inside the `agg()` method.

In the next section, you will explore a way to build custom aggregations by using your own functions, also known as user-defined aggregation functions.

15.3 *Building custom aggregations with UDAFs*

In the previous sections, you had a quick refresher on aggregating data, performed ideal operations on a simple dataset, and finally worked with real-life data (and its pesky annoyances). In those operations, you used standard aggregation operations including `max()`, `avg()`, and `min()`. Spark does not implement all possible aggregations you can do on data.

In this section, you will extend Spark by building your own aggregation function. Custom aggregations can be performed thanks to user-defined aggregation functions (UDAFs).

Imagine the following use case: you are an online retailer who wants to give loyalty points to your customers. Each customer gets one point per item ordered, but a maximum of three points per order.

One way to solve this problem could be to add a point column to your order dataframe and match the point-attribution rule, but you are going to solve this problem using an aggregation function (you can easily do the solution with the point column on your own).

Figure 15.6 shows the dataset you are going to use. It is similar to the one used in the first section of this chapter, section 15.1.

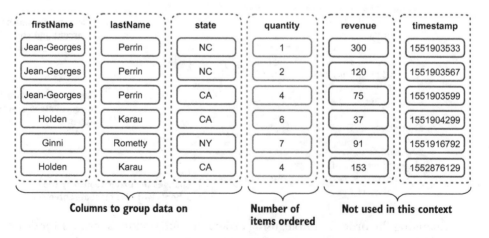

Figure 15.6   Orders on which you will apply a custom UDAF to calculate how many loyalty points each customer is getting per order

The result of the operation is a list of customers with their associated points, as in the following listing.

Listing 15.23 Customers with their associated points

```
+------------+--------+-----+-------------+-----+
|   firstName|lastName|state|sum(quantity)|point|
+------------+--------+-----+-------------+-----+
|       Ginni| Rometty|   NY|            7|    3|
|Jean-Georges|  Perrin|   NC|            3|    3|
|      Holden|   Karau|   CA|           10|    6|
|Jean-Georges|  Perrin|   CA|            4|    3|
+------------+--------+-----+-------------+-----+
```

LAB The code for this lab is in the net.jgp.books.spark.ch13.lab400_udaf package. The application is called PointsPerOrderApp.java, and the UDAF code is isolated in PointAttributionUdaf.java.

Calling a UDAF is not more complex than calling any aggregation function. There are a couple of steps:

1 Register the function in the Spark session by using the udf().register() method.
2 Call the function by using the callUDF() function.

The following listing shows the process to call the UDAF.

Listing 15.24 Registering and calling a UDAF

```
package net.jgp.books.spark.ch13.lab400_udaf;

import static org.apache.spark.sql.functions.callUDF;      ◁─── Used to call the UDAF
import static org.apache.spark.sql.functions.col;          │ Used in the aggregation
import static org.apache.spark.sql.functions.sum;
import static org.apache.spark.sql.functions.when;

import org.apache.spark.sql.Dataset;
import org.apache.spark.sql.Row;
import org.apache.spark.sql.SparkSession;

public class PointsPerOrderApp {
  public static void main(String[] args) {
    PointsPerOrderApp app = new PointsPerOrderApp();
    app.start();
  }

  private void start() {
    SparkSession spark = SparkSession.builder()
        .appName("Orders loyalty point")
        .master("local[*]")
        .getOrCreate();
```

```
        spark
            .udf().register("pointAttribution", new PointAttributionUdaf());
        Dataset<Row> df = spark.read().format("csv")
            .option("header", true)
            .option("inferSchema", true)
            .load("data/orders/orders.csv");

        Dataset<Row> pointDf = df
            .groupBy(col("firstName"), col("lastName"), col("state"))
            .agg(
                sum("quantity"),
                callUDF("pointAttribution", col("quantity")).as("point"));
        pointDf.show(20);
    }
}
```

Loads the orders →

Registers the user-defined function ←

Performs the group by on the firstName, lastName, and state columns →

Performs a sum ←

Performs the pointAttribution UDAF on the quantity column, and renames the resulting column to point ←

Calling a UDAF is as easy as this:

```
callUDF("pointAttribution", col("quantity"))
```

In this situation, your UDAF takes only one parameter, but the function can take more than one if necessary. If your UDAF needs more parameters, simply add the parameters: add them to both your call and the input schema (see listing 15.24).

Before drilling into the code, let's understand the architecture of a UDAF. Each row will be processed, and the result can be stored in an aggregation buffer (on the worker nodes). Note that the buffer does not have to reflect the structure of the incoming data: you will define its schema, and it can store other elements. Figure 15.7 illustrates the mechanism of an aggregation with its result buffer.

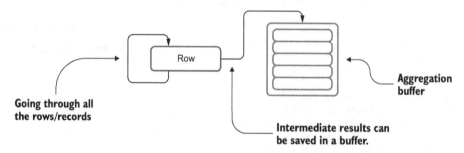

Going through all the rows/records

Row

Intermediate results can be saved in a buffer.

Aggregation buffer

Figure 15.7   As your code is analyzing each row of your dataset, the intermediary results can be saved in a buffer.

Now, let's look at how to implement the UDAF itself. The function is a function when it is called from your application; however, it is a full class when it comes to its implementation. The class must extend UserDefinedAggregateFunction (in the org.apache .spark.sql.expressions package).

As a consequence, the class implementing the UDAF must implement the following methods:

- `bufferSchema()`—Defines the schema of the buffer.
- `dataType()`—Indicates the datatype coming from the aggregation function.
- `deterministic()`—As Spark executes by splitting data, it processes the chunks separately and combines them. If the UDAF logic is such that the result is independent of the order in which data is processed and combined, the UDAF is deterministic.
- `evaluate()`—Calculates the final result of this UDAF based on the given aggregation buffer.
- `initialize()`—Initializes the given aggregation buffer.
- `inputSchema()`—Describes the schema of input sent to the UDAF.
- `merge()`—Merges two aggregation buffers and stores the updated buffer values back. This method is called when we merge two partially aggregated data elements together.
- `update()`—Updates the given aggregation buffer with new input data. This method is called once per input row.

You now have all the elements to build your UDAF, as shown in listing 15.25. Note that the class extends `UserDefinedAggregateFunction`, which implements `Serializable`. You will need to define a `serialVersionUID` variable, but, most importantly, every element of the class will need to be serializable too.

> ### Listing 15.25 Focus on the UDAF: PointAttributionUdaf.java

```
package net.jgp.books.spark.ch13.lab400_udaf;

import java.util.ArrayList;
import java.util.List;

import org.apache.spark.sql.Row;
import org.apache.spark.sql.expressions.MutableAggregationBuffer;
import org.apache.spark.sql.expressions.UserDefinedAggregateFunction;
import org.apache.spark.sql.types.DataType;
import org.apache.spark.sql.types.DataTypes;
import org.apache.spark.sql.types.StructField;
import org.apache.spark.sql.types.StructType;

public class PointAttributionUdaf
    extends UserDefinedAggregateFunction {

  private static final long serialVersionUID = -66830400L;      ◁──── A UDAF is serializable, hence the need for an identifier.
  public static final int MAX_POINT_PER_ORDER = 3;
```

The `inputSchema()` method defines a schema of the data sent to the function. In this case, you are receiving an integer representing the original number of items in the

order. A schema in Spark, which you've used a few times, is implemented using a
StructType:

Converts
a list of
fields to a
StructType

Creates a list that will
contain the field definition

_c0 is the
default name of
the first column
in a dataframe.

```
@Override
public StructType inputSchema() {
    List<StructField> inputFields = new ArrayList<>();
    inputFields.add(
        DataTypes.createStructField("_c0", DataTypes.IntegerType, true));
    return DataTypes.createStructType(inputFields);
}
```

The bufferSchema() method defines the aggregation buffer's schema, which is used
for storing the intermediate results. In this case, you will need only one column storing an integer. You may need more columns for more-complex aggregation processes.

```
@Override
public StructType bufferSchema() {
    List<StructField> bufferFields = new ArrayList<>();
    bufferFields.add(
        DataTypes.createStructField("sum", DataTypes.IntegerType, true));
    return DataTypes.createStructType(bufferFields);
}
```

```
@Override
public DataType dataType() {
    return DataTypes.IntegerType;
}
```

Datatype of
the final result

```
@Override
public boolean deterministic() {
    return true;
}
```

This function does not care
about the order of execution.

Fairly enough, the initialize() method initializes the internal buffer. In this situation, as it is a fairly simple aggregation, the buffer will be set to 0.

Nevertheless, the contract fulfilled by the class needs to follow this basic rule.
Applying the merge() method on two initial buffers should return the initial buffer
itself; for example, merge(initialBuffer, initialBuffer) equals initialBuffer.

```
@Override
public void initialize(MutableAggregationBuffer buffer) {
    buffer.update(
        0,
        0);
}
```

Column number, starting at 0

Initial value for this column

The action takes place in the update() method. This is where you will process the
data. You receive a buffer that may or may not contain data, so it must not be ignored:
in the first call, it will not contain data other than the initialized data. However, in sub-
sequent calls, the data will already be in the buffer, so it should not be ignored:

```
@Override
public void update(MutableAggregationBuffer buffer, Row input) {
    ...
    int initialValue = buffer.getInt(0);
    int inputValue = input.getInt(0);
    int outputValue = 0;
    if (inputValue < MAX_POINT_PER_ORDER) {
        outputValue = inputValue;
    } else {
        outputValue = MAX_POINT_PER_ORDER;
    }
    outputValue += initialValue;

    buffer.update(0, outputValue);
}
```

Extracts the initial value from the buffer → `int initialValue = buffer.getInt(0);`

Calculates the number of points earned with this order

Adds the points previously earned → `outputValue += initialValue;`

Stores the new value in column #0 of the aggregation buffer ← `buffer.update(0, outputValue);`

The `merge()` method merges (who could tell?) two aggregation buffers and stores the updated buffer values back in the aggregation buffer. In this scenario, when you have two buffers containing loyalty points, you simply add them:

```
@Override
public void merge(MutableAggregationBuffer buffer, Row row) {
    buffer.update(0, buffer.getInt(0) + row.getInt(0));
}
```

Finally, the `evaluate()` method calculates the final result of this UDAF based on the given aggregation buffer:

```
@Override
public Integer evaluate(Row row) {
    return row.getInt(0);
}
}
```

In this section, you have used and built your own user-defined aggregation function, which is a little tricky. The use case you followed is a simple loyalty point attribution, but you can imagine other kinds of scenarios.

If you are interested in understanding a little more about how the aggregation works, you can activate trace logging in the Log4j.properties file. Change the line

```
log4j.logger.net.jgp=DEBUG
```

to

```
log4j.logger.net.jgp=TRACE
```

On your next execution, you will then have verbose output:

```
...alize(PointAttributionUdaf.java:79): -> initialize() - buffer as 1 row(s)
...alize(PointAttributionUdaf.java:79): -> initialize() - buffer as 1 row(s)
...pdate(PointAttributionUdaf.java:92): -> update(), input row has 1 args
...pdate(PointAttributionUdaf.java:97): -> update(0, 1)
...
```

Summary

- Aggregations are a way to group data so you can look at the data from a higher, or macro, level.
- Apache Spark can perform aggregations on dataframes with Spark SQL (by creating a view) or the dataframe API.
- The `groupBy()` method is the equivalent of the SQL GROUP BY statement.
- Data needs to be prepared and cleaned before performing aggregations. Those steps can be done via transformations (chapter 12).
- Aggregations can be performed by methods chained after the `groupBy()` method, or by static functions inside the `agg()` method.
- Spark's aggregations can be extended by custom user-defined aggregation functions (UDAFs).
- A UDAF must be registered by name in your Spark session.
- A UDAF is called using the `callUDF()` method and the UDAF name.
- A UDAF is implemented as a class, which should implement several methods.
- Use the `agg()` method to perform aggregations on multiple columns at once.
- You can use the `sum()` method and static function to calculate a sum of a set.
- You can use the `avg()` method and static function to calculate an average of a set.
- You can use the `max()` method and static function to extract the maximum value of a set.
- You can use the `min()` method and static function to extract the minimum value of a set.
- Other aggregation functions include many statistical methods, such as these: `approx_count_distinct()`, `collect_list()`, `collect_set()`, `corr()`, `count()`, `countDistinct()`, `covar_pop()`, `covar_samp()`, `first()`, `grouping()`, `grouping _id()`, `kurtosis()`, `last()`, `mean()`, `skewness()`, `stddev()`, `stddev_pop()`, `stddev_samp()`, `sumDistinct()`, `var_pop()`, `var_samp()`, and `variance()`.

Part 4

Going further

Y ou're hitting the last part of this book. However, your journey is only about to start, or, if you have started it, it will become even more exciting. That's why the next three chapters will bring knowledge and answers to a lot of your questions but will also trigger more questions and guide you to more sources of knowledge. This is also the time that you can start to put everything together, in an integrated way, like building complete pipelines.

There is no doubt: Apache Spark is fast. However, performance is driven not only by the engine, but also by how you use the engine. Chapter 16 focuses primarily on two optimization techniques called *caching* and *checkpointing*. After seeing an example using theoretical data to explain caching, you will take a deep dive with real-life data and analytics. I will conclude by giving more hints and resources on further optimizing Spark.

Up to now, with the exception of chapter 2, you have been ingesting, processing, and simply showing onscreen the result of transformations and actions. Isn't it about time we do something with this data, like exporting it to files? Chapter 17 focuses on those operations and explains the impact of partitions on this project. Be careful, as chapter 17 may also include a not-so-subtle reference to the *Hitchhiker's Guide to the Galaxy*, a must for any computer book, no? Chapter 17 will also help you explore using cloud services with Spark.

Finally, finally, Chapter 18 concludes this journey—but not your journey—by focusing on the reference architectures needed for deployment. Deployment requires better understanding of the resources needed in the context of big data, as you deal with clusters and other types of resources such as network and cloud-based resources. You will also learn how to share data and files more easily. Chapter 18 is not designed to turn you into a Spark security expert, but will give you the keys to becoming one if you so wish!

Cache and checkpoint: Enhancing Spark's performances

This chapter covers

- Caching and checkpointing to enhance Spark's performance
- Choosing the right method to enhance performance
- Collecting performance information
- Picking the right spot to use a cache or checkpoint
- Using collect() and collectAsList() wisely

Spark is fast. It processes data easily across multiple nodes in a cluster or on your laptop. Spark also loves memory. That's a key design for Spark's performance. However, as your datasets grow from the sample that you use to develop applications to production datasets, you may feel that performance is going down.

In this chapter, you'll get some foundational knowledge about how Spark uses memory. This knowledge will help you in optimizing your applications.

You will first use caching and checkpointing in an application with dummy data. This step will help you better understand the various modes you can use to optimize your applications.

You will then switch to a real-life example with real-life data. In this second lab, you will run analytical operations against a dataset containing economic information from Brazil.

Finally, you will read about other considerations when optimizing workloads. I also share some hints on increasing performance as well as pointers to go further.

LAB Examples from this chapter are available in GitHub at https://github .com/jgperrin/net.jgp.books.spark.ch16.

16.1 *Caching and checkpointing can increase performance*

In this first section, you will explore caching and checkpointing in the context of Apache Spark. You'll then run a lab on dummy data, executing a process using no cache, using caching, and using both eager and non-eager checkpoints. During this process, you will also learn how to collect performance data and see that collected data in a visual representation.

Apache Spark offers two distinct techniques for increasing performance:

- Caching, via `cache()` or `persist()`, which can save your data and the data lineage
- Checkpointing, via `checkpoint()`, to save your data, without the lineage

---

Data lineage is your data's timeline

In my history classes in elementary school, the teacher would make us work on a history timeline (in French: *frise chronologique*) by having each student write a historical event on the timeline.

With data, it is exactly the same scenario: you want to be able to trace the history and provenance of your data. If there is a problem with the data, you want to be able to pinpoint where the problem comes from. Likewise, if you need to add an application to an existing architecture, data lineage will help you pick the most judicious place to plug in this new app.

In an organization, the *data lineage* indicates where the data originates, where it is going, and what modifications it goes through on this journey. Data lineage is essential in modern, relatively complex enterprise applications, because it guarantees that you have *trusted data in your system*.

In the theoretical example in the following diagram, a point-of-sale terminal generates data, which is transferred via a Perl app to a local Informix database. The local data is replicated to the HQ master database. There, several apps can consume the aggregated data, including a Node.js microservice. The microservice is being used by several clients.

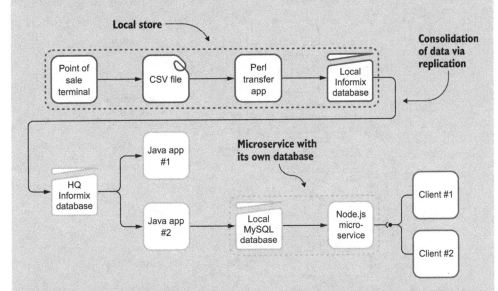

Example of a data lineage: data originates from the point-of-sale terminal and is consolidated in the local Informix database, which is replicated in the headquarters. Part of this data is then extracted from this master database and stored in a MySQL database used by a Node.js microservice.

In the context of Spark, data lineage is represented by the directed acyclic graph (DAG). You learned about the DAG in chapter 4. The diagram at the top of the next page represents the DAG used in chapter 4.

In chapter 4, you worked on lab #200, where you loaded an initial dataset, copied it 60 times, created one column based on an expression (computation of an average), duplicated two columns, and deleted the three columns.

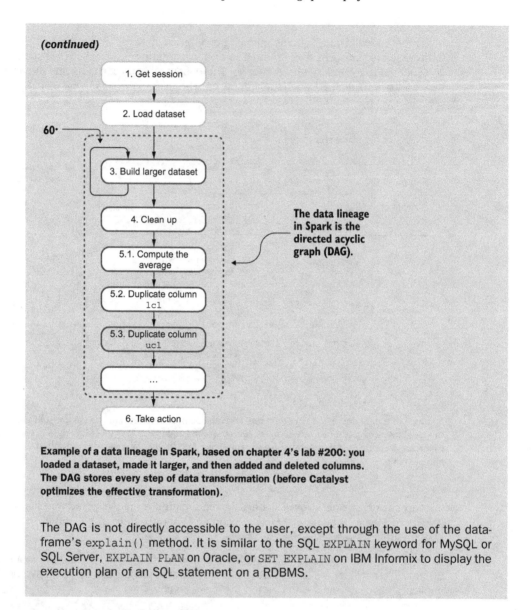

(continued)

Example of a data lineage in Spark, based on chapter 4's lab #200: you loaded a dataset, made it larger, and then added and deleted columns. The DAG stores every step of data transformation (before Catalyst optimizes the effective transformation).

The DAG is not directly accessible to the user, except through the use of the dataframe's `explain()` method. It is similar to the SQL `EXPLAIN` keyword for MySQL or SQL Server, `EXPLAIN PLAN` on Oracle, or `SET EXPLAIN` on IBM Informix to display the execution plan of an SQL statement on a RDBMS.

16.1.1 *The usefulness of Spark caching*

Let's start by understanding what caching has to offer and how it works in the context of Apache Spark. You'll also learn about caching's multiple storage levels, allowing you to fine-tune caching.

Caching can be used to increase performance. Caching will persist the dataframe in memory, or disk, or a combination of memory and disk. Caching will also save the lineage of the data. Saving the lineage is useful only if you need to rebuild your dataset from scratch, which will happen if one of the nodes of your cluster fails.

Spark offers two methods for caching: `cache()` and `persist()`. They work the same, except that `persist()` enables you to specify the storage level you wish to use. When using an argument, `cache()` is a synonym for `persist(StorageLevel.MEMORY_ONLY)`. There are no other reasons for using one versus the other. Available storage levels with the `persist()` method are as follows:

- `MEMORY_ONLY`—This is the default level. It will store the RDD composing the dataframe as deserialized Java objects in the JVM. If the RDD does not fit in memory, Spark will not cache the partitions; Spark will recompute as needed. You will not be notified.
- `MEMORY_AND_DISK`—Similar to `MEMORY_ONLY`, except that when Spark runs out of memory, it will serialize the RDD on disk. It is slower, as disk is slower, but performance will vary depending on the storage class you may have on your node (NVMe drives versus mechanical drives, for example).
- `MEMORY_ONLY_SER`—Similar to `MEMORY_ONLY`, but the Java objects are serialized. This should take less space, but reading will consume more CPU.
- `MEMORY_AND_DISK_SER`—Similar to `MEMORY_AND_DISK` with serialization.
- `DISK_ONLY`—Stores the partitions of the RDD composing the dataframe to disk.
- `OFF_HEAP`—Similar behavior to `MEMORY_ONLY_SER`, but it uses off-heap memory. Off-heap usage needs to be activated (see subsection 16.1.3 for more details on memory management).

`MEMORY_AND_DISK_2`, `MEMORY_AND_DISK_SER_2`, `MEMORY_ONLY_2`, and `MEMORY_ONLY _SER_2` are equivalent to the ones without the _2, but add replication of each partition on two cluster nodes. You would use those settings when you need replicated data to increase availability.

You can use `unpersist()` to free the cache, as well as `storageLevel()` to query the dataframe's current storage level. The `unpersist()` method will clear the cache whether you created it via `cache()` or `persist()`. You clear the cache when you're not using this dataframe anymore, so you can free up memory for processing of other datasets. When the dataframe is not cached/persisted, `storageLevel()` returns `Storage-Level.NONE`. If you do not free the memory manually, it will be cleared when the session ends, thus keeping your memory unavailable for more data or processing.

You can find more details on the storage levels at http://mng.bz/MOEE and http://mng.bz/adnx.

16.1.2 *The subtle effectiveness of Spark checkpointing*

Checkpoints are another way to increase Spark performance. In this subsection, you'll learn what checkpointing is, what kind of checkpointing you can perform, and how it differs from caching.

The `checkpoint()` method will truncate the DAG (or logical plan) and save the content of the dataframe to disk. The dataframe is saved in the checkpoint directory. There are no default values for the checkpoint directory: it must be set with

SparkContext's setCheckpointDir(), as illustrated in listing 16.1. If you do not set a checkpoint directory, checkpointing will fail and your application will stop.

A checkpoint can be eager or lazy. When eager, which is the default, the checkpoint will be created right away. If you use false with the checkpoint() method, the checkpoint will be created when an action is called. Your usage will vary depending on your goals: building a checkpoint eagerly (or right now) requires time up front, but then you can use the checkpointed dataframe in a more efficient way. If you can wait, your checkpoint will be built later, when needed by an action; the availability of the checkpoint may not be predictable.

To learn more about the logical plan and optimizer, see "Deep Dive into Spark SQL's Catalyst Optimizer" by Michael Armbrust et al. (http://mng.bz/gVMZ).

16.1.3 *Using caching and checkpointing*

In this subsection, you will put caching and checkpointing into practice through a simple application. In this scenario, you will collect performance measurements and see how performance differs.

In lab #100, you will compare the performance difference between caching and checkpointing data. To have a relatively precise measure, you need to use similar datasets. The best way to do this is to use a record generator: it will eliminate the discrepancies you may have in files, and you can more precisely define key attributes such as number of records, fields, and data types. Once loaded, the dataframe will contain books, authors, rating, year of publication (within the last 25 years), and language. Table 16.1 shows the record's structure and some random values coming from the data generator.

Table 16.1 The book record with author's name, title, rating, year published, and language

Name	Title	Rating	Year	Lang
Rob Tutt	My Worse Trip	3	2005	es
Jean-Georges Perrin	Spark in Action, 2e	5	2020	en
Ken Sanders	A Better Work	3	2018	fr

You will first keep (or filter) only the books with a rating of 5 (this is a good hint for the rating you could give this book on the Manning website and Amazon). From this dataframe of "top books," you will count the books per year and per language. Figure 16.1 illustrates the operation.

Don't get too excited: if you expect to see whether French authors get more or fewer five-star ratings than Brazilian authors, this is generated data, so the distribution is pretty much equal. If you want to perform more-sophisticated book analytics, look at lab #900 and the Goodreads dataset in the repository.

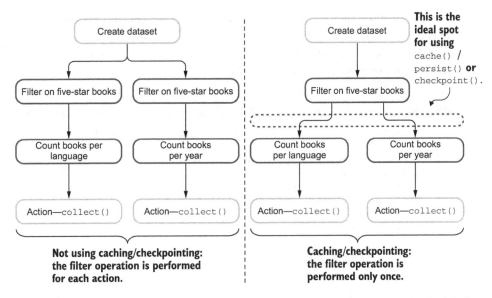

Figure 16.1 Visual representation of the transformation: if you do not put a cache or checkpoint after the filter, the filter will be recomputed every time.

The result of the application should be something like the following:

```
...
1995 ... 1337

Processing times
Without cache .............. 3618 ms
With cache ................. 2559 ms
With checkpoint ............ 1860 ms
With non-eager checkpoint ... 1420 ms
```

The code starts with CacheCheckpointApp in the net.jgp.books.spark.ch16.lab100 _cache_checkpoint package. (A reminder that this is lab #100.)

To enumerate the various execution scenarios, I will use an enumeration (enum) to designate each mode the application is going through. Those modes are without cache, with cache, and with checkpoint.

As with all labs we've gone through so far, you start a SparkSession. However, in this lab, you will learn how to specify some parameters passed to the executor, and to the driver when Spark runs the application in cluster mode (more details in chapter 6). Some of the most advanced configuration can be done at the SparkContext level (SparkSession was introduced in Spark v2 to provide a nicer abstraction). Setting the path indicating where you want the checkpointed files to be saved is done through SparkContext's setCheckpointDir(). Note that this path should be visible from the executors, not the driver: the executor will perform the checkpointing operation on the worker node, not the driver.

You will then build a function that will do all the processing based on the number of records to create and the caching mode (from the enumeration of modes).

Let's look at the code. As a reminder, I like to leave the import sections in the listing so you can easily refer to those packages.

Listing 16.1 CacheCheckpointApp: Setting the environment and running the workloads

```java
package net.jgp.books.spark.ch16.lab100_cache_checkpoint;

import static org.apache.spark.sql.functions.col;
import java.util.List;
import org.apache.spark.SparkContext;
import org.apache.spark.sql.Dataset;
import org.apache.spark.sql.Row;
import org.apache.spark.sql.SparkSession;

public class CacheCheckpointApp {
  enum Mode {
    NO_CACHE_NO_CHECKPOINT, CACHE, CHECKPOINT, CHECKPOINT_NON_EAGER
  }

  private SparkSession spark;

  public static void main(String[] args) {
    CacheCheckpointApp app = new CacheCheckpointApp();
    app.start();
  }

  private void start() {
    this.spark = SparkSession.builder()
        .appName("Lab around cache and checkpoint")
        .master("local[*]")
        .config("spark.executor.memory", "70g")
        .config("spark.driver.memory", "50g")
        .config("spark.memory.offHeap.enabled", true)
        .config("spark.memory.offHeap.size", "16g")
        .getOrCreate();
    SparkContext sc = spark.sparkContext();
    sc.setCheckpointDir("/tmp");

    int recordCount = 10000;
    long t0 = processDataframe(recordCount, Mode.NO_CACHE_NO_CHECKPOINT);
    long t1 = processDataframe(recordCount, Mode.CACHE);
    long t2 = processDataframe(recordCount, Mode.CHECKPOINT);
    long t3 = processDataframe(recordCount, Mode.CHECKPOINT_NON_EAGER);

    System.out.println("\nProcessing times");
    System.out.println("Without cache .............. " + t0 + " ms");
    System.out.println("With cache ................. " + t1 + " ms");
    System.out.println("With checkpoint ............ " + t2 + " ms");
    System.out.println("With non-eager checkpoint ... " + t3 + " ms");
  }
```

Annotations:

- **Creates a session (as usual)** → `this.spark = SparkSession.builder()`
- **Specifies that the executor memory is 70 GB. (You can run this on a machine with less.)** → `.config("spark.executor.memory", "70g")`
- **Specifies that the driver memory is 50 GB; if you run this app in local mode, you're already running the driver, so you can't change its memory.** → `.config("spark.driver.memory", "50g")`
- **Tells Spark to use the memory off heap** → `.config("spark.memory.offHeap.enabled", true)`
- **Specifies the size of the memory off the heap** → `.config("spark.memory.offHeap.size", "16g")`
- **Gets the SparkContext instance from the session** → `SparkContext sc = spark.sparkContext();`
- **Sets the path for checkpoint (on the executor)** → `sc.setCheckpointDir("/tmp");`
- **Specifies the number of records to generate** → `int recordCount = 10000;`
- **Creates and processes the records without cache or checkpoint** → `long t0 = processDataframe(recordCount, Mode.NO_CACHE_NO_CHECKPOINT);`
- **Creates and processes the records with cache** → `long t1 = processDataframe(recordCount, Mode.CACHE);`
- **Creates and processes the records with an eager checkpoint** → `long t2 = processDataframe(recordCount, Mode.CHECKPOINT);`
- **Creates and processes the records with a lazy checkpoint** → `long t3 = processDataframe(recordCount, Mode.CHECKPOINT_NON_EAGER);`

A couple of things to remember:

- Even if you set values of memory higher than the available memory, the JVM will simply not be able to use it.
- When you are running in local mode, you are executing the driver: you will not be able to change the memory allocated to the driver after it is started. That's just how the JVM works. However, when you `spark-submit` a job to a cluster, Spark will spawn the JVM and then will use the provided parameters.

Heap space issues? Are we back to the MS DOS 640 KB?

The *heap space* is a memory zone that the Java Virtual Machine (JVM) dynamically allocates for the application's objects. Some JVMs implement an *off-heap space*, also called *permanent generation* (or *permgen*). This permgen space is used for metadata and other internal JVM needs.

Default values vary from implementation to implementation. You can use the `-Xmx` parameter on the JVM command line to specify the heap space, and the `-XX:Max-PermSize` parameter to set the permgen size.

Java is one of the languages that runs on the JVM, but Scala also relies on the JVM with the same constraints. Figure 16.2 illustrates the memory model.

Wikipedia's article on the JVM describes pretty well the constraints and architecture of the virtual machine (https://en.wikipedia.org/wiki/Java_virtual_machine).

As a quick look back, in the 1980s, the Intel 8088 was used to power the first IBM PC. The processor could address 2^{20} bytes, or 1 MB. When IBM and Microsoft designed the architecture and MS DOS, they decided that the first ten 64 KB segments would be user allocable, while the last six would be used by the system. This 640 KB barrier has annoyed legions of developers and was later solved in systems like OS/2, Windows NT, and Linux . . . until 32-bit systems hit the 3 GB barrier. . . .

In conclusion, it seems that our industry, which keeps reinventing itself, is always facing the same problems again and again—memory being one of them.

To learn more about conventional memory and MS DOS, start at Wikipedia (https://en.wikipedia.org/wiki/Conventional_memory).

As you implemented the lab, you saw that Spark has important configuration entries for memory. Figure 16.2 illustrates how memory is used with a JVM and how it relates to Apache Spark.

The reference page for configuring Apache Spark (including memory) is https://spark.apache.org/docs/latest/configuration.html. To further understand Spark's memory management, you can read "Deep Understanding of Spark Memory Management Model" (https://www.tutorialdocs.com/article/spark-memory-management.html).

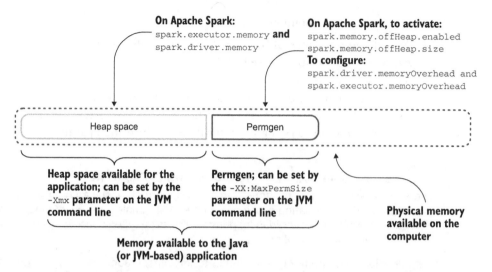

Figure 16.2   The JVM memory model with the heap space and the permanent generation (or permgen). Note that the JVM may not implement a permgen or nonheap memory area.

After this short divergence on memory management, let's get back to the application and focus on creating the record, filtering, caching and checkpointing, and assessing performance.

The `processDataframe()` method first creates a large dataframe by using a utility method you can write. This utility method builds a dataframe from a schema but uses random values for each record. The benefit is that you will have a new dataframe for each of your lab experiments, but the dataframes will be very similar. You can tweak the utility tool to build whatever record you desire. It's a simpler version of the record generator you used with structured streaming in chapter 10. Here, you will generate a record mimicking a book, containing name, title, rating, year, and language.

The first operation will be to filter all the books with a rating of five. Then you can perform an aggregation on the `lang` column to count the number of books for each language. Finally, you can perform the same operation for the year of publication.

In every example and lab so far, you've always let the executor be in charge of the outcome of the process: in most labs, I simply `show()`-ed the dataframe or dumped in a database, as in chapter 2 (and chapter 17). What if you needed to process some of the data at the driver level, not at the executor level? An example could be to use Spark to do some heavy lifting on the data and use the result of this processing with local resources to the driver (for example, sending an email with all the data or displaying it in a UI). For those scenarios, I always think of the *Hitchhiker's Guide to the Galaxy*: you send all the data to Deep Thought (or Spark), and you get back a very, very short answer: 42.[1]

---

[1] Deep Thought is a fictional computer that appears in *The Hitchhiker's Guide to the Galaxy* (the 1979 novel, as well as in the eponym 2005 movie). The computer was designed to come up with the "Answer to the Ultimate Question of Life, the Universe, and Everything." After 7.5 million years of calculation (they were obviously not using Spark), the answer turns out to be 42.

That is how you should envision the use of collect() and collectAsList(). Figure 16.3 illustrates what happens when you collect() data from the executor.

The collect() method returns an array that contains each row in this dataframe as a Java Object, while collectAsList() will return a Java List of Object, and those objects will be Row in the case of dataframes (as in List<Row>).

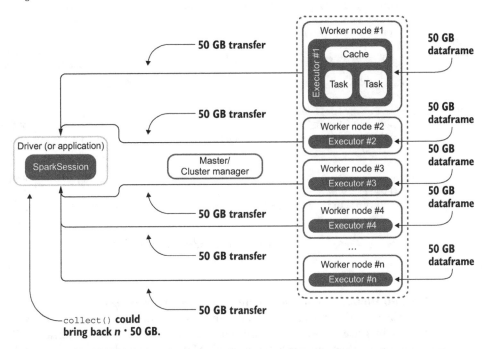

Figure 16.3 At this stage, the data resides in the worker nodes. The collect() method will bring back the dataframe's content from all the executors to the driver. If you have 100 executors (on 100 worker nodes), and your dataframe contains 50 GB, your network will endure 100 transfers of 50 GB, and your driver will need 5 TB of memory, as the collect operation will bring a list of objects in the heap memory of the driver's JVM.

Let's walk through the code in the following listing.

Listing 16.2 CacheCheckpointApp: Filtering and aggregating the data

```
private long processDataframe(int recordCount, Mode mode) {
  Dataset<Row> df =
      RecordGeneratorUtils.createDataframe(this.spark, recordCount);

  long t0 = System.currentTimeMillis();          ← Starts the timer
  Dataset<Row> topDf = df.filter(col("rating").equalTo(5));   ← Filters
  switch (mode) {
    case CACHE:
      topDf = topDf.cache();     ← When in cache mode,
      break;                        caches the dataframe
```

Creates the dataframe with the specified number of records

```
    case CHECKPOINT:
        topDf = topDf.checkpoint();        When in checkpoint
        break;                              mode, checkpoints       Counts books
    }                                       the dataframe           per language
                                                                    and collects
    List<Row> langDf =
        topDf.groupBy("lang").count().orderBy("lang").collectAsList();
    List<Row> yearDf =
        topDf.groupBy("year").count().orderBy(col("year").desc())
            .collectAsList();
    long t1 = System.currentTimeMillis();        Counts books per year of
                                                  publishing and collects

    System.out.println("Processing took " + (t1 - t0) + " ms.");

    System.out.println("Five-star publications per language");     Prints the content
    for (Row r : langDf) {                                         of the language
      System.out.println(r.getString(0) + " ... " + r.getLong(1)); aggregate
    } #I

    System.out.println("\nFive-star publications per year");       Prints the content
    for (Row r : yearDf) {                                         of the year-of-
      System.out.println(r.getInt(0) + " ... " + r.getLong(1));    publication
    }                                                              aggregate

    return t1 - t0;        Returns the consumed time
  }
}
```

Stops the timer → `long t1 = System.currentTimeMillis();`

LEAVE NO TRACE Cache uses memory. Checkpoints are saved in files. You got that. Cache will be cleaned when the session ends (or sooner). However, checkpoints are never clean and will stay on disk as Java serializable files, which means they can easily be opened. Make sure you leave no trace: delete your files.

You can clearly see that I used the *Hitchhiker's Guide to the Galaxy* (or HG2G) effect. I can process 20 million books (see figure 16.4) but will always return a very small fraction of the original dataset:

- The language aggregate will always contain at most six records composed of a short string and a long, as you are randomly generating the book language from six different languages.
- Because each year of publication was in the last 25 years, the aggregate will always contain at most 25 records composed of an integer and a long.

I ran this application with a record count from 1 to 20 million on a couple of computers. The raw results are in table 16.2, and figures 16.4 and 16.5 offer a graphical representation of the result. In this lab's repository, you will also find an Excel sheet, which you can use for your own benchmarks.

As you can see in table 16.2, using cache is a win as soon as you process more than one record, which is really an edge effect when you use Spark. The most interesting conclusion is certainly to observe that after 500,000 records, the performance is constant.

Table 16.2 Time to process a single record, in various modes (cache vs. checkpoint), time in μs (microseconds, unless stated otherwise)

Mode	Records								
	1	100	10K	100K	1M	5M	10M	15M	20M
No cache, no checkpoint	260 ms	21 ms	267.05	28.74	18.60	19.74	16.46	16.04	16.65
Caching	2158 ms	13 ms	118.33	19.80	12.95	12.87	10.62	10.74	10.84
Eager checkpoint	1352 ms	11 ms	109.78	14.41	9.69	8.82	7.86	9.85	9.02
Non-eager, or lazy, checkpoint	795 ms	10 ms	120.50	14.13	10.43	8.10	7.20	9.18	11.85

Nothing forbids you from combining caching and checkpointing, but I did not find any use case for that.

Figure 16.4 illustrates the ratio of time spent processing the data, specifically in the different modes: no cache/no checkpoint, with cache, with checkpoint, and with a lazy checkpoint.

You can conclude that the optimization method you pick is pretty much consistent whatever the optimization technology you choose, regardless of the number of records (except edge cases like 1 to 10). However, there is no absolute rule (for example, that lazy checkpointing is always better than caching): this will depend on your dataset, volume, and environment.

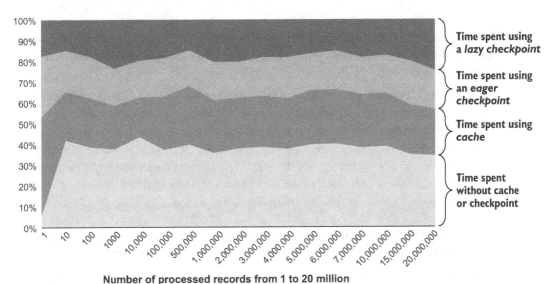

Number of processed records from 1 to 20 million

Figure 16.4 Time spent processing records in various modes: except for the edge cases, the performance is consistent per optimization method for this type of dataset, infrastructure, and hardware.

Figure 16.5 illustrates the time needed to process one record as the number of records is growing. You can conclude here too that the technology you pick delivers about the same performance, whether you are dealing with 100,000 records or 10,000,000 records.

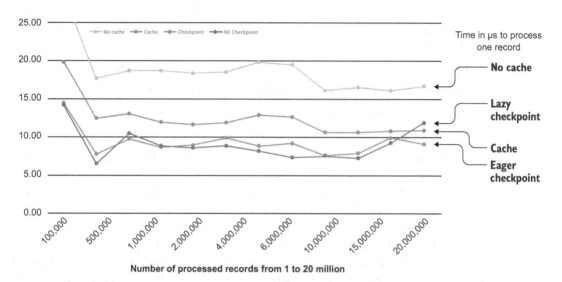

Figure 16.5   Time spent in μs (microseconds) to process a single record using no caching, cache, checkpoint, and a lazy checkpoint for this dataframe in this configuration

In this simulated environment, both checkpointing techniques are faster than caching, but both are clearly faster than no caching. How can you explain those results? Consider the following:

- Thanks to caching/checkpointing, the filtering operation is done only once. When there is no cache/checkpoint, the filtering is done once for the language aggregate and once for the year-of-publication aggregate.
- The difference between caching and checkpointing is caused mainly by whether you are keeping the lineage. The performance will be dependent on your infrastructure. Even if the checkpoint is reading the data to the disk, you will have to look at the hardware. In this situation, working on both a laptop (MacBook Pro 2015 with 16 GB of RAM, NVMe drive) and a desktop (iMac 2014 with 32 GB of RAM and a Fusion drive), data is checkpointed locally on a fast local drive, and even at 20 million records, it remains small data.

In the next section, you will apply caching in an example that is closer to real life.

16.2 Caching in action

In the previous section, you learned which kinds of optimization you can perform and how to use them. In this section, you will put this knowledge into practice on a real dataset with a real goal.

Brazil is the fifth largest country in the world (third in the Americas). It is divided into 26 states, 1 federal district (combined as 27 federative units) and 5,570 municipalities. Statistics from those 5,570 municipalities are described in the Kaggle datasets you are going to work on, which is maintained by Cristiana Parada at www.kaggle .com/crisparada/brazilian-cities. The dataset is pretty wide and contains 81 columns containing the population, the area, various economic criteria including number of hotels, hotel beds, agriculture revenue, and more.

The economic indicators from the dataset are at the municipality level. This level is too detailed to understand the macro economics of such an immense country. Therefore, you are first going to aggregate the data, then cache it, and then perform detailed operations to better understand the economics of Brazil's 27 federative units.

From this dataset, you will extract the five federative units that have the following:

- The highest population
- The biggest area
- The most McDonald's restaurants per capita
- The most Walmart supermarkets per capita
- The highest gross domestic product (GDP) per capita
- The number of post offices per capita and per area
- The number of vehicles per capita
- The percentage of agriculture land over the entire federative unit

I will call those *experiments* in the lab.

LAB This is lab #200. The source code is in the net.jgp.books.spark.ch16 .lab200_brazil_stats package. The application is called BrazilStatisticsApp.

Note that I do not endorse any brand or company noted in the datasets: these are often used in such economics-oriented datasets as an indicator of economic growth, particularly over time. This is particularly true in emerging and dynamic economies like Brazil's.

The output is in listing 16.3: I have voluntarily reduced the output in the book as it is pretty long! The full output is available online at http://mng.bz/eD2w.

Listing 16.3 Brazil economics: output

```
***** Raw dataset and schema
+--------------------+-----+-------+------------+----------------+...
|                CITY|STATE|CAPITAL|IBGE_RES_POP|IBGE_RES_POP_BRAS|...
+--------------------+-----+-------+------------+----------------+...
|           São Paulo|   SP|      1|    11253503|        11133776|...
```

```
|         Osasco|  SP|    0|    666740|        664447|...
|  Rio De Janeiro|  RJ|    1|   6320446|       6264915|...
|         Jundiaí|  SP|    0|    370126|        368648|...
...
root
 |-- CITY: string (nullable = true)
 |-- STATE: string (nullable = true)
 |-- CAPITAL: integer (nullable = true)

 |-- LONG: string (nullable = true)
 |-- LAT: string (nullable = true)
...
 |-- HOTELS: integer (nullable = true)
 |-- BEDS: integer (nullable = true)
...
 |-- Cars: integer (nullable = true)
 |-- Motorcycles: integer (nullable = true)
 |-- Wheeled_tractor: integer (nullable = true)
 |-- UBER: integer (nullable = true)
 |-- MAC: integer (nullable = true)
 |-- WAL-MART: integer (nullable = true)
 |-- POST_OFFICES: integer (nullable = true)
```

This is the raw dataset and its schema. The next step is to purify (or clean) the data so you will have quality data. During this step, you will also perform the aggregations:

```
***** Pure data
+-----+----------+----------+-----------+--------+-------------------+...
|STATE|      city|pop_brazil|pop_foreign|pop_2016|           gdp_2016|...
+-----+----------+----------+-----------+--------+-------------------+...
|   AC|Rio Branco|    732629|        930|  816687|   4757012.914863586|...
|   AL|    Maceió|   3119722|        772| 3358963|4.5452747180238724E7|...
...
Aggregation (ms) .................. 2368
```

Here you can see the results of the performed analytics:

```
***** Population
+-----+--------------+--------+
|STATE|          city|pop_2016|
+-----+--------------+--------+
|   SP|     São Paulo|44749699|
|   MG|Belo Horizonte|20997560|
|   RJ|Rio De Janeiro|16635996|
...
Population (ms) ................... 613
***** Area (squared kilometers)
+-----+--------------+----------+
|STATE|          city|      area|
+-----+--------------+----------+
|   AM|        Manaus|1503340.96|
|   PA|         Belém|1245759.35|
|   MT|        Cuiabá| 903207.13|
...
```

```
|   DF|      Brasília|    5760.78|
...
Area (ms) ....................... 615
```

Now let's have a look at the retail industry:

```
***** McDonald's restaurants per 1m inhabitants
+-----+-------------+--------+------------+----------+
|STATE|         city|pop_2016|mc_donalds_ct|mcd_1m_inh|
+-----+-------------+--------+------------+----------+
|   DF|      Brasília| 2977216|          28|       9.4|
|   SP|     São Paulo|44749699|         315|      7.03|
|   RJ|Rio De Janeiro|16635996|         103|      6.19|
...
Mc Donald's (ms) .................. 589
***** Walmart supermarket per 1m inhabitants
+-----+------------+--------+-----------+--------------+
|STATE|        city|pop_2016|wal_mart_ct|walmart_1m_inh|
+-----+------------+--------+-----------+--------------+
|   RS|Porto Alegre|11286500|         52|           4.6|
|   PE|      Recife| 9410336|         22|          2.33|
|   SE|     Aracaju| 2265779|          5|           2.2|
...
Walmart (ms) ..................... 577
```

And here are some other economic indicators, such as GDP, the number of post offices, and vehicles:

```
***** GDP per capita
+-----+-------------+--------+-------------------+----------+
|STATE|         city|pop_2016|           gdp_2016|gdp_capita|
+-----+-------------+--------+-------------------+----------+
|   DF|      Brasília| 2977216|         2.35497104E8|     79099|
|   SP|     São Paulo|44749699|1.7657257060075645E9|     39457|
|   RJ|Rio De Janeiro|16635996| 6.148317895841064E8|     36957|
...
GDP per capita (ms) .............. 617
****  Per 1 million inhabitants
+-----+-------------+--------+---------------+------------------+
|STATE|      capital|pop_2016|post_offices_ct|post_office_1m_inh|
+-----+-------------+--------+---------------+------------------+
|   TO|       Palmas| 1532902|            151|              98.5|
|   MG|Belo Horizonte|20997560|           1925|             91.67|
|   RS|  Porto Alegre|11286500|            972|             86.12|
...
****  per 100000 km2
+-----+-------------+---------------+------------------+--------------------
     +
|STATE|      capital|post_offices_ct|
     area|post_office_100k_km2|
+-----+-------------+---------------+------------------+--------------------
     +
|   RJ|Rio De Janeiro|            544| 43750.46017074585|
   1243.41|
```

```
|  DF|      Brasília|              60|   5760.77978515625|
    1041.52|
|  ES|       Vitória|             308|   46074.50023651123|
    668.48|
...
Post offices (ms) ................ 1404 / Mode: NO_CACHE_NO_CHECKPOINT
***** Vehicles
+-----+------------+--------+--------+-------+----------+
|STATE|        city|pop_2016| cars_ct|moto_ct|veh_1k_inh|
+-----+------------+--------+--------+-------+----------+
|   SC|Florianópolis| 6910553| 2942198|1151969|    592.45|
|   SP|   São Paulo|44749699|18274046|5617982|     533.9|
|   PR|    Curitiba|11242720| 4435871|1471749|    525.46|
|   DF|    Brasília| 2977216| 1288107| 211392|    503.65|
...
Vehicles (ms) .................... 547
```

Let's conclude by looking at agriculture, focusing on land usage:

```
***** Agriculture - usage of land for agriculture
+-----+------------+------+---------+------------+
|STATE|     capital|  area| agr_area|agr_area_pct|
+-----+------------+------+---------+------------+
|   PR|    Curitiba|199305|105806.85|        53.0|
|   SP|   São Paulo|248219| 88242.08|        35.5|
|   RS|Porto Alegre|278848| 90721.48|        32.5|
...
Agriculture revenue (ms) ......... 569
```

Finally, you can display the performance by using no cache or checkpoint, cache, checkpoint, and a non-eager checkpoint:

```
***** Processing times (excluding purification)
Without cache .............. 5460 ms
With cache ................. 1074 ms
With checkpoint ............ 2114 ms
With non-eager checkpoint ... 742 ms
```

It is interesting to notice that, as Brasília is the capital, it concentrates the highest GDP per capita and the most McDonald's per inhabitant. Similarly, the state of São Paulo is the economic powerhouse with a higher GDP and many of those restaurants. The economy of the southern Brazilian state of Paraná, whose capital is Curitiba, is geared more toward agriculture. And you can discover a lot more insights.

Let's have a look at the application, and then you will look at the performance. Listings 16.4, 16.5, and 16.6 show the complete application.

You will first start with the classics:

1 Import your packages and all the transformation functions.
2 Define the various execution modes.
3 Open a session.

4 Read the CSV file.
5 Call a method for performing the aggregation and analytics for each mode.
6 Display the results.

As you are going to load the data, it's always a good idea to look at the file. Here is a quick look at the first couple of lines of the dataset in CSV:

```
CITY;STATE;CAPITAL;IBGE_RES_POP;IBGE_RES_POP_BRAS;IBGE_RES_POP_ESTR;
  IBGE_DU;IBGE_DU_URBAN;IBGE_DU_RURAL;IBGE_POP;IBGE_1;IBGE_1-4;
  IBGE_5-9;IBGE_10-14;…
Abadia De Goiás;GO;0;6876;6876;0;2137;1546;591;5300;69;318;438;517;
  3542;416; 319;1843;1689;0.708;0.687;0.83;0.622;-49.44054783;
  -16.75881189;893.6;360;842;…
```

You can see that the separator is the semicolon (;), the decimal separator is the dot (.), and so on.

In listing 16.4, I simplified the import, but you could replace

```
import static org.apache.spark.sql.functions.*;
```

with

```
import static org.apache.spark.sql.functions.col;
import static org.apache.spark.sql.functions.expr;
import static org.apache.spark.sql.functions.first;
import static org.apache.spark.sql.functions.regexp_replace;
import static org.apache.spark.sql.functions.round;
import static org.apache.spark.sql.functions.sum;
import static org.apache.spark.sql.functions.when;
```

because you are going to use only those functions: col(), expr(), first(), regexp _replace(), round(), sum(), and when().

Listing 16.4   Initialization and ingestion

```
package net.jgp.books.spark.ch16.lab200_brazil_stats;

import static org.apache.spark.sql.functions.*;

import org.apache.spark.SparkContext;
import org.apache.spark.sql.Dataset;
import org.apache.spark.sql.Row;
import org.apache.spark.sql.SparkSession;

public class BrazilStatisticsApp {
  enum Mode {
    NO_CACHE_NO_CHECKPOINT, CACHE, CHECKPOINT, CHECKPOINT_NON_EAGER
  }
…
  private void start() {                                        Creates a session
    SparkSession spark = SparkSession.builder()      ←──────┘  on a local master
        .appName("Brazil economy")
        .master("local[*]")
```

```
         .getOrCreate();
    SparkContext sc = spark.sparkContext();
    sc.setCheckpointDir("/tmp");
                                                    Reads a CSV file with header;
    Dataset<Row> df = spark.read().format("csv")    stores it in a dataframe
        .option("header", true)
        .option("sep", ";")
        .option("enforceSchema", true)
        .option("nullValue", "null")
        .option("inferSchema", true)
        .load("data/brazil/BRAZIL_CITIES.csv");
    System.out.println("***** Raw dataset and schema");
    df.show(100);                                   Creates and processes
    df.printSchema();                               the records with cache

    long t0 = process(df, Mode.NO_CACHE_NO_CHECKPOINT);
    long t1 = process(df, Mode.CACHE);              Creates and processes
    long t2 = process(df, Mode.CHECKPOINT);         the records with a
    long t3 = process(df, Mode.CHECKPOINT_NON_EAGER); checkpoint

    System.out.println("\n***** Processing times (excluding purification)");
    System.out.println("Without cache .............. " + t0 + " ms");
    System.out.println("With cache ................. " + t1 + " ms");
    System.out.println("With checkpoint ............ " + t2 + " ms");
    System.out.println("With non-eager checkpoint ... " + t3 + " ms");
}
```

Creates and processes the records
(without cache or checkpoint) — *Creates and processes the records without cache or checkpoint*

Creates and processes the records with a non-eager checkpoint

The next step is to purify (prepare) the data so you can use the dataframe. To have a suitable dataframe to perform analytics on, you will perform about 25 operations, detailed in listing 16.5. In production, I would recommend using constants for field names.

In previous versions of this dataset, the GDP was formatted using the European locale: the period (.) is used as a thousands separator, and the comma (,) as the decimal separator. In the following listing, I'll show you how you can transform such a value to be understood by Spark as a float.

Listing 16.5   Processing of the dataset in various modes

```
long process(Dataset<Row> df, Mode mode) {
    long t0 = System.currentTimeMillis();
                                                Replaces commas with periods
    df = df                                     in a string, so the field can be
        .orderBy(col("CAPITAL").desc())         converted to a float
        .withColumn("WAL-MART",
            when(col("WAL-MART").isNull(), 0).otherwise(col("WAL-MART")))
        .withColumn("MAC",
            when(col("MAC").isNull(), 0).otherwise(col("MAC")))
        .withColumn("GDP", regexp_replace(col("GDP"), ",", "."))
        .withColumn("GDP", col("GDP").cast("float"))
        .withColumn("area", regexp_replace(col("area"), ",", ""))
```

Replaces null values with 0 — *Replaces null values with 0*

```
        .withColumn("area", col("area").cast("float"))
        .groupBy("STATE")                              ←——— Groups by state
        .agg(
            first("CITY").alias("capital"),
            sum("IBGE_RES_POP_BRAS").alias("pop_brazil"),
            sum("IBGE_RES_POP_ESTR").alias("pop_foreign"),
            sum("POP_GDP").alias("pop_2016"),
            sum("GDP").alias("gdp_2016"),
            sum("POST_OFFICES").alias("post_offices_ct"),
            sum("WAL-MART").alias("wal_mart_ct"),
            sum("MAC").alias("mc_donalds_ct"),
            sum("Cars").alias("cars_ct"),
            sum("Motorcycles").alias("moto_ct"),
            sum("AREA").alias("area"),
            sum("IBGE_PLANTED_AREA").alias("agr_area"),
            sum("IBGE_CROP_PRODUCTION_$").alias("agr_prod"),
            sum("HOTELS").alias("hotels_ct"),                   Converts hectares to
            sum("BEDS").alias("beds_ct"))             ┌——— square kilometers
        .withColumn("agr_area", expr("agr_area / 100"))  ←——┘
        .orderBy(col("STATE"))
        .withColumn("gdp_capita", expr("gdp_2016 / pop_2016 * 1000"));  ←——┐
    switch (mode) {                                              Computes the
        case CACHE:          ←——┐                                GDP per capita
            df = df.cache();      Further operations will be
            break;               done on a cached dataframe.

        case CHECKPOINT:         ←——┐ Further operations will be done
            df = df.checkpoint();      on a checkpointed dataframe.
            break;

        case CHECKPOINT_NON_EAGER:  ←——┐ Further operations will be done on a
            df = df.checkpoint(false);   non-eagerly checkpointed dataframe.
            break;
    }
    System.out.println("***** Pure data");
    df.show(5);
    long t1 = System.currentTimeMillis();
    System.out.println("Aggregation (ms) ................. " + (t1 - t0));
```

Switches on mode (annotation pointing to `switch (mode) {`)

You can now perform analytics on the dataset. Because there are quite a few operations, I removed some of them to keep the listing short. Nevertheless, the whole listing is at http://mng.bz/py4E. The listing will focus on the following:

- The population per state
- The number of Walmart stores per million inhabitants
- The number of post offices per million inhabitants and area

In the first analytics in the following listing, you will simply use the master dataframe, remove some unneeded columns, and sort by population.

Listing 16.6 Analytics: finding the population

```
System.out.println("***** Population");
Dataset<Row> popDf = df
    .drop(
        "area", "pop_brazil", "pop_foreign", "post_offices_ct",
        "cars_ct", "moto_ct", "mc_donalds_ct", "agr_area", "agr_prod",
        "wal_mart_ct", "hotels_ct", "beds_ct", "gdp_capita", "agr_area",
        "gdp_2016")
    .orderBy(col("pop_2016").desc());
popDf.show(30);
long t2 = System.currentTimeMillis();
System.out.println("Population (ms) .................. " + (t2 - t1));
```

In the second analytics experiment, in listing 16.7, you will find out how many Walmart supermarket stores exist per million inhabitants. Note that to have a precision of two decimal points, you can use round() or can multiply by 100, get the integer value, and divide by 100.

Listing 16.7 Analytics: counting the Walmart stores

```
System.out.println("***** Walmart supermarket per 1m inhabitants");
Dataset<Row> walmartPopDf = df
    .withColumn("walmart_1m_inh",
        expr("int(wal_mart_ct / pop_2016 * 100000000) / 100"))
    .drop(
        "pop_brazil", "pop_foreign", "post_offices_ct", "cars_ct",
        "moto_ct", "area", "agr_area", "agr_prod", "mc_donalds_ct",
        "hotels_ct", "beds_ct", "gdp_capita", "agr_area", "gdp_2016")
    .orderBy(col("walmart_1m_inh").desc());
walmartPopDf.show(5);
long t5 = System.currentTimeMillis();
System.out.println("Walmart (ms) .................... " + (t5 - t4));
```

The next listing shows the last experiment. You will compute the number of post offices per million inhabitants, as well as per 100,000 km². Then you will refine the results.

Listing 16.8 Analytics: Where are the post offices?

```
System.out.println("***** Post offices");
Dataset<Row> postOfficeDf = df
    .withColumn("post_office_1m_inh",
        expr("int(post_offices_ct / pop_2016 * 100000000) / 100"))
    .withColumn("post_office_100k_km2",
        expr("int(post_offices_ct / area * 10000000) / 100"))
    .drop(
        "gdp_capita", "pop_foreign", "gdp_2016", "gdp_capita",
        "cars_ct", "moto_ct", "agr_area", "agr_prod", "mc_donalds_ct",
        "hotels_ct", "beds_ct", "wal_mart_ct", "agr_area", "pop_brazil")
    .orderBy(col("post_office_1m_inh").desc());
switch (mode) {
  case CACHE:
```

⎤ **Caches or checkpoints the**
⎦ **intermediate dataframe**

```
      postOfficeDf = postOfficeDf.cache();
      break;
   case CHECKPOINT:
      postOfficeDf = postOfficeDf.checkpoint();       Caches or checkpoints the
      break;                                           intermediate dataframe
   case CHECKPOINT_NON_EAGER:
      postOfficeDf = postOfficeDf.checkpoint(false);
      break;
}
System.out.println("****  Per 1 million inhabitants");
Dataset<Row> postOfficePopDf = postOfficeDf        Calculates the number
      .drop("post_office_100k_km2", "area")          of post offices per
      .orderBy(col("post_office_1m_inh").desc());     million inhabitants
postOfficePopDf.show(5);
System.out.println("****  per 100000 km2");
Dataset<Row> postOfficeArea = postOfficeDf         Calculates the number of
      .drop("post_office_1m_inh", "pop_2016")        post offices per 100,000 km²
      .orderBy(col("post_office_100k_km2").desc());
postOfficeArea.show(5);
long t7 = System.currentTimeMillis();
System.out.println(
      "Post offices (ms) ................ " + (t7 - t6) +
      " / Mode: " + mode);
...
```

The interesting part is that by caching/checkpointing the intermediate results for the calculation around the post offices, you will also be able to increase performance:

```
Post offices (ms) ................ 1301 / Mode: NO_CACHE_NO_CHECKPOINT
Post offices (ms) ................ 351 / Mode: CACHE
Post offices (ms) ................ 1580 / Mode: CHECKPOINT
Post offices (ms) ................ 361 / Mode: CHECKPOINT_NON_EAGER
```

Figure 16.6 gives a visual representation of the number of operations that Spark has to do for each analytics experiment. Each little square represents an operation, regardless of its complexity or duration. Darker squares indicate data preparation (intrinsically providing less value), while light squares are specific operations for the experiment and provide a higher apparent value.

Finally, when you look at the overall performance, it varies from 742 ms to 5460 ms. In this lab, compared to lab #100 in section 16.1, caching is faster than using an eager checkpoint. There are no specific rules to follow. However, analytics jobs seem to repeat themselves, so after you find a better optimization, it will very likely be consistent.

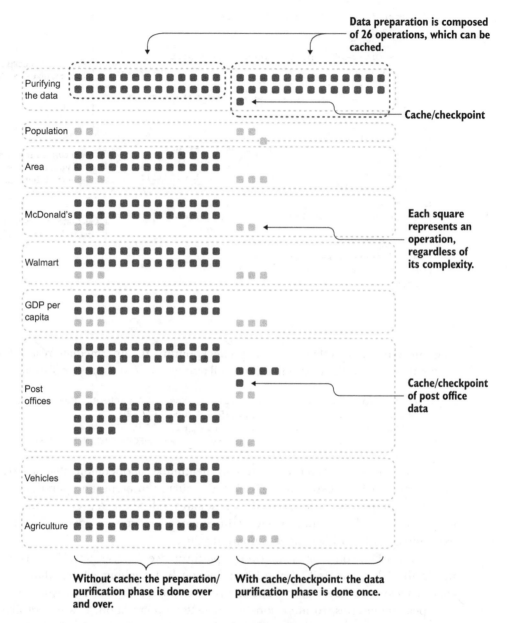

Figure 16.6 Representation of the number of operations Spark has to do to run all the analytics experiments in this lab. Each square represents an operation. You can quickly see the benefits of caching and/or checkpointing in this context.

16.3   *Going further in performance optimization*

Before wrapping up this chapter, I want to give you more hints about increasing the performance of your Spark applications.

A lot of the issues can come from key skewing (or data skewing): the data is so fragmented among partitions that a join operation becomes very long. In this situation, you may want to investigate repartitioning the data by using `coalesce()`, `repartition()`, or `repartitionByRange()`. Repartitioning is most likely to be an expensive operation but it will increase the performance for the join afterward. Data skewing is not a Spark-specific problem; it can arise from any distributed dataset.

This book focuses on dataframes as the API and storage container. However, if you inherit an existing Spark application, you may want to replace the RDDs with dataframes because Catalyst (the Spark optimizer) will thrive with dataframes. RDDs are known to be slower than dataframes.

If you are into benchmarks and performance measurement, you may find that the methodology used in this chapter may not be precise enough. Therefore, I recommend you have a look at CODAIT's open source tool, Spark-Bench. It is defined as a flexible system for benchmarking and simulating Spark jobs. You can find its documentation and download it from https://codait.github.io/spark-bench/.

Here are some interesting resources to help you go further:

- Spark documentation on tuning: https://spark.apache.org/docs/latest/tuning.html.
- *High Performance Spark: Best Practices for Scaling and Optimizing Apache Spark* by Holden Karau and Rachel Warren (O'Reilly, 2017).
- My friend Jacek Laskowski maintains a GitBook, *The Internals of Apache Spark*, which has a section on performance tuning: https://books.japila.pl/apache-spark-internals/apache-spark-internals/2.4.4/spark-tuning.html.

Summary

- As one way to increase performance, Spark offers caching, eagerly checkpointing, and non-eagerly (or lazy) checkpointing.
- Caching keeps the lineage data. You can trigger the cache by using `cache()` or `persist()`. Caching offers various levels of storage combining memory and disk.
- Checkpointing does not keep the lineage and saves the content of the dataframe to disk.
- Lack of heap memory can become an issue with large datasets; Spark can use the off-heap/permgen space.
- Keep in mind the *Hitchhiker's Guide to the Galaxy* (or HG2G) effect when you use `collect()`, as you are bringing back data from the executors to the driver.

- Data lineage is your data transformation timeline; it identifies the source, the destination, and all the steps in between. This is part of the fundamental concepts of data governance.
- Caching can use a combination of memory and disk.
- Checkpointing helps increase performance by saving the data contained in the dataframe to disk. An eager checkpoint performs the operation right away, while a non-eager or lazy operation will wait for an action.
- A checkpoint directory has to be set in the `SparkContext`, which you can get from the `SparkSession`. There is no default value for the checkpoint directory.
- Performance depends on many factors; there is no one-size-fits-all solution.
- Brazil has 27 federative units: 26 states and 1 federal district.

Exporting data and building full data pipelines

This chapter covers

- Exporting data from Spark
- Building a complete data pipeline, from ingestion to export
- Understanding the impact of partitioning
- Using Delta Lake as a database
- Using Spark with cloud storage

As you are reaching the end of this book, it is time to see how to export data. After all, why did you learn all this if it was just to keep data within Spark, right? I know, I do appreciate learning as a hobby, but it is even better when you can actually bring some business value, right?

This chapter is divided into three sections. The first section covers exporting data. As usual, you will use a real dataset, ingest it, and then export it. You will impersonate a NASA scientist and start exploiting data coming from satellites.

Those datasets can be used to prevent wildfires. This is the first step of using code for good! In this section, you will also see the impact of partitioning on exporting data.

In the second part of this chapter, you will experiment with Delta Lake, a database that sits within the core of Spark. Delta Lake can radically simplify your data pipeline, and you will see how and why.

Finally, I will share resources about using Apache Spark with cloud storage providers including AWS, Microsoft Azure, IBM Cloud, OVH, and Google Cloud Platform. Those resources are mainly aimed at helping you navigate in those ever-moving cloud offerings.

Appendix Q is a companion for this chapter. Whereas the chapter focuses on teaching you how to export data, the appendix is a reference that will be useful as you walk through the labs and implement Spark applications.

> **LAB**   Examples from this chapter are available in GitHub at https://github.com/jgperrin/net.jgp.books.spark.ch17. Appendix Q is a reference for exporting data.

17.1   Exporting data

This section will walk you through the main concepts of exporting (or writing, in the Spark terminology) the data contained in the dataframes. You will build a workflow, perform transformations, and then export data to files. At the end of the section, you will dig a bit deeper into what happens behind the scenes.

In chapter 2, you exported a dataframe to a database. Now that you are more skilled, let's export the content of a dataframe after transformation.

> **LAB**   This section relies on chapter 17's lab #100, called ExportWildfiresApp, in the net.jgp.books.spark.ch17.lab100_export package. The datasets come from NASA, found via IBM's Call for Code.

17.1.1   Building a pipeline with NASA datasets

In this section, you will discover the scenario of this chapter's first lab. You will then perform the now-traditional and routine (in the context of this book, as you have done it many times) data observation and data mapping steps. Along the way, you will learn how to download datasets automatically and learn about one of my favorite best practices when I code in Java: using constants.

Imagine this scenario. You are a participant at IBM's Call for Code (https://callforcode.org), an international competition in which coders are invited to use their skills to do good on the planet. You are focusing on wildfires (http://mng.bz/O9O2). Your idea is to use multiple data sources to identify regions that have a higher risk of wildfires.

You will start by analyzing NASA's wildfire data, which can be downloaded from http://mng.bz/YeEe. In this context, you want to create a data pipeline: you'll download files from two systems, ingest the data, create a unified data file, and save the results. Figure 17.1 illustrates the data pipeline you are building.

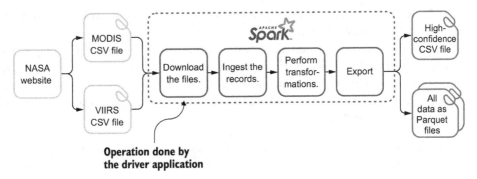

Figure 17.1 Data pipeline taking the raw data from the NASA website to local storage

You will save the records with high confidence in a CSV file, and will save all the data aggregated and cleaned in Parquet files. There are a lot of similarities between exporting data and ingesting from files, which you studied in chapter 7. If you are not familiar with Parquet, you will find more information about it and other file formats in that chapter.

The output will be files in /tmp, as illustrated in the next listing. If you are using Windows, you will need to modify the export path to match the filesystem. Your output will also differ a little bit from that shown here.

Listing 17.1 Output of the export data app

```
$ ls -l /tmp/fires_parquet
total 9592
...         0 ... _SUCCESS
...   3321231 ... part-00000-364a9bfd-c976-4a99-b1e4-f11b37e40...-c000.snappy.parquet
...    649907 ... part-00001-364a9bfd-c976-4a99-b1e4-f11b37e40...-c000.snappy.parquet
$ ls -l /tmp/high_confidence_fires_csv
total 2256
...         0 ... _SUCCESS
...   1154373 ... part-00000-59d63211-5088-4cf9-8357-11a8c7621246-c000.csv
```

Let's first go through our data discovery. NASA provides two types of files based on different equipment and providing different resolutions:

- The Moderate Resolution Imaging Spectroradiometer (MODIS) has a resolution of 1,000 meters You can discover the MODIS data catalog at http://mng.bz/G4QV.
- The Visible Infrared Imaging Radiometer Suite (VIIRS) data comes from a sensor on the joint NASA/NOAA Suomi (Finland) national polar-orbiting partnership (Suomi-NPP) satellite. It offers a resolution of 375 meters. The VIIRS data catalog is available at http://mng.bz/zlYr.

When NASA receives the data, the administration makes it available at http://mng.bz/YeEe. On this website, you can download a rolling dataset of the last 24 hours,

48 hours, or seven days of the satellite data. You will download the data from both data sources for the last 24 hours.

Listing 17.2 contains the K class with constants. I love using constants; they impose rigor. I usually have my constants in a class named K. Why K, do you ask? *K* is the first letter of *Konstante,* the German word for a *constant.* And who are probably the most rigorous people? Germans. So, it makes sense to have a class called K containing all the *Konstanten,* right?

Listing 17.2   Constants

```
package net.jgp.books.spark.ch17.lab100_export;

public class K {
  public static final String MODIS_FILE = "MODIS_C6_Global_24h.csv";
  public static final String VIIRS_FILE = "VNP14IMGTDL_NRT_Global_24h.csv";
  public static final String TMP_STORAGE = "/tmp";
}
```

Name of the VIIRS file

Name of the MODIS file

Temporary storage location

The whole download mechanism is in the following listing.

Listing 17.3   Downloading files using Java NIO: beginning the data pipeline

```
private boolean downloadWildfiresDatafiles() {
  String fromFile =
      "https://firms.modaps.eosdis.nasa.gov/data/active_fire/c6/csv/"
          + K.MODIS_FILE;
  String toFile = K.TMP_STORAGE + "/" + K.MODIS_FILE;
  if (!download(fromFile, toFile)) {
    return false;
  }

  fromFile =
      "https://firms.modaps.eosdis.nasa.gov/data/active_fire/viirs/csv/"
          + K.VIIRS_FILE;
  toFile = K.TMP_STORAGE + "/" + K.VIIRS_FILE;
  if (!download(fromFile, toFile)) {
    return false;
  }

  return true;
}

private boolean download(String fromFile, String toFile) {
  try {
    URL website = new URL(fromFile);
    ReadableByteChannel rbc = Channels.newChannel(website.openStream());
    FileOutputStream fos = new FileOutputStream(toFile);
    fos.getChannel().transferFrom(rbc, 0, Long.MAX_VALUE);
    fos.close();
    rbc.close();
```

Downloads the MODIS data file

Downloads the VIIRS data file

Downloads code using Java NIO (nonblocking I/O)

```
  } catch (IOException e) {
...
    return false;
  }
...
  return true;
}
```

Once you have downloaded the files, you will need to modify their schemas so you can union them, as shown in figure 17.2.

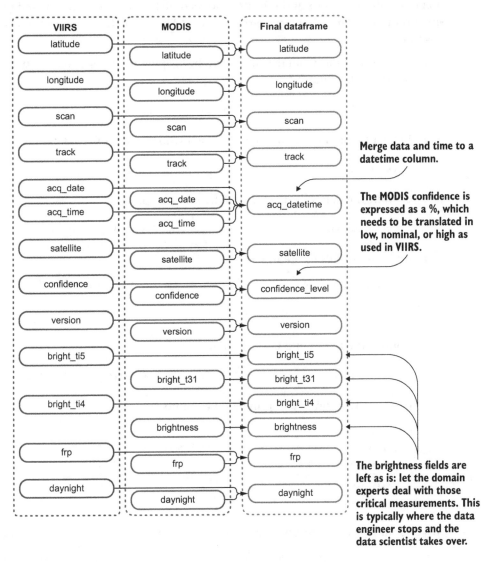

Figure 17.2 Data mapping between the VIIRS, MODIS, and final datasets

These mapping and transformation operations are similar to any transformation, so let's go through them diligently in the next subsection.

17.1.2 *Transforming columns to datetime*

The benefits of using real-world datasets comes with a price: you also have to adapt to their incongruences and work around them. In this subsection, you will manipulate dates and timestamps to get the right format in the final dataset.

The files include the date field as *YYYY-MM-DD* (the ISO standard), and time as an integer combining hours and minutes (no seconds). The time zone is based on UTC, which is the standard for all space-related data. The way I choose to do this operation is as follows:

1 Extract the hour from the time field, by keeping the integer part of the division by 100 of the dataset's time:

```
.withColumn("acq_time_hr", expr("int(acq_time / 100)"))
```

2 Extract the minute as the modulo of a division by 100 of the dataset's time:

```
.withColumn("acq_time_min", expr("acq_time % 100"))
```

3 Convert the dataset's date to a UNIX timestamp:

```
.withColumn("acq_time2", unix_timestamp(col("acq_date")))
```

4 Add the seconds to the timestamp:

```
.withColumn(
    "acq_time3",
    expr("acq_time2 + acq_time_min * 60 + acq_time_hr * 3600"))
```

5 Convert the timestamp back to a date:

```
.withColumn("acq_datetime", from_unixtime(col("acq_time3")))
```

6 Drop the temporary and unneeded columns:

```
.drop("acq_date")
.drop("acq_time")
.drop("acq_time_min")
.drop("acq_time_hr")
.drop("acq_time2")
.drop("acq_time3")
```

This operation is done for both datasets.

17.1.3 *Transforming the confidence percentage to confidence level*

Now, you will perform another transformation: turning an integer value into a textual explanation. You will use more of Spark's static functions for this operation.

Another transformation on the MODIS dataset is turning the confidence expressed as a percentage into a confidence level as expressed in the VIIRS dataset. I picked the following values:

- If the confidence is less than or equal to 40%, the level is low.
- If the confidence is more than 40%, but below 100%, then the level is nominal.
- Any other value (100%) is high.

The way to do this is to use conditional functions such as when() and otherwise(). If the confidence is less than or equal to 40, the confidence level is low. Otherwise, the confidence level is null:

```
int low = 40;
int high = 100;
...
    .withColumn(
        "confidence_level",
        when(col("confidence").$less$eq(low), "low"))
```

If the confidence is greater than 40 and less than 100, the confidence level is nominal. Otherwise, the confidence level remains at its current value (at this stage, the confidence level can be low or null):

```
    .withColumn(
        "confidence_level",
        when(
            col("confidence").$greater(low)
                .and(col("confidence").$less(high)),
            "nominal")
                .otherwise(col("confidence_level")))
```

If the confidence level is null, set it to high:

```
    .withColumn(
        "confidence_level",
        when(isnull(col("confidence_level")), "high")
            .otherwise(col("confidence_level")))
.drop("confidence")
```

17.1.4 *Exporting the data*

In this section, you'll finally write (export) the data. You will first get accustomed to the key method for exporting data: write(). You will then go through the code to export the data contained in the dataframe in two sets of files, both Parquet and CSV.

The write() method is the counterpart method to load(), which you have been using extensively in this book. The write() method returns a DataFrameWriter,

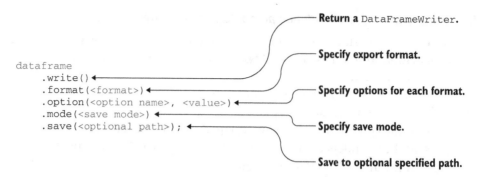

Figure 17.3   The `write()` method syntax, where you can specify the format, options, save mode, and save location

whose reference is available at http://mng.bz/07Nm. Figure 17.3 illustrates the write() syntax.

Appendix Q lists the available formats for exporting data from Spark, as well as the various write options. Those are the built-in formats, but, as you can expect, you can build your own writer, as you built your own reader in chapter 9.

You will first save the entire dataframe as a Parquet file, overwriting any existing files. Then, you can filter the data to get only records with the highest confidence levels. To make sure you have only one file, you will need to repartition to one partition and then save the file. Toward the end of listing 17.4, you can see the write() calls and process.

The save() method takes a directory path in which the file(s) will be written. Here, I used /tmp/fires_parquet and /tmp/high_confidence_fires_csv. The exported files will be in those directories. In the next subsection, you will review in more detail what is happening.

You can now focus on the whole pipeline code, as illustrated in the next listing. As usual, I will show all the import statements so you can see which packages and functions are being used.

Listing 17.4   Building the data pipeline

```
package net.jgp.books.spark.ch17.lab100_export;

import static org.apache.spark.sql.functions.col;
import static org.apache.spark.sql.functions.expr;
import static org.apache.spark.sql.functions.from_unixtime;
import static org.apache.spark.sql.functions.isnull;
import static org.apache.spark.sql.functions.lit;
import static org.apache.spark.sql.functions.round;
import static org.apache.spark.sql.functions.unix_timestamp;
import static org.apache.spark.sql.functions.when;
import java.io.FileOutputStream;
import java.io.IOException;
```

```
import java.net.URL;
import java.nio.channels.Channels;
import java.nio.channels.ReadableByteChannel;

import org.apache.spark.sql.Dataset;
import org.apache.spark.sql.Row;
import org.apache.spark.sql.SaveMode;
import org.apache.spark.sql.SparkSession;
...

public class ExportWildfiresApp {
...
  private boolean start() {
    if (!downloadWildfiresDatafiles()) {          ⟵── Downloads the files
      return false;
    }

    SparkSession spark = SparkSession.builder()    ⟵── Gets a session
        .appName("Wildfire data pipeline")
        .master("local[*]")
        .getOrCreate();
                                                              Loads and formats
    Dataset<Row> viirsDf = spark.read().format("csv")    ⟵─┘ the VIIRS dataset
        .option("header", true)
        .option("inferSchema", true)
        .load(K.TMP_STORAGE + "/" + K.VIIRS_FILE)
        ...
        .withColumnRenamed("confidence", "confidence_level")
        .withColumn("brightness", lit(null))
        .withColumn("bright_t31", lit(null));
```

Loads and formats the MODIS dataset

Turns the date and time columns into a datetime column (see section 17.1.2)

```
    int low = 40;
    int high = 100;
    Dataset<Row> modisDf = spark.read().format("csv")
        .option("header", true)
        .option("inferSchema", true)
        .load(K.TMP_STORAGE + "/" + K.MODIS_FILE)
        ...
        ...
        .withColumn("bright_ti4", lit(null))
        .withColumn("bright_ti5", lit(null));
```

Turns the confidence into a confidence level (see 17.1.3)

Unions (or merges) the two datasets

```
    Dataset<Row> wildfireDf = viirsDf.unionByName(modisDf);

    log.info("# of partitions: {}", wildfireDf.rdd().getNumPartitions());  ⟵
```

Displays the number of partitions in the merged datasets

```
    wildfireDf                      ⟵── Writes the dataframe
        .write()                        to Parquet files
        .format("parquet")
        .mode(SaveMode.Overwrite)
        .save("/tmp/fires_parquet");
```

Filters on high level of confidence

```
    Dataset<Row> outputDf = wildfireDf       ⟵
        .filter("confidence_level = 'high'")
        .repartition(1);                     ⟵
```

Repartitions the data in only one partition

```
outputDf
    .write()                         ◄───┐  Writes the data to
    .format("csv")                       │  a single CSV file
    .option("header", true)
    .mode(SaveMode.Overwrite)
    .save("/tmp/high_confidence_fires_csv");

return true;
}
```

After the file(s) have been successfully exported, Spark will add a _SUCCESS file to the directory, allowing you to monitor whether the operation, which can be lengthy, has completed as expected.

17.1.5 Exporting the data: What really happened?

In the previous subsections, you built and ran the application. The data is now exported. Now you will learn about what really happened, as understanding the initial result may not be straightforward. You will first have another look at the output, and then dive into the Spark implementation and learn more about partitions.

When you look closely at the collection result at http://mng.bz/zlYr, you will see two files in the Parquet directory and one file in the CSV directory, as shown in the following listing. You will also have a _SUCCESS file that indicates that the process has successfully ended.

Listing 17.5   Output files

```
$ ls -l /tmp/fires_parquet
total 9592
...         0 ... _SUCCESS
...   3321231 ... part-00000-364a9bfd-c976-4a99-b1e4-f11b37e40...-c000.snappy.parquet
...    649907 ... part-00001-364a9bfd-c976-4a99-b1e4-f11b37e40...-c000.snappy.parquet
$ ls -l /tmp/high_confidence_fires_csv
total 2256
...         0 ... _SUCCESS
...   1154373 ... part-00000-59d63211-5088-4cf9-8357-11a8c7621246-c000.csv
```

When you load two datasets, they will be stored in two dataframes. Each dataframe will have at least one partition. As you perform a union operation on those dataframes, you will have one resulting dataframe, but the partitions will now be two. Figure 17.4 illustrates the mechanism.

The filtering operation, which removes the nominal and low confidence levels to keep the records with high confidence, does not modify the structure of the partitions: you will still have two. However, when you repartition to one partition, Spark will move the data to a single partition.

This process explains why you have two Parquet files and one CSV file in the end.

Partitions are not directly attached to the dataframe; they are attached to the RDD. Therefore, to access them, you will have to use the rdd() (or javaRDD()) method of

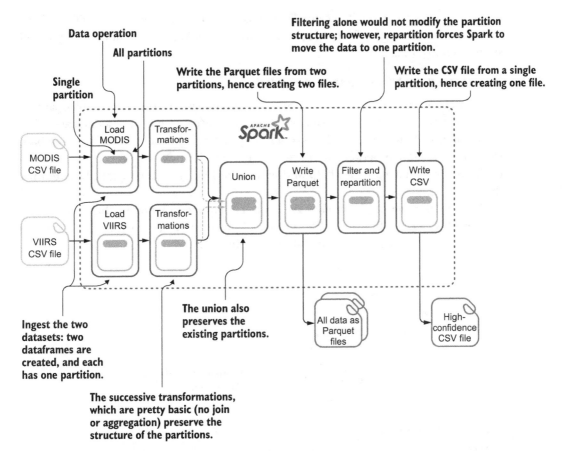

Figure 17.4 Follow the data: as the data is ingested and transformed, it is physically stored in a partition, and as the union is performed, partitions are kept until a repartition operation.

the dataframe. There, you can call methods such as `getNumPartitions()` to get the number of partitions, or even `getPartitions()` to access the partition.

Lab #100 uses `repartition()`, but you may see in documentation and source code the `coalesce()` method, which does the same thing. Other signatures for the `repartition()` method allow you to fine-tune the repartition operation, using column expressions, ranges, and more. More information is available at http://mng.bz/9wZa.

17.2 Delta Lake: Enjoying a database close to your system

Delta Lake is a database at the heart of the Spark infrastructure. You will first learn what Delta Lake is, why it is needed, and in which contexts it should be used. You will then build your first application to feed Delta Lake. You will finish with two smaller applications that consume data stored in the database.

Delta Lake was initially known as Databricks Delta and was available in the Databricks cloud offering. At Spark Summit in May 2019, Databricks open sourced Delta under an Apache license: it became Delta Lake (https://delta.io/). You will not have to download anything, as Delta Lake simply installs as a Maven dependency, as you will see in section 17.2.2.

17.2.1 Understanding why a database is needed

In early chapters, I often compared Spark to a database, in order to draw a parallel between Spark and more traditional concepts. However, Spark is not a database; it's a powerful distributed and analytics operating system. As such, it lacks a database to stage data, share it between applications, and give it more persistence. This section explains how a database can help and why Delta Lake is (almost) ideally suited for the job.

One of Spark's security models relies on a complete isolation of the data per session, as illustrated in figure 17.5. You can find more about security in chapter 18 and at https://spark.apache.org/docs/latest/security.html.

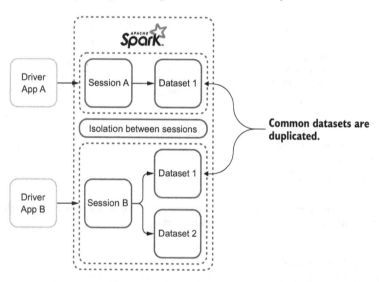

Figure 17.5   One aspect of the Spark security model: isolating the data at the session level

Based on this model, how could you share information between two applications? Before Delta Lake, you could save your dataframes to files or a database, as you just practiced in section 17.1. But even if you can do that, imagine applications that update simultaneously and need that data. Delta Lake is a permanent database that can sit in the middle and can help you share data. Figure 17.6 illustrates the use of Delta Lake to share a dataset between two applications.

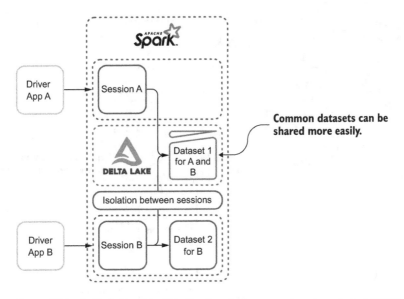

Figure 17.6   Delta Lake sits within Spark and allows sessions to access datasets.

17.2.2 *Using Delta Lake in your data pipeline*

In this subsection, you will implement Delta Lake in your pipeline. You will discover the dataset to use, ingest it, apply basic data quality rules, and then save the results in the database (write the data to the database).

Between January and March 2019, as one of the responses to France's social unrest, President Emmanuel Macron organized *Le Grand Débat* (the Great Debate). The idea was to have an open discussion channel between the people and their government. Those discussions were organized throughout the country (and internationally, for French citizens residing abroad). As you can imagine, a lot of data has been collected and, as it should be in 21st-century democracies, the data has been made available as open data.

To know more about this initiative, you can find the official site at https://grand-debat.fr/ (you can see on this site that, in French, *open data* translates as *open data*). A Google search on "great debate France" will bring you a lot of articles. However, as you can imagine, they are often politically loaded. Your job is not to be distracted by politics and analyze the data.

Figure 17.7 shows the data pipeline you are going to build. Additionally, you will build two applications that will consume the data from Delta Lake to perform some analytics: calculating the number of meetings per *department* (an administrative subdivision similar to the United States' *counties*) and a basic analysis of the types of organizers.

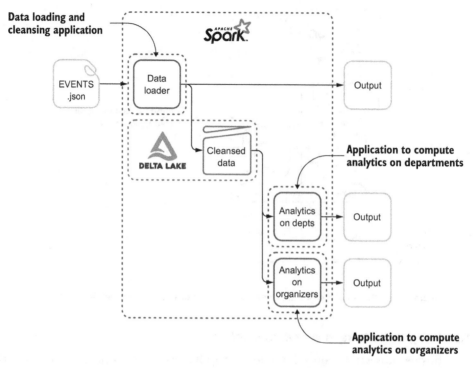

Figure 17.7   The data loader application takes a JSON file containing the events, cleanses the data, and stores it in Delta Lake. The two analytics applications can now take the data from there.

The output of the data loader is fairly simple: it will display a snapshot of the dataframe, its schema, and the number of rows that are inserted in the Delta Lake database, as illustrated in the following listing.

Listing 17.6   Output of the data loader

```
+--------------------+...+--------------------+...+----------+
|            authorId|...|               title|...|authorDept|
+--------------------+...+--------------------+...+----------+
|VXNlcjplYWE1OTUzM...|...| Grand débat citoyen|...|        25|
|VXNlcjowODM3NGZjN...|...|Fiscalité et dépe...|...|        64|
...

root #B
 |-- authorId: string (nullable = true)
 |-- authorType: string (nullable = true)
 |-- authorZipCode: integer (nullable = true)
 |-- body: string (nullable = true)
 |-- createdAt: timestamp (nullable = true)
 |-- enabled: boolean (nullable = true)
 |-- endAt: timestamp (nullable = true)
 |-- fullAddress: string (nullable = true)
 |-- id: string (nullable = true)
```

Content of the dataframe

Schema

```
|-- lat: double (nullable = true)
|-- link: string (nullable = true)
|-- lng: double (nullable = true)
|-- startAt: timestamp (nullable = true)         Schema
|-- title: string (nullable = true)
|-- updatedAt: timestamp (nullable = true)
|-- url: string (nullable = true)
|-- authorDept: integer (nullable = true)
```

9501 rows updated.   ⟵—— **Number of rows stored in Delta Lake**

Over the past chapters, you have experienced many similar scenarios, where you ingest files and process them. The first part of this lab is similar. You will need a schema to associate the proper datatypes with columns, and you will ensure that the data quality rules are applied before storing the data in Delta Lake.

In this lab, the only data quality we are going to apply is on the postal code. Like many western countries, France introduced postal codes in the 1960s, with a few updates in the 1970s bringing the system to its quasi final state. French postal codes are similar to German and US postal codes: they contain five digits.

Trivia about postal codes

Postal codes always seem to generate a lot of passion and debate among developers. I do not wish to add to this debate, so I've just added a few facts here.

ZIP codes in the United States were created by the United States Postal Service (USPS). They originally started with five digits, but, in 1983, the ZIP+4 extension turned the US ZIP code into nine digits (though the last four are not required and remain less used).

An interesting fact about the French ones is that the first two digits represent the department number. They contain a few oddities (for instance, for managing PO boxes, mail orders, or contests), but that information is not needed here. However, if you want to know more, go to https://en.wikipedia.org/wiki/Postal_codes_in_France. Postal code values cannot exceed 98000, except for specific commercial operations.

You are going to create a new column with the department number after you have cleaned the postal code. Remember, the process is only about extracting the first two digits of the postal code. You can also find more information at https://en.wikipedia .org/wiki/Departments_of_France.

Finally, you are going to save the data in Delta Lake by overwriting the existing data. Of course, at first, there'll be no data in Delta Lake, but if you rerun the lab several times, you want to have consistency.

To add support for Delta Lake, you simply have to add a reference to it in your pom.xml, as shown in the following listing.

Listing 17.7   pom.xml addition for Delta Lake

```xml
<properties>
  <scala.version>2.11</scala.version>
  <delta.version>0.3.0</delta.version>
...
</properties>

<dependencies>
  <dependency>
    <groupId>io.delta</groupId>
    <artifactId>delta-core_${scala.version}</artifactId>
    <version>${delta.version}</version>
  </dependency>
...
</dependencies>
```

Listing 17.8 shows the data loader application. Despite its early version number, 0.5.0 at the time of writing, Delta Lake is already used by Databricks customers to store petabytes of data.

LAB   This is lab #200. The application is called FeedDeltaLakeApp from the net.jgp.books.spark.ch17.lab200_feed_delta package.

Listing 17.8   Data loader

```java
package net.jgp.books.spark.ch17.lab200_feed_delta;

import static org.apache.spark.sql.functions.col;
import static org.apache.spark.sql.functions.expr;
import static org.apache.spark.sql.functions.when;

import org.apache.spark.sql.Dataset;
import org.apache.spark.sql.Row;
import org.apache.spark.sql.SparkSession;
import org.apache.spark.sql.types.DataTypes;
import org.apache.spark.sql.types.StructField;
import org.apache.spark.sql.types.StructType;

public class FeedDeltaLakeApp {
...
  private void start() {
    SparkSession spark = SparkSession.builder()          Creates
        .appName("Ingestion the 'Grand Débat' files to Delta Lake")   a session
        .master("local[*]")                              on a local
        .getOrCreate();                                  master

    StructType schema = DataTypes.createStructType(new StructField[] {   ◄──
        DataTypes.createStructField(
            "authorId",                               Builds a schema
            DataTypes.StringType,                  specifically for this file
            false),
...
```

```
DataTypes.createStructField(
    "createdAt",
    DataTypes.TimestampType,
    false),
...
```

Notes the use of the timestamp type

```
Dataset<Row> df = spark.read().format("json")
    .schema(schema)
    .option("timestampFormat", "yyyy-MM-dd HH:mm:ss")
    .load("data/france_grand_debat/20190302 EVENTS.json");

df = df
    .withColumn("authorZipCode",
        col("authorZipCode").cast(DataTypes.IntegerType))
    .withColumn("authorZipCode",
        when(col("authorZipCode").$less(1000), null)
            .otherwise(col("authorZipCode")))
    .withColumn("authorZipCode",
        when(col("authorZipCode").$greater$eq(99999), null)
            .otherwise(col("authorZipCode")))
    .withColumn("authorDept", expr("int(authorZipCode / 1000)"));
df.show(25);
df.printSchema();
```

Reads a JSON file called 20190302 EVENTS.json

Specifies the timestamp format

Applies data quality rules—here, cleansing the postal code

Shows at most 25 records

Prints the schema

Extracts the department number from the postal code

```
df.write().format("delta")
    .mode("overwrite")
    .save("/tmp/delta_grand_debat_events");

System.out.println(df.count() + " rows updated.");
    }
}
```

Writes the content of the dataframe to Delta

Overwrites all existing data

Specifies the path where Delta will store its files, on the worker node

Displays the number of rows in the dataframe

As you noticed, the format used for writing the data is delta, but when saved on disk, the data is written in the efficient Apache Parquet file format, which you worked with in chapter 7. The data is saved on the worker node. The next step is to consume the data from Delta Lake.

17.2.3 Consuming data from Delta Lake

As expected, this subsection covers ingestion (or loading) of data from Delta Lake by two small applications. Those small analytics applications will use the database you created with Delta Lake in the previous subsection, 17.2.2. The applications will do the following:

- Count the number of meetings per department
- Count the number of meetings per type of organizer

Figure 17.8 illustrates the process.

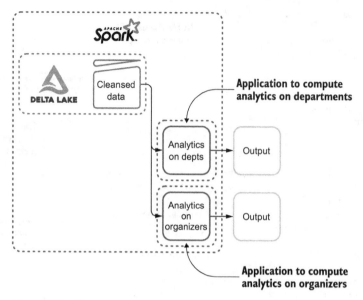

Figure 17.8   Two applications are going to consume data from Delta Lake to produce analytics.

NUMBER OF MEETINGS PER DEPARTMENT

This is lab #210, which focuses on counting the number of meetings per department during France's great debate. The output of the application will look like the following listing: a simple list of departments with the number of meetings, in descending order.

Listing 17.9   Number of meetings per department

```
+----------+-----+
|authorDept|count|
+----------+-----+
|        75|  489|
|        59|  323|
|        69|  242|
|        33|  218|
...
```

The application is going to be fairly easy:

1 Open a session.
2 Load the data.
3 Perform an aggregation.
4 Display the result.

The following listing shows the code to perform the operation.

Listing 17.10 Counting the number of meetings per department

```
package net.jgp.books.spark.ch17.lab210_analytics_dept;

import static org.apache.spark.sql.functions.col;

import org.apache.spark.sql.Dataset;
import org.apache.spark.sql.Row;
import org.apache.spark.sql.SparkSession;

public class MeetingsPerDepartmentApp {
...
  private void start() {
    SparkSession spark = SparkSession.builder()
        .appName("Counting the number of meetings per department")
        .master("local[*]")
        .getOrCreate();

    Dataset<Row> df = spark.read().format("delta")        Reads the Delta Lake dataset
        .load("/tmp/delta_grand_debat_events");           from the specified path

    df = df.groupBy(col("authorDept")).count()
        .orderBy(col("count").desc_nulls_first());
...
```

As you can see in this short application, reading the data from Delta Lake is simple: you use the `delta` format with the `read()` method. There is no need to specify a schema or options. Spark will find all that information directly from the database.

NUMBER OF MEETINGS PER TYPE OF ORGANIZER

This is lab #220, which describes how to count the number of meetings per type of organizer during France's great debate. As you can imagine, the output (in listing 17.11) and the code (in listing 17.12) will be similar to the previous example, when you counted the number of meetings per department.

Listing 17.11 Number of meetings per type of organizer

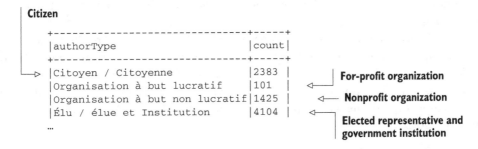

```
Citizen

+------------------------------+-----+
|authorType                    |count|
+------------------------------+-----+
|Citoyen / Citoyenne           |2383 |     For-profit organization
|Organisation à but lucratif   |101  |  ◁── Nonprofit organization
|Organisation à but non lucratif|1425 | ◁── 
|Élu / élue et Institution     |4104 |  ◁── Elected representative and
...                                          government institution
```

Listing 17.12   Counting the number of meetings per type of organizer

```
...
Dataset<Row> df = spark.read().format("delta")
    .load("/tmp/delta_grand_debat_events");
df = df.groupBy(col("authorType")).count()
    .orderBy(col("authorType").asc_nulls_last());
...
```

As you can see, the operation is similar; the major change is the request itself.

17.3   Accessing cloud storage services from Spark

This section looks at the major cloud providers' offerings for cloud storage (in general) and gives you pointers to more resources. I include links to examples, tutorials, and reference material so you can investigate each in more depth. In this section, I'll provide an overview of the following:

- Amazon Simple Storage Service (S3)
- Google Cloud Storage
- IBM Cloud Object Storage (COS)
- Microsoft Azure Blob Storage
- OVH Object Storage

It's probably no surprise to you that you will probably deploy your application in the cloud. You may have to read data from cloud storage solutions, and, eventually, write your processed data there. One typical use case is to ingest data from an on-premises database, and write the data into cloud storage (for example, Amazon S3). You can also imagine multicloud aggregation and more.

Those scenarios are completely feasible with Apache Spark. You will need to connect to each cloud vendor to access your data. Every cloud vendor offers a solution, and, as you might guess, they all have different names. You can read more about most cloud services at https://spark.apache.org/docs/latest/cloud-integration.html.

AMAZON S3

Amazon is definitely a leader and pioneer in cloud computing, with its Amazon Web Services (AWS). *S3* is the cloud storage service offered by AWS. It is probably the most well-known service. Amazon, like some other vendors, combines Spark and Hadoop in its offering.

You will need to use the Hadoop AWS module, which is part of Apache Hadoop, to access data on Amazon S3. Be careful about the dependencies (there are quite a few). Make sure you will have those dependencies in your deployment environment. My experience with AWS libraries is that you can end up in JAR hell pretty rapidly. More information on Apache Hadoop's integration with AWS can be found at http://mng.bz/j5qy.

GOOGLE CLOUD STORAGE

Google's offering is called *Google Cloud Platform* (*GCP*). GCP offers several storage components, and Cloud Storage is the file and online storage you can use with Spark. One of the benefits of Cloud Storage is that its API lets you access several classes of storage, from highly available for recent data, to older data being archived.

IBM COS

IBM acquired Cleversafe in 2015 and uses its Dispersed Storage Network (dsNet) product for storing data in the cloud. *Cloud Object Storage* (*COS*) is the name of the postacquisition offering in IBM's portfolio and can be accessed via the S3 API.

Documentation on IBM COS is a little scarce, so here are a couple of pointers:

- You can access IBM COS from Spark as a Service, http://mng.bz/WOWx. Note that this uses Spark as a Service on IBM COS, but it is easily transferable in a local environment.
- An efficient way to connect to COS is via IBM Watson Studio, at http://mng.bz/E1vl.

MICROSOFT AZURE BLOB STORAGE

Microsoft Azure also offers a storage service in the cloud called *Azure Blob Storage*. Refer to http://mng.bz/Nep2 for more information.

OVH OBJECT STORAGE

OVH, which might not be as well known as the other providers, is a European leader in hosting services and now has a strong cloud offering (OVHcloud). Its cloud storage solution, *OVH Object Storage*, is described at https://www.ovh.com/world/public-cloud/object-storage/. OVH uses the OpenStack Swift API. For more information on how to use Apache Spark with OpenStack Swift, check out http://mng.bz/DNn9.

Summary

- Just as Apache Spark can ingest data from multiple formats, it can export data in multiple formats.
- The key method for writing data from a dataframe to a file or database is write().
- The write() method behaves similarly to the read() method: you can specify the format() and several options via option().
- The save() method, which is linked to the dataframe's write() method, is a counterpart to the read() method, which is linked to the dataframe's load() method.
- You can specify the write mode with the mode() function.
- Exporting data will export data from each partition, potentially resulting in several files being created.

- Delta Lake is a database that lives in the Spark environment. You can persist your dataframes in Delta Lake. More information on Delta Lake can be found at https://delta.io/.
- You can use the `coalesce()` method or the `repartition()` method to reduce the number of partitions.
- Apache Spark can access data stored in cloud providers including Amazon S3, Google Cloud Storage, IBM Cloud Object Storage, Microsoft Azure Blob Storage, and OVH Object Storage by using the S3 and OpenStack Swift APIs.
- Appendix Q contains reference material for exporting data.
- Spark's static functions offer several ways to manipulate the date and time.
- You can download a file using Java NIO and ingest it in Spark.
- I often store constants in a class called K, standing for *Konstante*, the German for *constant*.

18

Exploring deployment constraints: Understanding the ecosystem

This chapter covers

- Learning key concepts behind deploying big data applications
- Learning the roles of resource and cluster managers
- Sharing data and files with Spark's workers
- Securing both network communication and disk I/O

In this last chapter of the book, you will explore the key concepts required to grasp the infrastructure constraints of deploying a big data application. This chapter explores the constraints of deployment, not the deployment process itself or installing Apache Spark in a production environment. That essential information is covered in chapters 5 and 6, as well as appendix K.

Apache Spark lives in an ecosystem, where it shares resources, data, security, and more with other applications and components. Spark lives in an open world, and this chapter also explores the constraint of being a good citizen in this world.

In my experience with Spark, I have met two kinds of people: the ones who came from an Apache Hadoop background and the rest of us. Until recently, Apache Hadoop was the most popular implementation of big data storage and processing. You do not need Hadoop knowledge to understand this chapter, as you will learn about some key concepts familiar to Hadoop users, architects, and engineers. You will also learn about Hadoop technologies that can be used with Apache Spark. This knowledge will help you design reference architectures or integrate within existing big data projects within your organization.

At this point in time, the focus is all about managing resources. The resources I am talking about are the ones you would expect: CPU, memory, disk, and network. Therefore, you will first learn about the role of resource managers. So far, you have been using Spark's built-in resource manager, but, as you design and integrate Spark in more-complex architectures, you will be exposed to other resource managers including YARN, Mesos, Kubernetes, and others.

Spark needs access to data, as you found when experimenting with the countless labs throughout the book. Section 18.2 will help you define the right strategy for sharing files with Spark.

Finally, the last section, 18.3, focuses on key security concepts in order to help you understand whether any of your data is at risk on the network or on disk. This is an overview of security; more reading and study will be required on your end if you want to be an expert!

Although this chapter doesn't contain examples, it contains a lot of reference architecture diagrams to help you design your cluster and securely deploy Spark applications.

18.1 Managing resources with YARN, Mesos, and Kubernetes

In this section, you will discover Spark resources and learn why you need to manage them. You will then have a look at the various resource managers available in the context of Spark. By the end of this section, you will have the knowledge to pick the right resource manager for your needs when you need to build a cluster.

The following is a nonexhaustive list of the main resource managers:

- The built-in Spark resource manager
- YARN
- Mesos
- Kubernetes

In a traditional laptop or desktop (a single box) environment, the OS manages those resources, which are a combination of the hardware components (from CPU to network). In a cluster environment, you have many of those boxes, and you want them to work uniformly. Resource managers do this job above the individual box OS. You typically have one resource manager to manage your cluster. Specific implementations will vary by type of resource manager. You can replace those physical boxes (bare metal) by virtual machines or containers. Using those technologies is a valid solution too, but both virtual machines and containers need to be managed.

You have a few options for managing resources with Spark. Let's look at them briefly.

18.1.1 *The built-in standalone mode manages resources*

The easiest resource manager to learn and use comes built-in as Spark's standalone cluster manager. Spark's standalone mode is the easiest system to deploy, as you learned in chapter 5. You will have to install Spark on each node, manually elect a master, and start the workers on each node. Figure 18.1 illustrates this architecture.

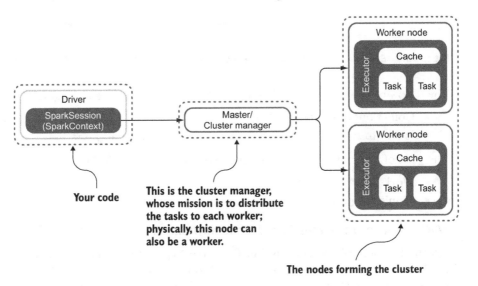

Figure 18.1 Using Spark with its own cluster manager: the worker nodes are managed by the master, which sends the tasks to each executor; the binary code of the application is also being shared.

Spark provides a basic web interface to monitor what is going on. You can see resource allocations, tasks, and so on. By default, the web interface is accessible on port 8080 of the master, as shown in figure 18.2.

In a production environment, you may want to build high availability (HA), so you build a more robust system. You can build HA with Apache ZooKeeper, which aims to keep configurations in a central location.

Chapter 5 covers the standalone mode in more detail. Appendix K can also help, as it is a reference for using Spark in production. Full documentation for setting up a cluster by using Apache Spark in standalone mode is available at http://mng.bz/1omM.

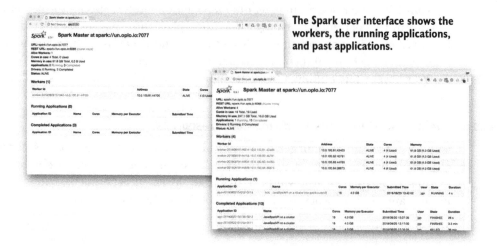

The Spark user interface shows the workers, the running applications, and past applications.

Figure 18.2   **Example of the monitoring screens you will experience when connecting to Apache Spark**

The following are some pros of using Spark as its own resource manager:

- Comes out of the box with Spark
- Is easy to set up, as it does not require any external components

The cons of using Spark as its own resource manager are as follows:

- Works only with Spark.
- Monitoring is limited to Spark resources.

18.1.2 *YARN manages resources in a Hadoop environment*

Apache Hadoop *YARN* (Yet Another Resource Negotiator) is a resource manager that has been fully integrated with Apache Hadoop since Hadoop version 2. YARN is a key component of a Hadoop deployment; it is not independent. If your organization already operates Hadoop clusters, it will most likely run Apache Spark on the same (or adjacent) cluster, through YARN.

Alibaba Cloud Elastic MapReduce (or E-MapReduce), Amazon EMR, Google Cloud Platform's Dataproc, IBM Analytics Engine, Microsoft Azure HDInsight, and OVH Data Analytics Platform are managed offerings from the big cloud players. They are all based on Hadoop and include YARN as part of their cluster-to-go offering, making deployment easier. Figure 18.3 illustrates a combined Spark and YARN architecture.

In September 2019, Google announced that Dataproc will also use Kubernetes with Spark. Google is the first to go to production with a cloud-based Spark hosting without a strong dependency on YARN. Others will most certainly follow.

YARN offers more features than running Spark in standalone mode, in terms of process isolation and prioritization, which can result in better security and performance.

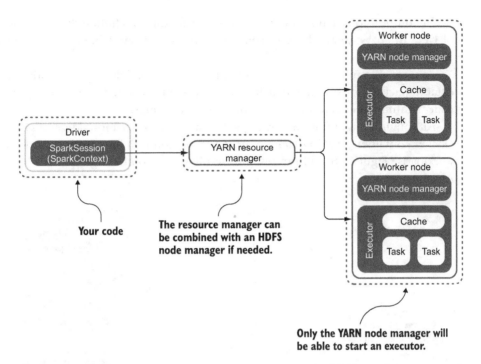

Figure 18.3 Architecture combining Hadoop YARN and Spark. The YARN resource manager works with the YARN node manager to manage the executors. Every YARN-based architecture shares a similar pattern.

You can find more on using YARN with Spark at http://mng.bz/BY6g and http://mng.bz/dxRX.

Here are the pros of using Hadoop YARN as a resource manager:

- Comes out of the box with Hadoop since v2; if you use Hadoop in your organization, it is likely that you use YARN.
- Has more features, including prioritization and isolation.

The cons of using Hadoop YARN as a resource manager are as follows:

- Involves high dependency on Hadoop, which may not be desired.
- Has limited support for the Spark shell. In some YARN installations, you may connect to Spark via its shells when on the edge nodes. In some versions of (at least) AWS or GCP, you cannot connect to the cluster via the shell from a remote host.

18.1.3 Mesos is a standalone resource manager

Mesos is an Apache project offering a standalone and general-purpose cluster manager, designed independently from its consumers. Mesos can indeed be used by any application willing to access cluster resources. Mesos supports Spark, but also Hadoop, Jenkins, Marathon, and more.

In addition to isolation, Mesos offers other features including dynamic allocation of CPU in coarse-grained mode (fine-grained mode is available but deprecated for Spark as of v2.0).

As a quick reminder, a Docker container image is a lightweight, standalone, executable package of software that includes everything needed to run an application: code, runtime, system tools, system libraries, and settings.

Although it might not directly impact your Spark application, Mesos also supports Docker containers, making Mesos a more flexible solution for managing most types of workloads. Figure 18.4 illustrates the architecture combining Apache Spark with Apache Mesos.

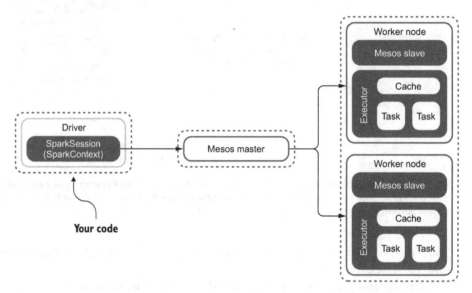

Figure 18.4   Your application can use a Mesos master to manage the Mesos workers and Spark executor.

To learn more about implementing Mesos for Spark, read the online documentation at http://mng.bz/rPXZ. You can find more about Mesos in Roger Ignazio's *Mesos in Action* (Manning, 2016, https://livebook.manning.com/book/mesos-in-action). Manning also offers numerous resources on Docker, including *Docker in Action* by Jeff Nickoloff and Stephen Kuenzli (Manning, 2019, https://livebook.manning.com/book/docker-in-action-second-edition).

The pros of using Mesos as a cluster manager include the following:

- Mesos is an independent resource and cluster manager, with its own life cycle and dependencies. Unlike YARN, Mesos is not linked to Hadoop. Mesos has more features, including dynamic allocation or support for Docker containers.

The cons of using Mesos as a cluster manager include the following:

- It is yet another product you will have to learn and maintain.

Matei Zaharia contributed to Spark and Mesos

Matei Zaharia is one of the brains behind Spark. He started the Spark project back in 2009 at the University of California, Berkeley, in the prestigious AMPLab. He later cofounded Databricks in 2014, which operates and sells a hosted version of Spark accessible through notebooks. Prior to Spark, Zaharia cocreated Mesos, at that time named Nexus.

The legend says that Spark started as a project for testing Mesos. This should motivate people to do more test-driven development (TDD). It also explains why you may find some similarities between the Spark and Mesos architectures and vocabularies.

18.1.4 Kubernetes orchestrates containers

Kubernetes (often abbreviated *K8s*) is a container platform developed by Google and open sourced in 2014. Kubernetes is not a classic resource manager per se; however, the Apache Spark team started adding support for Kubernetes in Spark v2.3.

Kubernetes support has been a high priority for the Spark team, and its experimental status was removed in Spark v3. The overall idea of Kubernetes is to handle Docker containers. To use Kubernetes with Spark, you have to build (or reuse) a Docker container with a Spark installation, which is the standard expectation when using Kubernetes. Figure 18.5 shows a typical reference architecture for using Apache Spark with Kubernetes.

Kubernetes schedules operations via its scheduler and manages processing via pods. When you use the `spark-submit` tool (as described in chapter 5), the Spark-on-Kubernetes scheduler will create a Kubernetes pod containing your driver application.

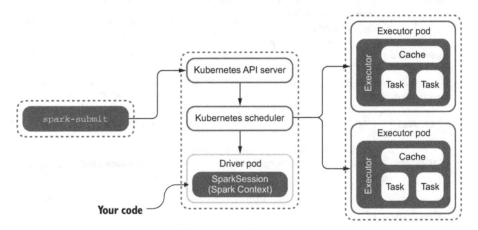

Figure 18.5   Kubernetes in an Apache Spark infrastructure: the application and the executors are running in pods, orchestrated by the Kubernetes scheduler

To learn more about installing Kubernetes with Spark, read the online documentation at http://mng.bz/VPjO. For a more step-by-step approach, see http://mng.bz/xlpY. You can find more about Kubernetes in Marko Lukša's *Kubernetes in Action* (Manning, 2017, https://www.manning.com/books/kubernetes-in-action).

Here are the pros of using Kubernetes as a resource manager for Spark:

- Kubernetes is an independent product, with its own life cycle and dependencies.
- Kubernetes is a complete solution for executing Docker containers.

The cons of using Kubernetes as a resource manager for Spark include the following:

- It is yet another product you will have to learn and maintain.

18.1.5 *Choosing the right resource manager*

When you use Spark in production, you have many options when it comes to choosing a resource or cluster manager. An organization that comes from a Hadoop background may be tempted to continue along the line of YARN, but other choices are summarized in table 18.1.

In table 18.1, the HA component indicates the element that will need to be taken care of, as all the tools listed are designed to support the failure of a node. Basically, the HA tools should take care of the single point of failure (SPOF). Hopefully it is a single point, right?

As you can see in this table, Apache ZooKeeper can be an important element when you are trying to build an HA cluster. More information can be found at https://zookeeper.apache.org/.

Table 18.1 Comparison of resource/cluster managers for Spark

	Spark in standalone mode	YARN	Mesos	Kubernetes
Spark support	All versions	All versions	All versions	v2.3.0 and later
Base technology	Resource manager	Resource manager	Cluster and container manager	Container manager
License	Apache 2.0	Apache 2.0	Apache 2.0	Apache 2.0
Highlight	Works out of the box	Comes with Apache Hadoop	Standalone product, not dedicated to Spark	Standalone product, not dedicated to Spark
Deployment complexity	Low	High	High	High
High-availability component	Master	Resource manager	Master	N/A

Table 18.1 Comparison of resource/cluster managers for Spark *(continued)*

	Spark in standalone mode	**YARN**	**Mesos**	**Kubernetes**
High availability	Requires Zoo-Keeper or specific configuration	Active/standby strategy managed by ZooKeeper	Leader/backup nodes managed by ZooKeeper	Managed by the K8s `kubeadm`
Security	Lower	Higher	Higher	Higher

18.2 Sharing files with Spark

In this section, you will learn how Spark can get data from the world, so Spark can transform that data and provide insights, and can save the resulting data back to files. Accessing files is a fundamental part of the input/output (I/O) operations of Spark.

Figure 18.6 illustrates file sharing in Spark:

- Accessing data contained in files from the workers
- Using distributed filesystems
- Using shared drives or file servers
- Using file-sharing services
- Other and hybrid solutions

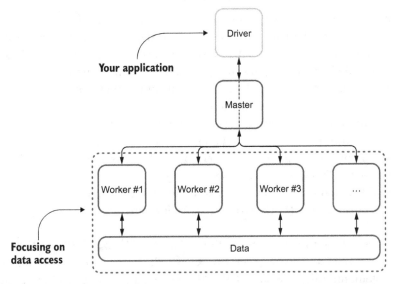

Figure 18.6 Spark's workers must be able to access the data. The data can be in files, databases, or streams. Files can be problematic because they may be spread logically around organizations and physically around servers and clusters.

18.2.1 Accessing the data contained in files

To perform an ingestion, Spark needs to access the data contained in files; more specifically, each executor on the worker nodes needs to access the data. Typically, data can be stored in files on disk, stored in databases, or come from streams, which you have studied in detail in chapters 7, 8, and 10, respectively. In this section, let's have a look at the architectural constraints for accessing files.

Each worker needs to access the data. Each needs to access the *same file*. Remember that workers are most likely going to run on different nodes, which may not share filesystems with one another. Let's analyze the options of getting the same file to the executors.

> **THE SAME FILE**   When I started working with Apache Spark, I thought that each node would ingest a part of the file, so I took a 10 MB or so file and sliced it. I can assure you that this was not a good idea: you're just making extra work for yourself, and the results are simply not what you want. Make sure that Spark has access to the same file on each node and let Spark do the heavy lifting (slicing and distribution) for you.

You can make the same file available to all nodes by using a distributed filesystem, a file-sharing service, or shared drives.

18.2.2 Sharing files through distributed filesystems

A *distributed filesystem* is a filesystem on which you can access files in a distributed environment. The Hadoop Distributed File System (HDFS) is not the only distributed filesystem, but it is definitely one of the most popular in the context of big data. In this subsection, you will learn how Spark lives in an HDFS environment.

A distributed filesystem shares the files (or part of the files) on the different nodes to ensure both access and data replication.

HDFS is one of the components of the Hadoop ecosystem. HDFS is designed to store large files with a write-once, read-many paradigm. As a consequence, HDFS is slower at writing or updating, but optimized for read access. It is not designed for low-latency write access, unlike what you would expect from an analytics system, which needs to access data quickly. This is why some implementations use redundant array of independent disks (RAID) for striping, as redundancy is built through the HDFS cluster itself.

HDFS uses blocks to store information. The default size is 128 MB. Blocks are spawned over several servers in several racks, which requires you to be aware of the physical implementation. This size of 128 MB also means that if you have a bunch of 32 KB files, performance and physical storage will be impacted: for every 32 KB file, 128 MB will be used on your disks.

The Spark worker nodes can be combined with the Hadoop HDFS data nodes where the data is stored, if the load is such that both services can run on the same server.

Spark can then be a reading and writing client to HDFS. Remember that HDFS does not perform very well when it needs to update data; it's mostly a read-oriented filesystem.

Figure 18.7 summarizes a Spark-on-HDFS infrastructure.

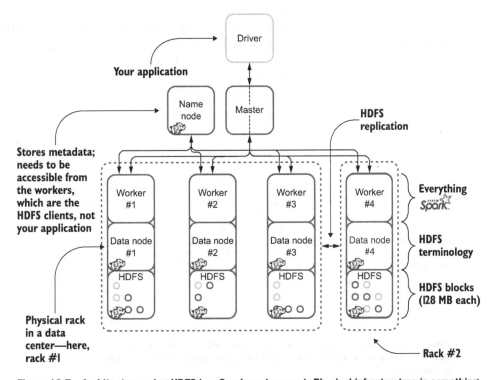

Figure 18.7 Architecture using HDFS in a Spark environment. Physical infrastructure is something to care about in an HDFS/Hadoop deployment. The elephants symbolize Hadoop-related software components.

The following are pros of using HDFS to share files with Spark:

- Very popular, easy to find documentation and resources
- Suitable for large and very large files (ideally around or over the block size)

Here are the cons of using HDFS to share files with Spark:

- Not that easy to deploy.
- Performance is degraded with small files.

18.2.3 *Accessing files on shared drives or file server*

Another way to share data on your network is via a shared drive on a file server, like your good old Windows network (or even NetWare for those born some time ago).

Implementations for shared drives vary: Common Internet File System (CIFS), Server Message Block (SMB), Samba, Network File System (NFS), Apple Filing Protocol (AFP, the evolution of AppleTalk), and many more. However, despite the various (and often incompatible) implementations, the idea stays the same: you have a server, and clients connect to the server and then transfer the files as those clients need them.

Figure 18.8 illustrates a shared drive scenario with Spark: each worker will access the file server where the files are stored. Naturally, the mounting point needs to be the same; otherwise, workers will not be able to find the files from one worker to the other, as the master will transmit the same path to each worker.

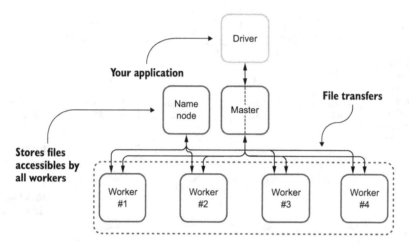

Figure 18.8   Using a file server in a Spark environment to give access to the data stored in files: each worker needs to access the file server through the same mounting point.

The pros of using a file server to share files with Spark are as follows:

- Very popular, easy to find documentation and resources
- Suitable for small- to medium-sized files
- Easy to deploy, probably already exists in your company

Here are the cons of using a file server to share files with Spark:

- Will increase network traffic
- Not designed for very large files

18.2.4 *Using file-sharing services to distribute files*

A third option for sharing files is to use a file-sharing service like Box, Dropbox, ownCloud/Nextcloud, Google Drive, and others. In this subsection, you will see the typical architectures and benefits of using such services.

The system works as a publisher/subscriber: when you drop a file in a directory, it is copied to all subscribers. This system is convenient for distributing files to a lot of

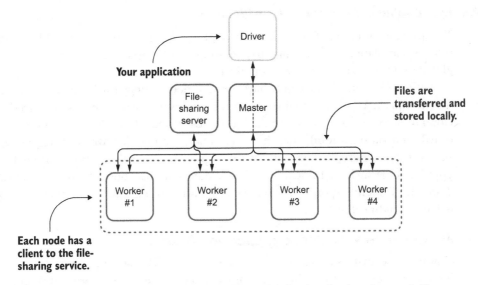

Figure 18.9 Using a file-sharing service like Box or Dropbox in a Spark environment: files are automatically published to each node, allowing an easy share of each file.

nodes, each node being a subscriber. Figure 18.9 illustrates the mechanism in a Spark environment.

Here are some pros of using a file-sharing service:

- Suitable for small- to medium-sized files
- Easy to deploy
- Limits network traffic as the files are physically copied to the disk of each worker node, because files are copied once and there is no random access to the files

The cons of using a file-sharing service include the following:

- Not designed for very large files

18.2.5 Other options for accessing files in Spark

To finalize the tour of options for accessing big data through files in Spark, you need to keep in mind cloud options such as these:

- Amazon S3 is a popular AWS service to access files stored in the cloud. Files are stored in buckets (equivalent to shared drives) and folders.
- IBM COS, formerly Cleversafe, can be used as a valid storage option.

More details on cloud options and vendors can be found in chapter 17.

18.2.6 Hybrid solution for sharing files with Spark

The previous sections, from 18.2.1 through 18.2.5, gave an overview of the various solutions available when it comes to accessing files via Spark. Let's think about a more global and integrated way in an organization.

Ultimately, you will probably have a combined strategy for bringing your big data files to Spark. You can imagine that your data warehouse extracts are saved to the cloud in Amazon S3. Your reference files, whose update frequencies are slow, could be distributed via ownCloud to each node. Finally, you could save your aggregates in a shared drive. There, business analysts can grab them for their visualizations by using popular tools such as Tableau or Qlik or data scientist tools like Jupyter or Apache Zeppelin. Depending on your organization and existing assets, you may have to help make the right call.

18.3 Making sure your Spark application is secure

Nowadays, security is more and more of a concern. This section gives you a thorough high-level overview of the things you need to be aware of to secure your components in a production environment.

Spark has built-in security features, but by default, they are *not activated*. It is your responsibility to turn on security within your cluster based on your organizational constraints.

When data is within dataframes in Spark, it is isolated per session. There is no way to connect to an existing session, so data isolation guarantees no easy tampering or even read access.

So instead you need to worry about the following:

- *Data being transferred over the network*—You can think of snooping data, altering data, denial-of-service attacks, and more.
- *Data being permanently or temporarily stored on disk*—Someone could have access to the data.

18.3.1 Securing the network components of your infrastructure

In this subsection, you will go through a holistic view of the network infrastructure, specifically when you use Spark's built-in cluster manager. From there, you can secure each component.

Figure 18.10 illustrates the various data flows between the components in a rather simple implementation of Spark.

Spark components rely on remote procedure calls (RPCs) between the components. To secure your infrastructure, you can do the following:

- Add authentication between the components, using the `spark.authenticate.*` series of configuration entries.
- Add encryption using the `spark.network.crypto.*` entries in the configuration file.

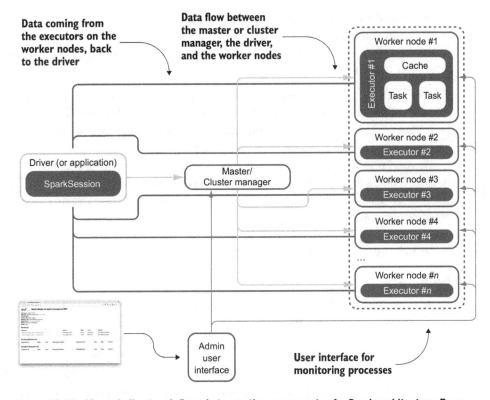

Data coming from the executors on the worker nodes, back to the driver

Data flow between the master or cluster manager, the driver, and the worker nodes

User interface for monitoring processes

Figure 18.10 View of all network flows between the components of a Spark architecture. Every arrow represents data transfer, which could be eavesdropped on.

The user interface (UI) can be secured via authentication and SSL encryption.

The last component, the Spark history server, can be accessed through the UI of the monitoring. The Spark history server can also be secured independently via authentication and SSL encryption.

For more information about network security, such as precise settings and values, you can refer to Apache Spark's page on security at https://spark.apache.org/docs/latest/security.html.

If Spark needs to get data from a network service such as a database, check the database parameters for encryption on the wire and authentication.[1]

18.3.2 Securing Spark's disk usage

In this subsection, let's have a look at how Apache Spark uses disk storage and how it can be secured. There are two types of disk usage to consider:

---

[1]*Encryption on the wire* is the process of protecting sensitive data by using encryption while the data is being sent from one source over the network or the internet to its destination.

- *Normal I/O*—When your application uses `read()`/`load()`, `write()`/`save()`, or when you `collect()` the data to the driver and write the result to disk
- *Overflow and temporary I/O*—When Spark needs to write something to disk without you asking

For the normal I/O operations, it is your entire responsibility to manage the life cycle of the artifacts your save to disk. There is no provision within Spark to clean up after you. The `write()` method does not have options to encrypt data using the normal writers (as you saw in chapter 16 and appendix Q).

As you know by now, Apache Spark heavily uses memory to process data. However, in cases like ingesting data bigger than the available memory, Spark will store those files on disk. To activate encryption for those files, you can use the `spark.io.encryption.*` set of configuration entries.

For more information about disk encryption, you can refer to Apache Spark's page on security at https://spark.apache.org/docs/latest/security.html.

Summary

- The role of the underlying operating system is to manage resources locally. However, when dealing with a cluster, you need a cluster manager or a resource manager.
- Spark comes with its own resource manager called standalone mode, allowing you to build a cluster without depending on other software components.
- YARN, a resource manager inherited from the Hadoop world, remains a popular choice, especially in hosted cloud environments.
- Mesos and Kubernetes are standalone cluster managers, freeing you from the Hadoop dependencies.
- Support for Kubernetes in Spark has been added in version 2.3 and is constantly improving.
- All cluster managers support high availability.
- When dealing with files, all Spark's workers need to have access to the same file or copy of the file.
- HDFS is one option for large files. Files can be distributed over the cluster by using HDFS, part of Hadoop.
- Smaller files can be shared via a file server or a file-sharing service such as Box or Dropbox.
- Object stores like Amazon S3 or IBM COS can also be used to store large files.
- By default, security is not activated in Spark.
- For network communication, you can fine-tune the security per component. Most components accept both specific authentication and encryption on the wire.
- Temporary storage from Spark can be encrypted using the `spark.io.encryption.*` set of configuration entries.

appendix A
Installing Eclipse

This appendix covers installing Eclipse on macOS and Windows. The installation process is similar on Linux.

Eclipse is a well-known development studio (aka an integrated development environment, or IDE) used for Java (and many other development languages). You probably have heard of Eclipse. If you are an Eclipse user, this appendix is not for you. This appendix is a five-minute tutorial on downloading, installing, and getting around in Eclipse.

In this book, I have used Eclipse Oxygen, as the support for Git and Maven have been greatly improved over the previous versions of Eclipse. If you already use Eclipse Oxygen, you will probably not learn anything here. If you are using another IDE, such as IntelliJ IDEA or NetBeans, or an older version of Eclipse, you will find a lot of similarities.

A.1   Downloading Eclipse

Eclipse can be downloaded from www.eclipse.org. You will quickly spot a Download link. Simply click the link.

On Windows, download eclipse-inst-win64.exe. It is about 50 MB. Once it is downloaded, double-click the installer.

On the Mac platform, download eclipse-inst-mac64.tar.gz. It is about 50 MB. Once it is downloaded, double-click the archive; Eclipse Installer.app will appear in your finder. Double-click the installer.

Both the Eclipse IDE for Java EE Developers and Eclipse IDE for Java Developers will work. However, it is more likely that your project will use the Enterprise Edition (EE). All examples and screenshots in this appendix are based on the EE distribution. Click the Eclipse IDE for Java EE Developers option, shown in figure A.1.

411

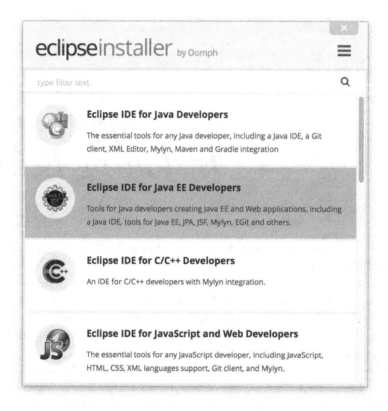

Figure A.1   Eclipse Installer offers installation options. I recommend Eclipse IDE for Java EE Developers.

The next step of the wizard, shown in figure A.2, asks you for the installation path. The proposed/default option is good.

On Windows, the installer will not install Eclipse in the Program Files folder, but in your personal space. Every user on your Windows machine will need to install Eclipse.

Note that on the Mac platform, Eclipse does not install in the Applications folder but in the Users folder. This means that if you share your Mac with other people, they will not see Eclipse and will have to perform the installation again.

Click the Install button.

Figure A.2 Select the Eclipse installation path (the default is usually a good option).

Let the installer work. It may take a little time as it will download additional packages and install them. When it has finished, you can launch Eclipse by clicking the Launch button, shown in figure A.3.

Figure A.3   With the installation complete, you are now ready to launch Eclipse.

A.2   *Running Eclipse for the first time*

In this section, you will learn about the vocabulary used within Eclipse and a few essential operations to make your life easier. When Eclipse starts, it asks for the workspace where you want to work, as shown in figure A.4.

The *workspace* is a physical folder on your computer where Eclipse will save projects as well as some files it needs internally. It is easy to have multiple workspaces for different projects, different customers, and so forth. For example, as I wrote this book, I used a dedicated workspace to isolate my work on the book from other labs, projects, commercial work, and so on.

As you get to the welcome screen, you'll see many options, including tutorials and samples. Click the upper-left Workbench icon, circled in figure A.5, to access the *workbench* (the work area).

Figure A.6 shows what your screen looks like when you access Eclipse's workbench for the first time.

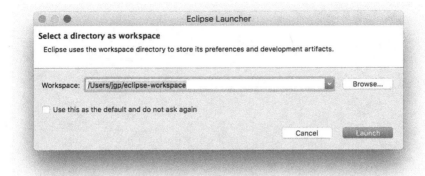

Figure A.4   When you start Eclipse, it asks for your workspace, where it will save projects and files.

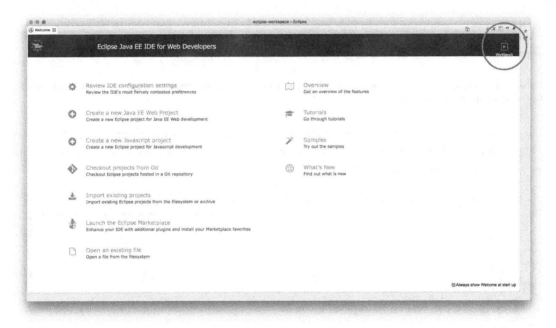

Figure A.5   The Eclipse welcome screen presents a lot of options, but you can skip to the workbench by clicking the Workbench icon in the upper-right corner.

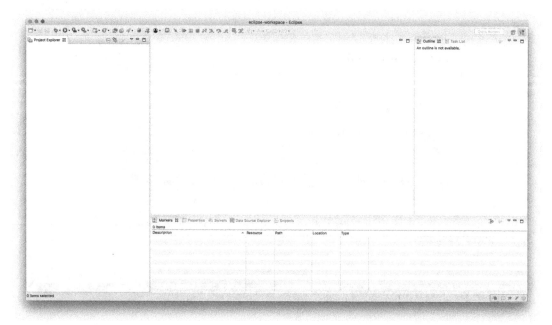

Figure A.6   An empty Eclipse workbench is probably as inspirational as an empty word processor document when you start a new chapter of your book.

Next, figure A.7 shows the workbench after a project has been imported. This shows you a little bit better where we are going! (Refer to appendix D for how to import existing projects into Eclipse.)

Figure A.7   A "working" workbench with the default views in the Java perspective

Eclipse isolates topics you are working on in *perspectives*. Figure A.7 shows the Java perspective, and figure A.8 shows the Git perspective. (Appendix C explains how to install Git if you need to use the command line. It is not required for Eclipse.)

You can learn more about Eclipse at www.eclipse.org/getting_started/.

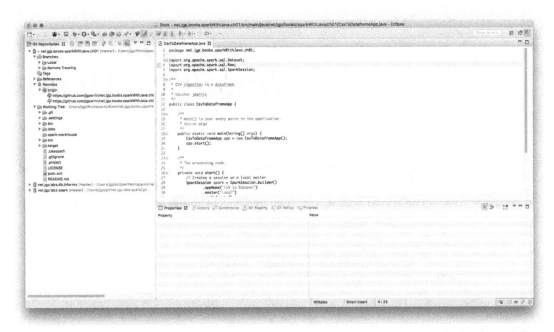

Figure A.8 The Git perspective in Eclipse

appendix B
Installing Maven

Apache Maven is a build automation tool largely available in the Java world, and you've probably used it without even knowing it. It replaced Apache Ant, and similar tools include Gradle, sbt, and Apache Ivy. This book uses Maven exclusively, so this appendix covers quick ways to install it.

> **ECLIPSE AND MAVEN** Maven comes with some Eclipse installations and plugins, but they might not be easily accessible, and you may want to control Maven's version within Eclipse yourself.

After you have installed Maven, you can learn more about it in appendix H.

B.1 Installation on Windows

For Windows, the easiest way to install Maven is to refer to https://maven.apache.org/install.html. Make sure Maven's bin folder is in your path.

B.2 Installation on macOS

On Mac, you can either install Maven the manual way (see section B.5) or use the Homebrew package manager. I recommend Homebrew, as it is much easier to install and maintain.

Check whether you have the packager on your Mac by calling brew -v. If you do not have Homebrew on your Mac, go to https://brew.sh/ and follow the one-line installation process, which I paste here for your convenience:

```
/usr/bin/ruby -e "$(curl -fsSL https://raw.githubusercontent.com/
➥ Homebrew/install/master/install)"
```

Then install Maven:

```
$ brew install maven
==> Downloading https://www.apache.org/dyn/closer.cgi?path=maven/
    maven-3/3.5.4/binaries/apache-maven-3.5.4-bin.tar.gz
==> Best Mirror http://ftp.wayne.edu/apache/maven/maven-3/3.5.4/[CA]
      binaries/apache-maven-3.5.4-bin.tar.gz
########################################################################
     100.0%
?  /usr/local/Cellar/maven/3.5.4: 104 files, 10.2MB, built in 6 seconds
```

Call the mvn command to see that the installation went well:

```
$ mvn -version
Apache Maven 3.5.4 (1edded0938998edf8bf061f1ceb3cfdec cf443fe;
    2018-06-17T14:33:14-04:00)
...
```

B.3   *Installation on Ubuntu*

First, check that Maven is not already installed on your Ubuntu system. Ubuntu is one of those systems that might have Maven out of the box, especially if you installed other Java elements. Check that by calling the mvn command:

```
$ mvn -version
Apache Maven 3.3.9
Maven home: /usr/share/maven
Java version: 1.8.0_181, vendor: Oracle Corporation
Java home: /usr/lib/jvm/java-8-oracle/jre
Default locale: en_US, platform encoding: UTF-8
OS name: "linux", version: "4.4.0-131-generic", arch: "amd64", family: "unix"
```

If Maven is not installed, install it by using APT:

```
$ sudo apt install maven
```

And check that it worked by calling the mvn command:

```
$ mvn -version
Apache Maven 3.3.9
...
```

B.4   *Installation on RHEL / Amazon EMR*

Out of the box, the Amazon Elastic MapReduce (EMR) cluster is missing a few tools. It is based on Red Hat Enterprise Linux (RHEL). You will need to deploy and run your application. In this section, you will first connect to the server, update it, and install the missing tools (maven and git—Git installation is described in appendix C).

Connecting to an EMR cluster can be done via ssh. The default user is hadoop, and you will need a Privacy-Enhanced Mail (PEM) key, a Base64-encoded certificate.

Check with your Amazon Web Services (AWS) administrator to get one if you were not given one.

Here is the syntax:

```
ssh hadoop@<hostname>.amazonaws.com -i /<path to key>/key.pem
```

Here's an example:

```
$ ssh hadoop@ec2-145-237-75-23.us-west-2.compute.amazonaws.com -i ~/emr.pem
```

Because EMR is based on Red Hat Linux, you can use the yum package manager to update the system:

Updates your system (optional)   **Adds an external repository to yum and configures it**

```
$ sudo yum -y update
$ sudo wget https://repos.fedorapeople.org/repos/dchen/apache-maven/
  epel-apache-maven.repo -O /etc/yum.repos.d/epel-apache-maven.repo
$ sudo sed -i s/\$releasever/6/g /etc/yum.repos.d/epel-apache-maven.repo
$ sudo yum install -y apache-maven
```

Installs Maven

Unfortunately, installing Maven in this way will also install Java v1.7, so you will need to switch back to Java v1.8. To do that, use the `alternatives` command for `java` (runtime):

```
$ sudo alternatives --config java

There are 2 programs which provide 'java'.

  Selection    Command
-----------------------------------------------
   1           /usr/lib/jvm/jre-1.8.0-openjdk.x86_64/bin/java
*+ 2           /usr/lib/jvm/jre-1.7.0-openjdk.x86_64/bin/java

Enter to keep the current selection[+], or type selection number: 1
```

And for the Java compiler:

```
$ sudo alternatives --config javac

There are 2 programs which provide 'javac'.

  Selection    Command
-----------------------------------------------
   1           /usr/lib/jvm/java-1.8.0-openjdk.x86_64/bin/javac
*+ 2           /usr/lib/jvm/java-1.7.0-openjdk.x86_64/bin/javac

Enter to keep the current selection[+], or type selection number: 1
```

Check that everything went well:

Maven is correctly installed.

```
$ mvn -version
Apache Maven 3.5.2 (138edd61fd100ec658bfa2d307c43b76940a5d7d;
   2017-10-18T07:58:13Z)
Maven home: /usr/share/apache-maven
Java version: 1.8.0_171, vendor: Oracle Corporation
Java home: /usr/lib/jvm/java-1.8.0-openjdk-1.8.0.171-8.b10.38.amzn1.x86_64/
     jre
Default locale: en_US, platform encoding: UTF-8
OS name: "linux", version: "4.14.47-56.37.amzn1.x86_64",
   arch: "amd64", family: "unix"
```

Java vl.8 is the default JVM.

B.5 *Manual installation on Linux and other UNIX-like OSes*

For manual installation, the easiest way is to refer to https://maven.apache.org/install.html. Make sure Maven's bin folder is in your path.

appendix C
Installing Git

Git is a version control system for tracking changes in files and coordinating work on those files among multiple people. It can be used for deployment.

C.1 Installing Git on Windows

To install Git on Windows, go to https://git-scm.com/download/win and follow the instructions.

C.2 Installing Git on macOS

For your Mac, you have several options to choose from:

- Go to https://git-scm.com/download/mac and follow the instructions. This is the default way.
- Open a terminal and type `git`. You will be prompted to install Xcode and its command-line tools. Xcode is a bit of a heavy installation, but this is the recommended way.
- Use Homebrew (installation covered in appendix B) and install Git via `brew install git`.

C.3 Installing Git on Ubuntu

Use `git --version` to check that Git is not installed. If Git is not installed already, use the following:

```
$ sudo apt install git
```

C.4 *Installing Git on RHEL / Amazon EMR*

Use `git --version` to check that Git is not installed. If Git is not installed already, use the following:

```
$ sudo yum install -y git
```

C.5 *Other tools to consider*

Here are a few tools to consider on your journey with Git:

- My favorite graphical frontend for Git is Atlassian's Sourcetree. It is available for Windows and macOS. It is free to install and use. Check it out at https://www.sourcetreeapp.com/.
- For Windows, you can use TortoiseGit (https://tortoisegit.org/). TortoiseGit integrates with Windows Explorer. It is recommended by one of the book's technical editors, Rambabu Posa.
- Eclipse Oxygen integrates pretty seamlessly with the Git repository for most operations. However, sometimes it gets weird, and Sourcetree comes to the rescue.
- GitHub (now a Microsoft company) is offering the Git repository as a service; all the examples, labs, and data from this book are stored there.
- Documentation and tutorials can be found at https://git-scm.com/doc.

appendix D
Downloading the code and getting started with Eclipse

This appendix explains how to download the code used for the labs in the book and access it in Eclipse. This appendix focuses on chapter 1's code, but you can easily extrapolate to the rest of the chapters.

The source code is in a public repository on GitHub. While you are looking at the code on GitHub, feel free to star it; it always helps (thanks!). Every chapter has its own repository. The URL of the source code repository is formatted like this:

https://github.com/jgperrin/net.jgp.books.spark.ch{chapter number}.git

The *{chapter number}* is the chapter number in two digits. For example, the URL of the source code repository for chapter 1 is as follows:

https://github.com/jgperrin/net.jgp.books.spark.ch01.git

Chapter 6 is an exception: it uses chapter 5's examples.

For this appendix, I initially used Eclipse Oxygen.2 December 2017. Newer versions, and especially the new quarterly based Eclipse versions, work even better, as Git and Maven support within Eclipse is becoming more and more seamless.

D.1 Downloading the source code from the command line

If you are familiar with the command line, open a terminal or command prompt and run this:

```
$ git clone https://github.com/jgperrin/net.jgp.books.spark.ch01.git
```

See appendix C for information on installing the command-line Git on your Mac, Ubuntu, Windows, RHEL, or Amazon EMR systems.

D.2   Getting started in Eclipse

To get started in Eclipse, open the Git perspective by choosing Window > Perspective > Open Perspective > Other. From the list, select Git, as shown in figure D.1.

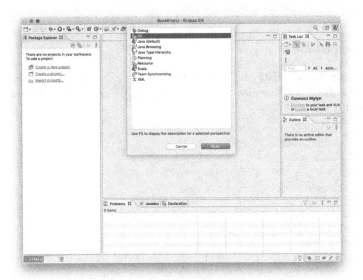

Figure D.1   Choosing the Git perspective in Eclipse to easily download the source code

On the next screen, shown in figure D.2, click the Clone a Git Repository link. If your screen does not display the same thing, look for the icon in the center of the left pane, shown in figure D.3.

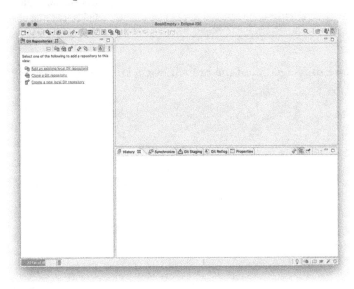

Figure D.2   In this empty Git perspective in Eclipse, you can easily clone a project and work on it. Click the Clone a Git Repository link on the left.

Figure D.3   The Clone a Git Repository icon

To set up your repository, set the following values, as shown in figure D.4:

- URI: `https://github.com/jgperrin/net.jgp.books.spark.ch01.git`
- Host: `github.com`
- Repository path: `/jgperrin/net.jgp.books.spark.ch01.git`
- Protocol: `https`

Then click the Next button.

> **HINT** If you have the full URI on your clipboard (for example, by copying it from GitHub or the e-book version of this book), Eclipse automatically populates all the fields for you!

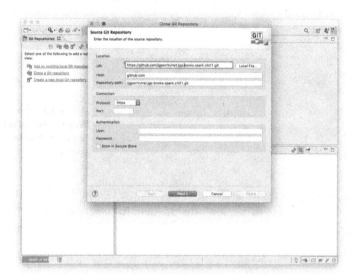

Figure D.4 If you copy the URI of the repository, Eclipse will automatically fill in the fields from the copied value during setup.

You can safely ignore the selection of the branch by clicking Next on the next screen, shown in figure D.5.

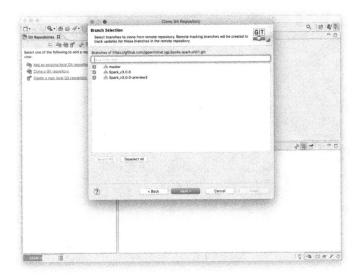

Figure D.5   You can safely ignore the branch selection. Click the Next button.

The last step of the wizard asks where you want to store the project, as shown in figure D.6. Make sure you click Finish after ensuring that the Directory option is correct.

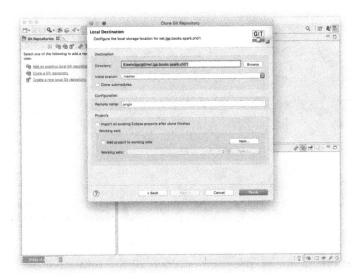

Figure D.6   Make sure you have the right location and then click the Finish button.

The next step is to import the project in Eclipse. Select the repository in the list, right-click, and select Import Projects, as shown in figure D.7.

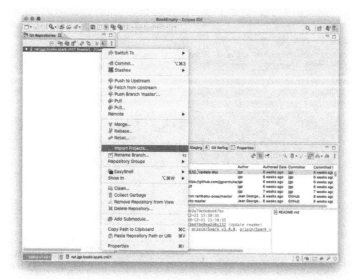

Figure D.7   Importing the newly cloned project in Eclipse

As you can see in figure D.8, Eclipse finds the Maven project. You can now click Finish.

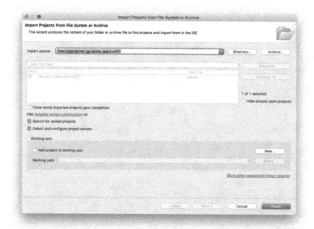

Figure D.8   Eclipse finds the project, so click Finish.

Don't freak out: at this point, Eclipse will download all the software it needs for an Apache Spark project, and there is a lot. You can click the progress bar icon at the right of the status bar in Eclipse to see what is going on.

Switch back to the Java perspective, shown in figure D.9, by choosing Window > Perspective > Open Perspective > Other. Select Java EE from the list and then click Open.

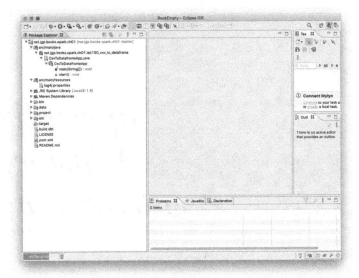

Figure D.9 Eclipse with the project tree in the Project Explorer

appendix E
A history of
enterprise data

I got my first computer when I was 12. It was an exciting Atari 800XL, and I loved coding in BASIC without any GO TO. Soon after I got it, I started thinking of a project that would be considered a big data/IoT project nowadays: connecting traffic lights, cameras, parking meters, and other city devices. To understand a little better how we can now imagine smart cities, beyond my childhood's wandering thoughts, let me share (a personal interpretation of) the history of data storage in the context of the enterprise.

E.1   The enterprise problem

A lot of the data in enterprises comes from transactional systems. When you shop at your local grocery store, for instance, you perform a *transaction*. The register at your local Walmart sends data to a local server, and that data is transferred to Bentonville, Arkansas.

Once all the data is collected, you can start performing *analytics*. This was easily doable in the 1990s, when you had a limited number of data sources and synced them once a day. However, nowadays, you're adding web data, advertising data, TV data, and real-time store data, and you start seeing the problem.

E.2   The solution is—hmmm, was—the data warehouse

The traditional databases—the famous relational database management systems (RDBMSs) including Informix, Oracle, MySQL, Db2, and SQL Server—started to slowly give up on the analytics tasks. It was time for a new concept called the *data warehouse*.

To make sure you would not confuse your home data warehouse with your business data warehouse, the industry (read: marketing) came up with the term *enterprise data warehouse*, or *EDW*.

Why are schemas so important?

As you know, data can take many forms. When data is stored in a relational database, a *schema* represents the structure of the data you are storing. That schema can contain more data about the data, such as indices, foreign keys, and other traditional relational database constructs. This data about the data is called *metadata*. Schemas are part of the metadata.

Consider this example of a schema: a table `book`, with a column `title`, a column `releaseDate`, and a column `ISBN`.

The ISBN (International Standard Book Number) is a unique numeric commercial book identifier. An ISBN is assigned to each edition and variation of a book. It is composed of 13 digits (it used to be 10). For example, this book's ISBN is 9781617295522.

The schema would define the following:

`title` is of type `VARCHAR(255)`, a string of characters whose length is smaller than 255. This column cannot be `NULL` (undefined value). A book must have a title.

`releaseDate` is of type `DATE`. This value can be `NULL`, as a book takes a long time to write, so you may not have the date from the beginning.

Even if the `ISBN` column is a numeric value, it will probably be defined as a `CHAR(13)`. It can be `NULL` if the book does not yet have an ISBN.

As you can see, even for three simple fields, it takes time and business knowledge to define a good schema.

Despite having an ugly name (who wants their data in a warehouse? I want mine in a vault or palace), data warehouses came with complex IT management such as an enforced schema: the data warehouse needed to know what data to expect. In a brick-and-mortar warehouse, if you don't know what goods are coming in, you will have problems storing them. Similarly, in a data warehouse, you have to know what data is coming in, in order to know where to store it.

However, with data coming from different business units, acquired companies, and external sources, implementing a data warehouse was becoming a never-ending story. And the performance was not at the rendezvous point.

E.3 *The ephemeral data lake*

As data warehouses were failing and the digital age was bringing more data, the enterprise was ready for a new buzzword: big data.

Although Hadoop is not the only big data solution, it quickly became the de facto standard. Hadoop is open source, backed by companies such as Cloudera, Hortonworks, IBM, and MapR, and available on platforms including AWS and Azure.

A key characteristic of data warehouses is a *schema-on-read* approach, or, as they put it in the West, "Store first, ask questions later."

Schema-on-read versus schema-on-write

As you know, if you want to insert data into a database or a data warehouse, you have to know the schema. If you want to insert a book's title in a character field, that will work; but if the type is a date, the insertion will fail.

Systems with schema-on-read will automatically build the schema when you read the data, inferring the schema.

On paper, schema-on-read seems to be the perfect solution, but you have to trust that the inferring algorithm will analyze a fragment of your data. To avoid risks, the inferring algorithm will default to String, which is difficult to optimize or work with. If your system ingests two dates, for example, OCT051971 would be placed alphabetically after MAY162004, even though the date is earlier.

The market was ready for this technology and even a new buzzword: data lake. A *data lake* is a storage repository that holds a vast amount of raw data in its native format until it is needed. What could go wrong?

E.4   *Lightning-fast cluster computing*

Hadoop seemed to be the solution for big data challenges. However, its design mainly uses disk, which is good when you need to store data, but not when you need to process it. And processing? Well, it uses primarily an algorithm called map-reduce, which is powerful but not intellectually approachable by anyone.

Finally, a lot of data lakes were becoming data swamps, as organizations understood the "store first, ask questions later" concept, but simply forgot to ask the *right* questions after.

The industry was ready for new functionalities and not-another-buzzword under the big data umbrella—lightning-fast cluster computing—and for a product: Apache Spark. Apache Spark works with both disk and memory, is agnostic to algorithms (SQL, API, map-reduce), and supports several programming languages.

E.5   *Java rules, but we're okay with Python*

When Matei Zaharia and his team started the Spark project, they needed a robust enterprise-class platform, so that's probably why they picked the Java Virtual Machine (JVM). However, they decided to implement Spark in a new(er) language called Scala, not Java. As you know, the JVM supports not only Java as a language, but also Scala, Clojure, Ruby, Python (via Jython), and a few others.

As a result, the JVM opens Spark to many languages: Scala, of course, Python, R, and Java.

I know it may create some controversy and give fuel to the programming language war, but, as a fact, Python and Java are the most widely sought languages for enterprise-level applications,[1] and Python is the most popular language among data scientists.[2]

Some urban legends claim that you need to learn Scala to use Spark. Others insist you must master Hadoop before starting Spark. To all those, my answer is simple: *que nenni!*[3]

This is what I want to teach through this book: focus on learning Apache Spark, with your Java and RDBMS skills. There is no need to lean Hadoop and its myriad of components or a new programming language.

---

[1] See the annual IEEE studies by Stephen Cass on the top programming languages for 2017 (http://mng.bz/MON2), 2018 (http://mng.bz/adW), and 2019 (http://mng.bz/gVZR).

[2] See "The Most Popular Language for Machine Learning and Data Science Is . . ." by Jean-Francois Puget (IBM), 2016, at KDnuggets, http://mng.bz/eDrJ.

[3] *Que nenni*, first used in chapter 1, is a medieval French expression meaning *of course not.* As Zig Ziglar said, "Repetition is the mother of learning, the father of action, which makes it the architect of accomplishment."

appendix F
Getting help with
relational databases

This appendix covers help and resources for installing relational databases that we use throughout this book. This appendix gives you hints about installing, procuring, and downloading relational databases you can use with Spark. Databases are listed alphabetically.

Every engineer and architect I've met has a bias for a particular database, often linked proportionally to the time worked with it and inversely proportionate to the number of issues that person had to deal with. Having said that, I worked a lot with Informix and had few issues with it, but I've also used a lot of other great databases throughout my career.

F.1   IBM Informix

Informix was one of the first commercial relational databases, created and launched in the 1980s. Bought by IBM in 2001, Informix is still kicking, thanks to a vibrant user community.

F.1.1   Installing Informix on macOS

To install IBM Informix on your Mac, you can read *Informix 12.10 on Mac 10.12 with a Dash of Java 8: The Tale of the Apple, the Coffee, and a Great Database* by this author (e-book on Amazon, http://amzn.to/2H6cReC).

F.1.2   Installing Informix on Windows

For help installing Informix on Windows, you can read "IDS on Windows Series: Installing IDS on XP" (www.jgp.ai/informix-windows), also by this author. Although a little old, the article is still up-to-date for the most part.

The JDBC driver is now available via Maven repositories. However, you can still read my article, "Installing the Informix JDBC driver on Windows Vista" (http://jgp.ai/2007/04/16/installing-the-informix-jdbc-driver-on-windows-vista/).

F.2 MariaDB

MariaDB is a fork of MySQL. MySQL was bought by Sun Microsystems, Sun Microsystems was bought by Oracle, and this situation was enough for the founders of MySQL to start MariaDB as a fork of MySQL. You can find more at https://mariadb.org.

F.2.1 Installing MariaDB on macOS

For macOS, you can download only the commercial version of MariaDB at https://mariadb.com/downloads/mariadb-tx. If you like Homebrew (the macOS package manager), you can find installation instructions at http://mng.bz/YeQ7.

I installed MariaDB TX v10.2.12 on macOS v 10.13.3. The direct download link is https://go.mariadb.com/download.

If you get an alert as shown in figure F.1, simply right-click the package file, select Open, and then click Continue.

Figure F.1 To avoid this security alert, indicating that MariaDB can't be opened because it is from an unidentified developer, right-click and select Open instead of double-clicking.

Follow the instructions in the installation wizard. At the end, you can access MariaDB by running `/usr/local/mariadb/server/bin/mariadb` on the command line.

F.2.2 Installing MariaDB on Windows

You can download the package from https://downloads.mariadb.org/ and follow the instructions.

F.3 MySQL (Oracle)

MySQL remains "the world's most popular open source database," as its slogan says. You can access MySQL resources at www.mysql.com.

F.3.1 Installing MySQL on macOS

You can download the community edition of MySQL at https://dev.mysql.com/down-loads/mysql/.

I installed MySQL v5.7.21-1 on macOS v 10.13.3; the direct download link is https://dev.mysql.com/downloads/file/?id=475582.

At the end of the installation process, the installer generates a password for root. In this situation, it is `NkZvElnfC1&j`, as you can see in figure F.2.

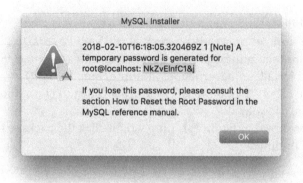

Figure F.2 MySQL installer generates a password for root.

To change it:

```
$ /usr/local/mysql/bin/mysql -uroot -p          Enter the password you
Enter password:                          ◄────── got from the installation.
mysql> SET PASSWORD FOR 'root'@'localhost' = PASSWORD('Spark<3Java');
```

F.3.2 Installing MySQL on Windows

MySQL offers an entire set of tools for Windows, which you can access at https://dev.mysql.com/downloads/windows/.

The full process of installing MySQL on Windows is available at http://mng.bz/zldZ.

F.3.3 Loading the Sakila database

MySQL's demo database is called *Sakila* and contains (among other things) actors and movies. You will use this database for examples using MySQL and MariaDB. Follow these steps to load the database:

1 Download the file from https://dev.mysql.com/doc/index-other.html. Pick either the ZIP or TGZ file; you will have to de-archive it. For your convenience, in March 2018 (Sakila does not have a version number), I downloaded and copied the files to the chapter 8 repository at https://github.com/jgperrin/net.jgp.books.spark.ch08.

2 Follow the installation process at http://mng.bz/07az. The tutorial is written for Windows but can be easily understood and adapted for macOS and Linux.

Once downloaded and unzipped, to install it on my system, I ran the following:

```
$ /usr/local/mysql/bin/mysql -uroot -p
Enter password: Spark<3Java
mysql> SOURCE /Users/jgp/Downloads/sakila-db/sakila-schema.sql;
```

I removed lots of boring results from SQL commands:

```
mysql> SOURCE /Users/jgp/Downloads/sakila-db/sakila-data.sql;
```

I removed more boring results from SQL commands:

```
mysql> show databases;
+--------------------+
| Database           |
+--------------------+
| information_schema |
| mysql              |
| performance_schema |
| sakila             |
| sys                |
+--------------------+
```

F.4 PostgreSQL

PostgreSQL is a mature relational database that also integrates NoSQL features. Postgre-SQL, which defines itself as "the world's most advanced open source database" and the fourth most popular database, has been available for more than 20 years. It is an object-oriented database that is fully ACID-compliant and highly extensible, enabling the community to add new features and capabilities as workload demands evolved. It integrates a lot of the features Informix offers with a little delay.

F.4.1 Installing PostgreSQL on macOS and Windows

You can download PostgreSQL for macOS and Windows from http://mng.bz/KEjn. EnterpriseDB is a company offering commercial support and downloads. More options and downloads can be found at www.postgresql.org/download/.

F.4.2 Installing PostgreSQL on Linux

Refer to the package manager specific to your distro to find out how to install packages, etc. You can then follow the Linux links from www.postgresql.org/download/.

F.4.3 GUI clients for PostgreSQL

PostgreSQL comes with a cross-platform graphical client for Windows and macOS, called *pgAdmin* (as you may have guessed, a lot of the tools are prefixed by *pg*). Other tools include SQLPro (macOS and Windows) and Aqua Data Studio (multiplatform).

appendix G
Static functions ease
your transformations

Static functions are a fantastic help when you are performing transformations. They help you transform your data within the dataframe.

This appendix is a comprehensive reference that can be used to find the functions you will need. The appendix contains the list of functions per category. This is an abbreviated version of the full guide to static functions, which you can download from the Manning website's resources section at http://jgp.ai/sia.

There are 405 functions. I've classified them into the following categories:

- *Popular functions*—Frequently used functions.
- *Aggregate functions*—Perform data aggregations.
- *Arithmetical functions*—Perform simple and complex arithmetical operations.
- *Array manipulation functions*—Perform array operations.
- *Binary operations*—Perform binary-level operations.
- *Byte functions*—Perform byte operations.
- *Comparison functions*—Perform comparisons.
- *Compute function*—Performs computation from a SQL-like statement.
- *Conditional operations*—Perform conditional evaluations.
- *Conversion functions*—Perform data and type conversions.
- *Data shape functions*—Perform operations relating to modifying the shape of the data.
- *Date and time functions*—Perform date and time manipulations and conversions.
- *Digest functions*—Calculate digests on columns.
- *Encoding functions*—Perform encoding/decoding.
- *Formatting functions*—Perform string and number formatting.

- *JSON functions*—Transform to and from JSON documents and fragments.
- *List functions*—Perform data collection operations on lists.
- *Map functions*—Perform map manipulation and conversion.
- *Mathematical functions*—Perform mathematical operations on columns. Check out the mathematics subcategories as well: trigonometry, arithmetic, and statistics.
- *Navigation functions*—Allow referencing of columns.
- *Parsing functions*—Allow parsing of data in a column.
- *Partition functions*—Help partition on dataframes.
- *Rounding functions*—Perform rounding operations on numerical values.
- *Sorting functions*—Perform column sorting.
- *Statistical functions*—Perform statistical operations.
- *Streaming functions*—Perform window/streaming operations.
- *String functions*—Perform common string operations.
- *Technical functions*—Inform on dataframe technical/meta information.
- *Trigonometry functions*—Perform trigonometric calculations.
- *UDF helpers*—Provide help with manipulating UDFs.
- *Validation functions*—Perform value type validation.
- *Deprecated functions*—Functions that you should not use and, if you see them, you should consider replacing with the newer versions.

G.1   Functions per category

This section lists, per category, all the functions. Some functions can be in several categories, which is typically the case for mathematical functions (subdivided into arithmetical, trigonometry, and statistical). Functions are listed in each category and subcategory; they may appear several times.

G.1.1   Popular functions

These functions are popular. This popularity is probably subjective: these are functions my teams and I use a lot and are frequently queried about on Stack Overflow.

There are six functions in this category: `col()`, `concat()`, `expr()`, `lit()`, `split()`, and `to_date()`.

G.1.2   Aggregate functions

Aggregate functions allow you to perform a calculation on a set of values and return a single scalar value. In SQL, developers often use aggregate functions with the GROUP BY and HAVING clauses of SELECT statements.

There are 26 functions in this category: `aggregate()`, `approx_count_distinct()`, `collect_list()`, `collect_set()`, `corr()`, `count()`, `countDistinct()`, `covar_pop()`, `covar_samp()`, `first()`, `grouping()`, `grouping_id()`, `kurtosis()`, `last()`, `max()`, `mean()`, `min()`, `skewness()`, `stddev()`, `stddev_pop()`, `stddev_samp()`, `sum()`, `sumDistinct()`, `var_pop()`, `var_samp()`, and `variance()`.

G.1.3   *Arithmetical functions*

Arithmetical functions perform operations like computing square roots.

There are 13 functions in this category: cbrt(), exp(), expm1(), factorial(), hypot(), log(), log10(), log1p(), log2(), negate(), pmod(), pow(), and sqrt().

G.1.4   *Array manipulation functions*

Array functions manipulate arrays when they are in a dataframe's cell.

There are 27 functions in this category: array(), array_contains(), array _distinct(), array_except(), array_intersect(), array_join(), array_max(), array_min(), array_position(), array_remove(), array_repeat(), array_sort(), array_union(), arrays_overlap(), arrays_zip(), element_at(), exists(), filter(), forall(), map_entries(), map_from_arrays(), reverse(), shuffle(), size(), slice(), sort_array(), and zip_with().

G.1.5   *Binary operations*

Thanks to binary functions, you can perform binary-level operations, like binary not, shifting bits, and similar operations.

There are five functions in this category: bitwiseNOT(), not(), shiftLeft(), shiftRight(), and shiftRightUnsigned().

G.1.6   *Byte functions*

Byte functions allow manipulation of data at the byte level.

There is one function in this category: overlay().

G.1.7   *Comparison functions*

Comparison functions are used to compare values.

There are two functions in this category: greatest() and least().

G.1.8   *Compute function*

This function is used to compute values from a statement. The statement itself is SQL-like.

There is one function in this category: expr().

G.1.9   *Conditional operations*

Conditional functions are used to evaluate values on a conditional basis.

There are two functions in this category: nanvl() and when().

G.1.10   *Conversion functions*

Conversion functions are used for converting various data into other types: date, JSON, hexadecimal, and more.

There are 16 functions in this category: conv(), date_format(), from_csv(), from_json(), from_unixtime(), from_utc_timestamp(), get_json_object(), hex(), schema_of_csv(), schema_of_json(), to_csv(), to_date(), to_json(), to_time-stamp(), to_utc_timestamp(), and unhex().

G.1.11 *Data shape functions*

These functions modify the data shape; for example, creating a column with a literal value (`lit()`), flattening, mapping, and more.

There are 24 functions in this category: `coalesce()`, `explode()`, `explode_outer()`, `flatten()`, `lit()`, `map()`, `map_concat()`, `map_filter()`, `map_from_arrays()`, `map_from_entries()`, `map_keys()`, `map_values()`, `map_zip_with()`, `monotonically_increasing_id()`, `posexplode()`, `posexplode_outer()`, `schema_of_json()`, `sequence()`, `struct()`, `transform()`, `transform_keys()`, `transform_values()`, `typedLit()`, and `zip_with()`.

G.1.12 *Date and time functions*

Date and time functions manipulate dates, time, and their combinations; for example, finding the current date (`current_date()`), adding days/months/years to a date, and more.

There are 32 functions in this category: `add_months()`, `current_date()`, `current_timestamp()`, `date_add()`, `date_format()`, `date_sub()`, `date_trunc()`, `datediff()`, `dayofmonth()`, `dayofweek()`, `dayofyear()`, `days()`, `from_unixtime()`, `from_utc_timestamp()`, `hour()`, `hours()`, `last_day()`, `minute()`, `month()`, `months()`, `months_between()`, `next_day()`, `quarter()`, `second()`, `to_date()`, `to_timestamp()`, `to_utc_timestamp()`, `trunc()`, `unix_timestamp()`, `weekofyear()`, `year()`, and `years()`.

G.1.13 *Digest functions*

Digest functions create digests from values in other columns. Digests can be MD5 (`md5()`), SHA1/2, and more.

There are eight functions in this category: `base64()`, `crc32()`, `hash()`, `md5()`, `sha1()`, `sha2()`, `unbase64()`, and `xxhash64()`.

G.1.14 *Encoding functions*

Encoding functions can manipulate encodings.

There are three functions in this category: `base64()`, `decode()`, and `encode()`.

G.1.15 *Formatting functions*

Formatting functions format strings and numbers in a specified way.

There are two functions in this category: `format_number()` and `format_string()`.

G.1.16 *JSON functions*

JavaScript Object Notation (JSON) functions help the conversion and JSON manipulation functions.

There are five functions in this category: `from_json()`, `get_json_object()`, `json_tuple()`, `schema_of_json()`, and `to_json()`.

G.1.17 List functions

With list functions, you can manipulate lists through collecting the data. The meaning of the data collected is based on the dataset/dataframe's collect() method; chapter 16 explains collect() and collectAsList().

There are two functions in this category: collect_list() and collect_set().

G.1.18 Map functions

Map functions allow manipulation and conversion of maps.

There are 11 functions in this category: map(), map_concat(), map_entries(), map_filter(), map_from_arrays(), map_keys(), map_values(), map_zip_with(), transform(), transform_keys(), and transform_values().

G.1.19 Mathematical functions

The range of mathematical functions is broad, with subcategories in trigonometry, arithmetic, statistics, and more. They usually behave like their java.lang.Math counterparts.

There are 37 functions in this category: abs(), acos(), asin(), atan(), atan2(), avg(), bround(), cbrt(), ceil(), cos(), cosh(), covar_pop(), covar_samp(), degrees(), exp(), expm1(), factorial(), floor(), hypot(), log(), log10(), log1p(), log2(), negate(), pmod(), pow(), radians(), rand(), randn(), rint(), round(), signum(), sin(), sinh(), sqrt(), tan(), and tanh().

G.1.20 Navigation functions

Navigation functions perform navigation or referencing within the dataframe.

There are four functions in this category: col(), column(), first(), and last().

G.1.21 Parsing functions

Parsing functions perform data transformation from a format that can be parsed, like JSON or CSV, to a usable column.

There are four functions in this category: from_csv(), schema_of_csv(), schema _of_json(), and to_csv().

G.1.22 Partition functions

Partition functions help Spark by giving it hints for partitioning based on criteria such as dates.

There are four functions in this category: days(), hours(), months(), and years().

G.1.23 Rounding functions

Rounding functions perform rounding of numerical values.

There are five functions in this category: bround(), ceil(), floor(), rint(), and round().

G.1.24 Sorting functions

Sorting functions are used for sorting of elements within a column.

There are 12 functions in this category: array_sort(), asc(), asc_nulls _first(), asc_nulls_last(), desc(), desc_nulls_first(), desc_nulls_last(), greatest(), least(), max(), min(), and sort_array().

G.1.25 Statistical functions

Statistical functions cover statistics; for example, calculating averages, variances, and more. They are often used in the context of window/streaming or aggregates.

There are 11 functions in this category: avg(), covar_pop(), covar_samp(), cume_dist(), mean(), stddev(), stddev_pop(), stddev_samp(), var_pop(), var_samp(), and variance().

G.1.26 Streaming functions

Streaming functions are used in the context of window/streaming operations.

There are nine functions in this category: cume_dist(), dense_rank(), lag(), lead(), ntile(), percent_rank(), rank(), row_number(), and window().

G.1.27 String functions

String functions allow manipulation of strings, like concatenation, extraction and replacement based on regex, and more.

There are 31 functions in this category: ascii(), bin(), concat(), concat_ws(), date_format(), date_trunc(), format_number(), format_string(), get_json _object(), initcap(), instr(), length(), levenshtein(), locate(), lower(), lpad(), ltrim(), overlay(), regexp_extract(), regexp_replace(), repeat(), reverse(), rpad(), rtrim(), soundex(), split(), substring(), substring_index(), translate(), trim(), and upper().

G.1.28 Technical functions

Technical functions give you meta information on the dataframe and its structure.

There are six functions in this category: broadcast(), bucket(), col(), column(), input_file_name(), and spark_partition_id().

G.1.29 Trigonometry functions

Trigonometry functions perform operations such as sine, cosine, and more.

There are 12 functions in this category: acos(), asin(), atan(), atan2(), cos(), cosh(), degrees(), radians(), sin(), sinh(), tan(), and tanh().

G.1.30 UDF helpers

User-defined functions (UDFs) are functions in their own right. They extend Apache Spark. However, to use the UDF in a transformation, you will need these helper functions. Chapter 14 covers using and building UDFs. The counterpart to UDFs for aggregations are user-defined aggregate functions (UDAFs), detailed in chapter 15.

There are two functions in this category: callUDF() and udf().

G.1.31 *Validation functions*

Validation functions allow you to test for a value's status; for example, whether it's not a number (NaN) or null.

There are two functions in this category: isnan() and isnull().

G.1.32 *Deprecated functions*

These functions are still available, but are deprecated. If you are using them, check for their replacements at http://mng.bz/WPqa.

There are two functions in this category: from_utc_timestamp() and to_utc _timestamp().

G.2   *Function appearance per version of Spark*

This section lists all the functions in reverse order of appearance (or update) per version of Apache Spark.

G.2.1   *Functions in Spark v3.0.0*

There are 26 functions in this category: add_months(), aggregate(), bucket(), date_add(), date_sub(), days(), exists(), filter(), forall(), from_csv(), hours(), map_entries(), map_filter(), map_zip_with(), months(), overlay(), schema_of_csv(), schema_of_json(), split(), to_csv(), transform(), transform _keys(), transform_values(), xxhash64(), years(), and zip_with().

G.2.2   *Functions in Spark v2.4.0*

There are 25 functions in this category: array_distinct(), array_except(), array_intersect(), array_join(), array_max(), array_min(), array_position(), array_remove(), array_repeat(), array_sort(), array_union(), arrays _overlap(), arrays_zip(), element_at(), flatten(), from_json(), from_utc _timestamp(), map_concat(), map_from_entries(), months_between(), schema _of_json(), sequence(), shuffle(), slice(), and to_utc_timestamp().

G.2.3   *Functions in Spark v2.3.0*

There are nine functions in this category: date_trunc(), dayofweek(), from_json(), ltrim(), map_keys(), map_values(), rtrim(), trim(), and udf().

G.2.4   *Functions in Spark v2.2.0*

There are six functions in this category: explode_outer(), from_json(), posexplode _outer(), to_date(), to_timestamp(), and typedLit().

G.2.5   *Functions in Spark v2.1.0*

There are 11 functions in this category: approx_count_distinct(), asc_nulls _first(), asc_nulls_last(), degrees(), desc_nulls_first(), desc_nulls_last(), from_json(), posexplode(), radians(), regexp_replace(), and to_json().

G.2.6 Functions in Spark v2.0.0

There are 10 functions in this category: `bround()`, `covar_pop()`, `covar_samp()`, `first()`, `grouping()`, `grouping_id()`, `hash()`, `last()`, `udf()`, and `window()`.

G.2.7 Functions in Spark v1.6.0

There are 22 functions in this category: `collect_list()`, `collect_set()`, `corr()`, `cume_dist()`, `dense_rank()`, `get_json_object()`, `input_file_name()`, `isnan()`, `isnull()`, `json_tuple()`, `kurtosis()`, `monotonically_increasing_id()`, `percent_rank()`, `row_number()`, `skewness()`, `spark_partition_id()`, `stddev()`, `stddev_pop()`, `stddev_samp()`, `var_pop()`, `var_samp()`, and `variance()`.

G.2.8 Functions in Spark v1.5.0

There are 76 functions in this category: `add_months()`, `array_contains()`, `ascii()`, `base64()`, `bin()`, `broadcast()`, `callUDF()`, `concat()`, `concat_ws()`, `conv()`, `crc32()`, `current_date()`, `current_timestamp()`, `date_add()`, `date_format()`, `date_sub()`, `datediff()`, `dayofmonth()`, `dayofyear()`, `decode()`, `encode()`, `factorial()`, `format_number()`, `format_string()`, `from_unixtime()`, `from_utc_timestamp()`, `greatest()`, `hex()`, `hour()`, `initcap()`, `instr()`, `last_day()`, `least()`, `length()`, `levenshtein()`, `locate()`, `log2()`, `lpad()`, `ltrim()`, `md5()`, `minute()`, `month()`, `months_between()`, `nanvl()`, `next_day()`, `pmod()`, `quarter()`, `regexp_extract()`, `regexp_replace()`, `repeat()`, `reverse()`, `round()`, `rpad()`, `rtrim()`, `second()`, `sha1()`, `sha2()`, `shiftLeft()`, `shiftRight()`, `shiftRightUnsigned()`, `size()`, `sort_array()`, `soundex()`, `split()`, `sqrt()`, `substring()`, `to_date()`, `to_utc_timestamp()`, `translate()`, `trim()`, `trunc()`, `unbase64()`, `unhex()`, `unix_timestamp()`, `weekofyear()`, and `year()`.

G.2.9 Functions in Spark v1.4.0

There are 33 functions in this category: `acos()`, `array()`, `asin()`, `atan()`, `atan2()`, `bitwiseNOT()`, `cbrt()`, `ceil()`, `cos()`, `cosh()`, `exp()`, `expm1()`, `floor()`, `hypot()`, `lag()`, `lead()`, `log()`, `log10()`, `log1p()`, `mean()`, `ntile()`, `pow()`, `rand()`, `randn()`, `rank()`, `rint()`, `signum()`, `sin()`, `sinh()`, `struct()`, `tan()`, `tanh()`, and `when()`.

G.2.10 Functions in Spark v1.3.0

There are 23 functions in this category: `abs()`, `asc()`, `avg()`, `coalesce()`, `col()`, `column()`, `count()`, `countDistinct()`, `desc()`, `explode()`, `first()`, `last()`, `lit()`, `lower()`, `max()`, `min()`, `negate()`, `not()`, `sqrt()`, `sum()`, `sumDistinct()`, `udf()`, and `upper()`.

appendix H
Maven quick cheat sheet

Maven is a powerful tool for building projects, including compiling, testing, generating documentation, packaging, and so on. This appendix provides a few tips and tricks for using Maven, stuff that's hard to find on the internet and that's useful for both Java and Spark development.

H.1 Source of packages

Packages and artifacts are cataloged on several sites. The most popular is MVN Repository at https://mvnrepository.com/.

H.2 Useful commands

Here are a few commands that are useful to know (but not to have to memorize) when you use Maven:

- `$ mvn clean`—Cleans everywhere; allows you to start from a clean slate, which is useful sometimes.
- `$ mvn compile`—Compiles the code.
- `$ mvn package`—Creates a package but leaves it in the target directory.
- `$ mvn install`—Creates a package and copies it in the repository. There are options for creating various types of Java packages, but you are going to use only JARs here.
- `$ mvn install -Dmaven.test.skip=true`—Installs your project without running the tests (I know, no comment on this one).

H.3 Typical Maven life cycle

Maven builds your application as a life cycle. That means you can do any of the operations, and Maven will do the previous operations for you. The typical life cycle is as follows:

- validate—Makes sure the project is correct and all necessary information is available
- compile—Compiles the source code
- test—Tests the compiled source code by using a suitable unit-testing framework
- package—Takes the compiled code and packages it, such as a JAR
- verify—Runs any checks on results of integration tests
- install—Installs the package into the local repository, for use as a dependency in other local projects
- deploy—Done in the build environment; copies the final package to the remote repository for sharing with other developers and projects

Two commands are not part of the life cycle:

- clean—Cleans the project
- site—Builds the project's website, including documentation

H.4 Useful configuration

When configuring Maven, you can add plugins to automate repetitive tasks. This section details a few of the ones I like that may not be obvious.

H.4.1 Built-in properties

In your pom.xml file, you may already use some properties. In all of this book's examples, I have properties to specify the version of Spark I use and the version of Scala it is built on, so I can easily change a bunch of artifacts' versions.

Here is the definition of the properties:

```
<properties>
...
  <scala.version>2.11</scala.version>
  <spark.version>2.3.1</spark.version>
</properties>
```

And here is their usage:

```
<dependency>
  <groupId>org.apache.spark</groupId>
  <artifactId>spark-core_${scala.version}</artifactId>
  <version>${spark.version}</version>
</dependency>

<dependency>
  <groupId>org.apache.spark</groupId>
  <artifactId>spark-sql_${scala.version}</artifactId>
  <version>${spark.version}</version>
</dependency>

<dependency>
```

```
      <groupId>org.apache.spark</groupId>
      <artifactId>spark-mllib_${scala.version}</artifactId>
      <version>${spark.version}</version>
   </dependency>
```

Maven also has a list of built-in properties you can use in the pom.xml file, enabling you to avoid hardcoding elements such as the project's name or version, which you can call through `${project.name}` and `${project.version}`, respectively

The complete list of built-in properties can be found in *Maven, The Complete Reference* by Tim O'Brien et al. (Sonatype, 2010) at http://mng.bz/8pGz.

H.4.2   Building an uber JAR

An uber (or fat) JAR contains all the classes of your application and its dependencies. It is discussed in chapter 5. Here is an example of the Shade plugin syntax, which can build the uber JAR:

```
<plugin>
   <groupId>org.apache.maven.plugins</groupId>           ┐ Definition of
   <artifactId>maven-shade-plugin</artifactId>           │ the plugin
   <version>3.1.1</version>
   <executions>
     <execution>
       <phase>package</phase>          ◁──┐ Shade will be executed
       <goals>                            │ during packaging.
         <goal>shade</goal>
       </goals>
       <configuration>
         <minimizeJar>true</minimizeJar>        ◁──┐ Removes all classes that are not
         <artifactSet>                              │ used by the project, reducing the
Exclusions ──▷  <excludes>                          │ size of the JAR
             <exclude>org.apache.spark</exclude>
             <exclude>org.apache.hadoop</exclude>
   Allows a     <exclude>*:xml-apis</exclude>
  suffix for    <exclude>log4j:log4j:jar:</exclude>
 name of the  </excludes>
   uber JAR  </artifactSet>                                    ┐ Suffix added to
          └─▷ <shadedArtifactAttached>true</shadedArtifactAttached>  │ the generated
             <shadedClassifierName>uber</shadedClassifierName>  ◁──┘ uber JAR
       </configuration>
     </execution>
   </executions>
</plugin>
```

You can build the uber JAR by calling the following:

```
$ mvn package
```

The name of the uber JAR will be suffixed by *uber*.

H.4.3 Including the source code

While deploying, including the application's source code in the repository can be useful, to ensure that you have the exact version of the source code that is being deployed. This topic is discussed in chapter 5.

Here is the plugin definition:

```
<plugin>
  <groupId>org.apache.maven.plugins</groupId>           Definition of
  <artifactId>maven-source-plugin</artifactId>          the plugin
  <version>3.0.1</version>
  <executions>
    <execution>
      <id>attach-sources</id>
      <phase>verify</phase>
      <goals>
        <goal>jar-no-fork</goal>      ◁──── No forking during
      </goals>                              the packaging
    </execution>
  </executions>
</plugin>
```

You can build the source JAR by calling the following:

```
$ mvn install
```

The packaging is done during the verify phase, which is before the install phase. The name of the JAR will be suffixed by *sources*.

H.4.4 Executing from Maven

Executing a Java application can be painful. Where's my JVM installed? What's the class path? You could build a shell, which needs to be maintained, or directly use Maven. You can directly run your application from Maven by using the following:

```
$ mvn exec:exec
```

To do so, you can include this plugin in your build section:

```
<plugin>
  <groupId>org.codehaus.mojo</groupId>                  Definition of
  <artifactId>exec-maven-plugin</artifactId>            the plugin
  <version>1.6.0</version>
  <configuration>
    <executable>java</executable>    ◁──── Name of the executable
    <arguments>
      <argument>-Dlog4j.configuration=file:src/main/java/
  log4j.properties</argument>
      <argument>-classpath</argument>                Automatically replaced by the
      <classpath />                      ◁───────── value of the class path (yeah!)
      <argument>net.jgp.books.AnApp</argument>    ◁─┐
    </arguments>                                      Your application's main class
  </configuration>
</plugin>
```

appendix I
Reference for transformations and actions

This appendix lists the transformations and actions supported by Spark in a Java context. The online documentation covers them from a Scala viewpoint.

LAB Examples from this appendix are available in GitHub at https://github.com/jgperrin/net.jgp.books.spark.ch12. Chapter 12 focuses on transformations (records, documents, and joins).

I.1 Transformations

Transformations modify data only after an action. Table I.1 lists the available transformations. This list is based on Spark documentation and adapted to Java.

This is not an exhaustive list of transformations, but rather the primitives being used by higher-level functions: any higher-level function using one or more transformations is a transformation.

In Java, the function used as a parameter can be a *lambda function* or a *class*. Although a little more verbose, the code is a lot clearer and more maintainable when you use a class (which you will instantiate) rather than a lambda function. Online documentation does not list the class signatures, so I added them here as examples, after the table.

The inspiration for table I.1 is the list of transformations found in the Apache Spark programming guide, specifically the RDDs at http://mng.bz/EdEd.

Table I.1 Transformations with class signature

Transformation	Description

map (*func*, *encoding*)	Returns a new distributed dataset formed by passing each element of the source through a function *func*.
	
	Usage example:
	
	``
	Dataset<String> dfString = df.map(
	    new CountyFipsExtractorUsingMap(),
	    Encoders.STRING());
	``
	
	See listing I.1 for implementation.

filter (*func*)	Returns a new dataset formed by selecting those elements of the source on which *func* returns true.
	
	Usage example:
	
	``
	Dataset<Row> dfFilter = df.filter(
	    new SmallCountiesFilter());
	``
	
	See listing I.2 for implementation.

flatMap (*func*, *encoding*)	Similar to map, but each input item can be mapped to 0 or more output items. *func* should return an Iterator in Java or a Seq in Scala rather than a single item.
	
	Usage example:
	
	``
	Dataset<String> dfFlatMap = df.flatMap(
	    new CountyStateExtractorFlatMap(),
	    Encoders.STRING());
	``
	
	See listing I.3 for implementation.

mapPartitions (*func*, *encoding*)	Similar to map, but runs separately on each partition (block) of the RDD, so *func* must be of type Iterator<T> => Iterator<U> when running on an RDD of type T.
	
	Usage example:
	
	``
	Dataset<String> dfMapPartitions =
	dfPartitioned.mapPartitions(
	    new FirstCountyUsingMapPartitions(),
	    Encoders.STRING());
	``
	
	See listing I.4 for implementation.

mapPartitionsWithIndex (*func*)	Similar to mapPartitions, but also provides *func* with an integer value representing the index of the partition, so *func* must be of type (Int, Iterator<T>) => Iterator<U> when running on an RDD of type T. Although this method is mentioned in the online documentation, there was no implementation in Spark v2.3.1 (and maybe earlier).
sample (*withReplacement*, *fraction*, *seed*)	Samples a *fraction* of the data, with or without replacement, using a given random number generator seed. Chapter 12 describes the statistical notion of replacement.
union (*otherDataset*)	Returns a new dataset that contains the union of the elements in the source dataset and the argument. The number and type of columns must be matching.

Table I.1   Transformations with class signature *(continued)*

Transformation	Description
intersection (*otherDataset*)	Returns a new RDD that contains the intersection of elements in the source dataset and the argument.
distinct ()	Returns a new dataset that contains the distinct elements of the source dataset.

groupByKey (*func*, *encoding*)	When called on a dataset of (K, V) pairs, returns a dataset of (K, Iterable<V>) pairs.
	
	Note: If you are grouping in order to perform an aggregation (such as a sum or average) over each key, using reduceByKey or aggregateByKey will produce better performance.
	
	Usage example:
	
	`KeyValueGroupedDataset<String, Row> dfGroupByKey =`
	`    df.groupByKey(`
	`        new StateFipsExtractorUsingMap(),`
	`        Encoders.STRING());`
	
	See listing I.5 for implementation.

reduceByKey (*func*, [*numPartitions*])	When called on a dataset of (K, V) pairs, returns a dataset of (K, V) pairs, where the values for each key are aggregated using the given reduce function *func*, which must be of type (V, V) => V. Although this method is mentioned in the online documentation, there was no implementation in Spark v2.3.1 (and maybe earlier).
aggregateByKey (*zeroValue*) aggregateByKey (*seqOp*, *combOp*, [*numPartitions*])	When called on a dataset of (K, V) pairs, returns a dataset of (K, U) pairs, where the values for each key are aggregated using the given combine functions and a neutral "zero" value. Allows an aggregated value type that is different from the input value type, while avoiding unnecessary allocations. As in groupByKey, the number of reduce tasks is configurable through an optional second argument. Although this method is mentioned in the online documentation, there was no implementation in Spark v2.3.1 (and maybe earlier).

agg(<*multiple signature*>)	Performs an aggregation on the entire dataset.
	
	Usage example:
	
	`Dataset<Row> countCountDf =`
	`    countyStateDf.agg(count("County"));`

sortByKey ([*ascending*], [*numPartitions*])	When called on a dataset of (K, V) pairs, where K implements Ordered, returns a dataset of (K, V) pairs sorted by keys in ascending or descending order, as specified in the Boolean ascending argument.
join (*otherDataset*, [*numPartitions*])	When called on datasets of type (K, V) and (K, W), returns a dataset of (K, (V, W)) pairs with all pairs of elements for each key. Joins can be inner, cross, outer (full, full_outer), left_outer (left), right_outer (right), left_semi, or left_anti. Joins are described in chapter 12 and appendix M.

Table I.1 Transformations with class signature (*continued*)

Transformation	Description
cogroup (otherDataset, [*numPartitions*])	When called on datasets of type (K, V) and (K, W), returns a dataset of (K, (Iterable<V>, Iterable<W>)) tuples. This operation is also called groupWith.
cartesian (*otherDataset*)	When called on datasets of types T and U, returns a dataset of (T, U) pairs (all pairs of elements).
pipe (*command*, [*envVars*])	Pipes each partition of the RDD through a shell command; for example, a Perl or bash script. RDD elements are written to the process's stdin, and lines output to its stdout are returned as an RDD of strings.
coalesce (*numPartitions*)	Decreases the number of partitions in the RDD to numPartitions. Useful for running operations more efficiently after filtering down a large dataset.
repartition (*numPartitions*)	Randomly reshuffles the data in the RDD to create either more or fewer partitions and balance it across them. This always shuffles all data over the network.
repartitionAndSort-WithinPartitions (*partitioner*)	Repartitions the RDD according to the given partitioner and, within each resulting partition, sorts records by their keys. This is more efficient than calling repartition() and then sorting within each partition: the sorting is pushed down into the shuffle machinery.

Listing I.1 map() usage and implementation

Output:
```
map()
+-----+
|value|
+-----+
|   01|
|   03|
|   05|
|   07|
|   09|
+-----+
only showing top 5 rows
```

Usage:
```
System.out.println("map()");
Dataset<String> dfMap = df.map(new CountyFipsExtractorUsingMap(),
    Encoders.STRING());
dfMap.show(5);
```

Implementation:
```
import org.apache.spark.api.java.function.MapFunction;
...
private final class CountyFipsExtractorUsingMap
    implements MapFunction<Row, String> {
  private static final long serialVersionUID = 26547L;

  @Override
```

```
public String call(Row r) throws Exception {
  String s = r.getAs("id2").toString().substring(2);
  return s;
  }
}
```

Listing I.2 `filter()` usage and implementation

Output:
```
filter()
+-------------+----+--------------------+--------+------------+...
|           id| id2|           Geography|real2010|estimate2010|...
+-------------+----+--------------------+--------+------------+...
|0500000US01005|1005|Barbour County, A...|   27457|       27332|...
|0500000US01007|1007|Bibb County, Alabama|   22915|       22872|...
|0500000US01011|1011|Bullock County, A...|   10914|       10880|...
|0500000US01013|1013|Butler County, Al...|   20947|       20944|...
|0500000US01019|1019|Cherokee County, ...|   25989|       25973|...
+-------------+----+--------------------+--------+------------+...
only showing top 5 rows
```

Usage:
```
System.out.println("filter()");
Dataset<Row> dfFilter = df.filter(new SmallCountiesUsingFilter());
dfFilter.show(5);
```

Implementation:
```
import org.apache.spark.api.java.function.FilterFunction;
...
private final class SmallCountiesFilter implements FilterFunction<Row> {
  private static final long serialVersionUID = 17392L;

  @Override
  public boolean call(Row r) throws Exception {
    if (r.getInt(4) < 30000) {
      return true;
    }
    return false;
  }
}
```

Listing I.3 `flatMap()` usage and implementation

Output:
```
flatMap()
+--------------+
|         value|
+--------------+
|Autauga County|
|       Alabama|
|Baldwin County|
|       Alabama|
|Barbour County|
+--------------+
```

```
only showing top 5 rows
```

Usage:
```
System.out.println("flatMap()");
Dataset<String> dfFlatMap = df.flatMap(
    new CountyStateExtractorFlatMap(),
    Encoders.STRING());
dfFlatMap.show(5);
```

Implementation:
```
import org.apache.spark.api.java.function.FlatMapFunction;
...
public class CountyStateExtractorFlatMap
    implements FlatMapFunction<Row, String> {
  private static final long serialVersionUID = 63784L;

  @Override
  public Iterator<String> call(Row r) throws Exception {
    String[] s = r.getAs("Geography").toString().split(", ");
    return Arrays.stream(s).iterator();
  }
}
```

Listing I.4 `mapPartitions()` usage and implementation

Output:
```
mapPartitions()
Input dataframe has 3220 records
Result dataframe has 20 records        ◁  Two records for each partition,
+----------------+                        repartitioned in ten partitions
|           value|
+----------------+
|Caledonia County|
|         Vermont|
|    Boone County|
|        Nebraska|
|Hillsdale County|
+----------------+
only showing top 5 rows
```

Usage:
```
System.out.println("mapPartitions()");
Dataset<Row> dfPartitioned = df.repartition(10);
Dataset<String> dfMapPartitions = dfPartitioned.mapPartitions(
    new FirstCountyAndStateOfPartitionUsingMapPartitions(),
    Encoders.STRING());
System.out.println("Input dataframe has " + df.count() + " records");
System.out.println("Result dataframe has " + dfMapPartitions.count()
    + " records");
dfMapPartitions.show(5);
```

Implementation:
```
import org.apache.spark.api.java.function.MapPartitionsFunction;
...
public class FirstCountyAndStateOfPartitionUsingMapPartitions
```

```
    implements MapPartitionsFunction<Row, String> {
  private static final long serialVersionUID = -62694L;

  @Override
  public Iterator<String> call(Iterator<Row> input) throws Exception {
    Row r = input.next();
    String[] s = r.getAs("Geography").toString().split(", ");
    return Arrays.stream(s).iterator();
  }
}
```

Listing I.5   groupByKey() usage and implementation

Output:
```
groupByKey()
+-----+--------+
|value|count(1)|
+-----+--------+
|   51|     133|
|   15|       5|
|   54|      55|
|   11|       1|
|   29|     115|
+-----+--------+
only showing top 5 rows
```

FIPS state #29 is Missouri, which has 114 counties and one city (St. Louis).

Usage:
```
System.out.println("groupByKey()");
KeyValueGroupedDataset<String, Row> dfGroupByKey =
    df.groupByKey (
        new StateFipsExtractorUsingMap(),
        Encoders.STRING());
dfGroupByKey.count().show(5);
```

Implementation:
```
import org.apache.spark.api.java.function.MapFunction;
...
private final class StateFipsExtractorUsingMap
    implements MapFunction<Row, String> {
  private static final long serialVersionUID = 26572L;

  @Override
  public String call(Row r) throws Exception {
    String id = r.getAs("id").toString();
    String state = id.substring(9, 11);
    return state;
  }
}
```

I.2   Actions

Actions are the real trigger of the processing. In chapter 4, I described the concept of the directed acyclic graph (DAG) and the laziness of Spark, which was awakened/triggered by an action. This section lists the low-level actions.

Note that some higher-level operations may trigger actions, but you may not see them because they are hidden in those operations.

In Java, the function used as a parameter can be a *lambda function* or a *class*. Although a little more verbose, the code is a lot clearer and more maintainable when you use a class rather than a lambda function. Online documentation does not list the class signatures, so I added them here as examples, after the table.

The inspiration for table I.2 is the list of transformations found in the Apache Spark programming guide, specifically the RDDs at https://spark.apache.org/docs/latest/rdd-programming-guide.html#actions.

Table I.2   List of actions with Java signature

Action	Description

reduce(*func*)	Aggregates the elements of the dataset by using a function *func* (which takes two arguments and returns one), also known as a *reduce operation*. The function should be commutative and associative so that it can be computed correctly in parallel.
	
	Usage example:
	
	`String listOfCountyStateDs = countyStateDs`
	`    .reduce(`
	`        new CountyStateConcatUsingReduce());`
	
	See listing I.6 for implementation.

collect()	Returns all the elements of the dataset as an array at the driver program. This is usually useful after a filter or other operation that returns a sufficiently small subset of the data.
count()	Returns the number of elements in the dataset.
first()	Returns the first element of the dataset (similar to take(1)).
take(n)	Returns an array with the first *n* elements of the dataset.
takeSample(*withReplacement, num, [seed]*)	Returns an array with a random sample of *num* elements of the dataset, with or without replacement, optionally pre-specifying a random number generator seed. See chapter 12 for an explanation of the notion of replacement in statistics.
takeOrdered (*n, [ordering]*)	Returns the first *n* elements of the RDD by using either their natural order or a custom comparator.
saveAsTextFile (*path*)	Writes the elements of the dataset as a text file (or set of text files) in a given directory in the local filesystem, HDFS, or any other Hadoop-supported filesystem. Spark will call toString() on each element to convert it to a line of text in the file.
saveAsSequenceFile (*path*)	Writes the elements of the dataset as a Hadoop SequenceFile in a given path in the local filesystem, HDFS, or any other Hadoop-supported filesystem. This is available on RDDs of key/value pairs that implement Hadoop's Writable interface. In Scala, it is also available on types that are implicitly convertible to Writable. Spark includes conversions for basic types like Int, Double, String, and so on.

Table I.2   List of actions with Java signature (continued)

Action	Description
saveAsObjectFile (*path*)	Writes the elements of the dataset in a simple format by using Java serialization, which can then be loaded using SparkContext.objectFile().
countByKey()	Available only on RDDs of type (K, V). Returns a hashmap of (K, Int) pairs with the count of each key.
foreach (*func*)	Runs a function *func* on each element of the dataset. This is usually done for side effects such as updating an accumulator or interacting with external storage systems. Note: Modifying variables other than accumulators outside the foreach() may result in undefined behavior. See "Understanding Closures" at https://spark.apache.org/docs/latest/rdd-programming-guide.html#understanding-closures- for more details. Usage example: df.foreach(new DisplayCountyPopulationForeach()); See listing I.7 for implementation.

Listing I.6   reduce() usage and implementation

Output:
```
reduce()
Autauga County, Alabama, Baldwin County, Alabama, Barbour County, Alabama,
     Bibb County, Alabama, Blount County, Alabama, Bullock County, Alabama,
     Butler County, Alabama, Calhoun County, Alabama, Chambers County,
     Alabama, Cherokee County, Alabama, Chilton County,
...
```

Usage:
```
System.out.println("reduce()");
String listOfCountyStateDs = countyStateDs
    .reduce(new CountyStateConcatenatorUsingReduce());
System.out.println(listOfCountyStateDs);
```

Implementation:
```
private final class CountyStateConcatenatorUsingReduce
    implements ReduceFunction<String> {
  private static final long serialVersionUID = 12859L;

  @Override
  public String call(String v1, String v2) throws Exception {
    return v1 + ", " + v2;
  }
}
```

Listing I.7   foreach() usage and implementation

```
Output:
foreach()
Autauga County, Alabama had 54571 inhabitants in 2010.
```

Baldwin County, Alabama had 182265 inhabitants in 2010.
Barbour County, Alabama had 27457 inhabitants in 2010.
Bibb County, Alabama had 22915 inhabitants in 2010.
Blount County, Alabama had 57322 inhabitants in 2010.
Bullock County, Alabama had 10914 inhabitants in 2010.
Butler County, Alabama had 20947 inhabitants in 2010.
Calhoun County, Alabama had 118572 inhabitants in 2010.
Chambers County, Alabama had 34215 inhabitants in 2010.
Cherokee County, Alabama had 25989 inhabitants in 2010.

Usage:
```
System.out.println("foreach()");
df.foreach(new DisplayCountyPopulationForeach());
```

Implementation:
```
import org.apache.spark.api.java.function.ForeachFunction;
...
private final class DisplayCountyPopulationForeach
    implements ForeachFunction<Row> {
  private static final long serialVersionUID = 14738L;
  private int count = 0;

  @Override
  public void call(Row r) throws Exception {
    if (count < 10) {
      System.out.println(r.getAs("Geography").toString()
          + " had "
          + r.getAs("real2010").toString()
          + " inhabitants in 2010.");
    }
    count++;
  }
}
```

appendix J
Enough Scala

This appendix lists the few Scala concepts and methods you may need throughout your Apache Spark with Java venture.

I am convinced that you do not need to be a Scala expert (or even a Scala rookie) to embark on your Spark journey. Nevertheless, some methods return or expect Scala types and/or objects, and your code will naturally use their Java equivalents. This appendix gives you a few hints so you'll know enough Scala to get through.

J.1 *What is Scala*

Scala is a general-purpose programming language providing support for object-oriented programming and functional programming in a strong static type system. Designed to be concise, many of Scala's design decisions are aimed to address criticisms of Java.

Scala source code is intended to be compiled to Java bytecode so that the resulting executable code runs on a Java Virtual Machine. Scala provides language interoperability with Java, so libraries written in both languages may be referenced directly in Scala or Java code.

The name *Scala* is a portmanteau of *scalable* and *language*. Scala was developed by the Programming Methods Laboratory of the École Polytechnique Fédérale de Lausanne (Switzerland) by Martin Odersky, who serves as the chairman and chief architect of Lightbend, a company that provides commercial support, training, and services for Scala.

If you really, really want to know more about Scala, you can have a look at www.scala-lang.org, www.lightbend.com, and https://en.wikipedia.org/wiki/Scala _(programming_language)#Criticism.

J.2   Scala to Java conversion

This section shows how to convert datatypes between Scala and Java.

J.2.1   General conversions

Scala data collections don't use the same collections as Java. Therefore, in some situations when using Spark functions in methods, you will have to convert the collections from one language to the other.

Scala provides methods for performing the conversions. Those utilities come with Scala and are available in the `scala.collection.JavaConverters` class. Conversions may vary a lot with each version of Scala you are using, even if you are implicitly using Scala through Spark.

As you know, Spark relies on Scala. Throughout the versions of Spark, the supported versions of Scala have changed: for example, Spark v1.2.1 supported both Scala v2.10 and Scala v2.11. Fast-forward to Spark v2.4.4, which supported both Scala v2.11 and Scala v2.12. As of now, Spark v3 supports Scala v2.12, and the last version of Scala is v2.13.

If you need help in converting collections, remember that those conversions are outside the scope of Spark: you will not need to have Spark as part of your keywords in your search engine.

J.2.2   Maps: Conversion from Scala to Java

This small section provides an easy example of converting a Scala map to a Java map. Scala maps can be converted to Java maps by using `mapAsJavaMapConverter()`, as in this example used in chapter 9:

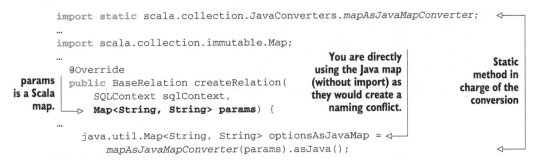

```
import static scala.collection.JavaConverters.mapAsJavaMapConverter;     ◁
...
import scala.collection.immutable.Map;
...
    @Override
    public BaseRelation createRelation(
        SQLContext sqlContext,
        Map<String, String> params) {
...
        java.util.Map<String, String> optionsAsJavaMap =     ◁
            mapAsJavaMapConverter(params).asJava();
```

params is a Scala map.

You are directly using the Java map (without import) as they would create a naming conflict.

Static method in charge of the conversion

appendix K
Installing Spark in production and a few tips

This appendix describes the following:

- Installing Spark under several operating systems
- Learning about the various tools you are installing
- Discovering key elements of the configuration

Although some of this content is presented elsewhere in the book, some of it is adapted from online content that may not be easy to find or put together. Putting it all together in a convenient place is the goal of this appendix. This appendix is up-to-date for Spark v3.

K.1   Installation

In most of the book, you will never need to install Spark because all the examples are designed to work in Spark's local mode (see chapter 5). When you run a Spark application in local mode using Maven, Maven will download the required files the first time, and then your application will take control. Therefore, installing Apache Spark is something you want to consider only when you get closer to production or if you want to use Python or Scala in the Spark shell (see chapter 5). Nevertheless, installation of Spark is a pretty straightforward process.

K.1.1   Installing Spark on Windows

This section describes how to install Apache Spark on a freshly updated Windows 10. The only prerequisites are as follows:

1   Install a Java Development Kit (JDK) from http://mng.bz/NKnn. A Java Runtime Environment (JRE) will not be sufficient. Java 11 is not supported by Spark prior to v3.

2   Install Python from www.python.org/downloads/. Select the latest version in the list and pick the "Windows x86-64 executable installer" package.

Go to http://spark.apache.org/downloads.html. Although Spark is not linked to Hadoop, Spark uses some of its libraries, hence some dependencies. You will not have to install Hadoop because Spark is self-sufficient. Download the full archive and then follow the next steps at a command prompt:

tar is part of Windows 10.

Assuming you downloaded the executable as spark-2.3.1-bin-hadoop2.7.gz in C:\Users\jgp\Downloads

```
C:\Users\jgp>cd \
C:\>md opt
C:\>cd opt
C:\opt>tar xvzf C:\Users\jgp\Downloads\spark-2.3.1-bin-hadoop2.7.gz
C:\opt>ren spark-2.3.1-bin-hadoop2.7 apache-spark
C:\opt>cd apache-spark\bin
```

Download a Hadoop binary for Windows called winutils.exe. You can get it from https://github.com/steveloughran/winutils. This tool is maintained by Steve Loughran, a member of the Cloudera technical staff and active member of the Apache Software Foundation. Make sure you pick the matching version on which Spark has been built—in this installation, Hadoop v2.7.1 for Spark v2.3.1. You can directly download the binary without Git.

In this installation, because I do not plan to use any other Hadoop components, I simply install the tool in the Spark binary directory:

```
C:\opt\apache-spark\bin>copy \Users\jgp\Downloads\winutils.exe
C:\opt\apache-spark\bin>set HADOOP_HOME=c:\opt\apache-spark
C:\opt\apache-spark\bin>spark-shell.cmd
```

And you should get this:

```
2018-08-26 14:33:54 WARN  NativeCodeLoader:62 - Unable to load
➥ native-hadoop library for your platform... using builtin-java classes
➥ where applicable
Setting default log level to "WARN".
To adjust logging level use sc.setLogLevel(newLevel). For SparkR, use
➥ setLogLevel(newLevel).
Spark context Web UI available at http://172.16.217.131:4040
Spark context available as 'sc' (master = local[*],
➥ app id = local-1535308443594).
Spark session available as 'spark'.
Welcome to
      ____              __
     / __/__  ___ _____/ /__
    _\ \/ _ \/ _ `/ __/  '_/
   /___/ .__/\_,_/_/ /_/\_\   version 2.3.1
      /_/

Using Scala version 2.11.8 (Java HotSpot(TM) 64-Bit Server VM,
➥ Java 1.8.0_181)
Type in expressions to have them evaluated.
Type :help for more information.
```

To exit the Spark shell, you can type the `:exit` command.

> **SCRIPTS ON WINDOWS FINISH WITH .CMD** Remember that all the scripts on Windows finish with `.cmd` for Spark (you may find `.bat` for other tools).

K.1.2 *Installing Spark on macOS*

On macOS, you can install Spark like a UNIX application, without using a package manager. However, I highly recommend using Homebrew, which you can install from https://brew.sh/. This section will assume you use Homebrew. This section shows how to install Spark v2.3.1, but it is the same for any Spark version.

Open a terminal window:

```
$ brew install apache-spark
==> Downloading https://www.apache.org/dyn/closer.lua?path=spark/
➥ spark-2.3.1/spark-2.3.1-bin-hadoop2.7.tgz
==> Best Mirror http://apache.mirrors.tds.net/spark/spark-2.3.1/spark-2.3.1-
    bin-hadoop2.7.tgz
################################################################### 100.0%
? /usr/local/Cellar/apache-spark/2.3.1: 1,018 files, 243.8MB,
➥ built in 1 minute 49 seconds
```

For v2.3.1, Apache Spark's home directory will be in /usr/local/Cellar/apache-spark/2.3.1/libexec.

To check that the installation went well, you can try to run the Spark shell:

```
$ cd /usr/local/Cellar/apache-spark/2.3.1/libexec
$ cd bin
$ ./spark-shell
```

Press Ctrl-C to exit (or refer to the examples in chapter 5).

K.1.3 *Installing Spark on Ubuntu*

Spark is not available in a Ubuntu repository, so you will have to install it manually. This section shows how to install Spark v2.3.1, but it is the same for any Spark version.

Prerequisite: make sure Java is installed by calling `java -version`. If Java is not already installed, install it via `sudo apt-get install default-jdk`.

You need the download URL, which could be a little tricky to get if your Ubuntu is a server without a graphical browser. On your Mac or Windows machine, go to http://spark.apache.org/downloads.html. Pick the version and the package type, and then click the download link, as illustrated in figure K.1.

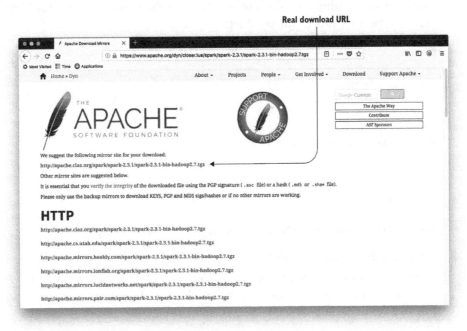

Figure K.1 Getting the real download URL for Apache Spark so you can copy it to your command line

In your shell, simply type the following:

```
$ cd /opt
$ sudo wget http://apache.claz.org/spark/spark-2.3.1/
  spark-2.3.1-bin-hadoop2.7.tgz
--2018-08-25 10:42:16--  http://apache.claz.org/spark/spark-2.3.1/
  spark-2.3.1-bin-hadoop2.7.tgz
Resolving apache.claz.org (apache.claz.org)... 216.245.218.171
Connecting to apache.claz.org (apache.claz.org)|216.245.218.171|:80...
  connected.
HTTP request sent, awaiting response... 200 OK
Length: 225883783 (215M) [application/x-gzip]
```

```
Saving to: 'spark-2.3.1-bin-hadoop2.7.tgz'

spark-2.3.1-bin-hadoop2.7.tgz
100%[=======================================>] 215.42M 43.0MB/s in 5.1s

2018-08-25 10:42:21 (42.3 MB/s) - 'spark-2.3.1-bin-hadoop2.7.tgz'
saved [225883783/225883783]
$ sudo tar xvzf spark-2.3.1-bin-hadoop2.7.tgz
```

I like my Apache products to start with apache-, so add the following:

```
$ sudo mv spark-2.3.1-bin-hadoop2.7 apache-spark-2.3.1-bin-hadoop2.7
```

To easily have multiple versions of the same product installed on a machine, I usually create a symbolic link to the product:

```
$ sudo ln -s apache-spark-2.3.1-bin-hadoop2.7 apache-spark
```

Finally, clean up:

```
$ sudo rm spark-2.3.1-bin-hadoop2.7.tgz
```

You can test your installation:

```
$ cd /opt/apache-spark
$ cd bin
$ ./spark-shell
```

Press Ctrl-C to exit (or refer to the examples in chapter 5).

K.1.4   Installing Spark on AWS EMR

There is nothing to do for Amazon Web Services (AWS) EMR, as everything you need is preinstalled. Some limitations exist, but AWS updates EMR frequently, so check at https://aws.amazon.com/emr/details/spark/.

K.2   Understanding the installation

Spark is installed in a directory that can be revealed via SPARK_HOME. You do not need to configure this environment variable unless you have multiple Spark installations on the same machine. I will use SPARK_HOME here to illustrate the directory in which your installation has been done.

Therefore, using SPARK_HOME, type the following:

```
$ ls $SPARK_HOME
```

You will get this:

```
bin  conf  data  examples  jars  kubernetes  LICENSE  licenses  logs
NOTICE  python  R  README.md  RELEASE  sbin  work  yarn
```

Table K.1 describes the content of each directory and the most important files.

Table K.1 Directories and files in Spark installation

Directory/file	Description
bin/	Binaries used by Spark such as `spark-submit` or `spark-shell`. In the Windows installation, this is also where I installed the winutils.exe binary.
+- beeline	Starts beeline, used for testing JDBC connections (more at http://mng.bz/D2zR).
+- docker-image-tool.sh	Builds and pushes Docker images when run from a release of Spark with Kubernetes support; more details in chapter 18.
+- find-spark-home	Attempts to find a proper value for SPARK_HOME. Should be included by using the `source` directive.
+- load-spark-env.sh	Loads spark-env.sh if it exists, and ensures it is loaded only once. spark-env.sh is loaded from SPARK_CONF_DIR if set, or within the current directory's conf/ subdirectory.
+- pyspark	Starts the Python shell. Use `quit()` or Ctrl-D to exit.
+- run-example	Runs examples.
+- spark-class	Utility script.
+- sparkR	Runs the R shell. Use `quit;` to exit.
+- spark-shell	Runs the Scala shell. Use `:exit` or Ctrl-C to exit.
+- spark-sql	Runs the Spark SQL shell. Use `exit;` or Ctrl-C to exit.
+- spark-submit	Submits a job to Spark.
conf/	All configuration files (not all configuration files are described in this table).
+- log4j.properties.template	Logging configuration file.
+- spark-defaults.conf.template	Default system properties included when running `spark-submit`. This is useful for setting default environmental settings.
+- spark-env.sh.template	This file is sourced when running various Spark programs. Copy it as spark-env.sh and edit the renamed file to configure Spark for your installation.
data/	Sample data.
examples/	Examples in Java, Python, R, and Scala.
jars/	Libraries used by Apache Spark; these libraries will be available on your system when you deploy your application and should not be in your uber JAR (if this is your deployment preference, see chapter 5). You can also add your own libraries in this directory to make them available to Spark.
kubernetes/	Kubernetes stuff.

Table K.1   Directories and files in Spark installation (*continued*)

Directory/file	Description
licenses/	Licenses for specific third-party products bundled with Spark.
logs/	Log files.
python/	Python stuff.
R/	R stuff.
sbin/	Server binaries including start-master.sh and start-slave.sh.
+- slaves.sh	Runs a shell command on all worker hosts.
+- spark-config.sh	All the Apache Spark scripts call this script. It should not be executed directly.
+- spark-daemon.sh	Runs a Spark command as a daemon.
+- spark-daemons.sh	Runs a Spark command on all worker hosts.
+- start-all.sh	Starts all spark daemons, starts the master on this node, and starts a worker on each node specified in the $SPARK_HOME/conf/slaves file.
+- start-history-server.sh	Starts the history server on the machine that this script is executed on.
+- start-master.sh	Starts the master on the machine that this script is executed on.
+- start-mesos-dispatcher.sh	Starts the Mesos cluster dispatcher on the machine that this script is executed on.
+- start-mesos-shuffle-service.sh	Starts the Mesos external shuffle server on the machine that this script is executed on.
+- start-shuffle-service.sh	Starts the external shuffle server on the machine that this script is executed on.
+- start-slave.sh	Starts a worker on the machine that this script is executed on. You can start more than one worker on each machine using the SPARK_WORKER_INSTANCES environment variable. The default is 1, and I assume that in the book. You need to specify the master's URL when you call this script; for example: `start-slave.sh spark://un:7077.`
+- start-slaves.sh	Starts a worker instance on each machine specified in the $SPARK_HOME/conf/slaves file.
+- start-thriftserver.sh	Starts the Spark SQL Thrift server.
+- stop-all.sh	Stops all spark daemons. Run this on the master node.
+- stop-history-server.sh	Stops the history server on the machine that this script is executed on.
+- stop-master.sh	Stops the master on the machine that this script is executed on.

Table K.1 Directories and files in Spark installation *(continued)*

Directory/file	Description
+- stop-mesos-dispatcher.sh	Stops the Mesos cluster dispatcher on the machine that this script is executed on.
+- stop-mesos-shuffle-service.sh	Stops the Mesos external shuffle service on the machine that this script is executed on.
+- stop-shuffle-service.sh	Stops the external shuffle service on the machine that this script is executed on.
+- stop-slave.sh	Stops all workers on this worker machine.
+- stop-slaves.sh	Stops all workers.
+- stop-thriftserver.sh	Stops the thrift server on the machine that this script is executed on.
work/	Working directory.
yarn/	YARN stuff (see chapter 6).

K.3   Configuration

As in all complex systems, configuration is rich and unveils potential performance gains. The goal of this section is to summarize the key properties you are more likely to use on a regular basis. You will find the common syntax for property values, application and environment configuration, and a link to the full online reference to configuration.

This content is mostly inspired by and summarized from http://spark.apache.org/docs/latest/configuration.html.

K.3.1   Properties syntax

Properties follow a standard syntax across the board. This syntax applies to memory/disk size and time duration.

Properties that specify a byte size should be configured with a particular unit. The following format is accepted:

- 1b (bytes)
- 1k or 1kb (kibibytes = 1,024 bytes)
- 1m or 1mb (mebibytes = 1,024 kibibytes)
- 1g or 1gb (gibibytes = 1,024 mebibytes)
- 1t or 1tb (tebibytes = 1,024 gibibytes)
- 1p or 1pb (pebibytes = 1,024 tebibytes)

Although numbers without units are generally interpreted as bytes, a few are interpreted as KiB or MiB. See documentation of individual configuration properties. Specifying units is desirable where possible.

Properties that specify a time duration should be configured with a unit of time. The following format is accepted:

- 25ms (milliseconds)
- 5s (seconds)
- 10m or 10min (minutes)
- 3h (hours)
- 5d (days)
- 1y (years)

K.3.2   *Application configuration*

Table K.2 describes the key properties for application configuration. You can use them on the command line of some tools (listed in section K.2) or in the option parameters of your application when you start a Spark session. Note that some parameters cannot be modified after Spark has started.

Table K.2   Properties and default values of application configuration

Property name	Default value	Description
spark.app.name	(None)	Name of your application. This will appear in the UI and in log data.
spark.driver.cores	1	Number of cores to use for the driver process, only in cluster mode.
spark.driver.maxResultSize	1g	Limit of total size of serialized results of all partitions for each Spark action (for example, collect()) in bytes. Should be at least 1M, or 0 for unlimited. Jobs will be aborted if the total size is above this limit. Having a high limit may cause out-of-memory errors in driver (depends on spark.driver.memory and memory overhead of objects in JVM). Setting a proper limit can protect the driver from out-of-memory errors.
spark.driver.memory	1g	Amount of memory to use for the driver process, where SparkContext is initialized, in MiB unless otherwise specified (for example, 1g, 2g). In client mode, this config cannot be set through the SparkConf (or SparkSession) directly in your application, because the driver JVM has already started at that point. Instead, set this through the --driver-memory command-line option or in your default properties file.
spark.driver.memoryOverhead	spark.driver.memory * 0.10, with minimum of 384	The amount of off-heap memory to be allocated per driver in cluster mode, in MiB unless otherwise specified. This is memory that accounts for things like VM overheads, interned strings, other native overheads, and so on. This tends to grow with the container size (typically 6–10%). This option is currently supported on YARN and Kubernetes.

Table K.2 Properties and default values of application configuration

Property name	Default value	Description
`spark.executor.memory`	`1g`	Amount of memory to use per executor process, in MiB unless otherwise specified (for example, 2g, 8g).
`spark.executor.memoryOverhead`	`spark.executor .memory * 0.10,` with minimum of 384	The amount of off-heap memory to be allocated per executor, in MiB unless otherwise specified. This is memory that accounts for things like VM overheads, interned strings, and other native overheads. This tends to grow with the executor size (typically 6–10%). This option is currently supported on YARN and Kubernetes.
`spark.extraListeners`	(None)	A comma-separated list of classes that implement `SparkListener`; when initializing `SparkContext`, instances of these classes will be created and registered with Spark's listener bus. If a class has a single-argument constructor that accepts a `SparkConf`, that constructor will be called; otherwise, a zero-argument constructor will be called. If no valid constructor can be found, the `SparkContext` creation will fail with an exception.
`spark.local.dir`	`/tmp`	Directory to use for scratch space in Spark, including map output files and RDDs that get stored on disk. This should be on a fast, local disk in your system (like a local NVMe drive). It can also be a comma-separated list of multiple directories on different disks. Note: This will be overridden by `SPARK_LOCAL_DIRS` (standalone, Mesos) or `LOCAL_DIRS` (YARN) environment variables set by the cluster manager.
`spark.logConf`	`false`	Logs the effective `SparkConf` as `INFO` when a `SparkContext` is started.
`spark.master`	(None)	The cluster manager to connect to. See the list of allowed master URLs at http://mng.bz/lGX2.
`spark.submit.deployMode`	(None)	The deploy mode of the Spark driver program, either `client` or `cluster`, which means to launch the driver program locally (`client`) or remotely (`cluster`) on one of the nodes inside the cluster.
`spark.log.callerContext`	(None)	Application information that will be written into YARN RM log/HDFS audit log when running on YARN/HDFS. Its length depends on the Hadoop configuration `hadoop.caller.context.max .size`. It should be concise and typically can have up to 50 characters.

Table K.2   Properties and default values of application configuration

Property name	Default value	Description
`spark.driver.supervise`	`false`	If `true`, restarts the driver automatically if it fails with a nonzero exit status. Has an effect only in Spark standalone mode or Mesos cluster deploy mode.

K.3.3   Runtime configuration

Table K.3 describes the key properties for configuring your Spark installation in a Java environment. Note that some parameters cannot be modified after Spark has started.

Table K.3   Properties and default values of environment configuration

Property name	Default value	Description
`spark.driver.extraClassPath`	(None)	Extra class path entries to prepend to the class path of the driver. Note: In client mode, this config must not be set through the `SparkConf` directly in your application, because the driver JVM has already started at that point. Instead, set this through the `--driver-class-path` command-line option or in your default properties file.
`spark.driver.extraJavaOptions`	(None)	A string of extra JVM options to pass to the driver. For instance, garbage collector (GC) settings or other logging. Note 1: It is illegal to set maximum heap size (`-Xmx`) with this option. Maximum heap size can be set with `spark.driver.memory` in cluster mode and through the `--driver-memory` command-line option in client mode. Note 2: In client mode, this config must not be set through the `SparkConf` directly in your application, because the driver JVM has already started at that point. Instead, set this through the `--driver-java-options` command-line option or in your default properties file.
`spark.driver.extraLibraryPath`	(None)	Sets a special library path to use when launching the driver JVM. Note: In client mode, this config must not be set through the `SparkConf` directly in your application, because the driver JVM has already started at that point. Instead, set this through the `--driver-library-path` command-line option or in your default properties file.
`spark.driver.userClassPathFirst`	`false`	(Experimental) Whether to give user-added JARs precedence over Spark's own JARs when loading classes in the driver. This feature can be used to mitigate conflicts between Spark's dependencies and user dependencies. This is used in cluster mode only.

Table K.3 Properties and default values of environment configuration

Property name	Default value	Description
spark.executor.extraClassPath	(None)	Extra class-path entries to prepend to the class path of executors. This exists primarily for backward-compatibility with older versions of Spark. Users typically should not need to set this option.
spark.executor.extraJavaOptions	(None)	A string of extra JVM options to pass to executors. For instance, GC settings or other logging. Note: It is illegal to set Spark properties or maximum heap size (-Xmx) with this option. Spark properties should be set using a SparkConf object or the spark-defaults.conf file used with the spark-submit script. Maximum heap size can be set with spark.executor.memory.
spark.executor.extraLibraryPath	(None)	Sets a special library path to use when launching the executor JVMs.
spark.executor.logs.rolling.maxRetainedFiles	false	Sets the number of latest rolling log files that will be retained by the system. Older log files will be deleted. Disabled by default.
spark.executor.logs.rolling.enableCompression	false	Enables executor log compression. If it is enabled, the rolled executor logs will be compressed. Disabled by default.
spark.executor.logs.rolling.maxSize	(None)	Sets the maximum size of the file in bytes by which the executor logs will be rolled over. Rolling is disabled by default. See spark.executor.logs.rolling.maxRetainedFiles for automatic cleaning of old logs.
spark.executor.logs.rolling.strategy	(None)	Sets the strategy of rolling of executor logs. By default, it is disabled. It can be set to time (time-based rolling) or size (size-based rolling). For time, use spark.executor.logs.rolling.time.interval to set the rolling interval. For size, use spark.executor.logs.rolling.maxSize to set the maximum file size for rolling.
spark.executor.logs.rolling.time.interval	daily	Sets the time interval by which the executor logs will be rolled over. Rolling is disabled by default. Valid values are daily, hourly, minutely, or any interval in seconds. See spark.executor.logs.rolling.maxRetainedFiles for automatic cleaning of old logs.
spark.executor.userClassPathFirst	false	(Experimental) Same functionality as spark.driver.userClassPathFirst, but applied to executor instances.
spark.executorEnv.[EnvironmentVariableName]	(None)	Adds the environment variable specified by EnvironmentVariableName to the Executor process. The user can specify multiples of these to set multiple environment variables.

Table K.3   Properties and default values of environment configuration

Property name	Default value	Description
`spark.redaction.regex`	`(?i)secret` `|password`	Regex to decide which Spark configuration properties and environment variables in driver and executor environments contain sensitive information. When this regex matches a property key or value, the value is redacted from the environment UI and various logs such as YARN and event logs.
`spark.files`	(None)	Comma-separated list of files to be placed in the working directory of each executor. Globs are allowed.[a]
`spark.jars`	(None)	Comma-separated list of JARs to include on the driver and executor class paths. Globs are allowed.
`spark.jars.packages`	(None)	Comma-separated list of Maven coordinates of JARs to include on the driver and executor class paths. The coordinates should be `groupId:artifactId:version`. If `spark.jars.ivySettings` is given, artifacts will be resolved according to the configuration in the file; otherwise, artifacts will be searched for in the local Maven repository, then in Maven Central, and finally in any additional remote repositories given by the command-line option `--repositories`. For more details, see advanced dependency management.[b]
`spark.jars.excludes`	(None)	Comma-separated list of `groupId:artifactId`, to exclude while resolving the dependencies provided in `spark.jars.packages` to avoid dependency conflicts.
`spark.jars.ivy`	(None)	Path to specify the Ivy user directory, used for the local Ivy cache and package files from `spark.jars.packages`. This will override the Ivy property `ivy.default.ivy.user.dir`, which defaults to `~/.ivy2`. Note: This book does not use Ivy.
`spark.jars.ivySettings`	(None)	Path to an Ivy settings file to customize resolution of JARs specified using `spark.jars.packages` instead of the built-in defaults, such as Maven Central. Additional repositories given by the command-line option `--repositories` or `spark.jars.repositories` will also be included. Useful for allowing Spark to resolve artifacts from behind a firewall; for example, via an in-house artifact server such as Artifactory or Nexus. Details on the settings file format can be found at http://mng.bz/B2E1. Note: This book does not use Ivy.
`spark.jars.repositories`	(None)	Comma-separated list of additional remote repositories to search for the Maven coordinates given with `--packages` or `spark.jars.packages`.

a. Globs are explained on Wikipedia at https://en.wikipedia.org/wiki/Glob_(programming).
b. For more information on advanced dependency management, see http://mng.bz/dywo.

K.3.4   Other configuration points

There are a lot of configuration parameters. Table K.4 describes some key properties outside the application or runtime configurations. Note that some parameters cannot be modified after Spark has started.

Table K.4   Properties and default values of environment configuration

Property name	Default value	Description
spark.driver.port	Random value	Port for the driver to listen on. This is used for communicating with the executors and the standalone master.
spark.memory.*		Set of values to configure memory management, as you may encounter some memory issues from time to time. Chapter 16 explains some of those parameters.

The full configuration documentation can be found on the Spark website: http://spark.apache.org/docs/latest/configuration.html.

appendix L
Reference for ingestion

This appendix can be used as a reference for all things ingestion: datatypes, options for XML, CSV, JSON, and more. As you develop data ingestion in Spark, this appendix will be very useful!

L.1 Spark datatypes

Spark datatypes are used to build the schema, which is associated with the data-frame. Table L.1 lists each datatype with its name, description, equivalent in Java, and range of values. Note that data is managed by a component called *Tungsten* in Spark. Tungsten does not use the classic Java encoding for types, so a direct correlation does not always exist between a type in Spark (Tungsten) and a type in Java.

Table L.1 Standard Apache Spark datatypes and their equivalents in Java

Type in the DataTypes class	Description	Java equivalent	Min/max or other value
BinaryType	Storage of binary or unidentified content		
BooleanType	Storage of Boolean	boolean (primitive type)	true/false
ByteType	Storage of signed byte, 8 bits	byte (primitive type)	-128 / 127
CalendarIntervalType	Storage of calendar interval, internally implemented as months and seconds		
DateType	Storage of date, using the java.sql package, not java.util	java.sql.Date	

Table L.1 Standard Apache Spark datatypes and their equivalents in Java

Type in the DataTypes class	Description	Java equivalent	Min/max or other value
DoubleType	Storage of double on 8 bytes/64 bits, with 15 significant digits (IEEE 754)	double (primitive type)	≈±1.798+308
FloatType	Storage of float on 4 bytes/32 bits, with 15 significant digits (IEEE 754)	float (primitive type)	
IntegerType	Storage of signed integer values, based on 32 bits/4 bytes	int (primitive type)	-2,147,483,648 / 2,147,483,647
LongType	Storage of signed long values, based on 64 bits/8 bytes	long (primitive type)	-263 / 263-1 -9,223,372,036, 854,775,808 / 9,223,372,036, 854,775,807 ±9.223e18
NullType	Type for null value	N/A	
ShortType	Storage of signed short values, based on 16 bits/2 bytes	short (primitive type)	-32,768 / 32,767
StringType	Storage of string values	String	
TimestampType	Storage of timestamps	java.sql .Timestamp	

L.2 *Options for CSV ingestion*

Table L.2 lists options that Spark may use for ingesting CSV files. Options are not case-sensitive.

Prior to version 2 of Spark, you needed an open source plugin from Databricks (aka com.databricks.spark.csv). The older version of the plugin is not described here. The last reference document should be available at http://mng.bz/rr2J.

Table L.2 Options for CSV ingestion

Option name	Default value	Description	Appeared/ modified in version
sep	,	Sets the single character as a separator for each field and value.	v2.0.0
encoding	UTF-8	Decodes the CSV files by the given encoding type.	v2.0.0

Table L.2   Options for CSV ingestion *(continued)*

Option name	Default value	Description	Appeared/ modified in version
quote	"	Sets the single character used for escaping quoted values, where the separator can be part of the value. If you would like to turn off quotations, you need to set an empty string. If you want a double quote to be the quotation symbol, you do not have to specify anything.	v2.0.0
escape	\	Sets the single character used for escaping quotes inside an already quoted value. This will have to be in the data you plan to ingest.	v2.0.0
charToEscape QuoteEscaping	default escape or \0	Sets a single character used for escaping the escape for the quote character. The default value is the escape character when escape and quote characters are different, and \0 otherwise.	v2.3.0
comment	Empty string	Sets the single character used for skipping lines beginning with this character. By default, it is disabled: there is no support for comments.	v2.0.0
header	false	Uses the first line as names of columns. Two-line headers are not supported.	v2.0.0
enforceSchema	true	If it is set to true, the specified or inferred schema will be forcibly applied to data-source files, and headers in the CSV files will be ignored. If the option is set to false, the schema will be validated against all headers in CSV files when the header option is set to true. Field names in the schema and column names in CSV headers are checked by their positions, taking into account spark.sql. caseSensitive. Though the default value is true, it is recommended to disable the enforceSchema option to avoid incorrect results.	v2.4.0
inferSchema	false	Infers the input schema automatically from data. It requires one extra pass over the data. If Spark cannot infer, it will assume a string.	v2.0.0
samplingRatio	1.0	Inferring a schema can be an expensive operation on a large dataset, hence defining a fraction of rows used for schema inferring. The default value of 1.0 means 100% of the dataset.	v2.4.0
ignoreLeading WhiteSpace	false	Flag indicating whether leading whitespaces from values being read should be skipped.	v2.0.0
ignoreTrailing WhiteSpace	false	Flag indicating whether trailing whitespaces from values being read should be skipped.	v2.0.0

Table L.2 Options for CSV ingestion *(continued)*

Option name	Default value	Description	Appeared/ modified in version
nullValue	Empty string	Sets the string representation of a null value. Since v2.0.1, this applies to all supported types, including the string type.	v2.0.0
emptyValue	Empty string	Sets the string representation of an empty value.	v2.4.0
nanValue	NaN	Sets the string representation of a non-number value.	v2.0.0
positiveInf	Inf	Sets the string representation of a positive infinity value.	v2.0.0
negativeInf	-Inf	Sets the string representation of a negative infinity value.	v2.0.0
dateFormat	yyyy-MM-dd (RFC 3339)	Sets the string that indicates a date format. Custom date formats follow the formats at java.text.SimpleDateFormat.	v2.0.0
timestamp Format	yyyy-MM-dd'T' HH:mm:ss.SSSXXX (RFC 3339)	Sets the string that indicates a timestamp format. Custom date formats follow the formats at java.text.SimpleDateFormat.	v2.1.0
maxColumns	20480	Defines a hard limit for the number of columns a record can have.	v2.2.0
maxCharsPer Column	-1	Defines the maximum number of characters allowed for any given value being read. By default, it is -1, meaning unlimited length. In v2.0.0, the default was 1000000; it became -1 in v2.1.0.	v2.0.0
mode	PERMISSIVE	Allows a mode for dealing with corrupt records during parsing. It supports the following case-insensitive modes: PERMISSIVE—Sets other fields to null when it meets a corrupted record and puts the malformed string into a field configured by columnNameOfCorruptRecord. To keep corrupt records, you can set a string type field named columnNameOfCorruptRecord in a user-defined schema. If a schema does not have the field, it drops corrupt records during parsing. When a length of parsed CSV tokens is shorter than an expected length of a schema, it sets null for extra fields. DROPMALFORMED—Ignores all corrupted records. You will not know which records were malformed. FAILFAST—Throws an exception when it meets a corrupted record. You cannot recover.	v2.0.0

Table L.2   Options for CSV ingestion *(continued)*

Option name	Default value	Description	Appeared/ modified in version
columnNameOf CorruptRecord	Value specified in spark.sql .columnNameOf CorruptRecord	Allows renaming the new field that has a malformed string created by PERMISSIVE mode. This overrides spark.sql.columnNameOfCorruptRecord.	v2.2.0
multiLine	false	Parses one record, which may span multiple lines.	v2.2.0
locale	en-US	Sets a locale as language tag in IETF BCP 47 format. This is used while parsing dates and timestamps.	v3.0.0
lineSep	Covers all \r, \r\n, and \n	Defines the line separator that should be used for parsing. The maximum length is one character.	v3.0.0

L.3   *Options for JSON ingestion*

JSON ingestion has been part of Spark since version 1.4.0. Since version 2.2.0, Spark has supported multiline JSON; it was limited to JSON Lines in previous versions. Options to parse JSON appeared throughout its development, as stated in table L.3.

The last version of this reference document is available at http://mng.bz/Vg8y.

Table L.3   Options for JSON ingestion

Option name	Default value	Description	Appeared/ modified in version
primitivesAsString	false	Infers all primitive values as a string type.	v1.6.0
prefersDecimal	false	Infers all floating-point values as a decimal type. If the values do not fit in decimal, it infers them as doubles.	v2.0.0
allowComments	false	Ignores Java/C++-style comments in JSON records.	v1.6.0
allowUnquotedFieldN ames	false	Allows unquoted JSON field names.	v1.6.0
allowSingleQuotes	true	Allows single quotes in addition to double quotes.	v1.6.0
allowNumericLeading Zeros	false	Allows leading zeros in numbers (for example, 00012).	v1.6.0
allowBackslash EscapingAnyCharacter	false	Accepts quoting of all characters using the backslash quoting mechanism.	v2.0.0

Table L.3 Options for JSON ingestion (continued)

Option name	Default value	Description	Appeared/ modified in version
allowUnquoted ControlChars	false	Indicates whether JSON strings can contain unquoted control characters (ASCII characters with values less than 32, including tab and line-feed characters).	V2.3.0
mode	PERMISSIVE	Allows a mode for dealing with corrupt records during parsing: PERMISSIVE—Sets other fields to null when it meets a corrupted record and puts the malformed string into a new field configured by columnNameOfCorruptRecord. When a schema is set by the user, it sets null for extra fields. Applicable only to the field, not the entire record. DROPMALFORMED—Ignores all corrupted records. FAILFAST—Throws an exception when it meets corrupted records.	v2.0.0
columnNameOfCorrupt Record	The value specified in spark.sql.column NameOfCorruptRecord	Allows renaming the new field that has a malformed string created by PERMISSIVE mode. This overrides spark.sql .columnNameOfCorruptRecord.	v2.0.0
dateFormat	yyyy-MM-dd (RFC 3339)	Sets the string that indicates a date format. Custom date formats follow the formats at java.text.SimpleDateFormat. This applies to date type.	v2.1.0
timestampFormat	yyyy-MM-dd'T' HH:mm:ss.SSSZZ (RFC 3339)	Sets the string that indicates a timestamp format. Custom date formats follow the formats at java.text.SimpleDateFormat. This applies to timestamp type.	v2.1.0
multiLine	false	Parses one record, which may span multiple lines, per file.	v2.2.0
encoding		Allows forcibly setting either standard basic or extended encoding for the JSON files. For example, UTF-16BE, UTF-32LE. If the encoding is not specified and multiLine is set to true, it will be detected automatically.	v2.4.0
lineSep	default covers all \r, \r\n and \n	Defines the line separator that should be used for parsing.	v2.4.0
samplingRatio	1.0 (= 100%)	Defines fraction of input JSON objects used for schema inferring.	v2.4.0

Table L.3   Options for JSON ingestion *(continued)*

Option name	Default value	Description	Appeared/modified in version
dropFieldIfAllNull	false	Indicates whether to ignore column of all null values or empty array/struct during schema inference.	v2.4.0
locale	en-US	Sets a locale as language tag in IETF BCP 47 format. This is used while parsing dates and timestamps.	v3.0.0

L.4   Options for XML ingestion

Table L.4 lists the various options you can use with Spark to ingest XML files. Options are not case-sensitive.

The last version of this reference document is available on GitHub at https://github.com/databricks/spark-xml.

Table L.4   Options for XML ingestion

Option name	Default value	Description	Appeared/modified in version
rowTag	ROW	The row tag of your XML files to treat as a row. For example, in the fragment <books> <book> </book> ...</books>, the appropriate value would be book. At the moment, rows containing self-closing XML tags are not supported. Check with your XML generator if this is the case.	v0.3.0
samplingRatio	1	Sampling ratio for inferring schema (0.0 ~ 1). Possible types are StructType, ArrayType, StringType, LongType, DoubleType, BooleanType, TimestampType and NullType, unless you provide a schema. If you know your XML content, you may need just a little bit; if it is completely unknown to you or changes often, leave the default value.	v0.3.0
excludeAttribute	false	Indicates whether to exclude attributes in elements.	v0.3.0
treatEmptyValues AsNulls	false	Indicates whether to treat whitespaces in values as a null value. Deprecated as of version 0.4.0: use nullValue set to " ".	v0.3.0
failFast	false	Indicates whether you want the program to fail when it fails to parse malformed rows in XML files, instead of dropping the rows. The XML does not have to be on a single line. Deprecated as of version 0.4.0: use mode.	v0.3.0

Table L.4 Options for XML ingestion *(continued)*

Option name	Default value	Description	Appeared/modified in version
mode	PERMISSIVE	The mode for dealing with corrupt records during parsing: PERMISSIVE—Sets other fields to null when it meets a corrupted record, and puts the malformed string into a new field configured by columnNameOfCorruptRecord. When a schema is set by the user, it sets null for extra fields. DROPMALFORMED—Ignores all corrupted records. FAILFAST—Throws an exception when it meets corrupted records.	v0.4.0
columnNameOf CorruptRecord	_corrupt_record	The name of the new field where malformed strings are stored.	v0.4.0
attributePrefix	_	The prefix for attributes so that we can differentiate attributes and elements. This will be the prefix for field names. Prior to version 0.4.0, the default value was @.	v0.3.0
valueTag	_VALUE	The tag used for the value when there are attributes in the element having no child. Prior to version 0.4.0, the default value was #VALUE.	v0.3.0
charset	UTF-8	Decodes the XML files by the given encoding type.	v0.3.0
ignoreSurrounding Spaces	false	Defines whether surrounding whitespaces from values being read should be skipped. In CSV, you can specify leading and trailing spaces, but it does not make sense in XML.	v0.4.0
rowValidationXSD Path	None	Defines the path to an XML schema (XSD) file, used to validate XML for each row individually. Rows that fail to validate are treated like parse errors (see mode).	v0.8.0

L.5 *Methods for building a full dialect*

Dialects are described in chapter 8, but I covered only the detection and conversion of a SQL datatype to Spark. Table L.5 lists the other methods you may need to implement. The full Javadoc is available at http://mng.bz/xWrd.

Table L.5 Additional methods that may need to be implemented to build a full dialect

Method	Description
void beforeFetch (java.sql.Connection connection, scala.collection.immutable.Map<String, String> properties)	Overrides connection-specific properties to run before an SQL SELECT is made.

Table L.5 Additional methods that may need to be implemented to build a full dialect *(continued)*

Method	Description
`abstract boolean canHandle(String url)`	Checks if this dialect instance can handle a certain JDBC URL. See example in chapter 8.
`Object compileValue(Object value)`	Converts value to SQL expression.
`scala.Option<DataType> getCatalystType (int sqlType, String typeName, int size, MetadataBuilder md)`	Gets the custom datatype mapping for the given JDBC metadata, including type, name, size, and other meta information. See example in chapter 8.
`scala.Option<JdbcType> getJDBCType(DataType dt)`	Retrieves the JDBC/SQL type for a given Spark datatype.
`String getSchemaQuery(String table)`	The SQL query that should be used to discover the schema of a table. Dialects can override this method to return a query that works best in a particular database. The query should look like SELECT * . . . based on the given table name.
`String getTableExistsQuery(String table)`	Gets the SQL query that should be used to find whether the given table exists. Dialects can override this method to return a query that works best in their associated database.
`String getTruncateQuery(String table)`	The SQL query that should be used to truncate a table.
`scala.Option<Object> isCascadingTruncateTable()`	Returns the following: Some[true]—If TRUNCATE TABLE causes cascading. Some[false]—If TRUNCATE TABLE does not cause cascading. None—The behavior of TRUNCATE TABLE is unknown (default).
`String quoteIdentifier(String colName)`	Quotes the identifier. This is used to put quotes around the identifier if the column name is either a reserved keyword or contains characters that require quotes (for example, space).

L.6   *Options for ingesting and writing data from/to a database*

You can use various options to ingest data and write data back to a database. Table L.6 lists those options for connecting, reading, and writing data The full reference is available at http://mng.bz/AAzo.

Table L.6 Options for ingesting and writing data from/to a database

Option	Description
url	The JDBC URL to connect to. The source-specific connection properties may be specified in the URL. For example: `jdbc:postgresql://localhost/analytics?user=pg&password=secret`. See chapter 8 for examples.

Table L.6 Options for ingesting and writing data from/to a database *(continued)*

Option	Description
dbtable	The JDBC table that should be read. Anything that is valid in a FROM clause of an SQL query can be used. Instead of a table, you could also use a subquery in parentheses. See chapter 8 for examples.
driver	The class name of the JDBC driver to use to connect to this URL. See chapter 8 for examples.
partitionColumn, lowerBound, upperBound	These options must all be specified if any of them is specified. In addition, numPartitions must be specified. They describe how to partition the table when reading in parallel from multiple workers. partitionColumn must be a numeric column from the table in question. Note that lowerBound and upperBound are used to decide the partition stride, not to filter rows in the table. All rows in the table will be partitioned and returned. This option applies only to reading. See chapter 8 for examples.
numPartitions	The maximum number of partitions that can be used for parallelism in table reading and writing. This also determines the maximum number of concurrent JDBC connections. If the number of partitions to write exceeds this limit, Spark decreases it to this limit by calling coalesce(numPartitions) before writing. See chapter 8 for an example on reading.
fetchsize	The JDBC fetch size, which determines how many rows to fetch per round trip. This can help performance on JDBC drivers that default to low fetch size (for example, Oracle with 10 rows). This option applies only to reading.
batchsize	The JDBC batch size, which determines how many rows to insert per round trip. This can help performance on JDBC drivers. This option applies only to writing. It defaults to 1000.
isolationLevel	The transaction isolation level, which applies to the current connection. It can be NONE, READ_COMMITTED, READ_UNCOMMITTED, REPEATABLE_READ, or SERIALIZABLE, corresponding to standard transaction isolation levels defined by JDBC's Connection object, with a default of READ_UNCOMMITTED. This option applies only to writing. Refer to the documentation in java.sql.Connection.
sessionInitStatement	After each database session is opened to the remote database and before starting to read data, this option executes a custom SQL statement (or a PL/SQL block). Use this to implement session initialization code. Example: `option("sessionInitStatement", """BEGIN execute immediate 'alter session set "_serial_direct_read"=true'; END;""")`

Table L.6   Options for ingesting and writing data from/to a database *(continued)*

Option	Description
truncate	When `SaveMode.Overwrite` is enabled, this option causes Spark to truncate an existing table instead of dropping and re-creating it. This can be more efficient and prevents the table metadata (for example, indices) from being removed. However, it will not work in some cases, such as when the new data has a different schema. It defaults to `false`. This option applies only to writing.
createTableOptions	If specified, this option allows setting of database-specific table and partition options when creating a table. This option applies only to writing. Example: `CREATE TABLE t (name string) ENGINE=InnoDB`
createTableColumnTypes	The database column datatypes to use, instead of the defaults, when creating the table. Datatype information should be specified in the same format as `CREATE TABLE` column syntax; for example: `name CHAR(64)`, `comments VARCHAR(1024)`. The specified types should be valid Spark SQL datatypes. This option applies only to writing.
customSchema	The custom schema to use for reading data from JDBC connectors. For example, `id DECIMAL(38, 0)`, `name STRING`. You can also specify partial fields, and the others use the default type mapping; for example: `id DECIMAL(38, 0)`. The column names should be identical to the corresponding column names of the JDBC table. Users can specify the corresponding datatypes of Spark SQL instead of using the defaults. This option applies only to reading.

L.7   *Options for ingesting and writing data from/to Elasticsearch*

Elasticsearch has a pretty huge number of options you can use to ingest data and write data. Table L.7 lists some of those options for connecting, reading, and writing data. elasticsearch-hadoop is the name of the driver. The full reference is available at http://mng.bz/Z2rR.

Table L.7   Options for ingesting and writing data from/to Elasticsearch

Option	Default	Description
es.resource		Elasticsearch resource location, where data is read and written to. Requires the format `<index>/<type>`.
es.resource.read	Defaults to `es.resource`	Elasticsearch resource used for reading (but not writing) data. Useful when reading and writing data to different Elasticsearch indices within the same job.
es.resource.write	Defaults to `es.resource`	Elasticsearch resource used for writing (but not reading) data. Used typically for dynamic resource writes or when writing and reading data to different Elasticsearch indices within the same job.

Table L.7 Options for ingesting and writing data from/to Elasticsearch *(continued)*

Option	Default	Description
es.nodes	localhost	List of Elasticsearch nodes to connect to. When using Elasticsearch remotely, *do* set this option. Note that the list does *not* have to contain *every* node inside the Elasticsearch cluster; these are discovered automatically by elasticsearch-hadoop by default (see next table entry). Each node can also have its HTTP/REST port specified individually (for example, mynode:9600).
es.port	9200	Default HTTP/REST port used for connecting to Elasticsearch. This setting is applied to the nodes in es.nodes that do not have any port specified.
es.mapping.join		The document field/property name containing the document's join field. Constants are not accepted. Join fields on a document must contain either the parent relation name as a string, or an object that contains the child relation name and the ID of its parent. If a child document is identified when using this setting, the document's routing is automatically set to the parent ID if no other routing is configured in es.mapping.routing.
es.scroll.size	50	Number of results/items returned by each individual per request.
es.scroll.limit	-1	Number of total results/items returned by each individual scroll. A negative value indicates that all documents that match should be returned. Do note that this applies per scroll, which is typically bound to one of the job tasks. The total number of documents returned is LIMIT * NUMBER_OF_SCROLLS (OR TASKS).
es.net.http.auth.user		Basic authentication username.
es.net.http.auth.pass		Basic authentication password.

To configure SSL, proxy, and serialization, refer to http://mng.bz/Z2rR.

appendix M
Reference for joins

In this appendix, you will find the reference material for joins. The idea is to help you go through the various types of joins with quick examples, so you can quickly pick the right one (or left one, if my editors allow me a little joke), based on your needs.

The labs in this appendix are based on chapter 12, where you learned more about transformations. Two labs explore joins: labs #940 and #941.

This appendix does not mention the `union()` and `unionByName()` methods, which can be used to combine (union) dataframes together. Those methods are used in chapters 3, 15, and 17.

> **LAB** Examples from this chapter are available in GitHub at https://github.com/jgperrin/net.jgp.books.spark.ch12.

M.1 Setting up the decorum

In this preamble section, I want to set the environment (or decorum) in which joins will be performed. You will have a look at the datasets to use. I will also introduce the two labs before you perform all the joins.

Tables M.1 and M.2 show the datasets we are going to use. The datasets are similar in lab #940 and #941. As you know, I like to use datasets that have meaning. But in this scenario, I do not know of a meaningful dataset that would be applicable that has all the types of joins and would still retain meaning after the joins.

Table M.1 Dataset used for the left side

Identifier	Value
1	Value 1
2	Value 2

Table M.1 Dataset used for the left side

Identifier	Value
3	Value 3
4	Value 4

Table M.2 Dataset used for the right side

Identifier	Value	Note
3	Value 3	
4	Value 4	The identifier is the same for both rows. Spark is not a relational database, where you can have unicity constraints on a column.
4	Value 4_1	
5	Value 5	
6	Value 6	

The Java source code is divided into two small applications: AllJoinsApp (lab #940) and AllJoinsDifferentDataTypesApp (lab #941). Both labs will execute each type of join, one after the other. Lab #940 performs the joins on columns with the same datatype, while lab #941 performs the joins on columns with different names and datatypes. Both labs also have a special case for the cross-join, which should not take any column as a parameter.

Figure M.1 illustrates a typical join scenario.

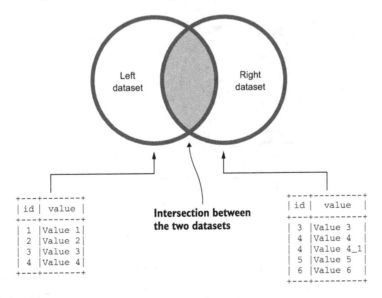

Figure M.1 Illustration of a join operation between two datasets

M.2   *Performing an inner join*

Inner joins are the default behavior in Apache Spark. An *inner join* selects all rows from the left dataset and the right dataset, where the join condition is met. Figure M.2 illustrates an example.

In this situation, you can see what happens when you have two identifiers (4) in the right datasets: rows are duplicated, as shown in the following listing.

Listing M.1   Output of an inner join

```
INNER JOIN
+---+-------+---+---------+
| id|  value| id|    value|
+---+-------+---+---------+
|  3|Value 3|  3|  Value 3|
|  4|Value 4|  4|  Value 4|
|  4|Value 4|  4|Value 4_1|
+---+-------+---+---------+
```

The join is performed on the id identifier column, as shown in the next listing. In lab #940, both identifiers are the same type; in #941, they are different types.

Listing M.2   Performing an inner join

```
Dataset<Row> df = dfLeft.join(
    dfRight,
    dfLeft.col("id").equalTo(dfRight.col("id")),
    "inner");
```

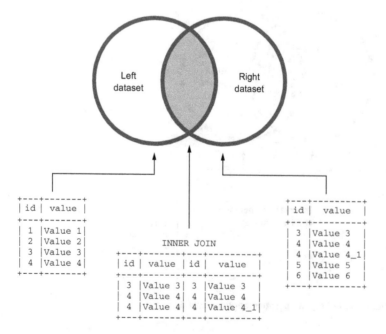

Figure M.2   An inner join between two datasets on the id column

M.3   *Performing an outer join*

Outer joins select data from both datasets based on the join condition, and add `null` when data is missing from the left or right dataset. Figure M.3 shows an example. For Spark, an *outer* join, a *full* join, and a *full-outer* join are the same thing. The following listing shows the output of an outer join.

Listing M.3   Output of an outer, full, and full-outer join

```
OUTER JOIN

...

FULL JOIN

...

FULL_OUTER JOIN
+----+-------+----+---------+
|  id|  value|  id|    value|
+----+-------+----+---------+
|null|   null|   5|  Value 5|
|null|   null|   6|  Value 6|
|   1|Value 1|null|     null|
|   2|Value 2|null|     null|
|   3|Value 3|   3|  Value 3|
|   4|Value 4|   4|  Value 4|
|   4|Value 4|   4|Value 4_1|
+----+-------+----+---------+
```

The join is performed on the `id` identifier column, as shown in the following listing. In lab #940, both identifiers are the same type; in #941, they are different types.

Listing M.4   Performing an outer, full, and full-outer join

```java
Dataset<Row> df = dfLeft.join(
    dfRight,
    dfLeft.col("id").equalTo(dfRight.col("id")),
    "outer");
Dataset<Row> df = dfLeft.join(
    dfRight,
    dfLeft.col("id").equalTo(dfRight.col("id")),
    "full");
Dataset<Row> df = dfLeft.join(
    dfRight,
    dfLeft.col("id").equalTo(dfRight.col("id")),
    "full_outer");
```

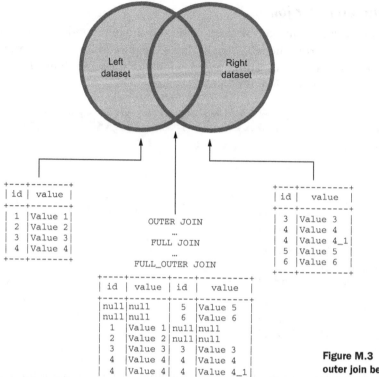

```
+---+-------+
| id| value |
+---+-------+
| 1 |Value 1|           OUTER JOIN
| 2 |Value 2|               ...
| 3 |Value 3|            FULL JOIN
| 4 |Value 4|               ...
+---+-------+          FULL_OUTER JOIN
```

```
+---+---------+
| id|  value  |
+---+---------+
| 3 |Value 3  |
| 4 |Value 4  |
| 4 |Value 4_1|
| 5 |Value 5  |
| 6 |Value 6  |
+---+---------+
```

```
+----+-------+----+---------+
| id | value | id |  value  |
+----+-------+----+---------+
|null|null   |  5 |Value 5  |
|null|null   |  6 |Value 6  |
| 1  |Value 1|null|null     |
| 2  |Value 2|null|null     |
| 3  |Value 3|  3 |Value 3  |
| 4  |Value 4|  4 |Value 4  |
| 4  |Value 4|  4 |Value 4_1|
+----+-------+----+---------+
```

Figure M.3   An outer, full, or full-outer join between two datasets on the `id` column

M.4   *Performing a left, or left-outer, join*

The *left join*, shown in figure M.4, selects the following:

- All rows from the left dataset
- All rows from the right dataset for which the join condition is met

Left and *left-outer* are synonyms; the following listing shows an example of the output.

Listing M.5   Output of a left, or left-outer, join

```
LEFT JOIN

...

LEFT_OUTER JOIN
+---+-------+----+---------+
| id|  value| id|    value|
+---+-------+----+---------+
|  1|Value 1|null|     null|
|  2|Value 2|null|     null|
|  3|Value 3|  3| Value 3|
|  4|Value 4|  4|Value 4_1|
|  4|Value 4|  4| Value 4|
+---+-------+----+---------+
```

The join is performed on the `id` identifier column, as shown in the following listing. In lab #940, both identifiers are the same type; in #941, they are different types.

Listing M.6   Performing a left, or left-outer, join

```
Dataset<Row> df = dfLeft.join(
    dfRight,
    dfLeft.col("id").equalTo(dfRight.col("id")),
    "left");
Dataset<Row> df = dfLeft.join(
    dfRight,
    dfLeft.col("id").equalTo(dfRight.col("id")),
    "left_outer");
```

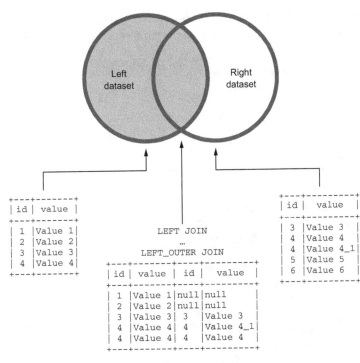

Figure M.4   A left, or left-outer join, between two datasets on the `id` column

M.5   *Performing a right, or right-outer, join*

The *right join*, shown in figure M.5, selects the following:

- All rows from the right dataset
- All rows from the left dataset for which the join condition is met

Right and *right-outer* are synonyms; the following listing shows the output of a right join.

Listing M.7   Output of a right, or right-outer, join

```
RIGHT JOIN
...
RIGHT_OUTER JOIN
+----+-------+---+---------+
| id| value| id|    value|
+----+-------+---+---------+
|null|   null|  5|  Value 5|
|null|   null|  6|  Value 6|
|   3|Value 3|  3|  Value 3|
|   4|Value 4|  4|  Value 4|
|   4|Value 4|  4|Value 4_1|
+----+-------+---+---------+
```

The join is performed on the `id` identifier column, as shown in the following listing.
In lab #940, both identifiers are the same type; in lab #941, they are different types.

Listing M.8   Performing a right, or right-outer, join

```java
Dataset<Row> df = dfLeft.join(
    dfRight,
    dfLeft.col("id").equalTo(dfRight.col("id")),
    "right");
Dataset<Row> df = dfLeft.join(
    dfRight,
    dfLeft.col("id").equalTo(dfRight.col("id")),
    "right_outer");
```

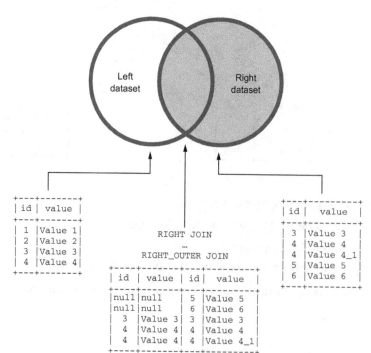

**Figure M.5   A right,
or right-outer, join
between two datasets
on the `id` column**

M.6   *Performing a left-semi join*

A *left-semi join* selects rows from only the left dataset for which the join condition is met, as shown in figure M.6. The following listing shows the output.

Listing M.9   Output of a left-semi join

```
LEFT_SEMI JOIN
+---+-------+
| id|  value|
+---+-------+
|  3|Value 3|
|  4|Value 4|
+---+-------+
```

The join is performed on the id identifier column, as shown in the following listing. In lab #940, both identifiers are the same type; in #941, they are different types.

Listing M.10   Performing a left-semi join

```java
Dataset<Row> df = dfLeft.join(
    dfRight,
    dfLeft.col("id").equalTo(dfRight.col("id")),
    "left_semi");
```

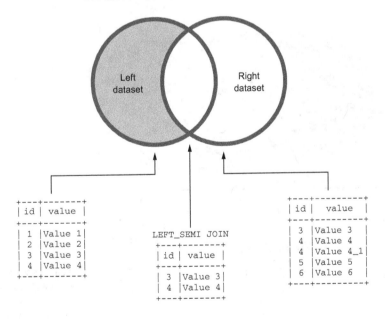

Figure M.6   A left-semi join between two datasets on the id column

M.7   *Performing a left-anti join*

A *left-anti join*, illustrated in figure M.7, selects rows from only the left dataset for which the join condition is *not* met. It's the complementary dataset to the semi-join; the following listing shows the output.

Listing M.11   Output of a left-anti join

```
LEFT_ANTI JOIN
+---+-------+
| id|  value|
+---+-------+
|  1|Value 1|
|  2|Value 2|
+---+-------+
```

The join is performed on the id identifier column, as shown in the following listing. In lab #940, both identifiers are the same type; in #941, they are different types.

Listing M.12   Performing a left-anti join

```
Dataset<Row> df = dfLeft.join(
    dfRight,
    dfLeft.col("id").equalTo(dfRight.col("id")),
    "left_anti");
```

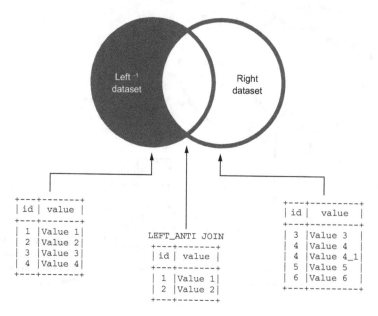

Figure M.7   A left-anti join between two datasets on the id column

M.8 *Performing a cross-join*

A *cross-join*, illustrated in figure M.8, performs a Cartesian join of both datasets. As a reminder, a *Cartesian join* (also sometimes called a *Cartesian product*) is a join of every row of one table to every row of another table.

As an example, when the dataset on the left that has 500 rows is joined with the dataset on the right with 1,000 rows, the cross-join will return 500,000 rows. The following listing shows the output.

Listing M.13 Output of a cross-join

```
CROSS JOIN
+---+-------+---+---------+
| id|  value| id|    value|
+---+-------+---+---------+
|  1|Value 1|  4|Value 4_1|
|  1|Value 1|  3|  Value 3|
|  1|Value 1|  5|  Value 5|
|  1|Value 1|  4|  Value 4|
|  1|Value 1|  6|  Value 6|
|  2|Value 2|  3|  Value 3|
|  2|Value 2|  4|Value 4_1|
|  2|Value 2|  6|  Value 6|
|  2|Value 2|  4|  Value 4|
|  2|Value 2|  5|  Value 5|
|  3|Value 3|  4|  Value 4|
|  3|Value 3|  4|Value 4_1|
|  3|Value 3|  5|  Value 5|
|  3|Value 3|  6|  Value 6|
|  3|Value 3|  3|  Value 3|
|  4|Value 4|  3|  Value 3|
|  4|Value 4|  4|  Value 4|
|  4|Value 4|  4|Value 4_1|
|  4|Value 4|  6|  Value 6|
|  4|Value 4|  5|  Value 5|
+---+-------+---+---------+
```

The join is performed on the id identifier column, as shown in the following listing. In lab #940, both identifiers are the same type; in #941, they are different types.

Listing M.14 Performing a cross-join

```
Dataset<Row> df = dfLeft.join(
    dfRight,
    dfLeft.col("id").equalTo(dfRight.col("id")),
    "cross");
```

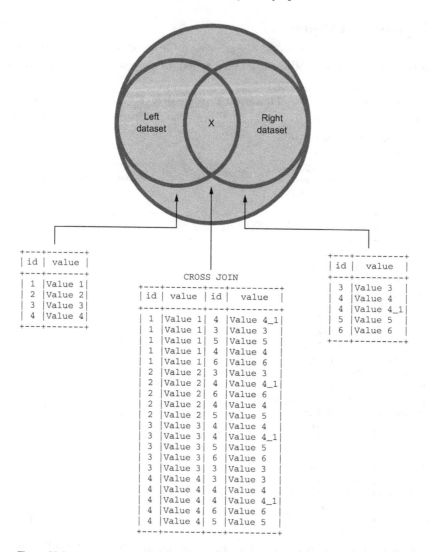

Figure M.8   A cross-join between two datasets on the `id` column

appendix N
Installing Elasticsearch and sample data

This appendix explains how to install Elasticsearch and a sample dataset. Elasticsearch is a very interesting database, especially as its authors do not consider it a database but a search engine based on Lucene. Nevertheless, it's part of the general family of databases.

It provides a distributed, multitenant-capable, full-text search engine with an HTTP web interface and schema-free JSON documents. *Multitenancy* refers to a software architecture in which a single instance of software runs on a server and serves multiple tenants (which seems pretty obvious for a database). Elasticsearch is developed in Java and is released as open source under the Apache License.

We use Elasticsearch as an ingestion source in chapter 8.

N.1   Installing the software

Installation is pretty straightforward for all systems, and the online documentation is really helpful. Nevertheless, on macOS, I recommend using Homebrew, the package manager.

N.1.1   All platforms

Go to www.elastic.co/downloads/elasticsearch and follow the directions for installation.

N.1.2   macOS with Homebrew

Homebrew is a package manager for macOS, like APT for Debian and Ubuntu, or rpm for RedHat and SUSE. It drastically simplifies the installation of a lot of products on the Mac platform. You can find out more about Homebrew, including its very easy installation, at https://brew.sh/.

Once you have Homebrew working, you can do the following:

```
$ brew install elasticsearch
```

You will also need the wget utility:

```
$ brew install wget
```

To have launchd (Mac equivalent of init.d on Unix) start Elasticsearch now and restart automatically at login, use this command:

```
$ brew services start elasticsearch
```

Or, if you don't want/need a background service you can just run this:

```
$ elasticsearch
```

To see if it works with your browser, go to http://localhost:9200/. You should see something similar to this:

```
{
  "name" : "0AvECY3",
  "cluster_name" : "elasticsearch_jgp",
  "cluster_uuid" : "sPIEZi0YQ7-1YOO4mhanpw",
  "version" : {
    "number" : "6.2.1",
    "build_hash" : "7299dc3",
    "build_date" : "2018-02-07T19:34:26.990113Z",
    "build_snapshot" : false,
    "lucene_version" : "7.2.1",
    "minimum_wire_compatibility_version" : "5.6.0",
    "minimum_index_compatibility_version" : "5.0.0"
  },
  "tagline" : "You Know, for Search"
}
```

You're done! I really wish everything was that easy!

N.2   *Installing the NYC restaurant dataset*

Now, we need data, so let's get the NYC restaurants. The full process is explained at http://mng.bz/jgo9, but I simplified it here. In the command line (Terminal, iTerm), simply type the following:

```
$ cd
$ mkdir data
$ cd data
$ mkdir elastic_restaurants
$ cd elastic_restaurants
```

```
$ wget -v http://download.elasticsearch.org/demos/nyc_restaurants/
➡ nyc_restaurants-5-4-3.tar.gz
$ tar -xvf nyc_restaurants-5-4-3.tar.gz
$ rm nyc_restaurants-5-4-3.tar.gz
```

Next, you need to modify Elasticsearch's configuration. You will need the path, so let's make sure you have yours:

```
$ pwd
/Users/jgp/data/elastic_restaurants
```

Edit the configuration file. If vi is not your favorite command-line text editor, pick yours, but you need to acknowledge that we disagree on something:

```
$ vi /usr/local/etc/elasticsearch/elasticsearch.yml
```

Locate the path.repo entry. If you do not have one, add one; it should look like this:

```
path.repo: ["/Users/jgp/data/elastic_restaurants/nyc_restaurants"]
```

If you already have a repository path in your configuration file (for example, /path0), the entry should look like this:

```
path.repo: ["/path0",
➡    "/Users/jgp/data/elastic_restaurants/nyc_restaurants"]
```

> **ON WINDOWS** The paths on Windows include the drive, so if your repository path is C:\appdata\elastic_restaurants\nyc_restaurants, your configuration file should look like path.repo: ["c:/appdata/elastic_restaurants/nyc_restaurants"].

Restart Elasticsearch.

Register a filesystem repository for the snapshot and make sure the location matches your filesystem. You will use curl, which is a standard command-line tool on Macs (and on most Unix systems). Before running the query, double-check the path in the location settings:

```
$ curl -H "Content-Type: application/json" -XPUT
➡ 'http://localhost:9200/_snapshot/restaurants_backup' -d '{
    "type": "fs",
    "settings": {
        "location":
➡ "/Users/jperrin/data/elastic_restaurants/nyc_restaurants/",
        "compress": true,
        "max_snapshot_bytes_per_sec": "1000mb",
        "max_restore_bytes_per_sec": "1000mb"
    }
}'?
{"acknowledged":true}
```

Restore the index data into your Elasticsearch instance:

```
$ curl -XPOST "localhost:9200/_snapshot/restaurants_backup/snapshot_1/
➥ _restore" ?
{"accepted":true}
```

You can then check that everything is correct by running the following query:

```
$ curl -H "Content-Type: application/json" -XGET
➥ localhost:9200/nyc_restaurants/_count -d '{
  "query": {
        "match_all": {}
  }
}'?
{"count":473039,"_shards":{"total":5,"successful":5,"skipped":0,"failed":0}}
```

N.3   Understanding Elasticsearch terminology

Many technologies use different terms to define similar concepts. Elasticsearch is no exception to this regrettable rule. Table N.1 compares the terminology used in a traditional RDBMS database with that used by Elasticsearch.

Table N.1   Comparison of terms used in a relational database and Elasticsearch

Concept in a relational database	Equivalent concept in Elasticsearch
Database	Index (plural: indices)
Partition	Shard
Table	Type
Row	Document
Column	Field
Schema	Mapping
SQL	Query DSL
View	Filtered alias
Trigger	Watch API (via X-Pack)

From an RDBMS terminology standpoint, there are no index, constraint, and keys (primary, foreign) in Elasticsearch.

N.4   Working with useful commands

Elasticsearch provides a REST API for all its operations; therefore, `curl` (or `wget`) is very useful. GUI tools also are available (including Postman and SoapUI).

N.4.1   *Get the server status*

In this subsection, you will see how to check the status of an Elasticsearch server. If you are familiar with a tool like Postman, you can use it instead of using `curl`. For example, to check whether Elasticsearch is running, simply type this:

```
$ curl -H "Content-Type: application/json" http://localhost:9200
```

And you should get something like the following:

```
{
  "name" : "0AvECY3",
  "cluster_name" : "elasticsearch_jgp",
  "cluster_uuid" : "sPIEZi0YQ7-1YOO4mhanpw",
  "version" : {
    "number" : "6.2.1",
    "build_hash" : "7299dc3",
    "build_date" : "2018-02-07T19:34:26.990113Z",
    "build_snapshot" : false,
    "lucene_version" : "7.2.1",
    "minimum_wire_compatibility_version" : "5.6.0",
    "minimum_index_compatibility_version" : "5.0.0"
  },
  "tagline" : "You Know, for Search"
}
```

N.4.2   *Display the structure*

In this section, you'll see how to display the structure of an index within the Elasticsearch index. To see the structure of an index, you can type the following:

```
$ curl -H "Content-Type: application/json"
   http://localhost:9200/nyc_restaurants | python -m json.tool
```

And you will get this:

```
{
    "nyc_restaurants": {
        "aliases": {},
        "mappings": {
            "inspection": {
                "_all": {
                    "enabled": true
                },
                "properties": {
                    "Action": {
                        "type": "keyword"
                    },
                    "Address": {
                        "fielddata": true,
                        "fields": {
                            "keyword": {
                                "ignore_above": 256,
```

```
                                "type": "keyword"
                            }
                    },
                        "type": "text"
                    },
                    "Boro": {
                        "type": "keyword"
                    },
    ...
    }
```

N.4.3   *Count documents*

To count the number of documents in a type, you can use this command:

```
curl -H "Content-Type: application/json"
➥ http://localhost:9200/nyc_restaurants/_count | python -m json.tool
```

And you'll get the following:

```
{
    "_shards": {
        "failed": 0,
        "skipped": 0,
        "successful": 5,
        "total": 5
    },
    "count": 473039
}
```

appendix O
Generating
streaming data

This appendix explains how to use the streaming data generator introduced in chapter 10.

O.1   *Need for generating streaming data*

By definition, streaming data cannot be found in a file. Streaming data can be dropped as a file into a directory or via a network. You need to generate streaming data.

   To illustrate streaming data, I built a small generator API, which you need to call in your application.

   LAB Examples from this appendix are available in GitHub at https://github.com/jgperrin/net.jgp.books.spark.ch10.

O.2   *A simple stream*

The following application will generate up to 10 records at a time, in an interval between 2.5 seconds and 7.5 seconds, for 60 seconds. The record will simulate a person with an age and a Social Security number (SSN),[1] used to uniquely identify a person in the United States.

   The result will look like the following listing.

---

[1] They are all generated and fake, so no need to call the FBI for a data breach of some kind.

Listing O.1 Output of the stream

```
2018-11-01 06:27:27.289 -DEBUG --- [            main] ure.getRecords(RecordS
➡ tructure.java:106): Generated data:
Briggs,Nadia,Tutt,72,200-29-2107
Case,Alora,Mills,93,126-32-0414
Skylar,Amiyah,Haque,63,338-49-4094
Kaya,Jorge,Christie,40,257-19-6822
Maria,Ramona,Foster,40,652-40-1413
Lilian,Dylan,Kumar,3,177-05-6531
Azalea,Armani,Kahn,103,134-23-7273
Landry,Dustin,Haque,26,743-37-6985
Zahra,Roger,Sanders,97,714-37-6811

2018-11-01 06:27:27.293 - INFO --- [            main]   erUtils.write(Record
➡ WriterUtils.java:16): Writing in: /var/folders/v7/3jv0_jbj7lz360_472wvf
➡ j5r0000gn/T/streaming/in/contact_1541068047254.txt
2018-11-01 06:27:30.983 -DEBUG --- [            main] ure.getRecords(RecordS
➡ tructure.java:106): Generated data:
Vera,Sabrina,Smith,108,438-94-0711
Leif,Kira,Tutt,85,576-09-6749
Shepard,Sridyvia,Kahn,80,739-86-5223
...
```

Records generated in the first batch

Log information, safe to ignore

Records generated in the second batch

To produce this output, you will have to create a small program by using the data generator. The following listing illustrates how to do this.

Listing O.2 RecordStreamApp.java

Streaming duration in seconds

```
package net.jgp.books.sparkInAction.ch10.x.utils.streaming.app;

import net.jgp.books.sparkInAction.ch10.x.utils.streaming.lib.*;

public class RecordStreamApp {

    public int streamDuration = 60;
    public int batchSize = 10;
    public int waitTime = 5;

    public static void main(String[] args) {
        RecordStructure rs = new RecordStructure("contact")
            .add("fname", RecordType.FIRST_NAME)
            .add("mname", RecordType.FIRST_NAME)
            .add("lname", RecordType.LAST_NAME)
            .add("age", RecordType.AGE)
            .add("ssn", RecordType.SSN);

        RecordStreamApp app = new RecordStreamApp();
        app.start(rs);
    }

    private void start(RecordStructure rs) {
```

Maximum number of records sent at the same time

Wait time between two batches of records, in seconds

The record contains a field called fname, of type FIRST_NAME.

The record contains a middle name field called mname, of type FIRST_NAME.

Creates a record

The record contains a field called lname, of type LAST_NAME.

The record contains a field called age, of type AGE.

The record contains a field called ssn, of type SSN.

```
                    long start = System.currentTimeMillis();
    Writes          while (start + streamDuration * 1000 > System.currentTimeMillis()) {
    records           int maxRecord = RecordGeneratorUtils.getRandomInt(batchSize) + 1;
    to a file         RecordWriterUtils.write(
                        rs.getRecordName() + "_" + System.currentTimeMillis() + ".txt",
     Creates          rs.getRecords(maxRecord, false));
   maxRecord        try {
    records            Thread.sleep(RecordGeneratorUtils.getRandomInt(waitTime * 1000)
    without                + waitTime * 1000 / 2);
     header        } catch (InterruptedException e) {
     (false)         // Simply ignore the interruption
                   }
                 }
               }

             }
```

Creates maxRecord records without header (false)

Waits a random number of milliseconds between waitTime / 2 and waitTime x 1.5

You can tweak the record definition and the parameters to see how they change. Section O.4 describes the various field types you can use.

O.3 Joined data

The data generator has been designed to create joined data structures, so you can easily create books written by authors, orders containing line items, and more.

The following listing shows the output of generated data. From this snippet, you can tell that Lucia Wojtaszek, born May 24, 1971, wrote *My Job, Their Nebulous Work,* and *The Colorful Job.*

Listing O.3 Joined records output

```
...
id,fname,lname,dob
29869,Alivia,Papazian,02/10/1916
13968,Cruz,Gutzmer,09/11/1954
1048,Lucia,Wojtaszek,05/24/1971

...
id,title,authorId
23589,Their Terrific Beach,13968
56625,A Fantastic Sky,29869
19362,My Job,1048
43658,Their Trip,13968
41754,Their Nebulous Work,1048
12374,The Colorful Job,1048
...
```

The following listing shows you how to achieve similar results.

Listing O.4 RandomBookAuthorGeneratorApp.java

```
package net.jgp.books.sparkInAction.ch10.x.utils.streaming.app;

import net.jgp.books.sparkInAction.ch10.x.utils.streaming.lib.*;
```

Creates a record for the author →

```
public class RandomBookAuthorGeneratorApp {

  public static void main(String[] args) {
    RecordStructure rsAuthor = new RecordStructure("author")
        .add("id", FieldType.ID)
        .add("fname", FieldType.FIRST_NAME)
        .add("lname", FieldType.LAST_NAME)
        .add("dob", FieldType.DATE_LIVING_PERSON, "MM/dd/yyyy");

    RecordStructure rsBook = new RecordStructure("book", rsAuthor)
        .add("id", FieldType.ID)
        .add("title", FieldType.TITLE)
        .add("authorId", FieldType.LINKED_ID);

    RandomBookAuthorGeneratorApp app = new RandomBookAuthorGeneratorApp();
    app.start(rsAuthor, RecordGeneratorUtils.getRandomInt(4) + 2);
    app.start(rsBook, RecordGeneratorUtils.getRandomInt(10) + 1);
  }

  private void start(RecordStructure rs, int maxRecord) {
    RecordWriterUtils.write(
        rs.getRecordName() + "_" + System.currentTimeMillis() + ".txt",
        rs.getRecords(maxRecord, true));
  }

}
```

Creates a record for book, linked to the author record structure →

Defines a field of type LINKED_ID →

Will generate two to five authors →

Will generate 1 to 10 books →

You can create more-complex structures with more tables by using the same technique.

O.4   *Types of fields*

This section briefly describes the types of fields you can use when you define a record you will use in the generator. The types of fields are listed in table O.1.

To extend the types of fields, add the field type to the FieldType enumeration and add an entry in the switch statement of the getRecords() method in the Record-Structure class.

Table O.1   Types of fields supported by the generator

Field type	Description
FIRST_NAME	Generates a first name, equal chance of being female or male. Also used for middle names.
LAST_NAME	Generates a last name.
AGE	Generates an integer from 1 to 115, even distribution. Upper bound defined by RecordGeneratorK.MAX_AGE.
SSN	Generates a Social Security number as defined by the US Social Security Administration.

Table O.1 Types of fields supported by the generator

Field type	Description
ID	Generates an integer ID, from 0 to 60,000. Each identifier is unique to the record, so there is no collision. It also means that you cannot generate more than 60,000 records without changing the value in `RecordGeneratorK.MAX_ID`.
TITLE	Generates a title such as a book or film title.
LINKED_ID	Generates a linked identifier, useful for building joints. This requires a linked record. Check out the example in section O.3 to see how you can build a joint record.
DATE_LIVING_PERSON	Generates a date of birth of a living person. Upper bound defined by `RecordGeneratorK.MAX_AGE`.

appendix P
Reference for streaming

This appendix contains reference material for streaming. Ingestion via streaming is covered in chapter 10. This appendix extends and summarizes key information from the Spark reference documentation at http://mng.bz/RAMZ.

LAB Examples from this appendix are available in GitHub at https://github.com/jgperrin/net.jgp.books.spark.ch10.

P.1 Output mode

The *output mode* will tell the query how to behave when it receives new data. Table P.1 provides details of the output modes. The reference can be found in Spark's Javadoc at http://mng.bz/2XWg.

Table P.1 Output modes for streaming queries

Output mode	Constant	Description
Append (default)	OutputMode.Append()	Only the new rows are added to the result table, because the last trigger is outputted to the sink. This is supported for only those queries with rows added to the result table that are never going to change. Hence, this mode guarantees that each row will be output only once. This is the default mode.
Complete	OutputMode.Complete()	The whole result table is outputted to the sink after every trigger. A good use case is aggregation.
Update	OutputMode.Update()	Only the rows in the result table that were updated since the last trigger are outputted to the sink. Available since Spark v2.1.1.

510

P.2 Sinks

The *sink* is the destination of the data. Each sink is demoed in at least one example or lab, which is part of chapter 10's repository. Table P.2 provides details of the output sinks. The reference can be found in Spark's documentation at http://mng.bz/1zgX.

Table P.2 Output sinks

Sink	Format	Description	Example
File	`parquet, orc, json, csv`	Outputs to a file of the specific format into a directory.	Lab #900; see listings P.1, P.2, and P.3.
Kafka	`kafka`	Outputs to a Kafka topic.	Lab #910; see listing P.4.
Foreach (single and batch)	`N/A`	Processes each record through a `for each`. You can process a record at a time or a batch of records. As of Spark v2.4.0, batch processing is still considered experimental.	Lab #920; see listings P.5, P.6, and P.7.
Console	`console`	Dumps the content on the console (std-out). Use with caution and only in debugging mode.	Lab #1xx, #2xx, and #3xx; see listings in chapter 10.
Memory	`memory`	Outputs the content in an in-memory table. Be cautious because the data will be stored in the driver's memory and, as such, can easily create an out-of-memory error. Use only in debugging mode.	Lab #930, see listing P.8.

P.3 Sinks, output modes, and options

Sinks have technology constraints, which limits some output modes. Sinks also have some required and optional options. Table P.3 summarizes this information. Sinks were described previously in table P.2, and output modes were described in table P.1.

Table P.3 Sinks, supported output modes, and options

Sink	Supported output modes	Options	Fault-tolerant
File	Append	`path`: path to the output directory, must be specified. For file-format-specific options, see the related methods in `DataFrameWriter` (see http://mng.bz/PA1w).	Yes (exactly once).
Kafka	Append, Update, Complete	See the Kafka Integration Guide at http://mng.bz/Jyxo.	Yes (at least once).
Foreach	Append, Update, Complete	N/A	Depends on `ForeachWriter` implementation.

Table P.3   Sinks, supported output modes, and options *(continued)*

Sink	Supported output modes	Options	Fault-tolerant
ForeachBatch	Append, Update, Complete	N/A	Depends on the implementation.
Console	Append, Complete	numRows—Number of rows to print every trigger (default: 20). truncate—Whether to truncate the output if too long (default: true). Prior to Spark v3, Console accepted the update mode.	No.
Memory	Append, Complete	N/A	No. But in complete mode, restarted query will re-create the full table.

P.4   *Examples of using the various sinks*

This section lists code examples associated with the scenarios described in table P.2. The first example saves stream data in a file, on another stream using Apache Kafka, then processing each record, and, finally, in memory. Because the console is used in so many examples in chapter 10, it did not make sense to copy the examples here.

To optimize your reading experience, only the first example (in listing P.1) contains all of the code. The next labs contain only an abstract of the code. Of course, in the repository, all the source code is provided in its entirety.

P.4.1   *Output in a file*

Listing P.1 outputs the content of a stream, read by records, and saves the content in a Parquet file. There is no console output outside the debug lines. The outputted file is in /tmp/spark. You may need to change this value on a Windows system.

The data stream can be generated using chapter 10's RecordsInFilesGeneratorApp in your IDE or via mvn compile package install exec:java@generate-records-in-files on the command line.

Listing P.1   **StreamRecordOutputParquetApp.java**

```
package net.jgp.books.spark.ch10.lab900_parquet_file_sink;

import java.util.concurrent.TimeoutException;

import org.apache.spark.sql.Dataset;
import org.apache.spark.sql.Row;
import org.apache.spark.sql.SparkSession;
import org.apache.spark.sql.streaming.OutputMode;
import org.apache.spark.sql.streaming.StreamingQuery;
import org.apache.spark.sql.streaming.StreamingQueryException;
import org.apache.spark.sql.types.StructType;
import org.slf4j.Logger;
```

```
import org.slf4j.LoggerFactory;

import net.jgp.books.spark.ch10.x.utils.streaming.lib.StreamingUtils;

public class StreamRecordOutputParquetApp {
  private static Logger log =
      LoggerFactory.getLogger(StreamRecordOutputParquetApp.class);

  public static void main(String[] args) {
    StreamRecordOutputParquetApp app = new StreamRecordOutputParquetApp();
    try {
      app.start();
    } catch (TimeoutException e) {
      log.error("A timeout exception has occured: {}", e.getMessage());
    }
  }

  private void start() throws TimeoutException {
    log.debug("-> start()");

    SparkSession spark = SparkSession.builder()
        .appName("Read lines over a file stream")
        .master("local")
        .getOrCreate();

    StructType recordSchema = new StructType()
        .add("fname", "string")
        .add("mname", "string")
        .add("lname", "string")
        .add("age", "integer")
        .add("ssn", "string");

    Dataset<Row> df = spark
        .readStream()
        .format("csv")
        .schema(recordSchema)
        .csv(StreamingUtils.getInputDirectory());

    StreamingQuery query = df
        .writeStream()
        .outputMode(OutputMode.Append())
        .format("parquet")
        .option("path", "/tmp/spark/parquet")
        .option("checkpointLocation", "/tmp/checkpoint")
        .start();
    try {
      query.awaitTermination(60000);
    } catch (StreamingQueryException e) {
      log.error(
          "Exception while waiting for query to end {}.",
          e.getMessage(),
          e);
    }

    log.debug("<- start()");
  }
}
```

The record structure must match the structure of your generated record.

Reading the record is always the same.

Format is Apache Parquet

File output supports only append mode

Spark needs a checkpoint directory.

Output directory— you do not specify the filename; Spark will do that for you.

Spark will need a checkpoint directory to store its intermediate states and checkpoints (you'll learn more about checkpoints in chapter 14). You can specify it here per output streams or globally at the `SparkSession` level by using `SparkSession.conf.set` (`"spark.sql.streaming.checkpointLocation", ...`).

You do not have to create any of the directories. Spark will create them for you (assuming Spark has the right to do so, of course).

After the execution, you should see a file in /tmp/spark/parquet. Between executions, you will have to clear the checkpoint directory or generate new data.

You can also export as JSON; the following listing shows a small abstract of the file.

Listing P.2   Excerpt from JSON output file

```
{"fname":"Delilah","mname":"Easton","lname":"Matis","age":36,
  "ssn":"620-99-5349"}
{"fname":"Jackson","mname":"Moshe","lname":"Walrod","age":15,
  "ssn":"045-01-6452"}
{"fname":"Presley","mname":"Harlan","lname":"Estel","age":56,
  "ssn":"892-04-6618"}
{"fname":"Sariyah","mname":"Atticus","lname":"Cousar","age":41,
  "ssn":"823-38-0945"}
{"fname":"Ellie","mname":"Cooper","lname":"Bettinger","age":62,
  "ssn":"218-04-1235"}
{"fname":"Skylar","mname":"Gianni","lname":"Wixon","age":38,"ssn":
  "397-89-1192"}
...
```

The following listing shows the modification to export the data as JSON. This is lab #901.

Listing P.3   StreamRecordOutputJsonApp.java

```
...
    StreamingQuery query = df
        .writeStream()
        .outputMode(OutputMode.Append())          Output format
        .format("json")                           is now JSON
        .option("path", "/tmp/spark/json")
        .option("checkpointLocation", "/tmp/checkpoint")
        .start();
...
```

P.4.2   *Output to a Kafka topic*

You can also publish the content of your stream to a Kafka topic, as illustrated in listing P.4. The base of the application is similar to listing P.1, so listing P.4 shows only what differs. This is lab #910. More details about Kafka integration can be found at http//mng.bz/Jyxo.

The data stream can be generated using chapter 10's RecordsInFilesGeneratorApp in your IDE or via mvn compile package install exec:java@generate-records-in-files on the command line.

Listing P.4   StreamRecordOutputKafkaApp.java

```
...
    StreamingQuery query = df
        .writeStream()
        .outputMode(OutputMode.Update())
        .format("kafka")
        .option("kafka.bootstrap.servers", "host1:port1,host2:port2")
        .option("topic", "updates")
        .start();
...
```

← **Format is now Apache Kafka**

P.4.3   *Processing streamed records through foreach*

In this lab, you will process records coming from a stream and process each one individually. This is lab #920.

The data stream can be generated using chapter 10's RecordsInFilesGeneratorApp in your IDE or via mvn compile package install exec:java@generate-records-in-files on the command line.

The following listing shows an abstract of the output.

Listing P.5   Partial output of StreamRecordThroughForEachApp

```
...main] t(StreamRecordThroughForEachApp.java:31): -> start()
...sk 0] ugger.process(RecordLogDebugger.java:40): Record #1 has 5 column(s)
...sk 0] ugger.process(RecordLogDebugger.java:41): First value: Delilah
...sk 0] ugger.process(RecordLogDebugger.java:40): Record #2 has 5 column(s)
...sk 0] ugger.process(RecordLogDebugger.java:41): First value: Jackson
...sk 0] ugger.process(RecordLogDebugger.java:40): Record #3 has 5 column(s)
...sk 0] ugger.process(RecordLogDebugger.java:41): First value: Presley
...sk 0] ugger.process(RecordLogDebugger.java:40): Record #4 has 5 column(s)
...
```

The following listing illustrates the definition of the query. Each record will be processed in a dedicated class.

Listing P.6   StreamRecordThroughForEachApp.java

```
...
    StreamingQuery query = df
        .writeStream()
        .outputMode(OutputMode.Update())
        .foreach(new RecordLogDebugger())
        .start();
...
```

← **foreach() replaces format().**

The following listing describes the class you will need in order to implement the writer itself. The writer will open and close a communication channel and process each row.

Listing P.7   RecordLogDebugger.java

```java
package net.jgp.books.spark.ch10.lab920_for_each_sink;

import org.apache.spark.sql.ForeachWriter;
import org.apache.spark.sql.Row;
import org.slf4j.Logger;
import org.slf4j.LoggerFactory;

public class RecordLogDebugger extends ForeachWriter<Row> {
  private static final long serialVersionUID = 4137020658417523102L;
  private static Logger log =
      LoggerFactory.getLogger(RecordLogDebugger.class);
  private static int count = 0;

  @Override
  public void close(Throwable arg0) {         Implement this method to
  }                                           close your sink; for example,
                                              disconnect from a service.

  @Override
  public boolean open(long arg0, long arg1) {    Implement this method to
    return true;                                 open your sink; for example,
  }                                              connect to a service.

                      If you return false, process()
                      will not be called.

  @Override
  public void process(Row arg0) {            Processes the row
    count++;
    log.debug("Record #{} has {} column(s)", count, arg0.length());
    log.debug("First value: {}", arg0.get(0));
  }
}
```

This example simply increments the number of records, counts the number of columns in the row, and logs the first value.

P.4.4   *Output in memory and processing from memory*

Spark's structured streaming can also have a query output in memory, creating a virtual table that is directly usable by SQL statements. In this lab, #930, you are going to discover how to use the memory sink.

This sink is unfortunately reserved for debugging operations, as all the data is brought back to the driver's memory, which will not use the cluster's capacity.

The data stream can be generated using chapter 10's RecordsInFilesGeneratorApp in your IDE or via mvn compile package install exec:java@generate-records-in-files on the command line.

The output is abstracted in the following listing. The code is illustrated in listing P.9.

Listing P.8 Partial output of StreamRecordInMemoryApp

```
…main] p.start(StreamRecordInMemoryApp.java:30): -> start()
…
…main] p.start(StreamRecordInMemoryApp.java:64): Pass #2,
   dataframe contains 276 records
+----------+---------+----------+---+-----------+
|     fname|    mname|     lname|age|        ssn|
+----------+---------+----------+---+-----------+
|     Emmet|  Tristian|   Spencer| 33|193-46-9248|
|     Ellis|     Olive|     Huang| 57|302-14-0038|
…
+----------+---------+----------+---+-----------+
only showing top 20 rows

…main] p.start(StreamRecordInMemoryApp.java:64): Pass #3,
   dataframe contains 283 records #A
+----------+---------+----------+---+-----------+
|     fname|    mname|     lname|age|        ssn|
+----------+---------+----------+---+-----------+
|     Emmet|  Tristian|   Spencer| 33|193-46-9248|
…
…main] p.start(StreamRecordInMemoryApp.java:64): Pass #10,
   dataframe contains 286 records #A
+----------+---------+----------+---+-----------+
|     fname|    mname|     lname|age|        ssn|
+----------+---------+----------+---+-----------+
|     Emmet|  Tristian|   Spencer| 33|193-46-9248|
…
…main] p.start(StreamRecordInMemoryApp.java:64): Pass #13,
   dataframe contains 293 records #A
+----------+---------+----------+---+-----------+
|     fname|    mname|     lname|age|        ssn|
+----------+---------+----------+---+-----------+
|     Emmet|  Tristian|   Spencer| 33|193-46-9248|
…
```

As time passes, the dataframe grows.

Spark will first create a virtual table, so you can use SQL directly. Spark SQL is detailed in chapter 11. When the table is created, you can use SQL. The table will be filled as time goes on. You will not use awaitTermination(), which is blocking. But a loop is not and allows you to work directly with the data. You will read the data, through an SQL statement, every two seconds for a minute. The following listing details the code you need.

Listing P.9 StreamRecordInMemoryApp.java

```java
package net.jgp.books.spark.ch10.lab930_memory_sink;

import java.util.concurrent.TimeoutException;
```

```
import org.apache.spark.sql.Dataset;
import org.apache.spark.sql.Row;
import org.apache.spark.sql.SparkSession;
import org.apache.spark.sql.streaming.OutputMode;
import org.apache.spark.sql.streaming.StreamingQuery;
import org.apache.spark.sql.types.StructType;
import org.slf4j.Logger;
import org.slf4j.LoggerFactory;

import net.jgp.books.spark.ch10.x.utils.streaming.lib.StreamingUtils;

public class StreamRecordInMemoryApp {
  private static Logger log =
      LoggerFactory.getLogger(StreamRecordInMemoryApp.class);

  public static void main(String[] args) {
    StreamRecordInMemoryApp app = new StreamRecordInMemoryApp();
    try {
      app.start();
    } catch (TimeoutException e) {
      log.error("A timeout exception has occured: {}", e.getMessage());
    }
  }

  private void start() throws TimeoutException {
    log.debug("-> start()");

    SparkSession spark = SparkSession.builder()
        .appName("Read lines over a file stream")
        .master("local")
        .getOrCreate();

    StructType recordSchema = new StructType()
        .add("fname", "string")
        .add("mname", "string")
        .add("lname", "string")
        .add("age", "integer")
        .add("ssn", "string");

    Dataset<Row> df = spark
        .readStream()
        .format("csv")
        .schema(recordSchema)
        .csv(StreamingUtils.getInputDirectory());

    StreamingQuery query = df
        .writeStream()
        .outputMode(OutputMode.Append())
        .format("memory")
        .option("queryName", "people")
        .start();

    Dataset<Row> queryInMemoryDf;
    int iterationCount = 0;
    long start = System.currentTimeMillis();
    while (query.isActive()) {
```

The virtual table will be called people. →

The format is memory. ←

You will use a dataframe with the streamed data. ←

← While the query is active

```
queryInMemoryDf = spark.sql("SELECT * FROM people");
iterationCount++;
log.debug("Pass #{}, dataframe contains {} records",
    iterationCount,
    queryInMemoryDf.count());
queryInMemoryDf.show();
if (start + 60000 < System.currentTimeMillis()) {
  query.stop();
}
try {
  Thread.sleep(2000);
} catch (InterruptedException e) {
  // Simply ignored
}
}

log.debug("<- start()");
}
}
```

Creates a dataframe with the content of the SQL query.

When the query has been active for more than a minute, stop it.

appendix Q
Reference
for exporting data

You can use this appendix as a reference for all-things-export: main formats, options for Parquet, CSV, JSON, and more. Because you will need to export data in Spark, this appendix will be very useful. It has some similarities with appendix L (for ingestion). The content is aggregated from several web pages, providing an easy one-stop shop for all developers.

The general syntax for exporting data is illustrated in figure Q.1.

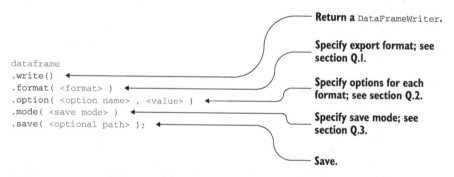

Figure Q.1 General syntax for exporting data from a dataframe, with format, option, and mode

Q.1 Specifying the way to save data

Spark supports numerous saving modes (`SaveMode`). Table Q.1 summarizes these modes and their behavior. Save modes are in the org.apache.spark.sql.SaveMode enumeration.

Table Q.1   Save modes for Apache Spark

Save mode	Description	Appeared/modified in version
Append	When saving a dataframe to a data source, if the data/table already exists, contents of the dataframe are expected to be appended to existing data. See "Exporting data to a database via JDBC" later in this appendix when using with JDBC.	v1.3.0
ErrorIfExists	When saving a dataframe to a data source, if data already exists, an exception is expected to be thrown. Not supported on Delta Lake.	v1.3.0
Overwrite	When saving a dataframe to a data source, if the data/table already exists, existing data is expected to be overwritten by the contents of the dataframe. This is not a merge operation: your existing data will be erased.	v1.3.0
Ignore	When saving a dataframe to a data source, if data already exists, the save operation is expected to —Not save the contents of the dataframe —Not change the existing data Not supported on Delta Lake.	v1.3.0

When you are appending data from a dataframe to an existing table, if your destination table has a primary key, then appending will not add the data from rows having the same ID. Lab #900 in chapter 17 illustrates this principle.

The reference for save mode, as well as one of the sources used to build this section, is http://mng.bz/MdXW.

Q.2   *Spark export formats*

Spark can export in several formats out of the box and has external writers. Table Q.2 lists the main formats and references for more information.

Table Q.2   Out-of-the-box and other formats for data export in Spark

Format	Description
csv	Comma-Separated Values. Options are listed in table Q.3.
json	JavaScript Object Notation. Options are detailed in table Q.4.
parquet	Apache Parquet. Details are in table Q.5. Parquet is described in chapter 7.
orc	Apache Optimized Row Columnar. Details are in table Q.6.
xml	Extensible Markup Language. Details are in table Q.7.
text	Text. Details are in table Q.8.

Table Q.2   Out-of-the-box and other formats for data export in Spark *(continued)*

Format	Description
jdbc	Export to a database using Java Database Connectivity. As importing (ingestion) and exporting share a lot of common behaviors for databases, details are in appendix L. Details are in Q.9.
Elasticsearch	Use format `org.elasticsearch.spark.sql`. Details are in table Q.10.
delta	Delta Lake. Details are in table Q.11.

Q.3   Options for the main formats

This section details the options you can use for exporting data in the main formats: CSV, JSON, Parquet, ORC, XML, and text.

Q.3.1   Exporting as CSV

Options are available to export data from your dataframe as a CSV file. Table Q.3 lists all the options. The latest reference is available at http://mng.bz/aRo7.

Table Q.3   CSV options for exporting data from Spark

Option name	Default value	Description	Appeared/ modified in version
`sep`	,	Sets a single character as a separator for each field and value.	v2.0.0
`quote`	"	Sets a single character used for escaping quoted values, where the separator can be part of the value. If an empty string is set, it uses u0000 (Unicode `null` character).	v2.0.0
`escape`	\	Sets a single character used for escaping quotes inside an already quoted value.	v2.0.0
`charToEscape QuoteEscaping`	escape or \0	Sets a single character used for escaping the escape for the quote character. The default value is the escape character when escape and quote characters are different; \0 otherwise.	v2.3.0
`escapeQuotes`	true	Flag indicating whether values containing quotes should always be enclosed in quotes. Default is to escape all values containing a quote character.	v2.0.0
`quoteAll`	false	Flag indicating whether all values should always be enclosed in quotes. Default is to escape only values containing a quote character.	v2.0.0

Table Q.3   CSV options for exporting data from Spark

Option name	Default value	Description	Appeared/modified in version
`header`	`false`	Writes the names of columns as the first line.	v2.0.0
`nullValue`	Empty string	Sets the string representation of a `null` value.	v2.0.0
`emptyValue`		Sets the string representation of an empty value.	v2.4.0
`encoding`	Not set	Specifies the encoding (charset) of saved CSV files. If no encoding is set, the UTF-8 charset will be used.	v2.4.0
`compression`	`null`	Sets the compression codec to use when saving to file. This can be one of the known case-insensitive shortened names (`none`, `bzip2`, `gzip`, `lz4`, `snappy`, and `deflate`).	v2.0.0
`dateFormat`	`yyyy-MM-dd`	Sets the string that indicates a date format. Custom date formats follow the formats at java.text.SimpleDateFormat. This option applies to the date type.	v2.1.0
`timestampFormat`	`yyyy-MM-dd'T'HH:mm:ss.SSSXXX`	Sets the string that indicates a timestamp format. Custom date formats follow the formats at java.text.SimpleDateFormat. This option applies to the timestamp type.	v2.1.0
`ignoreLeadingWhiteSpace`	`true`	Flag indicating whether leading whitespaces from values being written should be skipped.	v2.2.0
`ignoreTrailingWhiteSpace`	`true`	Flag indicating whether trailing whitespaces from values being written should be skipped.	v2.2.0
`lineSep`	`\n`	Defines the line separator that should be used for parsing. The maximum length is one character.	v3.0.0

Q.3.2   *Exporting as JSON*

Options are available to export data from your dataframe as a JSON file. Table Q.4 lists all the options. The latest reference is available at http://mng.bz/gyoV.

Table Q.4   JSON options for exporting data from Spark

Option name	Default value	Description	Appeared/ modified in version
compression	null	Specifies the compression codec to use when saving to file. This can be one of the known case-insensitive shortened names (none, bzip2, gzip, lz4, snappy, and deflate).	v2.1.0
dateFormat	yyyy-MM-dd	Sets the string that indicates a date format. Custom date formats follow the formats at java.text.SimpleDateFormat. This option applies to the date type.	v2.1.0
timestampFormat	yyyy-MM-dd'T' HH:mm:ss.SSSXXX	Sets the string that indicates a timestamp format. Custom date formats follow the formats at java.text.SimpleDateFormat. This option applies to the timestamp type.	v2.1.0
encoding	Not set	Specifies the encoding (charset) of saved JSON files. If no encoding is set, the UTF-8 charset will be used.	v2.4.0
lineSep	\n	Defines the line separator that should be used for writing.	v2.4.0
ignoreNullFields	true	Indicates whether to ignore null fields when generating JSON objects.	v3.0.0

Q.3.3   Exporting as Parquet

Only one option is available to export data from your dataframe as a Parquet file. Table Q.5 details that option. The latest reference is available at http://mng.bz/eQ5Q.

Table Q.5   Parquet option for exporting data from Spark to a database

Option name	Default value	Description	Appeared/ modified in version
compression	Value specified in spark.sql.parquet .compression.codec	Specifies the compression codec to use when saving to file. This can be one of the known case-insensitive shortened names (none, uncompressed, snappy, gzip, lzo, brotli, lz4, and zstd). This will override the spark.sql.parquet.compression.codec value in the configuration file.	v2.0.0

Q.3.4   Exporting as ORC

Only one option is available to export data from your dataframe as an Apache ORC file. Table Q.6 details that option. The latest reference is available at http://mng.bz/pBVz.

Table Q.6 ORC option for exporting data from Spark to a database

Option name	Default value	Description	Appeared/ modified in version
compression	Value specified in spark.sql.orc .compression.codec	Specifies the compression codec to use when saving to file. This can be one of the known case-insensitive shortened names (none, snappy, zlib, and lzo). This will override orc.compress and spark.sql.orc.compression.codec. If orc.compress is given, it overrides spark.sql.orc.compression.codec.	v2.0.0

Q.3.5 Exporting as XML

Options are available to export data from your dataframe as an XML file. Table Q.7 lists all the options available.

The XML export feature is not available out of the box. You will need the same configuration as for ingesting XML, and you will find more details in chapter 7. The latest version of this reference document is available on GitHub at https://github.com/databricks/spark-xml.

Table Q.7 XML options for exporting data from Spark to a database

Option name	Default value	Description	Appeared/ modified in Spark XML version
path		Location to write files.	v0.3.0
rowTag	ROW	The row tag of your XML file to treat as a row. For example, in the XML<books> <book><book> ... </books>, the appropriate value would be book.	v0.3.0
rootTag	ROWS	The root tag of your XML file to treat as the root (document). For example, in the XML <books> <book><book> ...</books>, the appropriate value would be books.	v0.3.0
nullValue	null (as a string)	The value to write a null value. When this is null, it does not write attributes and elements for fields.	v0.3.0
attributePrefix	_	Prefix used for attributes so you can differentiate attributes and elements. This will be the prefix for field names.	v0.3.0
valueTag	_VALUE	The tag used for the value when there are attributes in the element having no child.	v0.3.0
compression	Not set	Specifies the compression codec to use when saving to file. Should be the fully qualified name of a class implementing org.apache.hadoop.io.compress .CompressionCodec or one of the case-insensitive shortened names (bzip2, gzip, lz4, and snappy).	v0.3.0

Q.3.6   Exporting as text

Options are available to export data from your dataframe as a text file. Table Q.8 lists all the options available. The latest reference is available at http://mng.bz/OMEE.

Table Q.8   Text options for exporting data from Spark

Option name	Default value	Description	Appeared/ modified in version
compression	null	Specifies the compression codec to use when saving to file. This can be one of the known case-insensitive shortened names (none, bzip2, gzip, lz4, snappy, and deflate).	v2.0.0
lineSep	\n	Defines the line separator that should be used for writing.	v2.4.0

Q.4   Exporting data to datastores

In this subsection, you will find important resources for exporting data from Apache Spark to datastores like relational databases (via JDBC), Elasticsearch, and Delta Lake.

Q.4.1   Exporting data to a database via JDBC

Once your data has been processed by Spark, you may want to export it to a relational database. JDBC options are described in chapter 2 and chapter 8.

As described in chapters 2 and 8, you can use the Java properties mechanism as well. This section only looks at the options, as in listing Q.1.

Listing Q.1   Listing Q.1 Excerpt of exporting data using JDBC using options

```
df.write()
    .mode(SaveMode.Overwrite)
    .option("dbtable", "ch02lab900")
    .option("url", "jdbc:postgresql://localhost/spark_labs")
    .option("driver", "org.postgresql.Driver")
    .option("user", "jgp")
    .option("password", "Spark<3Java")
    .format("jdbc")
    .save();
```

Table Q.9 provides a summary of the options.

Table Q.9   JDBC options for exporting data from Spark

Option name	Default value	Description	Appeared/ modified in version
dbtable	None	Name of the table to save to	v1.4.0
url	None	URL-like JDBC connection string	v1.4.0
driver	None	Class name of the driver	v1.4.0
user	None	Name of the user	v1.4.0

Table Q.9   JDBC options for exporting data from Spark

Option name	Default value	Description	Appeared/ modified in version
`password`	None	Password for the specified user	v1.4.0
Any other	None	Directly passed to the JDBC driver—for example, `useSSL` or `serverTimezone` for MySQL	N/A

Q.4.2   Exporting data to Elasticsearch

To export to Elasticsearch, simply use `org.elasticsearch.spark.sql` as the format. You will also need two options, as mentioned in table Q.10. The version indicates the version of Elasticsearch (note that it could have appeared earlier).

Table Q.10   Elasticsearch options for exporting data from Spark

Option name	Default value	Description	Appeared/modified in version
`es.nodes`	`localhost`	List of nodes to save to	v6.8
`es.port`	`9200`	Port of the server	v2.2

Q.4.3   Exporting data to Delta Lake

Options are available to export data from your dataframe to Delta Lake. Table Q.11 lists all the options available. No online reference exists (yet), but most options are described at http://mng.bz/YrqA.

Table Q.11   Delta Lake options for exporting data from Spark

Option name	Default value	Description	Appeared/ modified in Delta Lake version
`replaceWhere`	None	Specifies a condition to apply the write on. For example: `date >= '2017-01-01' AND date <= '2017-01-31'`.	v0.2.0
`mergeSchema`	`false`	When set to `true`, columns present in the dataframe but missing from the table are automatically added as part of a write transaction.	v0.2.0
`overwriteSchema`	`false`	By default, overwriting the data in a table does not overwrite the schema. When overwriting a table using `mode("overwrite")` without `replaceWhere`, you may still want to override the schema of the data being written. You can choose to replace the schema and partitioning of the table by setting this to `true`.	v0.2.0

appendix R
Finding help
when you're stuck

This appendix contains basic troubleshooting tips as well as links to external resources. The first section contains tips and tricks for when you have a problem starting or running an application. The second section contains links to external resources that can provide additional help.

R.1   Small annoyances here and there

This section lists small annoyances that you may encounter while developing with Spark.

R.1.1   Service sparkDriver failed after 16 retries . . .

While trying to run Spark, you get a connection error at startup: *Can't assign requested address: Service 'sparkDriver' failed after 16 retries (on a random free port)! Consider explicitly setting the appropriate binding address for the service 'sparkDriver' (for example spark.driver.bindAddress for SparkDriver) to the correct binding address.*

The message comes with an exception dump:

```
2018-07-09 17:38:34.545 -ERROR --- [            main]
➥ Logging$class.logError(Logging.scala:91): Error initializing
    SparkContext.
java.net.BindException: Can't assign requested address: Service
➥ 'sparkDriver' failed after 16 retries (on a random free port)! Consider
➥ explicitly setting the appropriate binding address for the service
➥ 'sparkDriver' (for example spark.driver.bindAddress for SparkDriver) to
➥ the correct binding address.
    at sun.nio.ch.Net.bind0(Native Method)
    at sun.nio.ch.Net.bind(Net.java:433)
    at sun.nio.ch.Net.bind(Net.java:425)
    ...
```

This means that Spark cannot bind to the local address when you are calling:

```
SparkSession spark = SparkSession.builder()
    .appName("Restaurants in Durham County, NC")
    .master("local[*]")          ◄─────┐  Calling localhost
    .getOrCreate();
```

A solution is to add your hostname as a synonym to localhost in your /etc/hosts file. In a command prompt/terminal, type this:

```
$ hostname
WKSMAC21201
```

Make a backup copy of your /etc/hosts file and then edit it so it looks like the following:

```
127.0.0.1.  localhost WKSMAC21201    ◄─────    WKSMAC21201 is now a synonym
::1         localhost WKSMAC21201    ◄─────    for localhost in IPv4.
```

You can run your application again.   WKSMAC21201 is now a synonym
                                                                for localhost in IPv6.

R.1.2 *Requirement failed*

If you ever get a strange message like *Requirement failed: Can only call getServletHandlers on a running MetricsSystem* as you are trying to connect to your master, it may mean that the network has an issue.

Check the master line when you create a session:

```
SparkSession spark = SparkSession
    .builder()
    .appName("JavaSparkPi on a cluster")
    .master("spark://un:7077")       ◄─────  The URL of the master node
    .config("spark.executor.memory", "16g")
    .getOrCreate();
```

The driver may not be able to connect to it. One action is to try this:

```
$ ping un
PING un (10.0.100.81): 56 data bytes
64 bytes from 10.0.100.81: icmp_seq=0 ttl=64 time=0.379 ms
64 bytes from 10.0.100.81: icmp_seq=1 ttl=64 time=0.322 ms
```

Or try this:

```
$ telnet un 7077
Trying 10.0.100.81...
Connected to un.
Escape character is '^]'.
```

If you do not get similar output, check your network connection (one good way is to use the ping command).

R.1.3   Class cast exception

You may also encounter a class cast exception looking like this: *java.lang.ClassCast-Exception: cannot assign instance of scala.collection.immutable.List to field type scala.collection .Seq.*

Although class cast exceptions can happen, this one could come from a missing JAR. Remember deployment in chapters 5 and 18: you need all your files (data, JAR, binaries) to be available to the driver and workers. It is possible that you do not have the right version of your JAR, a missing JAR, and so on.

You can add the missing JARs by using `spark-submit` at the command line (if this is applicable to your case), adding it to the global class path (which may not be possible on your installation), or adding it to the session creation code:

```
SparkSession spark = SparkSession
    .builder()
    .appName("JavaSparkPi on a cluster")
    .master("spark://un:7077")
    .config(
        "spark.jars",
        "/home/jgp/.m2/repository/net/jgp/books/spark-
➥ chapter05/1.0.0-SNAPSHOT/spark-chapter05-1.0.0-SNAPSHOT.jar")
    .getOrCreate();
```

R.1.4   Corrupt record in ingestion

When you ingest files, you may get an additional, unexpected column, called `_corrupt _record`:

```
+--------------------+
|     _corrupt_record|
+--------------------+
|                [ {|
|       "tag" : "A1",|
|  "geopoliticalar...|
+--------------------+
only showing top 3 rows
```

Check your ingestion parameters. I've often seen this column because I messed up; for example, forgetting the `multiline` option when you ingest JSON.

R.1.5   Cannot find winutils.exe

When you run Spark on Windows, you get an exception: *Could not locate executable null\bin\winutils.exe in the Hadoop.*

This error is well known and not directly linked to Spark (it is a Hadoop error, and Spark uses some Hadoop elements). You can read more about the error at https:// issues.apache.org/jira/browse/SPARK-2356.

You can download the binary from Steve Loughran's GitHub repository at https:// github.com/steveloughran/winutils. Loughran is not just a random guy with a few repos; he is one of the committers on Apache Hadoop, and you can trust the binaries and source over there. Don't worry if the date seems old; it's really just a utility library that does not move that much.

Copy the file in a (sub)directory called bin, and then set the HADOOP_HOME environment variable to its parent directory, so that DIR %HADOOP_HOME%\bin will show winutils.exe.

R.2 *Help in the outside world*

This book does not have all the solutions to all the problems you may encounter with Spark. I hope this is not shocking news to you, especially if you've read from page 1 to now. Here are some sources of additional information.

R.2.1 *User mailing list*

The Apache Spark user mailing list is my favorite place to get help: it sure is the "older" way of getting help, through a community, but it is vibrant and allows more personal contact.

Connect to user@spark.apache.org for usage questions, help, and announcements. Send a blank email/subject to user-subscribe@spark.apache.org to subscribe and, if ever you want to unsubscribe (who knows why you would), send an email to user-unsubscribe@spark.apache.org. Archives can be consulted at http://apache-spark-user-list.1001560.n3.nabble.com/ (but they did not prove to be very reliable for me).

Here are some quick tips when using the mailing list, the basic email etiquette that everybody has a tendency to forget:

- Prior to submitting questions, please do the following:
  - Search Stack Overflow at https://stackoverflow.com/questions/tagged/apache-spark to see if your question has already been answered.
  - Search the Nabble archive at http://apache-spark-user-list.1001560.n3.nabble.com/.
- Tagging the subject line of your email will help you get a faster response; for example, [Spark SQL]: Does Spark SQL support LEFT SEMI JOIN?
- Tags may help identify a topic:
  - *Component*—Spark Core, Spark SQL, ML, MLlib, GraphFrames, GraphX, TensorFrames, and so on
  - *Language*—Java, Scala, Python, R
  - *Level*—Beginner, Intermediate, Advanced
  - *Scenario*—Debug, How-to

R.2.2 *Stack Overflow*

If you do not know Stack Overflow, I am really honored to introduce you to the most dynamic mutual aid developer platform, available for free at https://stackoverflow.com/.

Each question should have tags:

- Always use the apache-spark tag when asking questions.
- Use a secondary tag to specify components so subject matter experts can more easily find them. Examples include java, pyspark, spark-dataframe, spark-streaming, spark-r, spark-mllib, spark-ml, spark-graphx, spark-graphframes, spark-tensorframes, and so on.
- Avoid the dataframe tag because it refers to Python's dataframes. Instead, use the spark-dataframe tag.

index